MEGARRY'S MANUAL

OF

THE LAW OF REAL PROPERTY

A MANUAL OF

THE LAW OF
REAL PROPERTY

BY

THE RT. HON. SIR ROBERT MEGARRY,
M.A., LL.D. (Cantab.), Hon. LL.D. (Hull, Nottingham,
The Law Society of Upper Canada, and London),
Hon. D.U. (Essex), F.B.A.
*an Honorary Fellow of Trinity Hall, Cambridge;
a Bencher of Lincoln's Inn; sometime the
Vice-Chancellor of the Supreme Court
(1910–2006)*

NINTH EDITION

BY
Philip Rainey QC
LLB (Hons), MCI Arb, of the Middle Temple, One of Her Majesty's Counsel

Michael Walsh
*LLB (Hons), Barrister of the Middle Temple, Visiting Lecturer in Property Law,
King's College London*

Piers Harrison
LLB (Hons), Barrister of Gray's Inn

Daniel Dovar
LLB (Hons), Barrister of Gray's Inn

SWEET & MAXWELL

 THOMSON REUTERS

First Edition	1946	By R.E. Megarry
Second Impression, revised	1947	" "
Third Impression, revised	1949	" "
Fourth Impression	1951	" "
Second Edition	1955	" "
Second Impression	1960	" "
Third Edition	1962	" "
Second Impression	1967	" "
Fourth Edition	1969	By P.V. Baker
Second Impression	1972	" "
Third Impression	1973	" "
Fifth Edition	1975	" "
Sixth Edition	1982	By D.J. Hayton
Second Impression	1989	" "
Seventh Edition	1993	By R.E. Megarry and M.P. Thompson
Second Impression	1994	" " " "
Eighth Edition	2002	By A.J. Oakley

Published in 2014 by Sweet & Maxwell
part of Thomson Reuters (Professional) UK Limited
(Registered in England and Wales, Company No. 1679046. Registered Office and address for service:
Aldgate House, 33 Aldgate High Street, London EC3N 1DL)

For further information on our products and services, visit
www.sweetandmaxwell.co.uk

Typeset by Servis Filmsetting Ltd, Stockport, Cheshire
Printed in Great Britain by Ashford Colour Press, Gosport, Hants

No natural forests were destroyed to make this product;
only farmed timber was used and re-planted

A CIP catalogue record for this book is available from the British Library.

ISBN: 978-0-414-03206-4

FOREWORD

I am delighted at the publication of this new edition of *Megarry's Manual of the Law of Real Property*. It is a tribute to the original vision and high standards of the late Sir Robert Megarry that the Manual continues to be in demand nearly 70 years after it was first published by him. He was the most eminent land law scholar of his time and an outstanding Vice Chancellor of the Chancery Division of the High Court. The continued high reputation of the Manual undoubtedly also rests on the expertise of those eminent editors who have been responsible for successive editions since 1969. Not least among them is the late Tony Oakley, who was the editor of the last edition and, like Sir Robert, was both a distinguished academic and a practising barrister.

The co-editors of the present edition are all members of Tanfield Chambers. They have brought to the task their deep knowledge of the subject and the practical expertise that comes with litigation experience. They are to be congratulated on completing the difficult task of bringing the text up to date in the light of so much relevant new law over the past 12 years. The significant reorganisation of the text has allowed this to be achieved without any increase in the overall size of the work. There is every reason to feel confident that this new edition will be as much valued by both students and members of the profession as its predecessors.

The Right Honourable Sir Terence Etherton
Chancellor of the High Court

ACKNOWLEDGMENTS

Grateful acknowledgement is made to the Land Registry for permission to reproduce their sample Title Register and form TR1.

While every care has been taken to establish and acknowledge copyright, and contact the copyright owners, the publishers tender their apologies for any accidental infringement. They would be pleased to come to a suitable arrangement with the rightful owners in each case.

PREFACE

It has been 12 years since the last edition of *The Manual* was published. In that time its author, Sir Robert Megarry, passed away on October 11, 2006 and the editor of the eighth edition, Tony Oakley, passed away in 2011. It has been both a great honour and a heavy responsibility for us to follow in their footsteps in editing the ninth edition. We hope it would meet with their approval.

This edition sees a significant reorganisation of the book, which has allowed us to achieve a slimmer text. This was the aim of Sir Robert Megarry when he and Professor William Wade wrote the foreword to the first edition of *Megarry & Wade: The Law of Real Property* in 1957:

> "The publication of this work completes the original scheme for two books of a common design but different scope. Those who in students days have become familiar with the *Manual* should be able to turn with ease to the greater amplitude of this book; and the similarity of design will, we hope, not only assist teachers of law in their tasks, but also make it possible for future editions of the *Manual* to become a little slimmer."

Registered Title is now contained in its own chapter, which reinforces its importance in the modern system of ownership of land in England and Wales. At the time the last edition went to press the Land Registration Act 2002 had been enacted into law but was not yet in force. More than 11 years have now passed since its enactment and so this edition considers the effect it has had in greater detail than was possible in the eighth edition. Whilst the importance of unregistered title is diminishing it is key to the understanding of the development of land law. It is discussed in Chapters 4 and 6.

Proprietary Estoppel (Chapter 9) and Licences (Chapter 10) have been separated into their own chapters, which recognises the developments in the law, specifically in relation to the former. There is detailed analysis of the House of Lords decisions in *Cobbe v Yeoman's Row Management Ltd* [2008] 1 W.L.R. 1752 and *Thorner v Major* [2009] 1 W.L.R. 776.

The scope of the discussion of covenants relating to freehold land has been expanded to include positive covenants, and not just those that are restrictive. Accordingly, Chapter 16 is renamed as Freehold Covenants.

The title of Chapter 7 has been changed from "Settlements" to "Trusts and Real Property" to better describe the content of the discussion in that Chapter. This edition sees the removal of large parts of the text relating to the Settled Land Act 1925. A summary of its application is available but it no longer warrants the detail given to it in previous editions.

Chapter 8 contains a detailed discussion of the importance of the House of Lords decision in *Stack v Dowden* [2007] 2 A.C. 432 and the Supreme Court decision in *Jones v*

Kernott [2011] UKSC 53 on the law relating to co-ownership of the home in the domestic context.

Finally, we have removed the chapter on future interests and the sections relating to wills, intestacy, personal representatives and disabilities. Where relevant these have been reincorporated in other parts of the text.

We would like to offer our thanks to our research assistant Georgia Fullarton, and to Amanda Strange, Jill Harper and Katherine Batchelor of Sweet & Maxwell. Any errors or omissions in this work are our own.

The law has been stated as of January 31, 2014, although it has been possible to make some minor additions during the proofing stage.

PRQC
MW
PH
DD

Tanfield Chambers
April 28, 2014

CONTENTS

Chapter 7   TRUSTS AND REAL PROPERTY

Chapter 8   CO–OWNERSHIP

Chapter 9   PROPRIETARY ESTOPPEL

Chapter 10   LICENCES

Chapter 15   EASEMENTS, PROFITS AND INCORPOREAL HEREDITAMENTS

Chapter 16   FREEHOLD COVENANTS

Chapter 17   MORTGAGES

TABLE OF CASES

TABLE OF STATUTES

TABLE OF STATUTORY INSTRUMENTS

ABBREVIATIONS

STATUTES

AEA: Administration of Estates Act
AHA: Agricultural Holdings Act
CA: Conveyancing Act
C & LRA: Commonhold and Leasehold Reform Act
ECHR: European Convention on Human Rights
HA: Housing Act
IEA: Intestates' Estates Act
JA: Supreme Court of Judicature (Consolidation) Act
LCA: Land Charges Act
LPA: Law of Property Act
LP(Am.)A: Law of Property Amendment Act
LP(MP)A: Law of Property (Miscellaneous Provisions) Act
LRA: Land Registration Act
LRH & UDA: Leasehold Reform, Housing and Urban Development Act
LRR: Land Registration Rules
L & TA: Landlord and Tenant Act
L & T(C)A: Landlord and Tenant (Covenants) Act
RPA: Real Property Act
SLA: Settled Land Act
TA: Trustee Act
TLATA: Trusts of Land and Appointment of Trustees Act

CASES

B.S.: Building Society
D.C.: District Council
I.R.C.: Commissioners of Inland Revenue
In b.: (*In bonis*) In the Goods of, In the Estate of
L.B.C.: London Borough Council
R.D.C.: Rural District Council
S.E.: Settled Estate(s)
S.T.: Settlement Trust(s)
W.T.: Will Trust(s)

BOOKS AND PERIODICALS

Bl. Comm.: Blackstone's Commentaries on the Laws of England (15th edn, 1809)

C.L.J.: Cambridge Law Journal

Challis R.P.: Challis's Law of Real Property (3rd edn, 1911)

Co.Litt.: Coke's Commentary upon Littleton (19th edn, 1832)

Conv. (N.S.) (or Conv.): The Conveyancer, New Series, 1936–

Conv. (O.S.): The Conveyancer, Old Series, 1916–1936

Conv. Y.B.: Conveyancers' Year Book

Cru.Dig: Cruise's Digest of the Laws of England respecting Real Property (4th edn, 1835)

Gray, *Perpetuities*: Gray's Rule against Perpetuities (4th edn, 1942)

Halsbury: Halsbury's Laws of England (5th edn)

Harv.L.R.: Harvard Law Review

H.E.L.: Holdsworth's History of English Law, 1922–1966 (see (1945) 61 L.Q.R. 346)

Law Com.: Law Commission

Litt.: Littleton's Tenures: see Co.Litt.

L.J.News.: Law Journal Newspaper

L.Q.R.: Law Quarterly Review

L.R.Ann.Rep.: Land Registry Annual Report

L.S.G.: The Law Society's Gazette

Maitland, *Equity*: Maitland's Equity (2nd edn, 1936)

Forms of Action: Maitland's Forms of Action at Common Law, 1936

M.L.R.: Modern Law Review

M. & W.: Megarry & Wade's Law of Real Property (8th edn, 2012)

N.L.J.: New Law Journal

P. & M.: Pollock & Maitland's History of English Law (2nd edn, 1898: reprinted with new introduction 1968)

Preston, *Estates*.: Preston's Elementary Treatise on Estates (1820–27)

Ruoff & Roper: Ruoff & Roper's Law and Practice of Registered Conveyancing (Looseleaf)

Sanders, *Uses*: Sanders' Essay on Uses and Trusts (5th edn, 1844)

Shep.: Sheppard's Touchstone of Common Assurances (7th edn, 1820)

S.J.: Solicitors' Journal

Theobald, *Land*: Theobald's Law of Land (2nd edn, 1929)

Tudor L.C.R.P.: Tudor's Selection of Leading Cases on Real Property, Conveyancing and the Construction of Wills and Deeds (4th edn, 1898)

Williams R.P.: Williams' Principles of the Law of Real Property (23rd edn, 1920)

V. & P.: Williams' Treatise on the Law of Vendor & Purchaser (4th edn, 1936)

W.P.: Working Paper

GLOSSARY

The object of this glossary is to provide a ready source of reference to the meanings of some of the more troublesome technical expressions used in the text. For the most part, brief but not necessarily exhaustive definitions have been given.

Abstract of title: an epitome of documents and facts showing ownership.

Ademption: the failure of a gift by will, e.g. because the property ceases to exist or belong to the testator.

Ad hoc settlement, trust for sale or trust of land: one with special overreaching powers.

Administrators: persons authorised to administer the estate of an intestate; compare Executors.

Advowson: a right of presenting a clergyman to a vacant benefice.

Alienation: the act of disposing of or transferring.

Allodial land: land not held of a lord.

Ante-nuptial: before marriage.

Appendant: attached to land by operation of law; compare Appurtenant.

Approvement: the appropriation of a portion of the manorial waste free from rights of common.

Appurtenant: attached to land by act of parties; compare Appendant.

Assent: an assurance by personal representatives vesting property in the person entitled.

Assignment: a disposition or transfer, usually of a lease.

Assurance: the documentary or other evidence of a disposition or transfer.

Beneficial owner: a person entitled for his own benefit and not, e.g. as trustee.

Beneficiaries: those entitled to benefit under a trust or will.

Bona vacantia: goods without an owner.

Cestui que trust: a beneficiary under a trust.

Cestui que use: a person to whose benefit property was conveyed.

Cestui que vie: a person for whose life an estate *pur autre vie* lasted.

Charge: an incumbrance securing the payment of money.

Commonhold: a freehold tenure which enables freeholds to be acquired by the owners of individual units in buildings which are divided horizontally.

Consolidation: a requirement that a mortgagor shall not redeem one mortgage without another.

Contingent: operative only upon an uncertain event; compare Vested.

Conversion: a change in the nature of property either actually or notionally.

Conveyance: an instrument (other than a will) transferring property.

Corporeal: accompanied by physical possession; contrast Incorporeal.

Covenant: a promise contained in a deed.

Deed: a document which shows that it is intended to be a deed and has been signed and delivered.

Deed poll: a deed with only one party; compare Indenture.

Defeasance: the determination of an interest on a specified event.

Demise: a transfer, usually by the grant of a lease.

Determine: terminate, come to an end.

Devise: a gift of real property by will.

Distrain, distress: the lawful extra-judicial seizure of chattels to enforce a right, e.g. to the payment of rent.

Dominant tenement: land to which the benefit of a right is attached; compare Servient tenement.

Emblements: crops still growing which an outgoing tenant may take.

Engross: prepare a fair copy.

En ventre sa mère: conceived but not born.

Equities: equitable rights.

Equity of redemption: the sum of a mortgagor's rights in the mortgaged property.

Escrow: a document which upon delivery will become a deed.

Estate:
1. the *quantum* of an interest in land.
2. an area of land.
3. the whole of the property owned by a deceased person.

Estovers: wood which a tenant may take for domestic or other purposes.

Execute:
1. to perform or complete, e.g. a deed.
2. to convert, e.g. to transform the equitable interest under a use into a legal estate.

Executors: persons appointed by a testator to administer his estate; compare Administrators.

Executory trust: a trust the details of which remain to be set out in some further document.

Fee: base, conditional, determinable, simple, tail.

Feoffee to uses: a person holding property to the use of another.

Feoffment: a conveyance by livery [delivery] of seisin.

Fine: a premium or a lump sum payment, e.g. for the grant of a lease.

Foreclosure: proceedings by a mortgagee which free mortgaged property from the equity of redemption.

Freehold:
1. socage tenure.
2. commonhold tenure.
3. an estate of fixed but uncertain duration.

General equitable charge: an equitable charge on a legal estate not protected by a deposit of documents of title.

Good consideration: natural love and affection for near relatives.

Hereditaments: inheritable rights in property.

Heritable issue: descendants capable of inheriting.

Hold over: remain in possession after the termination of a tenancy.

Hotchpot: the bringing into account of benefits already received before sharing in property.

Human rights: the rights conferred by the European Convention on Human Rights.

Improved value: the value of land together with improvements to it.

In capite: in chief, immediately holding of the Crown.

Inclosure: the appropriation of the whole of a manorial waste free from rights of common.

Incorporeal: not accompanied by physical possession; contrast Corporeal.

Incumbrance: a liability burdening property.

Indenture: a deed between two or more parties; compare Deed poll.

Infant: a person under 18 years of age.

In gross: existing independently of a dominant tenement.

Instrument: a legal document.

Intestacy: the failure to dispose of property by will.

Issue: descendants of any generation.

Jointure: provision by a husband for his widow, usually under a settlement.

Jus accrescendi: right of survivorship.

Lapse: the failure of a gift.

Letters of administration: the authorisation to persons to administer the estate of a deceased person.

Licence: a permission, e.g. to enter on land.

Limitation, words of: words delimiting the estate granted to some person previously mentioned; compare Purchase, words of.

Marriage articles: the preliminary agreement for a marriage settlement.

Mere equities: rights to equitable relief that fall short of being rights in land.

Merger: the fusion of two or more estates or interests.

Mesne: intermediate, middle.

Minor: see Infant.

Minority: the state of being an infant.

Nuncupative: oral (of wills).

Overreach: to transfer rights from land to the purchase money paid for the land.

Parol: by word of mouth.

Particular estate: an estate less than a fee simple.

Per capita: by heads; one share for each person; compare *Per stirpes*.

Personal representatives: executors or administrators.

Per stirpes: by stocks of descent: one share for each line of descendants; compare *Per capita*.

Portions: provisions for children, especially lump sums for the younger children under a settlement.

Possibility of reverter: the grantor's right to land if a determinable fee determines.

Post-nuptial: after marriage.

Prescription: the acquisition of easements or profits by long user.

Privity of contract: the relation between parties to a contract.

Privity of estate: the relation between landlord and tenant under a legal lease.

Probate: the formal confirmation of a will, granted by the court to an executor.

Puisne mortgage: a legal mortgage not protected by a deposit of title deeds.

Pur autre vie: for the life of another person.

Purchase, words of: words conferring an interest on the person that they mention ; compare Limitation, words of.

Purchaser: a person who takes land by virtue of a disposition by another person and not by operation of law.

Que Estate: dominant tenement.

Remainder: the interest of a grantee subject to a prior particular estate.

Rent: chief rent, fee farm rent, ground rent, quit rent, rack rent, rent of assize, rentcharge, rent seck, rent service.

Restrictive covenant: a covenant restricting the use of land.

Reversion: the interest remaining in a grantor after granting a particular estate.

Riparian owner: the owner of land adjoining a watercourse.

Root of title: a document from which ownership of unregistered land is traced.

Satisfied term: a term of years created for a purpose which has since been fulfilled.

Seisin: the feudal possession of land by a freeholder.

Servient tenement: land burdened by a right such as an easement; compare Dominant tenement.

Settlement: provisions for persons to enjoy property in succession (or the instruments making such provisions).

Severance: the conversion of a joint tenancy into a tenancy in common.

Severance, words of: words showing that a property is to be held in undivided (distinct) shares.

Spes or *Spes successionis*: a possibility of succeeding to property.

Squatter: a person occupying land without any title to it.

Statutory owner: persons with the powers of a tenant for life under the Settled Land Act 1925.

Statutory trusts: certain trusts imposed by statutes, especially—

　　1.　the trust for sale of land under co-ownership before 1997.

　　2.　the trust of land under co-ownership after 1996.

　　3.　the trusts for issue on intestacy.

Sub-mortgage: a mortgage of a mortgage.

Sui juris: "of his own right", i.e. subject to no disability.

Tenement: anything which may be held by a tenant.

Tenure: the set of conditions upon which a tenant holds land; compare Estate.

Term of years: a period with a defined minimum for which a tenant holds land.

Terre tenant: a freehold tenant in possession.

Title: the evidence of a person's right to property.

Trust: bare, completely constituted, constructive, executed, executory, express, implied, incompletely constituted, precatory, resulting.

Trust corporation: one of certain companies with a large paid-up capital, or one of certain officials.

Undivided share: the interest of a tenant in common.

Use: benefit.

User: use, enjoyment (Note: *not* the person who uses).

Vested: unconditionally owned; compare Contingent.

Vesting assent, declaration, deed, instrument.

Voluntary conveyance: a conveyance not made for valuable consideration.

Volunteer: a person taking under a disposition without having given valuable consideration.

Waste: ameliorating, equitable, permissive, voluntary.

Chapter 1

INTRODUCTION

WHAT IS "THE LAW OF REAL PROPERTY"?

What is generally described as the English law of real property, or "land law", applies to all   **1–001** land in England and Wales. It has never applied to any other part of the United Kingdom, although it has provided the basis for the systems of many countries in the common law world, from Ireland and the common law jurisdictions of the United States of America to Australia and New Zealand.

THE MEANING OF "REAL PROPERTY"

Property can be divided into two classes: "real property" (or "realty") and personal prop-   **1–002** erty. Land is immoveable and thus is real property, whereas this book, for example, is moveable and is personal property. *Megarry's Manual* is essentially a book about land law, but the concept of "real property" only approximately corresponds to the distinction between land and other property. This topic is explored in a section of its own later in this Chapter.

HOW TO APPROACH THE LAW OF REAL PROPERTY—"READ FAST, READ OFTEN"

It is pointless to deny that the subject, traditionally described by Oliver Cromwell as "an   **1–003** ungodly jumble", is justly recognised as a difficult one for beginners. This is partly because of the intricate interlocking of its component parts and partly because of the complexity of the language, which involves the use of many technical terms. An excellent illustration of both these difficulties is the precise meaning of the expression "real property" itself.[1] On the other hand, real property law is richly satisfying once understood.

For these reasons, those coming new to the subject must not expect to understand everything at a first reading. In this subject, more than any other, it is economical of time and effort to read fast and often. Much that is almost incomprehensible at first will become clear on a second reading and perhaps obvious on a third. In order to understand complex ideas expressed in unfamiliar language it is necessary to master the language as soon as possible, and for this purpose a generous use should be made of the glossary.

---

[1] See below, paras 1–045–1–049.

REAL PROPERTY VERSUS CONVEYANCING

1–004   It is not easy to distinguish accurately a boundary between the law of real property and conveyancing. In general, it can be said that the former is static, the latter dynamic; real property deals with the rights and liabilities of landowners, conveyancing with the practicalities of creating and transferring rights in land. Inevitably the two overlap, and often the exact place at which to draw the line is ultimately a matter of taste. It is best to regard real property and conveyancing not as two separate though closely related subjects, but as two parts of the one subject of land law; it is convenience of teaching rather than any essential difference of nature that dictates the division.

THE SIGNIFICANCE OF LEGAL HISTORY IN THE STUDY OF THE LAW OF REAL PROPERTY

1–005   History plays a significant part in the study of real property law, for two reasons. First and foremost, land law is arguably the part of English law which still owes most to its development in the Middle Ages. Land was the most valuable commodity in the Middle Ages, so the law governing the creation and transfer of interests in land, and the rights and liabilities of landowners was of paramount importance. Consequently, it became a developed and complex system at a comparatively early stage[2] and the great reform of real property law in 1925 (see below) is built on those early foundations.

Secondly, conveyancing makes it essential to include some historical element. This is because a conveyancer must deal with both ownership and incumbrances. In other words, he must see not only that his client gets what he has agreed to buy but also that he gets it free from any burdens such as mortgages or rights of way which would make it less valuable. A conveyancer acting for a client who is purchasing unregistered land must investigate the title to the land, both as to ownership and as to incumbrances. Incumbrances binding the land may well have been created considerably more than a hundred years before the transaction in question, and the ownership of the land sometimes has to be investigated for at least the preceding 15 years. It is necessary to know the law not only as it is but to have some understanding of the law as it was.

REGISTERED AND UNREGISTERED LAND

1–006   Modern real property law is based upon the 1925 property legislation, which came into force on January 1, 1926. The Land Registration Act 1925 introduced a country-wide system of land registration and created a distinction between unregistered land and registered land. The distinctions have been magnified by the Land Registration Act 2002 which has replaced the old 1925 Act.

The title to land may either be registered at the Land Registry, or else be unregistered. In the case of registered land, the register of titles sets out, subject to various classes of

---

[2]   Compare the law of negligence, which in modern form dates back only to *Donoghue v Stevenson* in 1932.

interests which override registration,[3] the current state of the title, and only to an extremely limited extent is any knowledge of the pre-1926 law required. Comparatively little attention therefore will be paid to it on subjects that fall within the system of registration of title.[4] In the case of unregistered land, although a purchaser now need only investigate the vendor's title as far back as a good "root of title" (such as a conveyance on sale) at least 15 years old,[5] it is of course perfectly possible for the root of title in question to pre-date the 1925 legislation. Further, it is also necessary to investigate the incumbrances binding the land, one particular type of which (covenants restricting the use of the land[6]) will not infrequently have been created in the latter part of the nineteenth century. It is nevertheless relatively uncommon for any detailed knowledge of the pre-1926 law to be required, although attention will be paid to such parts of it as are likely to be relevant. However, now that any transfer of unregistered land on sale or by way of gift obliges the transferee to register the title, registered land is increasingly predominant,[7] and so the emphasis of this edition of this book is on registration of title.

THE COMMON LAW BASIS OF THE SUBJECT

The law of real property is part of the common law of England. The phrase "common law" or "at law", which will frequently be encountered, is used in three senses: **1–007**

- (i) in contrast with local custom;
- (ii) in contrast with statute law; and
- (iii) in contrast with equity.

The third is the most usual sense, the second less usual, and the first comparatively rare: the context will normally make it plain which is meant.

A word must be said on the third meaning. As will be seen later,[8] certain rights could be enforced in the common law courts (i.e. the King's ordinary courts), and these were known as legal rights. Other rights were not protected by the common law courts, but in time came to be protected by the Chancellor (later Lord Chancellor), the King's Chief Minister, exercising a residual jurisdiction of the Crown to intervene where the common law courts could not or would not do justice, if he deemed this to be equitable. It was the Chancellor who first compelled trustees to carry out their trusts, and remedied wrongs which the common law courts would not redress because of non-compliance with some formal requirement. Rights enforced by the Chancellor were known as equitable rights, for the court presided over by the Chancellor, the Court of Chancery, was often described as the Court of Equity. Equitable rights were (and, in the case of unregistered land, still are) inferior to legal rights, in that a legal right would be enforced against everyone, whereas an equitable right would

---

[3] See below, paras 1–030, 5–022 et seq.
[4] Where more detailed knowledge is required, see the fifth (1984) or earlier editions of *Megarry & Wade: The Law of Real Property,* or the seventh (1993) or earlier editions of this book.
[5] Below, para.1–025.
[6] See below, Ch.16.
[7] 80 % of land is now registered (according to the Land Registry website).
[8] Below, Ch.3.

be enforced only against a person whom the Chancellor considered was unable in good conscience to deny liability (the enforceability of rights in registered land does not normally depend on whether they are legal or equitable). Thus not only would a trustee be compelled to carry out his trust but also, if he gave or sold the trust property to a third person who knew that the trustee was committing a breach of trust, the equitable rights of the beneficiaries under the trust would be enforced against that third person, who would thus be compelled to carry out the trust.

Ultimately, by virtue of what is known as the equitable doctrine of notice, equitable rights became enforceable against the whole world except a bona fide purchaser for value of a legal estate without notice of the equitable right, or someone claiming title under such a person.[9] In the language of more spacious days, he was "equity's darling", the one person whom equity preferred to the holder of an equitable right. Legal rights, on the other hand, were enforceable against everyone, without this exception. Rights in unregistered land continue to be governed by these rules, although some equitable rights now have to be protected by registration to be enforceable against a purchaser for value.[10] On the other hand, rights in registered land are enforceable against a purchaser for value, or someone claiming title under such a person, only if they have been protected on the register or fall within one of the limited classes of interests which override registration.

The common law affecting real property has in the course of time been profoundly affected by equity. Today most questions on real property law, if they reach the High Court, will be assigned to the Chancery Division of the High Court, which is the successor to the Court of Chancery; yet this arrangement must not be allowed to obscure the common law basis of the law of real property, though much affected by statute law.

THE COMPLEX FUNCTIONS OF LAND

1–008   A principal reason for the complexity of the law of real property lies in the physical nature of land itself:

(i)   land is both virtually indestructible and uniquely immovable, with the result that various people can have different interests in it and rights over it;

(ii) land is also especially apt for satisfying concurrent needs;

(iii) land may be subject to binding third party rights and restrictions on use which can be enforced by third parties;

(iv) land provides ideal security for loans;

(v)   land may readily be divided up into smaller parcels. Buildings on land may readily be divided both vertically and horizontally; and

(vi) the supply of land and buildings is limited and inelastic.

None of those things is generally true in the case of chattels. If a person wants to buy a car, there will be plenty to choose from. If a person buys a car, he does not find that it is subject to obligations such as a prohibition on driving it to Exeter, or a limit to what can be carried in

---

[9]   See below, paras 3–010 et seq., where this is more fully discussed.

[10] See below, paras 6–068 et seq.

it or what alterations he may make to it. He may, of course, by contract impose such obligations on himself, but they will not flow from his ownership of the car. Nor will such a person find that by reason of owning the car he has acquired rights over other people's property, such as a right to drive over their land. Again, he will not find that the boundaries of his car are uncertain or that it is liable to be compulsorily purchased. Nor will he find that another person has a life interest in the car or a 99-year tenancy or a 21-year sub-tenancy of it. Nor can the car be divided up while remaining a functioning car.

In contrast, because of the nature of land, it is quite feasible that an owner of land may be concerned with matters of this nature. Land may be settled upon A for life, then to A's eldest son for life and, finally to A's eldest grandson absolutely. Alternatively, it may be leased to X for 99 years, X may sub-lease it to Y for 21 years, and Y may further sub-lease it to Z for a year. Laws have to regulate not only the relationships both between A and those entitled to the land after him (who are generally described as remaindermen), and between X, Y and Z, but also the position of a purchaser of the property in which they are interested.

Land is also especially apt for satisfying concurrent needs, whether of spouses or businessmen. Land may be owned by H and W as joint tenants or by P and Q as tenants in common. In the former case, by virtue of what is known as the *jus accrescendi* (right of survivorship), the survivor of the two will become the sole owner; whereas in the latter instance the share of the first to die will pass under his will or, if he has left no will, under the rules governing his intestacy.

Land may also be subject to rights of others which may be adverse to the landowner. For example, a neighbour may have a right of way over the land. The land may also be subject to covenants restricting its user, as by limiting the number of buildings that may be erected upon it or prohibiting their use except as private dwellings.

Land also provides ideal security for a loan of money where it is lent on the basis of a mortgage or charge of it.

Land and any buildings thereon, which are treated as part of the land under the maxim *quicquid plantatur solo, solo cedit* (whatever is attached to the soil becomes part of it), are divisible vertically (such as into semi-detached or terraced houses) or horizontally (such as into maisonettes and flats), thus creating many problems as to mutual rights and obligations.

Further difficulties arise from the unique inelasticity of the supply of land, something which has provoked much legislation.

A balance of interests

Following on from that, another reason for the complexity of land law is that many different **1–009** human needs have to met. Many needs require many rights to meet those needs. Rights require rules to govern their operation, and complexity is the result. A single plot of land may be subject to a wide variety of rights, and the extent and validity of these rights may be tested from time to time, especially when the land is sold.

The interests of a purchaser would be served if all such rights were made void against him if not registered. The interests of a mortgage lender would be best served if his mortgage had priority over everything else. Yet such provisions would be oppressive, not only in the scale of registration that would be required but also in respect of rights that could not reasonably be expected to be registered. The question is therefore one of balance, and the development of the law of real property in recent times can be seen as a continuing search to achieve an appropriate balance between competing interests.

LEGAL ESTATES AND INTERESTS AND EQUITABLE INTERESTS

1–010   Before 1926, there were many different legal estates and legal interests that could exist in land, and a corresponding range of estates and interests could exist in equity. Since 1925, only two legal estates in land can exist, and the number of legal interests has been limited. The two legal estates are the "fee simple absolute in possession" and the "term of years absolute". In lay terms, A will be called the "owner" of Greenacre. In legal terminology, A holds the fee simple absolute in possession in Greenacre. If A has granted a lease to T (for instance for 21 years), A's fee simple is still "in possession", for "possession" includes the right to receive the rent from the land. Although T has a "term of years absolute" in the land, he will commonly be called the leaseholder or tenant of it.

Legal interests are rights over someone else's land, such as easements (for example rights of way), legal charges (mortgages), rentcharges (i.e. rights to a rent where there is no lease or tenancy), and rights of entry (i.e. the right reserved by the grantor of a lease to enter the land and end the lease if the tenant fails to comply with his obligations thereunder).

All other interests are equitable. These include the right to enforce restrictive covenants (such as an undertaking that the land will not be built upon) and interests under trusts. Further, any of the estates and interests that can exist at law may instead exist in equity, something which will occur where they have been created without the necessary formalities.

For unregistered land, legislation has reduced the number of estates and interests which will bind a purchaser of the land without notice of them. For registered land, as mentioned above, the enforceability of rights does not normally depend on whether they are legal or equitable.

THE ESTATE OWNER AND OVERREACHING

1–011   Before 1926, the legal estate in land could be divided between two or more persons in succession, so that X might have a legal life estate and Y the fee simple subject to that life estate. Since 1925, this is no longer possible. The entire legal estate in fee simple will be vested in one or more persons and the life interest can exist only in equity behind a trust of the legal estate. However, by following the correct procedure, the owner of the fee simple can sell the land free from the rights that others have in it; but their rights will not be destroyed, for they will be transferred to the purchase money and this will be held by the trustees of the trust. The process whereby rights in the land are detached from it and attached instead to the proceeds of sale is known as "overreaching".[11] This is quite distinct from the process whereby equitable rights are held to be void as against a purchaser of unregistered land without notice of them or a purchaser of registered land when such rights are neither overriding interests nor protected on the register of titles. That process destroys the equitable rights in question, whereas rights that are overreached are merely transferred, not invalidated.

_____

[11] Below, para.4–028.

Settlements

Some of the complications of land law arise from cases where land has been settled upon a succession of persons. A somewhat complex (and not very realistic) example may be taken so as to give a bird's eye view of the matter, though many readers will probably not fully comprehend the example until most of this book has been read. Until 1997, such settlements could take effect either in accordance with the provisions of the Settled Land Acts or behind an express trust for sale. Since 1996 it is no longer possible to create settlements in accordance with the Settled Land Acts. Although existing settlements of this type nevertheless continue, the choice now is between an express trust for sale and a trust of land which is not a trust for sale.

1–012

An example

Example: By his will a testator leaves Greenacre to his son H for life, subject thereto to H's wife W for life, and subject thereto for such child of H and W as H shall appoint by deed during his lifetime or by his will absolutely, but in default of appointment to the first of the sons of H and W to attain 21 years of age absolutely. The following consequences arise on this example:

1–013

Beneficial interests

(i) This provision gives H what is known as a life interest in possession and W what is known as a life interest in remainder.

(ii) H is also given what is known as a special power of appointment which enables him to appoint Greenacre to any child of H and W absolutely, for an estate in fee simple. Each child of H and W is what is known as an "object" of the power of appointment, taking no estate or interest in the land but having a mere hope (often known as a *spes*, the Latin word for hope) that the power will be exercised in his or her favour.

(iii) Each of the sons of H and W has what is known as a contingent absolute interest in remainder, the contingency being the attainment of 21 years of age; and the interest of each son is subject to the exercise of the power of appointment and to the interest of any older sons. When a son attains the age of 21, he acquires what is known as a vested absolute interest in remainder. This is subject to the interests of H and W and to any exercise of the power of appointment.

(iv) Because the testator has not disposed of the whole of his estate in fee simple (it is possible that H and W will die without any children or without any son who attains the age of 21 and without H exercising his power of appointment), the testator retains what is known as an estate in fee simple in reversion; if none of the children of H and W obtains an estate in fee simple, the land will fall back into the estate of the testator and will devolve in accordance with the remaining provisions of his will or, if they do not deal with the land, it will pass under the rules of intestacy, which determine who inherits the assets of someone who dies without leaving a will.

(v) Given the number of different beneficial interests in Greenacre thus created, the land would be virtually unsaleable if a purchaser had to deal with everyone who

1–014

had any such interest in it: hence the need for the settlement to take effect in one of the ways already mentioned.

Settlements under the Settled Land Acts

1–015   Continuing to illustrate the workings of the law by reference to the example above, the Settled Land Acts made it possible for a purchaser to acquire Greenacre in fee simple, free from the interests of H, W, their children, and the testator's estate, without having to deal with anyone except the tenant for life for the time being (initially H and, after his death, W).

Under the Settled Land Act 1925 the estate in fee simple is vested in the tenant for life on trust for himself and all the other beneficiaries under the settlement. He therefore has full powers of management and control of the land, including the power to convey the estate vested in him to any purchaser. However, the purchaser will take free from the interests of the other beneficiaries only if those interests are protected by being overreached, i.e. transferred from the land into the proceeds of sale. This requires the purchaser to pay the purchase moneys to the trustees of the settlement (who must be at least two in number or a trust corporation) rather than to the tenant for life for the time being. As will be seen below, rights in the land existing outside the settlement, such as easements and mortgages, will not be overreached and will not be affected.[12] As already mentioned, no further settlements of this type can now be created.

Express trusts for sale

1–016   The alternative to settlements under the Settled Land Act 1925 were express trusts for sale, which can still be created.[13] Such trusts enable exactly the same beneficial interests to take effect. The difference is that the estate in fee simple is vested in the trustees for sale rather than in the tenant for life for the time being. An express trust for sale is created by conveying the land to two, three or four trustees (or to a trust corporation) to hold it on trust to sell it but with a power to postpone sale. Normally the trustees will be expected to retain the land under the power of postponement, rather than to sell it, but by refusing to concur in exercising the power to postpone sale, any one trustee can compel the others to sell. While the trustees do retain the land, they will have full power to manage and control it. When they do sell it, they will convey to the purchaser the estate in fee simple that is vested in them and will receive and hold the purchase money on trust for all the beneficiaries under the trust for sale. The interests of the latter will thus be overreached into the purchase money provided that it has been paid to the trustees, being at least two in number or a trust corporation. Rights in the land existing outside the express trust for sale, such as easements and mortgages, will not be overreached and will not be affected.[14] In the days when there was a choice between creating a settlement under the Settled Land Acts and an express trust for sale, an important factor in the decision was who the creator of the settlement wished to be able to make decisions and exercise powers. This is not a factor in the present choice between an express trust for sale and a trust of land other than an express trust for sale.

---

[12] See generally below, para.4–039.
[13] Although they are within the category of a trust for land since the coming into force of the Trusts of Land and Appointment of Trustees Act 1996 (TLATA 1996); see s.1 of that Act.
[14] See generally below, para.4–033.

Trusts of land

Since 1996 it has been possible for exactly the same beneficial interests to take effect under **1–017** a trust of land which is not an express trust for sale. Such a trust works in exactly the same way as an express trust for sale. The difference is that the trustees now have only a power rather than a duty to sell the land so that the agreement of all the trustees is necessary for a sale: one alone cannot force a sale. This is obviously likely to be an important factor in the choice between the two.

Rights not overreached

In the case of all three types of settlements that have been discussed, rights in the land **1–018** existing outside the settlement are not affected by the process of overreaching and are therefore potentially binding on any purchaser of the land. He will therefore be as concerned to discover the existence of any such rights as a purchaser of land which is not settled. Thus tenancies, mortgages, easements and other rights existing when the settlement was made will continue to bind the land even when it has been sold by the tenant for life or by the trustees; a purchaser will take free from them only if he can do so under the rules which have already been discussed.[15] A purchaser for value of registered land will be able to do so only if the rights in question have not been protected on the register of titles and are not within one of the classes of interests which override registration. A purchaser for value of unregistered land will be able to do so only if the rights in question are equitable interests of which he has no notice. The position is exactly the same in respect of any such rights created by the tenant for life or trustees in the course of managing the land while it was settled and in respect of any beneficial interests which have not been overreached because the purchase money was not paid to the requisite number of trustees.[16]

Co-ownership

Preliminary

As well as being held for persons in succession, land may be held for persons concurrently: **1–019** in a sense ownership may be divided not only vertically but also laterally. Even though Greenacre may be free from any successive interests in it, it may be held by two or more co-owners. There may of course be both successive interests and co-ownership of some or all of the successive interests.

Joint tenancy or tenancy in common?

There are two types of co-ownership: joint tenancy and tenancy in common. The use of **1–020** the word "tenancy" in this context refers to all forms of tenure; it does not refer simply to leaseholds. At risk of over-simplification, joint tenants hold an undivided share in the land, in other words they jointly hold 100 per cent and the respective proportions of that

---

[15] Above, para.1–007.
[16] See below, paras 4–028–4–042.

100 per cent to which they may be entitled is not decided. Tenants in common hold divided shares, in other words it is decided what percentage each of them is entitled to.

This gives rise to an important difference in the treatment of their interest when one of the co-owners dies. In joint tenancy, there is a right of survivorship (*jus accrescendi*) so the interest of the deceased joint tenant passes to the surviving joint tenant(s). There is no such effect in co-ownership.

Fragmentation of title

1–021   There might be dozens of co-owners of the fee simple in Greenacre, either as joint tenants or tenants in common. Joint tenants tended to become reduced in numbers, for when one died, the *jus accrescendi* (right of survivorship) would in effect carry his interest to his fellow joint tenants. On the other hand, tenants in common tended to increase in number, since when one died his interest would pass under his will or intestacy, perhaps to his ten children. Land might be owned by dozens of tenants in common living in different parts of the world; and even if all of them could be traced, some might be children or patients suffering from mental incapacity. Until 1926, a would-be purchaser of such land might face such formidable and expensive difficulties that he would abandon his venture.

Integration of title

1–022   In 1925 the problem was resolved by two fundamental reforms[17]:

  (i) there can never now be more than four co-owners of the legal estate;
  (ii) the legal estate can only be co-owned as joint tenants, so that on death the legal estate remains in the survivors, by the *jus accrescendi*.

The surviving legal joint owners can appoint others to be joint tenants of the legal estate with themselves, but only so long as their number does not exceed four. Consequently, a would-be purchaser of land only ever has to deal with a maximum of four joint owners of the legal estate. There can be any number of co-owners of the beneficial interest, and the beneficial interest can be, and often is, held as a tenants in common, but the beneficial interests can be overreached by the joint owners of the legal estate.

The Law of Property Act 1925[18] provided that the legal estate should be held by the joint tenants on trust for sale with power to postpone sale, thus enabling the property to remain unsold for a long time. However, as a result of the Trusts of Land and Appointment of Trustees Act 1996,[19] all such trusts for sale have, since the end of 1996, been converted into trusts of land and all subsequent joint tenancies also take effect as trusts of land. Consequently, the legal estate is now held by the joint tenants as trustees of the land with *power* to sell it but no longer on any *trust* for sale. The discretion whether to sell or retain the land continues but the emphasis is now on retention rather than sale. Both before and after this reform, the joint tenants have held and may hold the legal estate on trust for any number of co-owners. They may be children or patients suffering from mental incapacity,

---

[17] Below, paras 8–012–8–034.
[18] Law of Property Act 1925 (LPA 1925) ss.34–36.
[19] TLATA 1996 s.1.

or live in remote countries, and have equitable interests which may be joint tenancies or tenancies in common. So long as a purchaser pays his purchase moneys to the joint tenants holding the legal estate as trustees and takes a conveyance of the legal estate from them, he obtains a good legal title, free from all the equitable interests of the beneficial co-owners. They are instead overreached and become interests in the proceeds of sale.[20]

Undisclosed co-ownership

Difficulties can, however, arise when there is an undisclosed co-owner of a beneficial inter-   **1–023**
est. If H purchases a house and his wife W contributes one-third of the purchase price, the course envisaged by the draftsmen of the 1925 property legislation was that the house should be conveyed to H and W as joint tenants to hold on trust for sale (now, of course, under a trust of land) for themselves as tenants in common in equity, as to two-thirds and one-third respectively. The draftsmen did not envisage, or at any rate did not specifically provide for, the possibility of the house instead being conveyed to H alone with nothing to reveal W's contribution. She will still be entitled to a one-third share as a tenant in common in equity but there will be nothing to disclose this to a purchaser of the legal estate.

If such a purchaser, P, pays the purchase moneys to H, thinking him to be solely entitled, W's equitable rights will not be overreached, for the purchase moneys will not have been paid to the necessary number of trustees (either at least two persons or a trust corporation). In these circumstances, not envisaged by the 1925 property legislation, the courts have decided that W's rights will bind P unless he has taken free of them under the relevant general principles.[21]

If the land in question is registered land, P will take free from W's rights unless they fall within one of the classes of interests which override registration or have been protected on the register of titles. If W is in actual occupation of the land, she will have such an interest by virtue of her actual occupation, and so her rights will bind P.[22] But if the marriage has broken up and she has left the house permanently, she will not have such an interest and her rights will bind P only if she has protected them on the register. If, on the other hand, the land in question is unregistered land, P will take free from W's rights only if he can show that he is a bona fide purchaser for value of the legal estate without notice of them.[23] P will obviously have had no actual knowledge of W's rights, for otherwise he would have paid the purchase moneys to the appropriate number of trustees in order to overreach her rights. However, he will be treated as having notice of those rights if they would have come to his knowledge had he made such inquiries and inspections as he ought reasonably to have made.[24]

These concepts have produced difficulties with both registered and unregistered land. In the case of registered land, the limits of actual occupation are still unclear. While it is clear that W will still be regarded as being in actual occupation during a temporary absence, as while in hospital or away on holiday, it is unclear whether and, if so, for how long she will be regarded as being in actual occupation if she left intending never to return. In the case of unregistered land, the courts have encountered difficulties in deciding what inquiries and

---

[20] *City of London B.S. v Flegg* [1988] A.C. 54.
[21] *Caunce v Caunce* [1969] 1 W.L.R. 286; *Williams & Glyn's Bank v Boland* [1981] A.C. 487.
[22] *Williams & Glyn's Bank v Boland* [1981] A.C. 487.
[23] *Caunce v Caunce* [1969] 1 W.L.R. 286.
[24] *Kingsnorth Finance Co Ltd v Tizard* [1986] 1 W.L.R. 783.

inspections P ought reasonably to have made. These difficulties are considered more fully later.[25]

However, it must be stressed that they only arise where there is a sole legal owner other than a trust corporation. Where the purchaser has paid the purchase moneys either to at least two persons or to a trust corporation, the rights of all co-owners will be overreached whether or not they are in actual occupation of the land and whether or not their presence on the land is inconsistent with the trustees being the sole owners.[26] Consequently, if the house had instead been conveyed to H and a third party T, payment by P of the purchase moneys to H and T would overreach W's rights into the proceeds of sale even if she was completely unaware of the transaction or wholly opposed to it. Her rights would not bind P and she would have to give up possession of the house to him.

The modern system of unregistered conveyancing

1–024   In order to understand why the successive reforms of land law, and the system of land registration, developed as they did, it is necessary to have some understanding of the investigations of title necessary when transferring unregistered land.

Investigation of a vendor's title

1–025   A purchaser of land must investigate the title of the vendor in order to confirm that the vendor is able to convey it. Where the land in question is unregistered land, he does this by examining the documents under which the vendor holds the land, going back to a "good root of title" at least 15 years old. A good root of title is a document which deals with the whole legal and equitable interest in the land, describes the land adequately, and contains nothing to throw any doubt on the title. If the title consists of a series of conveyances on sale made 4, 14 and 30 years ago, the purchaser must go back to the 30-year-old conveyance. If he fails to do this (such as by accepting the 14-year-old conveyance as the root of title), he will be fixed with constructive notice of all that he would have discovered had he investigated the title for the full period.

Investigation of third party rights in the land

1–026   In addition to confirming that the vendor has power to convey the land, the purchaser must see that there are no burdens on the land such as tenancies, easements or mortgages that will affect him. For this purpose, he must consider any third party rights which are disclosed by his investigation of title, and also inspect the land and make due inquiries of any tenant or other person in occupation of it.[27] In addition, he must search two registers which despite the similarity of name are quite separate: the land charges register and the appropriate local land charges register.

Land charges: The existence of the Land Charges Register is intended to avoid many of the difficulties of the equitable doctrine of notice by making certain equitable rights in unregistered

---

[25] Below, paras 3–014 et seq.
[26] *City of London B.S. v Flegg* [1988] A.C. 54.
[27] *Hunt v Luck* [1902] 1 Ch. 428.

land readily discoverable by being registered therein. This system, begun in a very restricted form in 1839, was much extended in 1888, and further important extensions were made in 1925. The present statute is the Land Charges Act 1972, replacing the Land Charges Act 1925. If such a right is duly registered, all persons are deemed to have actual notice of it for all purposes.[28] If it is not registered, it will normally be void against a purchaser for value, even if he knows of it.[29] What is decisive is thus the indisputable state of the register and not the arguable state of the purchaser's mind. Equitable interests registrable in this way include equitable easements, mortgages and restrictive covenants. In addition, the system has been extended to certain legal interests, such as mortgages not protected by a deposit of the title deeds. Such interests do not, of course, depend on notice for their existence, but nevertheless they are made void against a purchaser for value if they are not registered. Land charges are registered against the names of the persons who created them, in a national computerised system.

The Land Charges Register, being a names register, sometimes creates very considerable difficulties for a purchaser obliged to search it. He will be bound by all the land charges registered against the name of anyone who has held the legal title to the land in question since 1925; registration remains valid indefinitely. He will know the names of all the estate owners back to the good root of title at least 15 years old with which the vendor has to provide him and so he can search against their names. But usually he will not know and cannot discover who were the estate owners prior to the root of title and so he cannot search against their names; yet he will be bound by land charges registered against those names. Since 1969, however, a person who is adversely affected by such a charge may obtain compensation out of public funds.[30]

Local land charges: The existence of the system of Local Land Charges Registers, one of which is maintained by each district council in England and Wales, each London borough, and the Common Council of the City of London, is intended to make charges of a local public nature over both registered and unregistered land equally discoverable by being registered therein. The present statute is the Local Land Charges Act 1975 (replacing provisions in the Land Charges Act 1925). Charges so registrable include prohibitions or restrictions on the use of land under planning law, and charges for the cost of making up a private road. Registration is against the address of the land and not the name of the landowner.

The system of registered conveyancing

Investigation of a vendor's title and of third party rights in the land

A purchaser of registered land is equally obliged to investigate the title of the vendor in order to confirm that the vendor is able to convey it and to ensure that there are no burdens on the land such as tenancies, easements or mortgages that will affect him. His obligation to inspect the land and make due inquiries of any tenant or other person in occupation of the land and to search the Local Land Charges Register is the same as that of the purchaser of unregistered land. But the obligations to examine the documents under which the vendor holds the land, going back to a "good root of title" at least 15 years old,

1–027

---

[28] See Judgments Act 1839; Land Charges Registration and Searches Act 1888; LPA 1925 s.198.
[29] LPA 1925 s.198.
[30] LPA 1969 s.25.

and to search the land charges register are, in the case of registered land, replaced by the obligation to examine the register of titles.

The rationale and history of the system

1–028   Although modern legislation has to some extent mitigated the defects of the ancient system of investigating title to unregistered land, in other respects it has aggravated them, particularly because of the extensions made to the system of registration of land charges in 1925. Further, the system of unregistered conveyancing has always involved much duplication of work; a purchaser has to investigate the title anew even though many previous purchasers have fully investigated it and found it satisfactory. Under the system of registration of title, there is an official investigation of title on first registration and thereafter the land can be transferred without any further investigation of title. The register also notes certain rights held for the benefit of the land, and contains entries that protect certain rights adverse to the land.

The first attempts to introduce a system of registration of title merely provided for the voluntary registration of titles.[31] However, in 1897 the registration of title on dealings with land in the County and City of London became compulsory.[32] Not until the Land Registration Act 1925 came into force did the compulsory registration of title on dealings with land become more extensive and the system was not greatly extended until after the Second World War. Since then, the system has been gradually extended throughout England and Wales, so that 80 per cent of land is now registered, and it is expected that given enough time the system will entirely replace unregistered conveyancing. This extension made it possible to end the limited and unsatisfactory system for the registration of deeds for land in Middlesex and Yorkshire that had been established early in the eighteenth century as a safeguard against the loss, destruction or suppression of deeds; and these registers were closed in, respectively, 1940 and 1976.

Registrable interests

1–029   At present two estates in land are capable of being registered: the fee simple absolute in possession, and a term of years absolute which has more than seven years to run. A legal rentcharge can also be registered. Any legal interests in land which are not registrable interests either fall within one of the classes of interests which override registration or have to be protected on the register of titles. On registration, the owner of the estate or interest in question becomes the "registered proprietor" of it. He then becomes the holder of the legal estate or interests subject only to any interests which override registration and any interests protected by entries on the register of titles, and free from all other interests. The register of title is maintained by the Land Registry and can be searched on-line by anyone. The register is divided into three parts.

    (i) The property register: this describes the property by reference to a filed plan, and notes certain rights held for the benefit of the property.

    (ii) The proprietorship register: this sets out the name of the registered proprietor. It

---

[31] Land Registry Act 1862; Land Transfer Act 1875.
[32] Land Transfer Act 1897.

also records any restrictions on his powers of disposition (such as that no disposition will be effective unless the purchase money is paid to at least two trustees or a trust corporation).

(iii) The charges register: this notes the existence of subsidiary registered titles, such as a lease of seven years or longer and of the type of mortgage used in registered conveyancing, the registered charge. It also contains notices protecting certain incumbrances on the title, such as other types of leases and mortgages, restrictive covenants and easements.

Interests which override registration

These are various classes of interests that will bind a purchaser even though they have not been protected by any entry on the register of titles. In general, they are rights which usually can easily be discovered by inspecting the land, making inquiries of occupiers and searching the local land charges register (as has been mentioned, the land charges register plays no part in registered conveyancing). Interests which override registration include: certain types of easements; leases which are not long enough to be registrable interests; and local land charges. The categories of overriding interests were reduced by the Land Registration Act 2002 and there is power further to reduce them.

1–030

Conclusiveness of registration

A further important difference between the two systems of conveyancing lies in the greater security of title given to the owner of registered land. If a vendor V forges deeds that show him to be the owner of unregistered land when in fact he has no title thereto, a conveyance by V to a purchaser P vests nothing in P; a person cannot transfer what is not his (*nemo dat quod non habet*). But the result is different if the land is registered and V forges a transfer of it in his favour or uses the forged deeds to become the first registered proprietor of the land. In that case if he later sells the registered land to P, on registration of the transfer P will become the estate owner, and both his title and the title of any third party to whom he sells it will be valid. This is because, subject to the possibility of the register being rectified, the registration of P as the registered proprietor is conclusive.

1–031

Rectification and indemnity

As has just been indicated, the court and the registrar have wide powers to rectify the register where there has been an error or omission, although these powers are considerably restricted if the registered proprietor is in possession, as P is likely to be in the example just considered.[33] On the other hand, there are corresponding provisions for compensation out of public funds if any person suffers loss by reason of any rectification of the register, or by reason of an error or omission in the register which is not rectified.[34] There are no similar provisions for compensation in the case of unregistered land.

1–032

---

[33] See the unreported *Haigh* case, discussed in *Ruoff & Roper: The Law and Practice of Registered Conveyancing* 6th edn (London: Sweet & Maxwell, 1991) (cited as "Ruoff & Roper"), para.2–08 (murderer dissolves victims in acid bath and obtains registered title to a victim's land by forgery).

[34] See below, paras 5–040 et seq.

The concurrent systems of conveyancing

1–033   In principle, the intention is that all land will ultimately become registered land. After successive extensions over nearly a century, the whole of England and Wales is now subject to the compulsory registration of title. This has been the case since 1990. But unregistered land vested in companies or other corporations or bodies, which of course may never die, may remain unsold for centuries and the obligation to register the title may never arise. A knowledge of both systems of law will thus be needed for a while yet.

HISTORICAL OUTLINE

1–034   The history of the law of property in land can be divided into six periods.

Formulation of principles

1–035   This was the early period during which the courts of common law formulated many of the fundamental rules of land law. A number of important statutes were passed during this period, which extended from the Norman Conquest to the end of the fourteenth century.

Growth of equity

1–036   This was the period from about 1400 to 1535, when the jurisdiction of the Chancellor to give relief in cases not covered by the common law rules was firmly established and developed.

The Statute of uses

1–037   This was the period from 1535 to the middle of the seventeenth century, when the great changes made by the Statute of Uses 1535 were being worked out.

Development of trusts and the rules against remoteness

1–038   This encompassed the end of the seventeenth century and the eighteenth century, when trusts, which had been considerably restricted by the Statute of Uses 1535, were once more enforced. The modern form of a strict settlement of land, by which land was "kept in the family" from one generation to another, was fully developed during this period, as were rules preventing interests vesting in persons at remote future dates.

Statutory reforms

1–039   This period consists of the nineteenth and twentieth centuries, when far-reaching reforms were made by Parliament. Many reforms were made during the nineteenth century, particularly between 1832 and 1845 and again between 1881 and 1890. Yet, important though these were, they could not rival the 1925 property legislation in complexity and comprehensiveness. The Law of Property Act 1922 laid the foundation for the Acts of 1925, but most of it, together with extensive amendments of the law made by the Law of Property (Amendment) Act 1924, was repealed and replaced before it came into force. The provisions of these two Acts and of much of the earlier reforms were consolidated and divided up into six Acts. These Acts and the unrepealed portions of the Act of 1922 all came into force on January 1, 1926.

The great reform of 1925

Summary

What is known as "the 1925 property legislation" thus consisted of: **1–040**

- the few unrepealed portions of the Law of Property Act 1922;
- the Settled Land Act 1925;
- the Trustee Act 1925;
- the Law of Property Act 1925;
- the Land Registration Act 1925;
- the Land Charges Act 1925; and
- the Administration of Estates Act 1925.

Construing the 1925 property legislation

The genesis of the 1925 property legislation is important when construing it. The Acts of   **1–041**
1925 are all consolidating Acts, and a consolidating Act is presumed to change the law no more than the language necessarily requires. However, the Acts of 1922 and 1924 are professedly amending Acts, so that the presumption is not that the Acts of 1925 have not changed the old law, but that they have not changed the changes in that law made by the Acts of 1922 and 1924. Accordingly, where the Acts of 1922 and 1924 have left the old law unchanged, the Acts of 1925 are presumed not to have changed the law.[35] But where the Acts of 1922 and 1924 have changed the old law, it is those provisions which, though repealed, must first be construed.[36]

Subsequent changes

The Land Charges Act 1925 has been replaced by the Land Charges Act 1972 and the Local   **1–042**
Land Charges Act 1975, and the Land Registration Act 1925 has been replaced by the Land Registration Act 2002, but it is a tribute to the draftsmen of the 1925 property legislation that, although amended from time to time, the rest remains in force.

Since 1925 a number of other statutes directed to specific reforms have appeared. These include:

- the Perpetuities and Accumulations Act 1964 (now itself repealed by the Perpetuities and Accumulations Act 2009;
- the Law of Property (Joint Tenants) Act 1964;
- the Matrimonial Homes Acts 1967;

---

[35] See, e.g. *Beswick v Beswick* [1968] A.C 58.
[36] *Re Turner's W.T.* [1937] Ch. 15; *Grey v Inland Revenue Commissioners* [1960] A.C. 1; *Lloyds Bank Ltd v Marcan* [1973] 1 W.L.R. 339 at 344 (affirmed [1973] 1 W.L.R. 1387).

- the Law of Property Act 1969;
- the Charging Orders Act 1979;
- the Limitation Act 1980;
- the Insolvency Act 1985;
- the Law of Property (Miscellaneous Provisions) Act 1989;
- the Landlord and Tenant (Covenants) Act 1995;
- the Family Law Act 1996; and
- the Trusts of Land and Appointment of Trustees Act 1996.

Social control and registration of title

1–043   This period overlaps the last. It dates back to the Increase of Rent and Mortgage Interest (Restrictions) Act 1920 which was the real beginning of security of tenure for residential tenants, and continued through successive Rent Acts to the modern-day Housing Acts 1985 and 1988. During this period Parliament enacted drastic provisions, sometimes varying with the political party in power, which curtailed and restricted the rights of landowners in the interests of tenants and the public.

Planning control, in its modern form, was introduced by the Town and Country Planning Act 1947 (now Town and Country Planning Act 1990).

During this period there has also been a great extension of the compulsory registration of title, especially since 1965, culminating, as has already been seen, in the whole of England and Wales becoming subject to compulsory registration in 1990.

MEANING OF "REAL PROPERTY"

Land

1–044   The natural division of physical property is into land (sometimes called "immovables") and other objects known as chattels or "movables". This simple distinction is inadequate. In the first place chattels may become attached to land so as to lose their character of chattels and become part of the land itself.[37] Secondly, a sophisticated legal system of property has to provide not simply for the ownership of physical property, but also for the ownership of a wide variety of interests in such physical property, and also for the ownership of interests in non-physical or intangible property such as shares in companies or copyright.[38] Thirdly, for historical reasons English law has developed a distinction between "real property" (or "realty") and personal property (or "personalty") which only approximately corresponds to that between land and other types of property.

History

1–045   In early law, property was deemed "real" if the courts would restore to a dispossessed owner the thing itself, the "res", and not merely give compensation for the loss.[39] Thus if

---

[37] For "fixtures", see below, para.2–037.
[38] For interests in land, see below, para.1–050.
[39] 3 H.E.L. 3, 4; and see T.C. Williams (1888) 4 L.Q.R. 394.

X forcibly evicted Y from land which was classified as "freehold" under the feudal system of landholding imposed on all land in England after the Norman Conquest in 1066,[40] Y could bring a "real" action whereby he could obtain an order from the court that X should return the land to him. But if X took Y's sword or glove from him, Y could bring only a personal action which gave X the choice of either returning the article or paying the value of it. Consequently, a distinction was made between real property, which could be specifically recovered, and personal property, which was not thus recoverable. The classification of property as realty or personalty might have been expected to be that of nature, between immovable and movable property, in other words between land and chattels. The early lawyers did indeed draw this distinction, but in accordance with what they regarded as interests in land. They regarded leasehold interests in land as falling outside the feudal system of landholding and, consequently, only freehold interests in land were classified as real property, leases being classified, along with chattels, as personal property.

Reasons for distinction

In early times there were no opportunities for investing in stocks and shares such as there are today. Money was therefore often employed in buying land and letting it out on lease on order to obtain an income from the capital, or in buying a lease for a lump sum which could be recovered out of the produce of the land. Further, the relationship between landlord and tenant was regarded as being mainly contractual, the tenant agreeing to pay rent and the landlord agreeing to allow the tenant to occupy the land.[41] These conceptions were far removed from the feudal system of landholding, which at least initially was based on a personal relationship between feudal lord and feudal tenant that was totally absent from the relationship between freehold landlord and leasehold tenant. Hence, leaseholds remained outside that system and so were classified as personalty[42]; indeed, for a long time they were hardly regarded as being rights in the land at all.

1–046

Subsequent developments

As a result of the classification of leaseholds as personalty, at first a dispossessed lease-holder had no right to recover his land from anyone except the lessor who had granted him the lease. Against third parties, he remained without remedy until late in the thirteenth century, when he was enabled to recover damages but not possession. This did not prejudice the investor lessee, who was basically only interested in his monetary investment. Not until 1468 was this rule seriously questioned. By that time the number of leasehold tenants had substantially increased as a result of changes made to the feudal system of landholding in 1290. The typical tenant had become a subsistence farmer who had insufficient capital to purchase a freehold; his need for continued possession of his land was imperative. But when subsequently in 1499 it was finally decided that leasehold tenants were entitled to recover the land itself from anyone,[43] leaseholds had become too firmly established as

1–047

---

[40] See below, Ch.2
[41] See 3 H.E.L. 213–216.
[42] 2 P. & M. 106.
[43] 2 Challis R.P. 63.

personalty for this change to make any difference to their status. This produces the curious result that, even today, if a testator dies leaving a will giving all his realty to R and all his personalty to P, the leaseholds will be included in the property passing to P, the reason lying in a rule which ceased to exist some 500 years ago.

Formal classification

1–048   Although leaseholds are still classified as personalty, they differ from most of the other kinds of personalty in that they fall under the heading of "land" or "immovables" as opposed to "pure personalty" or "movables" such as furniture or stocks and shares. They are accordingly classified as "chattels real", the first word indicating their personal nature (cattle were the most important chattels in early days, hence the name), the second showing their connection with land.[44] The three types of interests may therefore be classified thus:

Land	{	(i) Realty.
		(ii) Chattels real.[45]
Personalty	{	(iii) Pure personalty.

Although, strictly speaking, a book with a title that refers only to real property should exclude leaseholds, it has long been customary and convenient to include them, and that course is adopted here.

Declining importance of the distinction

1–049   Before 1926 the classification of leaseholds as personalty had a number of significant consequences. For example, if a person died intestate (i.e. without a will), all his realty passed to his heir, while his personalty was divided between certain of his relatives. Again, realty could be the subject-matter of a now virtually obsolete estate known as an estate in fee tail or entail, under which the land in question could descend only to the descendants of the original tenant in fee tail, while personalty could not. However, the property legislation of 1925 abolished most of the remaining differences between the law governing realty and that governing personalty.[46] Consequently, since 1925 realty and personalty both pass on intestacy to certain relatives of the deceased; and until the end of 1996, after which time entails could no longer be created, both kinds of property could be entailed. Thus the modern emphasis is on the distinction between land and other property, though the term "real property" still has some significance and is still widely used.

---

[44]   See *Ridout v Pain* (1747) 3 Atk. 486 at 492.
[45]   For other chattels real, of no importance today, see Co. Litt. 118b and *Megarry & Wade: The Law of Real Property* 5th edn (London: Sweet & Maxwell, 1984), p.16.
[46]   See Administration of Estates Act 1925 (AEA 1925) ss.45–47; LPA 1925 ss.60, 130.

TENURES AND ESTATES

Basic doctrines

There are two basic doctrines in the law of real property. These are known as: **1–050**

(i) the doctrine of tenure: all land is held of the Crown, either directly or indirectly, on one or other of the various tenures; and

(ii) the doctrine of estates: a subject cannot own land, but can merely own an estate in it, authorising him to hold it for some period of time.

In short, the tenure answers the question "How is the land held?"; the estate answers the question "For how long is it held?". The way in which these doctrines emerged is explained below.

All land is held of the Crown

The underlying basis of English land law is that all land in England and Wales is held from **1–051** the Crown. This was a direct consequence of the imposition after the Norman Conquest of England in 1066 of what is known as the feudal system, a system progressively extended to Wales thereafter. Obviously only a very small part of this land is in the actual occupation of the Crown; the rest is occupied by freehold and leasehold tenants who hold either directly or indirectly from the Crown.[47]

This principle is embodied in the Norman French maxim: *Nulle terre sans seigneur* (no land without a lord). There was never in England and Wales (as there was in other countries in which a feudal system was imposed) any land owned by a subject which was not held of some lord: in technical terms, there has never been any allodial land in England and Wales.[48] That is why a freehold is so-called: it is still held of the Crown. It is possible for a freehold to be determined, as when a foreign company which owns freehold land is dissolved. The freehold then escheats back to the Crown.

Lord and tenant

The basis of the imposition of the feudal system in 1066 was that the victorious Norman **1–052** Conqueror, William I, regarded, at least for this purpose, the whole of England as his by right of conquest. To reward his principal followers (and also to give them some incentive for staying in England and thereby enabling him to preserve his military force more or less intact), he granted each of them certain lands to be held by them from him as their over-lord. He also confirmed on this same basis the landholdings of the relatively few members of the Anglo-Saxon aristocratic classes who had survived the Conquest and had submitted to him.[49]

---

[47] 1 P. & M. 232, 233.
[48] Co. Litt. 1b.
[49] Williams R.P. 12.

Tenures

1–053   These lands were not granted in the way in which land is usually sold today, by way of an out-and-out transfer, but were to be held from the Crown in return for and subject to the performance of certain services. Thus, a large area of land in (say) Lancashire might be granted to X on terms that he did homage and swore fealty to the King (an entirely formal but nevertheless important condition) and that he provided the King with fifty armed horsemen to fight for the Crown for 40 days in each year; it was by means of grants of this type that the King preserved his military force. A larger area of land in (say) Yorkshire might be granted to Y on similar terms with the additional condition that he supported the King's train in his coronation. X and Y would, in practice, grant some of the land granted to them on to their own principal followers in return for being or providing the necessary number of horsemen, and would also grant other land to agricultural labourers in return for carrying out the necessary work on the land retained by them.

At the lower end of the feudal ladder, the basic agricultural unit was a manor, held by the lord of the manor, usually a Norman, from his immediate feudal lord in return for providing (say) five horseman. Smallholdings of land on the manor would be granted by the lord to his own immediate servants and to agricultural labourers in return for the services which he himself needed. In days when land and its rents and profits constituted nearly the whole tangible wealth of the country,[50] it was more usual to secure the performance of services by the grant of land in return for those services than it was to secure them by payment; the whole social organisation was based on landholding in return for services.[51]

Within this system, those who held directly of the King (such as X and Y in the example above) were known as "tenants in capite" or "tenants in chief". Those who in fact occupied the land, whether tenants in chief or agricultural labourers, were called "tenants in demesne", whereas those persons (if any) who occupied the rungs on the feudal ladder between the King and the tenant in demesne were called "mesne lords" or "mesnes".[52] Each feudal lord, from the King down to the lord of the smallest manor, had an obligation to hold a court for his feudal tenants, which was the forum for disputes between them over their respective landholdings. It was from the court of this type that the King held for his tenants in chief that a centralised system of justice and the first royal law courts (the courts which later became known as the courts of common law) subsequently began to emerge about a hundred years after the Conquest.

Services

1–054   In the decades following the Conquest the services mentioned in the example above became standardised to a considerable extent. In descending order of importance, there was one set of services known as grand sergeanty, which included the performance of some honourable service for the King in person; there was another set of services known as knight service which included the provision of armed horsemen for battle; and there

---

[50] Challis R.P. 1.
[51] Williams R.P. 10.
[52] Pronounced "demain" (domain) and "mean".

was a set of services known as socage,[53] which included performing agricultural services of a fixed type and duration. Each set of services was known as a tenure, for it showed how the land was held (*tenere*, to hold). All of those who held by grand sergeanty and most of those who held by knight service were Normans rather than Anglo-Saxon. The basic tenure for the non-military classes of both nationalities was therefore socage, one form of which (common socage) constituted a residuary category applicable in the absence of proof to the contrary. All these tenures, together with the tenures by which land was held by ecclesiastical corporations, were eventually classified as "free tenures", which is the origin of the modern expression "freehold".

Once the royal law courts had evolved about a hundred years after the Conquest, tenants with free tenures were encouraged by the Crown to take disputes over their landholdings to the royal courts. As a result, the courts held by their feudal lords for this purpose were progressively undermined and virtually disappeared. However, for long they retained exclusive jurisdiction over some other forms of tenure, with sets of services which included the obligation simply to carry out agricultural work for a feudal lord without restriction of type or time. These tenures were originally held by common serfs, and the most common form at that time was known as "villeinage"; in contrast with the tenures already discussed, they were classified as "unfree tenures". In the absence of any protection by the royal courts, the tenant was protected only by the custom of the manor in question as laid down in that manor's feudal court. It gradually came to be established that land held on an unfree tenure could be transferred only by a surrender and admittance made in the lord's court. The transaction was recorded on the court rolls and the transferee was given a copy of the entry to prove his title; he thus held "by copy of the court roll", and the tenure became known as "copyhold".

Estates

A further essential variant was obviously the length of time for which the land in question was actually held. The grants made by William the Conqueror were in principle only for the tenant's lifetime, although he and his successors usually in practice had little option other than to renew the grant to the tenant's heir after his death. Such a grant of land for life (for as long as the tenant lives) has always been possible and still is. It subsequently also became accepted that land could be granted in fee tail (for as long as the tenant or any of his descendants lives), something which remained possible until 1996, or in fee simple (for as long as the tenant or any of his heirs, whether descendants or not, lives). This last form of grant is now overwhelmingly predominant.

1–055

Each of these possible lengths of tenancy was known as an estate, a word derived from status.[54] Thus the Crown might grant land to A for an estate in fee simple and A might in turn grant that land to B for the latter to hold for his lifetime. But the Crown remained entitled to that land as feudal overlord; A was both tenant in chief of the Crown and B's mesne lord, while B was tenant in demesne. Both A and B owned estates in land, yet neither owned any of the land itself: each continued to hold it from the Crown. Indeed, until the Statute of Quia Emptores 1290, a feudal tenant had no right to grant land in the modern sense,

---

[53] From "soc" meaning either "plough-share" or, more probably, "seek", for the tenant must seek his lord's "soke" or court.

[54] 2 H.E.L. 351, 352.

by out-and-out transfer. All he could do as of right was to turn himself into a feudal lord. However, that statute, which is still in force, prevented a feudal tenant from granting his land to a tenant to hold from him ("sub-infeudation"). Instead, he had to transfer his whole interest to someone who would replace him in the existing feudal tenancy of the land. The Statute enabled him to do this as of right and so drop out of the feudal ladder. As a result, although all the land in England and Wales is still held from the Crown, ownership of the largest estate in land, the fee simple, has come more and more to resemble ownership of the land itself. Even today, however, it is technically true to say that a subject can own only an estate, not the land itself.

For the sake of completeness, it should be mentioned that, in both popular speech and legal parlance, the word "estate" is often used in other senses. Thus it may describe an area of land ("the Blank Estate is for sale") or assets generally ("the testator left a net estate of £50,000"). The context will usually leave little doubt about which sense is intended.

EFFECTS OF THE DOCTRINES OF TENURE AND ESTATES

1–056   This doctrine of estates, coupled with the permanence of land as opposed to mere destructible chattels, is a further reason why the law relating to land is so much more complex than the law governing chattels. At common law, it can in general be said that only two distinct legal rights can exist at the same time in chattels, namely possession and ownership. If A lends his watch to B, the ownership of the watch remains vested in A, while B has possession of it. But in the case of land, a large number of legal rights could and still can exist at the same time. Thus the position of Greenacre in 1920 might have been that A was entitled to the land for life, B to a life estate in remainder (i.e. after A's death), and C to the fee simple in remainder. At the same time, D might own a lease for 99 years, subject to a sub-lease in favour of E for 21 years, and the land might be subject to a mortgage in favour of F, a rentcharge in favour of G, easements such as rights of way in favour of H, J and K, and so on, almost *ad infinitum*. Before 1926, all these estates, and interests could exist as legal rights and most, but not all, can exist as legal rights today.

It may thus be said that in the case of pure personalty, the unit of ownership is the chattel or other thing itself; either it is owned by one person (or several persons jointly or in common with each other), or it is not owned at all. In the case of land, however, the unit of ownership is not the land itself (which is necessarily held from the Crown) but the estates and interests which have been artificially created in the land. In popular speech, one may refer to X's ownership of Greenacre, but technically one should speak of X owning a lease of Greenacre, or holding Greenacre in fee simple. This conception of the subject-matter of ownership being an abstract estate rather than the corporeal land was a remarkable and distinctive achievement of early English legal thought; it contributed greatly both to the triumphant flexibility of the English system and to its undoubted complexity.

The modern significance of tenure and estates

1–057   The modern significance of the doctrine of tenure, which is now greatly attenuated, will be briefly described here. The modern significance of the doctrine of estates, which is still substantial, is considered in much greater detail in the next chapter.

Free feudal tenures

Today, only one free feudal tenure survives, the original residuary category of common socage. With the benefit of hindsight, the process of reducing the number of tenures may be seen as beginning with the Statute Quia Emptores 1290, still in force today, which prohibited the creation of any new tenures by anyone except the Crown. The first tenures actually to be abolished, by the Tenures Abolition Act 1660, were grand sergeanty and knight service; they therefore became common socage, a fate which the 1925 property legislation, by means of the Law of Property Act 1922, also imposed on all the other free tenures and all the regional variations of common socage. The process of attrition of tenures also brought about the disappearance of all intermediate tenures, and so the courts will now readily act on the presumption that all land held by free tenure (now universally described as "freehold land") is held directly of the Crown.[55]

1–058

Unfree feudal tenures

Prior to the 1925 property legislation, provision had already been made by a series of statutes during the nineteenth century for the enfranchisement of the only surviving unfree feudal tenures, copyholds, by converting them into land held by common socage. But the various copyhold tenures themselves remained substantially unaltered until 1926 when the Law of Property Act 1922[56] converted all remaining copyhold land into land of freehold tenure. However, while virtually all the incidental rights conferred on the parties to free tenures had become irrelevant centuries before the 1925 property legislation and they could therefore simply be abolished,[57] some of the incidental rights conferred on the parties to unfree tenures remained important and effective in 1925 and could not be abolished without causing injustice, particularly to feudal lords. Some were abolished forthwith subject to the payment of compensation.[58] Others were preserved for 10 years. But a few will continue indefinitely unless and until they are abolished by written agreement between lord and tenant; they should therefore be listed here. They are:

1–059

(i) any rights of the lord or tenant to mines and minerals;

(ii) any rights of the lord in respect of fairs, markets and sporting;

(iii) any tenant's rights of common (such as to pasture beasts on the waste land of the manor); and,

(iv) any liability of lord or tenant for the upkeep of dykes, ditches, sea walls, bridges and the like.

---

[55] See, e.g. *Re Lowe's W.T.* [1973] 1 W.L.R. 882.

[56] s.128 Sch.12 para.1.

[57] A survival is escheat where the trustee in bankruptcy of a landowner disclaims, or a corporation holding land is dissolved.

[58] LPA 1922 Sch.12 para.1; Sch.13 Pt II, as amended.

Present freehold tenures

1–060   The developments outlined above have ensured that only one feudal tenure is left today, namely common socage, now universally described as freehold tenure; little or nothing now remains of the former rights and obligations between feudal lord and tenant.

It is perhaps arguable that the status of commonhold, introduced by the Commonhold and Leasehold Reform Act 2002, is a new form of freehold tenure, given that it is only able to be created in respect of registered land held for an estate in fee simple and subjects the freehold to a complex statutory regime. However, this innovation has not been a success, only a very few commonholds exist at present, and thus it is unnecessary to consider in any detail.

Present leasehold tenures

1–061   In contrast with feudal freehold tenures, leasehold land has greatly increased in importance,[59] with rights and obligations between landlord and tenant that are always important and sometimes complex and extensive. Although leaseholds have always stood outside the feudal system of tenures, they have long been the only important estate in which tenure is significant.

---

[59] See below, para.2–007 and Ch.11.

Chapter 2

ESTATES AND FIXTURES

CHAPTER SUMMARY

The nature of an estate has already been discussed[1]; it is essentially an interest in land of defined duration. It is now necessary to consider the different kinds of estate. In doing this, much of the discussion will be in the past tense, for as will be seen[2] some of the estates can no longer exist as such, although some, but not all, of the corresponding rights can still exist as interests (instead of estates) in land. The structure of modern land law is set out in Ch.4 and this chapter should be regarded as an introduction which explains key concepts and sets them in their historical background. This Chapter also discusses the concept of fixtures, namely things which are not land but which may become part of the land, such as a building.

PART 1   CLASSIFICATION

Estates were divided into two classes: 2–001

    (i) estates of freehold; and
    (ii) estates less than freehold.[3]

It should be noted that "freehold" here is used here as shorthand for a fee simple estate in land of freehold tenure. The principal estate less than freehold is the leasehold. It is also necessary to consider the concept of "seisin" which was formerly an important distinction between the two classes of estate.

---

[1] Above, paras 1–055 et seq.
[2] Below, para.2–002.
[3] 1 Preston, Estates, 22.

ESTATES OF FREEHOLD

The three estates of freehold

2–002 The three estates of freehold were:

(i) a fee simple;
(ii) a fee tail; and
(iii) a life estate.[4]

In modern land law, the fee simple is the usual freehold estate which is encountered, and a practising lawyer using the word "freehold" almost invariably means a fee simple absolute.[5] But that was not always so. The basic feudal estate was the life estate. The grants made by William the Conqueror were in principle only for the tenant's lifetime, although he and his successors usually in practice had little option other than to renew the grant to the tenant's heir after his death. It has always remained possible to create life estates and life interests are not uncommon even today. However, the basic feudal estate became heritable in the course of the twelfth century and became alienable as a result of the Statute Quia Emptores 1290; only thereafter is it really appropriate to describe it as a fee simple. The fee tail had in the meantime been introduced by statute in 1285[6]; it was abolished prospectively by statute with effect from the end of 1996,[7] although a very few existing fees tail nevertheless continue. Before considering the estates in any detail a brief account of each must be given.

Fee simple

2–003 Originally a fee simple was an estate which endured for as long as the original tenant or any of his heirs survived. "Heirs" comprised any blood relations, although originally ancestors were excluded; not until the Inheritance Act 1833 could a person be the heir of one of his descendants. Thus when the basic feudal estate first became heritable, it would terminate if the original tenant died without leaving any descendants or collateral blood relations (such as brothers or cousins), even if before his death the land had been conveyed to another tenant who was still alive, something which at that stage required the permission of the feudal lord. But by 1306, it was settled that where a tenant in fee simple alienated the land, which by then[8] did not require the permission of anyone,[9] the fee simple would continue as long as there were heirs of the new tenant and so on, irrespective of any failure of the original tenant's heirs.[10] Thenceforward a fee simple was virtually eternal.[11]

---

4 Co. Litt. 43b.
5 The characteristics of the fee simple, and the other estates, are considered below.
6 Statute De Donis Conditionalibus 1285.
7 Trusts Of Land and Appointment of Trustees Act 1996 (TLATA 1996).
8 As a result of the Statute Quia Emptores 1290.
9 Save in the case of tenants in chief who, because the Statute Quia Emptores 1290 did not bind the Crown, continued to require the permission of the King until 1326, when Edward III conceded the point.
10 Y.B. 33-35 Edw. I (R.S.) 362.
11 1 Preston, Estates, 429; but see T. Cyprian Williams (1930) 69 L.J. News. 369, 385; 70 L.J. News. 4, 20; (1931) 75 S.J. 843 at 847.

Fee tail

A fee tail was an estate which continued for as long as the original tenant or any of his descendants survived. Thus if the original tenant died leaving no relatives except a brother, a fee simple would continue, but a fee tail would come to an end. The terms "fee tail", "estate tail", "entail" and "entailed interest" are often used interchangeably, although "fee tail" was the correct expression for legal entails,[12] which could only be created prior to 1926, and "entailed interest" is usually reserved for equitable entails, which all existing fees tail necessarily are.[13]

2–004

Life estate

As its name indicates, a life estate lasted only for the length of the life or lives in question. The name "life estate" usually denoted that the measuring life was that of the life tenant or tenants, for example when the grant was to A for life or to A and B for their joint lives or to A and B until the death of the survivor. The alternative form of life estate, where the measuring life was that of some person other than the tenant or tenants, is known as an estate *pur autre vie* (pronounced "per *oh*ter vee", and meaning "for the life of another"), for example to A for so long as B lives.

2–005

A common feature of all estates of freehold was that the duration of the estate was fixed but uncertain.[14] Nobody could say when the death would occur of a man and his heirs, or a man and all his descendants, or a man alone. But the duration was not wholly indefinite; the estate was bound to determine if some pre-ordained event occurred. In the case of the fee simple and the fee tail, the word "fee" denoted (a) that the estate was an estate of inheritance, i.e. an estate which, on the death of the tenant, was capable of descending to his heir[15]; and (b) that the estate was one which might continue for ever.[16] A life estate, on the other hand, was not a fee. It was not an estate of inheritance and it could not continue for ever. On the death of the tenant, an ordinary life estate determined, and an estate *pur autre vie* did not descend to the tenant's heir, but until 1926 passed under the special rules of "occupancy"[17]; since then it has devolved under the tenant's will or intestacy. Life estates were sometimes called "mere freeholds" or "freeholds", as opposed to "freeholds of inheritance".

Each estate of freehold could exist in a number of varied forms which will be considered in due course.

Reversions and remainders

Before it became possible, as a result of the Statute Quia Emptores 1290, to alienate an estate in fee simple without the permission of the tenant's feudal lord, a tenant who granted a lesser estate, such as a life estate or estate in fee tail would have done so

2–006

---

[12] Litt. 13; 1 Preston, Estates, 420; Challis R.P. 60.
[13] See below, para.3–024.
[14] Williams R.P. 65.
[15] 1 Preston, Estates, 262, 419; Challis R.P. 218.
[16] 1 Preston, Estates, 419, 480.
[17] See *Megarry & Wade: The Law of Real Property* 5th edn (London: Sweet & Maxwell, 1984), pp.93–94.

by granting a feudal tenancy to the prospective life tenant or tenant in fee tail and so become the latter's feudal lord. This process, known as subinfeudation, was prohibited by the Statute. Thereafter, a tenant in fee simple who created a life estate or an estate in fee tail had to carve the lesser estate out of his own estate. The estate thus created was called a "particular" estate in fee simple, as it was a mere part (*particula*) of the estate in fee simple. The estate in fee simple remained vested in the tenant, and was known as a "reversion", since the land would revert into his possession by operation of law when the life estate or fee tail ended. If instead some further life estate or fee tail had been created by the tenant in fee simple, subject to the particular estate and so taking effect when it expired, that further estate was classified as a "remainder", since the land remained away from the tenant in fee simple instead of reverting to him. Estates in land could thus be said to be held either "in reversion" or "in remainder". There could be many estates in remainder, but only one in reversion. An estate is said to be held "in possession" when the tenant has an immediate right either to the possession and enjoyment of the land itself or to receive the rents and profits of it, as under a lease or tenancy of the law.

LEASEHOLD ESTATES

2–007   At first, the three estates of freehold were the sole estates recognised by law; the only other lawful right to the possession of land was known as a tenancy at will,[18] under which the tenant could be ejected at any time, and which therefore hardly ranked as an estate at all. During this period a tenancy for life was regarded as a freehold estate and not a leasehold estate. Leasehold estates, that is terms of years, grew up outside this system of freehold estates and were regarded as inferior; closer to a contract than an estate in real property. A lack of protection given to them by the courts, and early doubts whether terms for longer than 40 years were valid,[19] placed leaseholders in a position of inferiority from which recovery was slow. Although by the sixteenth century terms of years had become recognised as legal estates[20] and were fully protected, yet they ranked below the three estates of freehold.[21] Leaseholders were regarded as holding their land in the name of their landlords, the possession of the leasehold tenant being regarded as the possession of the landlord.[22]

Like the estates of freehold, leasehold estates may be held in possession, in reversion or in remainder. The grant of a lease of land that is already held on lease takes effect as a lease of the reversion, giving the right to possession of the land only when the prior lease ends. Such leases are called "reversionary leases". When instead a leaseholder grants a sub-lease of the land (which cannot last longer than his own lease), he is said to hold the "leasehold reversion" while the sub-lease still exists. It should also be noted that the right of the free-holder to his estate in fee simple while that estate is the subject-matter of a lease is also a reversion, usually described as a "freehold reversion" (this does not prevent the freehold estate from being an estate in possession in the meantime).

---

[18] Challis R.P. 63.
[19] See Co. Litt. 45b, 46a.
[20] Challis R.P. 64.
[21] Co. Litt. 43b; and see *Re Russell Road Purchase Moneys* (1871) L.R. 12 Eq. 78 at 84.
[22] 1 Preston, Estates, 205, 206.

Today, the various forms of leasehold estate are of the first importance. They are dealt with more fully later.[23] The principal categories are as follows.

Fixed term of certain duration

The tenant may hold the land for a fixed term of certain duration,[24] as under a lease for 99 years. The possibility of the term being extended or curtailed under some provision in the lease to this effect does not affect the basic concept, which is one of certainty of duration in the absence of steps being taken for extension or curtailment. A lease "for 99 years if X so long lives" also fell under this head; it was not an estate of freehold,[25] for although X might well die before the 99 years had run, the maximum duration of the lease was fixed. For all practical purposes, there was no chance of X outliving the 99 years, so that the duration of the lease would be the same as an estate granted "to X for life"; yet in law the former was less than freehold and the latter freehold. Partly as a result of the intervention of statute, such leases are comparatively rare today.[26]

2–008

Term of indefinite duration capable of being rendered certain (periodic tenancy)

A lease of land "to A from year to year", with no other provision as to its duration, will continue indefinitely unless either landlord or tenant takes some step to determine it. Such a lease is known as "a yearly periodic tenancy". But either party can give half a year's notice to determine it at the end of a year of the tenancy, and thus ensure its determination on a fixed date. This, coupled with the fact that originally the lease was for an uncertain term of uncertain duration, classifies the estate as less than freehold. The same applies to shorter periodic tenancies such as quarterly, monthly, and weekly periodic tenancies, save that in their case the notice to determine them is a full period rather than half a period.[27] It is not possible for a periodic tenancy to have a period of more than a year.

2–009

Uncertain period of uncertain duration

A tenancy at will arises where a landlord agrees that to a tenant occupying the land indefinitely until his right to do so is determined by either of them at any time: it is thus less than freehold. In the same way, a tenancy at sufferance, which arises where a tenant remains in occupation of the leased property after the end of a lease without the permission of his landlord, is less than freehold.[28] Indeed, such tenancies are arguably not estates at all.[29] Either may be converted into the appropriate periodic tenancy if the landlord accepts rent from the tenant.[30]

2–010

---

[23] Below, Ch.11.
[24] 1 Preston, Estates 203.
[25] 1 Cru.Dig. 47.
[26] See below, para.11–002.
[27] For these tenancies see below, para.11–027.
[28] For these tenancies see below, para.11–028.
[29] Consider *Wheeler v Mercer* [1957] A.C. 416 at 427, 428; *Megarry & Wade: The Law of Real Property*, p.792.
[30] Depending on the presumed intention of the parties; *Doe d. Cheny v Batten (1775) 1 Cowp. 243*; *Javad v Aqil* [1991] 1 W.L.R. 1007 (CA).

Position of leaseholds today

2–011   As has been seen, leaseholds were at first regarded as mere contractual rights to occupy land.[31] Despite their subsequent recognition as legal estates, they always remained outside the feudal system of landholding. Today, it is possible to regard leasehold as a tenure. One distinction which remains is that only in the case of leaseholds does there now arise a relationship of lord and tenant which has any practical importance. Anyone who leases land to someone else is, for the purposes of the letting, their "lord", which is why a lessor is referred to as the "landlord".

SEISIN

Meaning

2–012   One distinction between freeholders and owners of estates less than freehold which was formerly of considerable importance was that only a freehold could carry seisin with it. It is difficult to define seisin satisfactorily.[32] It has nothing to do with the word "seizing", with its implication of violence. To medieval lawyers it suggested the very opposite: peace and quiet. A man who was put in seisin of land was "set" there and continued to "sit" there.[33] Seisin thus denotes quiet possession of land, but quiet possession of a particular kind.

Freeholder

2–013   Although at first the term was applied to the possession of a leaseholder as well as that of a freeholder, during the fifteenth century it became confined to those who held an estate of freehold.[34] A leaseholder merely had possession: only a freeholder could be seised.[35] And since the possession of a leaseholder was regarded as the possession of the freeholder from whom he held, a freeholder remained seised even after he had granted a term of years and had given up physical possession of the land: receipt of the rent was evidence of seisin. Further, only land of freehold tenure carried seisin with it. A copyholder could not be seised, even if he held a fee simple.

From this it will be seen that a person was seised only if:

(i)   he held an estate of freehold;
(ii)   the land was land of freehold tenure; and
(iii) either he had taken physical possession of the land, or a leaseholder or copyholder held the land from him.

---

[31] See para.1–046.
[32] See, generally, Maitland's *Collected Papers*, Vol.1, pp.329, 358, 407.
[33] 2 P. & M. 30.
[34] Challis R.P. 99.
[35] Litt. 324; Co. Litt. 17a, 200b.

Definition

Although it seems impossible to frame a satisfactory definition of seisin, to call it "that   **2–014**
feudal possession of land which only the owner of a freehold estate in freehold land could
have" is to express the most important elements. A man might be seised of many plots of
land at the same time, whether or not he had granted any leases of them, for the requirement of physical possession did not mean that the person seised had to be in continuous
occupation: seisin was not lost merely because he went away on a visit. Once seisin was
acquired, it continued until another person acquired it.

Importance

The original importance of seisin was that: **2–015**

(i)   feudal services could be claimed only from the tenant seised of the land[36];
(ii) real actions (ones in which the land itself could be recovered and not merely
      damages) could be brought only against the tenant seised (such actions were little
      used after the seventeenth century and had all been abolished by 1854)[37];
(iii) curtesy and dower (the rights of a surviving spouse under the rules for intestacy
      before 1926) could be claimed only out of property of which the deceased had
      been seised[38]; and
(iv) conveyances of freehold land could until the sixteenth century be made only by a
      "feoffment[39] with livery of seisin" this was a solemn ceremony carried out by the
      parties entering on the land, and the feoffor, in the presence of witnesses, deliver-
      ing the seisin to the feoffee either by some symbolic act, such as handing him a
      twig or sod of earth, or by uttering some words such as "Enter into this land and
      God give you joy", and leaving him in possession of the land.

For these and other reasons, the common law would not recognise an abeyance of seisin.
Any transactions whereby one person lost seisin without transferring it to another was
void.

Seisin survived the 1925 property legislation only to the extent that pre-existing rights to
curtesy and dower continued (all such rights must long since have ended as a result of the
death of the surviving spouse in question) and in respect of a few surviving feudal services
of a ceremonial nature, most of which have to do with the coronation (there have only been
two coronations since 1925; it remains to be seen whether future monarchs claim these
services).

---

[36] Challis R.P. 100.
[37] *Freeman d. Vernon v West* (1763) 2 Wils. K.B. 165 at 166.
[38] See *Megarry & Wade: The Law of Real Property* 5th edn (London: Sweet & Maxwell, 1984),
      pp.543–546.
[39] Pronounced "feffment"; and similarly for "feoffor" and "feoffee".

PART 2   ESTATES OF FREEHOLD

2–016   The two main points to be considered concerning estates of freehold are:

(i) the words required to create each of the estates; and
(ii) the characteristics of each estate.

WORDS OF LIMITATION

2–017   "Words of limitation" is the phrase used to describe the words which limit (i.e. delimit, or define) the estate to be taken. In the past these words were crucial to ensure that a transferor transferred what was intended, e.g. a fee simple rather than a mere life interest. As will be seen the law now presumes an intention to pass a fee simple. In a conveyance "to A in fee simple", the words "in fee simple" are words of limitation; for they show what estate A is to have.

Words of limitation for a fee simple

Conveyances inter vivos to natural persons

2–018   The rule at common law was that a freehold estate of inheritance could be created in a conveyance inter vivos (i.e. a transfer of land between living persons) only by a phrase which included the word "heirs". The proper expression to employ was "and his heirs" following the grantee's name, for example "to A and his heirs".[40] "Heir" in the singular would not do, and the word "and" could not be replaced by "or"[41]: "to A or his heirs" gave A a mere life estate, and so did expressions not containing the word "heirs", such as "to A for ever", or "to A in fee simple".[42] Since 1881 the words "in fee simple" have also sufficed to pass the fee simple.[43] Since 1925, there has been no need for any words of limitation whatever, since the grantee takes "the fee simple or other the whole interest which the grantor had power to convey in such land, unless a contrary intention appears in the conveyance".[44] However, in practice, the words "in fee simple" are always inserted to make it clear that there is no contrary intention; were they not, the document in question could never constitute a valid root of title because it would not show what estate was being transferred.

Conveyances inter vivos to corporations

2–019   At common law, different rules applied which depended on whether the corporation was a corporation aggregate or a corporation sole. A corporation aggregate consists of two or more persons united together under some name to form a new legal person potentially

---

[40] 2 Preston, Estates, 1.
[41] Co. Litt. 8b; Challis R.P. 221, 222.
[42] Litt. 1.
[43] Conveyancing Act 1881 s.51.
[44] LPA 1925 s.60(1).

having perpetual existence, such as a Dean and Chapter,[45] or a limited company. No words of limitation whatever were needed in such a case; a conveyance to the corporation, for instance "to the Alpha Co Ltd", sufficed to pass the fee simple, for there was no reason to give it any other estate.[46] A corporation sole, on the other hand, comprises only one natural person. Thus the Queen, a bishop or a parson are all corporations sole in their official capacities. In such cases, a life estate to the individual holder of the office was a conceivable alternative to a fee simple, and so to create a fee simple a formula had to be used which indicated that the corporation rather than the individual should benefit.[47] This formula was "and his successors", for example "to the Vicar of Bray and his successors".[48] Failure to use this phrase resulted in a mere life estate passing to the individual.[49] The statutory reforms of 1881 and 1925 also apply to corporations sole.[50]

Gifts by will before 1838

Before 1838, no formal words of limitation were required in a will, but it was necessary for the will to show an intent to pass the fee simple.[51] Thus "to A for ever", "to A and his heir", or "to A to dispose at will and pleasure" all sufficed to pass the fee simple.[52] But it was for the devisee to show that a fee simple was intended to pass; a devise "to A" prima facie carried merely a life estate.[53] **2–020**

Gifts by will after 1837

By the Wills Act 1837[54] the fee simple or other the whole interest of which the testator has power to dispose passes in a gift by any will made or confirmed after 1837[55] unless a contrary intention is shown. This is the same rule as that subsequently adopted for conveyances inter vivos after 1925. **2–021**

Words of limitation for a fee tail

Since no further entails have been able to be created fees since the end of 1996, either by deed or by will,[56] no detailed discussion of this topic is necessary. The rules were comparable to those for fees simple, with the additional complication that it was possible to restrict the descendants of the original tenant in fee tail who could take to his or her descendants of **2–022**

---

[45] Of a cathedral.
[46] 2 Preston, Estates, 43–47.
[47] See *Ex p. Vicar of Castle Bytham* [1895] 1 Ch. 348 at 354.
[48] Co. Litt. 8b, 94b; and see *Bankes v Salisbury Diocesan Council of Education Incorporated* [1960] Ch. 631.
[49] A gift "to the Vicar of Bray and his heirs" perhaps gave a fee simple to the current vicar as an individual rather than as a body corporate. 2 Preston, Estates, 48; Co. Litt. 94b, n.(5).
[50] LPA 1925 s.60(2).
[51] 2 Preston, Estates, 68.
[52] See, generally, 6 Cru.Dig., Ch.XI.
[53] 2 Preston, Estates, 78.
[54] s.28.
[55] s.34.
[56] TLATA 1996 Sch.1 para.5.

a particular sex or by a particular spouse, known as "a tail male", a "tail female" and "a tail special" respectively; an unrestricted fee tail was known as "a tail general".

Words of limitation for a life estate

Conveyances inter vivos

2–023   In a conveyance before 1926, a life estate was created either by words showing an intention to create a life estate, such as "to A for life", or by the use of expressions insufficient to create a fee simple or fee tail, such as "to A" or "to A for ever" or "to A and his seed".[57] After 1925, a fee simple (or the whole of the interest that the grantor has power to convey, if it is less than a fee simple) passes unless a contrary intention is shown.[58] Thus to create a life estate, words showing an intention to do so must normally be used, such as "to A for life".

Wills

2–024   Before the Wills Act 1837, a gift of land passed only a life estate unless an intention to create a fee simple or fee tail was shown. That Act provided that the fee simple passes unless a contrary intention is shown,[59] so that in this case also, words showing an intent to pass only a life interest are now essential.

NATURE OF THE ESTATES OF FREEHOLD

The fee simple

2–025   The fee simple is the most ample estate which can exist in land. Although in theory it still falls short of absolute ownership, in practice it amounts to this, for nearly all traces of the old feudal burdens have disappeared. A fee simple normally exists in a defined area of land, and all that is above or below it including the airspace immediately above the land and the sub-soil and minerals below it. A freehold can, however, exist in the upper storey of a building, without the soil beneath it[60] and the boundary may be subject to change as where the sea gradually invades or retreats.[61] A tenant in fee simple has long been free to dispose of his estate in whatever way he thinks fit, inter vivos since 1290[62] and by will since 1540.[63]

A fee simple (and for that matter a fee tail or a life estate) may be absolute or modified; a modified fee simple is any fee simple except a fee simple absolute; types of fee: a fee simple absolute; a determinable fee; a fee simple on condition; and a base fee.

---

[57] *Re Irwin* [1904] 2 Ch. 752.
[58] Above, para.2–018.
[59] s.28.
[60] Often referred to as a "flying freehold". This sort of estate is unsatisfactory because of the difficulty in enforcing covenants, as to which see Ch.16. That is why flats are usually leasehold.
[61] See Co. Litt. 48b; below.
[62] Tenants in chief could not do so until 1326.
[63] Subject to certain restrictions removed in 1661 and now subject to possible claims under the Inheritance (Provision for Family and Dependants) Act 1975.

Fee simple absolute

This is the type normally encountered in practice. It is an estate which can potentially con- **2–026** tinue for ever. "Fee" denotes inheritability,[64] "simple" excludes fees tail, and "absolute" distinguishes modified fees.

Determinable fee

A determinable fee is a fee simple which will automatically determine on the occurrence **2–027** of some specified event which may never occur. If the event is bound to happen at some time, the estate created is not a determinable fee. Thus before 1926 a grant "to A and his heirs until B dies" gave A an estate *pur autre vie*, and a grant "to C and his heirs" for a fixed term of years gave C a mere tenancy for a term of years. A grant to X and his heirs until a specified lease was made, or to Y and his heirs "as long as such a tree stands", however, created determinable fees.[65] The estates of X and Y might continue for ever, but if the specified state of affairs came about, the fee determined and the land reverted to the original grantor. The grantor thus had a "possibility of reverter", i.e. a possibility of having an estate at a future time. If the occurrence of the determining event became impossible, the possibility of reverter was destroyed and the fee simple became absolute,[66] as where land was given "to A and his heirs until B marries" and B died a bachelor.

Determinable fees are rarely encountered in practice. Since 1925 only a fee simple absolute may exist as a legal estate.[67]

A fee simple upon condition

In making a grant of a fee simple, a clause may be added providing that the fee simple is not **2–028** to commence until some event occurs, or that it is to determine on the occurrence of some event. Conditions of the first type are conditions precedent[68]: a gift "to X in fee simple if he attains 21" is a gift of a fee simple with a condition precedent that X must attain 21 before he can take the land. A condition subsequent is one which operates to defeat an existing interest, for example a devise of land to X "on the condition that he never sells it out of the family".[69] Here the land passes to X, but it is liable to be forfeited if the condition is broken: in such circumstances, X is said to have a vested interest, liable to be divested.

The distinction between a determinable fee and a fee simple upon condition

The difference between a determinable fee and a fee simple defeasible by condition subse- **2–029** quent is not always easy to discern. The essential distinction is that the determining event in a determinable fee is included in the words marking out the limits of the estate, whereas a condition subsequent is a clause added to a limitation of a complete fee simple absolute

---

[64] See above, para.2–003.
[65] *Idle v Cook* (1705) 1 P.Wms. 70 at 78.
[66] Challis R.P. 83, 254.
[67] Below, para.4–012.
[68] Pronounced "preeseedent" with the accent on the second syllable.
[69] *Re Macleay* (1875) L.R. 20 Eq. 186.

which seeks to defeat it. Thus a devise to a school in fee simple "until it ceases to publish its accounts" would create a determinable fee, whereas a devise to the school in fee simple "on condition that the accounts are published annually" creates a fee simple defeasible by condition subsequent.[70] Words such as "while", "during", "as long as", "until" and so on are apt for the creation of a determinable fee, whereas words which form a separate clause of defeasance, such as "provided that", "on condition that", "but if", or "if it happen that", operate as a condition subsequent.[71]

It will be seen that the difference is primarily one of wording; the determining event may be worked into the limitation in such a way as to create either a determinable fee or a fee simple defeasible by condition subsequent, whichever the grantor wishes. The question is whether the words limit the utmost time of continuance of the estate, or whether they mark an event which, if it takes place in the course of that time, will defeat the estate: in the first case the words form a limitation, in the second a condition. In short, a limitation marks the bounds or compass of the estate, a condition defeats the estate before it attains its boundary.

There are some practical differences between the two forms of fee.

Determination: A determinable fee automatically determines when the specified event occurs, for the natural limits of its existence have been reached.[72] A fee simple upon condition merely gives the grantor (or whoever is entitled to his realty, if the grantor is dead) a right to enter and determine the estate when the event occurs; until entry is made, the fee simple continues.[73]

Since a right of forfeiture arises from a condition subsequent, the condition is void (and so the grantee takes a fee simple absolute) unless it can be seen from the outset distinctly and precisely what events will cause a forfeiture.[74] The concepts of continuing to reside in Canada[75] and of marrying a person "not of Jewish parentage and of the Jewish faith"[76] have been held to be uncertain, whilst the concepts of continuing in permanent residence in England[77] and of being or becoming a Roman Catholic have been held to be sufficiently certain.[78] This strict rule for conditions subsequent may be contrasted with the more relaxed rule for conditions precedent, where the question is one not of forfeiture but of entitlement. Thus under a gift to the eldest son of X who is "a member of the Church of England",[79] or an option to purchase given to "any friends of mine",[80] the impossibility of defining who is or is not a "member" or "friend" will not invalidate the gift for any person who on any possible meaning of the words is indisputably a "member" or "friend". The courts are reluctant to hold a provision void for uncertainty.[81]

---

[70] See *Re Da Costa* [1912] 1 Ch. 337.
[71] See 1 Sanders, Uses 156; Shep. 121.
[72] *Newis v Lark* (1571) 2 Plowd. 403.
[73] *Matthew Manning's Case* (1609) 8 Co.Rep. 94b at 95b.
[74] *Sifton v Sifton* [1938] A.C. 656.
[75] *Sifton v Sifton* [1938] A.C. 656.
[76] *Clayton v Ramsden* [1943] A.C. 320.
[77] *Re Gape* [1952] Ch. 743: "permanent residence" is a concept used in the doctrine of domicile in the conflict of laws.
[78] *Blathwayt v Baron Cawley* [1976] A.C. 397.
[79] *Re Allen* [1953] Ch. 810.
[80] *Re Barlow's W.T.* [1979] 1 W.L.R. 278.
[81] See *Brown v Gould* [1972] Ch. 53 at 56.

Where the object of a condition subsequent is to secure payment of money or the performance of covenants, then the court has a jurisdiction to provide relief from forfeiture which may be exercised provided that the breach is not wilful and the default is made good.[82]

Remoteness: There are some minor differences in the treatment of determinable and conditional fees for the purpose of the rule against remoteness of vesting but that is beyond the scope of this book.

Existence at law: A determinable fee cannot, it seems, exist as a legal estate after 1925; but a fee simple subject to a condition subsequent apparently can.[83]

Flexibility: A determinable fee is more flexible than a fee simple upon condition. There are certain restrictions upon the conditions on which a fee simple may be made liable to be defeated. A condition subsequent will be void, and the fee simple will consequently be absolute, if the condition infringes any of the following rules.

(i)   It must not take away the power of alienation. One of the incidents of ownership is the right to sell or otherwise dispose of the property. A condition against alienation is said to be repugnant to this right, and contrary to public policy, if it substantially takes away the tenant's power of alienation; such conditions are thus void.[84] For example, conditions prohibiting all alienation, or all alienation during the life of some person, or alienation to anyone except X, have all been held void.[85] But certain partial restraints have been held valid; thus where land was devised to A "on the condition that he never sells it out of the family", the condition was held valid on the grounds that it did not prohibit any form of alienation except sale, it did not prohibit sales to members of the family, and it bound only A and not subsequent owners of the land.[86] Moreover, a mere covenant not to alienate is not repugnant to the power of alienation; the covenantee may recover damages (which might be nominal) for breach of the covenant, but the alienation is valid and gives rise to no right of forfeiture.[87]

(ii) It must not be directed against a course of devolution prescribed by law. A condition rendering a fee simple liable to be defeated if the tenant dies intestate, becomes bankrupt, or has the estate seized in execution, is void, for on each of these events the law prescribes that a fee simple shall devolve in a particular way, and this course of devolution cannot be altered by condition.[88]

(iii) It must not be illegal, immoral or otherwise contrary to public policy. The condition under this head most frequently encountered is a condition in restraint of marriage. Partial restraints, prohibiting marriage with a Papist, or a Scotsman, or a person who had been a domestic servant, have been held good.[89] But total restraints (or restraints which are virtually total, such as against marrying a person

---

[82] *Shiloh Spinners Ltd v Harding* [1973] A.C. 691.
[83] Below, para.4–012.
[84] *Bradley v Peixoto* (1797) 3 Ves. 324.
[85] See *Re Cockerill* [1929] 2 Ch. 131.
[86] *Re Macleay* (1875) L.R. 20 Eq. 186; cf. *Re Brown* [1954] Ch. 39; and see (1954) 70 L.Q.R. 15.
[87] *Caldy Manor Estates Ltd v Farrell* [1974] 1 W.L.R. 1303.
[88] *Re Machu* (1882) 21 Ch.D. 838 (bankruptcy).
[89] *Jenner v Turner* (1880) 16 Ch.D. 188 (domestic servant).

who has not freehold property worth £500 per annum in 1795) are void unless the intent is not merely to restrain marriage but simply to provide for the tenant until marriage,[90] or unless the tenant has already been married once.[91]

A determinable fee, on the other hand, is not so strictly confined. A devise of freeholds on trust for X "until he shall assign charge or otherwise dispose of the same or some part thereof or become bankrupt . . . or do something whereby the said annual income or some part thereof would become payable to or vested in some other person" has been held to give X a determinable fee.[92] On any of the events occurring X's estate would determine; if he died before any of them occurred, the fee simple would become absolute, for it would then cease to be possible for any of them to occur. But although a fee may thus be made determinable on alienation or on bankruptcy or on similar events, a limitation would probably be void if it were contrary to public policy for the fee to be determinable on the stated event, such as if the event is the return to X of his wife who is separated from him.

Effect of condition or limitation becoming void or impossible: If a condition subsequent is void or becomes impossible, the donee takes a fee simple absolute, free from any condition[93]; but if a fee is made determinable upon an event contrary to law, the whole gift fails.[94]

Alienation of modified fees

2–030   At common law a right of entry for breach of condition and a possibility of reverter to a determinable fee were inheritable but not alienable inter vivos. A right of entry may be disposed of by will or inter vivos since 1925.[95] It has been held that a possibility of reverter may be disposed of by will under s.3 Wills Act 1987. It is possible that it may also be disposed of by will or inter vivos under s.4(2)(a) Law of Property Act 1925.[96]

Nature of modified fees

2–031   In general, the owner of a modified fee has the same rights over the land as the owner of a fee simple absolute: thus the common law refused to restrain him from committing acts of waste,[97] such as opening and working mines. Equity, on the other hand, would intervene to prevent the commission of equitable waste, i.e. acts of wanton destruction,[98] whereas the owner of a fee simple absolute is under no such restraint.

At common law the owner of a modified fee could not convey a fee simple absolute but

---

[90] See *Jones v Jones* (1876) 1 QBD 279.
[91] *Newton v Marsden* (1862) 2 J. & H. 356.
[92] *Re Leach* [1912] 2 Ch. 422.
[93] *Re Greenwood* [1903] 1 Ch. 749.
[94] Consider *Re Moore* (1888) 39 Ch.D. 116 (personalty).
[95] LPA 1925 s.4(2)(b).
[96] See *Megarry & Wade: The Law of Real Property* 8th edn (London: Sweet & Maxwell, 2012), p.70 fn.333.
[97] For waste, see below, para.13–007.
[98] *Re Hanbury's S.E.* [1913] 2 Ch. 357 at 365.

merely a fee liable to determination, for a man cannot convey more than he has. Statute has qualified this position.[99] Further, such a fee may become enlarged into a fee simple absolute, for example by the determining event becoming impossible[100]; and there are special rules for the enlargement of base fees.[101]

The fee tail

As explained at the start of this chapter a fee tail was an estate which continued for as long as the original tenant or any of his descendants survived. Since no further fees tail can now be created, and there are very few in existence it is not necessary to explain the rules by which they were created and how the entail could be barred (i.e. how it could be converted into a fee simple).

2–031A

The life estate

Until 1926 an interest in land for life was able to exist as a legal estate but since 1925 it has not been able to do so and has therefore to take effect as an equitable interest.[102] In general, the law which governed legal life estates prior to 1926 equally applies to the corresponding life interests after 1925.

2–032

Types of life estate

The two types of life estate were the ordinary estate for the life of the tenant and the estate *pur autre vie*.

2–033

Estate for the life of the tenant

The normal type of life estate was one for the life of the tenant. This arose either:

2–034

   (i) by express limitation, as by a grant "to A for life"[103]; or
  (ii) by operation of law, as in the case of a surviving spouse's rights on an intestacy before 1926 to curtesy and dower.[104]

Estate pur autre vie

An estate *pur autre vie* was an estate for the life of someone other than the tenant,[105] the person whose life measured the duration of the estate being called the *cestui que vie* (pronounced "setty ker vee"). An estate *pur autre vie* could arise either:

2–035

---

[99] See *Megarry & Wade: The Law of Real Property* (2012), para.3–069.
[100] Above, para.2–029.
[101] See *Megarry's Manual on the Law of Real Property* (2002), pp.46–47.
[102] Below, 4–012.
[103] Above, 2–023.
[104] It is unlikely that any such tenancies now exist.
[105] See, generally, *Doe d. Jeff v Robinson* (1828) 2 Man. & Ry. 249.

(i) by the owner of a life estate assigning it to another: *nemo dat quod non habet* (nobody can give what he does not have), so that the assignor could create no interest which would last for longer than his own life; or

(ii) by express grant, for example "to A for the life of X".

Both types of life estate were estates of freehold, but neither was a freehold of inheritance, for they were not capable of descending to the tenant's heir on his death. A life estate ceased automatically when the tenant died, and although an estate *pur autre vie* continued during the life of the *cestui que vie* despite the tenant's death, before 1926 it did not descend to the tenant's heir as such but passed on intestacy according to special rules of occupancy. Since 1925 it passes like other property under a will or intestacy.

Both types of life estate could be made determinable or subject to conditions subsequent[106] and were in general subject to similar rights and burdens.

Commonhold

2–036   In an attempt to address the perceived problems[107] associated with leasehold tenure of flats, the Commonhold and Leasehold Reform Act 2002 introduced a new form of tenure called commonhold.[108] A commonhold is a freehold estate (fee simple absolute) in registered land but made subject to a complex statutory regime found in Pt 1 of the 2002 Act. The innovation has been an almost total failure: very few commonholds have been created and it is unnecessary to consider them further.

FIXTURES

2–037   In law, the word "land" extends to a great deal more than "land" in everyday speech. The general rule is *quicquid plantatur solo, solo cedit* (whatever is attached to the soil becomes part of it). Thus if a building is erected on land and objects are attached to the building, the word "land" prima facie includes the soil, the building and the objects affixed to it; and the owner of the land becomes the owner of the building, even if it was built with bricks stolen by the builder.[109] The word "fixtures"has traditionally been the name used to denote anything that has become so attached to land as to form in law part of the land. A mortgage or devise of Greenacre or a contract to sell it thus passes rights to the fixtures on Greenacre to the mortgagee or devisee or purchaser. In contrast, such transactions pass no such rights to chattels on the land which have not become fixtures. However, the courts now seem to be moving towards acceptance of a new threefold classification, dividing those elements which will pass with the land (chattels of course will continue not to do so) into fixtures, and objects which have become part and parcel of the land.[110] Confining the expression "fixtures" to its

---

[106] *Brandon v Robinson* (1811) 18 Ves. 429; and see *Re Evans's Contract* [1920] 2 Ch. 469; see also above, para.2–002.

[107] Including poor management by the landlord, excessive service charges, and the fact that leases lose value as the unexpired term becomes shorter.

[108] Alternatives to leasehold exist in other common law countries, such as strata title in Australia.

[109] *Gough v Wood & Co* (1894) 10 T.L.R. 318.

[110] *Elitestone Ltd v Morris* [1997] 1 W.L.R. 687 at 690–692.

everyday meaning, and consequently no longer having to describe buildings as "fixtures", will not only have linguistic advantages but may well also assist in resolving borderline cases.[111]

Objects that will pass with the land

The elements

In deciding whether or not an object has become a fixture (or, in the new terminology, part and parcel of the land), there are two main elements to be considered, namely: **2–038**

  (i) the degree of annexation; and
  (ii) the purpose of annexation.

Degree of annexation

The degree of annexation used unquestionably to be the primary element but, because of the ever-increasing technical skills of removing objects which are attached to buildings, it may well now have given way to the purpose of annexation,[112] except possibly in relation to buildings themselves. The test is whether some physical connection with the land, or with a building on it, can be shown. If, on the other hand, the object in question merely rests on the ground by its own weight, it will be regarded as a chattel; the traditional example of the latter is a "dutch barn", which rests on timber laid on the ground.[113] A building which cannot be removed from land without destroying it will be regarded as part and parcel of the land, even if it rests on concrete pillars and is not itself attached to the ground.[114] A pre-fabricated building which can be removed in sections may remain a chattel and be no fixture,[115] whereas an article attached to land may be a fixture even if it is not very difficult to remove it.[116] Although now less decisive, the degree of annexation remains important as showing where the burden of proof lies[117]: if the article is securely fixed, the burden lies on those who contend that it is not a fixture.   **2–039**

Purpose of annexation

The purpose of the annexation is now the main factor; the modern tendency, save possibly in the case of buildings, is to regard the degree of annexation as being chiefly of importance as evidence of the purpose of annexation.[118] The more securely an object is affixed and the more damage that would be caused by its removal, the more likely it is that the object was intended to form a permanent part of the land.[119] It therefore follows that an   **2–040**

---

[111] See *S. Bridge* [1997] C.L.J. 498.
[112] *Berkley v Poulett* [1977] 1 E.G.L.R. 86 at 89; *Hamp v Bygrave* [1983] 1 E.G.L.R. 174 at 177; *TSB Bank Plc v Botham* (1996) 73 P. & C.R. D1 at D2.
[113] See *Wiltshear v Cottrell* (1853) 1 E. & B. 674.
[114] See *Elitestone Ltd v Morris* [1997] 1 W.L.R. 687.
[115] *Potton Developments Ltd v Thompson* [1998] N.P.C. 49.
[116] See *Buckland v Butterfield* (1820) 2 Brod. & B. 54; *Jordan v May* [1947] K.B. 427.
[117] *Holland v Hodgson* (1872) L.R. 7 C.P. 328 at 335.
[118] *Leigh v Taylor* [1902] A.C. 157 at 162. See also *Hynes v Vaughan* (1985) 50 P. & C.R. 444.
[119] *Spyer v Phillipson* [1931] 2 Ch. 183 at 209, 210.

object which is not affixed at all is unlikely to be held to be a fixture.[120] In determining the purpose of annexation, the question to be asked is: "Was the intention to effect a permanent improvement of the land or building as such; or was it merely to effect a temporary improvement or to enjoy the chattel as a chattel?"[121] In the first case, the chattel is a fixture, in the second it is not. Thus, a wall composed of blocks of stone, or statues forming part of a general architectural design,[122] or movable dog-grates substituted for fixed grates,[123] or tapestries and portraits in a room designed as an Elizabethan room, have all been held to be fixtures.[124] In each case, the evident intention was to effect a permanent improvement to the land. But tapestry attached by tacks to wooden strips fastened to the wall by two-inch nails,[125] panelling screwed into wooden plugs let into the wall, a collection of stuffed birds attached to movable wooden trays in glass cases attached to the walls of a bird gallery,[126] and pictures recessed into panelling[127] have all been held not to form part of the premises. Although in these cases there was a substantial degree of annexation, the only way in which the chattels could be properly enjoyed was to attach them to the house in some way, and thus it was easy to infer an intent to affix them for the better enjoyment of them as chattels and not for the permanent improvement of the building.[128] So, too, a drainpipe serving a house and laid in adjoining land has been held not to be a fixture; it was put there for the commodious occupation of the house and not for the benefit of the land in which it lay.[129] Similar articles may in individual cases remain chattels or become fixtures, depending on the circumstances, such as tip-up seats fastened to the floor of a cinema or theatre,[130] statues, and tapestries.[131]

The right to remove objects which would normally pass with the land

2–041   If, according to the above rules, an article is a chattel, it can be removed by the person bringing it on to the land or by his successors in title. If, on the other hand, it is a fixture or has become part and parcel of the land, then prima facie it cannot be removed from the land and must be left for the owner in fee simple. However, there are some important exceptions to this rule. Questions of the right to remove fixtures arise between the following parties.

---

[120] *H.E. Dibble Ltd v Moore* [1970] 2 Q.B. 181; *Berkley v Poulett* [1977] E.G.D. 754; *Deen v Andrews* (1985) 52 P. & C.R. 17. *Contrast Hamp v Bygrave* [1983] E.G.D. 1000, not citing *Berkley v Poulett* [1997] E.G.D. 754.

[121] See *Hellawell v Eastwood* (1851) 6 Exch. 295 at 312.

[122] *DiEyncourt v Gregory* (1866) L.R. 3 Eq. 382. See now *Berkley v Poulett* [1977] E.G.D. 754.

[123] *Monti v Barnes* [1901] 1 Q.B. 205.

[124] *Re Whaley* [1908] 1 Ch. 615.

[125] *Leigh v Taylor* [1902] A.C. 157.

[126] *Viscount Hill v Bullock* [1897] 2 Ch. 482.

[127] *Berkley v Poulett* [1977] E.G.D. 754.

[128] See *Young v Dalgety Plc* [1987] 1 E.G.L.R. 116 (carpeting and light fittings).

[129] *Simmons v Midford* [1969] 2 Ch. 415; contrast *Montague v Long* (1972) 24 P. & C.R. 240 (bridge over river).

[130] *Contrast Lyon Co v London City Midland Bank* [1903] 2 K.B. 135 with *Vaudeville Electric Cinema Ltd v Muriset* [1923] 2 Ch. 74.

[131] Compare *Re Whaley* [1908] 1 Ch. 615 with *Leigh v Taylor* [1902] A.C. 157, and *D'Eyncourt v Gregory* (1866) L.R. 3 Eq. 382 with *Berkley v Poulett* [1977] E.G.D. 754.

Limited right of removal

Landlord and tenant

Prima facie, all fixtures that are attached by the tenant or become part and parcel of the land during his tenancy are "landlord;s fixtures", i.e. they must be left for the landlord. But the exceptions which have arisen nearly swallow up the rule, and articles which can be removed under these exceptions are known as "tenant's fixtures". These can be removed while the tenancy continues, and even after it has ended if the tenant remains in possession as a tenant under some statutory or other right.[132] If the tenancy is brought to an end by a notice which does not allow enough time for the tenant to remove his "tenant's fixtures", he is allowed a reasonable time in which to do so.[133] When removing them, the tenant must make good any damage that has been caused to the property either on their removal or on their original installation.[134]

2–042

The following articles have been held capable of being removed by a tenant, though in some cases it is not clear whether the article is removable because it has never become anything other than a chattel or because, although a fixture or part and parcel of the land, it is nevertheless a "tenant's fixture".

Trade fixtures: "Trade fixtures" are articles attached by the tenant for the purpose of his trade or business; these have long been removable by him.[135] Vats, fixed steam engines and boilers, a shed for making varnish, shrubs planted by a market gardener and the fittings of a public house have all been held to come within the category of trade fixtures.[136] A tenant does not surrender his right of removal by surrendering his existing tenancy in return for the grant of a new tenancy.[137] Nor is the value of any tenant's fixtures taken into account for the purposes of a rent review.[138]

Ornamental and domestic fixtures: The exception of what are known as "ornamental and domestic fixtures" appears to be rather more limited than the previous one. It seems to extend only to chattels perfect in themselves which can be removed without substantial injury to the building.[139] An article which can be moved entire is more likely to fall within this exception than one which cannot.[140] Thus while a conservatory on brick foundations has been held not to be removable, looking glasses, ornamental chimney pieces, window blinds, stoves, grates and kitchen ranges have all been held to be removable during the tenancy.

Agricultural fixtures: At common law, buildings and other articles used for the purposes of agriculture were not regarded as being removable by an agricultural tenant,[141] for

---

[132] *New Zealand Government Property Corp v H.M. & S. Ltd* [1982] Q.B. 1145.
[133] *Smith v City Petroleum Co Ltd* [1940] 1 All E.R. 260. See *G. Kodilinye* [1987] Conv. 253.
[134] *Mancetter Developments Ltd v Garmanson Ltd* [1986] Q.B. 1212.
[135] *Poole's Case* (1703) 1 Salk. 368.
[136] See M. & W. 14-318.
[137] *New Zealand Government Property Corp v H.M. & S. Ltd* [1982] Q.B. 1145.
[138] See *Young v Dalgety Plc* [1987] 1 E.G.L.R. 116.
[139] *Martin v Roe* (1857) 7 E. & B. 237 at 244.
[140] *Grymes v Boweren* (1830) 6 Bing. 437.
[141] *Elwes v Maw* (1802) 3 East 38.

agriculture was regarded as a normal use of land and not as a trade. But by statute[142] a tenant of an agricultural holding who has erected buildings or attached fixtures to the land for this purpose may remove them before, or within two months after, the determination of the tenancy, provided that the following conditions are observed:

(i) one month's written notice is given to the landlord;
(ii) all rent due is paid and all the tenant's obligations under the tenancy are satisfied by him;
(iii) no avoidable damage is done in the removal, and any damage done is made good; and
(iv) the landlord is allowed to retain the articles in question if he pays a fair price for them.

Tenant for life and remainderman

2–043   If land is settled on A for life with remainder to B, on the death of A the question arises whether articles which A has attached to the land or which have become part and parcel of the land during his lifetime can be removed and treated as part of A's estate or whether they must be left for B. The position here is similar to that between landlord and tenant. Prima facie, all such articles must be left for B, with the common law exceptions of trade, ornamental and domestic fixtures[143]; but the statutory exception for agricultural fixtures does not apply.

No right of removal

Devisee and personal representative

2–044   If the land is given by will, the rule is that all articles which are either fixtures or have become part and parcel of the land pass under the devise; the testator's personal representatives are not entitled to remove them for the benefit of those otherwise entitled to the testator's estate, whether they are ornamental, trade or any other kind of fixture.[144]

Vendor and purchaser

2–045   Without exception, all articles which are either fixtures or have become part and parcel of the land at the time of a contract of sale must be left for the purchaser[145] unless the contract contains an express stipulation to the contrary (a more informal agreement would now be likely to be void for lack of formality[146]). The transfer or conveyance will be effective to pass all such articles to the purchaser without express mention.[147] It will not, however, be

---

[142] Agricultural Holdings Act 1986 (AHA 1986) s.10, replacing provisions in statutes from LTA 1851 s.3, onwards.
[143] See *Re Hulse* [1905] 1 Ch. 406 at 410.
[144] See *Re Lord Chesterfield's S.E.* [1911] 1 Ch. 237.
[145] *Colegrave v Dias Santos* (1823) 2 B. & C. 76; *Phillips v Lamdin* [1949] 2 K.B. 33.
[146] Law of Property (Miscellaneous Provisions) Act 1989 (LP(MP) A 1989) s.2.
[147] LPA 1925 s.62(1); H.E. *Dibble Ltd v Moore* [1970] 2 Q.B. 181.

effective to pass structures or erections which are still chattels; these will only pass as the result of an express stipulation to this effect.

Mortgagor and mortgagee

If land is mortgaged, all articles which are either fixtures or have become part and parcel of the land are included within the security without any need for special mention; the exceptions as between landlord and tenant do not apply.[148] The mortgagor is not even entitled to remove any articles which he has affixed to the land after the date of the mortgage which are fixtures or have become part and parcel of the land, although he can of course remove articles afffixed to the land which have not become fixtures.[149]

2–046

FURTHER READING

- W. Holdsworth, *A History of English Law*, 7th edn (1956)
- G. Battersby, *Informally created interests in land* in Bright, S. and Dewar, J. (eds) *Land Law: Themes and perspectives* (Oxford: OUP, 1998)

---

[148] *Monti v Barnes* [1901] 1 Q.B. 205; LPA 1925 s.62(1).
[149] *Reynolds v Ashby & Son* [1904] A.C. 466.

Chapter 3

LAW AND EQUITY

CHAPTER SUMMARY

An understanding of the difference between legal and equitable principles is fundamental to understanding estates and interests in land. Until 1873 separate courts administered a dual system of law and equity. The former by judges of the courts of common law and the latter by the Chancellor in the Court of Chancery. Since the fusion of the courts of law and equity real property has continued to recognise two types of rights and ownership: legal and equitable. This chapter examines the interplay between law and equity and how it applies to modern land law.

PART 1   GENERAL PRINCIPLES

The difference between Law and Equity, which has already been mentioned in brief outline,[1] must now be considered in greater detail.   **3–001**

THE HISTORICAL BASIS OF EQUITY

The common law courts

The existence of equity can best be explained historically. At the end of the thirteenth century the principal courts were: (a) many local courts, organised on a geographical basis for each shire and hundred and some boroughs, where justice was dispensed on a communal basis; (b) the courts held by each feudal lord for his tenants, which dealt principally with disputes concerning land; and (c) the Royal courts, which had emerged from the feudal court held by the King for his tenants in chief (also known as the King's Council), and which by this time had become known as the Courts of Common Law, consisting of the Court of King's Bench, the Court of Common Pleas and the Court of Exchequer. These Courts, which   **3–002**

---

[1]   Above, para.1–007.

had initially only dealt with matters of interest to the King, had by this time begun to take over a substantial part of the jurisdiction of the local courts and the jurisdiction of the feudal courts relating to freehold tenures. Until the fifteenth century, each of the Royal courts had had its own proper sphere, but in the course of that century their jurisdiction came to overlap so much that a claimant could usually choose to litigate in any of the three of them. By this time, they had attracted virtually all the litigation of the country. Although many of the local courts survived into the eighteenth century, most of them were by then in decline, or moribund, while the feudal courts remained in existence only for the purpose of dealing with certain matters relating to unfree tenures.

The writ system

3–003   In general, no action could be commenced in any of the common law courts until a writ had been issued by the Chancellor. The Chancellor, who was usually an ecclesiastic, was the head of the King's Secretarial Department. As keeper of the Great Seal with which writs were sealed, he was at the head of the English legal system.

In medieval days the writs issued by the Chancellor differed for each different kind of action. Not only did each different kind of action have its own writ, often it had its own special procedure.[2] Often causes of action which seemed very similar in principle had separate writs. Thus if a tenant of land died and a stranger took it before his heir could enter the land, the heir could bring an action against the stranger for possession of the land. If the heir were a son of the tenant the action had to be started by a writ of *mort d'ancestor*; if he was a grandson a writ of *aiel* had to be used, while if he was the great-grandson a writ of *besaiel* was required. No action could succeed unless the correct writ was chosen.

The selection of the correct writ was thus of great importance. Sometimes there were two or more writs appropriate to the claimant's proceedings. Where this was so, one writ usually had procedural advantages over the other or others. A writ which had already been settled was known as a writ *de cursu*, a writ "of course", obtainable as a matter of course simply on paying the prescribed fee. But sometimes there was no known writ to fit the case, and the claimant would have to ask for the invention of a new writ.

At first new writs were invented with comparative freedom. But it did not follow that the courts would accept each new writ as being valid. Even if a suitor had surmounted the first obstacle by obtaining a writ from the clerks in the Chancellor's office he might still fall at the second fence by failing to obtain the court's recognition of its validity. Nevertheless the Register of Writs rapidly increased in size during the latter half of the twelfth century and the first half of the thirteenth, when many new writs became writs *de cursu*, duly recognised by the courts.

This power to invent new writs was assailed by the barons. Recognising that the power to invent new remedies was a power to create new rights and duties, they procured the making of the Provisions of Oxford 1258, in which the Chancellor swore that he would seal no writ, except a writ *de cursu*, without the command of the King and his Council. Had this undertaking remained fully effective, it would have stifled the growth of the common law. But the Statute of Westminster II 1285 provided in the famous Chapter 24, *In Consimili Casu*, that the clerks in Chancery should have a limited power to invent new

---

[2]   Maitland, Forms of Action, 5.

writs.[3] If there already existed one writ and in a like case (*in consimili casu*), falling under like law and requiring like remedy, there was none, the clerks in the Chancellor's office were authorised to agree in making a writ, otherwise they were to refer the matter to the next Parliament. Consequently, a suitor whose grievance was not covered by a writ *de cursu*, or one in *consimili casu*, was still left without a remedy unless he could persuade Parliament to intervene.

Petitions to the King referred to the Chancellor

The result of this was that there were a number of cases where claimants could obtain no   **3–004** remedy from the courts. In addition to the problems associated with writs, there was the possibility that a rich and powerful adversary would bribe or intimidate the members of the jury, which by this time had replaced earlier more archaic methods of trial as the means of deciding disputed issues of fact. The only way to obtain relief was then to petition the King's Council; for the King, as the Fountain of Justice, was regarded as having a residue of judicial power left in his hands after the Courts of Common Law had emerged from his Council. Such petitions were initially heard by the King's Council itself, of which the Chancellor was an important member. As keeper of the King's Conscience (at this stage he was usually a bishop), he was particularly well fitted to deal with such petitions, and during the reigns of Edward II and III (1307–1377) many petitions were referred to him for decision. Thereafter petitions were often addressed to the Chancellor alone rather than to the King's Council. Although the Chancery became recognised as a court during the fourteenth and fifteenth centuries, the Chancellor continued to take decisions on those petitions either in the name of the King's Council or else with the advice of the judges and the Serjeants-at-law. Not until 1474, it seems, did the Chancellor make a decree on his own authority; but after that date such decrees became frequent.[4]

The Court of Chancery

In this way there gradually came into existence what became known as the Court of   **3–005** Chancery, in which the Chancellor (later Lord Chancellor), acting independently of the King's Council, sat as a judge administering a system of justice which came to be called equity. By the middle of the sixteenth century the typical Chancellor was a lawyer rather than a bishop and no non-lawyer was appointed to the office of Chancellor after the end of the seventeenth century.[5] Initially the rules of equity had varied according to the views of each Chancellor, but under Lord Ellesmere (1596–1617) they began to develop into a code of principles, and the work of Lord Nottingham (1673–1682) in systematising the rules earned him the title of the Father of equity. By the time Lord Eldon retired in 1827 the rules of equity had become as fixed as those of the common law.

Over the course of time various subsidiary officials were appointed to assist the Chancellor (including the Master of the Rolls and, later, Vice-Chancellors), a system of appeals grew up,

---

[3] It is controversial how far the statute was responsible for this development: see S.F.C. Milsom, *Historical Foundations of the Common Law* 2nd edn (Oxford: OUP, 1981), pp.284, 344, collecting the literature.

[4] 1 H.E.L. 400–404.

[5] Until the appointment of Chris Grayling LLP as Lord Chancellor in 2012.

and finally in 1875 the Chancery system was merged with the common law courts to form a single Supreme Court of Judicature.[6] In short, what was once a method of petitioning the King for justice in exceptional cases gradually became a way of starting an action before a regular court of justice. There were important differences between Chancery and the common law courts. The latter decided cases according to strict common law rules, and technicalities often played an important part. Chancery, on the other hand, mitigated the rigour of the common law, deciding cases in the light of what had seemed just and equitable to generations of Chancellors, and technical pleas were usually unsuccessful. Further, the common law courts were mainly concerned with enforcing the strict rights of the claimant regardless of his conduct, whereas Chancery was a court of conscience. In Chancery, the court might cleanse the conscience of the parties, compelling a defendant to disgorge any ill-gotten gains by acting in personam (against his person), such as by imprisoning him. Equally, a remedy might be withheld from a claimant who was guilty of unconscionable conduct. There were also important differences in the remedies available. In the courts of common law a claimant might recover his land or be awarded damages, but he could not obtain orders for the specific performance of contracts, injunctions (orders compelling the defendant to do or not do something on pain of imprisonment) or various other remedies that were available only in Chancery. The Court of Chancery might even grant an injunction to restrain a claimant who had succeeded in a court of common law from inequitably enforcing his judgment.[7] There was thus a marked difference between legal rights, the name for rights enforced by the courts of law, and equitable rights, enforced only by equity. This will be examined later.[8]

Reform of the writ system

3–006   The Common Law Procedure Act 1852 replaced the old writs by a single form of writ for all actions. Since 1852, anyone claiming to be entitled to some remedy, such as the recovery of possession of land of which he had been dispossessed, or the payment of money owed to him, has been able to issue proceedings claiming the appropriate relief. From 1856 until April 25, 1999, he did so by issuing a writ in a form which left it to him to state his claim in his own words.[9] The same writ and claim form could be filled up with a claim for the possession of land as for payment of a debt, or damages for trespass to land. Since April 26, 1999,[10] he does so instead by issuing a claim form, which similarly leaves it to him to state his claim in his own words.

Nevertheless, until the Judicature Acts 1873–1875 came into force:

(i) it was still necessary to observe the form of action based on the old writs which was appropriate to the case;

(ii) the common law courts and the court of Chancery, and the administration of law and equity, remained separate.

---

[6] Now the "Senior Courts" of England and Wales; not to be confused with the Supreme Court of the United Kingdom created on October 1, 2009.

[7] Earl of Oxford's Case (1615) 1 Rep.Ch. 1.

[8] Below, paras 3–009 et seq.

[9] As a result of the Common Law Procedure Act 1852.

[10] As a result of the Civil Procedure Act 1997 and the Civil Procedure Rules 1998.

Fusion of the courts of law and equity

The Supreme Court of Judicature Act 1873,[11] (with effect from 1875) fused the superior courts of law and equity into one Supreme Court of Judicature, divided into a High Court and Court of Appeal. The final court of appeal, the House of Lords, remained outside the Supreme Court of Judicature. When in 2009 the Supreme Court of the United Kingdom replaced the House of Lords as the United Kingdom's final court of appeal the Supreme Court of Judicature was renamed the Senior Courts of England and Wales. For convenience,[12] the High Court was divided into five Divisions, broadly corresponding to the old common law courts, each of which had certain matters assigned to it. In 1880 the Common Pleas Division and Exchequer Division were merged into the Queen's Bench Division, and in 1972 the Probate, Divorce and Admiralty Division was re-named the Family Division, with some adjustments of jurisdiction. There are now three Divisions of the High Court:

(i) the Chancery Division,
(ii) the Queen's Bench Division, and
(iii) the Family Division.

The Queen's Bench Division primarily hears common law cases, the Chancery Division primarily hears equity cases, and the Family Division primarily deals with matrimonial matters and children, although overlaps between the Queen's Bench Division and the Chancery Division have become increasingly common. It is important to note, however, that the three are only divisions of one court, the High Court, and not separate courts. Each division of the High Court has jurisdiction to enforce both legal and equitable rights and give both legal and discretionary equitable remedies. This means that it is no longer necessary to go to two separate courts to enforce legal and equitable rights or to obtain legal and equitable remedies. If a point of equity arises in a claim in the Queen's Bench Division, for example, the court can deal with it and it will not be fatal to a claim if it is started in the wrong division, for the case can be transferred to the proper division if necessary.

Law and equity nevertheless remain distinct: the systems have not been fused, although they are now both administered by the same court.[13] Apart from registered land,[14] a legal right is still enforceable against a purchaser without notice, while an equitable right is not. Equitable rights in property of all types are still enforceable only by equitable remedies, though there is now power to award damages in place of or in addition to an order for

3–007

---

[11] Which, by the Supreme Court of Judicature (Commencement) Act 1874 s.2, came into force on November 1, 1875. See now Senior Courts Act 1981, which was originally enacted as the Supreme Court Act 1981 but was renamed by the Constitutional Reform Act 2005 s.59; Sch.11 Pt 1 para.1(1). The Act was renamed because the Supreme Court replaced the House of Lords as the final court of appeal in the United Kingdom.

[12] And because none of the five heads of the common law courts could lawfully be made to retire, as there was no retirement age in those days and Judges cannot otherwise be removed except for misconduct.

[13] *Salt v Cooper* (1880) 16 Ch.D. 544 at 549.

[14] Where enforceability does not depend on whether rights are legal or equitable; see above, para.1–010.

specific performance or an injunction.[15] Indeed, the distinction between the two systems is emphasised by the provision that where there is any conflict between the rules of law and those of equity, the rules of equity shall prevail. Conflicts rarely occur: but there have been cases where this provision has been operative, and the most important will be considered later.[16] The Court of Chancery is a ghost, but like many other English legal ghosts, its influence can be seen on every side.

EQUITY FOLLOWS THE LAW

3–008   In equity, there could exist a whole range of equitable estates or interests corresponding to the legal estates and interests in land. A fee simple, a fee tail, a life estate, a mortgage, an easement (such as a right of light) and nearly every other interest might be either legal or equitable. Thus if A granted a lease to B to hold on trust for C, B had a legal lease and C an equitable lease. If the fee simple owner of Greenacre granted Y a lease for 99 years, Y's lease would be legal if it was granted by deed and equitable if merely in writing. If a person held an equitable interest it would usually be found either that his interest arose under a trust or else that it was created without employing the formalities necessary at law.

Certain interests could exist only in equity. If Greenacre was bound by a restrictive covenant, this could never cast a legal burden on anyone who subsequently acquired the land, although it might well bind him in equity. But apart from these cases, there was a strict parallel in law and in equity. In most cases the maxim "equity follows the law" applied: the Chancery moulded equitable estates and interests after the fashion of the common law estates and interests.[17] The courts tended to treat an interest in the land in the same way whether it was legal or equitable.[18] Thus equitable fees tail had to be barred in the same way as legal fees tail[19]; equitable interests passed on intestacy to the same persons as legal estates; an equitable tenant for life was in the same position as regards equitable waste as a legal tenant for life, and so on. But in certain matters, equity considered that there was good reason for refusing to follow the law, often to avoid hardship. Thus equity allowed someone who mortgaged his land to secure the repayment of a loan made to him to recover the property which he had mortgaged if he paid all that was due. This was so even though he no longer had any right under the common law so to do because the due date for repayment had already passed.

With regard to words of limitation, equity followed the law in part only. If the grantor used informal words showing a clear intention to create a fee simple, such as a limitation on trust for A absolutely,[20] these were as effective to create a fee simple in equity as the formal words required by the common law. However, if strict conveyancing language was employed, the limitation was construed in the same way as a legal limitation and in the absence of proper words of limitation as at common law only a life estate passed. This was so even if a general

---

[15] Senior Courts Act 1981 (formerly the Supreme Court Act 1981) (SCA 1981) s.50, replacing Chancery Amendment Act 1858 (Lord Cairns' Act) s.2.
[16] Below, paras 11–018 et seq.
[17] Maitland, equity, 108.
[18] See *Re Somerville and Turner's Contract* [1903] 2 Ch. 583 at 588.
[19] *Kirkham v Smith* (1749) Amb. 518.
[20] *Re Arden* [1935] Ch. 326.

intention to pass some other interest could be gathered from the instrument,[21] although in this case if the court was asked to rectify the instrument and not merely construe it, words of limitation necessary to carry out the grantor's intention would be inserted.[22]

It will thus be seen that in some important points equity refused to follow the law. Nevertheless, it has been said with some justice that the cases where the analogy fails are not numerous and that there is scarcely a rule of law or equity of a more ancient origin, or which admits of fewer exceptions, than the rule that "equity followeth the law".[23]

THE NATURE OF EQUITABLE RIGHTS

Distinction between legal and equitable rights

At first sight it might seem that as long as a person had a right which would be enforced by some court, it mattered little which court it was. But there is a great difference between legal and equitable rights. This is sometimes expressed by saying that legal rights are rights in rem whereas equitable rights are rights in personam. A legal interest in unregistered land is a right in the land itself, so that whoever acquires the land is bound by that right, whether or not he knew of it. Equity, on the other hand, would enforce equitable rights only against certain persons. For example, if land was conveyed to T in fee simple on trust for A in fee simple, there was at first no court which would compel T to carry out his trust. The Chancellor, however, began to intervene on behalf of A if T was guilty of a breach of trust, and so A's interest, being enforceable in equity but not at law, was merely equitable. It was a right in personam enforceable against T alone, so that if he died or conveyed the land to another, the trust would not be enforced against the new tenant.

3–009

Then successive extensions were made. In 1465 it was laid down that a trust would be enforced against anyone who took a conveyance of the land with notice of the trust.[24] In 1483 the Chancellor said that he would enforce a trust against the trustee's heir,[25] and in 1522 it was said that a trust would be enforced against anyone to whom the land had been given.[26] After it had been decided that other persons, such as the executors and creditors of the trustees, would be bound by the trust, it finally became established as one of the most important rules of equity that trusts and other equitable rights would be enforced against everyone except a bona fide purchaser of a legal estate for value without notice of these rights, or somebody claiming through such a person. Equitable rights thus gradually came to look less and less like mere rights in personam and more and more like rights in rem. Although it is possible still to regard them as rights in personam, it is perhaps best to treat them as hybrids, being neither entirely one nor entirely the other. They have never reached the status of rights in rem, yet the class of persons against whom they will be enforced is too large for them to be regarded as mere rights in personam.

The difference between legal and equitable rights as regards a purchaser without notice of

---

[21] *Re Bostock's Settlement* [1921] 2 Ch. 469.
[22] *Banks v Ripley* [1940] Ch. 719.
[23] Co. Litt. 290b, n. 1, xvi.
[24] Y.B. 5 Edw. 4, Mich., pl. 16.
[25] Y.B. 22 Edw. 4, Pasch., pl. 18.
[26] Y.B. 14 Hen. 8, Mich., pl. 5, fo. 7.

unregistered land may be illustrated as follows. In 1920 X bought the fee simple in Greenacre. In 1921 he granted a legal easement, a right of way, across one corner to L, and a similar equitable easement of way across the other corner to E.[27] As long as X still owned Greenacre, no substantial difference appeared between the rights of L and E: both were enforceable against X. But as soon as the land was conveyed to a third party, Y, the distinction between the rights of L and E became apparent. Even if Y purchased the land without notice of L's easement, it bound him, for it was a right in rem.[28] But if Y could prove that he was a bona fide purchaser for value of a legal estate without notice of E's easement, he took free from it.

This doctrine of purchaser without notice, which has historically been so fundamental to property law (the "polar star of equity"[29]) and is still significant except in relation to registered land,[30] must now be considered more fully.

The purchaser without notice

3–010   The plea of bona fide purchase of a legal estate for value without notice is an absolute, unqualified, unanswerable defence.[31] The onus of proof lies on the person setting it up.[32] It is a single plea, and cannot be regarded as a plea of a purchase for value, to be met by a reply of notice.[33] The principal points are as follows.

Bona fide

3–011   The purchaser must act in good faith. Although this is a separate requirement from the absence of notice,[34] there is no clear example of it doing more than emphasising the requisite innocence of notice.

Purchaser for value

3–012   The words "for value" are included to show that value must have been given, because "purchaser" in its technical sense does not necessarily imply this. A "purchaser" is a person who acquires property by act of parties, as under a gift inter vivos or by will, and not by mere operation of law, as by descent on intestacy. "Value" includes money, money's worth (for example other land, or stocks and shares) and marriage (acquiring the land in consideration of entering into a particular marriage).[35] The value need not be full value,[36] but it must all have been actually paid or given before the purchaser receives

---

[27] Dates before 1926 have been used because an equitable easement of way created after 1925 over unregistered land requires registration as a land charge.

[28] See e.g. *Wyld v Silver* [1963] Ch. 243 (purchaser bound by undiscovered legal rights of others to hold an annual fair or wake on the land even though none had been held for over 80 years).

[29] *Stanhope v Earl Verney* (1761) 2 Eden 81 at 85, per Lord Henley L.C.

[30] Remembering that leases of 7 years or less remain unregistrable even if granted out of a registered title.

[31] *Pilcher v Rawlins* (1872) 7 Ch.App. 259 at 269.

[32] *Barclays Bank v Boulter* [1998] 1 W.L.R. 1 (HL).

[33] *Wilkes v Spooner* [1911] 2 K.B. 473 at 486.

[34] *Midland Bank Trust Co Ltd v Green* [1981] A.C. 513 at 528.

[35] *Wormald v Maitland* (1866) 35 L.J.Ch. 69 at 73.

[36] *Bassett v Nosworthy* (1673) Rep.t. Finch 102; *Midland Bank Trust Co Ltd v Green* [1981] A.C. 513.

notice of the equity.[37] "Money" or "money's worth" usually consists of some present consideration in the sense used in the law of contract, but it also includes the satisfaction of an existing debt.[38] "Marriage", however, extends only to a future marriage: an ante-nuptial agreement (i.e. a promise made in consideration of future marriage) is deemed to have been made for value, but a promise made in respect of a past marriage (a post-nuptial agreement) is not. When an ante-nuptial marriage settlement is made, valuable consideration is deemed to have been given both by the spouse and by the unborn issue of the marriage.[39] "Good consideration" (the natural love and affection which a person has for his near relatives, usually his children) formerly also amounted to value in certain circumstances but now no longer suffices; although it is sometimes still significant for other purposes. "Purchaser" is not confined to a person who acquires a fee simple; it includes, for example, mortgagees and lessees, who are purchasers pro tanto (to the extent of their interests).[40]

Of a legal estate

The purchaser must normally show that he has acquired some legal estate in the land and not merely an equitable interest.[41] If the purchaser acquires a mere equitable interest, that interest is necessarily later in time than any pre-existing equitable interests, and as between competing equitable interests the first in time normally prevails. Where part of the equitable interest is already vested in the owner of the pre-existing equitable interest, the subsequent purchaser can take only what remains.[42]   **3–013**

There are three qualifications to this rule.

Better right to legal estate: A purchaser without notice who acquires only an equitable interest will nevertheless take free from pre-existing equitable interests if his purchase gives him the better right to a legal estate. Thus if a legal estate is conveyed not to the purchaser but to a trustee on trust for him and the trustee is also without notice, the purchaser takes free from pre-existing equitable interests.[43]

Subsequent acquisition of legal estate: A purchaser without notice who at the time of his purchase fails to obtain either a legal estate or the better right to one will nevertheless prevail over a pre-existing equitable interest if he subsequently acquires a legal estate, even if by then he has notice of that equitable interest. As between himself and the owner of the prior equitable interest, there is equal equity, and the legal estate will prevail.[44] But if the purchaser knowingly acquires the legal estate in breach of trust, he will not take free from the interests of the beneficiaries under that trust.[45]

---

[37] *Tourville v Naish* (1734) 3 P.Wms. 307.
[38] See *Thorndike v Hunt* (1859) 3 De G. & J. 563.
[39] *Macdonald v Scott* [1893] A.C. 642 at 650.
[40] See *Goodright d Humphreys v Moses* (1774) 2 Wm.Bl. 1019.
[41] See *Pilcher v Rawlins* (1872) 7 Ch.App 259 at 268, 269.
[42] *Phillips v Phillips* (1862) 4 De G.F. & J. 208 at 216; *Cave v Cave* (1880) 15 Ch.D. 639.
[43] See *Assaf v Fuwa* [1955] A.C. 215.
[44] *Bailey v Barnes* [1894] 1 Ch. 25; and see below.
[45] *Harpham v Shacklock* (1881) 19 Ch.D. 207; *McCarthy & Stone Ltd v Julian S. Hodge & Co Ltd* [1971] 1 W.L.R. 1547.

Mere equities: Although a purchaser of an equitable interest without notice of prior equitable interests does not take free from them, he takes free from any "mere equities" of which he has no notice.[46] Mere equities fall short of being actual interests in the land, and in the main are rights to equitable relief in respect of property. They include the right to have a transaction set aside for fraud,[47] or to have an instrument rectified for mistake.[48] Mere equities are not purely personal rights. They are ancillary to the land, and the benefit of them will pass with the land to a purchaser.[49] The burden of them will also pass with the land, but they will not bind a purchaser of an equitable interest without notice of them as he is acquiring the entire equitable interest, and the mere equities are only burdens on that interest.[50] For brevity, equitable interests in unregistered land are often included in the term "equities", but they are not "mere" equities.[51]

Without notice

3–014   There are three kinds of notice.

Actual notice: A person has actual notice of all facts of which he has[52] actual knowledge, however, that knowledge was acquired; but he is not regarded as having actual notice of facts which have come to his ears only in the form of vague rumours.[53] Notice is not, however, simply a different word for knowledge[54]: so, for example, a person has actual notice of the content of a document which he has not bothered to read[55] and has actual notice of something he has subsequently forgotten.[56] Statute has made a number of rights over unregistered land registrable as land charges and registration of them constitutes actual notice.[57]

Constructive notice: A person has constructive notice of all facts of which he would have acquired actual notice had he made those inquiries and inspections which he ought reasonably to have made, the standard of prudence being that of men of business under similar circumstances.[58] A purchaser has constructive notice of a fact if he:

    (i) had actual notice that there was some encumbrance and a proper inquiry would have revealed what it was; or

---

[46] *Phillips v Phillips* (1862) 4 De G.F. & J. 208; *Cave v Cave* (1880) 15 Ch.D. 639 at 647; *Allied Irish Banks Ltd v Glynn* [1973] I.R. 188.

[47] *Ernest v Vivian* (1863) 33 L.J.Ch. 513.

[48] *Smith v Jones* [1954] 2 All E.R. 823; *Re Colebrook's Conveyance* [1972] 1 W.L.R. 1397.

[49] LPA 1925 s.63 *Boots the Chemist Ltd v Street* [1983] E.G.D. 251.

[50] See *National Provincial Bank Ltd v Ainsworth* [1965] A.C. 1175 at 1238, 1253; *Westminster Bank Ltd v Lee* [1956] Ch. 7; see also *Latec Investments Ltd v Hotel Terrigal Pty Ltd* (1965) 113 C.L.R. 265.

[51] In respect of registered land, the "mere equities" are elevated to the same level as other interests in land; LRA 2002 s.116(b).

[52] For facts forgotten, see *Re Montagu's Settlement* [1987] Ch. 264 at 284.

[53] *Lloyd v Banks* (1868) 3 Ch.App. 488; *Barnhart v Greenshields* (1853) 9 Moo.P.C. 18 at 36.

[54] *MCP Pension Trustees Ltd v AON Pension Trustees Ltd* [2010] EWCA Civ 377; [2012] Ch. 1 at [65].

[55] *Eagle Trust v SBC Securities* [1993] 1 W.L.R. 484 at 494.

[56] *MCP Pension Trustees Ltd v AON Pension Trustees Ltd* (above).

[57] Above, paras 1–028 et seq.

[58] LPA 1925 s.199; *Bailey v Barnes* [1894] 1 Ch. 25 at 35.

(ii) has, whether deliberately or carelessly, abstained from making those inquiries that a prudent purchaser would have made.[59]

A purchaser's duties of prudence fall under two main heads, namely inspecting the land and investigating the title.

Inspection of land

It has long been accepted that a purchaser should inspect the land with the object of discovering whether it is affected by any adverse interest (such as a right of way that is suggested by a footpath over the land) and whether any of the land is occupied by any other person.[60] A purchaser has constructive notice of all the equitable rights[61] of a tenant in occupation of any of the land, though not of the rights of that tenant's landlord.[62]

3–015

Where the vendor is not in sole occupation of the land himself but there are others who occupy it as well, there are sometimes questions as to whether a purchaser is to be treated as having constructive notice of the rights of those other occupants. At one time the view was that a purchaser was not required to make inquiries of any occupants whose presence was consistent with the vendor being in occupation. For example, the presence of the vendor's spouse would normally be explicable in terms of the vendor being in occupation, and as being a mere shadow of that occupation.[63] This view facilitated conveyancing by reducing the burden of inquiries that a purchaser had to make but it also failed to give proper protection to any rights that those occupants might have.[64] In particular, in recent years it has become increasingly common for a spouse or unmarried partner to be entitled some equitable interest in the matrimonial home (for example through having contributed to the purchase price), even though the house has been put in the husband or other partner's sole name; and the husband may sell or mortgage the house without disclosing his wife's interest.[65] This led to criticism of the "easy-going practice of dispensing with enquiries as to occupation beyond that of the vendor".[66]

Today, the approach is different. A purchaser who omits to inquire of any occupier of the land or any part of it will probably be held to have constructive notice of all the rights of that occupier so far as his occupation is in conflict with the vendor's title.[67] This approach has many difficulties for purchasers, especially mortgagees. Some homeowners have large families of varying ages, and some houses have "floating populations", making full inquiries

---

[59] *Jones v Smith* (1841) 1 Hare 43 at 55; *Oliver v Hinton* [1899] 2 Ch. 264.

[60] *Taylor v Stibbert* (1794) 2 Ves.Jun. 437 at 440; *Barnhart v Greenshields* (1853) 9 Moo.P.C. 18 at 32, 33.

[61] Including at least some mere equities: see *Green v Rheinberg* (1911) 104 L.T. 149 and *Blacklocks v J.B. Developments (Godalming) Ltd* [1982] Ch. 183 at 196, and contrast *Smith v Jones* [1954] 1 W.L.R. 1089.

[62] *Hunt v Luck* [1902] 1 Ch. 428.

[63] *Caunce v Caunce* [1969] 1 W.L.R. 286; *Bird v Syme-Thompson* [1979] 1 W.L.R. 440 at 444.

[64] See *Northern Bank Ltd v Henry* [1981] I.R. 1.

[65] See, e.g. *Hodgson v Marks* [1971] Ch. 892.

[66] See *Williams & Glyn's Bank Ltd v Boland* [1981] A.C. 487 at 508, per Lord Wilberforce; and see *Hodgson v Marks* [1971] Ch. 892.

[67] *Midland Bank Ltd v Farmpride Hatcheries Ltd* [1981] E.G.D. 985 (directors residing in their company's property).

burdensome. Again, a mortgagee may be held to have constructive notice of the rights of an estranged wife who only intermittently occupies the matrimonial home and is absent when the mortgagee inspects the house under an appointment arranged by the husband, the mortgagor.[68] The wide publicity given to cases in which the equitable interests of spouses have been held to bind mortgagees[69] has ensured that no mortgagee is likely to lend money on the security of residential property without at the very least the consent of the spouse or partner of the mortgagor. Indeed, mortgagors who have neither spouses nor partners encounter very considerable difficulties in convincing mortgagees of that fact. However, this has not resolved the position of mortgagees in respect of equitable interests held by other members of a family and by "floating populations". In at least the latter respects, the limits of the new approach have yet to be worked out.

Sometimes the position is affected by the doctrine of estoppel. Where an occupier has represented to the purchaser (whether by words, conduct or silence) that the property will pass free from any claim by the occupier, the occupier will be precluded from claiming any interest adverse to a purchaser who has relied on the representation.[70] Similarly, the owner of an equitable interest who permits the legal owner to mortgage the land without disclosing that interest will be precluded from claiming any priority for his interest over the mortgage.[71]

Investigation of title

3–016   A purchaser has constructive notice of all rights which he would have discovered had he investigated the title to the land for the period prescribed by law in the case of an open contract, i.e. one which inter alia prescribes no special length of title. This period was originally at least 60 years, but it has been successively reduced by statute: in 1874 to at least 40 years, in 1925 to at least 30 years, and in 1969 to at least 15 years.[72] The period is at least 15 years, so that the purchaser must call for a good root of title which is at least 15 years old and see all documents subsequent thereto which trace dealings with the property. A good root of title is a document which deals with the whole legal and equitable interest in the land, describes the property adequately and contains nothing to throw any doubt on the title. Thus if the title consists of a series of conveyances respectively 3, 14, 41 and 45 years old, as well as older deeds, a purchaser under an open contract (a contract which contains no express provision as to the title which the vendor is obliged to provide) can require the production of the conveyance 41 years old and all subsequent conveyances. If in fact he fails to investigate the title at all, or else investigates it for only part of this period (for example because he has agreed to accept a shorter title), he is fixed with constructive notice of everything that he would have discovered had he investigated the title for the full statutory period.[73]

---

[68] *Kingsnorth Finance Co Ltd v Tizard* [1986] 1 W.L.R. 783, a case in which there was notice of the wife's rights from other sources. See the criticism at [1986] Conv. 283 (M.P. Thompson).

[69] Particularly *Williams & Glyn's Bank Ltd v Boland* [1981] A.C. 487 (registered land).

[70] *Abigail v Lapin* [1934] A.C. 491; *Spiro v Lintern* [1973] 1 W.L.R. 1002; *Midland Bank Ltd v Farmpride Hatcheries Ltd* [1981] E.G.D. 985. See also *Wroth v Tyler* [1974] Ch. 30 at 47.

[71] *Bristol and West B.S. v Henning* [1985] 1 W.L.R. 778; *Paddington B.S. v Mendelsohn* (1985) 50 P. & C.R. 244 (registered land); *Abbey National B.S. v Cann* [1991] 1 A.C. 56 at 94. For criticism, see (1986) 49 M.L.R. 245; [1986] Conv. 57 (M. P. Thompson); (1986) 16 Fam.Law 315 (J. Martin).

[72] Vendor and Purchaser Act 1874 s.1; LPA 1925 s.44; LPA 1969 s.23.

[73] See *Re Cox and Neve's Contract* [1891] 2 Ch. 109 at 117, 118.

Imputed notice: If a purchaser employs an agent, such as a solicitor, any actual or constructive notice which the agent receives may be imputed to the purchaser.[74] Before the Conveyancing Act 1882, notice received by an agent in a previous transaction was occasionally imputed to a purchaser; but this discouraged the employment of local solicitors with knowledge of local affairs[75] and was modified by the Act. Only actual or constructive notice which the agent acquires as such in the particular transaction in question is now imputed to a purchaser.[76] Where the same solicitor acts for both parties, older cases suggested that any notice he acquires may be imputed to both parties,[77] (except where he enters into a conspiracy with one to conceal something from the other)[78] but the preponderance of recent authority is that what a Solicitor learns acting for one party is not imputed to the other.[79]

Successors in title

The protection given to a purchaser without notice extends also to his successors in title, even if they take with notice[80]; for otherwise the owner of the equitable interest could, by widely advertising his right, make it difficult for the purchaser without notice to dispose of the land for as much as he had paid for it. To this rule there is one exception, which prevents it being abused. If a person bound by the interest sells to a purchaser without notice and later acquires the property again, he cannot shelter behind the immunity of that purchaser.[81] But this exception can be evaded by the simple expedient of the property being reacquired by the person's wife or son,[82] provided, of course, that the latter actually provides the purchase money and is therefore not holding the property on trust for the person who was bound.

3–017

PART 2   SPECIES OF EQUITABLE RIGHTS

TRUSTS

Origin

Everyone today is familiar with the nature of trusts, whereby the ownership of property is vested in one or more persons (the trustees) who hold it for the benefit of others (the beneficiaries). The ancestor of the trust is the use, which had substantially the same nature. The word "use" was not derived from the Latin *"usus"* but from the Latin *"opus"* in the phrase

3–018

---

[74] *Re The Alms Corn Charity* [1901] 2 Ch. 750.
[75] See *Re Cousins* (1886) 31 Ch.D. 671.
[76] LPA 1925 s.199, replacing CA 1882 s.3. See *Kingsnorth Finance Co Ltd v Tizard* [1986] 1 W.L.R. 783.
[77] E.g. *Meyer v Chartres* (1918) 34 T.L.R. 589.
[78] *Sharpe v Foy* (1868) 4 Ch.App. 35; *Meyer v Chartres* (1918) 34 T.L.R. 589.
[79] See, e.g. *Barclays Bank v Thomson* [1997] 4 All E.R. 816.
[80] *Harrison v Forth* (1695) Prec.Ch. 51; *Wilkes v Spooner* [1911] 2 K.B. 473.
[81] *Gordon v Holland* (1913) 82 L.J.P.C. 81.
[82] See *Wilkes v Spooner* [1911] 2 K.B. 473.

"*ad opus*" (on his behalf) via the Old French "*al oes*" or "*al ues*" and hence "to the use of"; thus land was conveyed "to A and his heirs to the use of B and his heirs".[83]

Although there are records of uses having been created even before the Norman Conquest the only uses found for some time after the Conquest appear to have been merely temporary uses, so that a landowner could secure the protection of his land and his family while he went on a crusade. In about 1225 the Franciscan friars came to England. The rules of their Order prevented them from owning property, and so land was conveyed, for example, to some town to the use of the friars.[84] After this, uses of a permanent nature became more common, and by the middle of the fourteenth century they were frequent.

Enforced by equity

3–019   After early hesitations, the common law courts refused to recognise uses. If land was conveyed by A to B and C and their heirs to the use of D and his heirs, B and C were technically described as the feoffees to uses (there would usually be more than one to avoid the difficulties which would otherwise have arisen if a sole feoffee to uses had died) and D was technically described as the cestui que use (pronounced setty ker use). The common law courts therefore refused to compel B and C to hold the land for the benefit of D, B and C were the persons with the seisin,[85] and the common law would take notice only of their rights; D had no interest which the common law would recognise, for "uses were but imaginations".[86] Nevertheless, many uses were created in reliance on the honour and good faith of feoffees to uses, and sometimes they failed in their duty and committed breaches of trust. Towards the end of the fourteenth century the Chancellor's aid was sought, and although there is no record of a decree in favour of a cestui que use until 1446, relief was probably being given by the first quarter of the fifteenth century.[87]

Duties

3–020   The duties of the feoffees to uses towards their cestui que use were threefold: they were bound:

    (i) to permit him to take the profits of the land ("pernancy of profits");

    (ii) to dispose of the land in accordance with his instructions; and

    (iii) to take all necessary proceedings to protect or recover the land.[88]

Although at first the cestui que use was regarded as merely having a right to compel the feoffees to uses to carry out their duties, the rights of the cestui que use were so extensive that it was soon recognised that he had an estate in the land.[89] The legal estate was in the feoffees to uses, the equitable estate in the cestui que use: the former had the husk, the

---

[83]   Maitland, equity, 24.

[84]   2 P. & M. 231–238.

[85]   See above, para.2–013.

[86]   Chudleigh's Case (1595) 1 Co.Rep. 113b at 140a; and see Maitland, equity, 28.

[87]   Ames, Lectures on Legal History, 237.

[88]   4 H.E.L. 431.

[89]   *Brent's Case* (1583) 2 Leon. 14 at 18.

latter the kernel. With some qualifications, it could be said in Chancery that "the equity is the land."

Legal and equitable interests

Frequently the legal and equitable interests in property go together; a person who has had the legal fee simple in Blackacre conveyed to him normally receives the equitable fee simple as well. But although there is often no need to consider separately the legal and equitable estate in land, in some cases this is the only way to arrive at a proper understanding of the subject.[90] One of the fundamental principles of English law is the ability of the beneficial owner of a legal estate (i.e. someone who has the equitable interest as well as the legal estate for his own benefit) to separate the legal from the equitable interest.

3–021

The Statute of Uses 1535

By conveying lands to feoffees to uses it was possible to evade most of the feudal taxes to which feudal lords were in principle entitled, as these fell only upon the person or persons who were seised of land. All that was needed was the selection of suitable and sufficient feoffees so that the land was never vested in a single feoffee to uses whose death would give rise to the feudal taxes which had to be paid by anyone who inherited freehold land (these liabilities were particularly stringent if the person in question was an infant since the feudal lord then also acquired the right to manage the land for his own benefit during the infant's minority). The evasion seriously affected all feudal lords but principally the King, who alone was always lord and never tenant. After various manoeuvres, in 1535 "the Statute of Uses was forced upon an extremely unwilling parliament by an extremely strong-willed king".[91] The effect of this was to execute all uses to which it applied, taking the legal estate out of the feoffees to uses and converting the equitable interests of the cestui que use into corresponding legal estates. Thereafter, if land was conveyed by A to B and C and their heirs to the use of D and his heirs, the effect was to vest the legal fee simple in D, so that when D died or, if an infant, attained his majority, the relevant feudal taxes would all be payable.

3–022

The use upon a use

Soon after the statute was passed it was held that, where property was conveyed on two successive uses (a use upon a use), the second use was void at common law.[92] The final result of the decisions to this effect was that, if land was conveyed by A to B and C and their heirs to the use of D and his heirs to the use of E and his heirs, the first use was executed by the Statute of Uses but the second use was void. This gave the whole legal and equitable interest to D and nothing to B, C or E. Initially, successive uses were not created deliberately; in the cases which established this rule, the second use (that in favour of E and his heirs in the example above) had been created by implication. However, after the restoration of the monarchy in 1660, most of the relevant feudal taxes were abolished,[93] and so the purpose

3–023

---

[90] Consider, e.g. joint tenancies and tenancies in common; below, Ch.8.
[91] Maitland, equity, 34; the King in question was Henry VIII.
[92] *Tyrrel's Case* (1557) 2 Dy. 155a.
[93] Above, para.1–058.

for which the Statute of Uses had been passed became irrelevant. There was therefore no reason to prevent the situation which had existed prior to that statute from being recreated, and successive uses were intentionally employed for this purpose. Since the person entitled under the second use was then as unprotected at common law as all cestui que use had been before the Statute of Uses, by 1676 the Chancellor had come to enforce second uses as trusts.[94] Thereafter, the effect of the conveyance set out above was that D held the legal estate on trust for E. In time, the shorter formula unto and to the use of B and C and their heirs in trust for D and his heirs came to be employed as the usual means of creating trusts. The Statute of Uses nevertheless survived until its repeal by the Law of Property Act 1925[95] so this formulation continued to be necessary until 1926.

After 1925

3–024   A trust of land is now created by conveying land to A and B in fee simple in trust for the intended beneficiaries. The legal estate is thus in A and B, while those named as beneficiaries will have equitable interests.[96] Since 1925 life interests and entails have been able to exist only as equitable interests under a trust of the legal estate in fee simple.

OTHER EQUITABLE RIGHTS

3–025   The Chancellor did not confine his intervention to the enforcement of uses or trusts, though that always remained the most important part of his jurisdiction. There were other important areas of real property and leases in which he intervened.

Mortgages

3–026   If A conveyed his land to B as security for a loan, equity would allow A at any time after repayment of the loan fell due, despite any contrary provisions in the mortgage, to recover his land by paying B what was due to him under the loan, namely the outstanding principal sum, interest thereon and costs. The development of this equitable right of redemption, exercisable after expiry of the legal date for redemption, is described later.[97]

Restrictive covenants

3–027   The basic rule of common law, now modified by the Contracts (Rights of Third Parties) Act 1999, was that a contract is normally binding upon and enforceable by the parties alone. But during the nineteenth century it was held that if a landowner covenants for the benefit of neighbouring landowners not to use his land in a certain way, the restrictive covenant could be enforced in equity against successors in title of the covenantor, thus imposing an

---

[94] *Grubb v Gwillim* (1676) 73 S.S. 347; *Symson v Turner* (1700) 1 Eq. Ca. Abr. 383. For a full treatment of the Statute of Uses and developments therefrom, see *Megarry & Wade: The Law of Real Property* 5th edn (London: Sweet & Maxwell, 1984), pp.1164–1175.

[95] Sch.7.

[96] For the categories of trusts today, see below, Ch.7.

[97] Below, para.17–007.

equitable burden on his land.[98] This is confined to covenants that are negative in nature prohibiting certain acts, such as building on the land in question; it does not apply to positive covenants, requiring the landowner to carry out some action on the land in question, such as maintaining a garden.

Estate contracts

Where a person enters into a valid contract for the purchase of an estate in land, he is at once considered to have an equitable interest in that land, even before he has paid the price and has had the estate of the vendor conveyed to him.[99] This also applies to an option to purchase an interest in land, but not to a mere right of pre-emption or first refusal.[100] If P has an option to purchase land, he has the right, on exercising the option, to compel the landowner to sell the land to him in accordance with the terms of the option, and neither the landowner nor his successors in title can deal with the land in such a way as to defeat the option. If instead P has a right of pre-emption or a right of first refusal), he has no more than the right to be offered the land if the landowner decides to sell it; and although the right will become an interest in the land once the landowner makes an offer which cannot be withdrawn before the time by which it has to be accepted[101]; until then it is no more than a mere *spes* (hope).[102]

3–028

CREATION OF EQUITABLE RIGHTS

Equitable rights in land arose under three heads:

3–029

    (i)   lack of formality: where the proper formalities for the creation or conveyance of a legal estate were not observed;

   (ii)   lack of capacity: where the grantor had power only to create or convey an equitable interest; and

  (iii)   lack of intention: where the grantor provided that only an equitable interest should arise.

Lack of formality

At common law

At law, in order to create or transfer a legal estate, certain formalities had to be observed.

3–030

---

[98] Below, pp.397 et seq.

[99] *Lysaght v Edwards* (1876) 2 Ch.D. 499.

[100] *Pritchard v Briggs* [1980] Ch. 338. Rights of pre-emption or first refusal created after October 13, 2003 affecting registered land bind successors from the moment of registration: LRA 2002 s.115.

[101] *Pritchard v Briggs* [1980] Ch. 338; *Bircham & Co Nominees (2) v Worrall Holdings Ltd* (2001) 82 P. & C.R. 34; *Speciality Shops v Yorkshire & Metropolitan Estates* [2003] 2 P. & C.R. 410.

[102] See *Pritchard v Briggs* [1980] Ch. 338, criticised in this respect at (1980) 96 L.Q.R. 488 (H.W.R.Wade). The right of pre-emption is nevertheless registrable: below, para.6–069.

Freeholds: The original rule was that "Corporeal hereditaments lie in livery, incorporeal hereditaments lie in grant". A corporeal hereditament was an inheritable right in realty which was accompanied by physical possession of the land, for example a fee simple in possession; for such estates, a feoffment with livery of seisin was essential.[103] An incorporeal hereditament was an inheritable right in land not accompanied by physical possession, such as a fee simple in remainder or an easement; for such interests, a feoffment was inappropriate but a deed of grant was essential. By the beginning of the seventeenth century it had become possible to use a deed for both corporeal and incorporeal hereditaments, and feoffments with livery of seisin generally ceased to be employed. This practice was subsequently formalised, ultimately by the Real Property Act 1845,[104] which specifically provided that a deed was an alternative to a feoffment of corporeal hereditaments and that, if a feoffment was employed, it would be void unless evidenced by a deed. Feoffment by livery of seisin was finally abolished by the Law of Property Act 1925[105] and as a result no legal estate in freehold land can now be created otherwise than by deed.[106]

Leaseholds: Leases for a term of years were not hereditaments and at first could be created orally, but the Statute of Frauds 1677[107] made writing necessary in nearly all cases. The Real Property Act 1845[108] made a deed essential for most leases. This remains the position under the Law of Property Act 1925; a lease can be created otherwise than by deed only if it is for three years or less at a rent taking effect in possession immediately.[109]

Thus since the Real Property Act 1845 it has been substantially true to say that without a deed no legal estate can be created or transferred.[110]

In equity

3–031   Equity, on the other hand, was not so strict. In two important respects, what was ineffective at law might be effective in equity.

Contract: In accordance with the maxim "equity treats as done that which ought to be done", equity regarded a specifically enforceable contract to create or convey an interest in land as being as effective as if the transaction had been properly carried out. With certain exceptions, such as leases for three years or less at a rent taking effect in possession immediately, such a contract would not take effect at law because of the absence of a deed.[111] Equity, however, treated an attempt to convey or create a legal estate which failed at law through lack of a deed as being a contract to carry out the transaction, and thus, if it was specifically enforceable, as being effective in equity. Formerly, a transaction of this type would be specifically enforceable if it was supported either by sufficient evidence of it in writing (such as a letter referring to it) signed by the person against whom it was being

---

[103] Above, para.2–012.
[104] s.2.
[105] s.51.
[106] LPA 1925 s.52(1).
[107] s.1.
[108] s.3.
[109] LPA 1925 s.54(2).
[110] *Crago v Julian* [1992] 1 W.L.R. 372; see below, paras 11–016, 11–038.
[111] LPA 1925 ss.52(1), 54; for the leases, see below, para. 11–016.

enforced or by what was known as a sufficient act of part performance.[112] In this way, many informal transactions took effect in equity, including leases and mortgages by deposit of the relevant documents evidencing title (title deeds in the case of unregistered land; the land certificate in the case of registered land).[113] Now, however, under the Law of Property (Miscellaneous Provisions) Act 1989, contracts for the sale or disposition of land or any interest in land must actually be in writing, incorporating all the terms of the contract, and must be signed by all the parties.[114] Where these much more stringent requirements are satisfied, equity continues to regard the transaction as being as effective as if it had been properly carried out. But informal transactions which do not satisfy these requirements are no longer effective as such. This is the position of mortgages by deposit of the documents evidencing title, which no longer take effect as mortgages.[115] It is questionable whether Parliament would have adopted this oblique method of removing the theoretical foundation of an important range of long-established equitable interests if it had really intended to abolish them but it has clearly succeeded in doing so. In the Report which led to the 1989 Act, the Law Commission envisaged the adaptation of the doctrine of proprietary estoppel[116] so as to prevent informal transactions from losing their status in equity[117]; this has happened in appropriate circumstances where contracts have failed to comply with the requisite formalities[118] but not where other informal transactions have been entered into.[119]

Proprietary estoppel: Proprietary estoppel is an important equitable doctrine of considerable antiquity.[120] The essence of the doctrine is that if A has acted to his detriment in reliance on the belief or expectation that he owns or will acquire an interest in O's land, and has either encouraged that belief or expectation or has acquiesced in A's action, it is unconscionable for O to deny a proper fulfilment of A's belief or expectation.[121] An equity arises in A's favour and it is then in the court's discretion as to how that equity should be satisfied.[122] Thus if O knows that A is spending money on improving O's land in the belief that the land is A's, O's silence may result in the land being held to be A's,[123] or A may be held to have some lesser right.[124] Equity is at its most flexible here.[125] In the example just given, A is potentially prejudiced not by any lack of formality but by his own mistaken belief. However, the doctrine is equally applicable where a party to an informal contract has incurred detriment on the basis of an agreement that he would thereby acquire an interest in the land of the other party.[126] But the doctrine does not assist a person who has entered into some other form of

---

[112] LPA 1925 s.40.
[113] Below, para.17–028.
[114] s.2.
[115] *United Bank of Kuwait Plc v Sahib* [1997] Ch. 107.
[116] Below para.9–001.
[117] See (1987) Law Com. No.164, para.5.4.
[118] *Yaxley v Gotts* [2000] Ch. 162; *Thorner v Major* [2009] 1 W.L.R. 776.
[119] *United Bank of Kuwait Plc v Sahib* [1997] Ch. 107.
[120] See *Hunt v Carew* (1649) Nels. 47; *Hobbs v Norton* (1682) 1 Vern. 137.
[121] *Taylors Fashions Ltd v Liverpool Victoria Trustees Co Ltd* [1982] Q.B. 133N.
[122] *Crabb v Arun D.C.* [1976] Ch. 179.
[123] *Pascoe v Turner* [1979] 1 W.L.R. 431.
[124] *Inwards v Baker* [1965] 2 Q.B. 29.
[125] See *Crabb v Arun D.C.* [1976] Ch. 179 at 189. On the doctrine generally, see below, Ch.9.
[126] *Yaxley v Gotts* [2000] Ch. 162; *Thorner v Major* [2009] 1 W.L.R. 776.

informal transaction such as a mortgage by deposit of the documents evidencing his title.[127] Nor does the doctrine assist a person who has entered into a transaction which is formally valid but has subsequently failed to protect it in the appropriate way.[128]

Lack of capacity

3–032   If X owned only an equitable interest, such as a right under a trust, he had no power to create a legal interest out of it. So far as the common law was concerned, he had no interest in land at all, and thus could create nothing that the common law would recognise. But he could transfer his equitable interest or create a new equitable interest out of it, as by mortgaging it or declaring a sub-trust.

Lack of intention

3–033   Even if a deed was employed, and the grantor had power to create or convey a legal interest, no legal estate would pass if the grantor expressly provided that only an equitable interest should be created or transferred.

THE BORDERLINE BETWEEN PERSONAL AND PROPRIETARY RIGHTS

3–034   The boundary between rights that are merely personal and rights in the land itself is not always distinct. A fundamental rule of the common law was that a contract binds only the parties to it, creating merely personal rights and liabilities; and subject to the Contract (Rights of Third Parties) Act 1999, which permits someone who is expressly named in the contract as benefitting from it to enforce it, this is still the case. But as has been seen,[129] when equity intervened to grant specific performance of a contract to sell land, the purchaser's rights came to be treated as equitable rights in the land itself: the purchaser's personal rights became proprietary.[130]

This well-settled impact of remedies upon rights has now been carried further. Under the law of tort, merely personal rights may sometimes become enforceable against third parties, and so produce something of the same effect as if they were rights in land. The torts of inducing a breach of contract, causing loss by unlawful means,[131] and conspiracy,[132] are all applicable to contracts affecting land. A simple example is where someone takes an assignment or a sub-tenancy knowing full well that this is breach of covenant. In an appropriate case, an injunction can be granted requiring the transaction to

---

[127] *United Bank of Kuwait Plc v Sahib* [1997] Ch. 107.
[128] *Lloyds Bank Plc v Carrick* [1996] 4 All E.R. 630.
[129] Above, para.3–031.
[130] See *Swiss Bank Corp v Lloyds Bank Ltd* [1979] Ch. 548 at 565 (reversed on a different point: [1982] A.C. 584).
[131] See *OBG v Allan* [2007] UKHL 21, [2008] A.C. 1; also *Thames Valley Housing v Elegant Homes (Guernsey) Ltd* [2011] EWHC 1288 (Ch) which includes an excellent potted summary of the elements of the relevant economic torts in a land law context.
[132] For a classic example in the land law context see *Midland Bank Trust Co v Green (No.3)* [1982] Ch. 529—conspiracy to defeat an unregistered option.

be reversed.[133] A more complex but well known example arose in the context of a petrol station. If G Ltd, the owner of a garage, covenants with P Ltd that for five years G Ltd will sell only P Ltd's petrol at the garage (this is known as a "solus agreement"), and that if G Ltd sells the garage a similar covenant will be extracted from his purchaser, the obligations of G Ltd to P Ltd are merely personal. So if T Ltd then buys all the shares in G Ltd and makes G Ltd sell the garage to a subsidiary of T Ltd, the subsidiary, not being a party to the covenant, is not bound by it. Yet if T Ltd and its subsidiary have committed the tort of wrongful interference in the execution of the contract between G Ltd and P Ltd, the court may grant a mandatory injunction compelling the subsidiary to transfer the garage back to G Ltd, to be held subject to the covenant.[134] In this way the merely personal rights of P Ltd against G Ltd have in effect been enforced against third parties in respect of the garage. But mere uncertainties or suspicions about the contract are not enough[135]; actual knowledge must be shown.[136] Nor is there any tort if the interference is justifiable.[137] Thus if V contracts to sell land to X and then contracts to sell the same land to Y, X will be justified in requiring V to convey the land to him, despite the interference with Y's contract; for X has the prior right.[138] But interfering with a contract does not appear to be justified simply because the contract is void against purchasers for want of registration.[139]

Such cases are not yet recognised as forming part of property law, but they illustrate the effect of remedies on rights, and the need to look outside the sometimes narrow bounds of property law, for example in protecting the rights of contractual licensees.[140] In general, a right can be admitted to the category of property rights only if it is definable, identifiable by third parties, capable in its nature of being transferred to and taken over by third parties, and has some degree of permanence or stability.[141] What is relevant is the nature of the right and not the remedy which exists for its enforcement.[142]

FURTHER READING

- J.H. Baker, *An Introduction to English Legal History* (Butterworths, 2002)

---

[133] *Crestfort Ltd v Tesco* [2005 EWHC 805 (Ch); [2005] L&TR 20; *Test Valley BC v Minilec Engineering* [2005] 2 E.G.L.R. 113.

[134] The essential facts of *Esso Petroleum Co Ltd v Kingswood Motors (Addlestone) Ltd* [1974] Q.B. 142.

[135] *Smith v Morrison* [1974] 1 W.L.R. 659.

[136] *Greig v Insole* [1978] 1 W.L.R. 302; *Swiss Bank Corp v Lloyds Bank Ltd* [1979] Ch. 548 at 575 (reversed on other grounds [1982] A.C. 584). Actual knowledge includes wilful blindness ("blind-eye knowledge"): *OBG v Allan* (above) at [40].

[137] *Greig v Insole* [1978] 1 W.L.R. 302 at 340–342; and see (1977) 41 Conv.(N.S.) 318 (R.J. Smith).

[138] See *Pritchard v Briggs* [1980] Ch. 338 at 415.

[139] *Miles v Bull (No.2)* [1969] 3 All E.R. 1585 at 1590 suggests that such interference is not actionable but a conspiracy claim succeeded in *Midland Bank Trust Co v Green (No.3)* [1982] Ch. 529 after an option was held void for want of registration in *Midland Bank Trust Co Ltd v Green* [1981] A.C. 513.

[140] See below, para.10–016.

[141] *National Provincial Bank Ltd v Ainsworth* [1965] A.C. 1175 at 1248.

[142] *National Provincial Bank Ltd v Ainsworth* [1965] A.C. 1175 at 1248.

Chapter 4

THE STRUCTURE OF MODERN LAND LAW

CHAPTER SUMMARY

This Chapter examines the changes to the structure of real property brought about by the scheme of legislation enacted in 1925. Modern land law is governed principally by the Law of Property Act 1925, which brought about sweeping changes to the number of legal estates and interests that can subsist in land. The reforms started in the nineteenth century, and culminated in the great reforms of 1922, consolidated in 1925, and coming into force on January 1, 1926. Many old rules were swept away, the number of possible legal estates was reduced to two, and all other estates which had existed were for the future to be restricted to existence in equity, behind a trust.

The first part of this Chapter examines the scheme of legislation and then puts this into the context of registered and unregistered land. The aspects of land law that are relevant to both registered and unregistered title are then considered in detail.

Dealings in registered land are governed by the Land Registration Act 2002 and are examined in Ch.5. However, in recognition of its diminishing importance in practice unregistered land is not discussed in its own chapter. Instead, this book looks at aspects of unregistered conveyancing in the context of contracts for the sale of land in Ch.7.

PART 1   THE STRUCTURE PUT INTO PLACE BY THE 1925 LEGISLATION

The structure of modern land law was put into place by the 1925 legislation, whose domi-   **4–001** nant policy was to facilitate the transfer of land by easing the burden on purchasers without defeating the interests of others unfairly. A fundamental principle underlying the legislation, but nowhere explicitly stated in it, was to distinguish between commercial interests and family interests. Examples of commercial interests are leases, rights of way and mortgages; such rights are almost invariably created for money or money's worth. Examples of family interests are the rights of beneficiaries under a trust or settlement (this includes the beneficial rights of co-owners of land); such rights are not usually created for money or money's worth. This distinction between these two types of interests is largely historical in its nature because, as will be seen below, trusts are often employed in a commercial arrangement and some of the traditional "commercial" interests are concerned with family rights. Given that this distinction between "commercial" and "family" interests is largely historical, unlike previous editions of this book, they are given new nomenclature. The "commercial" interests are best described in a modern context as estates and interests, whether legal or equitable, as defined by s.1 of the Law of Property Act 1925 and "family" interests are described as interests under a trust.

Broadly speaking, with some exceptions intentionally created in 1925 and a few further exceptions not envisaged by the 1925 legislation which have been created subsequently by both the courts and the legislature, it was intended that:

(1) legal estates and interests should bind the successors in title of the person who created them; and

(2) interests under a trust should, upon sale or other disposition giving rise to the payment of a capital sum, be overreached, that is to say transferred from the land to that capital sum, and so should not bind the successors in title of the person who created them.

The different methods by which these objectives were achieved have already been considered in outline, but it is convenient to consider them together here. It has already been seen that the title to land may either be registered at the Land Registry or else be unregistered.[1] However, approximately 80 per cent of land in England and Wales is now registered.[2]

Interests in unregistered land

4–002   A purchaser of a legal estate in unregistered land for value without notice of adverse claims generally takes subject to those interests which are legal but free from those which are equitable. The dominant policy of the 1925 legislation was put into effect in two ways.

Reduction in number of legal estates

4–003   The reduction by the 1925 legislation of the number of legal estates and interests which can exist in land substantially improved the position of a purchaser of unregistered land for value.[3]

Extension of registration of land charges

4–004   The width of constructive and imputed notice sometimes made it difficult for the innocent purchaser of an interest for value to establish that he had no notice, and offered scope for argument. The extension of registration of land charges to three legal interests in unregistered land and the vast majority of equitable interests in unregistered land made the question not one of notice but one of the state of the register; and this was discoverable by a search. The extension of the system of registration of land charges often substituted certainty for contention. But some equitable interests in unregistered land were intention-

---

[1] Above, para.1–006.
[2] According to the Land Registry website.
[3] Above, para.3–009.

ally not made registrable and the courts have subsequently held not to be registrable some interests which the draftsmen of the 1925 legislation probably expected to be registrable. Interests in unregistered land which are not registrable continue to bind a purchaser without notice only if they are legal interests.[4]

Interests in registered land

Save for the fact that only legal estates and interests in land are capable of being registrable interests (interests registered on the Land Register with their own separate title),[5] the enforceability of rights in registered land does not normally depend on whether they are legal or equitable. The dominant policy of the 1925 legislation was put into effect and more recently extended by the Land Registration Act 2002 in the following ways.[6]   **4–005**

Protection of legal interests and leases

Some interests in registered land are registrable interests; an example is a legal lease for more than seven years.[7] Such interests are protected by virtue of the fact that their existence is noted on the register of the freehold title.[8] Most mortgages of registered land take effect as registered charges, which are protected by an entry on the register.[9] Other interests in registered land either automatically bind the successors in title of the registered proprietor (an example is shorter legal leases[10]) by overriding registration or only bind the successors in title of the registered proprietor if they are protected by an entry on the register (this is the way in which mortgages of registered land are protected under the Land Registration Act 2002). The purchaser of an interest who protects it in the appropriate way is completely protected. Further, registrable interests which have not been registered, and interests which should have been protected by registration but have not been will override registration and so automatically bind the successors in title of the registered proprietor if their holder is in actual occupation of the registered land.   **4–006**

Protection of purchasers

A purchaser of registered land for value is only bound by interests which override registration and by interests which have been protected by an entry on the register. Interests which should have been so protected but have not been (and which do override registration for the reason set out above) do not bind any purchaser for value, even if he has notice of them. This simplifies the task of a purchaser by enabling him to obtain the title to the land that is shown in the Land Register rather than the title which appears to him to be disclosed by his examinations of often bulky title deeds.   **4–007**

---

[4] Above, paras 1–025, 3–010 et seq.
[5] Leases for more than seven years, franchises and profits in gross are registrable under the LRA 2002.
[6] See below, Ch.5.
[7] LRA 2002 s.27.
[8] A registered lease will have its own title too.
[9] LRA 2002 s.27.
[10] Of seven years or less.

Interests under a trust

4-008 The dominant policy of the 1925 legislation was given effect to by making all interests under a trust in both registered and unregistered land overreachable. This was done in the following ways.

Extension of overreaching

4-009 When two or more persons are beneficially entitled to land (or for that matter to pure personalty) in succession (that is to say one after another) the property in question is said to be subject to a settlement; the simplest possible example of a settlement is where a testator leaves his property to his wife for life and subject to that to his children equally. The 1925 legislation made all the beneficial interests which arise under settlements of land overreachable. In other words, a purchaser for value of both registered and unregistered land will take free of all interests arising under any settlement of that land provided that he pays the purchase money to at least two trustees or a trust corporation. He is protected in this way, while the beneficiaries of the settlement are protected by the fact that their rights are thus overreached and so transferred to the purchase money received by the trustees or the trust corporation.

Simplification of title for co-ownership

4-010 The ownership of land by co-owners, and particularly by tenants in common (persons who hold undivided shares in land, of which there can be a large number of different sizes), often led to difficulties in making title to the land in question. These difficulties were met by a combination of prohibiting the ownership of a legal estate by tenants in common and providing for the legal estate instead to be vested in trustees on trust for sale (since 1996 on a trust of land[11]). The trustees could then make a good title to the land, and the rights of the co-owners would be overreached and so transferred to the purchase money received from the purchaser. This enables the purchaser to take free of the interests of all the co-owners, who are in turn protected by the fact that their rights are overreached.[12]

PART 2   REGISTERED AND UNREGISTERED LAND TODAY

4-011 In 1925 the majority of the land in England and Wales was unregistered. Although registration of title had been possible since 1862,[13] registration was on a voluntary basis and few titles were registered until the Land Transfer Act 1897 made registration compulsory in the County and City of London. Consequently, apart from those titles which had been registered voluntarily, only land in the County and City of London which had been the subject since 1897 of a transaction triggering first registration was registered.

---

[11] TLATA s.1.
[12] See above, para.1–015.
[13] Land Registry Act 1862.

The draftsmen of the 1925 legislation did not propose universal registration of title. They instead proposed that the much modified system of registered conveyancing introduced by the Land Registration Act 1925 should exist side by side with the equally modified system of unregistered conveyancing for an experimental period of 10 years, during which the two systems of conveyancing could be prepared.[14] This was because the legal profession was divided between those who accepted that universal registration of title was inevitable and those who thought that the already much amended system of unregistered conveyancing required only a little further amendment to make it perfect.[15] The proposed legislation was therefore designed to win the support of both sides, which it did.

During the 10-year review period only two county boroughs[16] became, at their own request, new areas of compulsory registration. After that period had concluded, the County of Middlesex and one further county borough[17] were designated areas of compulsory registration. No further extensions took place until 1952, by which time it had become accepted that registered conveyancing was the system of the future. By 1964 compulsory registration had been extended to three further counties[18] and 11 further county boroughs; and, following a decision in that year to accelerate the process, by 1978 the areas of compulsory registration covered three-quarters of the population of England and Wales. Finally, as from December 1, 1990, the whole of England and Wales became subject to compulsory registration.

This does not mean that all land in England and Wales is now registered. Until March 31, 1998, titles to land in areas of compulsory registration had to be registered only on the conveyance on sale of the fee simple absolute or the grant or assignment of a lease with more than 21 years to run. Since April 1, 1998, titles have also had to be registered if either of these estates is the subject of a first legal mortgage or a gift. This means that all land in England and Wales held directly by natural persons will become registered at the very latest on the death of those persons, effectively within a generation from 1998. Fee incentives have also been introduced to encourage voluntary first registration. Land that is the subject of a trust is now subject to compulsory first registration on the partition of the land or on the appointment of a new trustee.[19] Land vested in companies or other corporations or bodies (which of course may never die) may remain unsold and unmortgaged for centuries. Although an ever-increasing proportion of the land in England and Wales is now registered, the system of unregistered conveyancing remains in existence, admittedly to an ever-decreasing extent.

It is important to understand which parts of the 1925 legislation (and successor statutes) apply to which system of conveyancing.

(i) The Law of Property Act 1925, which contains the fundamental reforms to the pre-existing land law made by the 1925 legislation, applies to both registered and unregistered land.

---

[14] Memorandum prefixed to Law of Property Bill 1922: see 154 H.C.Deb (5th ser.) 102, 103 (1922).
[15] C. Sweet (1912) 28 L.Q.R. 24.
[16] Eastbourne and Hastings.
[17] Croydon.
[18] Surrey, Kent and Berkshire.
[19] By the amendment of the LRA 2002 s.4 by the Land Registration Act 2002 (Amendment) Order 2008 (SI 2008/2872).

   (ii) So do three other statutes which form part of the 1925 legislation:

       (a) the Settled Land Act 1925, which governs a form of settlement which has, since 1996, not been able to be created, although existing settlements continue;

       (b) the Trustee Act 1925, now substantially amended and supplemented by the Trustee Act 2000, which deals with the administrative powers of trustees; and

       (c) the Administration of Estates Act 1925, which deals with the administration of the property of deceased persons and contains the rules which determine who inherits the property of someone who dies without making a will.

  (iii) The Land Charges Act 1972, which has replaced the Land Charges Act 1925, which created the current system of registration of land charges, applies only to unregistered land.

  (iv) The Local Land Charges Act 1975, which deals with charges imposed on land by local authorities, either restricting the uses to which the land can be put or imposing financial liabilities relating to matters such as roads and sewers, applies to both registered and unregistered land (the similarity between the title of this Act and the Land Charges Act 1972, which applies only to unregistered land, is a frequent cause of confusion).

   (v) The Land Registration Act 2002, which has replaced the Land Registration Act 1925, applies only to registered land.

The basic rules of land law contained in the Law of Property Act 1925, the decided cases which have interpreted it, and the pre-existing and subsequent case law governing those aspects of those basic rules with which the Law of Property Act 1925 did not deal, therefore apply to both registered and unregistered land. It was the intention of the draftsmen of the 1925 legislation that these basic rules should be unaffected by whether the land in question was registered and unregistered. This remains the case, although, as will be seen in the remaining parts of this chapter, this objective was not achieved in a number of respects, probably by accident rather than by design. Moreover, the Land Registration Act 2002, which replaced the Land Registration Act 1925, has specifically changed a number of the basic rules of land law in respect of registered land only.

PART 3   ASPECTS COMMON TO BOTH REGISTERED AND UNREGISTERED LAND

REDUCTION IN THE NUMBER OF LEGAL ESTATES

4–012   Section 1 of the Law of Property Act 1925 reduced the number of legal estates that can exist in land to two, and the number of classes of legal interests to five. The distinction, broadly, is that a legal estate confers full rights to use and enjoy land as one's own, while a legal interest is a right over the land of another. The terms of the first three subsections of s.1 are as follows:

"1 (1) The only estates in land which are capable of subsisting or of being conveyed or created at law are:

(a) An estate in fee simple absolute in possession;

(b) A term of years absolute.

(2) The only interests or charges in or over land which are capable of subsisting or of being conveyed or created at law are:

(a) An easement, right, or privilege in or over land for an interest equivalent to an estate in fee simple absolute in possession or a term of years absolute;

(b) A rentcharge in possession issuing out of or charged on land being either perpetual or for a term of years absolute;

(c) A charge by way of legal mortgage;

(d) Land tax, tithe rentcharge,[20] and any other similar charge on land which is not created by an instrument;

(e) Rights of entry exercisable over or in respect of a legal term of years absolute, or annexed, for any purpose, to a legal rentcharge.

(3) All other estates, interests, and charges in or over land take effect as equitable interests."

It should be noted that the section does not provide that the estates and interests mentioned in subss.(1) and (2) are necessarily legal, but merely that they alone can be legal. If they are to be legal the proper formalities must be employed, i.e. a deed must be used except in the creation of leases at a rack rent taking effect in possession for a term not exceeding three years.[21]

The incidents of equitable interests are probably similar to those attaching to corresponding legal estates before 1926. Thus the position of a tenant for life as regards waste seems to have remained unchanged despite the conversion of his legal life estate into an equitable life interest at the beginning of 1926. There is no express provision on this point but "equity follows the law".[22]

The general scheme of the section is to deal with the legal rights of ownership in the land itself in subs.(1) and with legal rights over the land of another in subs.(2). However, this is complicated by the definition of "land" given by the Act. "Land" is defined as including, unless the context otherwise requires, any corporeal or incorporeal hereditament, and among the latter is mentioned an advowson.[23] An advowson is the right of presenting a clergyman to a living[24] and, oddly enough, is a species of real property. By reading subs.(1) in the light of the definition of "land", it seems clear that a fee simple absolute in possession in an advowson is a legal estate, and so is a term of years absolute in an advowson.

It will be noted that the rights mentioned in subs.(1) are called legal estates and those mentioned in subs.(2) are called legal interests or charges. This is a convenient distinction between rights over a person's own land and rights over the land of another, but both types

---

[20] These four words have been repealed: below, paras 4–020 et seq.

[21] LPA 1925 ss.52, 54; below, para.11–018.

[22] Above, para.3–008.

[23] LPA 1925 s.205(1)(ix).

[24] It is subject to important restrictions, e.g. no advowson may be sold after two vacancies of the benefice have occurred since July 14, 1924: see Benefices Act 1898; Benefices Act 1898 (Amendment) Measure 1923.

of right are referred to in the Act as "legal estates", and have the same incidents attached to them as attached to legal estates before 1926.[25] The title "estate owner" is given to the owner of a legal estate.[26] Before 1926, equitable rights in land were frequently and properly called equitable estates, but they should now be called equitable interests, and the name "estate" reserved for legal rights.

The various legal estates and interests must now be examined more closely.

"Fee simple absolute in possession"

4–013   The meaning of "fee simple" has already been considered.[27]

Absolute

4–014   "Absolute" is used to distinguish a fee simple which will continue for ever from a modified fee,[28] such as a determinable fee or a base fee.

A fee simple defeasible by condition subsequent[29] would also not be "absolute" but for the Law of Property (Amendment) Act 1926. A fee simple defeasible by condition subsequent used to arise most frequently in connection with rentcharges until the Rentcharges Act 1977 prohibited the creation of legal rentcharges in most cases. In some parts of the country, particularly Manchester and the north-west of England, it was a common practice to sell a fee simple for a comparatively small sum in cash and a perpetual rentcharge (an annual sum charged on the land). The remedies for non-payment of a rentcharge include a right to enter on the land temporarily in order to collect sufficient rents and profits to satisfy the annual payment; further, in a number of cases an express right of re-entry was reserved by the conveyance, entitling the grantor to enter and determine the fee simple, and thus regain his old estate, when the annual payment is a specified number of days in arrears. The express reservation of such a right of re-entry clearly made the fee simple less than absolute, and it was thought by some that even a temporary right of entry might have this effect. This meant that those who had purchased land in this way before 1926 and had obtained legal estates suddenly found that as from January 1, 1926 their estates might no longer be legal; indeed, where they were not, it was far from clear exactly who did have the legal estate. Further, the complicated provisions of the Settled Land Act 1925 probably applied.[30]

To remedy this state of affairs the Law of Property (Amendment) Act 1926[31] provided that "a fee simple subject to a legal or equitable right of entry or re-entry is for the purposes of [the Law of Property Act 1925] a fee simple absolute". While this undoubtedly meets the difficulty it was meant to deal with, the wide terms in which it was drawn appear to have done more than was intended. The effect of a condition subsequent annexed to a fee simple is to give rise to an implied right of re-entry exercisable on breach of the condition,

---

[25] LPA 1925 s.1(4).
[26] LPA 1925 s.1(4).
[27] Above, Ch.2.
[28] See above, para.2–025.
[29] Above, para.2–029.
[30] Below, paras 7–006 et seq.
[31] Sch.1, adding words to LPA 1925 s.7(1).

and until the right of re-entry is exercised the fee simple continues.[32] Consequently, by virtue of this amending Act, every fee simple defeasible by condition subsequent appears to rank as a legal estate (unless created under a trust), even though it is far from being "absolute" in the ordinary sense of the word. Further, by statute, certain land held for special purposes, such as schools or highways, is divested and reverts to (usually) the grantor when the special purpose is at an end. Such a fee simple was nevertheless declared to be absolute.[33] But, as a result of subsequent legislation, at the end of the special purpose the legal estate now remains vested in the existing owners, though they hold it on a trust of land for those entitled to the right of reverter.[34]

In possession

"In possession" means that the estate is a present estate and not in remainder or in reversion.[35] It includes not only physical possession of the land but also the receipt of rents and profits or the right to receive them, if any. Thus a fee simple is still "in possession" even though the owner has granted a lease, for he is entitled to the rent reserved by the lease. But if land has been granted "to A for life, remainder to B in fee simple", the interests of both A and B are necessarily equitable, for a life interest cannot now be legal and B's fee simple is not in possession.[36] However, a mortgagor's legal estate is not converted into an equitable interest merely by the mortgagee exercising his power to take possession of the mortgaged property.[37]

4–015

"Term of years absolute"

A term of years absolute is a lease which creates an interest in land.

4–016

Term of years

"Term of years" is defined as including a term of less than a year, or for a year or years and a fraction of a year, or from year to year.[38] In effect "term of years" means a term for any period having a fixed and certain duration as a minimum.[39] Thus, in addition to a tenancy for a specified number of years (such as "to X for ninety-nine years"), such tenancies as a yearly tenancy or a weekly tenancy are "terms of years" within the definition, for there is a minimum duration of a year or a week respectively. But a lease "for the life of X" cannot exist as a legal estate, and the same, perhaps, applies to tenancies at will or at sufferance (if they are estates at all[40]), for their duration is wholly uncertain.

4–017

---

[32] Above, para.2–029.

[33] LPA 1925 s.7(1).

[34] Reverter of Sites Act 1987 s.1, resolving the difficulty shown by *Re Clayton's Deed Poll* [1980] Ch. 99 and *Re Rowhook Mission Hall, Horsham* [1985] Ch. 62. See [1987] Conv. 408 (D. Evans).

[35] See *District Bank Ltd v Webb* [1958] 1 W.L.R. 148.

[36] See, however, the Welsh Church (Burial Grounds) Act 1945 s.1, for a curious qualification of LPA 1925 s.1.

[37] LPA 1925 s.95(4).

[38] LPA 1925 s.205(1)(xxvii).

[39] *Prudential Assurance Co Ltd v London Residuary Body* [1992] 2 A.C. 386; *Berrisford v Mexfield Housing Co-operative Ltd* [2012] 1 A.C. 955.

[40] See above, para.2–010.

Absolute

4–018 "Absolute" This word has very little effect since, by virtue of the definition section, a term of years is not prevented from being absolute merely by being liable to determination by notice, re-entry, operation of law or by a provision for cesser on redemption or in any other event (other than the dropping of a life, or the determination of a determinable life interest).[41] This means that a term of years may be absolute even if it contains a clause enabling the parties to determine it at certain specified periods, such as at the end of the first five or 10 years, or if it provides (as is almost always the case) that the landlord may determine it if the rent is not paid or a covenant is broken. A lease is determined by "operation of law" pursuant to the doctrine of satisfied terms[42] and to a proviso for cesser on redemption in a mortgage (although, today the type of mortgages which contain such provisos are virtually obsolete).[43]

It will be seen from this discussion that by the express provisions of statute a term of years absolute may consist of a tenancy which is neither a "term of years" nor "absolute" according to the natural meaning of the words, such as a monthly tenancy liable to be forfeited for non-payment of rent. "Absolute" really has very little meaning here.

Unlike a fee simple absolute, a term of years absolute may be a legal estate even though not "in possession". A lease to commence in five years' time may thus be legal, although there is now a 21-year limit to the length of time which may elapse between the grant of a lease and the commencement of the term.[44] There is no limit to the length of a term of years absolute; terms of 3,000 years can arise in the case of mortgages, although mortgages of this type are today virtually obsolete.[45] But there is no such thing as a lease in perpetuity.[46]

"An easement, right, or privilege in or over land for an interest equivalent to an estate in fee simple absolute in possession or a term of years absolute"

4–019 This head includes both easements and, it seems, profits á prendre.[47] An easement confers the right to use the land of another in some way, or to prevent it from being used for certain purposes. Thus rights of way, rights of water and rights of light may exist as easements. A profit á prendre gives the right to take something from the land of another, such as peat, fish or wood. These rights can be legal only if they are held for interests' equivalent to one of the two legal estates. Thus a right of way for 21 years may be legal but a right of way for life must be equitable.

---

[41] LPA 1925 s.205(1)(xxvii).
[42] Below, paras 12–022, 17–010.
[43] Below, para.17–010.
[44] Below, para.11–025.
[45] See LPA 1925 ss.85(2), 87(1).
[46] See *Sevenoaks, Maidstone and Tunbridge Ry v London, Chatham and Dover Ry* (1879) 11 Ch.D. 625 at 635.
[47] For easements and profits, see below, Ch.15.

"A rentcharge in possession issuing out of or charged on land being either perpetual or for a term of years absolute"

A rentcharge is a right which, independently of any lease or mortgage, gives the owner the right to a periodical sum of money, with the payment of which some land is burdened,[48] as where the fee simple owner of Blackacre charges the land with a payment of £50 per annum to X. With some exceptions,[49] no new legal rentcharges have been able to be created since August 21, 1977, and any existing legal rentcharges will be extinguished 60 years after they first became payable and in any case by July 22, 2037.[50]

4–020

"In possession"

Under the subsection, a rentcharge to start at a date subsequent to that on which it was granted could not be legal, even if it was perpetual or for a term of years absolute. But the Law of Property (Entailed Interests) Act 1932[51] declared that a rentcharge was "in possession" notwithstanding that the payments were limited to commence or accrue at a date subsequent to its creation, unless the rentcharge was limited to take effect in remainder after or expectant on the failure or determination of some other interest.[52] Thus if X conveyed land to Y in consideration of a perpetual rentcharge becoming payable one year after the conveyance, the rentcharge could nevertheless have been legal; but if a perpetual rentcharge was granted "to A for life, remainder to B absolutely", B's interest could only be legal after A's death.

4–021

Issuing out of or charged on land

"Land" includes another rentcharge.[53] Thus if P charged his fee simple estate in Blackacre with the payment to Q of £100 per annum in perpetuity, Q could, until August 21, 1977, have created a legal rentcharge of £50 per annum in favour of R, charged on his rentcharge of £100.

4–022

"Being either perpetual or for a term of years absolute"

"Perpetual" is used here in place of "fee simple absolute". This verbal difference seems to be of no practical importance.

4–023

"A charge by way of legal mortgage"

This needs no comment here save to point out that this is now the only permitted method of creating a legal mortgage today. The other method, to grant a term of years absolute

4–024

---

[48] For rentcharges, see below, paras 15–097 et seq.

[49] See estate rentcharges under the Rentcharges Act 1977 s.2(3)(c), (4) and (5); see also *Canwell Estate Co Ltd v Smith Brothers Farms Ltd* [2012] EWCA Civ 237; [2012] 1 W.L.R. 2626.

[50] Rentcharges Act 1977 ss.2, 3. See below, paras 15–097–15–125.

[51] s.2.

[52] See (1932) 73 L.J. News. 321.

[53] LPA 1925 ss.122, 205(1)(ix).

on certain conditions, is now abolished in the case of registered land by virtue of the Land Registration Act 2002. This is dealt with later.[54]

"Land tax, tithe rentcharge, and any other similar charge on land which is not created by an instrument"

4–025   This group comprises periodical payments with which land is burdened by operation of law (such as by statute) and not by some conveyance or other voluntary act of parties. The words "land tax, tithe rentcharge" have now been repealed,[55] but they are printed here in order to explain the word "similar".

Land tax was a small annual tax on land first imposed in 1692. It was abolished in 1963.[56]

Tithe rentcharge was abolished by the Tithe Act 1936. It was a type of rentcharge imposed by statute in lieu of the former right of parsons and others to one-tenth of the produce of land. Under the Act of 1936, tithe owners were compensated with government stock, and the land formerly burdened with tithe rentcharge was subjected to a "tithe redemption annuity" payable to the Crown; this was originally payable for 60 years[57] but the obligation was subsequently extinguished on October 2, 1977.[58] Although a tithe redemption annuity was not expressly stated to be a legal interest, it clearly fell within that category as being a "similar charge on land which is not created by an instrument".

"Rights of entry exercisable over or in respect of a legal term of years absolute, or annexed, for any purpose, to a legal rentcharge"

4–026   As already mentioned,[59] a legal term of years absolute is usually made subject to an express right of the landlord to re-enter if the tenant fails to pay rent or comply with the covenants (such a right will only rarely be implied). Such a right may be a legal right. This is also the case for any right of entry or re-entry attached to a legal rentcharge. If the rent is not paid, a temporary right of entry to collect payment out of the rents and profits is implied; and profits and many rentcharges have the benefit of an express right to re-enter and determine the legal estate of the person liable to pay the annual sum in the event of non-payment). By contrast, a right reserved on an assignment of a lease for the benefit of the assignor (who retains no other interest in the land enabling him to re-enter and retake the land in the event of a breach of covenant by the assignee is merely an equitable interest,[60] even, perhaps, if the right is reserved only for a defined or indefinite term.[61]

---

[54] See para.17–010.
[55] Tithe Act 1936 Sch.9; Finance Act 1963 Sch.14, Pt VI.
[56] Finance Act 1963 s.68, Sch.14, Pts V, VI.
[57] Tithe Act 1936 s.3.
[58] Finance Act 1977 s.56.
[59] Above, para.4–016.
[60] *Shiloh Spinners Ltd v Harding* [1973] A.C. 691. For assignments of leases, see below, para.11–038.
[61] *Shiloh Spinners Ltd v Harding* [1973] A.C. 691 at 726.

Concurrent legal estates

Any number of legal estates may exist concurrently in the same piece of land.[62] Thus A may
have the legal fee simple in Greenacre, subject to a legal mortgage in favour of B, a legal
rentcharge in favour of C, a legal lease in favour of D, and so on.

4–027

EXTENSION OF THE DOCTRINE OF OVERREACHING

It has already been seen that a fundamental principle underlying the 1925 legislation was
that all beneficial interests should be capable of being overreached into any capital sum
paid by way of purchase money for the legal estate in the land or a legal interest therein.

4–028

The scope of the doctrine

Settlements

It has already been seen that when two or more persons are beneficially entitled to property of any type in succession, that is to say one after another, the property in question
is said to be subject to a settlement. The 1925 legislation made all interests which arise
under settlements of land overreachable. A purchaser for value of both registered and
unregistered land will take free of all interests arising under settlements provided that he
pays the purchase money to at least two trustees or a trust corporation. If he does so, the
interests in question are overreached and transferred to the purchase money received from
the purchaser.

4–029

Settlements created after 1996 necessarily take effect under a trust of land. Before 1997,
settlements could take effect in two ways: under an express trust for sale under the Law of
Property Act 1925 and under the Settled Land Act 1925. Express trusts for sale, whenever
created, have since 1996[63] been trusts of land. Settlements which took effect under the
Settled Land Act 1925 before 1997 are still governed by that legislation. The overreaching
of interests arising under trusts of land is governed by s.2 of the Law of Property Act 1925.
The overreaching of interests arising under settlements under the Settled Land Act 1925 is
governed by that legislation.

Co-ownership

Co-ownership of land does not, without more, give rise to a settlement although it is obviously possible for individual interests under a settlement to be jointly owned. Thus where
a testator leaves his property to his wife for life and subject to that to his children equally,
the interest in remainder of the children is thus co-owned. However, the beneficial interests
of co-owners of land now take effect under an implied trust of land under which up to four
co-owners of the legal title in the land hold it on trust for all of the co-owners. Before 1997
these beneficial interests took effect behind an implied trust for sale but implied trusts for

4–030

---

[62] LPA 1925 s.1(5).
[63] When TLATA came into force.

sale that arose then now take effect as trusts of land.[64] Provided that a purchaser pays the purchase money to at least two trustees or a trust corporation, the rights of the co-owners are similarly overreached and transferred to the purchase money received from the purchaser. The overreaching of the beneficial interests of co-owners of land is also governed by s.2 of the Law of Property Act 1925.

Bare trusts

4–031   A bare, or simple, trust also does not constitute a settlement. Such a trust arises when a trustee or trustees hold property (whether legal or equitable) on trust for a person who is of full age and absolutely beneficially entitled, the nature of the trust not being prescribed by the settlor but being left to the construction of the law, as where X conveys land "to T in fee simple on trust for A in fee simple". In such a case, T is bound to permit A to occupy the land or receive the rents and profits and must obey A's instructions about the disposition of the land. A bare trust may also arise where on a purchase of land the money is provided by one person but the conveyance is made to another. Thus where P, wishing to keep his name out of the transaction, provides N with the money to buy the land, N holds on a bare trust for P.[65] Since 1996 beneficial interests arising under bare trusts have also been able to be overreached (prior to 1997 it was necessary for the beneficiary to join in the sale). This is because a bare trust is included in the definition of a trust of land.[66] Provided that a purchaser pays the purchase money to at least two trustees or a trust corporation, the rights of the beneficiary or beneficiaries are similarly overreached and transferred to the purchase money received from the purchaser. The overreaching of beneficial interests arising under bare trusts is therefore now also governed by s.2 of the Law of Property Act 1925.

Other examples

4–032   Overreaching also occurs:

(i)   where a mortgagee sells the mortgaged property in the exercise of a power of sale arising as a result of a default by the mortgagor in making his repayments or in some other respect, in which case the interests in the mortgaged property of the mortgagor and anyone claiming through him are overreached and transferred to the purchase money received from the purchaser (the mortgagee will of course first deduct from that purchase money the principal sum, interest and costs owed to him); and

(ii)   where the personal representatives of a deceased person sell land owned by him at the date of his death, in which case the potential beneficial interests of those entitled under his will or intestacy (it will not be known if they actually have any until the administration of the estate is completed and the net value of the deceased's assets is known) are overreached and transferred to the purchase money received from the purchaser.

---

[64]   TLATA 1996 s.1.
[65]   See *Dyer v Dyer* (1788) 2 Cox Eq. 92 at 93.
[66]   See TLATA 1996 s.1.

These last two examples of overreaching will be considered separately in the relevant chapters.

Overreaching under the Law of Property Act 1925

Where overreaching takes place under the Law of Property Act 1925, it will be the trustees who will be entering into the transaction by which the interests of the beneficiaries are overreached.

4–033

Until 1997

Until 1997 overreaching was only possible under the Law of Property Act 1925 under some form of trust for sale, either an express trust for sale or a trust for sale implied as a result of beneficial co-ownership. Indeed, in one sense, it could be said that a disposition by trustees for sale had no overreaching effect; for by the equitable doctrine of conversion, so long as the land remained unsold, the rights of the beneficiaries were already deemed to be rights in the purchase money into which it would ultimately be converted. It could thus be said that a sale or other transaction by trustees for sale did not transfer the rights of the beneficiaries from the land to the purchase money, for strictly they never were attached to the land in the first place. This view rather overstated the impact of the doctrine of conversion, particularly when the beneficiaries were in possession of the land, as was highly likely in the case of beneficial co-ownership.[67] It was therefore both convenient and less misleading to use the term "overreaching" as including the process by which the beneficiaries had their rights in what is money in theory but land in fact transferred to what is money both in theory and in fact.

4–034

Since 1996

Since 1996 overreaching has been possible under the Law of Property Act 1925 under a trust of land, which is defined[68] as including an express trust for sale of land, a bare trust of land and what is now implied as a result of beneficial co-ownership of land. The doctrine of conversion no longer exists, having been abolished except in respect of trusts created by will where the testator died before 1997,[69] and so, except in respect of the latter trusts, it can now no longer be argued that a disposition by express trustees for sale of land has no overreaching effect.

4–035

The effect of overreaching under the Law of Property Act 1925

A disposition by trustees of land under the Law of Property Act 1925 is effective to over-reach the equitable rights of the beneficiaries thereunder. There is no power to overreach legal estates, nor, apparently, to overreach rights already existing when the trust of land was created. A purchaser of a legal estate from the trustees is not concerned with the rents

4–036

---

[67] (1984) 100 L.Q.R. 86 (S. Anderson); and see below, para.8–045.
[68] TLATA 1996 s.1.
[69] TLATA 1996 s.3.

and profits of the land until sale or the proceeds of sale thereafter, even if the trusts are declared by the instrument which created the trust of land.[70]

Payment of capital money

4–037   For beneficial interests to be overreached,[71] the proceeds of sale or other capital money must be paid to or applied by the direction of:

(i) all the trustees of the trust of land, who must be either two or more in number or a trust corporation (the definition of "trust corporation" includes certain officials such as the Public Trustee and certain companies with sufficient paid-up capital (at present £250,000)[72]); or

(ii) a sole personal representative.[73]

There is no provision for payment into court. Overreaching will also occur where a transaction would normally give rise to the payment of capital money, even though no capital money is actually payable to or received by the trustees or personal representative in question. This has been held to occur where a mortgage secures only the existing indebtedness of the trust.[74] It would presumably also occur where no capital money was payable on the sale of an estate, either because the vendor had agreed to defer payment of the purchase price or, more implausibly, because the property was being leased back to the vendor and the lump sum payable for the lease back cancelled out the purchase price.

Where these requirements are satisfied, the interests of the beneficiaries will be overreached, whether or not they are aware of the transaction, and, if they are aware of the transaction, whether or not they are in favour of it[75]; the only exception to this rule is where the consent of the beneficiary in question is made a prerequisite of the transaction being entered into.[76] However, a beneficiary may obtain an injunction to restrain a sale if there is only one trustee[77]; one trustee will suffice if the transaction is of a type under which no capital money arises, such as the grant of a lease at a rent where no lump sum is payable.[78] Where capital money is paid to only one trustee, there is no overreaching; but if the land is registered land a beneficiary in actual occupation under a trust of land will have an interest which overrides registration and so will be binding upon the purchaser.[79] In the case of unregistered land, a purchaser will in all cases be bound by the beneficial interest unless he is a bona fide purchaser for value of a legal estate without notice.[80]

---

[70] LPA 1925 s.27; below, para.7–010.
[71] *City of London B.S. v Flegg* [1988] A.C. 54.
[72] LPA 1925 ss.2, 27.
[73] LPA 1925 ss.2, 27; LP(Am.)A 1926 Sch.
[74] *State Bank of India v Sood* [1997] Ch. 276.
[75] *City of London B.S. v Flegg* [1988] A.C. 54.
[76] See below, para.7–019.
[77] *Walker v Waller* [1967] 1 W.L.R. 451; for the appointment of additional trustees, see below, para.7–042.
[78] LPA 1925 s.27(2); LP(Am.)A 1926, Sch.
[79] *Williams & Glyn's Bank Ltd v Boland* [1981] A.C. 487.
[80] *Kingsnorth Finance Co Ltd v Tizard* [1986] 1 W.L.R. 783.

Capital money as land

Until 1997 proceeds of sale or other capital money arising under a trust for sale could be applied in the same way as capital money arising from settled land.[81] This did not convert the rights of the beneficiaries into rights in land; they remained rights in pure personalty[82] and any land acquired under this provision had to be conveyed to the trustees for sale to hold on trust for sale.[83] Since 1996, as a result of the abolition of the doctrine of conversion (except in respect of trusts created by will where the testator died before 1997),[84] the rights of the beneficiaries are rights in land even before sale and, after sale, remain rights in land in the event that further land is acquired with the proceeds of sale.

4–038

Overreaching under the Settled Land Act 1925

In settlements under the Settled Land Act 1925, the legal title to their subject-matter will be vested not in the trustees of the settlement but in what the Act describes as the "tenant for life", the person entitled under the settlement to an interest in possession for the time being, whether or not that interest is actually a life interest. If there is no such person or the person in question is an infant, the legal title will instead be vested in what are described as the "statutory owner", who usually will be the trustees of the settlement. It is therefore the tenant for life or statutory owner, rather than the trustees of the settlement as such, who will be entering into the transaction by which the interests of the beneficiaries are overreached.

4–039

Rights under the settlement[85]

A conveyance is effectual to pass the land or other interest concerned "discharged from all the limitations, powers, and provisions of the settlement, and from all estates, interests, and charges subsisting or to arise thereunder"; it is immaterial whether or not a purchaser has notice of these rights. In short, the purchaser takes the land free from all the rights under the settlement. The Act then makes certain qualifications to this rule: the land is to pass to the purchaser discharged from the above rights, "but subject to and with the exception of"[86]:

4–040

(i) All legal estates and charges by way of legal mortgage having priority to the settlement.

In nearly every case this provision is mere surplusage, for no power is given to overreach rights prior to the settlement and so the qualification is unnecessary. If X makes a legal mortgage of land and later settles the land, the tenant for life has no power to overreach the mortgage, which continues to bind the land.

---

[81] LPA 1925 s.28 (now repealed); *Re Wellsted's W.T.* [1949] Ch. 296. cf. *Re Wakeman* [1945] Ch. 177. See Thompson, *Co-ownership*, pp.7, 8.
[82] *Re Kempthorne* [1930] 1 Ch. 268.
[83] LPA 1925 s.28 (now repealed).
[84] TLATA 1996 s.3.
[85] SLA 1925 s.72.
[86] See *Re Dickin and Kelsall's Contract* [1908] 1 Ch. 213 at 221.

(ii) All legal estates and charges by way of legal mortgage which have been conveyed or created for securing money actually raised at the date of the deed.

This is a true exception, for it excludes something which otherwise would have been included in the overreaching provision. Thus if a tenant for life creates a legal mortgage to pay for improvements or raise portions, and the mortgagee has actually paid the money, the mortgage cannot be overreached even though it is an interest arising under the settlement. "Mortgagees who have actually lent their money on the security of the land are regarded as strangers to the settlement, and are not to have the security which they bargained for on the land itself transferred to the purchase money at the will of the tenant for life."[87] If the money has not in fact been paid (for instance, where a legal term of years has been created to secure portions which have not been raised) the right is overreached.[88]

(iii) All leases and grants of other rights (except annuities, limited owner's charges and general equitable charges[89]) which at the date of the deed are:
    (a) binding on the successors in title of the tenant for life; and
    (b) duly registered if capable of registration.

This also is a true exception, but unlike the previous provisions it is not confined to legal rights. It thus apparently applies to a restrictive covenant creating a mere equitable burden on the land.

Rights prior to the settlement

4–041 Having dealt with the exceptions to the rule that all rights arising under the settlement can be overreached, the Act proceeds to the converse case, namely the exceptions to the rule that rights prior to the settlement cannot be overreached. The Act[90] provides that:

(i) an annuity;
(ii) a limited owner's charge; and
(iii) a general equitable charge

will be overreached on a disposition under the Act even if they have been duly protected by registration; these rights are treated as if they had been created by the settlement even if in fact they arose before it came into existence. They are all rights which can be represented in terms of money and so will not suffer from being transferred to the purchase money.

Summary

4–042 It cannot be said that the overreaching provisions are very happily drawn. For those who wish to have a bird's eye view of their effect (necessarily at the expense of some accuracy) the position may be represented as follows:

---

[87] *Re Mundy and Roper's Contract* [1899] 1 Ch. 275 at 289 per Chitty L.J.
[88] See *Re Du Cane and Nettlefold's Contract* [1898] 2 Ch. 96 at 108.
[89] For these rights, see below, para.6–070.
[90] SLA 1925 s.72.

(i)   there is in general no power to overreach legal rights;

(ii) subject to the three exceptions set out above, there is no power to overreach equitable rights already existing when the settlement was made;

(iii) there is power to overreach all the equitable rights of the beneficiaries under the settlement, including derivative rights, such as the rights of a mortgagee of the beneficial interest of a tenant for life.

Payment of capital money

Notwithstanding anything to the contrary in the settlement, for beneficial interests to be overreached any capital money payable in respect of the transaction must be paid either: **4–043**

(i)   to, or by the direction of, all the trustees of the settlement, who must be either two or more in number or a trust corporation; or

(ii) into court.[91]

It is for the tenant for life to decide which of the two methods of payment is to be adopted.[92] Presumably, as in the case of trusts of land, overreaching will also occur where a transaction would normally give rise to the payment of capital money, even though no capital money is actually payable to or received by the trustees or paid into court.[93]

Where these requirements are satisfied, the interests of the beneficiaries will be overreached whether or not they are aware of the transaction and, if they are aware of the transaction, whether or not they are in favour of it; this is because, in the case of settlements under the Settled Land Act 1925, it is not possible to impose restrictions on the dispositive powers of the tenant for life.[94] If a purchaser fails to pay his money in accordance with these provisions, and pays it, for example, to the tenant for life, he will not get a good discharge and will be unable to make a good title to a subsequent purchaser.[95] Where no capital money arises on a transaction (as where a lease is granted at a rent where no lump sum is payable), a disposition in favour of a bona fide purchaser for value of a legal estate takes effect under the Act and thus has an overreaching effect even though there are no trustees.[96]

Capital money as land

The capital money and any investments representing it are for all purposes of disposition, transmission and devolution (but not otherwise, such as for fiscal purposes[97]) treated as land, and are held for and go to the same persons, in the same manner and for the same estates, interests and trusts, as the land whence they arise would have been held and have gone under the settlement.[98] Thus where a tenant for life had become absolutely entitled to   **4–044**

---

[91] SLA 1925 s.18.

[92] SLA 1925 s.75; *Hatten v Russell* (1888) 38 Ch.D. 334 at 345.

[93] By analogy with *State Bank of India v Sood* [1997] Ch. 276.

[94] See p.269 of the 8th edition of this work.

[95] *Re Norton and Las Casas' Contract* [1909] 2 Ch. 59.

[96] SLA 1925 s.110(4).

[97] Earl of *Midleton v Baron Cottesloe* [1949] A.C. 418.

[98] SLA 1925 s.75.

the land, a will of his that effectively disposed of personalty alone could not carry any capital money[99]; whereas an option under the settlement to purchase the land can be exercised so as to obtain the capital money.[100] In short, the state in which the settled property happens to be at any given moment, whether it is land, investments or money, cannot affect the rights of the beneficiaries or those claiming under them.

Under ad hoc settlements

4–045   The original intention of the 1925 legislation was that a conveyance under a settlement under a trust for sale or under the Settled Land Act 1925 should overreach not only the interests of the beneficiaries but also prior equitable interests as well. This provision was attacked in Parliament, and ultimately a workable scheme was produced and duly embodied in the 1925 legislation.

Clearly some equitable interests cannot be overreached; thus a restrictive covenant (such as against building) and an equitable easement (such as a right of way which takes effect only in equity) cannot become corresponding rights in the purchase money. But dispositions under certain special settlements under (until 1997) trusts for sale, under (since 1996) trusts of land, and under the Settled Land Act 1925, described in each case by the label "ad hoc", have a special wider overreaching effect than that set out above. Dispositions under ad hoc settlements overreach, in addition to the rights of the beneficiaries under the settlement, annuities, limited owner's charges and general equitable charges (dispositions under settlements under the Settled Land Act 1925 do this anyway, so that this is only an advantage in the case of, until 1997, ad hoc trusts for sale and of, since 1996, ad hoc trusts of land). Certain other equities, such as a widow's right of dower, which must by now be entirely obsolete are also overreached to obtain this wider effect the settlement in question must have "guaranteed" trustees, i.e. either trustees appointed or approved by the court, or a trust corporation. The idea is that such trustees are likely to be particularly trustworthy and that this will console those whose rights are overreached but would not normally have been overreached. That is the theory; in practice, because the additional overreaching powers are so meagre, little use has ever been made of such special settlements, which are effectively obsolete. It therefore seems inappropriate to consider them any further.

Summary of overreaching provisions

4–046   In broad outline, the position may be summarised as follows:

(i)   A conveyance until 1997 under an ordinary trust for sale or since 1996 under an ordinary trust of land overreaches the rights of the beneficiaries thereunder.

(ii)   A conveyance under an ordinary settlement under the Settled Land Act 1925 overreaches:

(a)   the rights of the beneficiaries thereunder; and

(b)   annuities, limited owner's charges and general equitable charges.

---

[99]   *Re Cartwright* [1939] Ch. 90.
[100]   *Re Armstrong's W.T.* [1943] Ch. 400.

(iii) A conveyance until 1997 under an ad hoc trust for sale or since 1996 under an ad hoc trust of land or under an ad hoc settlement under the Settled Land Act 1925 overreaches:
  (a) the rights of the beneficiaries thereunder;
  (b) annuities, limited owner's charges and general equitable charges; and
  (c) certain other equities, such as a widow's right of dower.

FURTHER READING

- M. Dixon, "Proprietary and non-proprietary rights in modern land law" in L. Tee (ed), *Land Law: Issues, Debates and Policy* (Devon: Willan, 2002)

Chapter 5

REGISTERED TITLE

CHAPTER SUMMARY

Registration of title is a fundamental change to the historical method of proving title to the rights in land in England & Wales. The objective of the Land Registration Act 2002 was that the register should be a complete and accurate reflection of the state of title of the land at any given time.[1]

The principle difference between registered and unregistered title is that, regardless of whether an estate or interest in land has been transferred into the name of a person, he does not become the legal owner until he is registered. This ensures that there is conclusiveness as to title and reduces the investigation of title required by purchasers. Furthermore, the State guarantees that, where the Register is mistaken, a person who suffers loss will be entitled to an indemnity.

This chapter explains the system of registered land in England & Wales and covers the following core areas:

- The history and development of registered land from the late nineteenth century, to the Land Registration Acts of 1925 and 2002.
- The fundamental principles that registration confers title and is conclusive.
- The classification of registrable estates and interests under the Land Registration Act 2002.
- The structure of the Register.
- Interests which override.
- Overreaching.
- Alteration, rectification and indemnity.

INTRODUCTION

History

Today, registration of title is of great and increasing importance; but it is by no means new. **5–001**
Acts were passed in 1862 and 1875,[2] providing for voluntary registration of title, but not

---

[1] See Law Commission Report, (2001) Law Com. No.271, para.1.5.
[2] Land Registry Act 1862 (LRA 1862); Land Transfer Act 1875 (LTA 1875).

until the Land Transfer Act 1897 made registration of title compulsory on dealings with land in the County of London were any substantial numbers of titles registered. The Land Registration Act 1925 was considered to be ill-drafted and consequently there was a series of amending Acts, which together were cited as the Land Registration Acts 1925 to 1997.[3] These Acts are supplemented by the Land Registration Rules 1925, as amended, and a number of other statutory rules. All this legislation was repealed by the Land Registration Act 2002, which came into force on October 13, 2003. In addition to the Land Registration Act 2002, the Land Registration Rules 2003 make detailed provision for the operation of the system of land registration under the Act. The LRA 2002 was a joint project between the Law Commission and the Land Registry.[4]

It is considered that the changes made by the Land Registration Act 2002 are so substantial that authorities on the law under the Land Registration Act 1925 are unlikely to be of much assistance.

Basis of the system

5–002   When land is described as "registered" it means that the title (the "estate" in the land held) of the registered proprietor (the owner) is documented on the individual register for that land, which is held by HM Land Registry. As has been discussed elsewhere in this book, the proprietor of land does not own the land itself, he owns an "estate" in the land, which, by virtue of the Law of Property Act 1925 may only be either an estate in fee simple or a term of years absolute.[5]

The basic idea was to replace the separate investigation of title that took place on every purchase by a title guaranteed by the State. In the case of unregistered land, a purchaser must satisfy himself from the abstract (also known as the epitome), the deeds, his requisitions on title,[6] his searches and his inspection of the land that the vendor has power to sell the land and that it is subject to no undisclosed incumbrances. In the case of registered land, on the other hand, the purchaser can discover from the mere inspection of the register whether the vendor has power to sell the land and what the more important incumbrances are; the other incumbrances must be investigated in much the same way as in the case of unregistered land. The complexity of rights in land is such as to render it impossible to make the transfer of registered land as simple as the transfer of shares registered in the books of a company, but the present system of registration of title may be said to go almost as far as is practicable.

Classification of rights

5–003   The system of registration of title in no way amounts to a separate code of land law although certain rules of the substantive law do differ depending on whether land is registered or unregistered. One example of this is in relation to the doctrine of notice. The

---

[3]   See Land Registration Act 1936 (LRA 1936); Land Registration Act 1966; Land Registration and Land Charges Act 1971; Land Registration Act 1986, Land Registration Act 1997. See also Administration of Justice Act 1977; Land Registration Act 1988; and certain Acts on special subjects, such as Housing Acts 1980 and 1985.

[4]   See Law Commission Report, (2001) Law Com. No. 271.

[5]   LPA 1925 s.1(1).

[6]   This is a questionnaire that relates to the sale of the property.

Land Registration Act 2002 (as did the 1925 Act) has abandoned the doctrine of notice and it does not apply to registered land when ascertaining if third-party rights affecting the land in question will bind a purchaser.[7] In the main, registration is concerned with the conveyancing aspects of land law, i.e. documenting title and dealing with actual or potential transfers of rights existing under the general law, and in the main it leaves the basis of this unaffected. In this connection, the differing classes of interests in land must be distinguished.

Unregistered land

In very broad terms, on a purchase of unregistered land, rights in the land fall into three main categories: **5–004**

    (i)   the estate or interest that the purchaser is buying;

   (ii)   rights adverse to the land which, being legal, will bind the purchaser except in the few cases where they are overreached or are void for want of registration; and

  (iii)   other rights adverse to the land which are equitable, and so, if not overreached or void for want of registration, will bind the purchaser unless he takes the estate for value in good faith without notice of them.

Registered land

On a purchase of registered land, there is a similar but not exactly corresponding division: **5–005**

    (i)   the estate or interest that the purchaser is buying will usually be a registrable interest: a legal estate or interest which is registrable with its own title (legal easements, profits á prendre, mortgages and rights of entry are not registrable interests and after completion the purchaser will have to protect them as minor interests on his vendor's registered title);

   (ii)   rights adverse to the land which will override registration and so, if they are not overreached, will bind the purchaser whether or not their existence is disclosed by the register or otherwise; and

  (iii)   other rights adverse to the land which will not bind the purchaser if they are over-reached or if he purchased for value under a registered disposition and they have not been protected by some entry on the register.

Other registrations

If the title to land is registered, there is no question of registration in the land charges register, for entries on the land register take the place of this. But entries must still be made in the local land charges registers. Further, most charges created by a company for securing money require registration in the companies charges register in addition to protection by an entry on the land register.[8]

---

[7] See para.1–007 for a discussion of the doctrine.

[8] CA 2006 Pt 25.

Open register

5–007   On December 3, 1990, the land register was opened to public inspection, with the right to obtain copies of it.[9] Previously, nobody could inspect it or obtain copies of the entries on the register without the authority of the registered proprietor of the land,[10] though on a sale or other disposition (except a lease or charge) the vendor was obliged to give the purchaser an authority to inspect the register.[11] Further, an index map, a parcels index and a list of pending applications were[12] (and still are) open to public inspection, making it possible to discover whether or not any particular property has been or is about to be registered.

Electronic conveyancing

5–008   The Land Registration Act 2002[13] has created a framework by which it will in due course be possible to create and to transfer interests in registered land electronically. The Act has done so by enabling the formal documents to be executed electronically[14] and by providing for an electronic communications network which will be secure.[15] Access to the network is to be controlled by the Land Registry. This is because the ultimate objective of the Land Registration Act 2002 is that the execution of the formal documents and their registration will be a simultaneous process to be initiated by conveyancers.[16] The Land Registry will also be obliged to make arrangements for access to the network by persons who wish to do their own conveyancing.[17] Both conveyancing practitioners and the Land Registry will have to develop new ways of working if the system is to be established. It is therefore envisaged that it will be introduced in stages, starting with only the simplest transactions and gradually progressing. This will be regulated by rules which the Act gives the Lord Chancellor power to make.[18] He has also been given power, subject to appropriate consultation, to make electronic conveyancing compulsory[19]; this is because some of the benefits of electronic conveyancing can be maximised only if it is used universally. However, compulsory electronic conveyancing will only become feasible when it has become the predominant way of carrying out transactions; consequently, this is likely to be many years away. Indeed, a pilot scheme was completed in 2008 but the aim to move to e-conveyancing is now "on hold".[20]

---

[9]   LRA 1988 s.1; SI 1990/1359.
[10]   LRA 1925 ss.112, 112A (repealed).
[11]   LRA 1925 s.110(1) (repealed).
[12]   LRR 2003 Pt 2.
[13]   LRA 2002 ss.91–95.
[14]   LRA 2002 s.91.
[15]   LRA 2002 s.92 and Sch.5.
[16]   LRA 2002 s.93.
[17]   LRA 2002 s.92 and Sch.5.
[18]   LRA 2002 s.95.
[19]   LRA 2002 s.93.
[20]   Land Registry Report on responses to e-conveyancing secondary legislation Pt 3.

Dispute resolution

The Land Registration Act 2002 created a new office, which did not exist under the Land Registration Act 1925, that of an Adjudicator to the Land Registry,[21] but this office was abolished on July 1, 2013 and its functions were transferred to the First-tier Tribunal (Property Chamber) Land Registration Division.[22] It is now the First-tier Tribunal which has jurisdiction to resolve disputes that arise under the LRA 2002. It is important to acknowledge the creation and abolition of this office because much of the case law will refer to the Adjudicator to HM Land Registry.

5–009

Fundamental principles

Two linked principles are fundamental to registered land.

5–010

Registration confers title

In unregistered conveyancing, the vendor's estate in the land passes to the purchaser as soon as the conveyance is executed. In registered conveyancing, the execution of the transfer by the vendor confers no estate on the purchaser. It is registration that vests legal title in the purchaser in accordance with the register.[23] Registration is treated as having effect from the time of the making of the application.[24]

5–011

Registration is conclusive

Registration is conclusive of title.[25] When a title is first registered, the registration confers a new statutory title on the registered proprietor, even if his previous title was defective or he had no title at all, as where he claims under forged title deeds. The act of registration confers the statutory title on the proprietor,[26] and gives him "a new root of title".[27] He holds this title subject to any interests protected by entries on the register and to any interests which override registration. In principle he holds free from all other interests,[28] even if he has full notice of them; the doctrine of notice for unregistered land has no application to registered land, even by analogy.[29] In practice, however, the first registered proprietor will have acquired title to the land in question under the system of unregistered conveyancing and he will continue to be bound by any interests to which he took subject under that system even if they neither override registration nor are protected on the register at the time of first registration. Subject to this qualification and to interests which override registration, the register is conclusive and can be relied on by subsequent registered proprietors. A second or subsequent registered proprietor who purchases the land for valuable consid-

5–012

---

[21] LRA 2002 s.107, which has now been repealed.
[22] Transfer of Tribunal Functions Order 2013 art.4.
[23] LRA 2002 s.58.
[24] LRA 2002 s.74.
[25] LRA 2002 s.58.
[26] LRA 2002 ss.9–10.
[27] *Kitney v MEPC Ltd* [1977] 1 W.L.R. 981 at 993.
[28] LRA 2002 ss.11–12.
[29] *Williams & Glynís Bank Ltd v Boland* [1981] A.C. 487 at 504.

eration which is other than nominal does indeed acquire title free from all interests other than those which are protected on the register or override registration but free from all other interests,[30] even if he has full notice of them. The one qualification to this doctrine is that there are limited powers to rectify the register in order to correct errors; but normally these are subject to the payment of compensation to any person thereby suffering loss.[31] Subject to this, a registered title is indefeasible.

INTERESTS IN REGISTERED LAND

5–013   The three types of interest in registered land (namely registrable interests, interests which override registration and interests which require protection on the register) will now be considered in turn.

Registrable estates and interests

Interests and estates which can be registered

5–014   The only interests in respect of which a proprietor can be registered are estates and interests capable of subsisting as legal estates.[32] The estates and interests capable of being registered are:

    (i)   a transfer of an estate, except a transfer on the death or bankruptcy of an individual proprietor or the dissolution of a company[33];

    (ii) the grant of a lease for a term of years absolute of more than seven years from the date of grant[34];

    (iii) the grant of a lease for a term of years absolute that takes effect in possession after the end of the period of three beginning with the date of grant[35];

    (iv) the grant of a lease for a term of years absolute under which the right is discontinuous[36];

    (v) the grant of a lease for a term of years absolute made pursuant to the statutory right to buy in Pt 5 of the Housing Act 1985[37];

    (vi) the grant of a lease for a term of years absolute by a private landlord to a former secure tenant, whose right has been preserved under s.171A of the Housing Act 1985[38];

    (vii) the grant of a lease of any duration where the registered estate is a franchise or manor[39];

---

[30] LRA 2002 ss.28–31, 129(1).
[31] See below, paras 5–037 et seq.
[32] LRA 2002 s.3.
[33] LRA 2002 ss.27(2)(a), 27(5)(a), 27(5)(b).
[34] LRA 2002 s.27(2)(b)(i).
[35] LRA 2002 s.27(2)(b)(ii).
[36] LRA 2002 s.27(2)(b)(iii).
[37] LRA 2002 s.27(2)(b)(iv).
[38] LRA 2002 s.27(2)(b)(v).
[39] LRA 2002 s.27(2)(c).

(viii) the express grant or reservation of an easement falling within s.1(2)(a) of the Law of Property Act 1925,[40] (but excluding easements created pursuant to s.62 of that Act[41]) but excluding easements capable of registration under the Commons Act 2006[42];

(ix) the express grant or reservation of a rentcharge falling within s.1(2)(b) or (e) of the Law of Property Act 1925[43]; and

(x) the grant of a legal charge.[44]

The register

The register for each individual registered title is divided into three parts. A specimen example of an official copy of the register of title (colloquially known as an "office copy entry" or "OCE") is reproduced at the end of this chapter.　**5–015**

The property register: This describes the land and the estate for which it is held, refers to a map or plan showing the land, and contains notes of interests held for the benefit of the land, such as easements or restrictive covenants of which the registered land is the dominant tenement, and other like matters. The boundaries shown on the map are general unless the boundary has been determined under s.60 of the 2002 Act.

The proprietorship register: This states the class of title, the name of the proprietor, his address for service and other matters prescribed by the rules.[45]

The charges register: This notes the incumbrances affecting the registered estate, such as registered charges and interests protected by notice.[46]

Compulsory and voluntary registration　**5–016**

The compulsory areas: During the years 1897 to 1990, the areas in which registration of title is compulsory were gradually extended, with a marked acceleration from 1965 onwards.[47] Since December 1, 1990, the whole of England and Wales has been subject to compulsory registration of title.[48]

Ambit of compulsory registration: By no means all the land in the country has a registered title. According to the Land Registry website[49] approximately 80 per cent of all land in England and Wales is now registered. Registration is compulsory in the following circumstances[50]:

---

[40] This section refers to an easement, right or privilege in or over land.
[41] LRA 2002 s.27(7).
[42] LRA 2002 s.27(2)(d).
[43] LRA 2002 s.27(2)(e).
[44] LRA 2002 s.27(2)(f).
[45] LRR 2003 r.8.
[46] LRR 2004 r.9.
[47] See the map in L.R.Ann.Rep. 1990–1991.
[48] SI 1989/1347.
[49] *http://www.landregistry.gov.uk/* [Accessed April 25, 2014].
[50] LRA 2002 s.4.

(a) the transfer of an unregistered legal estate;

(b) the grant of a lease out of unregistered land;

(c) the grant of a lease not in immediate possession;

(d) the grant of a first legal mortgage;

(e) transfers and leases of public sector housing;

(f) the grant of an estate out of demesne land of the Crown[51]; and

(g) on the partition of land the subject of a trust and the appointment of new trustees.

Extent of compulsory registration: As has been discussed, some 20 per cent of land is still unregistered. However, the introduction[52] of new triggers for compulsory first registration in the case of the partition of land subject to a trust and the appointment of new trustees, will greatly reduce the number of unregistered family estates as time progresses. This amendment to s.4 of the 2002 Act was made under the power, exercisable by statutory instrument, and after consultation, by which the Lord Chancellor may add the events that trigger first registration.[53]

Non-registration: Where registration is compulsory, the transaction will be void as to the legal estate unless application to register it is made within two months[54]; but the Registrar has power to extend this period for good reason to a date specified in his order.[55] In default of due registration, the vendor or lessor will hold the legal estate on a bare trust for the purchaser or lessee. Where the transfer is on the appointment of a new trustee, the legal estate reverts to the person in whom it was vested immediately before the transfer.[56] If an application for first registration is made, but is cancelled, the effect is as if no application had been made, and the statutory sanction applies.[57]

Voluntary registration: A voluntary application for registration may be made in respect of any registrable interest.[58]

Titles

5–017   There are four classes of title with which an applicant for registration may be registered[59]:

(i)   absolute;

(ii)   qualified;

(iii) possessory; or

(iv)   good leasehold.

---

[51] Demesne land is defined by LRA 2002 s.132 as land belonging to Her Majesty in right of the Crown which is not held for an estate in fee simple absolute in possession.

[52] By the amendment of the LRA 2002 s.4 by the Land Registration Act 2002 (Amendment) Order 2008 (SI 2008/2872).

[53] LRA 2002 s.5(1) and (4).

[54] LRA 2002 ss.6–7.

[55] LRA 2002 s.6(5).

[56] LRA 2002 s.7(2)(aa).

[57] *Sainsbury's Supermarket Ltd v Olympia Homes Ltd* [2005] EWHC 1235 at [67]–[71].

[58] LRA 2002 s.3.

[59] LRA 2002 ss.9, 10.

The first three of these apply to both freehold and leasehold titles. The fourth applies only to leasehold titles.[60]

Absolute: A person may be registered with absolute title if the Registrar is of the opinion that the person's title to the estate is such as a willing buyer could properly be advised by a competent professional adviser to accept.[61] A defect in title is not a bar to registration with an absolute title, provided that the Registrar considers that it will not cause the holding under it to be disturbed.[62] In the case of leasehold title, a person may be registered with absolute title if the Registrar is of the opinion that the person's title to the estate is such as a willing buyer could properly be advised by a competent professional adviser to accept, as is the case with absolute freehold title, and if the Registrar approves the lessor's title to grant the lease.[63]

In the case of freeholds, an absolute title vests in the first registered proprietor, by force of statute and without any conveyance, a fee simple in possession (in equity[64] as well as at law) together with all rights and privileges (such as easements) belonging thereto, subject only to:

(i)   entries on the register;

(ii) interests which override registration, except so far as the register states that the land is free from them;

(iii) interests acquired under the Limitation Act 1980 of which he has notice; and

(iv) as between himself and those entitled to interests which require protection on the register, to those interests of which he has notice, if he is not entitled to the land for his own benefit; thus trustees for sale who are registered as proprietors will still hold subject to the claims of the beneficiaries.[65]

In principle he holds free from all other interests,[66] even if he has full notice of them. In practice, however, the first registered proprietor will have acquired title to the land in question under the system of unregistered conveyancing and he will continue to be bound by any interests to which he took subject under that system even if they neither override registration nor have been protected on the register at the time of first registration.

In the case of leaseholds, an absolute title similarly vests the leasehold in the first registered proprietor subject to the rights set out above, and in addition to:

(v)   all the covenants, obligations and liabilities incident to the lease.[67]

An absolute title in the case of leaseholds guarantees not only that the registered proprietor is the owner of the lease but also that the lease was validly granted. Easements, restrictive covenants and other incumbrances affecting the superior title (but not mortgages or

---

[60] LRA 2002 ss.9(1) and 10(1).

[61] LRA 2002 s.9(2).

[62] LRA 2002 s.9(3)

[63] LRA 2002 s.10(2).

[64] The inference to the contrary from *Epps v Esso Petroleum Co Ltd* [1973] 1 W.L.R. 1071 at 1075, 1078, is very slender; and see (1974) 38 Conv.(n.s.) 236 (S.N.L. Palk).

[65] LRA 2002 s.11(2)–(5).

[66] LRA 2002 ss.11–12.

[67] LRA 2002 s.12(2)–(5).

charges) also appear on the leasehold title,[68] so that, in contrast with unregistered land,[69] a purchaser of the lease is free from the risk of being bound by incumbrances which he cannot discover.

Good leasehold: A good leasehold title applies only to leaseholds. It is the same as an absolute title, save that the lessor's right to grant the lease is not guaranteed.[70] If it appears that the lessor was never entitled to grant the lease, the lessee is protected if he has an absolute title, but unprotected if he has a good leasehold title. Since a lessee cannot investigate the freehold title unless he stipulates for this in the contract,[71] he usually cannot give the Registrar evidence of the freehold title where it is or appears to be unregistered, and so he can apply only for a good leasehold title. The Registrar may nevertheless be able to grant an absolute title if the title to the freehold is in fact registered, and, though unknown to the lessee, his landlord is the registered proprietor.

Qualified: In the case of freeholds, a qualified title has the same effect as an absolute title except that the property is held subject to some defect or right specified in the register. This title is granted when an absolute title has been applied for but the Registrar has been unable to grant it owing to some defect in the title. A qualified title to leaseholds has the same effect as an absolute or good leasehold title, as the case may be, except for the specified defect.[72]

Possessory: In the case of either freeholds or leaseholds, first registration with possessory title has the same effect as registration with an absolute title, save that the title is subject to all rights existing or capable of arising at the time of first registration.[73] In short, the title is guaranteed as far as all dealings after the date of registration are concerned, but no guarantee is given as to the title prior to first registration, which must accordingly be investigated by a purchaser in the same way as if the land were not registered.

Upgrading of titles

5–018   The Land Registration Act 2002 changed the name of the procedure previously known as conversion of title to "upgrading title" in order to emphasise that its purpose is to improve the quality of a registered title. Despite the change of name the general principles of conversion have been retained. Applications to upgrade title under the 2002 Act are made to the Registrar.[74]

Where there has been registration with any title other than absolute, the title may be upgraded subsequently, either on application by the proprietor or by the Registrar of his own motion. There are various categories.[75]

---

[68] See *Ruoff & Roper: Registered Conveyancing* (London: Sweet & Maxwell), para.56.003; and see *White v Bijou Mansions Ltd* [1937] Ch. 610 (affirmed [1938] Ch. 351). Cf. LRA 1925 ss.20,23 (repealed).

[69] See above, para.6–078.

[70] LRA 2002 s.12(6).

[71] Above, para.6–078.

[72] LRA 2002 ss.11(6), 12(7).

[73] LRA 2002 ss.11(7), 12(8).

[74] See LRA 2002 ss.62–63; LRR 2003 r.124

[75] LRA 2002 s.62.

Good leasehold: A good leasehold title may be upgraded to absolute if the Registrar is satisfied as to the title to the freehold and to any intermediate leasehold.

Possessory: A possessory title may be upgraded to absolute or (if leasehold) to good lease-hold if the Registrar is satisfied as to the title, or if the possessory title has been registered for at least 12 years and he is satisfied that the proprietor is in possession.

Qualified: A qualified title may be upgraded to absolute or (if leasehold) to good leasehold if the Registrar is satisfied as to the title.

Any person (other than the proprietor) who suffers loss by any upgrading of title is entitled to indemnity as if a mistake had been made in the register.[76]

Application for first registration

With the exceptions set out above, an application for registration may be made by any estate owner, including those holding the estate as a trustee. Further, anyone entitled to call for a legal estate to be vested in him (except a mere purchaser under a contract, or a mortgagee) can apply for registration.[77] Thus if A holds land on a bare trust for B, B can apply for registration without first requiring a conveyance to be executed in his favour, though normally A will have to join or concur in the application. In reality, B will find it difficult to obtain anything other than qualified title because of the evidential burden of proving that he is entitled to have the estate vested in him.[78]

The Registrar examines the title and inquires into any objections that may be made to the proposed registration. He has power to register an absolute title if he is of the opinion that the title is "such as a willing buyer could properly be advised by a competent professional adviser to accept"[79]; and in applying that test, he may disregard the fact that a title is defective if in his opinion it is "a title the holding under which will not be disturbed".[80] There is no appeal to the court from a refusal to register a title as absolute,[81] though it may be possible to challenge the Registrar's action or inaction on an application for judicial review.[82]

5–019

Cautions against first registration

Any person interested in unregistered land who thinks that he may be prejudiced by an application to register any title to it may lodge a caution against first registration with the Registrar.[83] This entitles him to be informed by the Registrar of any application to register the title. Thus a person who claims that the execution by him of a conveyance of his unregistered land was obtained by fraud may lodge a caution against first registration to prevent

5–020

---

[76] LRA 2002 Sch.8, para.1(2)(a); below, para.5–040.
[77] LRA 2002 s.3(2).
[78] See *Ruoff & Roper: Registered Conveyancing* (London: Sweet & Maxwell), para.9.003.
[79] LRA 2002 s.9(2).
[80] LRA 2002 s.9(3).
[81] *Dennis v Malcolm* [1934] Ch. 244, considered in *Quigly v Chief Land Registrar* [1992] 1 W.L.R. 834 at 837.
[82] *Dennis v Malcolm* [1934] Ch. 244 at 253; *Ruoff & Roper: Registered Conveyancing* (London: Sweet and Maxwell), para.6.002.02
[83] LRA 2002 ss.15–22.

the grantee registering the title without his knowledge. The notice given to the cautioner requires him to make his objections to the registration or conversion within a fixed time, usually 14 days. Abuse of this procedure is discouraged by a provision that any person who causes damage to another by unreasonably lodging a caution is liable to pay him compensation.[84] The Registrar is required to keep a register of cautions against first registration[85] and its existence will show on a search of the Land Registry's index map of the land in question subject to the caution. Cautions against first registration are sometimes registered by holders of registrable interests which are not subject to compulsory registration. All cautions of this and any other type which were in existence when the Land Registration Act 2002 came into force continue to be effective indefinitely.[86]

Registered charges

5–021   The only way in which a legal mortgage of registered land can be created, whether freehold or leasehold, is by way of charge by deed expressed to be by way of legal mortgage.[87] In order for the proprietor of the legal charge to maintain priority against other charges on the register the charge must be registered.[88] Under the Land Registration Act 1925, a charge certificate was issued to the mortgagee, and the land certificate was retained at the Land Registry for duration of the mortgage. This system has been abolished by the Land Registration Act 2002 and now registered charges are simply protected on the register in the same way as other interests which require protection by registration. Registered charges are discussed in more detail in Ch.17.

Interests which override registration

Nature

5–022   The Land Registration Act 2002 does not use the expression "overriding interests" but provides for two classes of interests which will have the same effect as overriding interests had under the Land Registration Act 1925. These are respectively called "unregistered interests which override first registration"[89] and "unregistered interests which override registered dispositions".[90] Interests which override registration bind the proprietor even though he has no knowledge of them and the register does not refer to them. In general, they are the kinds of rights which a purchaser of unregistered land would not expect to discover from a mere examination of the abstract and title deeds, but for which he would make inquiries and inspect the land. Many are legal rights but some are equitable. Yet it is to be emphasised that for incumbrances on registered land, the issue in deciding whether or not a purchaser is bound is not whether the rights are legal or equitable, but whether they override registration or require protection on the register.

---

[84] LRA 2002 s.77.
[85] LRA 2002 s.19.
[86] LRA 2002 Sch.12 para.16.
[87] LRA 2002 s.23
[88] LRA 2002 s.30.
[89] LRA 2002 ss.11, 12 and Sch.1.
[90] LRA 2002 ss.29, 30 and Sch.3.

Interests which override registration

Unregistered interests which override first registration: Schedule 1 to the Land Registration   **5–023**
Act 2002 sets out in 14 paragraphs a list of unregistered interests which will override first
registration. Only the most important of them will be considered here. Paragraphs 10 to 14
ceased to have effect on October 13, 2013, which was 10 years after the coming into force
of those paragraphs of Schedule 1.[91]

    (a) Paragraph 1: Legal leases for not more than seven years unless they take effect
       in possession more than three months after their grant or are granted pursuant
       to the Housing Act 1985[92] (the excluded categories are registrable interests). This
       paragraph therefore does not catch leases of this type created by signed writing
       unless they are for three years or less and take immediate effect in possession (the
       latter leases are legal even if created orally[93]). However, all leases where the lessee
       is in physical possession of the land, unless they are registrable interests which are
       entered on the register, will override registration under paragraph 2 below, even
       if they are for more than seven years.
    (b) Paragraph 2: Interests of every person in actual occupation, except for an interest
       in a settlement under the Settled Land Act 1925. This provision will be considered
       shortly.[94]
    (c) Paragraph 3: Legal easements and profits á prendre.
    (d) Paragraphs 4, 5 and 6: Customary rights, public rights and local land charges.

Unregistered interests which override registered dispositions: Schedule 3 to the Land
Registration Act 2002 also sets out in 14 paragraphs a list of unregistered interests which
override registered dispositions; however, the scope of several of the paragraphs is considerably more restricted. Only the most important of them will be considered here.
Paragraphs 10 to 16 ceased to have effect on October 13, 2013, which was 10 years after
the coming into force of those paragraphs of Schedule 1.[95]

    (a) Paragraph 1: Short leases. Legal leases for not more than seven years unless they
       take effect in possession more than three months after their grant or are granted
       pursuant to the Housing Act 1985[96] or are for some other reason registrable inter-
       ests. This paragraph therefore does not catch leases of this type created by signed
       writing unless they are for three years or less and take immediate effect in posses-
       sion (the latter leases are legal even if created orally[97]). However, all leases where
       the lessee is in physical possession of the land will, unless they are registrable
       interests which are entered on the register, will override registration under para.2
       below, even if they are for more than seven years.

---

[91] See LRA 2002 s.117(1).
[92] Either under s.171A or Pt 5.
[93] LPA 1925 s.54(2).
[94] Below, para.5–023.
[95] LRA 2002 s.117.
[96] Either under s.171A or Pt 5.
[97] LPA 1925 s.54(2).

(b) Paragraph 2: Persons in actual occupation. Interests of every person in actual occupation, except for:

    (i) an interest under a settlement subject to the Settled Land Act 1925;

    (ii) an interest of a person who failed to disclose the interest upon inquiry when he could reasonably have been expected to do so;

    (iii) an interest of a person whose occupation would not have been obvious on a reasonably careful inspection of the land and of which the purchaser had no actual knowledge; and

    (iv) a lease taking effect in possession more than three months after its grant which has not yet done so.

This provision will also be considered shortly.[98]

(c) Paragraph 3: Legal easements or profits á prendre. Legal easements or profits á prendre, except for those not registered under the Commons Registration Act 1965 of which the purchaser had no actual knowledge and which would which not have been obvious on a reasonably careful inspection of the land over which they are exercised; the exception does not apply where they have been exercised within the preceding year. This paragraph catches both legal and equitable profits á prendre whenever and however they are acquired, legal easements which existed at first registration, and easements acquired as a result of an implied grant or reservation and by prescription after first registration. However, a legal easement can only be acquired as a result of an express grant or reservation after first registration if it is created by registered disposition and therefore entered on the register (an easement created merely by deed will take effect only as an equitable easement); consequently, this paragraph does not catch any legal easements created by express grant or reservation after first registration.

(d) Paragraphs 4, 5 and 6: Customary rights, public rights and local land charges.

(e) Paragraph 16: Church chancels. A right in respect of the repair of a church chancel. This paragraph was inserted by a statutory instrument[99] because when the Land Registration Act 2002 was enacted the Court of Appeal had held[100] that the liability to repair the chancel of a church[101] contravened the European Convention on Human Rights. However, the House of Lords reversed this decision and so the Lord Chancellor exercised his power under the Land Registration Act 2002 s.134(1) to insert it as an overriding interest. In common with all other interests under paragraphs 10 to 16, after October 13, 2013, these rights must be protected by notice on the register and in default they will no longer be interests that override.[102]

---

[98] Below para.5–023.

[99] Land Registration Act 2002 (LRA 2002) (Transitional Provisions) (No.2) Order 2003.

[100] In *Aston Cantlow and Wilmcote with Billesley PCC v Wallbank* [2002] Ch. 51.

[101] Historically, this liability fell to the rector, with the parishioners responsible for maintaining the area of the church in which they sat (the nave). Following the dissolution of the monasteries the land was sold into the hands of institutions and individual and the liability passed with the land. For a history of chancel repairs see *Aston Cantlow and Wilmcote with Billesley PCC v Wallbank* [2004] 1 A.C. 546 at [97]–[109].

[102] LRA 2002 s.117.

(f) Public-private Partnership (PPP) leases.[103] These are leases of, for example, underground railways or stations that have been granted for 30 years. The impractical nature of mapping the demised premises means registration is not feasible and so they take effect as overriding interests, even though they are not mentioned in Schs 1 or 3 of the 2002 Act.

"Actual occupation" under the Land Registration Act 2002: The first point to note is that the Land Registration Act 2002 does not protect any interests by virtue of the fact that their holder is in receipt of rent and profits, save for when they were already protected when the 2002 Act came into force.[104]

The meaning of "actual occupation" under the s.70(1)(g) of the Land Registration Act 1925 was considered in many authorities, which must now be read in conjunction with the provisions of the Land Registration Act 2002. The following principles can be derived from the authorities to ascertain the meaning of "actual occupation"[105]:

  (i) it is a question of fact to be determined by reference to the circumstances of each case[106]:

 (ii) the words "actual occupation" are ordinary words of plain English and should be interpreted as such. The word "actual" emphasises that physical presence is required[107];

 (iii) the nature and extent of the physical presence required to constitute actual occupation can vary according to the type of property under consideration[108];

 (iv) it does not necessarily involve the personal presence of the person claiming to occupy. A caretaker or the representative of a company can occupy on behalf of his employer[109];

  (v) however, actual occupation by a licensee (who is not a representative occupier) does not count as actual occupation by the licensor[110];

 (vi) the mere presence of some of the claimant's furniture will not usually count as actual occupation[111];

 (ix) if the person said to be in actual occupation at any particular time is not physically present on the land at that time, it will usually be necessary to show that his occupation was manifested and accompanied by a continuing intention to occupy[112];

(vii) the courts are unwilling to strictly define the situations in which a person may be in actual occupation, or to lay down a code[113]; and

---

[103] LRA 2002 s.90(1). The definition of this type of lease is contained in the Greater London Authority Act 1999 s.218.

[104] LRA, Sch.12, para.8; see below.

[105] See the summary in *Thompson v Foy* [2009] EWHC 1076 (Ch), [2010] 1 P. & C.R. 308 at [127], which was approved in *Link Lending Ltd v Bustard* [2010] EWCA Civ 424; [2010] 2 E.G.L.R. 55 at [31].

[106] *Williams v Glyn's Bank v Boland* [1981] A.C. 487 at 504, 505.

[107] *Williams v Glyn's Bank v Boland* [1981] A.C. 487 at 504, 505.

[108] *Malory Enterprises Ltd v Cheshire Homes Ltd* [2002] EWCA Civ 151 at [80].

[109] *Abbey National Building Society v Cann* [1991] 1 A.C. 56 per Lord Oliver at 93.

[110] *Strand Securities Ltd v Caswell* [1965] Ch. 958 per Lord Denning M.R. at 981.

[111] *Strand Securities Ltd v Caswell* [1965] Ch. 958 per Russell L.J. at 984.

[112] *Thompson v Foy*, above.

[113] *Hodgson v Marks* [1971] Ch. 892 at 932 per Russell L.J. (a decision under the LRA 1925 s.70(1)(g).

(viii) the courts will look to the cases to provide guidance even though the matter is ultimately one of fact.[114]

The impact of actual occupation on first registration is broadly comparable with its impact under the Land Registration Act 1925, with the following four differences:

(i)   there is only one statutory exception: the interests of beneficiaries of a settlement under the Settled Land Act 1925;
(ii) the interests of occupiers which are not revealed on inquiry are to be protected;
(iii) actual occupation of only part of the land in the registered title protects only the interests held by the occupier in that part, not, as under the 1925 Act, the whole of it; and
(iv) a person will only be in actual occupation if he, or his agent or employee, is physically present there (the first two of these changes increases the impact of actual occupation, while the last two decreases it, when compared to the 1925 Act).

Transitional provisions: There are transitional provisions contained in Schedule 12 of the Land Registration Act 2002 dealing with interests which formerly overrode registration under the 1925 Act but no longer do so:

(i)   Easements, profits á prendre,[115] and leases[116] which overrode registration at the time when they came into existence[117] will continue to do so indefinitely despite the fact that they would not do so if they came into existence after the Land Registration Act 2002 came into force.
(ii) Legal easements and profits á prendre of any type which came into existence during the first three years after the Act came into force will also always override registration.[118]
(iii) And rights which overrode registration by virtue of the receipt of rents and profits at the time when the Act came into force[119] will continue to do so for as long as the person in question continues to receive the rents and profits.
(iv) Rights acquired by adverse possessors in land before the Act came into force, whether before or after the first registration of the land in question, do not take effect under a bare trust, as under the 1925 Act. Instead, the Land Registration Act 2002 confers on such adverse possessors a right to be registered as proprietors.[120]

---

[114] *Thompson v Foy*, above.
[115] LRA 2002 para.9.
[116] LRA 2002 para.12.
[117] Some easements and profits á prendre which came into existence within two years of the Act coming into force will also do so; LRA 2002 para.10.
[118] LRA 2002 para.10.
[119] LRA 2002 para.8.
[120] LRA 2002 Sch.12 para.18(1).

Interests which require protection on the register

Definition

The Land Registration Act 1925 Act described interests which required protection on the register as "minor interests"[121] and elaborately defined them; the Land Registration Act 2002 does not give any collective name to interests which require protection on the register.[122] Interests which override registration obviously do not require protection on the register and any registrable interests which have been registered and registered charges are necessarily on the register anyway. All other interests require protection by an entry on the register, otherwise they will not bind a purchaser for valuable consideration under a registered disposition of a registered or registrable estate or interest.[123]

5–024

Interests which require protection on the register are divided into two classes:

(i) those which will not bind a purchaser even when protected by an entry on the register, but which will be overreached, such as the equitable interests of beneficiaries of a settlement under the Settled Land Act 1925 or a trust of land (which includes both express trusts for sale and bare trusts); and

(ii) those which will bind a purchaser provided they are protected in the appropriate way, such as restrictive covenants.

The manner of protection on the register

The Land Registration Act 2002 has simplified the means of protecting interests. Minor interests can be protected by notices and restrictions. All entries on the register made before the Land Registration Act 2002 came into force will continue to have effect indefinitely so existing cautions against dealings and inhibitions remain valid.[124]

5–025

Notices

A notice is defined as an entry on the register in respect of the burden of an interest affecting a registered estate or charge.[125] Some interests cannot be protected by a notice[126]: these include interests under either a settlement under the Settled Land Act 1925 or a trust of land (because they will be overreached on a disposition); a lease granted for three years or less which is not a registrable interest (because it is an overriding interest); and covenants in a lease relating to the subject-matter of the lease (which are binding under the general law[127]).

5–026

The fact that the notice is registered will not mean that the interest in question is valid

---

[121] *Elias v Mitchell* [1972] Ch. 652.
[122] LRA 2002 s.29(1).
[123] *Miles v Bull (No.2)* [1969] 3 All E.R. 1585; contrast *Barclays Bank Ltd v Taylor* [1974] Ch. 137, where the purchaser took an equitable interest only.
[124] LRA 2002 Sch.12, paras 1–3.
[125] LRA 2002 s.32.
[126] LRA 2002 s.33.
[127] See below, paras 11–024 et seq.

but, if it is, its priority will be protected.[128] Notices can be agreed notices or unilateral notices. The former can only be registered on the application of or with the consent of the registered proprietor unless the Registrar is satisfied of the validity of the interest in question.[129] Following the registration of the latter, the Registrar will notify the registered proprietor of its registration.[130] He can apply to have the registration cancelled and, if the beneficiary of the notice does not object within a prescribed period, it will have to be cancelled.[131] Objections will be resolved in accordance with the dispute resolution procedures already discussed.[132] A person who fails to exercise reasonable care when applying for the entry of a notice will be potentially liable to anyone who suffers damage thereby.[133]

Restrictions

5–027   A restriction is defined as an entry in the register regulating the circumstances in which a disposition of a registered estate or charge may be the subject of an entry in the register.[134] It may prohibit any disposition or a specific type of disposition either indefinitely, for a specified period or until the occurrence of a specified event,[135] which include the giving of notice, the obtaining of consent and the making of an order by the court or Registrar.[136]

Once a restriction has been entered, no entry will be able to be made on the register otherwise than in accordance with the terms of the restriction, although the Registrar can, on the application of a person who appears to him to have a sufficient interest in the restriction, disapply or modify it.[137] The Registrar can enter a restriction if it appears to him that it is necessary or desirable to do so for the purpose of preventing invalidity or unlawfulness in relation to dispositions, protecting a right or claim or for securing compliance with the overreaching rules[138] and will have to do the latter when he registers two or more persons as registered proprietors.[139] Restrictions are notifiable unless they are registered on the application of or with the consent of the registered proprietor or the Registrar is satisfied of the validity of the interest in question.[140] Following the registration of a notifiable restriction, the Registrar must notify the registered proprietor of its registration.[141] As in the case of notices, objections will be resolved in accordance with the dispute resolution procedures already discussed.[142] A person who fails to exercise reasonable care when applying for the entry of a restriction will be potentially liable to anyone who suffers damage thereby.[143]

---

[128] LRA 2002 s.32.
[129] LRA 2002 s.34.
[130] LRA 2002 s.35.
[131] LRA 2002 s.36.
[132] Above, para.5–009.
[133] LRA 2002 s.77.
[134] LRA 2002 s.40(1).
[135] LRA 2002 s.40(2).
[136] LRA 2002 s.40(3).
[137] LRA 2002 s.41.
[138] LRA 2002 s.42.
[139] LRA 2002 s.44.
[140] LRA 2002 s.43(1).
[141] LRA 2002 s.45.
[142] Above, para.5–009.
[143] LRA 2002 s.77.

Official searches and "the registration gap"

Where there has been a disposition of land, which must be completed by registration in order to effect a transfer of legal title, either because the land is already registered or is subject to first registration, there is a gap between completion of the documents effecting the disposition and the completion of the disposition by registration. This is known as the "registration gap".[144] In order to protect the disponee, where the disposition is for valuable consideration,[145] the Land Registration Act 2002 provides for priority protection,[146] whereby the disponee can apply for an official search of the register with priority.[147] During the priority period[148] any application to change the register is postponed to the end of the period, thereby giving the disponee time to register the disposition. The Land Registration Rules 2003 makes provision for applications for an official search with priority.[149] It should be noted that it is possible to make an official search of the register with or without priority.[150]

5–028

DEALINGS WITH REGISTERED LAND

The registered proprietor can deal with or dispose of his land insofar as it is permitted by the general law. The Land Registration Act 2002 has created the concept of "owner's powers"[151] and states that the registered proprietor has the following powers:

5–029

    (i) to make a disposition of any kind permitted by the general law other than mortgages by lease or sub-lease, which have been abolished prospectively in respect of registered land[152]; and

    (ii) to charge his estate at law.[153]

In relation to a registered charge the proprietor may make a disposition of any kind permitted by the general rule, save that sub-mortgages of registered land are prohibited, no matter what type the mortgage is.[154]

The registerable dispositions prescribed by the Land Registration Act 2002 are set out above.[155]

---

[144] The registration gap will cease to exist if the provisions for e-conveyancing in the LRA 2002 are ever brought into force.

[145] It is a requirement that the disposition is for valuable consideration in order to apply for an official search with priority: see LRR 2003 rr.147(1) and 131.

[146] LRA 2002 s.72

[147] LRA 2002 s.70.

[148] Which is normally 30 business dates; LRR 2003 r.131.

[149] LRR 2003 rr.147–154.

[150] LRR 2003 r.147 (with priority) and r.155 (without priority).

[151] LRA 2002 s.23.

[152] A legal charge must be used.

[153] LRA 2002 s.23(1).

[154] LRA 2002 s.23(2). Sub-charges are permitted.

[155] See para.5–014. LRA 2002 s.27(1).

Transfer of an Estate in Registered Land

Transfer

5–030   The transfer of an Estate in registered land is effected by a simple form of transfer, which is prescribed by the Land Registration Rules.[156] Any application to be registered must comply with the rules and be lodged at the Land Registry.[157]

Where the proprietor is disposing of the whole or part of the registered estate, the successor in title must be registered as the proprietor.[158] Where the proprietor of an estate grants out of that estate a term of years absolute the grantee, or his successor in title, must be entered in the register as the proprietor of the lease[159] and a notice in respect of that lease must be entered in the register of the grantor's title.[160]

Title

5–031   No legal estate passes until the title is registered,[161] and registration is treated as having effect from the time of the making of the application.[162] Until the successor in title is registered as the proprietor the transfer takes effect in equity only. With the land, the transferee takes all easements and other rights for the benefit of the land. Correspondingly the transferee takes subject to all entries on the register and to interests which override registration. However, where the disposition is made for valuable consideration he takes free from all other estates and interests,[163] even if he has express notice of them.[164] A transfer made without valuable consideration has the same effect as a transfer for value, except that the transferee takes subject to any interests which require protection on the register that bind the transferor even if they have not been protected.[165] In these circumstances, the "basic rule" under the Land Registration Act 2002 applies.[166]

Charges

5–032   The Land Registration Act 2002 has abolished mortgages of registered land by lease or sub-lease[167] and sub-mortgages of registered land have also been prohibited, no matter what type the principal mortgage is.[168] These different types of mortgages are considered later.[169]

---

[156] See LRR 2003 Pt 6.
[157] See further *Ruoff & Roper: Registered Conveyancing*, (London: Sweet & Maxwell), para.18.010.
[158] LRA 2002 Sch.2, para.2(1).
[159] LRA 2002 Sch.2, para.3(2)(a).
[160] LRA 2002 Sch.2, para.3(2)(b).
[161] LRA 2002 s.74.
[162] LRA 2002 s.74.
[163] LRA 2002 s.29.
[164] *Hodges v Jones* [1935] Ch. 657 at 671; *De Lusignan v Johnson* [1974] E.G.D. 76 (cases under the LRA 1925).
[165] LRA 2002 s.29.
[166] LRA 2002 s.28. See also *Halifax Plc v Curry Popeck (A firm)* [2008] EWHC 1692 (Ch).
[167] LRA 2002 s.23(1).
[168] LRA 2002 s.23(2).
[169] See below, Ch.17.

Where a registered charge is created or transferred the chargee, or his successor in title, must be entered in the register as the proprietor of the charge.[170] In the case of the creation of a sub-charge, the sub-chargee, or his successor in title, must be entered in the register as the proprietor of the sub-charge.[171]

Transfer on death

This is one of the exceptions to the normal rule that the transfer of an estate must be registered.[172] On the death of a sole registered proprietor (or the last survivor of joint proprietors if the register has not been updated following earlier deaths), his personal representatives may either:

    (i) apply for registration themselves, on producing to the Registrar the grant of probate or letters of administration[173]; or

    (ii) without being themselves registered, transfer the land direct either to a purchaser or to the person entitled under the will or intestacy; in this case, both the transfer or assent and the probate or letters of administration must be lodged with the application for registration.[174]

5–033

The name of a joint proprietor will be removed from the register on proof of death.[175]

Bankruptcy

Another of the exceptions to the general rule under s.27 relates to bankruptcy. The steps at present taken on bankruptcy, so far as they affect registered land, are briefly as follows:

5–034

    (i) A bankruptcy petition is presented; the petition is then registered as a pending action under the Land Charges Act 1972.[176] Thereafter, as soon as practicable, the Registrar must enter in the register in relation to any registered estate or charge which appears to him to be affected a notice in respect of the pending action.[177] The notice will continue in force until either a restriction is entered in the register following the making of a bankruptcy order (see (ii), below), or the trustee in bankruptcy is registered as proprietor.[178] The court must notify the Chief Land Registrar of the existence of the petition[179] but breach of that obligation does not give rise to a cause of action at common law or for breach of statutory duty.[180]

    (ii) A bankruptcy order is made by which the registered proprietor is adjudged

---

[170] LRA 2002 Sch.2, paras 8 and 10.
[171] LRA 2002 Sch.2, para.11.
[172] LRA 2002 s.27(5).
[173] LRR 2003 r.163.
[174] LRR 2003 r.162(1).
[175] LRR 2003 r.164.
[176] LCA 1972 s.5(1)(b) and 3(b).
[177] LRA 2002 s.86(2).
[178] LRA 2002 s.86(3).
[179] Insolvency Rules 1986 r.6.13.
[180] *St. John Poulton's Trustee in Bankruptcy v Ministry of Justice* [2011] Ch 1.

bankrupt[181]; this is registered as such under the Land Charges Act 1972, and thereafter the Registrar must, in relation to any registered estate or charge which appears to him to be affected by the order enter in the register a restriction to reflect the effect of the Insolvency Act 1986.[182]

(iii) Once the registered proprietor is adjudicated bankrupt is trustee in bankruptcy (or, until a trustee is appointed, the official receiver) may be registered as proprietor in place of the bankrupt on production a copy of the bankruptcy order, a certificate of his appointment as trustee and a declaration that the land is part of the bankrupt's estate.[183]

Limitation and prescription

Limitation under the Land Registration Act 1925

5–035   Although the law relating to adverse possession in registered land has completely changed since the Land Registration Act 2002 has come into force, it is of some use to know how the system operated under the old law. Under the 1925 Act a title to registered land could be acquired under the Limitation Act 1980[184] in the same way as in the case of unregistered land. This occurs when a person, his predecessors in title, and earlier adverse possessors dispossessed by him or them having between them been in adverse possession for a continuous period of 12 years. The 12-year period starts to run again as against holders of superior titles when the inferior title would have determined but for the adverse possession and holders of interests under trusts which are not in possession have a further six-year period in which to recover the land after their interests come into possession. However, in the case of registered land under the 1925 Act, no legal title was acquired by the adverse possessor until he was registered as proprietor (of a new, possessory title); until then, the registered proprietor held his title to the land on trust for the squatter.[185]

Limitation under the Land Registration Act 2002

5–036   The Land Registration Act 2002 totally changed the previous law under the 1925 Act. This change has been made because of what the Law Commission had described[186] as "considerable public disquiet" over the operation of the existing law. Adverse possession of itself, for however long, does not bar the title of the registered proprietor.[187] The system under the Land Registration Act 2002 is discussed in detail in Ch.18 but it can briefly be summarised as follows.

Ten-year period: When a person is in adverse possession of registered land or has been evicted from that land during the last six months by the registered proprietor, and he

---

[181] IA 1986 ss.274(3)(b) and 278(a).
[182] LRA 2002 s.86(4).
[183] LRR 2003 r.168.
[184] LA 1980 s.15.
[185] LRA 1925 s.75 (repealed). Contrast unregistered land, where the adverse possessor acquires an entirely new estate: below, para.18–044.
[186] Law. Com. No. 271, para.24.
[187] LRA 2002 s.95(1).

and his predecessors in title (but not earlier adverse possessors dispossessed by him or them) have been in adverse possession for 10 years, he can apply to the Registrar to be registered as proprietor.[188] However, no application will be able to be made during any period while the registered proprietor is an enemy, detained in enemy territory, or is suffering from mental disability.[189] No one will be regarded as having been in adverse possession during any period while the land has been held for persons by way of succession.[190]

Procedure thereafter: The Registrar then notifies the registered proprietor, any registered chargee, and the registered proprietor of any superior title of the application.[191] Anyone who is notified can serve a notice on the Registrar within a period to be laid down by the new Rules.[192] If no one does so, the applicant will be registered as proprietor.[193] If a notice is served, the applicant can only be registered as proprietor at this stage in one of the following three circumstances: first, if it would be unconscionable because of an equity by estoppel for the registered proprietor to seek to dispossess the applicant and the circumstances are such that the applicant ought to be registered as proprietor; secondly, if he is for some other reason entitled to be registered as proprietor (for example, as being entitled under the will or intestacy of the deceased proprietor or having purchased the land without having taken a transfer); and, thirdly, if he is the owner of adjoining property, the boundary has not been determined, and for the 10-year period he reasonably believed that the land to which the application relates belonged to him.[194] If the applicant and the server of the notice cannot reach agreement as to whether any of these circumstances has arisen, the Registrar will have to refer the matter to the First-tier Tribunal in accordance with the dispute resolution procedures already discussed.[195]

Further two-year period: Save in these three circumstances, the registered proprietor then has a further period of two years from the date of the application to evict the adverse possessor. If he does not commence proceedings by then, a further application by the same applicant or his successors in title to be registered as proprietor after that two year period will be successful.[196]

Effect of registration: The adverse possessor will obtain the same class of title as the previous registered proprietor. Following registration, the priorities of existing interests in the registered land will be preserved save in the case of registered charges, which will only bind the adverse possessor if he is registered in one of the three circumstances set out above (the reason for the general exclusion of registered charges is that the chargee will be one of the persons entitled to be notified).[197]

---

[188] LRA 2002 Sch.6 para.1.
[189] LRA 2002 Sch.6 para.8.
[190] LRA 2002 Sch.6 para.12.
[191] LRA 2002 Sch.6 para.2.
[192] LRA 2002 Sch.6 para.3.
[193] LRA 2002 Sch.6 para.4.
[194] LRA 2002 Sch.6 para.5.
[195] Above, para.7–023.
[196] LRA 2002 Sch.6 paras 6, 7.
[197] LRA 2002 Sch.6 para.9.

Rectification and indemnity

5–037 Although in general it may be said that a registered proprietor has a title guaranteed by the State, the guarantee is not absolute but relative. There is power to alter the register so as to correct mistakes, and a registered proprietor may lose some or all of his land by alteration that amounts to rectification. Under the Land Registration Act 1925 any alteration of the register was known as "rectification" but under the Land Registration Act 2002 rectification is the term used where the alteration of the register to correct a mistake prejudicially affects the title of a registered proprietor.[198] In this situation he may have a right to compensation by way of indemnity. His title is, in effect, insured by the state: he will have either the land or compensation.

Rectification under the Land Registration Act 2002

5–038 The provisions of the Land Registration Act 2002 governing alteration of the register are contained in Schedule 4.[199] As discussed above, rectification has become just one particular form of alteration.

Alterations which do not amount to rectification

5–039 The court is able to order[200] and the Registrar can make[201] an alteration to the register as distinct from a rectification of it for the purposes of correcting mistakes, bringing the register up to date, and giving effect to any estate, right or interest excepted from the effect of registration; and the Registrar also has power to remove superfluous entries. Rules may make provision for the circumstances in which there is a duty to make alterations of this type.[202] This enables clerical errors to be amended but also enable effect to be given to interests which override registration, since such alterations do not prejudice the registered proprietor who is bound by such interests both before and after the alteration.

Alterations which do amount to rectification

5–040 The court[203] and the Registrar[204] are able to order rectification of the register. The importance of rectification lies in the fact that the person whose title has been prejudicially affected by the rectification of the register may claim an indemnity.

The definition of "mistake" is not given in the Act but it has been held that it is not limited in its scope to any procedural or official error. In *Baxter v Mannion*[205] the registration of the title of a person on the basis of his adverse possession where he had not in fact been in possession of the land for the required period was a mistake.

---

[198] LRA 2002 Sch.4 para.1.
[199] LRA 2002 s.65.
[200] LRA 2002 Sch.4 para.2.
[201] LRA 2002 Sch.4 para.5.
[202] LRA 2002 Sch.4 paras 4(a), 7(a); see LRR 2003 Pt 12.
[203] LRA 2002 Sch.4 para.3.
[204] LRA 2002 Sch.4 para.6.
[205] *Baxter v Mannion* [2011] EWCA Civ 120, [2011] 1 W.L.R. 1594.

It is important to note that the question of whether an entry in the register is a mistake depends on the circumstances at the time of registration. For example, the registration of title procured by a fraudulent instrument is void *ab initio*. Accordingly, the registration will be a mistake. However, where a person is registered with title that is *voidable* but not a *void*, and the transaction is not avoided at the date of registration, there will be no mistake until the transaction has been declared as void.

In the circumstances where a person has been registered with title following a void transaction and there has been a subsequent disposition by that registered proprietor, it is thought that this will be a mistake. For example, where A owns Greenacre and B fraudulently transfers A's estate to B and then charges that estate to C, A is entitled to rectification of the register as against B and C, despite the fact that B had the full powers to charge the estate to C by virtue of being the registered proprietor. In this scenario C is the innocent party but he will be entitled to an indemnity from the Land Registry. Although this point has not been conclusively decided it is thought that the registration of the charge will be a mistake because either the charge forms part of the original mistake, or it is a consequence of the original mistake and should accordingly be rectified.[206]

Registered proprietors not in possession: Unless there are exceptional circumstances which justify not doing so, the court and the Registrar are obliged to order rectification as against a registered proprietor who is not in possession.[207] Possession clearly means physical occupation since in the 2002 Act possession is not defined as including the receipt of rents and profits.

Registered proprietors in possession: The court and the Registrar will not be able to order rectification as against a registered proprietor who is in possession unless (i) he consents, (ii) he has by fraud or lack of proper care caused or substantially contributed to the mistake or (iii) it would for any other reason be unjust for rectification not to be made.[208] Where a person seeks rectification the burden of proof rests upon him.[209]

Effect of rectification: Rectification is of prospective effect.[210] Accordingly, any effect on the proprietor of a registered estate or charge takes effect from the date of rectification.[211]

Indemnity

Indemnity under the Land Registration Act 2002 is governed by Sch.8.[212] A person is entitled to be indemnified by the Registrar if he suffers loss in the following circumstances[213]:   **5–041**

    (a) rectification of the register;
    (b) a mistake whose correction would involve rectification of the register;
    (c) a mistake in an official search;

---

[206] See *Knight's Construction (March) Ltd v Roberto Mac Ltd* [2011] 2 E.G.L.R. 123, where the decision reached reflects the current approach taken by the Adjudicator (now the First-Tier Tribunal).
[207] LRA 2002 Sch.4 paras 3(3), 6(3).
[208] LRA 2002 Sch.4 paras 3(2), 6(2).
[209] *Sainsbury's Supermarkets Ltd v Olympia Homes Ltd* [2005] EWHC (Ch) at [90].
[210] LRA 2002 Sch.4 para.8.
[211] *Sainsbury's Supermarkets Ltd v Olympia Homes Ltd* [2005] EWHC (Ch) at [96].
[212] LRA 2002 s.102.
[213] LRA 2002 Sch.8 para.1.

    (d) a mistake in an official copy;

    (e) a mistake in a document kept by the Registrar which is not an original and is referred to in the register;

    (f) the loss or destruction of a document lodged at the registry for inspection or safe custody;

    (g) a mistake in the cautions register; or

    (h) failure by the Registrar to perform his duty under s.50.

Furthermore, if a person suffers loss by virtue of a change of title under s.62 of the Act he is regarded as having suffered a loss by reason of rectification of the register.[214]

Therefore, the right to indemnity falls under three heads: the entitlement, exceptions, and determination.

Entitlement

5–042   The grounds on which a person is entitled to claim indemnity may be put under four heads.

Rectification: Loss by reason of any rectification of the register.[215] There is no indemnity for rectification which does not cause any loss but merely gives effect to a loss previously suffered. However, where the title of a proprietor claiming in good faith under a forged disposition is rectified, he is deemed to have suffered loss by reason of the rectification and to be entitled to indemnity.[216] An indemnity may also be paid to a person in whose favour the register is rectified who nevertheless suffers loss. This is possible because the rectification has only prospective effect and so adverse terms of an overriding interest such as a lease created between the mistake and the rectification may continue to bind him after rectification.[217]

Non-rectification: Loss by reason of an error or omission in the register which is not rectified. Thus if F by forgery obtains registration as proprietor of A's land, and then sells it to B, A will be entitled to indemnity if he cannot obtain rectification against B because B is a registered proprietor in possession.

Upgrading of title: Loss suffered by anyone except the registered proprietor by reason of any entry made on the upgrading of titles.[218]

Errors: Loss by reason of various errors or omissions. These include errors in official searches or inaccuracies in various documents, and also the loss or destruction of documents lodged at the registry.[219]

Exceptions

5–043   The main provision is that no indemnity is payable where the applicant or a predecessor in title of his (except under a disposition for value protected on the register) has suffered loss

---

[214] LRA 2002 Sch.8 para.1(2)(a).
[215] LRA 2002 Sch.8 para.1(1)(a).
[216] LRA 2002 Sch.8 para.1(2)(b).
[217] For an example of this situation under the LRA 1925 see *Freer v Unwins Ltd* [1976] Ch. 288.
[218] LRA 2002 Sch.8 para.1(2)(a).
[219] LRA 2002 Sch.8 para.1(2)(c)–(h); see below.

wholly or partly as a result of his own fraud or wholly as a result of his own lack of proper care.[220] Any indemnity paid where the applicant has suffered loss partly as a result of his own lack of proper care is reduced to such extent as is just and equitable having regard to his share of the responsibility.[221] There are also exceptions for certain minerals and costs.[222]

Determination

Liability and amount are both determined either by proceedings in court[223] against the Registrar or by letter to the Registrar[224]; and payment is made out of moneys provided by Parliament. The indemnity is for the amount of the loss, together with a reasonable amount for costs and expenses properly incurred by the claimant, though not the costs of any proceedings brought by the claimant against third parties (such as those who caused the loss) without the Registrar's consent.[225] But where an estate or interest in land, or a charge on it, has been lost, the amount of the indemnity is restricted to its value. For rectification, the amount is the value immediately before rectification. For non-rectification it is the value when the error or omission causing the loss was made.[226] This may be much less than its present value[227] but the restriction is less harsh than it appears because the registry pays interest on the sum from the time that the mistake is made.[228] Claims for indemnity are barred after six years, though time begins to run only when the claimant knew of the existence of the claim, or but for his own default might have known of it.[229]

5–044

Where an indemnity is paid, the Registrar may recover the amount of it from any person who caused or substantially contributed to the loss by his fraud.[230]

SUMMARY OF KEY CASES

- *Abbey National Building Society v Cann* [1991] 1 A.C. 56
- *Norwich & Peterborough Building Society v Steed (No.2)* [1993] Ch. 116
- *Malory Enterprises Ltd v Cheshire Homes (UK) Ltd* [2002] Ch. 216
- *Derbyshire CC v Fallon* [2007] EWHC 1326 (Ch)
- *Sainsbury's Supermarkets v Olympia Homes* [2006] 1 P. & C. R. 17
- *Halifax Plc v Curry Popeck (A firm)* [2008] EWHC 1692 (Ch).

---

[220] LRA 2002 Sch.8 para.5(1), (3).
[221] LRA 2002 Sch.8 para.5(2).
[222] LRA 2002 Sch.8 para.2.
[223] LRA 2002 Sch.8 para.7.
[224] See Land Registry Practice Guide 39.
[225] LRA 2002 Sch.8 para.3(1).
[226] LRA 2002 Sch.8 para.6.
[227] See a case under the LRA 1925: *Epps v Esso Petroleum Co Ltd* [1973] 1 W.L.R. 1071 at 1081 (1959 values for non-rectification in 1973).
[228] LRR 2003 r.195.
[229] LRA 2002 Sch.8 para.1(8); Limitation Act 1980 Sch.3, para.1.
[230] LRA 2002 Sch.8 para.10.

FURTHER READING

- Law Commission, "Land Registration for the Twenty-first Century: A Conveyancing Revolution", (2001) Law Com. No. 271
- "The feudal system and the Land Registration Acts" [2008] L.Q.R.E. 586
- P. Matthews, "Registered Land, Fraud and Human Rights" (2008) 124 L.Q.R. 451
- M. Dixon, "The Reform of Property Law and the Land Registration Act 2002: A Risk Assessment" [2002] Conv. 136
- "Forgery and land registration: The decision in Malory Investments v Cheshire Homes" [2009] Conv. 127

This document is a sample created to illustrate an actual Title Register. The Title Number, names and addresses are fictitious.

Please note that each Title Register varies as to the amount of detail, some containing far more detail and others, less detail. Where there are no mortgages or charges affecting the property there may not be a C Section.

THIS TITLE IS DEALT WITH BY LAND REGISTRY, WALES OFFICE

TITLE NUMBER: NGL00119900

There is no application or official search pending against this title

A: Property Register

This register describes the land and estate comprised in the title. Except as mentioned below, the title includes any legal easements granted by the registered lease but is subject to any rights that it reserves, so far as those easements and rights exist and benefit or affect the registered land.

BRENT

1   (01.01.1991)   The Leasehold land shown edged with red on the plan of the above Title filed at the Registry and being Flat 1, 20 Long Road, Lewisham, London NW7 3HH, and Parking Space

Note: As to the part tinted blue on the filed plan only the first floor flat is included in the title

2   (01.01.1991) Short particulars of the lease(s) (or under-lease(s)) under which the land is held:

Date   : 6 December 1990
Term   : 125 years (less 3 days) from 22 December
Rent   1988
Parties   : £125 rising to £625 and additional rent
           : (1)   Wainwright Homes Lt
              (2)   Adam Smith

3   (01.01.1991)   There are excepted from the effect of registration all estates, rights, interests, powers and remedies arising upon, or by reason of, any dealing made in breach of the prohibition or restriction against dealings therewith inter vivos contained in the lease.

4   Unless otherwise mentioned the title includes any legal easements granted by the registered lease(s) but is subject to any rights that it

reserves, so far as those easements and rights exist and benefit or affect the registered land.

B: Proprietorship Register

This register specifies the class of title and identifies the owner. It contains any entries that affect the right of disposal.

TITLE ABSOLUTE

1   (12.12.1990) PROPRIETOR: ADAM SMITH of 37 Abraham Drive, London W11 6ZZ

C: Charges Register

This register contains any charges and other matters that affect the land

1   (01.01.91) The land is subject to the following rights reserved by a Conveyance dated 16 June 1967 made between (1) The Biochemical Commissioners for England and (2) Brian Lunt:

"Except nevertheless and reserving unto the Commissioners and their successors in title the owner or owners for the time being of the adjoining and neighbouring property

(a)   The free passage of water soil and other services from such adjoining land through any drains watercourses pipes and conduits now existing in or under the said property hereby conveyed or substituted therefor by the purchaser and

(b)   All such rights of way and such rights of user of air light and the passage thereof as the Commissioners their lessees or tenants now have or enjoy in through over and upon the said property or any part thereof to for or in respect of any adjoining property."

2   (01.01.91) REGISTERED CHARGE dated 6 December 1990 to secure the moneys including the further advances therein mentioned.

3   (01.01.91) Proprietor: NATIONAL BUILDING SOCIETY of National House, Knotty Ash, Liverpool L11 1ZZ

End of Register

Chapter 6

CONTRACTS FOR THE SALE OF LAND, CONVEYANCING AND LAND CHARGES

CHAPTER SUMMARY

Land may be disposed of in a variety of ways. The most common dispositions inter vivos are by sale, though gifts and settlements are sometimes made. On a sale, the formal conveyance or transfer of the land is almost always preceded by a contract for sale. The contract for sale and subsequent conveyance are the subjects of this chapter. This chapter also includes sections explaining land charges and local land charges.

The contract for sale needs to be distinguished from the actual transfer of the estate or interest itself to which different rules apply. The law governing contracts for the sale or disposition of any interest in land was substantially reformed in 1989, under the Law of Property (Miscellaneous Provisions) Act 1989. Contracts made before September 27, 1989, continue to be governed by the old law, but all other contracts are subject to the new law. Although the former law is now of very little importance, in order that historical decisions may be understood, it is briefly summarised before turning to the new law.

PART 1   CONTRACTS FOR THE SALE OF LAND

CONTRACTS IN PRACTICE

Cases where it is usual to have a contract

Whenever a transaction involves a payment of a capital sum, it is usual for it to be governed   6–001
by a contract. Thus where land is being sold in fee simple, or a lease is to be granted at a ground rent (a rent representing the value of the land without the buildings on it, or a nominal rent payable as a result of a purchase of a long lease of, typically, a flat for a lump sum premium (sometimes technically described as a "fine")) or is being assigned in consideration of a capital payment, a formal contract is normally made. If, on the other hand, no capital payment is involved, there is often no contract, such as on the grant or assignment of a lease at a rack rent (a rent representing the full value of the land and buildings).

A mortgage, although involving a capital payment, is rarely preceded by a contract as such, although some institutional lenders require the intending borrower to countersign and return a copy of their written offer, something which has the effect of creating a binding contract between them.

THE OLD LAW: CONTRACTS MADE BEFORE SEPTEMBER 27, 1989

6–002   Before September 27, 1989, a contract for the sale or disposition of land or any interest in land could be validly made in any way. Although such contracts were usually made in writing, an oral contract was perfectly valid. But unless an oral contract was sufficiently evidenced in writing, or supported by a sufficient act of part performance, it could not be enforced by action.[1] Although deprived of its most important remedy, such a contract remained valid, and it could be enforced by any means except an action, as where a vendor forfeited (i.e. kept) the deposit paid by a purchaser who later defaulted.[2] The law as to evidence in writing and part performance gave rise to much litigation and was widely regarded as unsatisfactory.[3]

Evidenced in writing

6–003   The law required the agreement, "or some memorandum or note thereof", to be in writing, and to be signed by or on behalf of "the party to be charged",[4] namely, the person against whom the action was to be brought. Any form of evidence of the contract sufficed if it was in writing; and it might come into existence long after the contract was made, and be made up of two or more connected documents. But the writing was required to state all the terms of the contract that the parties had agreed. Where the evidence in writing was signed by one party (V) but not by the other (P), V could not sue P, but P could sue V; for V was the party to be charged.

Part performance

6–004   If a party to an oral contract for the sale or disposition of land or any interest in land had carried out a sufficient act of part performance of that contract, equity would enforce it for him against the other party. The principle behind the doctrine[5] was that, if one party had partly performed the contract, it would have been fraudulent for the other party to plead the lack of evidence as a defence. The acts done raised an equity in that party's favour, and in satisfying that equity the court had to choose "between undoing what has been done (which is not always possible, or, if possible, just) and completing what has been left undone."[6] Part performance differed from evidence in writing in that the act of part performance had to have been done by the claiming party, whereas the evidence in writing had

---

[1]   LPA 1925 s.40.
[2]   *Monnickendam v Leanse* (1923) 39 T.L.R. 445.
[3]   See *Steadman v Steadman* [1976] A.C. 536; Law Com. No.164, para.1.9.
[4]   LPA 1925 s.40(1), replacing part of Statute of Frauds 1677 s.4.
[5]   Recognised by LPA 1925 s.40(2).
[6]   *Maddison v Alderson* (1883) 8 App.Cas. 467 at 476, per Earl of Selborne L.C.

to have been signed by the defendant. What was required for part performance was some act which sufficiently indicated that there was some contract of the kind alleged. Thus if V agreed to sell land to P, and then allowed P to take possession of the land, the handing over of possession was a sufficient act of part performance both by V and by P.

THE CURRENT LAW: CONTRACTS MADE AFTER SEPTEMBER 26, 1989

For any contract made after September 26, 1989, the Act of 1989 repealed the law both as to evidence in writing and part performance.[7] Instead, it provided that: **6–005**

> "a contract for the sale or other disposition of an interest in land can only be made in writing and only by incorporating all the terms which the parties have expressly agreed in one document or, where contracts are exchanged, in each."[8]

A contract which does not comply with this provision is wholly void, and not merely unenforceable by action. The terms of this provision will be considered in turn, together with the additional requirement as to signature. It is important to appreciate that the 1989 Act is concerned only with the contract, and not with the disposition which follows. A contract may be void, but if neither party takes that point and the transaction completes, the validity of the disposition is unaffected by the fact that contract was void.

Sale or other disposition

Transactions included

"The sale or other disposition" of an interest in land: **6–006**

    (i)   includes every type of disposition, whether sale, lease, mortgage or anything else[9]; and

    (ii) applies both to disposing of existing interests and to the creation of new interests.

Contracts of the following descriptions do not relate to a "sale or disposition" and are not caught:

    (i)   a lock-out agreement (an agreement not to sell property or not to deal with anyone except the other party)[10];

    (ii) an agreement by the vendor (V) with another party (X) to sell the property on the market (to whoever will buy) and account to X for the proceeds (whatever they may be)[11];

---

[7] LP(MP)A 1989 ss.2(1), (7), (8), 5(3), (4), Sch.2.
[8] LP(MP)A 1989 s.2(1).
[9] LP(MP)A 1989 s.2(6); LPA 1925 s.205(1)(ii).
[10] *Pitt v PHH Asset Management* [1994] 1 W.L.R. 327.
[11] *Nweze v Nwoko* [2004] EWCA Civ 379; [2004] 2 P. & C.R. 667.

(iii) a boundary agreement between neighbours defining the boundary between their land holdings.[12]

As to fixtures, a disposition includes the sale of fixtures separately from the land to a stranger,[13] but not the sale of fixtures to the landlord by a tenant who is entitled to remove them,[14] for in substance this is merely a waiver by the tenant of his right of removal, and so is no sale of either land or goods.[15]

Exceptions

6–007   There are three classes of contract for a sale or disposition to which these statutory provisions do not apply[16]:

(i)   short leases—a contract for the grant of a lease for not more than three years at the best rent reasonably obtainable without taking a fine[17];
(ii) public auctions—a contract made in the course of a public auction;
(iii) financial services—a contract regulated under the Financial Services and Markets Act 2000 other than a regulated mortgage contract[18]; this Act controls the conduct of investment business.

Interrelationship with trusts

6–008   These statutory provisions do not affect the creation or operation of resulting, implied or constructive trusts.[19] However, where after an oral agreement the parties still intended to enter into a formal written agreement or there were still terms that remained to be agreed, there could be no reliance on a constructive trust to overcome s.2.[20] An agreement which fails to comply with formalities may also be enforced through proprietary estoppel.[21] Consequently, if a party to an agreement with a landowner which does not satisfy the statutory formalities acts to his detriment on the strength of an assurance by the landowner that he will thereby acquire an interest in the land, he will be able to claim that interest on

---

[12] *Joyce v Rigoli* [2004] EWCA Civ 79 (which assumes that any land transferred by such an agreement is de minimis); *Yeates v Line* [2012] EWHC 3085, [2013] Ch. 363.
[13] See *Underwood Ltd v Burgh Castle Brick and Cement Syndicate* [1922] 1 K.B. 123.
[14] See above, para.2–042.
[15] *Lee v Gaskell* (1876) 1 QBD 700.
[16] LP(MP)A 1989 s.2(5).
[17] See below, para.11–016.
[18] As well as any *"regulated home reversion plan"*, *"regulated home purchase plan"* and *"regulated sale and rent back agreement"* all of which must be read with (a) s.22 of the Financial Services and Markets Act 2000, (b) any relevant order under that section, and (c) Sch.2 to that Act.
[19] LP(MP)A 1989 s.2(5).
[20] *Herbert v Doyle* [2010] EWCA Civ 1095, [2011] 1 E.G.L.R. 119.
[21] See *Whittaker v Kinnear* [2011] EWHC 1479 (QB), [2011] 2 P. & C.R. DG20 but note Lord Scott's comment in *Cobbe v Yeoman's Row Management Ltd* [2008] 1 W.L.R. 1752 and the distinction drawn in *Whittaker* between commercial and domestic cases. The impact of Proprietary estoppel is considered further in Ch.9.

the basis that the landowner is estopped from denying the existence of that interest and is therefore a constructive trustee of the land for him.[22]

Interest in land

"Interest in land" is widely defined as "any estate, interest or charge in or over land".[23] However, it does not include a contractual licence as such a licence is not an interest in land.   **6–009**

Made in writing

The Act requires the contract to be "made" in writing and not merely "evidenced" in writing.[24] An oral agreement is therefore void, and cannot constitute a binding contract. Under an option to buy land, it could be said that there is no contract of purchase until the purchaser has exercised his option; but for the purposes of the Act the option is treated as being a conditional contract to sell the land, to which the requirements of the Act apply. If the option satisfies the Act it is immaterial that the notice exercising it does not.[25] One consequence of this is that an option granted in 1988 and exercised in 2001 will be subject to the old law and not the new, even though no obligation arose to actually buy or sell until 2001.   **6–010**

All the terms

The terms

The signed contract document must incorporate "all the terms which the parties have expressly agreed".[26] It is a question of fact as to what constitutes the contract document.[27]   **6–011**

A failure to include all the terms expressly agreed will render the contract void.[28] This does not extend to terms implied by law, such as the term that on a sale with vacant possession, vacant possession must be given at completion[29]; and perhaps the omission of an express term to this effect would be no breach of the statute.[30]

Terms may be incorporated in a document either by being set out in it or by reference to some other document.[31] The reference may be quite vague.[32]

---

[22] *Yaxley v Gotts* [2000] Ch. 162.
[23] LP(MP)A 1989 s.2(6).
[24] LP(MP)A 1989 s.2(1).
[25] *Spiro v Glencrown Properties Ltd* [1991] Ch. 537.
[26] LP(MP)A 1989 s.2(1).
[27] *Firstpost Homes v Johnson* [1995] 1 W.L.R. 1567, where it was held that an accompanying plan was not, on the facts, part of the signed document.
[28] *Keay v Morris Homes (West Midlands) Ltd* [2012] 1 W.L.R. 2855; *Oun v Ahmad* [2008] EWHC 545 (Ch).
[29] See *Topfell Ltd v Galley Properties Ltd* [1979] 1 W.L.R. 446.
[30] See *Farrell v Green* (1974) 232 E.G. 587.
[31] LP(MP)A 1989 s.2(2).
[32] *Courtney v Corp Ltd* [2006] EWCA Civ 518 where a reference to "our formal terms and conditions" was sufficient, as it could be established by hearing evidence which were the relevant terms to which this was a reference.

Certainty

6–012   The terms of the contract are sufficiently stated if they fall within the principle *id certum est quod certum reddi potest* (that is certain which can be made certain).
The only three essential terms[33] are:

    (i) the parties;
    (ii) the property to be sold; and
    (iii) the price (which in the case of a contract to grant a lease, includes the rent).

All other necessary terms, such as the time for completion and the title to be shown by the vendor, can be implied by the general law.[34] Although the majority of contracts contain express provisions dealing with these and many other matters. A contract which contains no express provisions as to, for example, the title to be shown by the vendor, is described as a contract which is open as to title.

    (i) Certainty of the parties: while it is essential that the document should disclose each party to the contract, or his agent,[35] it is sufficient if, without being named, each party is so described that their identity cannot be fairly disputed,[36] such as if the document refers to the "proprietor"[37] of the property, or states that "the vendor will convey as legal personal representative".[38] But references to the "vendor"[39] or "landlord"[40] or "my clients"[41] are not sufficient by themselves, for these descriptions may fit many persons; the proprietor of land is not the only person who can be the vendor, for many other persons such as mortgagees or even complete strangers may enter into a contract to sell the land.[42]

    (ii) Certainty of the property to be sold: when the land to be sold is sufficiently described, parol evidence may be admissible to identify it and its boundaries.[43] Where a contract is to be completed in stages, it must be stated which part is to be conveyed first.[44] In the absence of any statement to the contrary, it is assumed that the vendor is contracting to sell an estate in fee simple free from incumbrances of which the purchaser is not already aware.[45] Where the contract states

---

[33] See *Chaitlal v Ramlal* [2003] UKPC 12; [2004] 1 P. & C.R. 1.
[34] *Perry v Suffields Ltd* [1916] 2 Ch. 187.
[35] *McLaughlin v Duffill* [2010] Ch. 1, CA; *Davies v Sweet* [1962] 2 Q.B. 300.
[36] *Carr v Lynch* [1900] 1 Ch. 613 at 615.
[37] *Rossiter v Miller* (1878) 3 App.Cas. 1124.
[38] *Fay v Miller, Wilkins & Co* [1941] Ch. 360; but see (1941) 57 L.Q.R. 452.
[39] *Potter v Duffield* (1874) L.R. 18 Eq. 4.
[40] *Coombs v Wilkes* [1891] 3 Ch. 77.
[41] *Lovesy v Palmer* [1916] 2 Ch. 233.
[42] *Donnison v People's Cafe Co* (1881) 45 L.T. 187.
[43] *Westvilla Properties Ltd v Dow Properties Ltd* [2010] EWHC 30 (Ch), [2010] 2 P. & C.R. 332 (although this was a case where by mistake the plans had been omitted from the draft lease, but followed in *Rabiu v Marlbray* [2013] EWHC 3272 (Ch) with the comment that parole evidence was admissible to identify the property that was the subject matter of the contract); *Plant v Bourne* [1897] 2 Ch. 281; *Harewood v Retese* [1990] 1 W.L.R. 333.
[44] *Bushwall Properties Ltd v Vortex Properties Ltd* [1976] 1 W.L.R. 591.
[45] *Timmins v Moreland Street Property Co Ltd* [1958] Ch. 110.

that something less than the vendor's entire interest in the property is to pass (such as where a lease is being sold), the contract must state exactly what interest the purchaser is buying.[46]

(iii) Certainty of the price: this will be sufficiently certain if it is stated by reference to a formula which the court is capable of applying[47] but not where the parties have merely agreed to agree the price.[48] If the parties refer the decision as to the price to a third party, they will be presumed to have intended the third party to determine a fair and reasonable price by objective criteria, thus enabling the court to do so in default.[49]

Any other express terms of the contract must equally be certain or be capable of being rendered certain. A lack of certainty as to any express term, whether essential or not, will render the entire contract void for uncertainty.

Rectification

Where a document does not satisfy the requirements of the Act of 1989, it can sometimes   **6–013** be rectified by the court so as to cure the defect. Thus a term omitted by mistake can be inserted or mistaken language altered; but strong and convincing proof of the mistake must be adduced.[50] Rectification normally operates retrospectively, so that the document takes effect as if it had originally been in its correct form; but where a contract satisfies the Act of 1989 only by reason of the rectification of one or more documents, the contract comes into being at the time specified in the order of the court.[51]

"One document"

Position where there is no exchange of contracts

Save where contracts are exchanged the terms expressly agreed must be incorporated in   **6–014** one document signed by both parties. However, the absence of terms which have been agreed will not invalidate the document provided that the parties intended to be bound without those terms and although related to the land transaction they could be treated separately from it.[52] As noted earlier, it is a question of fact as to what constitutes the contract document[53] and the agreed terms may be incorporated in a document either by being

---

[46] *Dolling v Evans* (1867) 36 L.J. Ch. 474; *Cox v Middleton* (1854) 2 Drew 209.

[47] *Smith v Jones* [1952] 2 All E.R. 907; *Brown v Gould* [1972] Ch. 53.

[48] *Courtney Ltd v Tolaini Brothers Ltd* [1975] 1 W.L.R. 297.

[49] *Sudbrook Trading Estate Ltd v Eggleton* [1983] 1 A.C. 444; *Re Malpass* [1985] 1 Ch. 42.

[50] *Joscelyne v Nissen* [1970] 2 Q.B. 86, CA; *Swainland Builders Ltd v Freehold Properties Ltd* [2002] EWCA Civ 560, [2002] 2 E.G.L.R. 71.

[51] LP(MP)A 1989 s.2(4).

[52] *North Eastern Properties Ltd v Coleman & Quinn Conveyancing* [2010] 1 W.L.R. 2715, CA (the use of an entire agreement clause was suggested as a means of clarifying that other related agreements were not part of the land transaction); *Keay v Morris Homes (West Midlands) Ltd* [2012] 1 W.L.R. 2855, CA; *Grossman v Hooper* [2001] 2 E.G.L.R. 82.

[53] *Firstpost Homes v Johnson* [1995] 1 W.L.R. 1567, where it was held that an accompanying plan was not, on the facts, part of the signed document.

set out in it or by reference to some other document,[54] so that the terms may be found in two or more documents provided one of them sufficiently refers to the others.

Exchange of contracts

6–015   Where contracts are exchanged, which is what generally occurs in order to enable each party to have a copy signed by the other party, the usual practice is to prepare identical documents, and then, when both parties are ready to bind themselves, to exchange the document signed by the vendor for the document signed by the purchaser.[55]

Where both parties are legally represented, traditionally the purchaser's solicitor sends the document signed by the purchaser to the vendor's solicitor together with any deposit payable, and on receipt the vendor's solicitor sends the document signed by the vendor to the purchaser's solicitor. However, because one or both parties is likely to be involved in a related sale or purchase in which contracts have to be exchanged more or less simultaneously, exchanges of contracts are now generally carried out over the telephone in accordance with Formulae laid down by The Law Society on the basis of undertakings by the solicitors involved.

True collateral agreements

6–016   However, whether contracts are exchanged or not, the statute does not invalidate an independent collateral warranty (for example as to title) given to induce the signing of the contract.[56] It has also been held that the statute does not invalidate an agreement which is supplemental to a contract (such as to grant a lease) which has been duly carried out and so is no longer executory[57] but this has since been doubted.[58]

Signed

6–017   "The document incorporating the terms or, where contracts are exchanged, one of the documents incorporating them (but not necessarily the same one) must be signed by or on behalf of each party to the contract."[59]

Signature

6–018   The words in brackets in this provision permit the continuance of the practice of exchanging contracts, with each part signed by only one party. Under the current law, both parties will normally sign at the same place at the beginning or end of the document or, where contracts are exchanged, on the part which is to be given to the other party. Under the previous law, when only a note or memorandum was required, the courts gave an extended meaning to the word "signed"; provided the name of the signatory appeared in some part of the

---

[54] LP(MP)A s.2(2).
[55] See *Eccles v Bryant* [1948] Ch. 93.
[56] *Record v Bell* [1991] 1 W.L.R. 853.
[57] *Tootal Clothing Ltd v Guinea Properties Management Ltd* [1992] 2 E.G.L.R. 452.
[58] *Grossman v Hooper* [2001] 2 E.G.L.R. 82.
[59] LP(MP)A 1989 s.2(3).

document in some form, whether in writing, typewriting, print or otherwise, there was a sufficient signature if that person had shown in some way that he recognised the document as an expression of the contract.[60] According to some authority there is a more restrictive approach to what will constitute a signature under s.2.[61] It must be written in manuscript and in a manner which makes it clear that the signing party intends to be bound by the agreement. However, the correctness of this has been doubted by some commentators who suggest that the previous law should still apply.[62]

Agents

Where a party does not himself sign the contract, a signature "by or on behalf of" him suffices. The Act does not affect the law of agency. A contract signed by an agent who has been duly authorised (either orally or in writing) to sign on his principal's behalf binds the principal.[63] No provision is made about the mode in which an agent must receive his authority, and so it need not be given in writing. But the mere existence of an agency is not enough; it must be shown that the agent had authority to sign the same kind of contract as that which in fact was signed.[64] The same person may be given authority to sign on behalf of both parties, as where a solicitor acts for both of them[65]; a course of conduct which is most unwise for the solicitor in question because of possible conflicts of interest. A solicitor must have actual authority to sign and a contract will not be binding on the basis of ostensible authority, although an unauthorised signature can be subsequently ratified and therefore bring into effect a binding contract.[66]

6–019

Variations of a contract

A variation of a contract is, technically, a fresh contract, and so variations must comply with the Act in the same way that the original contract must comply. A void variation may mean that the original valid contract subsists unvaried. Conversely, a contract void for non-compliance with the Act may become valid (as varied) if a subsequent variation agreement does comply with the Act.[67]

6–020

Consequences of the abolition of part performance

Although there has been no express abolition of the doctrine of part performance, which had developed uncertainties,[68] it is plain that that doctrine no longer exists. As an oral agreement for the sale or other disposition of an interest in land cannot be a contract,

6–021

---

[60] See *Halley v O'Brien* [1920] 1 I.R. 330 at 339; and see *Leeman v Stocks* [1951] Ch. 941.

[61] *Firstpost Homes Ltd v Johnson* [1995] 1 W.L.R. 1567, 1575, CA.

[62] See *Emmet & Farrand on Title* (London: Sweet & Maxwell), para.2.041.

[63] *McLaughlin v Duffill* [2010] Ch. 1 (C.A.).

[64] See *Thirkell v Cambi* [1919] 2 K.B. 590 at 598.

[65] *Gavaghan v Edwards* [1961] 2 Q.B. 220.

[66] *Smith v Webster* (1876) 3 Ch. D 49; *Koenigsblatt v Sweet* [1923] 2 Ch. 314, CA; *Simple v Chee* [2013] EWHC 4444 (Ch).

[67] *Rabiu v Marlbray Ltd* [2013] EWHC 3272 (Ch) at [168].

[68] See above, para.6–004.

there is no contract that can be partly performed. This may well cause hardship.[69] If V orally agrees to grant or sell some interest in land to P, V can refuse to perform the agreement, however many and costly the acts that P has done in part performance of the agreement. This may be mitigated in some degree by the doctrine of proprietary estoppel,[70] (to which the now abolished doctrine of part performance was related).[71] In such circumstances the court is obviously likely to regard the oral agreement, though void as a contract, as providing evidence of the appropriate way of satisfying P's equity and has indeed done so.[72] However, the court is not obliged to follow this course; the type of interest to be given to P depends on the court's discretion and, as a result, the doctrine of proprietary estoppel is more uncertain in its operation than the doctrine of part performance was since it will not necessarily lead to the enforcement of the agreement actually made between the parties.[73]

TYPES OF CONTRACT AND USUAL TERMS

Types of contract

6–022   There are three main types of contract.

Open contracts

6–023   As has already been seen, in these contracts only the essential terms (the parties, the property to be sold and the price) have been expressly agreed. The remaining terms, such as the time for completion and the title to be shown by the vendor, are left to implied by the general law. Such contracts are uncommon, for obvious reasons.

Contracts by correspondence

6–024   In the case of contracts by correspondence for the sale of land, the Law of Property Act 1925[74] provides that the Statutory Form of Conditions of Sale 1925, made by the Lord Chancellor, are to govern the contract, subject to any modification or contrary intention expressed in the correspondence.[75] Such contracts were comparatively infrequent even prior to the Act, and now that they must be in writing signed by both parties[76] they are likely to become even rarer; but they are not impossible, as where a copy of a letter signed by one party is signed by the other. However, it is no longer possible, as it was prior to the Act, for a valid contract to be formed by an exchange of letters because in this case there will be neither one contract signed by both parties nor two identical contracts signed by each of them.

---

[69] See also below, para.17–019
[70] See above, para.3–031 and Ch.9 below; Law Com. No. 164, paras 5.4, 5.
[71] See (1985) 36 N.I.L.Q. 358 at 359–364 (M. P. Thompson).
[72] In *Yaxley v Gotts* [2000] Ch. 162.
[73] See above, para.6–004.
[74] s.46.
[75] See (1974) 90 L.Q.R. 55 (A. M. Prichard).
[76] Above, para.6–005.

Formal contracts

It is always open to the parties to make a contract in such terms as they see fit, subject to **6–025**
the rule that certain provisions contrary to the policy of the law are void, such as any provision that the conveyance should be prepared by a solicitor appointed by the vendor.[77] In
practice, various standard forms of conditions have been settled, the most recent being the
Standard Conditions of Sale,[78] introduced in 1990 and subsequently amended on a number
of occasions. Standard forms of conditions, with such amendments as are desirable to fit
the particular case, are usually employed, since they avoid the labour of preparing a set of
conditions for each case. It is common for standard forms of conditions to be supplemented
by special conditions on a variety of matters, for example by precluding the purchaser from
objecting to certain specified defects in the vendor's title.[79]

This division of the types of contract is not rigid; thus the parties may agree a few special
conditions and leave the rest to the rules of the general law, thereby creating a contract
which is in part formal and as to the remainder an open contract. A contract which contains
no express provisions as to, for example, the title to be shown by the vendor, is described
as a contract which is open as to title. This is actually the position under the Standard
Conditions of Sale when the property to be sold is an estate in fee simple.

Terms of contract

The following are examples of the matters usually dealt with in a formal contract for the **6–026**
sale of land.

1. Provision for the payment of a deposit (usually 10 per cent of the purchase
   money[80]) and for the payment of interest on the purchase money if completion is
   delayed.
2. Where the title is unregistered, any variations to general law relating to the length
   and nature of the title to be deduced by the vendor, and any special conditions as
   to title, such as to making no objections to some specified defect in title or flaw in
   the evidence of title. Where the title is registered, the title number of the property, the class of title and copies of documents referred to on the register, such as
   those imposing restrictive covenants.[81]
3. The time within which the matters affecting the title must be dealt with.
4. The date and place for completion of the sale.
5. Power for the vendor to rescind the contract or re-sell the property in certain
   circumstances, such as the purchaser's insistence on objections to the title, or his
   failure to perform the contract.

---

[77] LPA 1925 s.48(1).
[78] These conditions were originally an amended conflation of *The Law Society's Conditions of Sale*
(20th edn) and the *National Conditions of Sale* (20th edn). The original version is discussed in [1990]
Conv. 179 (J. E. Adams). The current edition is the fifth. There is also a National Conveyancing
Protocol which sets out the steps to be taken by each party.
[79] As should have been done in *Faruqi v English Real Estates Ltd* [1979] 1 W.L.R. 963.
[80] Anything more than that is open to challenge; see *Workers Trust & Merchant Bank v Dojap
Investments* [1993] A.C. 573; although the basis for this rule is controversial.
[81] See *Faruqi v English Real Estates Ltd* [1979] 1 W.L.R. 963.

6. Power for either party to serve a notice to complete if the contract is not completed on the date specified in the contract. Such a notice sets a further period of time for completion and entitles the party serving the notice to rescind the contract in default of compliance.

EFFECT OF CONTRACT

6–027 Once a contract for the sale of land has been made, the parties have many rights and become subject to many obligations. One important aspect of this is the basis upon which land is held between the execution of the contract for sale and completion.

The purchaser as owner in equity

6–028 As soon as a specifically enforceable contract for the sale of land has been made, the purchaser becomes "the real and beneficial owner of it".[82] Nearly all contracts for the sale of land are specifically enforceable, and equity treats that as done which ought to be done. The purchaser is under many obligations, not least that of paying the purchase money at completion, and normally has no right to possession until then; but in equity (though not at law) the land is his.

The vendor as trustee

6–029 On the same grounds, the vendor becomes a trustee of the land for the purchaser, and so is under a duty to take reasonable care of it.[83] Thus he is liable to the purchaser if he damages the land himself,[84] or if he fails to take reasonable care to prevent it being damaged by third parties[85] or by natural events.[86] The vendor's trusteeship is of an unusual kind because it is heavily qualified by the various rights that he has, such as the right to retain possession until completion; but his powers to act as the owner in matters such as changing tenancies is suspended.[87]

Passing of risk

6–030 For similar reasons, the risk of anything happening to the property passes to the purchaser as soon as the contract is made, unless it otherwise provides. Thus, if a house is destroyed by fire between contract and completion, the purchaser must still pay the vendor the full price, for the risk was his.[88] The purchaser should therefore either insure the house himself or arrange to take over the benefit of the vendor's policy. However, the Standard Conditions of Sale that are generally used provide that the vendor retains the risk until

---

[82] *Shaw v Foster* (1872) L.R. 5 H.L. 321 at 338 per Lord Cairns.

[83] *Wilson v Clapham* (1819) 1 Jac. & W. 36 at 38; *Englewood Properties v Patel* [2005] 1 W.L.R. 1961.

[84] *Cumberland Consolidated Holdings Ltd v Ireland* [1946] K.B. 264 (abandonment of much rubbish on land).

[85] *Clarke v Ramuz* [1891] 2 Q.B. 456 (trespasser removes soil); *Davron Estates Ltd v Turnshire Ltd* (1982) 133 N.L.J. 937 (squatters).

[86] *Lucie-Smith v Gorman* [1981] C.L.Y. 2866 (burst pipe from failure to turn off water in winter).

[87] *Raffety v Scholfield* [1897] 1 Ch. 937 at 945.

[88] *Lysaght v Edwards* (1876) 2 Ch.D. 499 at 507; *Rayner v Preston* (1881) 18 Ch.D. 1. See criticisms at [1984] Conv. 43 (M. P. Thompson).

completion. The vendor is under no obligation to the purchaser to insure but in practice he will do so as the risk is his and because the purchaser is entitled to rescind if the physical state of the property has made it unusable for its purpose at the date of the contract. The vendor is also given a right, which does not arise other than by an express provision of this type, to rescind the contract if the physical state of the property has made it unusable for its purpose at the date of the contract but only if this arises as a result of damage against which the vendor could not reasonably have insured or which he cannot legally make good.[89]

PART 2   CONVEYANCING

INTRODUCTION

Conveyancing may be regarded as the application of the law of real property in practice. It is an immense subject, and only a very brief outline of a few of the chief features can be given here. Although conveyancing does not form part of the subject of real property, every student should have some idea of the relationship between the two subjects. The work of a conveyancer is twofold. First, they investigate title by examining documents and making inquiries and searches. Secondly, they draft conveyances and other legal documents. The drafting of legal documents demands great skill, though books of forms or "precedents" are widely used.

    The necessary steps taken after a contract has been made have changed over the years with the introduction of land registration under the Land Registration Act 1925 and then further changes under the Land Registration Act 2002. Yet further change will occur if and when e-conveyancing is introduced. The steps are considerably more complex when the title is unregistered than when it is registered, something which was one of the principal factors which led to the decision to make the system of registered conveyancing predominant. The roll out of e-conveyancing (the computerisation of the process) has not gone as smoothly as planned though.[90]

6–031

Necessity for a deed

A conveyance of a legal estate must be by deed.[91] Formerly a deed required to be signed, sealed and delivered, but now the requirement of sealing, which had become an unimportant formality, has been abolished.[92] Instead, an instrument will be a deed only if[93]:

6–032

---

[89] See para.5 of the Conditions.

[90] The Land Registry's plans may have been a little over ambitious – see Law Society Gazette, 18th October 2012 – "Hudson warning over failure to modernise conveyancing" and *Report on Responses to E-Conveyancing Secondary Legislation Part 3* (2011).

[91] LPA 1925 s.52(1).

[92] LP(MP)A 1989 s.1(1).

[93] LP(MP)A 1989 s.1(2)–(4).

(i) it makes it clear on its face that it is intended to be a deed, usually by using the expression "signed as a deed by" each person who is executing it;

(ii) it is signed either by the person making it (or one of the parties to it) in the presence of a witness who attests the signature, or else at his direction and in his presence and the presence of two witnesses who each attest the signature (however, if the signatory holds out the document as a deed, it does not matter if the purported witness did not actually attest the signature but signed later on provided that there is nothing to place the other party to the conveyance on inquiry[94]); and

(iii) it is delivered[95] as a deed by him or by a person authorised to do so on his behalf.

REGISTERED TITLE

From contract to completion

6–033   On the sale of a freehold estate in registered land by V to P, the sequence of steps (normally taken by their solicitors) is as follows.

Evidence of title

6–034   The Land Registration Act 2002 currently leaves it to the parties to determine what should be done after exchange of contracts to evidence title. Each title can be examined on the register, which is an open register.[96]

Investigation of title

6–035   The entries on the register must be examined to see that the purchaser will obtain what he is expecting. The register provides an instant title (subject to interests which override registration – evidence of these should be checked by pre contract enquiries, local and searches and an actual inspection of the property) so there is obviously no need to examine past history.

Requisitions on title

6–036   After investigating title, V is entitled to raise questions of P (known as requisitions) in relation to clarify and/or rectify unsatisfactory matters. The time for raising such queries is usually set out in the contract for sale.

Replies to requisitions

6–037   V then answers the requisitions. If his answers are unsatisfactory on any point then P may make further requisitions until he is satisfied that he is obtaining what he contracted to purchase.

---

[94] *Shah v Shah* [2002] Q.B. 35.
[95] For delivery, see below, para.6–065.
[96] See above, para.5–007.

Draft transfer

P next fills in a standard form of draft transfer deed[97] with such special clauses as he consid-   **6–038**
ers appropriate to give effect to the contract. He sends this to V for approval. When the
draft transfer has been agreed (usually an easy matter), P sends a fair copy to V to be used
as the engrossment for execution by V.

Searches

About seven days before the date fixed for completion P makes an official search with prior-   **6–039**
ity of the register to ensure that nothing has been entered against the title since the last
search. This not only checks that no new interests have been notified, but also protects P in
that one effect of the search is to give P priority over any interest notified within 30 days of
the search having been carried out.[98] P also must carry out a local land charges search; the
operation of the Local Land Charges Act 1975 is considered separately later.

Completion

Before expiry of the priority period of 30 working days afforded by the official search   **6–040**
certificate,[99] completion will take place. The date, time and method of completion are
agreed prior to the date set for completion. Where both parties are legally represented
completion normally takes place in accordance with The Law Society's Code for Completion
by Post. P's solicitor will transfer the necessary sum to V's solicitor's client account to be
held to the order of P's solicitor and, once the funds have arrived in that account or on the
agreed completion date, if later, V will complete the transaction, after which he will hold
the transfer rather than the funds to the order of P's solicitor, notify P's solicitor and send
the transfer to him by post or, in practice, through a document exchange service.

The passing of title

In contrast with unregistered land, the legal title does not pass until P is registered as pro-   **6–041**
prietor[100] and P must ensure that this is done before the priority period expires.

The transfer: precedent and details

A registered proprietor can dispose of his registered estate, or deal with it, only as authorised   **6–042**
by statute.[101] The forms set out in the Schedule to the Land Registration Rules 2002 must be
used.[102] The following is the present Land Registry Form (Form TR1) for the transfer of the
whole of a registered title (different forms are employed for other forms of transfer).[103]

---

[97] The form and effect of the transfer is dealt with below.
[98] Land Registration Rules 2002 rr.131, 147.
[99] See above, paras 5–028 and 6–039.
[100] LRA s.27.
[101] Most significantly, subject to a few exceptions, s.52 of the LPA provides for all conveyances of a
legal estate to be by deed.
[102] LRR r.206.
[103] All the necessary forms can be found and downloaded at *http://www.landregistry.gov.uk/profes-
sional/forms* [Accessed April 25, 2014].

Land Registry
Transfer of whole of registered title(s)

If you need more room than is provided for in a panel, and your software allows, you can expand any panel in the form. Alternatively use continuation sheet CS and attach it to this form.

Leave blank if not yet registered.	1	Title number(s) of the property:
Insert address including postcode (if any) or other description of the property, for example 'land adjoining 2 Acacia Avenue'.	2	Property:
	3	Date:
Give full name(s).	4	Transferor:
Complete as appropriate where the transferor is a company.		**For UK incorporated companies/LLPs** Registered number of company or limited liability partnership including any prefix: **For overseas companies** (a) Territory of incorporation: (b) Registered number in the United Kingdom including any prefix:
Give full name(s).	5	Transferee for entry in the register:
Complete as appropriate where the transferee is a company. Also, for an overseas company, unless an arrangement with Land Registry exists, lodge either a certificate in Form 7 in Schedule 3 to the Land Registration Rules 2003 or a certified copy of the constitution in English or Welsh, or other evidence permitted by rule 183 of the Land Registration Rules 2003.		**For UK incorporated companies/LLPs** Registered number of company or limited liability partnership including any prefix: **For overseas companies** (a) Territory of incorporation: (b) Registered number in the United Kingdom including any prefix:
Each transferee may give up to three addresses for service, one of which must be a postal address whether or not in the UK (including the postcode, if any). The others can be any combination of a postal address, a UK DX box number or an electronic address.	6	Transferee's intended address(es) for service for entry in the register:
	7	The transferor transfers the property to the transferee

Place 'X' in the appropriate box. State the currency unit if other than sterling. If none of the boxes apply, insert an appropriate memorandum in panel 11.	**8** **Consideration** ☐ The transferor has received from the transferee for the property the following sum (in words and figures): ☐ The transfer is not for money or anything that has a monetary value ☐ Insert other receipt as appropriate:
Place 'X' in any box that applies. Add any modifications.	**9** **The transferor transfers with** ☐ full title guarantee ☐ limited title guarantee

Where the transferee is more than one person, place 'X' in the appropriate box.
 	
Complete as necessary.
 	
The registrar will enter a Form A restriction in the register *unless*:
– an 'X' is placed:
  – in the first box, or
  – in the third box and the details of the trust or of the trust instrument show that the transferees are to hold the property on trust for themselves alone as joint tenants, *or*
– it is clear from completion of a form JO lodged with this application that the transferees are to hold the property on trust for themselves alone as joint tenants.
 	
Please refer to Land Registry's Public Guide 18 – *Joint property ownership* and Practice Guide 24 – *Private trusts of land* for further guidance. These guides are available on our website www.landregistry.gov.uk
	10 **Declaration of trust. The transferee is more than one person and**
	
	☐ they are to hold the property on trust for themselves as joint tenants
	
	☐ they are to hold the property on trust for themselves as tenants in common in equal shares
	
	☐ they are to hold the property on trust:

Insert here any required or permitted statement, certificate or application and any agreed covenants, declarations and so on.	**11** **Additional provisions**

The transferor must execute this transfer as a deed using the space opposite. If there is more than one transferor, all must execute. Forms of execution are given in Schedule 9 to the Land Registration Rules 2003. If the transfer contains transferee's covenants or declarations or contains an application by the transferee (such as for a restriction), it must also be executed by the transferee.

If there is more than one transferee and panel 10 has been completed, each transferee may also execute this transfer to comply with the requirements in section 53(1)(b) of the Law of Property Act 1925 relating to the declaration of a trust of land. Please refer to Land Registry's Public Guide *18 – Joint property ownership* and Practice Guide *24 – Private trusts of land* for further guidance.

12   Execution

CONTRACTS FOR THE SALE OF LAND, CONVEYANCING AND LAND CHARGES   141

Title number(s) of the property

This contains the title number or numbers of the Registered Title and the name of the   **6–043**
relevant District Land Registry.

Property

This contains the address of the Property.   **6–044**

Date

This contains the date on which the transfer takes effect (this is unlikely to be the date on   **6–045**
which the vendor signed it; the date is inserted when the sale is actually completed). As
between the parties to it, it takes effect from the date when it is signed and delivered.[104]
But no legal estate passes until the transfer is registered, though when it is, it takes effect
"as of" the date when the application for registration was lodged at the Land Registry.[105]

Transferor; transferee for entry on the register; transferee's intended address for service in the U.K. for entry on the register

These are self-explanatory. Where there are more than four joint vendors or joint pur-   **6–046**
chasers only four of their names will appear here; they will hold the Property on a trust of
land for themselves and the others. The address usually given is that of the property itself
although for various reasons (such as where the property is not intended to be occupied by
the purchaser) it may be prudent to give a home or business address or the address of the
transferee's solicitors. The address on the register is important because this is the address
to which the Land Registry will send notices, such as notice of an application to make an
adverse entry on the title.

The transferor transfers the property to the transferee

These are the Operative Words which give the Transfer its effect; they do not of course   **6–047**
pass the legal title but merely give the Transferee the right to be registered as proprietor
in place of the Transferor. The Transferee obtains whatever title the Transferor had in the
land described in the Register.

Consideration

The appropriate box must be ticked. If a payment has been made, this constitutes the   **6–048**
Transferor's receipt for the sum in question (it will be for the complete purchase price
rather than for the sum paid on completion; any deposit paid will have been deducted from
the complete purchase price and further credits and debits will have been made in respect
of the apportionment of outgoings). So far as the Transferee is concerned, a disposition

---

[104] *Spectrum Investment Co v Holmes* [1981] 1 W.L.R. 221.
[105] Above.

made without valuable consideration is subject not only to entries on the register and interests which override registration but also to all interests which require protection, even if not protected.[106]

The transferor transfers with

6–049   If covenants for title are being given, the appropriate box must be ticked and any modifications to the covenants implied by the Law of Property (Miscellaneous Provisions) Act 1994 written below.

Declaration of trust

6–050   Where there is more than one purchaser, they will, where there are four or less of them, hold the legal title as joint tenants on a trust of land for themselves as either joint tenants or tenants in common in equity. The first or second box is ticked accordingly. The third box is utilised where there are more than four joint purchasers (in which case, it will be stated that the four transferees whose names appear on the Transfer are holding for all the joint purchasers in the appropriate way) or where the trustees are not or are not all beneficiaries of the trust in question (in which case, the name if any of the settlement in question will be inserted).

Additional provisions

6–051   This will contain the details of any rights or obligations which are being created or reserved. Examples are where the vendor is reserving some right, such as a right of way, over the property or where the purchaser is entering into any covenants, whether restrictive or otherwise, with the vendor.

The Transferors and all other necessary parties should execute this transfer as a deed using the space below

6–052   Section 52 of the Law of Property Act 1925 requires conveyances of a legal estate to be by deed in most cases. The execution of the form as set out in prescribed transfer document will satisfy this requirement. All the parties who need to sign the Transfer will do so here in the manner appropriate to their juridical nature (companies execute deeds in a different manner from natural persons). No Transferees will need to sign unless a trust is being declared in (10) above or some obligation is being entered into with the Transferor in (11) above.

UNREGISTERED TITLE

6–053   Since 1990 it has been compulsory to register unregistered land on a conveyance. Consequently the procedure set out below will be increasingly rare.

---

[106] LRA ss.28(1), 29(1).

From contract to completion

Delivery of abstract or epitome of title

Within the time mentioned in the contract, V must deliver to P the abstract of title or **6–054**
epitome of title. Abstracts of title are now rare. These documents provide a consecu-
tive story of the derivation of the title, consisting in part of a condensed version of the
various documents and in part of a recital of the relevant events, such as the births,
deaths and marriages which affect the title. An abstract starts with a good root of title[107]
and traces the devolution of the property down to V. Thus a very simple abstract might
consist of:

    (i)   a summary of a conveyance by A to B;
    (ii) a recital of B's death;
    (iii) a recital of probate of B's will being granted to X and Y;
    (iv) a summary of the assent by X and Y in favour of V.

However, once photocopiers became commonly available, it became customary instead to
provide an epitome of the title, stating briefly the essential facts in the derivation of title,
and supporting this by photocopies of the documents mentioned in the epitome. Today
most epitomes of title consist of nothing more than a list in chronological order of the
documents which have been photocopied.

Consideration of abstract

P then examines the abstract or epitome of title and considers the validity of the title **6–055**
shown. If an epitome of title supported by photocopies of the title deeds has been sent, he
will be able to verify V's title at that stage. Where an abstract of title is used, this will not be
possible until the title deeds are produced at completion.

Requisitions on title

P's examination of the abstract or epitome usually discloses a number of points upon **6–056**
which he requires further information. This further explanation is obtained by means of
"requisitions on title", a series of written questions which P delivers to V. Requisitions
usually consist of a mixture of genuine objections or requests for information (example as
to the date of some death, or as to the existence of some incumbrance which the abstract
does not disclose), and statements of the obvious, such as that V, having agreed to sell
free from incumbrances, must discharge a mortgage or obtain the concurrence of the
mortgagee to the sale of the property free from the mortgage. Requisitions also usually
seek confirmation of the answers to the inquiries on draft contract sent before conclusion
of the contract.[108]

---

[107] Above, para.1–025.
[108] See para.6–025.

Replies to requisitions

6–057   V then answers the requisitions within the agreed time. If his answers are unsatisfactory on any point, P may make further requisitions.

Draft conveyance

6–058   P will prepare the draft conveyance. As, since 1990, the conveyance will trigger the first registration of the land, a registered land transfer is commonly used (see above), save that it will need some amendment to remove the reference to title number and provide a sufficient description of the property. P sends this draft to V for his approval who can make amendments and so on until the conveyance is agreed. P then engrosses the conveyance (i.e. prepares a fair copy of it) and sends it to V for execution.

Searches

6–059   A few days before the date fixed for completion, P carries out a Land Charges Department Search. Such a search gives a 15 business day priority period to the purchaser.[109] The operation of the Land Charges Act 1972 is considered separately later. P also must carry out a local land charges search; again the operation of the Local Land Charges Act 1975 is considered separately later.

Completion

6–060   Completion takes place in a similar manner to a conveyance of registered land.[110] It involves V delivering to P the engrossment of the conveyance duly executed by V; only if P is entering into some obligation towards V, as by binding himself to observe restrictive covenants, will the conveyance be executed by P as well. Unlike a registered conveyance, P is also entitled to receive the pre-existing title deeds. However, V may retain any deed which:

   (i)   relates to other land retained by him; or
   (ii) creates a trust which is still subsisting; or
   (iii) relates to the appointment or discharge of trustees of a subsisting trust.[111]

If V retains any deeds, he must give P an acknowledgment of P's rights to production of the deeds and, unless V is a mortgagee or trustee of the land, an undertaking for their safe custody.[112]

First registration

6–061   P must then make an application for first registration on form FR1 to the proper land registry office. Once the application and required documents are provided, the registrar will

---

[109] See above for the necessity and impact of the priority period paras 5–028 and 6–039.
[110] See above, para.6–040.
[111] LPA 1925 s.45(9).
[112] For the effect, see LPA 1925 s.64.

investigate title to determine what class of title can be given.[113] Once title is registered, legal title will pass to P.[114]

EFFECT OF A CONVEYANCE

Before summarising the effect of a conveyance of unregistered land on the legal and equitable interests in that land, the greater complexity of equitable interests requires them to be considered first; yet it must at all times be remembered that legal interests bind the whole world unless they can be overreached and, as between themselves, rank in the order of their creation.

6–062

Equitable interests

In determining whether or not a purchaser of land takes subject to equitable interests in it, there are three major heads to consider:

6–063

  (i)   overreaching;
  (ii) non-registration of land charges; and
  (iii) the purchaser without notice.

The broad picture is that the expansion of (i) and (ii) has reduced but not destroyed the importance of (iii).

Overreaching

The system of overreaching, whereby rights in land become corresponding rights in the purchase money, has been considered mainly in relation to settlements under the Settled Land Act 1925 and trusts of land.[115] But there are other overreaching conveyances which take effect if the purchase money is paid to trustees or others in accordance with the law.[116]

6–064

  (i)   If a mortgagee exercised his power of sale on some default by the mortgagor, this overreaches the rights of all subsequent mortgagees (even if legal) and of the mortgagor, and these become attached to the money in the hands of the mortgagee, under a trust, though subject to the mortgagee's right to repayment of his loan, interest thereon and costs.[117]
  (ii) A conveyance by personal representatives overreaches the rights of the beneficiaries under the will or intestacy.[118]

---

[113] See para.5–017.
[114] LPA s.11 (Freehold title) s.12 (Leasehold title).
[115] Above, paras 4–033 and 4–039.
[116] LPA 1925 s.2(1).
[117] LPA 1925 ss.2(1), 104, 105.
[118] This is outside the scope of this text.

(iii) A conveyance made under an order of the court, such as to remove incumbrances, overreaches all equitable interests and powers which are bound by the order.[119]

Non-registration of land charges

6–065   If a land charge is not duly registered it is void against a purchaser; the charge is overridden and destroyed, not overreached. The varying details of this are considered later.[120]

The purchaser without notice

6–066   The doctrine of purchaser without notice, though greatly reduced in its ambit, can still apply in a somewhat motley collection of cases, in all of which the equitable interests in question have been held to be capable of binding the whole world other than a bona fide purchaser for value of a legal estate without notice. The various situations can perhaps be classified as follows.

Excluded interests: Some interests have been expressly made not registrable, as apparently being otherwise protected.

(i) A mortgage protected by a deposit of documents relating to the legal estate affected is not registrable[121]; the absence of the deeds will normally put a subsequent purchaser on inquiry, and so, if the mortgage is equitable (as it will be if it is not created by deed), he cannot claim to be a purchaser without notice.

(ii) Restrictive covenants and equitable easements are not registrable if they arose before 1926, or, in the case of restrictive covenants, if they are between a lessor and a lessee,[122] when the lease will normally disclose them to a purchaser. However, where the covenant binds not the lessor's reversion in the land, but other land of his, a purchaser of that other land will usually not see the lease and so will take free of covenants in question (this result has been criticised).[123]

Omitted interests: Some interests, without being expressly excluded, have simply been omitted from the provisions for overreaching and registration.

(i) Equitable rights of entry have not been made registrable. Thus the grant of a right to enter land and remove fixtures from it is not registrable,[124] nor is a right reserved on an assignment of a lease for the assignor (who retains no interest in the land) to re-enter the land and retake it for breach of covenant.[125]

(ii) Until 1997, where A held land on trust for B absolutely (B being sui juris) there was nothing to make B's equitable interest under the bare trust either registrable or

---

[119] LPA 1925 ss.2(1), 50.
[120] See para.6–079.
[121] See paras 6–069 et seq.
[122] See para.6–070.
[123] *Dartstone Ltd v Cleveland Petroleum Co Ltd* [1969] 1 W.L.R. 1807.
[124] *Poster v Slough Estates Ltd* [1969] 1 Ch. 495.
[125] *Shiloh Spinners Ltd v Harding* [1973] A.C. 691.

overreachable.[126] However, since 1996 bare trusts are trusts of land and so can now be overreached.[127]

The fringes of overreaching and non-registration: Various equitable interests which appear to fall within the provisions for overreaching or non-registration will nevertheless been held to fall outside their operation.

(i) An overreachable interest will not be overreached if the statutory requirements are not observed,[128] as where the purchase money is not properly paid to the trustees.[129]

(ii) A registrable interest will not be void against a purchaser who merely gives value (such as marriage) where the statute requires money or money's worth to be given,[130] as for estate contracts and post-1925 restrictive covenants.[131]

(iii) An equitable easement for an uncertain period, such as so long as certain foundations stand on certain land, created by proprietary estoppel or acquiescence, has been held not to be registrable as an equitable easement on the ground that it could not have existed at law before 1926.[132]

Legal and equitable interests: a summary

In the briefest possible form, the effect of a conveyance on sale on legal and equitable interests in the land may be shown as follows.   **6–067**

The purchaser takes subject to all legal rights.

Exceptions: He takes free from:

(i) the few legal rights which are void against him for want of registration; and

(ii) the few legal rights which are overreached.

The purchaser takes subject to all equitable rights.

Exceptions: He takes free from:

(i) equitable rights which are void against him for want of registration: notice is irrelevant;

---

[126] Consider *Hodgson v Marks* [1971] Ch. 892. A must obey B's directions.

[127] TLATA 1996 s.1.

[128] Consider *Caunce v Caunce* [1969] 1 W.L.R. 286; (1969) 33 Conv. 240 (J. F. Garner); also *Williams & Glyn's Bank Ltd v Boland* [1981] A.C. 487.

[129] Consider *Kingsnorth Finance Co Ltd v Tizard* [1986] 1 W.L.R. 783.

[130] See *McCarthy & Stone Ltd v Julian S. Hodge & Co Ltd* [1971] 1 W.L.R. 1547 (no legal estate); [1976] *Current Legal Problems* 26 (D.J. Hayton).

[131] See para.6–078.

[132] *E. R. Ives Investment Ltd v High* [1967] 2 Q.B. 379. LPA 1925 ss.1(2)(a), 1(3), 4(1) (as cited at 395), seem to provide little support.

(ii) the many equitable rights which are overreached, such as under a settlement under the Settled Land Act 1925 or a trust of land: again, notice is irrelevant; and

(iii) other equitable rights, relatively few in number, in respect of which he can show either that he is a bona fide purchaser of a legal estate for value without notice, or else that he claims through such a person.

LAND CHARGES (UNREGISTERED CONVEYANCING ONLY)

Registration of land charges

6–068   The system of registration of land charges, already considered in outline,[133] must now be examined in some detail. The registers in question are maintained by the Land Charges Department of the Land Registry under the Land Charges Act 1972, replacing the Land Charges Act 1925. The two basic principles of the system of registration of land charges are that for any registrable interest:

(i) due registration of the interest constitutes actual notice of the interest registered[134]; and

(ii) non-registration makes the interest void against certain purchasers.[135]

Registrable interests

6–069   Five separate registers and an index are kept in the Land Charges Department of the Land Registry.[136] The first of these registers is much more important than the others.

Land charges

6–070   Land charges,[137] strictly so-called, are divided into six classes, A, B, C, D, E and F. The most important classes are C and D (which are subdivided) and F.[138] Most of the interests are equitable interests affecting another's land.

Class A: Class A consists of charges imposed on land by some statute, but which come into existence only when some person makes an application. Thus where a landlord who is not entitled to land for his own benefit has to pay compensation to an agricultural tenant, the landlord may apply to the Minister of Agriculture, Fisheries and Food for a charge on the land for the amount of compensation.[139] Class A charges are registrable whenever created.

Class B: Class B consists of charges which are similar to those in Class A except that they are not created on the application of any person, but are automatically imposed by statute.

---

[133] Above, para.1–026.
[134] LPA 1925 ss.198, 199.
[135] See below, paras 6–078 et seq. for the details.
[136] LCA 1972 s.1.
[137] LCA 1972 ss.2–4.
[138] LCA 1972 s.2.
[139] AHA 1986 s.86. For a full list of such charges, see LCA 1972 Sch.2.

Most charges thus imposed are registrable as local land charges, only a few are registrable as Class B land charges. An example is a charge on property recovered or preserved for a publicly funded litigant in respect of unpaid contributions.

Class C: Class C land charges are divided into four categories.

> *C(i): A puisne mortgage.* A puisne (pronounced "puny") mortgage is a legal mortgage not protected by a deposit of documents relating to the legal estate affected. This has been made registrable because, while a mortgagee who takes the title deeds puts a subsequent mortgagee or purchaser on inquiry by virtue of the fact that the mortgagor will not be able to produce them, a mortgagee who does not obtain the deeds does not do so. He thus needs to protect his mortgage and is able to do so by registering a land charge under this head.
>
> *C(ii): A limited owner's charge.* This is an equitable charge which a tenant for life or statutory owner acquires under any statute by discharging inheritance tax or other liabilities to which the statute gives special priority. Inheritance tax is payable on the death of a tenant for life of any form of settlement. If the land remains settled thereafter, the person next entitled to the land may prefer to find the money necessary to pay the inheritance tax out of his own pocket instead of leaving the burden to fall on the settled property itself, something which would normally require it to be sold. If he does pay the inheritance tax himself, he is entitled to a charge on the land in the same way as if he had lent money to the estate on mortgage.[140] Such a charge is registrable under this head.
>
> *C(iii): A general equitable charge.* This is any equitable charge which:
>   (i)   is not included in any other class of land charge;
>   (ii) is not protected by a deposit of documents relating to the legal estate affected; and
>   (iii) does not arise, or affect any interest arising, under a trust of land or settlement under the Settled Land Act 1925 (and so is overreachable).
>
> This is a residuary class which catches equitable charges not registrable elsewhere, such as the right of an unpaid vendor to a charge on the land for the unpaid purchase money (technically known as an unpaid vendor's lien).[141] It includes equitable mortgages of a legal estate and certain annuities created after 1925.[142] It does not include either equitable mortgages of an equitable interest under a settlement under the Settled Land Act 1925 or a trust of land or other charges on the proceeds of sale of land.[143]
>
> *C(iv): An estate contract.* This is a contract to convey or create a legal estate, made by a person who either owns a legal estate or is entitled at the date of the contract to have a legal estate conveyed to him. It suffices if the person who makes the contract owns any legal estate in the land, even if it is less substantial than the estate he has agreed to convey or create, as where a yearly tenant

---

[140] Inheritance Tax Act 1984 s.212(2); LCA 1972 s.2(4), as amended by Inheritance Tax Act 1984 Sch. 8 para.3. See Finance Act 1986 s.100.

[141] *Uziell-Hamilton v Keen* (1971) 22 P. & C.R. 655.

[142] See para.6-066.

[143] *Georgiades v Edward Wolfe & Co Ltd* [1965] Ch. 487 (estate agent's commission charged on proceeds of sale not a C(iii) land charge); and see *Thomas v Rose* [1968] 1 W.L.R. 1797.

agrees that if he acquires the reversion he will grant his sub-tenant a lease for 10 years.[144]

In addition to ordinary contracts, options to purchase, rights of pre-emption[145] and other like rights are expressly included by the statute. Thus an option given to a tenant to purchase the freehold reversion is registrable,[146] and so is an option to renew a lease, even though such an option runs with the land at law[147] so that there seems little point in making it registrable.[148] An obligation to offer to surrender a lease to the landlord before seeking to assign it is also included,[149] and so is a tenant's notice exercising his statutory right to purchase the freehold or take an extended lease.[150] However, rights of pre-emption do not become registrable until the vendor makes the purchaser an offer which cannot be withdrawn before the time by which it has to be accepted.[151] At least some conditional contracts seem to be registrable,[152] and it has been held that a contract with an agent to convey the land to whoever the agent directs is also included.[153] But a contract with an agent to make an estate contract is not registrable,[154] nor is a notice to treat under the process for the compulsory acquisition of land.[155] A boundary agreement is registrable only if it clearly transfers land.[156]

Class D: Class D land charges fall into three categories.

D(i): Inland Revenue charges.   Originally this class comprised charges for estate duty on death (often called "death duty"). But in 1975 estate duty was replaced by the different system of capital transfer tax,[157] and after 1984 this tax, in a revised form, was renamed "inheritance tax".[158] The tax creates a charge on land in favour of the Commissioners of Inland Revenue, though it does not apply to leaseholds or undivided shares in land under a trust of land which were owned by the deceased beneficially.[159] This type of charge is therefore chargeable only on freeholds, and must be registered in order to bind purchasers. However, in practice such charges have rarely been registered and today are normally no longer necessary. This is because the personal representatives of the deceased now have to pay whatever inheritance tax is due before they can obtain a grant of representation, so that

---

[144] *Sharp v Coates* [1949] 1 K.B. 285.
[145] See above, para.3–028.
[146] *Midland Bank Trust Co Ltd v Green* [1981] A.C. 513.
[147] *Phillips v Mobil Oil Co Ltd* [1989] 1 W.L.R. 888.
[148] See (1981) 125 S.J. 816 (M.P. Thompson).
[149] *Greene v Church Commissioners for England* [1974] Ch. 467.
[150] Leasehold Reform Act 1967 s.5.
[151] *Pritchard v Briggs* [1980] Ch. 338; *Bircham & Co Nominees (2) Ltd v Worrall* (2001) 82 P. & C.R. 34.
[152] See *Haslemere Estates Ltd v Baker* [1982] 1 W.L.R. 1109 at 1118; and see *Williams v Burlington Investments Ltd* (1977) 121 S.J. 424.
[153] *Turley v Mackay* [1944] Ch. 37, doubted in *Thomas v Rose* [1968] 1 W.L.R. 1797.
[154] *Thomas v Rose* [1968] 1 W.L.R. 1797.
[155] *Capital Investments Ltd v Wednesfield U.D.C.* [1965] Ch. 774.
[156] *Neilson v Poole* (1969) 20 P. & C.R. 909; *Joyce v Rigolli* [2004] EWCA Civ 79; *Yeates v Line* [2012] EWHC 3085, [2013] Ch. 363.
[157] Under Finance Act 1975 Pt III, Sch.4.
[158] Under Capital Transfer Act 1984, now named Inheritance Tax Act 1984: see Finance Act 1986 s.100.
[159] Inheritance Tax Act 1984 s.237; and see Sch.8 para.3.

by the time that HM Revenue &Customs discover that the deceased has died the tax will already have been paid. Consequently it is only where the personal representatives have under-declared the tax payable that there will be any need for the registration of this type of charge.

D(ii): Restrictive covenants.   Under this head, any covenant or agreement restrictive of the user of land may be registered, provided it:

  (i) was entered into after 1925; and
  (ii) is not between a lessor and a lessee.

Restrictive covenants in leases are never registrable as a land charge even where they relate not to the demised land but to adjoining land owned by the lessor[160] (this is the most natural interpretation of the legislation but may well not have been the intention of the legislature since it means that a tenant who is the holder of a restrictive covenant over adjoining land of his landlord has no effective way of protecting his rights thereunder against a subsequent purchaser).

As between landlord and tenant in respect of the land demised, the position depends on whether the lease was created before 1996 or after 1995.[161] Where the lease was created before 1996, the landlord and the tenant for the time being can always enforce restrictive covenants against one another provided that the tenant has a legal, rather than an equitable lease, and they can sometimes also do so as against the original tenant or landlord. As between landlord and equitable tenant and landlord and sub-tenant, the question, as usual, is one of notice. Where the lease was created after 1995, the landlord and the tenant for the time being can always enforce restrictive covenants against one another whether the tenant has a legal or an equitable lease, and they can occasionally also do so as against the original tenant or landlord but on fewer occasions than hitherto. The landlord can also always enforce restrictive covenants against sub-tenants.

All restrictive covenants made before 1926 (other than those in leases which are in the position set out above) also still depend upon notice and are therefore enforceable against everyone except a purchaser for value of a legal estate without notice. This rule is considerably more significant than most of those relating to the pre-1926 law since many thousands of restrictive covenants created in the second half of the nineteenth century remain in force today.

D(iii): Equitable easements. Any "easement, right or privilege over or affecting land" is registrable under this head, provided:

  (i) it is merely equitable; and
  (ii) it was created or arose after 1925.

Thus a perpetual easement created without using a deed and an easement for life, being equitable, are both registrable.[162] Similarly, a specifically enforceable contract to create an

---

[160] *Dartstone Ltd v Cleveland Petroleum Co Ltd* [1969] 1 W.L.R. 1807.
[161] i.e. whether it is an "old lease" or a "new lease" for the purposes of the Landlord and Tenant (Covenants) Act 1995; see Ch.14.
[162] See above, para.3–029.

easement is also registrable as an equitable easement,[163] or perhaps as an estate contract.[164] Equitable profit á prendre also seem to be included under this head.[165]

The apparent width of the term "right or privilege" is restricted by the context. The modern approach has been to construe this head narrowly. It has therefore been held, controversially, that this head does not include a requisition of land under Defence Regulations,[166] an interest arising under the doctrine of equitable proprietary estoppel,[167] a right to remove fixtures at the end of a lease[168] or an equitable right of entry to secure compliance with the covenants contained in an assignment of a lease.[169] The result is that a number of both formal and informal rights fall outside the system of registration of land charges and so remain within the scope of the old doctrine of notice. It is questionable whether this was the intention of the 1925 legislation.

Class E: Annuities created but not registered before 1926.[170] An annuity is a rentcharge or an annuity for life or lives, or for an estate determinable on a life or lives (such as to X for 99 years if he so long lives) not created by a marriage settlement or a will.[171] It is highly unlikely that anyone granted an annuity before 1926 can still be alive so this class must now be obsolete. It has already been seen that annuities of these types created after 1925 are registrable in Class C(iii) as general equitable charges.

Class F: A spouse's statutory right to occupy a house owned by the other spouse. In a series of cases in the 1950s,[172] a controversial[173] doctrine was evolved under which a wife who had been deserted by her husband was held to have an equitable right to remain in occupation of the matrimonial home vested in her husband. This right, which was held to be a mere equity[174] rather than an equitable interest, was enforceable against her husband and everyone else except a bona fide purchaser for value of a legal or equitable interest in the house.[175] In 1965, the House of Lords held that this "deserted wife's equity" did not exist, and that the wife had a mere personal right that would not bind a purchaser.[176] This led to the enactment of the Matrimonial Homes Act 1967 (now replaced by the Family Law Act 1996) which gave statutory rights of occupation to both husbands and wives.

The statutory "rights of occupation" conferred by the Act arise automatically, and are not dependent on desertion or anything else. The rights are given only to a spouse who has neither the legal fee simple nor a term of years in the matrimonial home, and either has no right to occupy it (whether by virtue of any estate, interest, contract or statute) or

---

[163] *E. R. Ives Investment Ltd v High* [1967] 2 Q.B. 379 at 403 (contrast at 395, 396); [1986] Conv. 31 at 34–37 (M.P. Thompson).

[164] *Huckvale v Aegean Hotels Ltd* (1989) 58 P. & C.R. 163 at 165; (1947) 11 Conv.(n.s.) 165 at 176 (E.O. Walford); and see *E. R. Ives Investment Ltd v High* [1967] 2 Q.B. 379 at 397.

[165] *E. R. Ives Investment Ltd v High* [1967] 2 Q.B. 379 at 395.

[166] *Lewisham Borough Council v Maloney* [1948] 1 K.B. 50.

[167] *E. R. Ives Investment Ltd v High* [1967] 2 Q.B. 379.

[168] *Poster v Slough Estates Ltd* [1969] 1 Ch. 495 at 506, 507.

[169] *Shiloh Spinners Ltd v Harding* [1973] A.C. 691.

[170] For annuities registered before 1926, see below, para.6–074.

[171] LCA 1972 s.17(1).

[172] *Bendall v McWhirter* [1952] 2 Q.B. 466; *Street v Denham* [1954] 1 W.L.R. 624.

[173] See (1952) 68 L.Q.R. 379 (R.E.M.).

[174] See para.3–013.

[175] *Westminster Bank Ltd v Lee* [1956] Ch. 7.

[176] *National Provincial Bank Ltd v Ainsworth* [1965] A.C. 1175.

else has only an equitable interest in it, or in the proceeds of sale.[177] The statutory rights are the right not to be excluded from the home, and the right, with the leave of the court, to enter into occupation of it.[178] The rights are a charge on the other spouse's estate or interest in the home as from the date when that spouse acquired the home, or the date of the marriage, or January 1, 1968, whichever is the latest.[179] These rights are registrable as a Class F land charge even before the court has granted any leave to enter into occupation of the home[180]; and once registered, the rights will bind purchasers, and also the trustee in bankruptcy of the owning spouse.[181] But a registration effected not for the protection of rights of occupation but for some ulterior purpose (such as to put financial pressure on the other spouse) is improper and will be set aside.[182]

The statutory rights of occupation are not absolute. They end when the marriage ends, and the court has wide powers at any time to restrict or terminate them, or to prohibit, suspend or restrict the exercise of the right of occupation by either spouse, including the owning spouse.[183] In making orders under the Act the court has a wide discretion, and must consider all the circumstances of the case, including in particular the financial resources of the spouses, the housing needs of and the effect of any order on the spouses and any relevant child.[184] The court may also take into account the position of a purchaser from the owning spouse[185] and may decline to make an order against him even if he has not taken the matrimonial home free of the Class F charge.[186]

While married couples are living together, it is unusual for any rights of occupation to be registered. Registration, when discovered, is likely to be seen as a hostile act, and it is not the practice of the Land Registry to inform the owning spouse of any registration.[187] This is liable to create difficulties for an owning spouse who sells the home without knowing that a Class F Charge has been registered; it is also possible for such a charge to be registered between contract and completion. In both cases, registration of the charge will in practice prevent the sale from being completed.[188] A prudent purchaser will therefore obtain the written concurrence of the non-owning spouse to any sale before contracting, both for this reason and in case that spouse claims some beneficial interest in the home.[189]

Companies: Most charges on land created by a company for securing money (including a charge created by deposit of title deeds[190]) require registration within 21 days in the Companies Register maintained under the Companies Act 2006.[191] For floating charges and

---

[177] Family Law Act 1996 s.30(1), (9).
[178] Family Law Act 1996 s.30(2).
[179] Family Law Act 1996 s.31(2), (3).
[180] *Watts v Waller* [1973] Q.B. 153; [1976] Current Legal Problems 26 at 31–33, 43–50 (D.J. Hayton).
[181] Insolvency Act 1986 s.336(2).
[182] *Barnett v Hassett* [1981] 1 W.L.R. 1385.
[183] Family Law Act 1996 s.33(3).
[184] Family Law Act 1996 s.33(6).
[185] Family Law Act 1996 s.34(2).
[186] *Kaur v Gill* [1988] Fam. 110, effectively codified by Family Law Act 1996 s.34(2).
[187] See *Ruoff & Roper: Registered Conveyancing*, (London: Sweet & Maxwell), para.39–11.
[188] See *Wroth v Tyler* [1974] Ch. 30.
[189] See *Williams & Glyn's Bank Ltd v Boland* [1981] A.C. 487; (1974) 38 Conv. 110 (D.J. Hayton).
[190] *Re Wallis & Simmonds (Builders) Ltd* [1974] 1 W.L.R. 391.
[191] Companies Act 2006 s.870.

charges created before 1970, this suffices, and takes effect as registration under the Land Charges Act 1972[192]; other charges require registration in both registers.[193]

Pending actions

6–071   This head comprises pending land actions and petitions in bankruptcy. A pending land action (often called a *lis pendens*) is any action or proceeding pending in court relating to land or any interest in land or charge on it.[194] This definition is not as wide as it may seem. It is confined to claims for some proprietary right in specific land.[195] This includes a claim to an easement over the land,[196] an application for an access order,[197] and an application for leave to bring proceedings for forfeiture of a lease which would terminate the lease.[198] But it does not include an action for damages for breach of a repairing covenant in a lease (even if coupled with a claim for a mandatory order to effect the repairs),[199] an action to restrain a nuisance emanating from land,[200] or a claim to restrain the sale of land[201] or to receive the proceeds of sale if it is sold.[202] Nor does it include a claim based on equitable proprietary estoppel brought merely in the hope that, if it succeeds, the court will satisfy the estoppel by granting some form of proprietary right in the land to the claimant.[203]

A claim in divorce proceedings for a property adjustment order is registrable if it specifies the particular land claimed,[204] or, if it does not, when the land is specified on the application for registration.[205] But there is no *lis pendens*, and so nothing is registrable, before the proceedings have been commenced[206]; and a registration will be vacated when the proceedings have terminated on the making of the order, even if other proceedings to set aside the order have been commenced.[207] Registration lasts for five years, and it may be renewed for successive periods of five years if the *lis* is still pending.[208]

---

[192] LCA 1972 s.3(7); see *Property Discount Corp Ltd v Lyon Group Ltd* [1981] 1 W.L.R. 300.

[193] See [1982] Conv. 43 (D. M. Hare and T. Flanagan).

[194] LCA 1972 ss.5, 17.

[195] *Calgary and Edmonton Land Co Ltd v Dobinson* [1974] Ch. 102; and see *Whittingham v Whittingham* [1979] Fam. 9.

[196] *Greenhi Builders Ltd v Allen* [1979] 1 W.L.R. 156.

[197] See below, para.15–096.

[198] *Selim Ltd v Bickenhall Engineering Ltd* [1981] 1 W.L.R. 1318 (under Leasehold Property (Repairs) Act 1938; below, para.12–017).

[199] *Regan & Blackburn Ltd v Rogers* [1985] 1 W.L.R. 870.

[200] See *Calgary and Edmonton Land Co Ltd v Dobinson* [1974] Ch. 102 at 105.

[201] *Calgary and Edmonton Land Co Ltd v Dobinson* [1974] Ch. 102.

[202] *Taylor v Taylor* [1968] 1 W.L.R. 378.

[203] *Haslemere Estates Ltd v Baker* [1982] 1 W.L.R. 1109. For proprietary estoppel, see above, Ch.9.

[204] *Whittingham v Whittingham* [1979] Fam. 9.

[205] *Perez-Adamson v Perez-Rivas* [1987] Fam. 89.

[206] *Kemmis v Kemmis* [1988] 2 F.L.R. 223 at 239.

[207] *Sowerby v Sowerby* (1982) 44 P. & C.R. 192.

[208] LCA 1972 s.8.

Writs and orders affecting land

This register[209] is confined to writs and orders enforcing judgments and orders of the court; it does not include writs commencing an action relating to land. There are three heads.   **6–072**

Writs and orders affecting land issued or made by a court for the purpose of enforcing a judgment or recognisance: This head includes access orders,[210] and also charging orders, whereby the land of a judgment debtor is charged with the payment of the money due.[211] A charging order may now be made against a beneficial interest under a trust of land.[212] Before 1997 such an interest was not "land",[213] and so a charging order against it still appeared not to be registrable[214] but since the abolition of the doctrine of conversion[215] such a charging order must now be registrable. What was formerly known as a *Mareva injunction*[216] and is now known as a freezing injunction,[217] is not registrable, for it merely prevents a litigant from disposing of his assets pending trial.[218]

An order appointing a receiver or sequestrator of land: Sometimes a receiver is appointed in cases where no charging order can be made[219]; and in a dispute between the landlord and tenants of a block of flats, a receiver may be appointed to manage the flats pending trial.[220]

A bankruptcy order: Such an order is registrable whether or not the bankrupt's estate is known to include land.[221]

Registration remains effective for five years, but may be renewed for successive periods of five years.[222]

Deeds of arrangement[223]

The Deeds of Arrangement Act 1914[224] elaborately defines deeds of arrangement. For the present purpose, a deed of arrangement may be taken as any document whereby control over a debtor's property is given for the benefit of his creditors generally, or, if he is   **6–073**

---

[209] LCA 1972 s.6.
[210] See para.15–096.
[211] Charging Orders Act 1979 s.3.
[212] Charging Orders Act 1979 ss.1, 2. See *National Westminster Bank Ltd v Stockman* [1981] 1 W.L.R. 67.
[213] See *Irani Finance Ltd v Singh* [1971] Ch. 59.
[214] *Contrast National Westminster Bank Ltd v Allen* [1971] 2 Q.B. 718 (joint judgment against both joint tenants).
[215] TLATA 1996 s.3.
[216] See *Mareva Compania Naviera S.A. v International Bulk Carriers S.A.* [1975] 2 Lloyd's Rep. 509.
[217] As a result of the Civil Procedure Rules 1998 Pt 25.1(f).
[218] *Stockler v Fourways Estates Ltd* [1984] 1 W.L.R. 25.
[219] See *Levermore v Levermore* [1979] 1 W.L.R. 1277; Senior Courts Act 1981 (SCA 1981) s.37(4).
[220] *Clayhope Properties Ltd v Evans* [1986] 1 W.L.R. 1223, but note that the Court does not have power to appoint a receiver where Pt 2 of the Landlord and Tenant Act 1987 applies (power to appoint a statutory manager).
[221] LCA 1972 s.6(1), as amended by Insolvency Act 1985 Sch.8 para.21.
[222] LCA 1972 s.8.
[223] LCA 1972 s.7.
[224] LCA 1972 s.1.

insolvent, for the benefit of three or more creditors. A common example is an assignment by a debtor of all his property to a trustee for all his creditors, made in the hope of his trading out of his actual or expected insolvency.

Registration is effective for five years and may be renewed for successive periods of five years.[225] The registration may be effected by the trustee of the deed or by any creditor assenting to or taking the benefit of the deed.[226]

Annuities[227]

6–074   This register, opened in 1855, was closed in 1925.[228] It is highly unlikely that anyone granted an annuity before 1926 can still be alive so this register must now be virtually, if not completely, obsolete.

Mode of Registration

Land charges

6–075   All land charges must be registered in the name of the estate owner whose estate is to be affected.[229] The estate owner is the owner of a legal estate.[230] Normally this does not give rise to any difficulty as the estate owner usually creates the charge. Charges created by beneficiaries of their beneficial interests under trusts are not registrable.[231] However in one common case there is a trap. If V contracts to sell land to P who then contracts to sell it to S, it is against V, the estate owner, and not P, that S must register his estate contract; registration against P will not be effective even if P later acquires the legal estate.[232] Yet S will often be ignorant of the identity and even the existence of V. To be safe S should stipulate for the name of the estate owner to be disclosed as soon as contracts are exchanged.[233]

Other registers

6–076   Pending actions and writs and orders affecting land are registrable in the name of the estate owner or other person whose estate or interest is intended to be or is affected.[234] It will be noted that this is not limited to estate owners. Deeds of arrangement are registrable in the name of the debtor.[235]

---

[225] LCA 1972 s.8.
[226] LCA 1972 s.7.
[227] LCA 1972 s.1 Sch.1.
[228] For the registration of annuities created after 1925, see above, para.6–070.
[229] LCA 1972 s.3(1).
[230] LCA 1972 s.17(1), applying the definition in LPA 1925 s.205(1)(v).
[231] See above, para.6–070.
[232] *Barrett v Hilton Developments Ltd* [1975] Ch. 237.
[233] See *Patman v Harland* (1881) 17 Ch.D. 353 at 359.
[234] LCA 1972 ss.5(4), 6(2).
[235] LCA 1972 s.7(1).

The name

Registration should be against the estate owner's full correct name as it appears in the con-   **6–077**
veyance to him, even if he is generally known by another name, or another name appears in
his birth certificate[236] (in the event of any doubt, there is no reason why registration should
not be made in more than one name). This ensures that the name will appear in its correct
place in the index and will be revealed on a search made in the correct name. A registration in a name which may fairly be described as a version of the correct name (for example
"Frank" for "Francis") is not a nullity but will bind all except those who make an official
search in the correct name and obtain a certificate which does not disclose the entry.[237] But
registration is ineffective if it omits one of the names of the estate owner.[238] If the estate
owner is dead and his estate has not yet been administered, registration should be effected
not against his name but against the names of his personal representatives or, if there are
none and he died intestate, against the Public Trustee.[239]

Effects of registration and non-registration

Effect of registration   **6–078**

Notice: By the Law of Property Act 1925,[240] registration under the Land Charges Acts constitutes actual notice of the interest registered to all persons and for all purposes connected
with the land affected. There are statutory exceptions to this rule[241] (in particular, it does
not apply to a purchaser entering into a contract for the sale of land, where only actual
or imputed knowledge suffices.[242] However, this exception only regulates the position as
between vendor and purchaser: if the purchaser completes such a contract, he will have
notice and so will be bound). But the general effect of this provision is to prevent any person
claiming to be a purchaser without notice of a registered interest.

Names register: The most serious defect of the system from the point of view of a purchaser is that the registers are registers of the names of persons; an incumbrance is registered against the name of the estate owner at the time and not against the land. Thus
on a purchase of 14 Newcastle Street it is not possible to search against 14 Newcastle
Street, and a search must be made against the names of all previous owners of the land.

---

[236] *Standard Property Investment Plc v British Plastics Federation* (1987) 53 P. & C.R. 25.
[237] See *Oak Co-operative B.S. v Blackburn* [1968] Ch. 730, where the system of indexing is described.
    See below for searches.
[238] *Diligent Finance Co Ltd v Alleyne* (1972) 23 P. & C.R. 346.
[239] See [1979] Conv. 249 (A.M. Prichard); [1986] Conv. 237 (J.E. Adams); (1986) 83 L.S.Gaz. 2127 (E.J.
    Pryer) but note that the vesting is now in the Public Trustee following the amendment of the
    Administration of Estates Act 1925 s.9 by the Law of Property (Miscellaneous Provisions) Act 1994.
    Previously the estate vested in the President of the Family Division. A reform proposed at one stage
    was to validate registration against the name of the deceased: (1989) Law Com. No.184, para.2.7.
[240] s.198.
[241] See below, para.17–037 (mortgage deeds).
[242] LPA 1969 s.24, removing for land charges (but not local land charges) the difficulty arising from *Re
    Forsey and Hollebone's Contract* [1927] 2 Ch. 379: see *Rignall Developments Ltd v Halil* [1987] 1
    E.G.L.R. 193.

The rights most likely to concern a purchaser, namely, Classes C, D and F, only became registrable after 1925 (Class F only in 1968), but in course of time the cost of searches has become considerable. It assists if each purchaser in turn preserves the certificate of the search he made when purchasing the land, and hands the certificates on with the title deeds so that the subsequent purchasers can rely upon them; there can of course now be only one more purchaser since any purchase will trigger compulsory registration of title.

Compensation scheme: In 1956, when 30 years had elapsed since 1926, it became possible that the names of persons against whom charges were registered were contained in documents of a date earlier than the root of title (which at that time had to be at least 30 years old) which the purchaser was consequently not entitled to see. This possibility increased with each passing year and the situation was further aggravated in 1969 when the minimum length of title which had to be shown was reduced to 15 years.[243] The problem is that, despite the fact that a purchaser may be unable to discover the relevant names, he will nevertheless be deemed to have actual notice of the charges registered against those names. Since it has at all times been impossible to reorganise the registers on a territorial basis, the only long-term solution was to press on with the extension of compulsory registration of title to reduce the amount of unregistered land.[244] As an interim measure financial compensation at public expense was introduced for purchasers saddled with registered but undisclosed and undiscoverable land charges. The two main requirements are that the purchaser should not have any actual or imputed knowledge of the charge (the deemed actual notice from registration is disregarded), and that the estate owner against whom the charge is registered should not be a party to any transaction in the title which the purchaser was entitled to see or be concerned with any event in its devolution.[245]

Lessees: The doctrine that registration constitutes notice per se may work especial hardship in the case of lessees. Where a lease is granted by a tenant in fee simple at a low rent in consideration of a lump sum ("fine" or premium), the lessee usually stipulates that he shall be entitled to investigate the lessor's title, whereas if the lease is granted at a rent which reflects the occupation value of the property (a "market rent", technically known as a "rack rent"), the lessee usually takes it for granted that the lessor is able to grant the lease and so does not investigate his title. Further, by statute,[246] under an open contract[247] for the grant of a lease the lessee is not entitled to investigate the freeholder's title; this is also the case when an existing lease is assigned. This causes two problems.

(i)   In respect of leases granted before 1926, of which there are many still in existence, an assignee of a lease is fixed with notice of all that he would have discovered had he made a full investigation of the freehold title (this is on the grounds that he could have insisted on a provision in the contract entitling him to investigate this

---

[243] LPA 1969 s.23; above, para.3–016.
[244] See Report of Committee on Land Charges 1956 (Cmd. 9825).
[245] LPA 1969 s.25. For the first claim, see Chief Land Registrar's Report (1988–1989) para.56.
[246] LPA 1925 s.44, replacing Vendor and Purchaser Act 1874 s.2.
[247] See para.6–023.

title). This rule, known as the rule in *Patman v Harland*,[248] has been abolished for leases granted after 1925.[249]

(ii)   In respect of all leases granted after 1925, the prospective lessee will be able to search against the name of the lessor, but if he is not entitled to investigate the lessor's title he will not know the names of the previous owners of the land and so will not be able to discover land charges such as restrictive covenants registered against their names. Nevertheless, since registration is notice to all persons and for all purposes connected with the land,[250] the lessee is deemed to have notice of the covenants and, to make matters worse, is excluded from the compensation scheme.[251]

(iii)   An assignee of any lease, whenever granted, will as of right know only the name of the person who was owner of the land at the time when the lease was granted (because this will be on the lease) and the current owner (who will be receiving the rent). Although he will therefore be able to search against those two names, he will not know the names of anyone else who has owned the land, whether before or after the grant of the lease; and since the person assigning the lease to him is unlikely to know them either, a contractual provision entitling the assignee to investigate the lessor's title may not help either. Consequently, the assignee will be even more vulnerable to undiscoverable land charges such as restrictive covenants.

The position may be summarised thus:

(i)   Lease and restrictive covenant both made before 1926: any assignee of the lease is caught by *Patman v Harland*.

(ii)   Lease and restrictive covenant both made after 1925: both the original lessee and any assignee of the lease are caught by the provisions for the registration of land charges.

(iii)   Restrictive covenant made before 1926, lease made after 1925: here alone is the position of the original lessee and any assignees improved; they are safe unless they have obtained notice in some other way, for *Patman v Harland* does not apply and the restrictive covenant, being made before 1926, is not registrable.[252]

Effect of non-registration   6–079

Categories: The effect of non-registration varies according to the interest. There are two main categories:

(i)   the incumbrance may be void against a purchaser for value of any interest in the land; or

---

[248] The rule to the contrary in *Patman v Harland* (1881) 17 Ch.D. 353 was abolished.
[249] LPA 1925 s.44(5).
[250] LPA 1925 s.198. This prevails over s.44(5): see *White v Bijou Mansions Ltd* [1937] Ch. 610 at 619.
[251] LPA 1969 s.25(9), (10). For the scheme see above.
[252] See, e.g. *Shears v Wells* [1936] 1 All E.R. 832.

(ii) the incumbrance may be void against a purchaser for money or money's worth of a legal estate in the land.

There are two differences between (i) and (ii): a purchaser of an equitable interest is protected by (i) but not by (ii); and, since marriage is "value" but is not "money or money's worth", in the case of land settled on an ante-nuptial marriage settlement the spouses and their issue will be protected by (i) but not by (ii). In each case "purchaser" has an extended meaning and includes a lessee, mortgagee or other person taking an interest in land for value.

Effect: The effect of non-registration may be expressed as follows[253]:

(i) In general, whichever register is concerned, non-registration of any registrable matter in the appropriate register makes it void against a purchaser for value of any interest in the land.

(ii) If, however, a land charge falls within Class C(iv) (estate contracts) or Class D, and was created after 1925, non-registration makes it void only against a purchaser of a legal estate for money or money's worth.

(iii) Bankruptcy petitions (registrable as pending actions) and the title of trustees in bankruptcy under bankruptcy orders (registrable as writs and orders) are void only against a bona fide purchaser of a legal estate for money or money's worth.

(iv) Any other pending action is void against a purchaser for value of any interest in the land, provided he had no express notice of it.

"Void": The courts have given full and literal effect to the word "void"; "void" really does mean void. An unregistered interest will be void against a purchaser even if he had full knowledge of it, even if he was not acting in good faith, and even though the owner of the interest was in possession of the land concerned.[254] In the leading case,[255] a son was the tenant of a farm owned by his father. The father then granted the son an option for 10 years to purchase the farm at a fixed price. Some six years later, after the farm had nearly doubled in value and family disputes had arisen, the father conveyed the farm to his wife for £500, with the common intention of defeating the son's option, which had not been registered. It was held that the option was void against the wife. The son had a claim for breach of contract against the father,[256] a claim for conspiracy against the father and the wife[257] (provided a sufficient intent to injure was shown[258]), and a claim against his solicitor for negligence in failing to register the option[259]: but he had no claim to the farm. Had the land been registered, the actual occupation of it by the son would have conferred adequate protection[260]; but there is no corresponding provision for unregistered land. A section of

---

[253] LCA 1972 ss.4, 5(7), (8), 6(4), (5), (6), 7(2), Sch.1, para.4, as amended by Insolvency Act 1985 Sch.8, para.21, Sch.10, Pt III.

[254] LPA 1925 s.199; *Midland Bank Trust Co Ltd v Green* [1981] A.C. 513.

[255] LPA 1925 s.199; *Midland Bank Trust Co Ltd v Green* [1981] A.C. 513.

[256] *Midland Bank Trust Co Ltd v Green* [1981] A.C. 513 at 526.

[257] *Midland Bank Trust Co Ltd v Green (No.3)* [1982] Ch. 529; but see [1985] C.L.J. 280 at 293–295 (M.P. Thompson).

[258] See *Lonrho Ltd v Shell Petroleum Co Ltd* [1982] A.C. 173 at 189.

[259] *Midland Bank Trust Co Ltd v Hett, Stubbs & Kemp* [1979] Ch. 384: see *Midland Bank Trust Co Ltd v Green* [1981] A.C. 513 at 526; but contrast *Bell v Peter Browne & Co* [1990] 2 Q.B. 495.

[260] See para.5–023.

the Law of Property Act 1925[261] provides that the interest of any person in possession or in actual occupation of land is not to be prejudiced by Part I of the Act; but Part I does not contain the provisions relating to land charges.[262] In any case, the section is confined to interests to which the person is entitled "in right of such possession or occupation", and that would not include the option above. By construing "void" simply and strictly all concerned are relieved of the burden of litigious inquiries into the motives and state of mind of the purchaser; a clear and definite system for the protection of title to land is not to be destroyed by reading into the Act provisions to protect a person who has failed to protect himself by registering his land charge.[263]

Searches and priority notices

Searches

The means by which an intending purchaser of land can discover registrable incumbrances is by a search. This may be made in person,[264] which today means travelling to Plymouth and looking at the screen on which the results of the computerised search of the Land Charges Register appear. However, it is advisable to obtain an official certificate of search, since: **6–080**

(i) it is conclusive in favour of a purchaser or intending purchaser whose application correctly specifies the persons[265] and the land,[266] and so frees him from registered rights which it fails to disclose[267];

(ii) it protects a solicitor or trustee who makes it from liability for any error in the certificate[268]; and

(iii) it provides protection against incumbrances registered in the interval between search and completion. If a purchaser completes his transaction before the expiration of the fifteenth working day after the date of the certificate he is not affected by any entry made after the date of the certificate and before completion, unless it is made pursuant to a priority notice[269] entered on the register before the certificate was issued.[270]

If the official certificate of search mistakenly fails to disclose a charge properly registered before the search, the owner of the charge will be wrongly deprived of his rights and may suffer loss. Damages for negligence against those responsible may be obtained,[271] though in the absence of fraud, individual employees of the Registry are not liable for any discrepancy

---

[261] s.14.
[262] Originally it did: see LPA 1922 ss.14, 32, Sch.7. The change seems to have been an oversight.
[263] See *Midland Bank Trust Co Ltd v Green* [1981] A.C. 513 at 528, 530.
[264] LCA 1972 s.9.
[265] See *Oak Co-operative B.S. v Blackburn* [1968] Ch. 730.
[266] See *Du Sautoy v Symes* [1967] Ch. 1146.
[267] LCA 1972 s.10(4): see *Stock v Wanstead and Woodford BC* [1962] 2 Q.B. 479 (local land charge).
[268] LCA 1972 s.12.
[269] See below.
[270] LCA 1972 s.11(5), (6).
[271] See *Ministry of Housing and Local Government v Sharp* [1970] 2 Q.B. 223 (local land charge), not invalidated by *Murphy v Brentwood D.C.* [1991] 1 A.C. 398: see at 486.

between what is shown by the official search certificate as the particulars in the request for search and those actually stated in the request for a search.[272]

A single search is effective for all divisions of all five registers: but this does not include local land charges which have to be the subject of a separate search of the registers maintained by the relevant local authority.

Priority notices

6–081   Special provision has been made to provide for a rapid sequence of transactions, such as the creation of a restrictive covenant followed immediately by the creation of a mortgage before there has been time to register the covenant. Thus if V is selling land to P, who is both raising the purchase money by means of a loan on mortgage from M and entering into a restrictive covenant back in favour of V, both the relevant documents, the conveyance of the land from V to P which will also contain the grant of the restrictive covenant by P to V, and the mortgage of the land by P to M, will have to take effect simultaneously. P will need the funds being lent to him by M in order to be able to pay the purchase price to V. M will not release the funds without his mortgage and V will not convey the land without having received the purchase money. In practice, both documents will be executed in advance and will be held in escrow (to the order of the party executing them) pending receipt of the sum in question.

In such a case, V cannot register the restrictive covenant against the name of P before the mortgage to M takes effect because the restrictive covenant and the mortgage come into existence simultaneously. On the face of things, that means that the restrictive covenant, although valid as against P, will be void against M, a purchaser for money or money's worth of a legal estate. However, V can avoid this result by availing himself of the machinery of the priority notice. To do this, he must give a priority notice to the registrar at least 15 days before the creation of the restrictive covenant, and then, if he registers his land charge within 30 days of the entry of the priority notice in the register, the registration dates back to the moment of the creation of the restrictive covenant, i.e. to the execution of the conveyance from V to P; once again, days on which the registry is not open to the public are excluded.[273] The priority notice must be given 15 days before completion in order to allow the expiry of the 15 days' period of protection given to those who made official searches before the priority notice was lodged.[274]

Priority notices are not, of course, confined to restrictive covenants, but apply to all land charges.

The vacation of entries

6–082   An entry on the various registers at the Land Registry may be effected merely by making an application in the proper form[275]; registration is automatic, without the Land Registry investigating whether there is anything to justify the entry. As registration may effectively paralyse dealing with the land by the owner, provision is made for the court to order the

---

[272] LCA 1972 s.10(6).
[273] LCA 1972 s.11.
[274] Above.
[275] Land Charges Rules 1974 rr.5, 6.

vacation (i.e. removal) of any entries on the registers. There is an inherent jurisdiction to do this,[276] and also a wide statutory jurisdiction which now applies to all the registers and not only the land charges register.[277] This jurisdiction may be used to vacate entries not only of unjustified claims but also of interests that have ceased to be effective, such as contracts which have expired or have been rescinded (however, in these cases the person registering the charge will usually apply to have the entry cancelled).[278] There is also power to vacate the entry of a pending land action if the proceedings are not being prosecuted in good faith.[279] Applications under this jurisdiction can be made speedily, without any need first to issue a claim form, by the owner making an application to the court, and the jurisdiction is exercised with a certain robustness.[280] Sometimes the court will refuse to order the entry to be vacated only if the person who has made the entry is prepared to undertake to pay the landowner damages if at the trial it is established that the entry was wrongly made.[281]

Registration of local land charges

A register of local land charges is kept by each district council, each London Borough, and the Common Council of the City of London.[282] These registers are divided into 12 Parts[283] and the charges are registered against the land itself.[284] Official searches may be made.[285] It is important to note that the system of local land charges:

6–083

(a) applies to both registered and unregistered land[286];
(b) is entirely distinct from the system of registration of land charges, which applies only to unregistered land and is operated on a national basis by the Land Charges Department of the Land Registry.[287]

Another particularly significant distinction is that local land charges are registered against the land, and so do not suffer from the defect of land charges being registered against the name of the person who is the owner of the relevant estate in it at the time of registration. There is a wide range of interests that are registrable as local land charges.[288] In general, these interests are charges acquired by statute by a local authority or, in some cases, by a government department or a water authority; and they have the general nature of being public rights, rather than the private rights registrable at the Land Registry against

---

[276] *Calgary and Edmonton Land Co Ltd v Dobinson* [1974] Ch. 102.
[277] LCA 1972 s.1(6); *Northern Developments (Holdings) Ltd v U.D.T. Securities Ltd* [1976] 1 W.L.R. 1230; and see *Tucker v Hutchinson* (1987) 54 P. & C.R. 106 at 112.
[278] See Land Charges Rules 1974 rr.9–12.
[279] LCA 1972 s.5(10).
[280] *The Rawlplug Co Ltd v Kamvale Properties Ltd* (1969) 20 P. & C.R. 32 at 40; *Woolf Project Management Ltd v Woodtrek Ltd* [1988] 1 E.G.L.R. 179.
[281] See *Tucker v Hutchinson* (1987) 54 P. & C.R. 106, citing the cases (all on registered land).
[282] Local Land Charges Act 1975 s.3.
[283] Local Land Charges Rules 1977 (SI 1977/985) r.3.
[284] Local Land Charges Rules 1977 (SI 1977/985) r.6.
[285] Local Land Charges Act 1975 s.9.
[286] Local land charges are overriding interests: LRA 2002 Sch.1 para.6; Sch.3 para.6.
[287] See para.6–068.
[288] Local Land Charges Act 1975 ss.1, 2. See J.F. Garner, *Local Land Charges* 10th edn, (Kent: Shaw & Sons Ltd, 1987).

registered title (in the case of registered land) or in the Land Charges Department (in the case of unregistered land). Local land charges may for the most part be classified as being either financial or restrictive. Examples include:

(a) charges for making up a road that are imposed on the frontagers;
(b) the cost of certain drainage and sewerage works and coast protection works;
(c) prohibitions or restrictions on the use of land imposed or enforceable by a local authority or government department;
(d) closing or demolition orders for houses;
(e) conditions in a planning permission; and
(f) tree preservation orders.

But some private rights are registrable, such as light obstruction notices.[289]

Effect of no registration

6–084   Failure to register a local land charge does not make it void against a purchaser.[290] Instead, the charge remains valid, but the purchaser is normally entitled to compensation for any loss that he suffers; and similarly for omissions from an official search certificate.[291]

FURTHER READING

- Sir Terence Etherton, "Time provisions at common law and equity" [2013] Conv. 355
- (1987) Law Commission No.164 Pt V (effect of failure to comply with formalities)
- G. Owen and O. Rees, "Section 2(5) of the Law of Property (Miscellaneous Provisions) Act 1989: a misconceived approach?" [2011] Conv. 495

---

[289] Local Land Charges Act 1975 s.1, Sch.1; Local Land Charges Rules 1977 r.10, Sch.1, Forms A, B.
[290] Under the previous law it was void: Land Charges Act 1925 s.15(1) (repealed).
[291] Local Land Charges Act 1975 s.10.

Chapter 7

TRUSTS AND REAL PROPERTY

CHAPTER SUMMARY

The Trusts of Land and Appointment of Trustees Act 1996 ("the 1996 Act") radically changed the way in which land is held on trust; in particular in relation to successive and concurrent interests.

These methods of beneficial ownership were governed by two separate types of trust before 1996. The first, under a strict settlement, was governed by the principles set down in the Settled Land Act 1925. The second under a trust for sale, was governed by the Law of Property Act 1925. The 1996 Act now governs both successive interests and concurrent co-ownership of the beneficial interests in land.

Before examining the brief history of the development of the law it is necessary to understand the difference between successive interests and concurrent interests in land. When two or more persons are beneficially entitled to land (or for that matter to pure personalty) in succession, that is to say one after another, the property in question is said to be subject to a settlement. An example of a successive interest in land under a trust may be where A leaves Greenacre to B for life and then to C thereafter in fee simple. An example of concurrent co-ownership in land is where A hold Greenacre on trust for himself and B, such as in the case of a matrimonial home or the home of unmarried partners.

This chapter looks first, in summary, at the historical creation of strict settlements and trusts for sale. However, although strict settlements created before 1996 continue to exists, their impact on trusts in real property do not warrant an in-depth analysis. For more detail see Ch.7 of the eighth edition of this work.[1]

---

[1] See also the appendix to *Megarry & Wade: The Law of Real Property*, 8th edn (London: Sweet & Maxwell, 2012).

PART 1   SUCCESSIVE INTERESTS

THE ORIGIN OF THE STRICT SETTLEMENT

7–001   A strict settlement was the type of settlement employed "to keep land in the family". Provided that the various rules of law and equity were observed, the settlor might create such limitations as he thought fit; but the type of settlement most frequently encountered was the marriage settlement, giving a life interest to the husband and estates in fee tail to the children in order of seniority. Provision was also made for the wife by giving her a jointure (an annual income during widowhood), and for the younger children whose estate in fee tail never vested in possession by giving them portions (lump sums of money to assist them in their careers and in matrimony). This form of settlement was adopted because it made provision for all the members of the family and yet preserved the land as a unit. The device of giving the husband a mere life estate with remainder to his son for an estate in fee tail (the son, of course, being unborn at the time of the settlement, which was made shortly before the marriage) was adopted as being the best way of keeping the land in the family. If an estate in fee tail had been given to the husband, he could at once have converted it into an estate in fee simple by barring it; and under what eventually became known as the rule in *Whitby v Mitchell*,[2] a succession of life estates to the husband, his son, the son's son and so on was invalid after the first gift to an unborn person.

Intervention of statute

7–002   In order to deal with the fact that settlements rarely provided necessary powers to properly deal with or dispose of the land, a series of statutes were passed in the nineteenth century. Starting with Acts such as the Settled Estates Drainage Acts 1840 and 1845 which contained certain limited improvements, the legislature proceeded to enact the Settled Estates Acts 1856 and 1877, which enabled the court to authorise a number of dealings, and even enabled the tenant for life to grant certain leases without application to the court. These comparatively timid measures remained the law until the enactment of the Settled Land Act 1882, which was passed as the result of a period of agricultural depression and had as its paramount object the well-being of settled land. "The leading purpose of the Legislature was to prevent the decay of agricultural and other interests occasioned by the deterioration of lands and buildings in the possession of impecunious life-tenants."[3] The general scheme of the Act was to give the tenant for life under the settlement wide powers of dealing with the land free from the limitations of the settlement without making any application to the court, and to protect the rights of the beneficiaries in the case of a sale by shifting the settlement from the land to the purchase money, which had to be paid into court or into the hands of the trustees. A purchaser was not concerned with the rights of the beneficiaries, even if he had full knowledge of them; those rights were not destroyed, but, being overreached, were transformed from rights in the land to rights in the money paid for it. This Act formed the basis of the current legislation, the Settled Land Act

---

[2]   (1890) 44 Ch.D. 85.
[3]   *Bruce v Marquess of Ailesbury* [1892] A.C. 356 at 363 per Lord Watson.

1925. However, that legislation governs only settlements created before 1997; no further settlements thereunder can now be created.[4]

TRUSTS FOR SALE

Compared with strict settlements, settlements by way of trust for sale are of comparatively recent origin.[5] It is true that trusts for sale created by will can be traced back for some 500 years, but most of the earliest of these trusts seem to have been designed to raise sums of money, for example for the payment of debts, rather than to provide for persons by way of succession. Trusts for sale created inter vivos are more recent in origin; it was less than 200 years ago that marriage settlements by way of trust for sale appear to have become at all common. The purpose of such trusts for sale usually differed greatly from that of a strict settlement. Where the property to be settled was a family estate on which the beneficiaries would reside and over which the tenant for life would wish to exercise direct control, the settlor usually employed a strict settlement which would keep the land in the family. Where, however, the property was in the nature of an investment, such as a row of shops, there would be no desire to keep it in the family in any particular form, nor would the tenant for life wish to live on it or manage it. In such cases, a trust for sale would be employed, the primary object of such a settlement being to produce a regular income for the beneficiaries.

7–003

Retention unsold

For these reasons, in a trust for sale the legal estate was vested in the trustees upon trust to sell the land and hold the income until sale and the proceeds thereafter upon specified trusts for the beneficiaries. The trustees were usually given power to postpone sale in their discretion, and to manage the land until sale. Thus as long as the land produced a satisfactory income, it could be retained, and the trustees did not have to sell until market conditions made an advantageous sale possible. Often the consent of the beneficiaries entitled in possession was made a prerequisite of any sale. And the purchase money arising on any sale was usually directed to be invested in stocks, shares and other securities.

7–004

Doctrine of conversion

The effect of creating a trust for sale was that even before sale, the rights of the beneficiaries were deemed to be rights in personalty. Equity treated that as done which ought to be done, and since there was a binding obligation to sell the land sooner or later, the beneficiaries were treated as having forthwith interests in the purchase money into which the land was to be converted: this is known as the equitable doctrine of conversion. For this reason, trusts for sale were often referred to as "personalty settlements", in common with settlements of stocks and shares and other personal property; and the doctrine (which has in this respect now been abolished[6]) had important consequences, not least in relation to wills.[7] They were

7–005

---

[4]   TLATA 1996 s.2(1).
[5]   See generally (1927) 3 Camb. L.J. 59 (J.M. Lightwood).
[6]   TLATA 1996 s.3.
[7]   Below, para.7–016.

also sometimes called "traders' settlements", since they were more appropriate to the urban property of business men than the rural estates of the landed gentry.

PART 2   THE SETTLED LAND ACT 1925[8]

7–006   The Settled Land Act 1925 governs those settlements created before 1997 which fell within the definition of settled land contained therein. Such settlements are better described as settlements under the Settled Land Act 1925 than strict settlements because the definition in that Act was broad enough to catch a number of arrangements which were not intended to have created settlements at all, never mind strict settlements. No further settlements under the Settled Land Act 1925 have been able to be created since 1996 since settlements created thereafter which fall within the definition of settled land instead take effect as trusts of land.[9] Existing settlements continue until no land or personal chattels, usually heirlooms, settled so as to devolve with it are subject to the settlement or until those settlements cease to fall within the definition of settled land as a result, for example, of the death of a life tenant and the vesting in possession of the interests of remaindermen who are absolutely beneficially entitled.

It should be noted that, in respect of this legislation, the term "settlement" sometimes means the documents by which the land was settled, but more usually means the state of affairs resulting from them[10]; the context usually indicates which.

The basic structure of a settlement under the Settled Land Act 1925 is that the legal estate in the settled land is virtually always[11] vested in the person interested in possession under the settlement for the time being; this person is described in the Act as "the tenant for life", whether or not his beneficial interest is actually a life interest. Only in two exceptional circumstances discussed below is the legal estate vested not in the tenant for life but in a person or persons described as "the statutory owner", usually but not always, the trustees of the settlement. Consequently, on the creation of the settlement, the legal estate in the settled land had to be conveyed to the tenant for life or to the statutory owner, unless, of course, it was already vested in the tenant for life,[12] as would be the case where the owner of property settled it upon himself as tenant for life, with remainders over. ("With remainders over" is a concise way of referring to the remainders following the life interest without setting them out in detail.) The legal estate did not have to be so vested before 1926 but, in the case of pre-1926 strict settlements, the legal estate in the settled land was automatically vested in the tenant for life or statutory owner at the first moment of 1926.[13]

The tenant for life has wide and unfettered powers of sale, exchange, leasing, mortgaging

---

[8]   See the eighth edition of this work for a detailed analysis of the operation of the Settled Land Act 1925.

[9]   TLATA 1996 s.2(1).

[10]   See *Re Spencer's S.E.* [1903] 1 Ch. 75 at 79; *Re Ogle's S.E.* [1927] 1 Ch. 229 at 233.

[11]   For the two exceptions, see below.

[12]   SLA 1925 s.4.

[13]   LPA 1925 Sch.1 Pt II para.6.

and otherwise dealing with the settled land. Those beneficially entitled under the settlement other than the tenant for life are protected by the fact that:

(1) the tenant for life is a trustee for those beneficiaries;

(2) in the case of the most important powers, the tenant for life must give notice to the trustees of his intention to exercise them;

(3) in a few exceptional cases the tenant for life must not exercise his powers without the leave of the trustees or an order of the court; and

(4) the other party to any transaction entered into with the tenant for life which gives rise to the payment of capital moneys will only obtain a title free from the interests of the other beneficiaries if he pays those moneys to the trustees of the settlement and so enables their beneficial interests to be overreached.

PART 3   TRUSTS FOR SALE AFTER 1925

WHAT IS A TRUST FOR SALE?

It has been seen[14] that after 1925 land could not be settled land if it was subject to an "immediate binding trust for sale". Between 1925 and 1977, whenever land was limited in trust for persons by way of succession or for some other reason fell within the definition of settled land, it was governed by the Settled Land Act 1925 (and still is if the settlement is still continuing) unless it could be shown that it was subject to a trust for sale of this nature. The meaning of the phrase was thus of great importance. Because many settlements created before 1997 are still in existence today, it is still necessary to establish whether they were subject to the Settled Land Act 1925, in which case they still will be. Consequently, this phrase must be examined closely.

7–007

There had to be a "trust" for sale

There had to be a true trust to sell and not a mere power of sale. Thus a conveyance to trustees on trust for persons in succession, giving the trustees a power of sale, made the land settled land; the conveyance operated as an imperfect settlement and the trustees could not and cannot sell.[15] However, a trust "to retain or sell the land"[16] in a disposition or settlement coming into operation after 1925 is construed as a trust for sale with power to postpone sale.[17]

7–008

---

[14] See the eighth edition of this work, p.253.
[15] See the eighth edition of this work, pp.260, 278.
[16] See the eighth edition of this work, p.250.
[17] LPA 1925 s.25 (now repealed by TLATA 1996 Sch.4).

The trust for sale had to be "immediate"

7–009   A trust to sell at some future date, such as when X attained the age of 25, did not prevent land from being settled land.[18] But if there was a trust for sale which was immediately operative, this took the land out of the Settled Land Act 1925, even if the trustees had power to postpone the sale and even if a sale could not be made without the request or consent of some person.[19]

The trust for sale had to be "binding"

7–010   The interpretation of the word "binding" gave rise to considerable difficulty, especially in cases where the land was first subject to the Settled Land Act 1925 and then to a trust for sale, as where it was limited to A for life with remainder to trustees for sale. Three views were put forward:

(i)   That it meant a trust for sale capable of binding, in the sense of overreaching, as many interests as possible. Thus if an equitable interest created under the earlier settlement could not be overreached by the trustees for sale then the trust for sale was not "binding".[20]

(ii) That the word "binding" was inserted to emphasise that a revocable trust for sale was excluded, or else that the word was mere surplusage.[21]

(iii) That a "binding" trust for sale was one which was capable of binding the whole legal estate which had been settled.[22] If the legal estate was vested in the trustees for sale as such, the trust for sale was "binding", even if equitable interests such as charges under a former settlement were still outstanding. But where such equitable charges were outstanding when the tenant for life died, this would normally prevent the trustees for sale from requiring the special personal representatives to vest the legal estate in them[23] and as a result the trust for sale would not be "binding".[24]

It seems safe to say that the first alternative is now generally recognised as being wrong,[25] and that although the second view is innocuous, the third is probably correct. The issue is largely technical: on any view there is clearly a power of sale and the sole question, which can of course still arise today, is as to who is able to exercise it.

How a trust for sale comes into being

7–011   Since 1996 the only way in which a trust for sale has been able to arise has been expressly, by land being deliberately limited on trust for sale. Before 1997, trusts for sale also arose

---

[18] *Re Hanson* [1928] Ch. 96; and see *Bevan v Johnson* [1990] 2 E.G.L.R. 33.
[19] LPA 1925 s.205(1)(xxix).
[20] *Re Leigh's S.E. (No.1)* [1926] Ch. 852. See above for ad hoc trusts for sale with wider overreaching powers.
[21] *Re Parker's S.E.* [1928] Ch. 247 at 261.
[22] See *Re Beaumont S.E.* [1937] 2 All E.R. 353; *Re Sharpe's Deed of Release* [1939] Ch. 51.
[23] SLA 1925 s.7(5).
[24] *Re Norton* [1929] 1 Ch. 84; and see *Re Parker's S.E.* [1928] Ch. 247.
[25] *Re Norton* [1929] 1 Ch. 84; and see *Re Parker's S.E.* [1928] Ch. 247.

by operation of statute in five situations. Since 1996 these situations have instead given rise to trusts of land and in four of the five situations statutory trusts for sale which were in existence on January 1, 1997 were converted into trusts of land.

Express trusts for sale

With a view to keeping the trusts off the title, the general practice for many years has been to employ two documents to create an express trust for sale, namely, a conveyance on trust for sale and a trust instrument; it was this practice which suggested the vesting deed and trust instrument of the Settled Land Act 1925. Although today two documents are almost invariably employed to create a trust for sale inter vivos, there is nothing in the 1925 legislation to make this essential. In the case of testamentary trusts for sale, the usual position before 1926 was that the will was the sole document concerned. After 1925, a written assent is required to vest the legal estate in the trustees for sale, so that now there will usually be two documents in such cases. But even if a trust for sale is created by a single document, it is now provided that a purchaser of the legal estate from the trustees for sale is not concerned with the trusts affecting the rents and profits of the land until sale and the proceeds of sale thereafter, whether or not the trusts are declared by the same instrument as that by which the trust for sale is created.[26]

7–012

Statutory trusts for sale before 1997

Until January 1, 1997 a trust for sale was imposed by statute in a number of cases. For example:

7–013

    (i) if two or more persons were entitled to land as joint tenants or tenants in common, a trust for sale was normally imposed by the Law of Property Act 1925[27];

    (ii) the Administration of Estates Act 1925 imposed a trust for sale on the property of a person dying intestate;

    (iii) if trustees lent money on mortgage and the property became vested in them free from the right of repayment (such as by foreclosure), they held it upon trust for sale[28] (this preserved the character of the trust property; the money was pure personalty, and under the doctrine of conversion, the rights of the beneficiaries under a trust for sale were treated as being interests in pure personalty, even if the subject-matter of the trust was land);

    (iv) land held for special purposes, such as schools or highways, was held on trust for sale for (usually) the grantor when the special purpose came to an end[29]; and

    (v) if the trustees of a personalty settlement invested trust funds in the purchase of land, they held it on trust for sale unless the settlement otherwise provided.[30]

---

[26] LPA 1925 s.27 (now amended by TLATA 1996 Sch.3 para.4(8)).
[27] Below, Ch.8.
[28] LPA 1925 s.31 (now amended by TLATA 1996 Sch.2 para1).
[29] Reverter of Sites Act 1987 s.1.
[30] Reverter of Sites Act 1987 s.32; see *Re Hanson* [1928] Ch. 96.

Statutory trusts for sale after 1996

7-014   Statutory trusts for sale which existed on January 1, 1997 were converted into trusts of land on that date[31] with the sole exception of statutory trusts for sale which had already arisen as a result of the trustees of a personalty settlement investing trust funds in the purchase of land.[32] Consequently, the only situation in which a statutory trust for sale can still be in existence is where land was purchased by the trustees of a personalty settlement prior to January 1, 1997; in such circumstances, unless the settlement otherwise provided, they held that land on statutory trust for sale from the outset and still do so.

Position of trustees for sale

7-015   Since 1996, a trust for sale of land has been a trust of land and the position of trustees for sale of land is therefore generally the same as that of all other trustees of land discussed below. However, in one respect the position of trustees for sale of land is not the same as that of other trustees of land. The very essence of a trust for sale is that a duty to sell is imposed on the trustees. Admittedly the Law of Property Act 1925 implied a power to postpone sale in every trust for sale of land, even one created before 1926,[33] in the absence of an express provision to the contrary and the 1996 Act also implies such a power to postpone, in this case even if there is an express provision to the contrary.[34] Consequently, trustees for sale can now never be liable in any way if they postpone sale indefinitely in the exercise of their discretion.[35]

Superficially this appears no different from the position under other trusts of land, where the trustees have all the powers of an absolute owner of land[36] and, consequently, a power of sale. However, there is in fact a difference. The exercise of powers requires unanimity whereas a duty can be imposed by a minority of the trustees on an unwilling majority.[37] Consequently, if any one of the trustees of an express trust for sale of land wishes to sell, the land has to be sold; unanimity is required for the exercise of their power to postpone. On the other hand, all the trustees of a trust of land which is not a trust for sale must agree before selling that land; they are under no duty to sell and unanimity is required for the exercise of their power to sell.

The authorities prior to 1997 established that a minority of the trustees could not force a sale where this sale would have defeated the spirit or object of the trust or amounted to a breach of contract,[38] an aspect which had become increasingly important in cases of beneficial co-ownership.[39] However, all these authorities concerned trusts for sale which were implied by statute to give effect to beneficial co-ownership; beneficial co-ownership now

---

[31] TLATA 1996 Sch.2, paras 1(7), 3(6), 4(4), 5(5), 6(6), 7.
[32] TLATA 1996 Sch.2 para.2(2).
[33] LPA 1925 s.25 (now repealed).
[34] TLATA 1996 s.4(1).
[35] TLATA 1996 s.4(1).
[36] TLATA 1996 s.6(1).
[37] *Re Mayo* [1943] Ch. 302. Contrast joint tenants for life of settlements under SLA 1925.
[38] See *Re Buchanan-Wollaston's Conveyance* [1939] Ch. 738; *Re Hyde's Conveyance* (1952) 102 L.J. News. 58; *Jones v Challenger* [1961] 1 Q.B. 176.
[39] Below, para.8–045.

gives rise to an implied statutory trust of land which is not a trust for sale. There has never been a reported case where the courts have taken into account these factors and denied a sale to a minority of the trustees of an express trust for sale. It is true that the court can now in principle order a postponement against the wishes of a minority, or for that matter of the majority, of the trustees on the application of any trustee or other person who has an interest in the property.[40] The 1996 Act lays down a list of matters which are relevant to the determining of the application.[41] However, it is likely that, if these matters are very evenly balanced, the court will be more likely to order a sale in the case of an express trust for sale than in the case of other trusts of land simply because the settlor or testator has expressly imposed a duty of sale upon trustees.

The doctrine of conversion

Until 1997 it was settled that the rights of a beneficiary under a trust for sale were to be regarded as being rights not in the land itself but in the proceeds of sale on the basis of the equitable maxim that equity looks on that as done which ought to be done. The trustees were bound by the trust for sale to convert the land into money, sooner or later; and so, on the simple principle that it would be wrong that the precise moment when the trustees carried out their administrative duty of selling should alter the devolution of the beneficial interests,[42] the nature of those interests remain unchanged throughout.[43] This doctrine had many important effects, particularly on the devolution of property on death. (Until 1926 realty and personalty devolved in different ways on an intestacy and until 1997, if a testator died leaving all his realty to R and all his personalty to P, it was P who took the testator's interests under an ongoing trust for sale[44] although R would do so if the trust for sale had in effect ended by the testator becoming solely entitled before his death.[45])

However, during the second half of the twentieth century there was some judicial reluctance to apply the doctrine relentlessly, particularly in relation to modern statutes drafted without overt regard to its impact[46] and also where the real concern of the beneficiaries of the trust for sale was with the land itself (as where it was their home) and not merely with the proceeds of sale under a trust for sale imposed by statute.[47] This culminated in the abolition of the doctrine of conversion by the 1996 Act in relation to trusts for sale arising both before and after its commencement[48] save for testamentary trusts for sale created by the will of a testator who died before 1997.[49] But both the doctrine of conversion and the equitable maxim on which it is based remain important in other areas of property law.

7–016

---

[40] TLATA 1996 s.14(1).
[41] TLATA 1996 s.15.
[42] *Re Richerson* [1892] 1 Ch. 379 at 383.
[43] See *Fletcher v Ashburner* (1779) 1 Bro.C.C. 497; *Megarry & Wade: The Law of Real Property*, 5th edn (London: Sweet & Maxwell, 1984), pp.315–317.
[44] *Re Kempthorne* [1930] 1 Ch. 268.
[45] *Re Cook* [1948] Ch. 212.
[46] *Elias v Mitchell* [1972] Ch. 652; *Re Bradshaw* [1950] Ch. 78; *Cooper v Critchley* [1955] Ch. 431.
[47] *Barclay v Barclay* [1970] 2 Q.B. 677 at 684, 685; *Williams and Glyn's Bank Ltd v Boland* [1981] A.C. 487 at 507.
[48] TLATA 1996 s.4(1), (3).
[49] TLATA 1996 s.4(2).

PART 4   TRUSTS OF LAND

WHAT IS A TRUST OF LAND?

7–017   The expression "trust of land" was given a statutory definition by the Trusts of Land and Appointment of Trustees Act 1996.[50] It embraces all trusts of property which consists of or includes land[51] other than (i) settlements under the Settled Land Act 1925 which were in existence prior to January 1, 1997 and are still in existence and (ii) land to which the Universities and College Estates Act 1925 applies.[52] It therefore includes express trusts for sale, bare trusts and the statutory trusts of land imposed in a number of situations which until January 1, 1997 gave rise to statutory trusts for sale, namely:

    (i)   if two or more persons are entitled to land as joint tenants or tenants in common, a trust of land is normally imposed by the Law of Property Act 1925,[53] as amended by the 1996 Act[54];

    (ii) the Administration of Estates Act 1925,[55] as amended by the 1996 Act,[56] imposes a trust of land on the land of a person dying intestate;

    (iii) if trustees lend money on mortgage and the property becomes vested in them free from the right of repayment (such as by foreclosure), they hold it on a trust of land[57];

    (iv) land held for special purposes, such as schools or highways, is held on a trust of land for (usually) the grantor when the special purpose comes to an end[58]; and

    (v) if the trustees of a personalty settlement invest trust funds in the purchase of land after December 31, 1996, they held it on a trust of land unless the settlement otherwise provides.[59]

The 1996 Act defines "beneficiaries" more restrictively than the general law by excluding from that category persons who are merely annuitants.[60] This must be borne in mind when considering both the powers of the trustees and the rights of the beneficiaries.

Powers of trustees of land

7–018   Trustees of land are given, subject to contrary stipulation in the trust instrument,[61] all the powers of an absolute owner[62] and it is specifically provided that they can purchase

---

[50] See [1997] Conv. 401 (A.J. Oakley); [1997] Conv. 411 (N. Hopkins); 61 M.L.R. (1998) 56 (A. Clements).
[51] TLATA 1996 s.1(1).
[52] TLATA 1996 s.1(3).
[53] LPA 1925 ss.34-36; below, Ch.8.
[54] TLATA 1996 Sch.2 paras 3, 4.
[55] AEA 1925 s.33(1).
[56] TLATA 1996 Sch.2 para.5.
[57] LPA 1925 s.31, as amended by TLATA 1996 Sch.2 para.1.
[58] Reverter of Sites Act 1987 s.1, as amended by TLATA 1996 Sch.2 para.6.
[59] LPA 1925 s.32, as amended by TLATA 1996 Sch.2 para.2; see *Re Hanson* [1928] Ch. 96.
[60] TLATA 1996 s.22(3).
[61] TLATA 1996 s.8(1).
[62] TLATA 1996 s.6(1).

land[63] by way of investment, for occupation by any beneficiary, or for any other reason.[64] They must, however, have regard to the rights of the beneficiaries,[65] although a purchaser need not be concerned to see that they have complied with this requirement.[66] They can also compel absolutely entitled beneficiaries to take a conveyance of the legal title.[67] The power which trustees for sale had before 1997 to partition land[68] now applies to all trusts of land,[69] again subject to contrary stipulation in the trust instrument.[70] This enables them to divide any land to which beneficiaries of full age are absolutely entitled in undivided shares[71] between those beneficiaries.[72] However, this requires either the consent of each of these beneficiaries,[73] although a purchaser need not be concerned to see that they have consented,[74] or, apparently, an order of the court.[75]

Curtailment of powers

It has already been seen that the trust instrument can reduce the powers of trustees from those of an absolute owner and take away the power to partition.[76] The trust instrument can also make the exercise of any of the powers of an absolute owner and the power to partition subject to the requirement that the consent of specified persons, usually but not necessarily beneficiaries, should first be obtained[77] (consent of the relevant beneficiaries is a prerequisite of partition anyway unless, apparently, it is ordered by the court). Any consent required from a minor must be obtained from one of his parents or his guardian[78] but any consent required from a mental patient can only be obtained from his receiver.[79]

7–019

If the consent of more than two persons is required, a bona fide purchaser for value is protected if the consent of any two such persons is obtained[80] and he need not concern himself with the consent of any minor[81] (but he will need the consent of the receiver of any mental patient unless two other persons have consented). But this protection is given only to such a purchaser: the trustees will be guilty of a breach of trust if they do not obtain the full number of consents stipulated from the appropriate persons. However, the court has power[82] to dispense with consents which cannot be obtained due to the absence of a

[63] TLATA 1996 s.6(3).
[64] TLATA 1996 s.6(4).
[65] TLATA 1996 s.6(5).
[66] TLATA 1996 s.16(1).
[67] TLATA 1996 s.6(2).
[68] Under LPA 1925 s.28 (which has been repealed).
[69] TLATA 1996 s.7.
[70] TLATA 1996 s.8(1).
[71] See below, paras 8–009 et seq.
[72] TLATA 1996 s.7(1).
[73] TLATA 1996 s.7(3).
[74] TLATA 1996 s.16(1).
[75] Under s.14; see *Rodway v Landy* [2001] Ch. 703, where partition was denied.
[76] TLATA 1996 s.8(1).
[77] TLATA 1996 s.8(2).
[78] TLATA 1996 s.10(3)(b).
[79] Under Mental Health Act 1983 s.99.
[80] TLATA 1996 s.10(1).
[81] TLATA 1996 s.10(3)(a).
[82] Under s.14(2)(a).

person or the lack of a receiver[83] or where consent is unreasonably refused.[84] Under the previous legislation it was not required that the need for a consent be explicitly stated. This was able to be inferred, where, for example, the trust instrument gave a beneficiary a right to the land itself at a future date.[85] However, the 1996 Act only envisages needs for consent to be required by the trust instrument so it may no longer be possible for their need to be inferred in this way.

Delegation

7–020   The trustees have a power, which cannot be taken away by the trust instrument, to delegate revocably or irrevocably by power of attorney to one or more of the beneficiaries of full age entitled to an interest in possession in land (other than persons who are merely annuitants[86]) any of their functions as trustees which relate to that land.[87] They must delegate jointly, although any one trustee can revoke a revocable delegation,[88] and if a delegate ceases to be beneficially entitled to an interest in possession a revocable delegation to him is revoked automatically.[89] It is presumed in favour of anyone dealing with a person to whom functions have so been delegated that that he qualified to be a delegate in the absence of knowledge to the contrary and that absence of knowledge is also conclusively presumed in favour of any purchaser whose interest depends on the validity of the delegation if he makes a statutory declaration to that effect not later than three months after the completion of the purchase.[90] Delegates are in the same position and have the same duties and rights as the trustees in respect of the functions delegated to them (although they cannot sub-delegate or give a good receipt for capital sums)[91] and the trustees are only liable for the acts of delegates if they did not exercise reasonable care in deciding to delegate the function in question to the delegate in question.[92]

Consultation

7–021   Subject to contrary stipulation in the trust instrument,[93] the trustees are under an obligation, when exercising any of their functions relating to land subject to the trust (other than their right to compel absolutely entitled beneficiaries to take a conveyance of the legal title[94]), so far as is practicable to consult the beneficiaries of full age entitled to interests in possession in the land (other than persons who are merely annuitants[95]). The trustees must, so far as is consistent with the general interests of the trust, give effect to the wishes

---

[83]   Mental Health Act 1983 s.96(1)(k).
[84]   *Re Beale's S.T.* [1932] 2 Ch. 15.
[85]   *Re Herklots' W.T.* [1964] 1 W.L.R. 583, considered in *Dodsworth v Dodsworth* [1973] E.G.D. 233.
[86]   TLATA 1996 s.22(3).
[87]   TLATA 1996 s.9(1).
[88]   TLATA 1996 s.9(3).
[89]   TLATA 1996 s.9(4).
[90]   TLATA 1996 s.9(2).
[91]   TLATA 1996 s.9(7).
[92]   TLATA 1996 s.9(8).
[93]   TLATA 1996 s.11(2)(a).
[94]   TLATA 1996 s.11(2)(c).
[95]   TLATA 1996 s.22(3).

of those beneficiaries or, in the event that they are not all in agreement, to the wishes of the majority by value.[96]

Before 1997 this obligation to consult was confined to trusts for sale which were implied by statute, in which case it could not be ousted by contrary stipulation, or which manifested an intention that the obligation was to apply.[97] This remains the position for trusts of land created by wills made before 1997.[98] It also remains the position for trusts of land which were created as trusts for sale before 1997 or which were created after 1996 by reference to trusts for sale created before 1997 unless the settlor (or the survivor(s) of joint settlors) executes a deed stating that the obligation is to apply[99] (once executed, such a deed is irrevocable[100]).

Even when the obligation to consult arises, the trustees are not actually obliged to follow the wishes of the beneficiaries, nor need a purchaser be concerned to see that the trustees have complied with the obligation.[101]

Occupation of the trust property

A beneficiary who is beneficially entitled to an interest in possession under a trust of land (other than a person who is merely an annuitant[102]) is entitled by reason of his interest to occupy the land at any time when the purposes of the trust include making the land available for his occupation or the land is held by the trustees so as to be so available.[103] This right does not extend to land which is either unavailable or unsuitable for occupation by any particular beneficiary.[104]

7–022

At common law, where two or more persons are entitled to occupy land, the basic rule is that each of them is entitled to physical possession of every part of the land and to the use and enjoyment of it "in proper manner".[105] From this rule is derived the further rule that such co-owners are not obliged to pay rent to one another simply because only one of them happens to be in occupation.[106] Hitherto it has only been in quite exceptional circumstances that the courts have refused to allow a co-owner to exercise his right to occupation and use.[107] However, where two or more beneficiaries of a trust of land are entitled to occupy land under the 1996 Act, the trustees may exclude or restrict the entitlement of any one or more of them but not of all of them.[108] It has been held that this provision entitles the trustees to permit or the court to order[109] occupation of different parts of the land by different beneficiaries where such distinct occupation is feasible.[110] This is done by restricting each

---

[96]   TLATA 1996 s.11(1).
[97]   LPA 1925 s.26 as amended by L.P.(Am.)A. 1926, Sch.
[98]   TLATA 1996 s.11(2)(b).
[99]   TLATA 1996 s.11(3).
[100] TLATA 1996 s.11(4).
[101] TLATA 1996 s.16(1); this was also the case prior to 1997 (LPA 1925 s.26 as amended by LP(Am)A 1926, Sch.)
[102] TLATA 1996 s.22(3).
[103] TLATA 1996 s.12(1).
[104] TLATA 1996 s.12(2).
[105] *Bull v Bull* [1955] 1 Q.B. 234 at 237.
[106] *Jones v Jones* [1977] 1 W.L.R. 438.
[107] *Chhokar v Chhokar* (1984) 5 F.L.R. 313.
[108] TLATA 1966 s.13(1).
[109] Under s.14.
[110] *Rodway v Landy* [2001] Ch. 703.

beneficiary from occupying specific parts of the land, thus enabling joint occupation of areas such as entrances, corridors, stairways and lifts and individual occupation of the remainder of the land by the different beneficiaries.[111] The trustees must not exercise the power to exclude or restrict occupation unreasonably[112] or so as to prevent any person who is in occupation from continuing to occupy the land unless he consents or the court so orders.[113]

The trustees may also from time to time impose reasonable conditions on any beneficiary in relation to his occupation of the land,[114] although not in a manner which is likely to result in the beneficiary ceasing to occupy the land unless he consents or the court so orders.[115] In particular the trustees may require the occupying beneficiary to pay outgoings and expenses,[116] to assume obligations in relation to the land or to any activity conducted thereon[117] and, where another beneficiary's entitlement to occupy has been excluded or restricted, to pay compensation to the latter either directly or by forgoing in his favour other benefits under the trust to which the occupying beneficiary would otherwise have been entitled.[118] Reasonable conditions also include requiring the beneficiaries to pay the costs of any necessary adaptation of any premises where different beneficiaries have been allowed to occupy different parts of them.[119]

In exercising these different powers, the trustees are to have regard to the intentions of the settlor or testator, the purposes for which the land is held, and the circumstances and wishes of each of the beneficiaries who is entitled to occupy the land.[120]

Dispute resolution

7–023   "Any person who is a trustee of land or has an interest in property subject to a trust of land" may apply to the court for an order relating to the exercise by the trustees of any of their functions, including an order directing them to consult or relieving them from their obligation to do so, or declaring the nature or extent of anyone's interest in the trust property.[121] This provision obviously extends to mortgagees, who have an interest in the mortgaged land; it also extends to a person who is merely an annuitant and to trustees in bankruptcy of beneficiaries and annuitants. It presumably also extends to a creditor who has a charging order against the interest of a beneficiary; under the previous legislation[122] the similar expression "person interested" was held to include such a creditor.[123] The 1996 Act specifically provides that the provision also extends to trusts of the proceeds of sale of land and the trustees of such trusts.[124]

---

[111] This was done in *Rodway v Landy* [2001] Ch.703.
[112] TLATA 1996 s.13(2).
[113] TLATA 1996 s.13(7)(a). The court did so order in *Rodway v Landy* [2001] Ch. 703.
[114] TLATA 1996 s.13(3).
[115] TLATA 1996 s.13(7)(b).
[116] TLATA 1996 s.13(5)(a).
[117] TLATA 1996 s.13(5)(b).
[118] TLATA 1996 s.13(6).
[119] *Rodway v Landy* [2001] Ch. 703.
[120] TLATA 1996 s.13(4).
[121] TLATA 1996 s.14.
[122] LPA 1925 s.30 (now repealed).
[123] *Midland Bank Plc v Pike* [1988] 2 All E.R. 434.
[124] TLATA 1996 s.17.

In determining an application by anyone other than a trustee in bankruptcy, the matters to which the court has to have regard include: first, the intentions of the settlor or testator; secondly, the purposes for which the land is held; thirdly, the welfare of any minor who occupies or might reasonably be expected to occupy any land subject to the trust as his home; and, fourthly, the interests of any secured creditor of any beneficiary[125] (other than a person who is merely an annuitant[126]). Where the application concerns the occupation of any trust property, the court must additionally have regard to the circumstances and wishes of each of the beneficiaries who is entitled to occupy the land.[127] In any other case other than one concerning the occupation of any trust property or one relating to the trustees' right to compel absolutely entitled beneficiaries to take a conveyance of the legal title,[128] the court must instead additionally have regard to the circumstances and wishes of the beneficiaries of full age entitled to interests in possession in the land[129] (other than persons who are merely annuitants[130]).

However, where the application is made by a trustee in bankruptcy, the court must instead make such order as it thinks just and reasonable having regard to the following matters: first, the interests of the bankrupt's creditors; secondly, where the application concerns a dwelling-house which is or has been the home of the bankrupt, his spouse or his former spouse, the conduct of the spouse or former spouse in so far as it contributed to the bankruptcy, the needs and financial resources of the spouse or former spouse, and the needs of any children; and, thirdly, all the circumstances of the case other than the needs of the bankrupt.[131] On any application made more than a year after the appointment of the trustee in bankruptcy, the court must assume, unless the circumstances of the case are exceptional, that the interests of the bankrupt's creditors outweigh all other considerations.[132]

It has been held that the matters to which the court is to have regard are not exclusive but inclusive and that other matters may also be of relevance.[133]

All the reported decisions to date concerning proceedings of this type have been disputes between or involving co-owners. It therefore seems more appropriate to deal with these decisions in the chapter on co-ownership.[134] It should, however, be emphasised at this stage that it has been held[135] that in disputes between husband and wife where there are no third party interests the only relevant legislation is the Matrimonial Causes Act 1973,[136] not the 1996 Act.

---

[125] TLATA 1996 s.15(1).
[126] TLATA 1996 s.22(3).
[127] TLATA 1996 s.15(2).
[128] This interpretation of was confirmed in *The Mortgage Corp v Shaire* [2000] 1 F.L.R. 973 at 991.
[129] TLATA 1996 s.15(3).
[130] TLATA 1996 s.22(3).
[131] Insolvency Act 1986 (IA 1986) s.335A(2).
[132] IA 1986 s.335A(3).
[133] *Bank of Ireland Home Mortgages Ltd v Bell* [2001] 2 F.L.R. 809 at 815, [24].
[134] Below, para.7–022.
[135] In *Tee v Tee* [1999] 2 F.L.R. 613.
[136] ss.22–25.

PART 5   TRUSTS AND TRUSTEES

7–024   Much of the law of trusts and trustees is more appropriate to textbooks on equity and trusts than to a book on real property. But some account must be given here of the general points that most concern the law of land, in addition to the special provisions for settled land and land held on trust for sale.

CLASSIFICATION OF TRUSTS

Conveyancing classification

7–025   From the point of view of a conveyancer, a trust whose subject-matter is land falls under one of two heads:

   (i)   trusts of land, which now include express trusts for sale and bare trusts; or
   (ii) settlements under the Settled Land Act 1925.

All these types of trusts have already been dealt with.

Equity's classification

7–026   In equity, trusts have been classified in a number of ways. A traditional classification which has a statutory basis[137] is to distinguish between express, resulting, implied and constructive trusts, however the distinctions between the latter three types of trust has blurred over the years with a tendency towards considering both resulting and implied trusts as not only synonymous but in fact a form of constructive trust. There are also trusts imposed by statute:

Trusts imposed by statute

7–027   Various trusts are imposed by statute. Thus:

   (i)   a statutory trust of land is imposed in the case of joint tenancies and tenancies in common (prior to 1997 what was imposed was a statutory trust for sale)[138];
   (ii) where a person dies intestate, in certain cases his personal representatives hold his property on a statutory trust of land for his surviving spouse and relatives (prior to 1997 what was imposed was a statutory trust for sale);
   (iii) from 1926 to 1996 an attempt to convey a legal estate to a minor operated as a contract for value to make a proper settlement under the Settled Land Act 1925 and in the meantime to hold the land in trust for the minor or minors[139];

---

[137] LPA 1925 s.53(2); LP(MP)A 1989 s.2(4).
[138] Below, Ch.8.
[139] SLA 1925 s.27(1) (a statutory exception to the equitable rule that an imperfect voluntary conveyance will not be treated as a declaration of trust).

(iv) since 1996, an attempt to convey a legal estate to a minor operates as a declaration of trust in favour of the minor[140]; and

(v) a statutory trust of land is created when property on the security of which trustees have lent money becomes vested in them by foreclosure, or where trustees of a personalty settlement exercise a power conferred thereby to invest money in the purchase of land.[141]

Both (i) and (ii) are referred to in the 1925 legislation as "the statutory trusts". Although other trusts imposed by statute are in a sense "statutory" trusts, they are usually not thus referred to, and to avoid confusion they are perhaps better called "trusts imposed by statute".

Express trusts

Express trusts are those expressly created by the settlor. Trusts created by a settlor must be formally valid, must satisfy the "three certainties", must have a human beneficiary capable of enforcing them, and must be completely constituted.   **7–028**

Formal validity: The formalities required for the creation of a trust and for the transfer of an interest under a trust are considered below.[142]

The three certainties[143]**:** The first certainty is that there must be imperative words of trust. At one time merely precatory words, expressing only a hope or request, were sometimes held to suffice. But today precatory words are no longer enough unless the instrument as a whole shows an intention to create a trust. The word "trust" need not be used, but there must be language showing an imperative obligation. Secondly, there must be certainty of subject-matter, both as to the property to be held on trust and as to the beneficial interest to be taken by each beneficiary. Thirdly, except in the case of charitable trusts, there must be certainty of objects. It must be possible to ascertain who the beneficiaries are. A trust for "my old friends" is uncertain as to the concept of the persons who are to be regarded as the donor's "old friends".[144]

The result of the absence of any of the certainties is as follows. If there is no certainty as to the subject-matter to be held on trust, the transaction is wholly ineffective. If that certainty is present, but there is no certainty of words, the person entitled to the property holds it beneficially, free from any trust. If both these certainties are present, but there is uncertainty of objects, there is a resulting trust for the settlor. The same applies where there is uncertainty of subject-matter as regards the beneficial interest, unless any beneficiary can establish a claim to the whole.

The beneficiary requirement[145]**:** Except in the case of charitable trusts and some further anomalous exceptions which will be applied but not extended, it is necessary that there is

---

[140] TLATA, Sch.1, paras 1 and 2.
[141] Below, para.17–025.
[142] Below, paras 7–032 and 7–033.
[143] See *Snell's Equity* (London: Sweet & Maxwell) para.22-012.
[144] See *Brown v Gould* [1972] Ch. 53 at 57.
[145] See *Snell's Equity* (London: Sweet & Maxwell) para.22–021.

some human beneficiary capable of enforcing the trust. The absence of any such beneficiary renders the trust ineffective and there is a resulting trust for the settlor.

Completely and incompletely constituted trusts: A trust is completely constituted as soon as the trust property is vested in the trustee upon the trusts; until then it is incompletely constituted. The importance of the distinction is that a completely constituted trust may be enforced by any of the beneficiaries, even if they have provided no consideration for the creation of the trust and are therefore what equity describes as volunteers. On the other hand, if the trust is incompletely constituted it cannot be enforced by volunteers but only by beneficiaries who have given valuable consideration, although volunteers may nevertheless be able to enforce a contract or covenant with the settlor to which they are parties or third parties[146] and thereby obtain financial compensation. A trust may be completely constituted either by the trust property being effectually vested in the trustees upon the requisite trusts, or else by a "present irrevocable declaration of trust" being made by the settlor. In the latter case the settlor need not expressly declare that he holds the property on trust, but he must do something equivalent to this. An ineffective transfer to trustees will not be construed as being a declaration of trust except where the settlor has done all in his power to vest the property in the trustees,[147] and so there is no equity to perfect an imperfect transfer.[148]

Implied and resulting trusts[149]

7–029   An implied or resulting trust is said to exist where, on a conveyance of property, a trust arises by operation of equity and is founded on a legal presumption about the intentions of the settlor. The term "resulting" describes the effect of the beneficial interest in the property in the trust reverting back to the person who transferred it. In the context of real property this may occur where A has contributed to the purchase price of Greenacre but he is not registered as the legal owner, and in the absence of that contribution being a gift or loan, A will be the beneficial owner in direct proportion to his contribution.

Three cases must be considered.

Trusts not exhaustive: Where a disposition of property is made by the owner and all or part of the equitable interest is not effectively disposed of, there is a resulting trust for the owner. If the property is conveyed expressly on trust, for example "to X on trust", there is no difficulty; a trustee can take no benefit from the fact that the declared trusts do not exhaust the beneficial interest, and so much of the equitable interest as is not disposed of results to the grantor. Thus if G conveys property to X on trust for a beneficiary who is dead, there is a resulting trust of the entire beneficial interest in favour of G. Similarly if G conveys property to X on trust for Y for life without specifying any gifts in remainder, there is a resulting trust of the beneficial interest in favour of G subject to Y's life interest. What a person fails effectually to dispose of remains automatically vested in him.[150]

---

[146] See Contracts (Rights of Third Parties) Act 1999.

[147] *Re Rose* [1952] Ch. 499.

[148] *Richards v Delbridge* (1874) L.R. 18 Eq. 11 (attempted gift of lease by indorsement). For a statutory exception see above.

[149] Implied and resulting trusts have previously been considered as forming two separate categories of trusts. However, they are now generally considered as synonymous.

[150] See *Re Vandervell's Trusts (No.2)* [1974] Ch. 269 at 288, 289, 294 (not affected on appeal).

Voluntary conveyance: Before 1926, on a conveyance by G to X made without any consideration and without expressing any use, there was a resulting use to G in fee simple which the Statute of Uses 1535 promptly executed, thereby making the conveyance totally ineffective. The Law of Property Act 1925[151] provides that, in a voluntary conveyance executed after 1925, no resulting trust for the grantor is to be implied merely by reason that the property is not expressed to be conveyed for the use or benefit of the grantee. Because of the presence in this provision of a double negative, its effect has been disputed. However, it has now been held that, as stated in previous editions of this work, its effect is to prevent any corresponding resulting trust of land arising after 1925.[152] However, this does not prevent a resulting trust for the grantor from arising where it appears that the grantee was intended to take as a trustee, as where the property is conveyed on express trusts which fails to exhaust the entire beneficial interest; and in other cases there will be presumed to be a resulting trust, though the presumption is easily rebutted.[153]

Purchase in the name of another: Where a conveyance is made to one person, but the purchase money is provided by another as purchaser, there is a resulting trust in favour of the person providing the purchase money. If V conveys land to P, A being the real purchaser and as such providing the purchase money, prima facie P holds on a resulting trust for A.[154] Nevertheless, this is only a presumption which can be rebutted by evidence that P was intended to benefit.[155] It may also be displaced by the presumption of advancement. That presumption arises if P is the wife, child or ward of A. It is itself rebuttable, and it does not apply to other relationships, as where A is the wife, child, mother, stepmother or aunt of P. It should be noted that the presumption of advancement will be abolished prospectively by s.199 of the Equality Act 2010 once it has been brought into force.

Constructive trusts

Constructive trusts are trusts which arise by operation of equity, usually but not always as a consequence of a breach of some pre-existing fiduciary relationship. The best known type of constructive trust arises where a trustee or other fiduciary makes a profit as a result of his fiduciary position. He will hold the profit on constructive trust for the person to whom he owes his fiduciary duty. If a person receives property knowing that it is subject to a trust and that the transfer to him was in breach of trust, he will hold it subject to the trusts as a constructive trustee. If instead he receives the property innocently but later, after getting knowledge of the trusts, he deals with it inconsistently with the trusts, he will similarly be a constructive trustee. Further, a person who dishonestly acts as an accessory to a trustee who commits a breach of trust is often said to be liable as a constructive trustee even if he receives none of the trust property; however, a trust cannot exist without any trust property so such a person is better described as being liable to account as a trustee.

    Although the principal categories of constructive trusts are those set out above, they

7–030

---

[151] s.60(3), (4).
[152] *Lohia v Lohia* [2001] W.T.L.R. 101.
[153] See *Re Vandervell's Trusts (No.2)* [1974] Ch. 269.
[154] See *Dyer v Dyer* (1788) 2 Cox Eq. 92 at 93.
[155] *Fowkes v Pascoe* (1875) 10 Ch.App. 343.

have expanded into other fields, including cases of fraud and, more recently, estoppel. Today there is a tendency for the courts to hold that a constructive trust exists in a variety of other cases where equity and good conscience require it. Indeed, some jurisdictions now treat constructive trusts as being a general remedy in cases of inequitable conduct[156] but English law has yet to adopt this approach and is unlikely to do so.

FORMALITIES FOR THE CREATION OF A TRUST

Pure Personalty

7–031   An enforceable trust of pure personalty can be validly created by word of mouth, whether the owner is declaring himself a trustee of the property or is transferring it to a third party on trust for the beneficiaries.[157]

Land

Evidenced by writing

7–032   Before 1677, a trust of land could be created by word of mouth, but since then the Statute of Frauds 1677[158] and more recently the Law of Property Act 1925[159] have provided that a declaration of trust respecting any land or any interest therein must be evidenced either by writing signed by some person able to declare the trust, or else by his will. The chief points to note on this provision are as follows:

   (i)   "Any land". This includes leaseholds (and included copyholds before they were abolished).
   (ii) "Evidenced". The actual words in both statutes are "manifested and proved". It is settled that this does not require that the declaration should actually be made in writing, but that it suffices if an oral declaration is supported by some signed acknowledgement or declaration in existence when the action is begun, such as a letter,[160] or a recital in a deed, even if this was made some time after the trust was declared.[161] The writing must show not only that there is a trust but also what its terms are.[162]
   (iii) "Some person able to declare the trust". This means the owner of the beneficial interest, so that if a trust is declared of an equitable interest held under an existing trust, the writing must be signed by the beneficiary; the signature of the trustees is not sufficient.[163] There is no provision for signature by an agent.[164]

---

[156] See *Re Sharpe* [1980] 1 W.L.R. 219 at 225.
[157] See *M'Fadden v Jenkyns* (1842) 1 Ph. 153.
[158] ss.7, 8.
[159] s.53(1)(b).
[160] *Childers v Childers* (1857) 1 De G. and J. 482.
[161] *Rochefoucauld v Boustead* [1897] 1 Ch. 196 at 206.
[162] *Smith v Matthews* (1861) 3 De G.F. and J. 139; and see above, para.6–003.
[163] *Kronheim v Johnson* (1877) 7 Ch.D. 60.
[164] Contrast transfers, below.

Failure to comply with these requirements renders the trust unenforceable rather than void. Consequently, the beneficiary can bring seek to enforce the trust and it is only if the absence of writing is pleaded that he will be unable to do so.[165]

Exceptions

To these requirements, there are two important exceptions:

7–033

Resulting, implied or constructive trusts: The statutory requirements do not affect the creation of resulting, implied or constructive trusts[166] (operation is restrictively interpreted; a disposition of an interest under one of these types of trust must nevertheless comply with the statutory requirements[167]). It has now been held that estoppel interests take effect behind a constructive trust.[168] Consequently, if a landowner declared orally that he was holding land on trust for another and that other acted to his detriment on the strength of that assurance, it appears that he would be able to enforce that trust against the landowner on the basis that the latter was estopped from denying the trust and was therefore a constructive trustee of the land for him.

Fraud: The court will not permit the statutory requirements to be used as an engine of fraud. "It is a fraud on the part of a person to whom land is conveyed as a trustee, and who knows it was so conveyed, to deny the trust and claim the land himself. Consequently, notwithstanding the statute, it is competent for a person claiming land conveyed to another to prove by parol evidence that it was so conveyed upon trust for the claimant, and that the grantee, knowing the facts, is denying the trust and relying upon the form of conveyance and the statute, in order to keep the land himself."[169] The grantee would therefore be an express trustee. It appears that the grantor could now alternatively rely on the doctrine of equitable proprietary estoppel to claim that the grantor was a constructive trustee for him.[170]

FORMALITIES FOR TRANSFERRING AN INTEREST UNDER A TRUST

By the Law of Property Act 1925,[171] a disposition[172] of an existing equitable interest or trust must either be in writing signed by the person disposing of it or his agent authorised in writing, or else be made by will. On this, the following points should be noted.

7–034

---

[165] *North v Loomes* [1919] 1 Ch. 378 (actually a decision on Statute of Frauds 1677 s.4 (subsequently LPA 1925 s.40) which also required only evidentiary writing).
[166] LPA 1925 s.53(2), replacing Statute of Frauds 1677 s.8.
[167] *Grey v I.R.C.* [1960] A.C. 1 (actually an authority on s.53(1)(c)).
[168] *Yaxley v Gotts* [2000] Ch. 162 (party to void contract for the sale of land estopped from denying its validity).
[169] *Rochefoucauld v Boustead* [1897] 1 Ch. 196 at 206 per Lindley L.J.
[170] Above.
[171] s.53(1)(c), replacing Statute of Frauds 1677 s.9.
[172] See *Grey v I.R.C.* [1960] A.C. 1 (oral direction); *Oughtred v I.R.C.* [1960] A.C. 206 (oral agreement); but see *Vandervell v I.R.C.* [1967] 2 A.C. 291 (oral directions extended to legal estate).

"In writing"

7–035   A parol assignment supported by evidence thereof in writing is not enough. Unlike the rule for the creation of trusts, the rule here requires the assignment itself to be written, and is thus not a mere rule of evidence.

Signed by the person disposing of it or his agent authorised "in writing"

7–036   This should be contrasted with:

   (i) the rule for the creation of a trust of land, where the signature of an agent is not enough[173]; and
   (ii) the rule for contracts for the disposition of land, where the signature of an agent suffices even if his authority was given only by word of mouth.[174]

Scope

7–037   The rule applies to pure personalty as well as land. Although a trust of pure personalty is enforceable even if it is not evidenced in writing, once the trust has been created, a disposition of any interest under it is void unless it is in writing. Whether a declaration of a sub-trust is a disposition is a matter of some controversy. The general view is that it is (and so requires writing) unless the sub-trustee has retained some interest under the trust or some active duties under the sub-trust.

Effect of non-compliance

7–038   Failure to comply with these requirements renders the disposition wholly void and its subject-matter remains vested in the person disposing of it.

Exceptions

7–039   To these requirements, there are the same two important exceptions:

Resulting, implied or constructive trusts: The statutory provisions do not affect the creation or operation of resulting, implied or constructive trusts[175] (as before operation is restrictively interpreted; a disposition of an interest under one of these types of trust must nevertheless comply with the requirements[176]). And if the holder of an equitable interest purported to assign it orally to someone who acted to his detriment on the strength of that purported assignment, it appears that he would be able to enforce that assignment on the basis that the assignor was estopped from denying its existence and therefore held the equitable interest on constructive sub-trust for him.[177]

---

[173] Above.
[174] Above, para.6–015.
[175] LPA 1925 s.53(2), replacing Statute of Frauds 1677 s.8.
[176] *Grey v I.R.C.* [1960] A.C. 1.
[177] By analogy with *Yaxley v Gotts* [2000] Ch. 162; above.

Fraud: The court will not permit the statutory provisions to be used as an engine of fraud. Consequently, if the owner of an equitable interest, such as the interest of a beneficial co-owner of land, purported to assign it for value and later sought to raise the statutory formalities in order to claim that he was still beneficially entitled, he would hold his beneficial interest on constructive sub-trustee for the person to whom he had purported to assign it. It appears that the assignee could now achieve the same result by relying on the doctrine of equitable proprietary estoppel.[178]

TRUSTEES

The Trustee Act 1925, as amended, makes general provision for the appointment, replacement, retirement and removal of trustees, and also for the vesting of the trust property when a change is made. These heads will be taken in turn.   **7–040**

APPOINTMENT OF TRUSTEES

Original appointment

Appointment

Trustees are usually appointed by the settlor when creating the trust. If he neither makes   **7–041** an appointment nor makes any provision for one, the court may appoint trustees; once the trust has been created, the settlor has no power of making an appointment unless he has reserved such a power. A person appointed trustee need not accept the trust even if he had agreed to do so before it was created, provided he disclaims the trust before he has accepted it either expressly or by acting as trustee.[179] A disclaimer should preferably be express but it may be inferred from conduct[180]; and although the presumption is in favour of acceptance, a person appointed a trustee who maintains a complete inactivity in relation to the trust for a long period may be held thereby to have disclaimed the trust.[181] Disclaimer retrospectively divests the person appointed both of his office and of the trust property.[182]

Maximum number

Since 1925 not more than four trustees of a settlement subject to the Settled Land Act 1925   **7–042** or, until 1997, a trust for sale or, since 1996, a trust of land have been able to be appointed. If more than four are named as trustees, the first four who are able and willing to act become trustees to the exclusion of the others.[183] These provisions apply only to land; and in general there is no limit to the number of trustees of pure personalty.

---

[178] Above.
[179] See *Noble v Meymott* (1851) 14 Beav. 471.
[180] *Re Birchall* (1889) 40 Ch.D. 436.
[181] *Re Clout and Frewer's Contract* [1924] 2 Ch. 230 (29 years' inactivity).
[182] *Re Martinez' Trusts* (1870) 22 L.T. 403.
[183] TA 1925 s.34(2).

Minimum number

7–043 There is no minimum number of trustees even in the case of land. But in the case of settlements under the Settled Land Act 1925 or trusts of land, a sole trustee cannot, notwithstanding any contrary provision, give a valid receipt for capital money unless that trustee is a trust corporation.[184] This restriction, however, does not affect the right of a sole personal representative acting as such to give valid receipts for purchase money,[185] for example where a sole administrator sells under the trust which is imposed on all the property of an intestate.

Replacement

7–044 Even if there are properly appointed trustees when the trust is created, it may later become necessary to appoint new trustees, such as owing to the death of trustees. The events upon which new trustees can be appointed may be specified in the trust instrument. This is not usual, however, and reliance is normally placed on the statutory provisions, which apply notwithstanding any such express provision[186] unless a contrary intention is shown.[187] By the Trustee Act 1925[188] a new trustee or trustees may be appointed if a trustee "is dead; or remains outside the United Kingdom for a continuous period exceeding 12 months; or desires to be discharged from all or any of his trusts or powers; or refuses to act; or is unfit to act; or is incapable of acting; or is a minor; or is removed under a power in the trust instrument".

Method of appointment

7–045 The appointment must be in writing and must be made[189]:

   (i) by the person or persons nominated by the trust instrument for the purpose of appointing new trustees; in default of there being any such person able and willing to act;

  (ii) by the remaining trustees; in default of any;

 (iii) by the personal representatives of the last remaining trustee; in default of any; and

 (iv) by the court.

Since 1996, if there is no person nominated by the trust instrument for the purpose of appointing new trustees and the beneficiaries under the trust are of full age and capacity and are between them absolutely entitled to the property subject to the trust,[190] they

---

[184] SLA 1925 s.18(1); LPA 1925 s.27(2); see above, paras 4–029 et seq.
[185] LPA 1925 s.27(2).
[186] See *Re Wheeler and De Rochow* [1896] 1 Ch. 315.
[187] TA 1925 s.69(2).
[188] s.36(1), replacing earlier provisions.
[189] TA 1925 ss.36(1), 41, replacing earlier provisions.
[190] TLATA 1996 s.19(1).

may give a direction to any trustee to retire[191] and/or give a direction to the trustees or to the personal representatives of the last trustee to appoint the persons specified in the direction.[192] Where a trustee is directed to retire, once reasonable arrangements have been made for the protection of any rights of his in connection with the trust, he must by deed retire provided that there will thereafter be either a trust corporation or two persons to act as trustees and either another person is to be appointed or the continuing trustees by deed give their consent.[193] Similar provisions apply where it is necessary to replace a trustee who is incapable of exercising his functions as such by reason of mental disorder and there is no one able and willing to appoint a replacement.[194]

Who may be appointed

It is expressly provided that the person making the appointment may appoint himself.[195] **7–046** Even if he appoints a person whom the court would not normally appoint, such as a beneficiary, or the husband of a beneficiary, or the solicitor to the trustees or beneficiaries, the appointment will not thereby be rendered invalid[196]; but an appointment of a minor as trustee, whether of realty or personalty, is void.[197] Where a single trustee was originally appointed, the appointment of a single trustee in his place is valid,[198] except that in the case of settlements under the Settled Land Act and of trusts of land, a sole trustee (not being a trust corporation) cannot be appointed under the statutory power if, after his appointment, he would be unable to give receipts for capital money,[199] as would be the case if there were no other trustee. There is never any obligation to appoint more than two trustees even if originally more than two were appointed.[200] The appointment may increase the number of trustees, provided that in the case of settlements under the Settled Land Act and of trusts of land, the number is not increased above four.[201]

Additional trustees

Even though no occasion has arisen for the appointment of new trustees, if there are not **7–047** more than three trustees and none of them is a trust corporation, one or more additional trustees may be appointed, provided the effect of the appointment is not to increase the number above four. The appointment must be made by the same persons and in the same way as an appointment of new trustees, except that there is no provision for an appointment by the personal representatives of the last remaining trustee, or for the appointor to appoint himself.[202]

---

[191] TLATA 1996 s.19(2)(a)
[192] TLATA 1996 s.19(2)(b).
[193] TLATA 1996 s.19(3).
[194] TLATA 1996 s.20.
[195] TA 1925 s.36(1).
[196] *Re Earl of Stamford* [1896] 1 Ch. 288.
[197] LPA 1925 s.20.
[198] TA 1925 s.37(1)(c), replacing earlier provisions.
[199] TA 1925 s.37(2).
[200] TA 1925 s.37(1)(c), replacing earlier provisions.
[201] TA 1925 s.34(2).
[202] TA 1925 s.36(6); *Re Power's S.T.* [1951] Ch. 1074.

RETIREMENT AND REMOVAL OF TRUSTEES

Retirement

7–048   A trustee may retire:

   (i) If another trustee is appointed in his place; this has already been considered.[203]

   (ii) If no new trustee is being appointed in his place, provided that after his discharge there will be left to act in the trust either a trust corporation or two or more persons (until 1997 it had to be two or more individuals). The retirement is effected by a deed declaring the trustee's desire to retire; this is executed by the retiring trustee, the continuing trustees and the person entitled to appoint new trustees, all of whom must concur in the retirement.[204]

   (iii) If authorised to do so by an express power in the trust instrument.

   (iv) With the consent of all the beneficiaries if they are all of full age and capacity and are between them absolutely entitled to the property subject to the trust (in these circumstances they can now of course direct him to retire if there is no person nominated by the trust instrument for the purpose of appointing new trustees[205]).

   (v) With the leave of the court; this method should be employed only in cases of difficulty, for if the trustee applies to the court without good cause he may have to pay his own costs.[206]

Removal

7–049   A trustee may be removed:

   (i) Under the power to appoint new trustees considered above.[207]

   (ii) Under any express power to do so contained in the trust instrument.

   (iii) Since 1996, the beneficiaries may remove any trustee if there is no person nominated by the trust instrument for the purpose of appointing new trustees and they are of full age and capacity and are between them absolutely entitled to the property subject to the trust.[208]

   (iv) Under the court's inherent jurisdiction to remove a trustee where it is necessary for the safety of the trust property or the welfare of the beneficiaries,[209] as where the trustee has been inactive for a long while, or his interests conflict with those of the beneficiaries, or there has been friction with the beneficiaries on the mode of administering the trust.[210]

---

[203] Above, para.7–044.
[204] TA 1925 s.39(1), replacing earlier provisions.
[205] TLATA 1996 s.19.
[206] *Porter v Watts* (1852) 21 L.J.Ch. 211.
[207] Above, para.7–044.
[208] TLATA 1996 s.19.
[209] *Re Wrightson* [1908] 1 Ch. 789 at 803.
[210] *Letterstedt v Broers* (1884) 9 App.Cas. 371.

VESTING OF TRUST PROPERTY

Some trustees have no property vested in them, as is often the case with trustees of set-   **7–050**
tlements subject to the Settled Land Act 1925; in such cases, no question of the devolution
of trust property arises. But where property is vested in trustees, questions of the transfer
of the trust property arise on their death, retirement or removal, or on the appointment of
new trustees.

On death

Where there is a plurality of trustees, they are always made joint tenants or joint owners   **7–051**
of the trust property, whether it is real or personal. The advantage of this is that on the
death of one trustee the estate or interest vested in him passes to the surviving trustees by
the doctrine of survivorship.[211] If a sole surviving trustee dies the estate or interest held on
trust vests in his personal representatives notwithstanding any provision in his will.[212] Until
new trustees are appointed, the personal representatives may exercise any power or trust
exercisable by the former trustee, without being obliged to do so[213]; and they may appoint
new trustees.[214]

On appointment of new trustees

Vesting declaration

On an appointment of new trustees, the trust property has to be vested in the new trustees   **7–052**
jointly with any continuing trustees. Formerly, a formal conveyance of the trust property
by the persons in whom it was vested was necessary; if A and B were trustees and C was
appointed a new trustee on A's death, B had to convey the trust property to himself and C
jointly.[215] But by s.40 of the Trustee Act 1925,[216] if an appointment of new trustees is made
by deed, a declaration therein by the appointor that the property shall vest in the trustees
(a "vesting declaration") is sufficient to vest the property in them. This applies to all deeds
executed after 1881[217]; and if the deed is executed after 1925, a vesting declaration is
implied in the absence of an express provision to the contrary.[218]

These provisions apply even if the trust property is not vested in the appointor. He has a
statutory power to transfer what he has not got. Thus where A and B are the trustees and X
has the power to appoint new trustees, if A dies and X appoints C a trustee in his place, the
deed of appointment will vest the property in B and C jointly.

---

[211] See below, para.8–002.
[212] AEA 1925 s.1.
[213] TA 1925 s.18(2).
[214] TA 1925 s.36(1).
[215] See *Megarry & Wade: The Law of Real Property* 4th edn (London: Sweet & Maxwell, 1975), p.458.
[216] Replacing earlier provisions.
[217] TA 1925 s.40(6).
[218] TA 1925 s.40(1).

Exceptions

7–053   In certain cases the trust property cannot be transferred by a vesting declaration, either express or implied. These cases are when the property consists of:

(i)   land which the trustees hold by way of mortgage for securing trust money;

(ii)   land held under a lease with a provision against assigning or disposing of the land without consent, unless the requisite consent has first been obtained, or the vesting declaration would not be a breach of covenant or give rise to a forfeiture;

(iii)   any share, stock or other property which is transferable only in books kept by a company or other body, or in a way directed by statute[219]; or

(iv)   registered land.

In these excepted cases the trust property must be transferred by the method appropriate to the subject-matter, such as in the case of shares and registered land, by a duly registered transfer.[220] The reason for the inclusion of (1) is to avoid bringing the trusts on to the title, for otherwise, when the borrower sought to repay the loan, he would have to investigate the trust documents to see that he was paying the right persons; and (2) is included to avoid accidental breaches of the terms of the lease.

Vesting orders

7–054   The court has a wide jurisdiction to make vesting orders where this is desirable.[221]

On retirement or removal

7–055   Where a trustee retires or is discharged from a trust without a new trustee being appointed, and the transaction is effected by deed, the trust property can be divested from the former trustee and vested solely in the continuing trustees by means of a vesting declaration. This applies only if the deed is executed by the retiring trustee, the continuing trustees and any person with power to appoint new trustees; if the deed is executed after 1925, a vesting declaration is implied.[222] There are the same exceptions as in the case of vesting declarations on the appointment of new trustees. This special provision is necessary since survivorship operates only on death and not on retirement.

PROCEDURE FOR SETTLEMENTS

One document

7–056   Although it is undesirable, a trust of land may be created by only one instrument. In this case, when a new trustee is appointed, the appointment may be made by a single

---

[219] TA 1925 s.40(4), replacing earlier provisions.
[220] See *Ruoff & Roper: Registered Conveyancing* (London: Sweet & Maxwell), para.37–011.
[221] TA 1925 ss.44–56.
[222] TA 1925 s.40(2), replacing earlier provisions.

document. This may be merely in writing. In the case of unregistered land it should be by deed so that the legal estate may be vested in the new and continuing trustees by virtue of s.40 of the Trustee Act 1925,[223] thus avoiding the necessity of a separate conveyance; in addition, a memorandum must be indorsed on or annexed to the instrument creating the trust of land, stating the names of those who are the trustees after the appointment is made,[224] and not merely the names of the new trustees. In the case of registered land, whether the appointment is made in writing or by deed, it will be necessary for the registered land to be transferred by the existing trustees into the names of the continuing and the new trustees (or, if there are no surviving trustees, by the personal representative of the last surviving trustee into the names of the new trustees or, in the last resort, by an order of the court).

Two documents

Normally, however, a trust of land is created by two documents. In this case, and in the case of land settled under the Settled Land Act 1925, the procedure is more complicated. There must be[225]:   **7–057**

- (i) An appointment to go with the trust instrument. This may be either in writing or by deed.[226]
- (ii) In the case of unregistered land:
  - (a) a deed to go with the conveyance creating the trust of land or the vesting instrument, which purchasers can see; and
  - (b) an indorsement on the conveyance creating the trust of land or on the vesting instrument, stating the names of those who are the trustees after the appointment.

SUMMARY OF KEY CASES

- *Rochefoucauld v Boustead* [1897] 1 Ch. 196 at 206
- *Re Mayo* [1943] Ch. 302
- *Re Buchanan-Wollaston's Conveyance* [1939] Ch. 738
- *Williams and Glyn's Bank v Boland* [1980] UKHL 4, [1981] A.C. 487
- *City of London BS v Flegg* [1987] UKHL 6, [1988] A.C. 54
- *Rodway v Landy* [2001] Ch. 703

---

[223] Above, para.7–052.
[224] TA 1925 s.35(3).
[225] TA 1925 s.35; SLA 1925 s.35(1); and see above, para.7–009.
[226] TA 1925 s.35; SLA 1925 s.35.

FURTHER READING

- N. Hopkins, "The Trusts of Land and Appointment of Trustees Act 1996" [1996] Conv. 411
- W. Swadling, "Explaining Resulting Trusts" (2008) 124 L.Q.R. 72
- N. Jackson, "Overreaching and Unauthorised Dispositions in Registered Land" [2007] Conv. 120

Chapter 8

CO-OWNERSHIP

CHAPTER SUMMARY

Little has so far been said about cases where two or more persons are entitled to the simultaneous enjoyment of land either by way of a joint tenancy or a tenancy in common. These are important, and must be considered in some detail.

We have already examined the fundamental characteristics of trusts in relation to real property in Ch.7. This chapter examines the use of trusts of land in co-ownership and considers the operation of the Trusts of Land and Appointment of Trustees Act 1996. There is also a detailed discussion of the development of the law relating to express, resulting and constructive trusts of land, with reference to the recent House of Lords decision in *Stack v Dowden* and the Supreme Court decision in *Jones v Kernott*, where the law of trusts and co-ownership, particularly in relation to the family home, were restated.

PART 1   JOINT TENANCY AND TENANCY IN COMMON

NATURE OF THE TENANCIES: JOINT TENANCIES

"A gift of lands to two or more persons in joint tenancy is such a gift as imparts to them, with respect to all other persons than themselves, the properties of one single owner."[1] Although as between themselves joint tenants have separate rights, as against everyone else they are in the position of a single owner.[2] The intimate nature of joint tenancy is shown by two principal features: the right of survivorship and the "four unities".

8–001

---

[1] Williams P.R. 143.
[2] Williams P.R. 145; *Hammersmith & Fulham LBC v Monk* [1992] 1 A.C. 478 at 492.

The right of survivorship

The right

8–002   The right of survivorship is the distinguishing feature of a joint tenancy. On the death of one joint tenant, his interest in the land passes to the other joint tenants by the *jus accrescendi* (right of survivorship), and this process continues until there is but one survivor, who then holds the land as sole owner, without the need for any action on his part.[3] This *jus accrescendi* takes precedence over any disposition made by a joint tenant's will, and the same principle applies if a joint tenant dies intestate; a joint tenancy cannot pass under a will or intestacy.[4] For this reason it has been said that each joint tenant holds nothing and yet holds the whole[5]: he will become entitled to nothing or to all, according to whether or not he survives his joint-tenants. Where there is doubt as to which co-owner survived the other, the matter is resolved by the Law of Property Act 1925 s.184 which establishes the commorientes ("simultaneous deaths") rule. Under this rule the younger co-owner is deemed to have survived the elder co-owner, thus providing that the younger co-owner's heirs inherit the whole of the property. However, a joint tenant may in his lifetime convert his interest into a tenancy in common which will accordingly bring an end to the right of survivorship.[6]

Corporations

8–003   The common law previously held that no joint tenancy could exist between a corporation and a natural person. This is because a corporation never died, thus effectively removing the natural person's right of survivorship. However, by way of the s.1(2), Bodies Corporate (Joint Tenancy) Act 1899, Parliament provided that a corporation could acquire and hold any property in joint tenancy in the same manner as if it were an individual.[7] The effect of survivorship in relation to corporations is that upon dissolution of that body the property passes to the other co-owner.

Trustees

8–004   Trustees are always made joint tenants because of the convenience of the trust property passing automatically by the *jus accrescendi* to the surviving trustees when one trustee dies. If trustees were made tenants in common, a conveyance of the trust property to the surviving trustees by the personal representatives of the deceased trustee would be necessary. Although the *jus accrescendi* of a joint tenancy is often unsuitable for beneficial owners because it introduces an element of chance, it is ideal for trustees.

For a joint tenancy to exist the four unities must be present

8–005   The four unities of a joint tenancy are the unities of:

---

[3]   Litt. 280.
[4]   Litt. 287.
[5]   *Murray v Hall* (1849) 7 C.B. 441 at 455n.: he holds *"per mie* [nothing] *et per tout"*.
[6]   Below, para.8–051.
[7]   Bodies Corporate (Joint Tenancy) Act 1899.

(a) possession;
(b) interest;
(c) title; and
(d) time.[8]

Unity of possession

Each joint tenant is as much entitled to possession of any part of the land as the others.[9]   **8–006**
No tenant can point to any part of the land as his own to the exclusion of the others; if he
could, there would be separate ownership and not joint tenancy. In this respect, the position is similar to that of partners; no partner can point to any particular asset of the business
as being his, for each is entitled to possession of all the assets.

Right to occupy: Unity of possession is common to both forms of co-ownership. If one co-
owner of land under a trust of land is in sole occupation of any or all of the land, the others
cannot evict him[10]; and he is not liable to pay any rent or compensation to them[11] unless
he excludes them from possession.[12] But if he lets the land, he must account to the others
if he receives more than his just share.[13] At common law, if he was not in occupation, he
appeared to have no right to insist on being let into possession, though the trustees might
in their discretion permit beneficiaries entitled in possession to occupy the land in lieu of
receiving the rents and profits.[14] However, under the Trusts of Land and Appointment of
Trustees Act 1996 ("the 1996 Act") a beneficiary who is beneficially entitled to an interest
in possession under a trust of land (other than a person who is merely an annuitant[15]) is
entitled by reason of his interest to occupy the land at any time when the purposes of the
trust include making the land available for his occupation or the land is held by the trustees
so as to be so available.[16] This right does not extend to land which is either unavailable or
unsuitable for occupation by any particular beneficiary.[17]

Right to exclude: Before 1997, it was only in exceptional circumstances that the courts
refused to allow a co-owner to exercise his right to occupation and use.[18] However, where
two or more beneficiaries of a trust of land are entitled to occupy land under the 1996 Act,
the trustees may exclude or restrict the entitlement of any one or more of them but not of
all of them.[19] It has been held that this provision entitles the trustees to permit occupation
of different parts of the land by different beneficiaries where such distinct occupation is

---

[8] See *A.G. Securities v Vaughan* [1990] 1 A.C. 417 at 474. Their initial letters form the convenient
mnemonic P.I.T.T.
[9] Litt. 288: *Bull v Bull* [1955] 1 Q.B. 234.
[10] *Bull v Bull* [1955] 1 Q.B. 234, criticised at [1955] C.L.J. 155, but accepted in *Williams & Glyn's Bank
Ltd v Boland* [1981] A.C. 487.
[11] *Jones v Jones* [1977] 1 W.L.R. 438.
[12] *Dennis v McDonald* [1982] Fam. 63.
[13] *Henderson v Eason* (1851) 17 Q.B. 701.
[14] See *Re Bagot's Settlement* [1894] 1 Ch. 177; *Re Landi* [1939] Ch. 828 at 836; (1955) 19 Conv. 146
(F.R. Crane).
[15] TLATA 1996 s.22(3).
[16] TLATA 1996 s.12(1).
[17] TLATA 1996 s.12(2).
[18] *Chhokar v Chhokar* (1984) 5 F.L.R. 313.
[19] TLATA 1966 s.13(1).

feasible.[20] The trustees must not exercise this power unreasonably[21] or so as to prevent any person who is in occupation from continuing to occupy the land unless he consents or the court so orders.[22] They may, however, from time to time impose reasonable conditions on any beneficiary in relation to his occupation of the land,[23] although not in a manner which is likely to result in the beneficiary ceasing to occupy the land unless he consents or the court so orders.[24] In exercising these different powers, the trustees are to have regard to the intentions of the settlor or testator, the purposes for which the land is held, and the circumstances and wishes of each of the beneficiaries who is entitled to occupy the land.[25]

Unity of interest

8–006A   The interest of each joint tenant is the same in extent, nature and duration, for in theory of law they hold but one estate. This means[26]:

(i)   that although in theory of law each joint tenant has the whole of the property, the rents and profits of the land are divided equally between all the joint tenants;

(ii) that there can be no joint tenancy between those with interests of a different nature, such as a freeholder and a leaseholder;

(iii) that there can be no joint tenancy between those whose interests are similar but of different duration, such as a tenant in fee simple and a tenant in fee tail; and

(iv) that any legal act, such as surrendering a lease or giving notice under a contractual power to determine it,[27] or giving a statutory notice,[28] can be done only by all the joint tenants jointly: one alone cannot effectually bind the estate, for the whole estate is not his. In the case of the type of leases known as periodic tenancies (such as leases from week to week or from year to year) this rule somewhat paradoxically means that a notice to quit may be valid even if given by only one of the joint periodic tenants[29]; this has been held to be the case even if an ouster injunction is in force against the giver of the notice.[30] This is because such leases expire at the end of each period unless all concerned, either expressly or tacitly, concur in their continuation,[31] and so a notice given by one of joint landlords[32] or one of joint leaseholders[33] shows that there is no unanimity in a continuation.

---

[20] *Rodway v Landy* [2001] Ch. 703.

[21] TLATA 1966 s.13(2).

[22] TLATA 1966 s.13(7)(a).

[23] TLATA 1966 s.13(3).

[24] TLATA 1966 s.13(7)(b).

[25] TLATA 1966 s.13(4).

[26] See Co.Litt. 188a; 2 Bl.Com. 181.

[27] *Leek and Moorlands B.S. v Clark* [1952] 2 Q.B. 788.

[28] *Newman v Keedwell* (1978) 35 P. & C.R. 393 (counter-notice under AHA 1948 s.24 below).

[29] *Hammersmith and Fulham LBC v Monk* [1992] 1 A.C. 478.

[30] *Harrow LBC v Johnstone* [1997] 1 All E.R. 929; see also *Notting Hill Housing Trust v Brackley* [2001] E.G. 106.

[31] Below, paras 8–055–11–028.

[32] *Doe d. Aslin v Summersett* (1830) 1 B. & Ad. 135; *Parson v Parsons* [1983] 1 W.L.R. 1390.

[33] *Hammersmith and Fulham LBC v Monk* [1992] 1 A.C. 478; *Harrow LBC v Johnstone* [1997] 1 All E.R. 929; *Notting Hill Housing Trust v Brackley* [2001] E.G. 106.

Unity of title

Each joint tenant must claim his title to the land under the same act or document.[34] This requirement is satisfied if all the joint tenants acquired their rights by the same conveyance or if they simultaneously took possession of land and acquired title to it by adverse possession.[35]

Unity of time

The interest of each joint tenant must vest at the same time. This does not necessarily follow from the existence of unity of title. It is difficult to find any realistic modern example of a situation where there is unity of title without unity of time. Before 1926, if land was conveyed "to A for life, remainder to the heirs of B and C as joint tenants" and B and C died at different times in A's lifetime, B's heir and C's heir took the remainder in fee simple not as joint tenants but as tenants in common; they could not take as joint tenants because, although there was unity of title, there was no unity of time.[36] Today the equivalent would be a remainder to the statutory next of kin of B and C as joint tenants but it is hardly likely that anyone would ever make a gift in such peculiar terms. The requirement for there to be unity of time has never applied to class gifts so if land is settled on trust for the children of D as joint tenants each will acquire an interest at birth; the disparity of time does not prevent them from taking as joint tenants.[37] However, in practice, class gifts are invariably made to persons as tenants in common.

NATURE OF THE TENANCIES: TENANCY IN COMMON

A tenancy in common differs greatly from a joint tenancy.

The tenants hold in undivided shares

Unlike joint tenants, tenants in common hold in undivided shares: each tenant in common has a distinct fixed share in property which has not yet been divided among the co-tenants.[38] There is no right of survivorship; the share of each tenant is fixed once and for all and is not affected by the death of one of his fellows. When a tenant in common dies, his interest passes under his will or intestacy, for his undivided share is his to dispose of as he wishes.[39]

Only the unity of possession is essential

Although the four unities of a joint tenancy may be present in a tenancy in common, the only unity which is essential is the unity of possession. In particular, it should be noted that

---

[34] Co. Litt. 189a, 299b.
[35] *Ward v Ward* (1871) 6 Ch.App. 789; below, Ch.18.
[36] Co. Litt. 188a; 2 Bl.Com. 181.
[37] *Ruck v Barwise* (1865) 2 Dr. & Sm. 510; *Doe d. Hallen v Ironmonger* (1803) 3 East 533.
[38] *Fisher v Wiggs* (1700) 12 Mod. 296 at 302.
[39] Challis R.P. 368.

the unity of interest may be absent and the tenants may hold unequal interests, so that one tenant in common may be entitled to a one-fifth share and the other to four-fifths, or one may be entitled for life and the other in fee simple.[40]

ESTATES IN WHICH THE TENANCIES CAN EXIST

8–012   In general, before 1926 joint tenancies and tenancies in common could both exist either at law or in equity (i.e. as legal estates or as equitable interests), and in possession or in remainder, in any of the estates of freehold or in leaseholds.[41] After the enactment of the Law of Property Act 1925, the position is substantially the same except that a tenancy in common can no longer exist at law; this is dealt with below.[42] Further, since only fees simple absolute in possession and terms of years absolute can exist at law, joint tenancies of all other estates must necessarily also be equitable.

Co-ownership of a life interest is not unusual. If land is given to A and B as joint tenants for their lifetimes, they enjoy it jointly for their joint lives and the survivor enjoys the whole for the rest of his life.[43] If A and B instead hold as tenants in common for their lifetimes or have converted their joint tenancy into a tenancy in common (a process which is known as severing the joint tenancy and which can have fiscal benefits), the survivor is entitled only to the appropriate proportion of the property for the rest of his life. And, if X and Y are joint tenants for the life of X (a situation which could either have been created expressly or have arisen as a result of X assigning his life interest to himself and Y), X becomes sole tenant of the whole for the rest of his life if he is the survivor, whereas Y takes nothing if he is the survivor; the estate which he acquires by survivorship is one which comes to an end at the moment he receives it.

MODE OF CREATING TENANCIES: GENERAL

8–013   The key to a proper understanding of joint tenancies and tenancies in common is always to consider the legal estate separately from the equitable interest.[44] Thus it may be found that at law A and B are joint tenants, while in equity they are tenants in common. In such a situation, the effect of A's death on the legal joint tenancy is that B becomes solely entitled. In equity, on the other hand, A's share passes under his will or intestacy. In the result, B holds the legal estate on trust for himself as to his share and for A's personal representatives as to A's share. The mode of creating joint tenancies and tenancies in common must now be considered.

---

[40] Co.Litt. 189a; Williams R.P. 148; 2 Bl.Com. 191.
[41] Williams R.P. 143.
[42] Below, para.8–017.
[43] *Moffat v Burnie* (1853) 18 Beav. 211.
[44] Despite *Re Selous* [1901] 1 Ch. 921, criticised in Williams V. & P. 501, 502.

MODE OF CREATING THE TENANCIES: AT LAW

Presumption of joint tenancy

At law, the presumption has always been in favour of a joint tenancy,[45] because before 1926 that had advantages for feudal lords, for tenants, and for conveyancers. The rule was thus that if land was conveyed to two or more persons a joint tenancy of the legal estate was created unless either one of the unities was absent or words of severance had been employed.

8–014

Absence of unities

The four unities have already been considered. If there was unity of possession but one or more of the other unities were missing, the parties took as tenants in common; if there was no unity of possession, the parties took as separate owners.

8–015

Words of severance

Any words in the grant showing that the tenants were each to take a distinct share in the property amounted to words of severance and thus created a tenancy in common. Words which have been held to have this effect include: "share and share alike"; "to be divided amongst"; "equally"; and "between". Further, words showing that the tenants were to take unequal interests (such as "two-thirds to A and one-third to B") sufficed to create a tenancy in common; and even if there were no clear words of severance, the gift taken as a whole might show that a tenancy in common was intended.[46] Thus, if under a settlement on children there was provision for making advances out of capital, any advance to a child would have to be debited against that child's share, and this could not be done unless the child was a tenant in common and so had a distinct share.[47]

8–016

A legal tenancy in common cannot exist after 1925

The absence of a unity or the presence of words of severance still leads to the creation of a tenancy in common but not at law. Since 1925, a tenancy in common has not been able to take effect at law[48]; for this reason a legal joint tenancy can no longer be severed and converted into a legal tenancy in common.[49] As explained below, a tenancy in common can still exist in equity, but at law the only form of co-ownership possible after 1925 is a joint tenancy. Thus a conveyance today "to A, B and C in fee simple as tenants in common" (all being of full age) will vest the legal estate in A, B and C as joint tenants, although in equity they will be tenants in common.[50] If A is a minor, his rights in equity will not be affected but

8–017

---

[45] *Morley v Bird* (1798) 3 Ves. 628.
[46] e.g. *Surtees v Surtees* (1871) L.R. 12 Eq. 400.
[47] See *L'Estrange v L'Estrange* [1902] 1 I.R. 467 at 468, 469; *Re Dunn* [1916] 1 Ch. 97.
[48] LPA 1925 ss.1(6), 34(1), 36(2); SLA 1925 s.36(4).
[49] Below, para.8–051.
[50] LPA 1925 s.34(2).

the legal estate will vest in B and C on trust for all three of them.[51] If A, B and C are all minors, the legal estate will now remain in the grantor who will hold it on trust for the minors or, if the purported conveyance was to them as trustees for other persons, on trust for those persons[52] (before 1996 the legal estate would equally have remained in the grantor but it was not clear whether he would have been deemed to have made an agreement for value to execute a settlement under the Settled Land Act 1925 in their favour and in the meantime to hold the land in trust for them, or whether the transaction would have been void[53]).

The legal estate is now held on a trust of land

The trusts imposed by the Law of Property Act 1925

8–018   From 1926 to 1996, subject to the special provisions relating to land subject to the Settled Land Act 1925,[54] land was held upon what were described in the Law of Property Act 1925 as the "statutory trusts" wherever there was beneficial co-ownership, in other words whenever it was conveyed to or held by two or more persons beneficially, whether as tenants in common[55] or joint tenants.[56] The "statutory trusts" could be summarised thus: upon trust to sell the land, and stand possessed of the net proceeds of sale and of the net rents and profits until sale upon such trusts and subject to such powers and provisions as may be requisite for giving effect to the rights of those interested in the land,[57] whether beneficially or as trustees.[58]

The trusts imposed by the 1996 Act

8–019   Since 1996, land is instead held on a trust of land[59] whenever it was conveyed to or held by two or more persons beneficially, whether as tenants in common[60] or joint tenants.[61] Statutory trusts for sale which were implied before 1997 now take effect as trusts of land.[62] The 1996 Act does not utilise the expression "statutory trusts" as such but that does not alter the fact that the trusts which it imposes are statutory.

Beneficial not fiduciary co-ownership

8–020   Both before 1997 and after 1996, the trusts in question are imposed by statute only where the co-ownership is beneficial and not merely fiduciary. Thus they apply where land is

---

[51] TLATA 1996 s.2(6), Sch.1 para.1(2). Although the law was less clear before 1997, this was thought also to have been the position then; see LPA 1925 s.19(2) (now repealed).
[52] TLATA 1996 s.296 Sch.1 para.1(1).
[53] See the eighth edition of this work, p.201.
[54] See the eighth edition of this work, p.326.
[55] LPA 1925 s.34(2).
[56] LPA 1925 s.36(1).
[57] LPA 1925 s.35 (now repealed).
[58] *Re Hayward* [1928] Ch. 367.
[59] TLATA 1996 Sch.2 paras 3, 4.
[60] LPA 1925 s.34(2).
[61] LPA 1925 s.36(1).
[62] TLATA 1996 s.5(1) and Sch.2 paras 3(6), 4(4).

conveyed to A and B to hold jointly, or to hold on trust for C and D jointly, but not where A and B are to hold on trust for E absolutely, for then the only co-ownership is not beneficial.

Scope of the trusts

While the trusts in question are imposed both where land is beneficially limited to and held in trust for persons as joint tenants,[63] on a literal interpretation of the legislation they are imposed only when land is "expressed" to be conveyed in undivided shares to persons of full age.[64] Theoretical difficulties therefore arose before 1997 where land was conveyed in undivided shares to persons who included a minor. However, this problem has now been resolved by the 1996 Act.[65] Such difficulties also arose before 1997 and still do today in a number of situations where the undivided shares arise extraneously; an example is where land is conveyed to A alone but he and B are beneficially entitled as tenants in common because they contributed to the purchase price in unequal shares[66] (the fact that these difficulties have survived the enactment of the 1996 Act is one of the very few respects in which that legislation may justifiably be criticised). However, without paying undue attention to these difficulties the courts have managed to carry out the evident general intention of the legislation by recourse to statutory provisions which, on their face, have nothing whatever to do with the matter.[67] As a result, it is now generally accepted that, despite the literal interpretation of the legislation, whenever there is beneficial co-ownership, however it arose, the land will be held on the trusts imposed by statute[68] unless the land is settled under the Settled Land Act 1925.[69]

8–021

The legal estate cannot be vested in more than four persons

The position here is clear in the case of tenancies in common and rather less clear in the case of joint tenancies; each type of tenancy will be dealt with separately.[70]

8–022

Tenancies in common

If land is conveyed to trustees on trust for tenants in common, the general prohibition against the number of trustees exceeding four applies.[71] If the conveyance is expressed to be made to the tenants in common themselves, and they are of full age, statute provides for it to operate as a conveyance "to the grantees, or, if there are more than four grantees, to the four first named in the conveyance, as joint tenants upon the statutory trusts."[72] Further, a gift

8–023

---

[63] LPA 1925 s.36(1).
[64] LPA 1925 s.34(2).
[65] See above, para.8–019.
[66] This occurred in *Bull v Bull* [1955] 1 Q.B. 234.
[67] LPA 1925 s.36(1), relied on in *Re Buchanan-Wollaston's Conveyance* [1939] Ch. 217 at 222 (Ch.D.), [1939] Ch. 738 at 744 (C.A.); SLA 1925 s.36(4), relied on in *Bull v Bull* [1955] 1 Q.B. 234.
[68] See *Williams & Glyn's Bank Ltd v Boland* [1981] A.C. 487; *City of London B.S. v Flegg* [1988] A.C. 54 at 77, 78.
[69] See the eighth edition of this work, p.326.
[70] Elaborate transitional provisions were enacted with the object of ensuring that the legal estate should vest in suitable persons on January 1, 1926.
[71] Trustee Act 1925 s.34.
[72] LPA 1925 s.34(2).

of land by will to, or in trust for,[73] tenants in common operates as a gift to the Settled Land Act trustees of the will, or, if, as is now virtually inevitable, there are none, to the testator's personal representatives, upon a trust of land[74]; and the number of Settled Land Act trustees or personal representatives cannot exceed four. If all the beneficiaries are of full age and absolutely entitled, they can instead require the legal estate to be vested in themselves (or not more than four of them) as joint tenants on trust for themselves as tenants in common.[75] Since 1997, in such circumstances, if there is no person appointed by the trust instrument for the purpose of appointing new trustees, they have also been entitled to require the legal estate to be vested in up to four other persons of their choice on the same trusts.[76]

Joint tenancies

8–024   There are no provisions dealing expressly with the number of persons in whom the legal estate can be vested when two or more persons are beneficially entitled as joint tenants. But the trust of land arising in such cases involves the general provision that, in a trust of land made or coming into operation after 1925, the number of trustees must not exceed four,[77] and "where more than four persons are named as such trustees, the first four named (who are able and willing to act) shall alone be the trustees".[78] In the case of a gift of land by will to joint tenants, the general prohibition against more than four trustees of land coupled with the fact that there is a trust of land prevents the personal representatives from vesting the legal estate in more than four persons. If all the beneficiaries are of full age and absolutely entitled, they can instead require the legal estate to be vested in themselves (or not more than four of them) as joint tenants, this time on trust for themselves as joint tenants.[79] Since 1997, in such circumstances, if there is no person appointed by the trust instrument for the purpose of appointing new trustees, they too have also been entitled to require the legal estate to be vested in up to four other persons of their choice on the same trusts.[80]

End of the trusts imposed by statute

8–025   The trusts imposed by statute will cease to affect the land in question if the beneficial interests are overreached into the proceeds of sale (although in these circumstances the trusts themselves will continue in respect of those proceeds of sale) and in the event that the land becomes vested legally and beneficially in one person.

Overreaching

8–026   The trusts of land created by statute in the case of beneficial co-ownership take effect in the same way as all other trusts of land in the manner already considered.[81] Further, the

---

[73] *Re House* [1929] 2 Ch. 166.
[74] LPA 1925 s.34(3).
[75] *Saunders v Vautier* (1841) Cr. & Ph. 240; LPA 1925 s.3(1)(b)(ii).
[76] TLATA 1996 s.19.
[77] TA 1925 s.34.
[78] TA 1925 s.34(2).
[79] *Saunders v Vautier* (1841) Cr. & Ph. 240; LPA 1925 s.3(1)(b)(ii).
[80] TLATA 1996 s.19.
[81] Above, paras 7–017 et seq.

overreaching provisions apply. Consequently, provided that a purchaser pays his purchase money to trustees of land (being at least two in number or a trust corporation) he will take free from the rights of the beneficiaries, irrespective of whether or not they are in occupation of the land.[82] To a purchaser who does this, it is immaterial whether in equity there are three or thirty people entitled, or whether they are joint tenants or tenants in common. However, in practice, on a conveyance of land to joint tenants or tenants in common, it is sometimes the conveyance is made on an express trust of land, in which case there is no need to have recourse to the trusts imposed by statute.[83]

Union in one person

If the whole legal estate and equitable interest becomes vested in one person, the trust imposed by statute comes to an end,[84] as where A and B are joint tenants at law and in equity and A dies. In such circumstances the Schedule to the Law of Property (Amendment) Act 1926 provides that nothing in the Law of Property Act 1925 is to affect the right of a survivor of joint tenants who is solely and beneficially interested to deal with his legal estate as if it were not held on what is now a trust of land. Thus B, as the sole legal and beneficial owner of the land, can make title by himself despite the fact that a sole trustee of land is unable to give a proper receipt for purchase money.

8-027

Potential severances: Formerly there was in these circumstances a practical difficulty in satisfying a purchaser that B was in fact solely beneficially entitled. An act of severance might have occurred in A's lifetime,[85] causing A and B to become tenants in common, so that what was then the trust for sale imposed by statute continued to exist after A's death. Because it was impossible for B to prove affirmatively that this had not happened, any purchaser was potentially at risk of being bound by any severed beneficial interest formerly held by A; such an interest would not be overreached by a conveyance from B alone and the purchaser could not claim to have taken free of it under the equitable doctrine of notice. Consequently, he would insist upon the appointment of a second trustee to receive the purchase money together with B.

Unregistered land: So far as unregistered land is concerned, this difficulty was overcome by the Law of Property (Joint Tenants) Act 1964, which is retrospective to January 1, 1926.[86] It provides that in favour of a purchaser of a legal estate, a survivor of two or more joint tenants is "deemed to be solely and beneficially interested if he conveys as beneficial owner[87] or the conveyance includes a statement that he is so interested."[88] Where the survivor has himself died, his personal representatives have similar powers. The Act does not apply if, before the conveyance by the survivor, a memorandum recording the severance is indorsed on or annexed to the conveyance which vested the land in the joint

---

[82] *City of London B.S. v Flegg* [1988] A.C. 54.

[83] Where no express trust is declared, either on the legal transfer (Land Registry Form TR1), or by other instrument, this has given rise to problems for the Court in declaring the parties interests: see *Stack v Dowden* [2007] 2 A.C. 432; *Jones v Kernott* [2011] UKSC 53.

[84] *Re Cook* [1948] Ch. 212.

[85] See below, paras 8-050 et seq.

[86] s.2.

[87] A conveyance with full title guarantee also suffices.

[88] s.1.

tenants[89]; in the absence of such a memorandum the purchaser can safely assume that no severance has occurred unless he has actual notice that there has been a severance.[90] Nor does the Act apply where a bankruptcy petition or bankruptcy order has been registered[91] against the name of the deceased joint tenant.

Registered land: The Law of Property (Joint Tenants) Act 1964 does not apply to registered land.[92] At the time when the legislation was enacted, it was assumed, wrongly as it turned out, that the interest of a beneficial co-owner under a trust for sale could not take effect as an interest which overrides registration and therefore would bind a purchaser only where it had been protected on the register. Consequently, it was thought that in the absence of any entry on the register any purchaser for value would take free of any severed beneficial interest that there might be. Further, the system put into place by the legislation could not have worked in the case of registered land since there would have been nothing on which any memorandum of severance could have been indorsed. However, it has now been established[93] that the interest of a beneficial co-owner under a trust for sale can override registration and since 1996 the interest of a beneficial co-owner under a trust of land has also been able to do so. An interest under a trust of land can be an overriding interest if it is supported by discoverable actual occupation.[94] Purchasers of registered land from a sole surviving trustee of land who have any reason to suspect that anyone other than him is in actual occupation of the land or in receipt of its rents and profits therefore have no alternative but to do what purchasers of unregistered land formerly had to do, namely to insist upon the appointment of a second trustee to receive the purchase money together with him. If a purchaser of the land completed without being given vacant possession, they would take the land subject to the beneficial interest of the occupier of the property, unless they had made enquiries of that person and they failed to disclose their rights when it was reasonable to do so.[95]

Benefit to purchaser

8–028   It will be noticed that the three main changes introduced by the 1925 legislation all assist the purchaser. The prohibition of a legal tenancy in common and the limitation of the number of tenants of the legal estate to four means that purchasers are no longer exposed to the burden of having to investigate the titles of each of, say, 30 legal tenants in common, some of whom might own a sixty-eighth share, and who might be so scattered about the world that it took six months to get all their signatures to the conveyance.[96] Further, the overreaching effect of a conveyance by trustees of land enables a purchaser to ignore the equitable rights of the beneficiaries.

---

[89] s.1.
[90] *Grindal v Hooper* [1999] E.G.C.S. 150.
[91] Above, para.6–070.
[92] s.3.
[93] In *Williams & Glyn's Bank Ltd v Boland* [1981] A.C. 487.
[94] LRA 2002 s.29 and Sch.3 para.2
[95] LRA 2002 s.29 and Sch.3 para.2(b).
[96] See (1929) 15 Conv. (O.S.) 83 (A.H. Cosway); and see *City of London B.S. v Flegg* [1988] A.C. 54 at 77.

MODE OF CREATING THE TENANCIES: IN EQUITY

Preference for tenancy in common

Despite the feudal and conveyancing advantages of a joint tenancy, equity did not favour **8–029** it. Equity looked to the beneficial interests of the co-tenants, and preferred the certainty and equality of a tenancy in common to the element of chance which the *jus accrescendi* of a joint tenancy introduced. "Survivorship is looked upon as odious in equity"[97]; not least is this the case because few laymen contemplate that a gift to two or more persons gives rise to such a right.[98] This preference for a tenancy in common was manifested by equity holding that a tenancy in common would exist in equity not only in those cases where it existed at law, but also in certain other cases where an intention to create a tenancy in common could be discerned. Tenancies in common can no longer exist at law but equity still holds that a tenancy in common will exist in the remaining cases. However, outside those cases, equity follows the law so that when legal title is transferred to two or more adult persons, they will be legal and beneficial joint tenants.[99]

Purchase money provided in unequal shares

If two or more persons together purchase property and provide the money in unequal **8–030** shares, the purchasers are presumed to take as tenants in common in shares proportionate to the sums advanced.[100] Thus if A finds one-third and B two-thirds of the price, they are presumed to be tenants in common as to one-third and two-thirds respectively. If, on the other hand, the purchasers provide the money in equal shares, they are presumed to be joint tenants. These presumptions can be rebutted by evidence of circumstances showing that those providing the purchase money equally intended to take as tenants in common or vice versa. The court can exercise its discretion to quantify the shares of the co-owners who have not expressly declared their beneficial interests. In order to do so the court will look at the parties' actual, inferred or imputed intention.[101]

Loan on mortgage

Where two or more persons advance money on mortgage, whether in equal or unequal **8–031** shares, equity presumes a tenancy in common in the land between the mortgagees. "If two people join in lending money upon a mortgage, equity says, it could not be the intention, that the interest in that should survive. Though they take a joint security, each means to lend his own and take back his own."[102] "It is obvious, however, that this proposition cannot be put higher than a presumption capable of being rebutted."[103] Yet it should be

[97] *R. v Williams* (1735) Bunb. 342 at 343.
[98] See *Re Woolley* [1903] 2 Ch. 206 at 211; *Stack v Dowden* [2007] 2 A.C. 432; *Jones v Kernott* [2011] UKSC 53.
[99] *Cowcher v Cowcher* [1972] 1 W.L.R. 425 at 430
[100] *Lake v Gibson* (1729) 1 Eq.Ca.Abr. 290 at 291.
[101] *Stack v Dowden* [2007] 2 A.C. 432; *Jones v Kernott* [2011] UKSC 53.
[102] *Morley v Bird* (1798) 3 Ves. 628 at 631 per Arden M.R.
[103] *Steeds v Steeds* (1889) 22 Q.B.D. 537 at 541 per Wills J.

noted that the "joint account clause" which is normally inserted in mortgages to make the mortgagees appear as joint tenants to the outside world and so simplify the mechanism of discharging the mortgage[104] does not affect this presumption of a tenancy in common in the relationship of the mortgagees as between themselves.[105]

Partnership assets

8–032   Where partners acquire land as part of their partnership assets, they are presumed to hold it as tenants in common.[106] *Jus accrescendi inter mercatores locum non habet*: the right of survivorship has no place between merchants. The rule extends to any joint undertaking with a view to a profit, even if there is no formal partnership between the parties. Equity adopted this view despite the fact that the legal estate was held on a joint tenancy (it of course now has to be anyway).[107] In equity the partners were nevertheless presumed to be entitled in undivided shares, so that the surviving partners (or whoever held the legal estate) would be compelled to hold the legal estate on trust for those entitled to the property of a deceased partner as far as his share was concerned.[108] This is also the case where a tenancy of business premises is granted to joint tenants for each to occupy separate but unequal areas.[109]

Executory trusts

8–033   A trust is said to be executory where some further act is required to be done by the author of the trust or the trustees to give it its full effect.

An example of such an executory trust are "marriage articles", which are the preliminary agreement for a marriage settlement and create executory trusts while the marriage settlement itself creates executed trusts. In such cases there was a tenancy in common where any intention to create such a tenancy could be found or presumed. "Joint tenancy as a provision for the children of a marriage, is an inconvenient mode of settlement",[110] for no child could rely upon having a distinct share for his family until he had severed his joint tenancy (i.e. converted it into a tenancy in common) nor could any advance to a child be set against his share until this had been done.[111] Accordingly the court would readily infer that a provision in marriage articles or other executory trusts for the benefit of a class of children was intended to be a provision for them as tenants in common, despite the absence of words of severance.[112]

---

[104] Below, para.17–078.
[105] *Re Jackson* (1887) 34 Ch.D. 732.
[106] *Lake v Craddock* (1732) 3 P.Wms. 158; *Malayan Credit Ltd v Jack Chia-MPH Ltd* [1986] A.C. 549.
[107] By virtue of the LPA 1925.
[108] See *Re Fuller's Contract* [1933] Ch. 652.
[109] *Malayan Credit Ltd v Jack Chia-MPH Ltd* [1986] A.C. 549.
[110] *Taggart v Taggart* (1803) 1 Sch. & Lef. 84 at 88.
[111] Above, para.8–016.
[112] See *Mayn v Mayn* (1867) L.R. 5 Eq. 150.

Nature of tenancies in common since 1925

Strictly speaking, "tenancies" in common have not existed since 1925 because those inter-   **8–034**
ested hold no estate or interest in the land but are entitled merely as the beneficiaries
under a trust of land; the 1925 legislation throughout refers not to "tenancies in common"
but to "undivided shares". In general, however, the rights of these beneficiaries correspond
to the rights of tenants in common before 1926, and the same applies to those entitled in
equity as joint tenants.

POSITION OF THE BENEFICIARIES

Extent of the beneficial interests

Express trusts

Many cases of co-ownership arise pursuant to an express trust, declared in the will or in   **8–035**
the conveyance to the co-owners or to trustees to hold for them. If the relevant document
states that the parties are to be beneficial joint tenants or are to be tenants in common,
showing the size of their shares, that conclusively determines the matter.[113] This is subject
only to any question of rescission or rectification[114]; and for this the burden of proof is
heavy.[115] Thus a conveyance to two or more persons expressly as joint tenants makes them
joint tenants, each with an equal potential share, even if their contributions to the purchase
money were not only unequal but wholly disproportionate.[116] As an express trust of land
must at least be evidenced in writing,[117] the question will normally be merely[118] one of construing the document or documents. Contradictory expressions such as "as beneficial joint
tenants in equal shares"[119] can usually be resolved without resort to the quaint rule that, if
all else fails, the first words prevail in a deed but the last in a will.[120]

Other types of trusts

In the absence of any express trust, a resulting, implied or constructive trust may neverthe-   **8–036**
less arise; and these are exempt from the statutory requirement of writing.[121]

---

[113] *Pettitt v Pettitt* [1970] A.C. 777 at 813; *Pink v Lawrence* (1978) 36 P. & C.R. 98; *Goodman v Gallant*
[1986] Fam. 106; *Turton v Turton* [1988] Ch. 542; *Roy v Roy* [1996] 1 F.L.R. 541.
[114] *Re Johns' Assignment Trusts* [1970] 1 W.L.R. 955; *Thames Guaranty Ltd v Campbell* [1985] Q.B. 210.
A party seeking rectification must prove that the terms of the conveyance did not record the true
intention of the parties: *Roy v Roy* [1996] 1 F.L.R. 541.
[115] See *Thames Guarantee Ltd v Campbell* [1985] Q.B. 210.
[116] *Goodman v Gallant* [1986] Fam. 106.
[117] Above, para.7–032.
[118] "Merely" is sometimes an overstatement.
[119] *Martin v Martin* (1987) 54 P. & C.R. 238 ("in equal shares" prevailed).
[120] *Slingsby's Case* (1587) 5 Co.Rep. 18b at 19a.
[121] See above, para.7–032.

Constructive trusts

8–037   Constructive trusts of this type are imposed by equity to prevent the holder of the legal title from reneging on some sort of agreement or bargain which he has made[122]; such constructive trusts are quite distinct from the traditional categories of constructive trusts which have already been considered.[123] In the context of co-ownership the law has developed substantially in the past 10 years, especially in cases of shared ownership of the home of unmarried couples. It must be noted that its application to real property in this context does not necessarily correlate with its application to other types of property in other areas of the law. The development of the constructive trust has been driven primarily by two decisions: *Stack v Dowden* in the House of Lords and *Jones v Kernott* in the Supreme Court.

In cases where there are two (as is usually the case) or more joint legal owners the dispute will centre on the quantum of each party's beneficial interest. In cases where there is only one legal owner a claimant, who is usually the owner's cohabitee, may seek to establish a beneficial interest in the property but will need to first establish that interest before determination of its quantum. In both cases the claimant (A) will be able to establish a constructive trust where A has acted to his or her detriment in reliance upon a common intention shared with B, that the A was to have a beneficial interest in the property, or in the case of joint legal ownership, a larger share of the property's equity. It must also be shown that by acting in detrimental reliance on this common intention, it would be inequitable for B to deny A an interest in the property.[124]

In such cases there must be two elements present: (i) common intention; and (ii) detrimental reliance.[125] Where these are established it is likely to be inequitable for B to deny A his interest in the property. These two elements will be examined in more detail.

Common Intention

8–038   The first and fundamental question referred to is "whether, independently of any inference to be drawn from the conduct of the parties in the course of sharing the house as their home and managing their joint affairs, there has at any time prior to acquisition, or exceptionally at some later date,[126] been any agreement, arrangement or understanding between them that the property is to be shared beneficially."[127]

The starting point in the modern cases is the House of Lords decision in *Lloyds Bank Plc v Rosset*,[128] where it was held that for a constructive trust to be created there must either be an express agreement or an inferred agreement.[129] *Rosset* took a narrow view on how the Court could ascertain the parties' common intention but was developed by *Stack v Dowden* and then later *Jones v Kernott*. In *Stack v Dowden* the House of Lords added to the two

---

[122] *Lloyds Bank Plc v Carrick* [1996] 4 All E.R. 630; *Clough v Killey* (1996) 72 P. & C.R. D22.
[123] Above, para.7–032.
[124] *Gissing v Gissing* [1971] A.C. 886 at 905.
[125] Which must be referable to the common intention: *Grant v Edwards* [1986] Ch. 638.
[126] As in *Clough v Killey* (1996) 72 P. & C.R. D22.
[127] *Lloyds Bank Plc v Rosset* [1991] A.C. 107 at 132.
[128] [1991] 1 A.C. 107.
[129] See Lord Bridge's opinion at [132].

ways in which the court will ascertain common intention by stating that it could look for the parties' (i) actual, (ii) inferred, or (iii) imputed intention.

An express agreement (actual intention) can be ascertained from any "agreement, arrangement or understanding reached between them that the property is to be shared beneficially". Such agreement, arrangement or understanding can only be based on evidence of express discussion between the parties.

The parties' inferred agreement must be "deduced objectively from their conduct".[130] For instance, by one party making direct contributions to the purchase price.[131] In *Stack v Dowden* the House of Lords expanded upon the narrower method of inferring common intention set down in *Lloyds Bank Plc v Rosset* and held that inferred intention can be deduced from the parties whole course of conduct in relation to the property.[132] This was, according to Lady Hale, as a result of the law having moved on in response to changing social and economic conditions.

Where the court cannot establish an express common intention, or infer one from the parties whole course of conduct it may impute an intention. An imputed intention is one "which is attributed to the parties, even though no such actual intention can be deduced from their actions and statements, and even though they had no such intention. Imputation involves concluding what the parties would have intended, whereas the inference involves concluding what they did intend".[133] In *Stack v Dowden* Lord Neuberger regarded imputing an intention to be not only wrong in principle, but also a departure from House of Lords authority.[134] His Lordship took the view that a court constructing an intention where none existed at the time would be subjective and uncertain.[135]

After the House of Lords judgment in *Stack v Dowden* there was considerable uncertainty as to whether the courts could impute an intention to the parties, and indeed whether there was a difference between an inference and an imputation. As to the latter question, in *Jones v Kernott* the Supreme Court accepted there was a difference between inferring an intention and imputing one: an imputed intention is one that the parties would have had if they had turned their minds to it.[136] Lord Walker and Lady Hale expressed the view that a common intention could be imputed where the parties had not turned their minds to the issue. However, this only applied to two situations: (i) where the classic resulting trust presumption applies (which is rare in the domestic context, but may arise where the partners were also business partners); and (ii) "where it is clear that the beneficial interests are to be shared, but it is impossible to divine a common intention as to the proportions in which they are to be shared".[137] It is likely that courts will interpret this decision as also allowing the imputation of the parties' common intention as to acquisition of beneficial shares in single name cases.

---

[130] *Jones v Kernott* at [51].
[131] *Lloyds Bank Plc v Rossett* at [132].
[132] See Lady Hale's opinion at [60].
[133] *Stack v Dowden*, Per Lord Neuberger at [126].
[134] In *Pettit v Pettit* [1970] A.C. 777 and *Gissing v Gissing* [1971] A.C. 886.
[135] At [125]–[127].
[136] *Jones v Kernott* at [34]. However, perhaps unhelpfully, Lord Collins observed at [65]: ". . .it is my view that in the present context the difference between inference and imputation will hardly ever matter (as Lord Walker and Lady Hale recognise at [34]), and that what is one person's inference will be another person's imputation."
[137] *Jones v Kernott* at [31].

In *Stack v Dowden* Baroness Hale stated that "the search is to ascertain the parties' shared intentions, actual, inferred, or imputed, with respect to the property in light of their whole course of conduct in relation to it".[138] However, agreements in this context do not necessarily correspond with contractual agreements and the presence or absence of express common intention is judged objectively.[139]

Detrimental reliance

8–039   As a general rule, when there is an agreement or express common intention that land is to be held on trust, a beneficiary cannot enforce any trust if the statutory requirement of evidence in writing is not satisfied.[140] But if the intended beneficiary, in reliance on the agreement or express common intention, acts to his detriment in relation to the property in the reasonable belief that he is entitled to a beneficial interest under the trust, it would be inequitable to allow the legal owner to rely on the statute as defeating the claim of the beneficiary.[141] Thus, the statute cannot be used as an instrument of fraud.[142] However, there has to be some link between the common intention and the acts of detriment relied on.[143] The court will accordingly give effect to the intended trust by imposing a constructive trust on the property to the same effect.[144] A common intention without detrimental reliance is no trust at all because to constitute a valid declaration of trust by way of gift (which does not require detrimental reliance) there is a requirement for it to be executed in writing in accordance with s.53(1) of the Law of Property Act 1925.[145] It is the detrimental reliance that triggers the operation of a resulting, implied or constructive trust and thus avoids the limitation of the statute.

Quantum of beneficial interest

8–040   The size of the interest taken by a beneficiary depends on what was agreed, either in fact, by interference, or imputation[146]; it does not, as in the case of resulting trusts, depend on the size of whatever contribution was made to the purchase or improvement of the property made by the beneficiary in reliance on the agreement.[147] Nor are the acts of reliance confined, as in the case of resulting trusts, to direct or indirect payments towards the purchase price. Instead, they include other acts carried out in reliance on the express common intention,[148] such as doing heavy work to the house and grounds,[149] making substantial contributions to the general household expenses, or even staying at home to look after

---

[138] [2007] 2 A.C. 432 at [58].

[139] *Lloyds Bank Plc v Rosset* [1991] A.C. 107 at 133; *Eves v Eves* [1975] 1 W.L.R. 1338; *Stack v Dowden* [2007] 2 A.C. 432 at [126].

[140] Above, paras 7–031 et seq.

[141] *Gissing v Gissing* [1971] A.C. 886 at 905; *Midland Bank Plc v Dobson* [1986] 1 F.L.R. 171.

[142] *Rochefoucauld v Boustead* [1897] 1 Ch. 196; *Bannister v Bannister* [1948] 2 All E.R. 133.

[143] *Grant v Edwards* [1986] Ch. 638.

[144] *Gissing v Gissing* [1971] A.C. 886; *Midland Bank Plc v Dobson* [1986] 1 F.L.R. 171; and see *Maharaj v Chand* [1986] A.C. 898 at 907.

[145] *Gissing v Gissing* at 905.

[146] *Jones v Kernott* [2012] 1 A.C. 776.

[147] See *Re Densham* [1975] 1 W.L.R. 1519 at 1524; *Eves v Eves* [1975] 1 W.L.R. 1338; and see *Ungarian v Lesnoff* [1990] Ch. 206 (life interest).

[148] *Clough v Killey* (1996) 72 P. & C.R. D22.

[149] *Eves v Eves* [1975] 1 W.L.R. 1338; *Clough v Killey* (1996) 72 P. & C.R. D22.

children.[150] Separate consideration needs to be given to situations where a constructive trust arises in cases of joint legal ownership and single legal ownership.

Joint legal ownership: In cases of joint legal ownership, where the parties have expressed their beneficial shares in a trust deed, or on the Land Registry transfer Form TR1, the court will generally uphold those shares,[151] except where there is good cause to do so or in the case of fraud or estoppel.[152] Where there is no executed document expressing the shares and a dispute arises on the sale of the property the presumption is that equity follows the law and the parties hold their beneficial shares equally.[153] This presumption can be rebutted by evidence of a contrary intention.[154] In *Jones v Kernott* the Supreme Court established the following five-stage approach[155]:

"(1) The starting point is that equity follows the law and they are joint tenants both in law and in equity.

(2) That presumption can be displaced by showing (a) that the parties had a different common intention at the time when they acquired the home, or (b) that they later formed the common intention that their respective shares would change.[156]

(3) Their common intention is to be deduced objectively from their conduct: "the relevant intention of each party is the intention which was reasonably understood by the other party to be manifested by that party's words and conduct notwithstanding that he did not consciously formulate that intention in his own mind or even acted with some different intention which he did not communicate to the other party" (Lord Diplock in *Gissing v Gissing* [1971] AC 886, 906). Examples of the sort of evidence which might be relevant to drawing such inferences are given in Stack v Dowden, at para 69.

(4) In those cases where it is clear either (a) that the parties did not intend joint tenancy at the outset, or (b) had changed their original intention, but it is not possible to ascertain by direct evidence or by inference what their actual intention was as to the shares in which they would own the property, "the answer is that each is entitled to that share which the court considers fair having regard to the whole course of dealing between them in relation to the property": Chadwick LJ in *Oxley v Hiscock* [2005] Fam 211, para 69. In our judgment, "the whole course of dealing . . . in relation to the property" should be given a broad meaning, enabling a similar range of factors to be taken into account as may be relevant to ascertaining the parties' actual intentions.

(5) Each case will turn on its own facts. Financial contributions are relevant but there are many other factors which may enable the court to decide what shares were either intended (as in case (3)) or fair (as in case (4))."

---

[150] *Grant v Edwards* [1986] Ch. 638; and see the wide language at 657. See also *Hammond v Mitchell* [1991] 1 W.L.R. 1127.

[151] *Goodman v Gallant* [1986] Fam. 106

[152] *Clough v Kinney* (1996) 72 P. & C.R. D22; *Clarke v Meadus* [2010] EWHC 3117 (Ch).

[153] *Stack v Dowden* at [33], [54] and [109].

[154] *Jones v Kernott* at [25].

[155] At [51].

[156] This is known as an ambulatory constructive trust: see *Stack v Dowden* at [62], referring to Lord Hoffman's discussion of it in the course of argument before the Judicial Committee.

A non-exhaustive list of factors that will give rise to a displacement of the presumption that equity follows the law was given by Baroness Hale in *Stack v Dowden*, which were expressly approved in *Jones v Kernott*[157]:

> "These include: any advice or discussions at the time of the transfer which cast light upon their intentions then; the reasons why the home was acquired in their joint names; the reasons why (if it be the case) the survivor was authorised to give a receipt for the capital moneys; the purpose for which the home was acquired; the nature of the parties' relationship; whether they had children for whom they both had responsibility to provide a home; how the purchase was financed, both initially and subsequently; how the parties arranged their finances, whether separately or together or a bit of both; how they discharged the outgoings on the property and their other household expenses. When a couple are joint owners of the home and jointly liable for the mortgage, the inferences to be drawn from who pays for what may be very different from the inferences to be drawn when only one is owner of the home. The arithmetical calculation of how much was paid by each is also likely to be less important. It will be easier to draw the inference that they intended that each should contribute as much to the household as they reasonably could and that they would share the eventual benefit or burden equally. The parties' individual characters and personalities may also be a factor in deciding where their true intentions lay. In the cohabitation context, mercenary considerations may be more to the fore than they would be in marriage, but it should not be assumed that they always take pride of place over natural love and affection. At the end of the day, having taken all this into account, cases in which the joint legal owners are to be taken to have intended that their beneficial interests should be different from their legal interests will be very unusual."[158]

Single legal owner: Where a party has established a common intention constructive trust the court must then determine the beneficial interest of the parties in cases of single legal owners. Whilst this quantification was formerly done by reference to contributions, it is now clear that the court's task is to look at the whole course of conduct between the parties in order to find the actual, inferred or imputed intention of the parties as to shares. This will usually be by reference to inference. However, where it is impossible to ascertain the size of the parties' beneficial interest by inference it is possible to do so by imputation. When doing so each party is entitled to that share which the court considers to be fair having regard to the whole course of dealings between them in relation to the property.[159]

Resulting trusts

8–041   The Supreme Court has put the position as to the existence of a resulting trust in the context of a family home beyond doubt: "The time has come to make it clear, in line with *Stack v Dowden* [2007] 2 AC 432 (see also *Abbott v Abbott* [2008] 1 FLR 1451), that in the case of

---

[157] At [51].
[158] *Stack v Dowden*, at [69].
[159] *Jones v Kernott* at [51], approving *Oxley v Hiscock* [2005] Fam. 211 at [69] per Chadwick L.J.

the purchase of a house or flat in joint names for joint occupation by a married or unmarried couple, where both are responsible for any mortgage, there is no presumption of a resulting trust arising from their having contributed to the deposit (or indeed the rest of the purchase) in unequal shares. The presumption is that the parties intended a joint tenancy both in law and in equity. But that presumption can of course be rebutted by evidence of a contrary intention, which may more readily be shown where the parties did not share their financial resources."[160]

However, in all other situations, including where two family members purchase a joint property for investments purposes,[161] the presumption of a resulting trust depends on a legal presumption about the intentions of the settlor. When property is purchased with money provided by A and B, and there is a common intention that each of them is to have a beneficial interest in it, there will be presumed to be a resulting trust for them in shares proportionate to their contributions, whether the property is conveyed to one or both of them or to some third party. Therefore, if a house, which is not purchased for joint occupation, is conveyed to A alone, but the price is provided as to nine-tenths by A and as to one-tenth by B, A will be presumed to hold the house on resulting trust as to nine-tenths for himself and as to one-tenth for B.[162] This will be the case whether the contributions are in cash or by way of mortgage advances for whose repayment A or B is solely responsible.[163] However, no resulting trust will be inferred where money is provided by way of gift or loan[164]; and the presumption of a resulting trust may be rebutted.

Common intention: It has already been seen that express common intention coupled with any act of detrimental reliance leads to the imposition of a constructive trust rather than the presumption of a resulting trust and to a quantum of beneficial interest potentially superior to that obtainable under a resulting trust. Consequently, it is only in the absence of an express common intention that any beneficiary will need to fall back on a resulting trust. Where the common intention instead has to be inferred, it will have to be inferred from the contributions and the circumstances in which they were made; the main weight is thus on the contributions. The question is what in fact the inferred common intention was, and not what the court considers it might or ought to have been.[165]

Direct contributions to the purchase price: Contributions to the purchase price are sometimes made outright (such as contributions to the deposit[166] and to other initial payments of funds found by the purchasers themselves) but often they take the form of regularly bearing a share of the mortgage repayments on the property; merely occasional payments are not enough.[167] However, minor contributions appear to suffice. Thus, where the deposit

---

[160] *Jones v Kernott* [2012] 1 A.C. 776 at [25], per Baroness Hale and Lord Walker.
[161] See for example *Laskar v Laskar* [2008] 1 W.L.R. 2695.
[162] *Re Rogers' Question* [1948] 1 All E.R. 328; *Walker v Hall* [1984] F.L.R. 126 (purchase in joint names).
[163] *Huntingford v Hobbs* [1993] 1 F.L.R. 736.
[164] *Hussey v Palmer* [1972] 1 W.L.R. 1286; *Re Sharpe (a Bankrupt)* [1980] 1 W.L.R. 219; contrast *Risch v McFee* (1991) 61 P. & C.R. 42 (loan becoming a contribution).
[165] *Gissing v Gissing* [1971] A.C. 886, esp. at 898; and see *Pettitt v Pettitt* [1970] A.C. 777. In *Jones v Kernott* at [29], Lord Walker and Lady Hale take the view that resulting trusts are "presumed", but arise by imputed intention.
[166] See *Midland Bank Plc v Cooke* [1995] 2 F.L.R. 915.
[167] *Gissing v Gissing* [1971] A.C. 886 at 900, 906. For endowment mortgages, see Thompson,

was provided by a husband's parents, the wife was held thereby to have made a direct contribution of one half of that deposit on the basis that that sum was a gift to both of them; it was then inferred that they had clearly "agreed to share everything" and she was held to be entitled to 50 per cent of the property.[168]

Indirect contributions to the purchase price: Indirect contributions to the purchase price also suffice. Thus where A purchased property out of the profits of a family business to which B's unpaid work in the business had substantially contributed, B was entitled to a beneficial interest in the property.[169]

Contributions of other types: At one time the court sometimes considered that contributions of other types, such as doing work on the house and grounds,[170] bearing some of the household expenses, purchasing chattels for use in the house, and even staying home to look after children, sufficed.[171] Such contributions constitute sufficient detrimental reliance for the imposition of a constructive trust. But, in the context of resulting trusts, it is now settled that nothing will do except contributions to the purchase of the property, whether direct or indirect.[172] Thus even very substantial sums expended or time spent on renovating, improving and redecorating the property, never mind relatively trivial sums expended on paying the rates, is not enough by itself.[173] However, some form of judicial relief from the harshness of this result is available to anyone who has actually made some form of contribution to the purchase price, no matter how trivial, since this apparently enables contributions of other types to be taken into account in determining what the common intention of the parties was.[174] An inferred arrangement that one party should bear all the household expenses in order to enable the other party to pay the mortgage instalments may well still be held to be sufficiently related to the acquisition of the property for the inference to be drawn that each party was intended to have a beneficial interest.[175]

Subsequent improvements: By statute,[176] subsequent contributions towards improvements to the property (as distinct from its original acquisition) may now be invoked[177] in order to alter the balance of beneficial ownership as between husband and wife, but not as between others. Any substantial contribution in money or money's worth made by a husband or wife to the improvement of real or personal property in which either or both of them have a beneficial interest will entitle the contributor to such a share or enlarged share as is agreed or, in default, as seems "just" in all the circumstances.

Co-ownership, 52. See also Curley v Parkes [2005] 1 P. & C. R. DG15, where the Court of Appeal decided mortgage payments were not enough to establish a beneficial interest.

[168] Midland Bank Plc v Cooke [1995] 2 F.L.R. 915.

[169] Re Cummins [1972] Ch. 62; Bothe v Amos [1976] Fam. 46.

[170] Eves v Eves [1975] 1 W.L.R. 1338.

[171] Hazell v Hazell [1972] 1 W.L.R. 301; Hussey v Palmer [1972] 1 W.L.R. 1286 at 1289, 1290 (constructive trust); Hall v Hall [1982] 3 F.L.R. 379 at 381. See generally (1976) 92 L.Q.R. 489 (F.Webb).

[172] Gissing v Gissing [1971] A.C. 886; Burns v Burns [1984] Ch. 317.

[173] Lloyds Bank Plc v Rosset [1991] A.C. 107; Hammond v Mitchell [1991] 1 W.L.R. 1127. See also Savage v Dunningham [1974] Ch. 181 (tenancy: rent).

[174] Midland Bank Plc v Cooke [1995] 2 F.L.R. 915.

[175] See Gissing v Gissing [1971] A.C. 886 at 903, 909. Also see the discussion in Lady Hale's opinion in Stack v Dowden at [69].

[176] Matrimonial Proceedings and Property Act 1970 (MPPA 1970) s.37.

[177] See Suttill v Graham [1977] 1 W.L.R. 819 at 824.

Protection of beneficiaries' interests

Where all the co-owners hold the legal title on trust for themselves, only they will be able to deal with the legal title and, while all remain alive, require no protection from one another. In the case of registered land, the interests of the beneficial co-owners will normally be protected by the entry of a restriction on the register.[178] This will ensure that on a sale the purchase money will be properly paid to the trustees and the beneficial interests of the co-owners will be overreached and become corresponding rights in the proceeds of sale.[179] Any purported conveyance[180] or mortgage[181] of the entire property, effected by one joint tenant forging the signature of the other or others takes effect only as against his own beneficial interest. The position where there is a sole survivor of joint tenants has already been considered.[182]

8–042

What is the position of beneficial co-owners who are not on the legal title, something which is highly likely where their beneficial interests have arisen under a resulting or constructive trust? The intention of the 1925 property legislation was that on any disposition of the land their beneficial interests would be overreached into the proceeds of sale. This will happen when there is a disposition by two trustees or a trust corporation whether the beneficiaries wish their interests to be overreached or not.[183] This is so as regards any of the beneficiaries who are in "actual occupation" of registered land (their interests, having been overreached, are no longer "subsisting" in the land, and so cannot override registration of the title of the purchaser[184]). In the case of registered land, the beneficial co-owners will therefore be completely protected where a restriction has been entered on the register. However, this is not particularly likely where their beneficial interests arise under a resulting or constructive trust unless the land was co-owned already and no similar protection is ever available in the case of unregistered land. Consequently, whenever there is a sole trustee of land, the interests of beneficial co-owners who are not on the legal title are potentially vulnerable.

The 1925 property legislation did not state the effect of a disposition by a sole trustee of land. However, the courts have decided that in these circumstances the overreachable but unoverreached interests of the beneficial co-owners are treated as if they were commercial interests rather than family interests.[185] Consequently, those interests will be destroyed if the land reaches the hands of a bona fide purchaser for value of a legal estate without notice in the case of unregistered land[186] and a bona fide purchaser for value claiming under a registered disposition in the case of registered land.[187]

In the case of unregistered land, there is no way in which a beneficial co-owner can

---

[178] LRA 2002 s.44(1). LRR 2003 r.94(1) sets out the circumstances where an application for a restriction must be made.

[179] See *City of London B.S. v Flegg* [1988] A.C. 54.

[180] *Ahmed v Kendrick* (1988) 56 P. & C.R. 121.

[181] *First National Securities Ltd v Hegerty* [1985] Q.B. 850.

[182] Above, para.8–027.

[183] See *City of London B.S. v Flegg* [1988] A.C. 54.

[184] *City of London B.S. v Flegg* [1988] A.C. 54; above.

[185] *Caunce v Caunce* [1969] 1 W.L.R. 286 (unregistered land); *Willliams & Glyn's Bank Ltd v Boland* [1981] A.C. 487 (registered land).

[186] *Caunce v Caunce* [1969] 1 W.L.R. 286.

[187] LRA 2002 s.29.

protect himself from the risk of his interest being destroyed as a result of a disposition by a sole trustee unless he goes to the court[188] and asks for a second trustee to be appointed.[189] However, most beneficiaries of resulting and constructive trusts will be in occupation of the land. If this is the case, it is only in the most exceptional circumstances (such as where the trustee has removed all signs of a beneficiary's existence) that a purchaser will not have constructive notice of his presence and a purchaser who has notice will obviously be unable to take free of his interest.

In the case of registered land, assuming that no restriction has been registered, the beneficial co-owner can also go to the court and ask for a second trustee to be appointed. In practice, however, all that is necessary for him to do is to register a restriction. Where this has not been done, the beneficial co-owner will nevertheless be protected when he is in actual occupation of the land, which most beneficiaries of constructive trusts will be, because in that case his beneficial interest will override the registration of any purchaser. Under the Land Registration Act 2002, the actual occupation must be obvious on a reasonably careful inspection of the land.[190] Consequently, it will then be possible, as in the case of unregistered land, for a purchaser to take free because the trustee has removed all signs of a beneficiary's existence.

Only in very exceptional circumstances will a beneficial co-owner be at risk when he is in occupation of the land. Generally speaking, therefore, it is only where the beneficial co-owners of land held by a sole trustee are not in occupation of the land that there is any serious risk that their interests will be destroyed.

Dispute resolution

Occupation trusts

8–043   The imposition from 1926 until 1996 of a trust for sale and, since 1996, of a trust of land in cases of co-ownership has meant that there have been many trusts holding land whose main purpose is not the provision of financial benefits but to provide the means of occupying the property, usually a house. Such trusts may, for brevity, be called "occupation trusts", in contrast with what may be called "financial trusts", trusts holding land whose main purpose is to provide financial benefits for their beneficiaries. This has been and is the purpose of most express trusts for sale, under which the beneficiaries obtain income until sale and capital thereafter. (There is no formal classification of this kind, but the distinction is useful in relation to the resolution of disputes over the property, usually but not exclusively over selling the property and over orders for sale.[191])

The 1996 Act

8–044   Under the 1996 Act, "any person who is a trustee of land or has an interest in property subject to a trust of land" may apply to the court for an order relating to the exercise by the trustees of any of their functions, including an order directing them to consult or relieving

---

[188] Under TLATA 1996 s.14(1); see above, para.7–022 and below.
[189] See *Walker v Waller* [1967] 1 W.L.R. 451.
[190] Above, para.5–022.
[191] Formerly under LPA 1925 s.30 (now repealed), now under TLATA 1996 s.14; see above, para.7–022.

them from their obligation to do so, or declaring the nature or extent of anyone's interest in the trust property.[192] Anyone who is, or claims to be, a beneficial co-owner of land is therefore entitled to apply to the court for an order establishing the existence and extent of his beneficial interest. Both the trustees and the beneficial co-owners are also entitled to apply to the court for an order relating to the way in which the trustees should exercise their functions. In practice, by far the most likely function in respect of which such an order will be sought is the trustees' power of sale (indeed, before 1997, this was the only function in respect of which such an order could be sought[193]). However, the powers conferred on trustees by the 1996 Act to partition the land[194] and to permit and restrict occupation[195] have also been the subject of applications and the trustees' obligations to consult the beneficiaries specifically referred to in this provision are obviously likely to be the subject of applications in the future.

In determining an application by anyone other than a trustee in bankruptcy, the matters to which the court is to have regard include:

(a)   the intentions of the settlor or testator;
(b)   the purposes for which the land is held;
(c)   the welfare of any minor who occupies or might reasonably be expected to occupy any land subject to the trust as his home; and
(d)   the interests of any secured creditor of any beneficiary.[196]

Where the application concerns the occupation of any trust property, the court must additionally have regard to the circumstances and wishes of each of the beneficiaries who is entitled to occupy the land.[197] In any case other than one concerning the occupation of any trust property or one relating to the trustees' right to compel absolutely entitled beneficiaries to take a conveyance of the legal title,[198] the court must additionally have regard to the circumstances and wishes of the beneficiaries of full age entitled to interests in possession in the land.[199]

However, where the application is made by a trustee in bankruptcy, the court must instead make such order as it thinks just and reasonable having regard to the following matters: first, the interests of the bankrupt's creditors; secondly, where the application concerns a dwelling-house which is or has been the home of the bankrupt, his spouse or his former spouse, the conduct of the spouse or former spouse in so far as it contributed to the bankruptcy, the needs and financial resources of the spouse or former spouse, and the needs of any children; thirdly, all the circumstances of the case other than the needs of the bankrupt.[200] On any application made more than a year after the appointment of the trustee in bankruptcy, the court must assume, unless the circumstances of the case are exceptional, that the interests of the bankrupt's creditors outweigh all other considerations.[201]

---

[192] TLATA 1996 s.14.
[193] Under LPA 1925 s.30 (now repealed).
[194] TLATA 1996 s.7, above para.7–017.
[195] TLATA 1996 s.13, above para.7–020.
[196] TLATA 1996 s.15(1); by s.22(3) "beneficiary" does not include an annuitant.
[197] TLATA 1996 s.15(2).
[198] This interpretation was confirmed in *The Mortgage Corporation v Shaire* [2000] 1 F.L.R. 973 at 991.
[199] TLATA 1996 s.15(3); by s.22(3) "beneficiary" does not include an annuitant.
[200] Insolvency Act 1986 s.335A(2), inserted by TLATA 1996 Sch.3 para.23.
[201] Insolvency Act 1986 s.335A(3), inserted by TLATA 1996 Sch.3 para.23.

It has been held that the matters to which the court is to have regard are not exclusive but inclusive and that other matters may also be of relevance.[202]

Sales

8–045   This is the situation in which occupation trusts differ most from financial trusts. In the case of a financial trust, none of the matters to which the court must have regard is likely to impede the trustees from exercising their power of sale if they wish to do so or if the majority of the beneficiaries of full age entitled to interests in possession of the land or a trustee in bankruptcy of a beneficiary wishes them to do so; the sale will merely convert one form of financial asset into another. Even more so is this the case where the financial trust in question is an express trust for sale; in such cases it is hard to envisage any reason why the trustees should not carry out their duty to sell the property in the event that they are no longer unanimous about continuing to exercise their power to postpone sale.[203] Where there is an occupation trust, a sale will often defeat the purpose of the trust by making one or more of the co-owners homeless and so different considerations apply.

Applications by a co-owner: The first point that must be made is that, where the dispute is between husband and wife in the course of divorce proceedings and there are no third party interests, the only relevant legislation is the Matrimonial Causes Act 1973,[204] not the 1996 Act (this was also the view generally adopted before 1997[205]).

Disputes usually arise between co-owners when a relationship breaks down, or where one party wishes to sell the property and the other does not. Either of them may apply to the court, which may make such order as it thinks fit in relation to the exercise by the trustees of any of their functions.[206]

On an application for sale made by one of the co-owners, other than in the course of divorce proceedings, the position before 1997 was as follows. The law started from the position that the purpose of an occupation trust was for occupation of the property by its co-owners; consequently, an occupying co-owner could not be evicted by the others.[207] However, where the purpose of the trust was the provision of a family or matrimonial home for a married or unmarried couple, that purpose was regarded as ending when the couple separated, and so it would no longer prevent a sale.[208] A sale was therefore usually, but not always, ordered unless the occupying co-owner paid a proper rent or compensation[209] for his occupation.[210] But where the purpose of the trust was to provide a family home for a man, woman and their children, the house would not cease to be occupied as a family home merely because the man left it; therefore he would be refused an order for sale.[211]

Although the authorities under the old law prior to 1997 will provide some guidance, the

---

[202] *Bank of Ireland Home Mortgages Ltd v Bell* [2001] 2 F.L.R. 809 at 815 ([24]).
[203] Above, para.7–014.
[204] ss.22–25; *Tee v Tee* [1999] 2 F.L.R. 613.
[205] *Williams v Williams* [1976] Ch. 278.
[206] TLATA 1996 s.14(1)–(2).
[207] *Bull v Bull* [1955] 1 Q.B. 234.
[208] *Jones v Challenger* [1961] 1 Q.B. 176; *Bernard v Josephs* [1982] Ch. 391.
[209] Above, para.8–006.
[210] *Dennis v McDonald* [1982] Fam. 63; contrast *Stott v Ratcliffe* (1982) 126 S.J. 310 (no order).
[211] *Re Evers' Trust* [1980] 1 W.L.R. 1327; and see *Chhokar v Chhokar* [1984] F.L.R. 313 at 327.

case law should be treated with caution. Neuberger J. (as he then was) said in *Mortgage Corporation v Shaire*[212] "although it would be wrong to reject the wealth of learning in the old authorities dealing with opposed applications for the sale of jointly owned property, given the change in the law introduced by section 15 of the 1996 Act, pre-1996 cases should be treated with caution". Neuberger J. took this approach despite the Law Commission's view that much of the law prior to 1996 would remain relevant when interpreting ss.14 and 15 of the Trusts of Land and Appointment of Trustees Act 1996.[213] It must be remembered that before the 1996 Act co-owned land was subject to a trust for sale, which carried with it a duty to sell.

It has been accepted that the 1996 Act has given scope for some change in the court's practice,[214] although this has been in the context of applications brought by secured creditors rather than by one of the co-owners. It seems that the court will continue to regard the purpose of providing a family home as at an end when a couple separate and there are no longer any infant children.[215] Where the court is unable or unwilling to order sale, it is possible instead for the land to be partitioned between the co-owners or for the occupation of different parts of it by different co-owners to be permitted.[216] A sale is also likely to be ordered if the land was purchased as an investment, rather than as a home. However, a sale may be resisted if there are children living at the property[217] or it can be postponed to a future date, such as when the co-owning occupier has finished her studies.[218]

Applications by creditors: Most creditors who make applications will be secured creditors, that is to say mortgagees of either the co-owned property or the beneficial interest of one of the co-owners. It is important to note that the liability of co-owners under a mortgage or a further advance may be different for a number of reasons: the advance may have been obtained as a result of the undue influence of one co-owner over the other[219] or behind the back of the other co-owner[220] or by forging the latter's signature.[221] In all such cases the mortgage or further advance takes effect only against the beneficial interest of the co-owner who obtained it but the beneficial interest of the other co-owner remains bound to the extent that any previous mortgage was binding on him.[222] The interests of secured creditors are one of the matters to which the court is directed to have regard. However, it is also possible that an application for sale may be made by an unsecured creditor who has obtained a charging order against either the co-owned property or the beneficial interest of one of the co-owners.[223] The interests of such a creditor are not one of the matters to which the court is directed to have regard and it is unlikely that they would order a sale on his

---

[212] [2001] Ch. 743 at 761.
[213] See Law Commission Report No. 181.
[214] *The Mortgage Corp v Shaire* [2000] 1 F.L.R. 973, not following *TSB Bank Plc v Marshall* [1998] 2 F.L.R. 769; *Bank of Ireland Home Mortgages Ltd v Bell* [2001] 2 F.L.R. 809.
[215] *Bank of Ireland Home Mortgages Ltd v Bell* [2001] 2 F.L.R. 809 at 815–816 ([28]).
[216] Below.
[217] *Edwards v Lloyds TSB* [2004] EWHC 1745 (Ch).
[218] *Chun v Ho* [2002] EWCA Civ 1075.
[219] *Royal Bank of Scotland Plc v Etridge (No.2)* [2001] 4 All E.R. 449.
[220] *Equity & Law Home Loans Ltd v Prestridge* [1992] 1 W.L.R. 137.
[221] *First National Securities Ltd v Hegarty* [1985] Q.B. 850; cp. *Paddington B.S. v Mendelsohn* (1985) 50 P. & C.R. 244.
[222] *Equity & Law Home Loans Ltd v Prestridge* [1992] 1 W.L.R. 137.
[223] Such a person presumably has an interest by analogy with the previous legislation ("person interested" held to be within LPA 1925 s.30 in *Midland Bank v Pike* [1988] 2 All E.R. 434).

application if the co-owner in question had other unsecured creditors, since to do so would give him a priority over them which he would not enjoy in the event of the co-owner's bankruptcy (mortgagees have an automatic priority over unsecured creditors).

On an application for sale made by a creditor, whether secured or unsecured, the position before 1997 was as follows. The court had a discretion whether to make the order, and had to balance the conflicting interests. The interests of the creditors usually prevailed over those of any other co-owners or occupants of the property and so an order for sale was normally made.[224] Only in exceptional circumstances did the interests of children and families in occupation prevail.

However, it has been held that the 1996 Act has given scope for some change in the court's practice in this respect since the interests of any secured creditor is merely one of the five factors to which the court has to have regard and the court is not directed to have regard to the interests of unsecured creditors at all. In particular, there is no indication that the interests of secured creditors are to be given priority over the welfare of any minor who occupies the property as his home.[225] Consequently, where the mortgage debt of a deceased co-owner exceeded the value of his 25 per cent beneficial interest so that that interest was, in effect, the property of the mortgagee, sale was not ordered provided that the other co-owner continued to discharge her own much lower mortgage debt and to pay interest at 1.25 per cent above base rate on the value of the beneficial interest of the other co-owner (not on the much higher amount of his mortgage debt).[226] On the other hand, sale was ordered where the mortgage debt exceeded the value of the entire property and the co-owner resisting sale had no possibility of compensating the mortgagee for being kept out of its money.[227] In neither of these two cases was the property occupied by minors as their home; where it is so occupied, it is clearly likely that even greater changes will be made to the court's previous practice. It remains to be seen how the courts will balance the interests of such minors against the interests of secured creditors; their interests will presumably prevail over the interests of unsecured creditors.

Applications by trustees in bankruptcy: On an application made by the trustee in bankruptcy of a bankrupt co-owner, the position before 1997 was the same as when an application was made by a creditor. The court equally had discretion whether to make the order and had to balance the conflicting interests. However, the interests of the creditors to whom the trustee in bankruptcy owed his fiduciary duties again usually prevailed over those of any other co-owners or occupants of the property, and so an order for sale was normally made.[228] Only rarely did the circumstances justify refusing an immediate order for sale, as by postponing the sale of a house for five years while children were being educated.[229] Further, statute provided that, where a bankrupt and his spouse or former spouse were the co-owners of a dwelling-house and the trustee in bankruptcy applied for an order for sale at least a year after the dwelling vested in him, the court had to assume (unless the

---

[224] *Lloyds Bank Plc v Byrne* [1993] 1 F.L.R. 369.

[225] *The Mortgage Corp v Shaire* [2000] 1 F.L.R. 973 at 988.

[226] *The Mortgage Corp v Shaire* [2000] 1 F.L.R. 973 at 994–995.

[227] *Bank of Ireland Home Mortgages Ltd v Bell* [2001] 2 F.L.R. 809 at 815–817.

[228] *Re Bailey* [1977] 1 W.L.R. 278; *Re Lowrie* [1981] 3 All E.R. 353; *Re Citro* [1991] Ch. 142.

[229] *Re Holliday* [1981] Ch. 405 (bankrupt's own petition: creditors not pressing for payment); contrast *Re Lowrie* [1981] 3 All E.R. 353 (immediate sale, completion only postponed for three months).

circumstances of the case are exceptional) that the interests of the bankrupt's creditors outweighed all other considerations.[230]

This provision has been re-enacted by the 1996 Act.[231] Consequently, whatever effect the courts give to the factors to which it has to have regard during the first year following bankruptcy[232] (which are different from those to which it has to have regard on applications by anyone other than a trustee in bankruptcy), thereafter the position is very clear.[233] The presence of exceptional circumstances is a necessary condition to displace the assumption that the interests of the creditors outweigh all other considerations but the presence of exceptional circumstances does not debar the court from making an order for sale.[234] Consequently, once a year has passed, it is almost inevitable that sale will be ordered.

In the modern cases the exceptional circumstances typically relate to the personal circumstances of one of the co-owners, such as a medical or mental condition.[235] In *Nicholls v Lan*[236] the schizophrenia of the creditor's wife was not considered to be exceptional circumstances since she owned other property. The circumstances were considered exceptional when the mother of children was an alcoholic and they required a stable support network and there was sufficient equity in the property, even if the sale were postponed.[237]

However, the categories of exceptional circumstances are not to be categorised or defined; the court must make a value judgment after looking at all the circumstances.[238] Neither the fact that the other co-owner has been keeping up the mortgage payments, thus benefitting the bankrupt's estate, nor the fact that the other co-owner has also applied for an order for sale in order to complete a sale which he has already negotiated, nor the fact that any delay in sale might cause a mortgagee to step in and sell at a lower price constitute exceptional circumstances.[239] In the absence of such circumstances, a sale can be ordered even though its effect will be that the entire proceeds of sale will be consumed by the trustee's fees and expenses; that is not an exceptional circumstance and such a sale is still for the benefit of the creditors.[240]

Where a co-owner of land is bankrupt, his trustee in bankruptcy will often wish to obtain a sale of the property. After three years, beginning on the date of the bankruptcy, any interest of the bankrupt in a dwelling house which, at the date of the bankruptcy, was the sole or principal residence of the bankrupt's spouse, ceases to be compromised in the bankrupt's estate.[241]

---

[230] Insolvency Act 1986 s.336(5).
[231] Insolvency Act 1986 s.335A(3), inserted by TLATA 1996 Sch.3 para.23.
[232] Insolvency Act 1986 s.335A(2), inserted by TLATA 1996 Sch.3 para.23.
[233] *Harrington v Bennett* (2000) New Law Online Case 200035003.
[234] *Re D.R. Raval* [1998] B.P.I.R. 389.
[235] *Judd v Brown* [1997] B.P.I.R. 470; *Re D.R. Raval* [1998] B.P.I.R. 389; *Claughton v Charalamabous* [1998] B.P.I.R. 588.
[236] [2006] EWHC 1255.
[237] *Martin-Sklan v White* [2006] EWHC 3313 (Ch).
[238] *Claughton v Charalamabous* [1998] B.P.I.R. 588.
[239] *Harrington v Bennett* (2000) New Law Online Case 200035003.
[240] *Trustee of the Estate of Bowe v Bowe* [1997] B.P.I.R. 747; *Harrington v Bennett* (2000) New Law Online Case 200035003.
[241] Insolvency Act 1986 s.283A, inserted by the Enterprise Act 2002 s.262.

Partition and divided occupation

8–046   In disputes between co-owners, it is possible for an application to be made for partition of the land[242] or for the co-owners to be permitted to occupy different parts of it.[243] Such an application may be made either outright or by way of counterclaim to an application for an order for sale. Where premises were owned by two doctors and occupied for the purposes of their medical practice, an application by one doctor for an order for sale was met by a counterclaim for partition or for an order that the two doctors be permitted to occupy different parts of the premises.[244] The court was unable to order sale[245] and did not order partition,[246] presumably because of the impossibility of partitioning the entrance and a central corridor. But each doctor was restricted from occupying specific parts of the premises, thus procuring joint occupation of the entrance and central corridor and individual occupation of the units on either side of the corridor.[247] The court also ordered the doctors to contribute to the costs of adapting the property.[248]

Determination of joint tenancies and tenancies in common

8–047   Joint tenancies and tenancies in common may be determined by partition or by union in a sole tenant; joint tenancies may also be determined by severance, which converts them into tenancies in common.

Partition

No power at common law

8–048   Joint tenants and tenants in common have always been able to make a voluntary partition of the land concerned if all agreed; their co-ownership thus comes to an end as a result of each of them becoming sole tenant of the piece of land allotted to him. But at common law there was no right to compel a partition.

Statutory powers

8–049   The 1996 Act,[249] extending similar powers given to trustees for sale by the Law of Property Act 1925[250] to all trusts of land, gives trustees of land power to divide any land to which beneficiaries of full age are absolutely beneficially entitled in undivided shares between those

---

[242] Under TLATA 1996 s.7; above, para.7–017.

[243] Under TLATA 1996 s.13; above, para.7–020.

[244] *Rodway v Landy* [2001] Ch. 703.

[245] National Health Service Act 1977 s.54(1) makes unlawful any sale of the goodwill of a medical practice.

[246] *Rodway v Landy* (2000) New Law Online Case 2001018801 (Ch.D.); the application for partition was not pursued on appeal.

[247] *Rodway v Landy* [2001] Ch. 703.

[248] *Rodway v Landy* [2001] Ch. 703.

[249] TLATA 1996 s.7.

[250] LPA 1925 s.28(3) (now repealed). This replaced the successive Partition Acts of 1539, 1540 and 1868.

beneficiaries. However, this requires either the consent of each of these beneficiaries,[251] although a purchaser need not be concerned to see that they have consented,[252] or, apparently, an order of the court.[253]

Union in a sole tenant

Joint tenancies and tenancies in common may be determined by the entirety of the land becoming vested in a sole tenant. Thus where one of two surviving joint tenants dies, the other becomes sole tenant and the joint tenancy is at an end. Similarly if one joint tenant or tenant in common acquires the interests of all his fellows, as by purchase, the co-ownership is at an end.

    Because in theory each joint tenant has the whole of the land, the appropriate way for one joint tenant to transfer his rights to another is by a release operating to extinguish rather than to convey any rights, and so requiring no words of limitation; but any sort of conveyance will be construed as a release,[254] and it has now been retrospectively provided that the transaction can also be effected by grant.[255] A tenant in common, on the other hand, cannot release his share to his fellows, but has to convey it by some assurance by which a sole tenant could have conveyed his land, for "a release supposes the party to have the thing in demand".[256]

    Co-ownership in land is also extinguished if the land is sold to a purchaser, for the co-ownership is transferred from the land to the proceeds of sale.

8–050

Severance

The common law mitigated the uncertainty of the *jus accrescendi* by enabling a joint tenant to destroy the joint tenancy by severance, thereby becoming a tenant in common. "The duration of all lives being uncertain, if either party has an ill opinion of his own life, he may sever the joint tenancy by a deed granting over a moiety [i.e. conveying one-half] in trust for himself; so that survivorship can be no hardship, where either side may at pleasure prevent it."[257] This right of severance is unrestricted and absolute save where a joint tenant has by his conduct estopped himself from severing, in which case any attempted severance will be ineffective.[258] The expression "severance" strictly includes partition, but the word is normally used to describe the process whereby a joint tenancy is converted into a tenancy in common, and it is used in this sense here. Although no joint tenant owned any distinct share in the land, yet each had a potential share equal in size to that of his companions, and so depending upon the number of joint tenants at the time in question. Thus if there were five joint tenants, each had the right to sever his joint tenancy and become tenant in common of one undivided fifth share; if one joint tenant died before the severance each of the survivors had a potential quarter share, and so on. The potential shares in land

8–051

---

[251] TLATA 1996 s.7(3).
[252] TLATA 1996 s.16(1).
[253] Under s.14; see *Rodway v Landy* [2001] Ch. 703, where partition was denied (above, para.8–046).
[254] See *Re Schar* [1951] Ch. 280.
[255] LPA 1925 s.72(4).
[256] Litt. s.304, n.1.
[257] *Cray v Willis* (1729) 2 P.Wms. 529, per Verney M.R.
[258] *Price v Hartwell* [1996] E.G.C.S. 98.

conveyed to two or more persons as beneficial joint tenants will always be equal, even if they contributed unequally to the purchase price. Consequently, if those interests are severed, their interests in common will also be equal.[259]

Before 1926, a joint tenancy could be severed both at law and in equity. Since 1925, a legal joint tenancy can never be severed so as to create a legal tenancy in common; but this does not prevent one joint tenant from releasing his interest to the others nor does it affect the right to sever a joint tenancy in equity.[260] A severance can be effected by any of the methods which would have been effective in equity in the case of personalty before 1926.[261] These methods all involve destroying one of the unities. Unity of time cannot be destroyed and severance of the unity of possession means partition; but severance of the unity either of title or of interest converts a joint tenancy into a tenancy in common. It is also now possible to use a further method of severance created by the Law of Property Act 1925.[262] A joint tenancy can therefore now be severed in the following ways.

By acquiring another estate in the land

8–052 Although it is not fatal to a joint tenancy that one of the tenants is initially given some further estate in the land than his joint tenancy, the subsequent acquisition of an additional estate in the land destroys the unity of interest and severs the joint tenancy.[263] Thus if land is granted to A, B and C as joint tenants for life, with remainder to C in fee simple, the mere existence of C's fee simple remainder does not destroy his tenancy for life. However, if A acquires C's fee simple, A's life estate merges in the fee simple and severs his joint tenancy for life (this will not of course affect the legal title which will continue to be held by A, B and C as joint tenants on a trust of land). It should be noted, however, that this method of severance requires that some estate different from the estate held in joint tenancy should be acquired. Thus, in the above example, if A instead releases his interest to B, B takes A's one-third share as a tenant in common, but his beneficial joint tenancy with C in the remaining two-thirds is not affected.

By alienation

8–053 If a joint tenant alienates his interest inter vivos,[264] his joint tenancy is severed and the person to whom the interest is transferred takes it as tenant in common with the other joint tenants, for he has no unity of title with them.[265] Such a severance does not affect the other joint tenants, who remain joint tenants inter se. Thus if A, B and C are joint tenants, and A sells his interest to X, X becomes beneficial tenant in common of one-third and B and C remain joint tenants of two-thirds. (This will again not affect the legal title which will continue to be held by A, B and C as joint tenants on a trust of land unless and until A, B and C convey it to B, C and X.) If B then dies, C alone profits by the jus accrescendi in equity, X

---

[259] *Goodman v Gallant* [1986] Fam. 106; *Roy v Roy* [1996] 1 F.L.R. 541.
[260] LPA 1925 s.36(2).
[261] LPA 1925 s.36(2).
[262] LPA 1925 s.36(2).
[263] *Wiscot's Case* (1599) 2 Co.Rep. 60b.
[264] Above, paras 8–001–8–004.
[265] *Partriche v Powlet* (1740) 2 Atk. 54; and see *Goddard v Lewis* (1909) 101 L.T. 528, collecting many of the authorities.

and C being left as tenants in common as to one-third and two-thirds respectively; but the legal title will be held by the survivors of whoever held it prior to B's death.

An involuntary alienation suffices, as where a joint tenant becomes bankrupt and his interest vests in his trustee in bankruptcy.[266] However, where the estate of a deceased person is insolvent, his administrator in bankruptcy cannot claim his share of a joint tenancy which was subject to the *jus accrescend* on his death.[267] Partial alienation is also enough, as where a joint tenant mortgages his beneficial interest or leases it, provided that the lease really does take effect as a lease rather than a licence.[268] A purported conveyance[269] or mortgage[270] of the entire property, effected by one joint tenant forging the signature of the other, severs the forger's joint tenancy and takes effect only as against his beneficial interest. However, this is not the case when the purported conveyance is in favour of a person who is aware of the forgery; such a conveyance is a total sham and has no effect whatever.[271]

By mutual agreement

Prior to the reform of the formalities rules governing contracts for the sale of land in 1989,[272] an agreement by a joint tenant to alienate his beneficial interest or simply to sever that interest severed his equitable joint tenancy if the agreement was specifically enforceable,[273] and even if it was not when it was made with the only other joint tenants instead of with a third party.[274] This remains the situation since the reform of those rules but such an agreement will in principle now only be valid if it is in writing and signed by all the parties to it.[275] However, it has now been held that estoppel interests take effect behind a constructive trust.[276] Consequently, if the other party to an oral agreement by a joint tenant to sever his interest acted to his detriment in reliance on that agreement, it appears that he would be able to enforce it on the basis that the joint tenant was estopped from denying the agreement and was therefore a constructive sub-trustee of the land for him. However, the agreement must be for an immediate severance, not a severance at some time in the future[277]; but the making of mutual wills, which are irrevocable in equity without the consent of the other party, does amount to a severance (those making mutual wills normally leave their assets to one another with a substitutionary gift to the same third party). Mere negotiations for an agreement have never been enough,[278] nor is a mere unilateral declaration of a desire to sever[279] unless it takes effect as a notice in writing under the Law of Property Act 1925.[280]

8–054

---

[266] Insolvency Act 1986 s.283; *Re Dennis* [1993] Ch. 72.

[267] *Re Palmer* [1994] Ch. 316.

[268] Below, paras 11–005 et seq.

[269] *Ahmed v Kendrick* (1988) 56 P. & C.R. 121.

[270] *First National Securities Ltd v Hegerty* [1985] Q.B. 850.

[271] *Penn v Bristol & West Building Society* [1996] 2 F.C.R. 729.

[272] Above.

[273] *Brown v Raindle* (1796) 3 Ves. 256.

[274] *Burgess v Rawnsley* [1975] Ch. 429. See [1976] C.L.J. 20 (D. J. Hayton).

[275] LP(MP)A 1989 s.2.

[276] *Yaxley v Gotts* [2000] Ch. 162 (party to oral contract for the sale of land estopped from denying its validity).

[277] *Harris v Goddard* [1983] 1 W.L.R. 203. *Edwards v Hastings* [1996] N.P.C. 87.

[278] *Gore v Carpenter* (1990) 60 P. & C.R. 456; but see *Burgess v Rawnsley* [1975] Ch. 429.

[279] See *Nielson-Jones v Fedden* [1975] Ch. 222, and contrast *Burgess v Rawnsley* [1975] Ch. 429.

[280] Below.

By a mutual course of dealing

8–055   A severance can be made by means of any course of dealing between all the joint tenants which sufficiently indicates an intention that they are to become tenants in common.[281] There has to be a course of dealing which shows that all concerned are treating their interests as being tenancies in common with immediate effect, as where the joint tenants authorise the trustees to pay one of the tenants his share.[282] The burden of proof lies on the person seeking to establish a severance,[283] and it is not enough merely to show that the joint tenants have engaged in lengthy negotiations about the possibility of one buying the other out,[284] or that the joint tenants of a house have converted it into maisonettes so that each can live separately,[285] or that partners have included the farmhouse and land which they hold as joint tenants in their partnership accounts.[286]

By homicide

8–056   Nobody can benefit in law by his crime.[287] Hence if one joint tenant is guilty of the murder or deliberate and violent manslaughter[288] of another joint tenant, the criminal is treated as having severed the joint tenancy and so he forfeits the interest which he would otherwise have taken by survivorship.[289] However, despite the severance, the Forfeiture Act 1982 gives the court the power to grant relief against forfeiture in cases of homicide other than murder[290] and has done so.[291] A survivor of a suicide pact is also within this principle but is entitled to relief in full.[292]

By notice in writing

8–057   This is the method created by the Law of Property Act 1925. "Where a legal estate (not being settled land) is vested in joint tenants beneficially, and any tenant desires to sever the joint tenancy in equity, he shall give to the other joint tenants a notice in writing of such desire", whereupon the parties concerned are to be treated in equity as if there had been an actual severance.[293] This provision is limited in its operation. Settled land is expressly excluded, thus preventing it becoming subject to a trust of land, and it appears to be confined to land, thus excluding pure personalty.[294] It plainly applies where A and

---

[281] *Williams v Hensman* (1861) 1 J. & H. 546 at 557; *Burgess v Rawnsley* [1975] Ch. 429 at 440, 447; *McDowell v Hirschfield Lipson & Rumney and Smith* [1992] 2 F.L.R. 126.

[282] *Williams v Hensman* (1861) 1 J. & H. 546.

[283] *Re Denny* [1947] L.J.R. 1029.

[284] *McDowell v Hirschfield Lipson & Rumney and Smith* [1992] 2 F.L.R. 126.

[285] *Greenfield v Greenfield* (1979) 38 P. & C.R. 570.

[286] *Barton v Morris* [1985] 1 W.L.R. 1257.

[287] See *b Hall* [1914] P.I.; *Re Pollock* [1941] Ch. 219.

[288] See *Re Pollock*; *Re Giles* [1972] Ch. 544; *Re Royce* [1985] Ch. 22.

[289] *Re K.* [1986] Ch. 180.

[290] Forfeiture Act 1982.

[291] *Re K* [1986] Ch. 180; *Re H* [1990] 1 F.L.R. 441.

[292] *Dunbar v Plant* [1998] Ch. 412.

[293] LPA 1925 s.36(2); *Harris v Goddard* [1983] 1 W.L.R. 203 at 209. *Grindal v Hooper* [1999] E.G.C.S. 150.

[294] *Nielson-Jones v Fedden* [1975] Ch. 222; but see below.

B hold the legal estate on trust for themselves jointly, but, read literally, not where they hold it on trust for themselves and others, or where other trustees hold it on trust for them. But the court may be able to read "vested in joint tenants beneficially" as being "vested in any persons for joint tenants beneficially", and so cure this strange omission. The suggestion[295] that joint tenancies of pure personalty could be severed in equity by a notice in writing before 1926 and consequently joint tenancies of both land and pure personalty still can be so severed would remove both these limitations but does not appear to be any acceptable way of doing so. A notice given to one but not all of the other joint tenants seems to be ineffective as having been given not to "the other joint tenants" but only to one of them.

No form for such a notice is prescribed. A notice which is posted is effective if the letter is delivered to the other joint tenant's last known abode or business address, even if he does not receive it[296] and a notice sent by registered post to one of these addresses is effective even if it is not delivered unless it is returned.[297] A writ or originating summons commencing legal proceedings, or an affidavit in the proceedings may suffice if a claim to an immediate interest in the property is asserted, even if the proceedings are not pursued.[298] However, a divorce petition which makes no immediate claim but prays for a property adjustment order to be made in the future is not enough.[299]

Operation of the present law

An example illustrating the present position may be useful. In 1997 X purported to convey land to A, B, C, D, and E in fee simple; all were of full age. The legal estate vested in A, B, C, and D on a trust of land; in equity, A, B, C, D and E were tenants in common if there were words of severance or if it was one of equity's special cases, but otherwise joint tenants. If they were joint tenants and A died, B, C, and D would then hold the legal estate on a trust of land for B, C, D and E as joint tenants; E would not automatically fill the vacancy at law, but could, of course, be appointed by the remaining trustees to be a new trustee in place of A. If B afterwards sold and transferred his interest to P, then B, C and D would continue to hold the legal estate but thereafter on trust for P as tenant in common of a quarter and C, D and E as joint tenants of three-quarters. If C then severed his joint tenancy (such as by agreement in writing with D and E), the legal estate would remain in B, C and D as before, on trust for P and C as tenants in common of one-quarter each, and D and E as joint tenants of half. On D's death, B and C would hold the legal estate on trust for P, C and E as tenants in common as to one-quarter, one-quarter and one-half respectively.

8–058

---

[295] *Burgess v Rawnsley* [1975] Ch. 429 at 440 per Lord Denning M.R.
[296] *Kinch v Bullard* [1999] 1 W.L.R. 423, applying LPA 1925 s.196(3).
[297] *Re 88 Berkeley Road, NW9* [1971] Ch. 648, applying LPA 1925 s.196(4).
[298] *Burgess v Rawnsley* [1975] Ch. 429 at 447.
[299] *Harris v Goddard* [1983] 1 W.L.R. 203.

SUMMARY OF KEY CASES

- *Goodman v Gallant* [1985] EWCA Civ 15, [1986] Fam. 106
- *Lloyds Bank Plc v Rosset* [1991] 1 A.C. 107
- *Gillett v Holt* [2001] Ch. 210
- *Stack v Dowden* [2007] 2 A.C. 432
- *Jones v Kernott* [2011] UKSC 53

FURTHER READING

- N. Hopkins, "The Trusts of Land and Appointment of Trustees Act 1996" [1996] Conv. 411
- "Constructive trusts and proprietary estoppel: the search for clarity and principle" [2009] Conv. 104
- M. Dixon, "The never-ending story—Co-ownership after Stack v Dowden" [2007] Conv. 456
- Law Commission, *Cohabitation: The Financial Consequences of Relationship Breakdown*, Report No.307, July 31, 2007
- M. Dixon, "To sell or not to sell: That is the Question" [2011] C.L.J. 579

Chapter 9

PROPRIETARY ESTOPPEL

CHAPTER SUMMARY

Proprietary estoppel is a form of equitable estoppel which affects or creates rights of property. It has developed out of the court of equity's jurisdiction to prevent unconscionable conduct. This chapter defines the doctrine, and explains when the courts will apply it and what remedy will be applied to give satisfaction to the claimant. Although there have been two House of Lords decisions on the doctrine in the last decade this is a developing area of law and there remain areas of uncertainty.

THE DOCTRINE

Traditional approach

The traditional approach of the judges has been that proprietary estoppels arise in three distinct situations, all governed by different rules: **9–001**

   (i)   where there has been an assurance by the owner of land ("O") that the claimant ("C") will have rights therein (the "imperfect gift" cases)[1];
   (ii) where O and C have consistently dealt with one another on the basis that O will acquire rights of some kind in C's land (the "common expectation" cases)[2]; and
   (iii) where O has stood by and allowed C to act to his detriment in the mistaken belief that C has rights over O's land (the "unilateral mistake" cases).[3]

Modern approach

Since 1976,[4] the traditional compartmentalised approach has been abandoned and the   **9–002**
courts have regarded these three situations as being governed by a single principle. They

---

[1]   *Dillwyn v Llewellyn* (1862) 4 De G.F. & J. 264; *Pascoe v Turner* [1979] 1 W.L.R. 431.
[2]   *Ramsden v Dyson* (1866) L.R. 1 H.L. 129 at 170 per Lord Kingsdown; *Inwards v Baker* [1965] 2 Q.B. 29.
[3]   *Ramsden v Dyson* (1866) L.R. 1 H.L. 129 at 140 per Lord Cranworth L.C.; *Willmott v Barber* (1880) 15 Ch.D. 96 at 105 per Fry J.
[4]   The date of the decision in *Taylors Fashions Ltd v Liverpool Victoria Trustees Co Ltd* (1976) [1982] 1 Q.B. 133N.

have adopted "a very much broader approach which is directed rather at ascertaining whether, in particular individual circumstances, it would be unconscionable for a party to be permitted to deny that which, knowingly or unknowingly, he has allowed or encouraged another to assume to his detriment than to inquiring whether the circumstances can be fitted within the confines of some preconceived formula serving as a universal yardstick for every form of unconscionable behaviour".[5] This broader approach has been developed into the principle that a proprietary estoppel requires:

(i)   an assurance or a representation by O;

(ii) reasonable reliance on that assurance or representation by C; and

(iii) some unconscionable disadvantage or detriment suffered by C.

These were referred to in *Thorner v Major* [2009] UKHL 18, as "the three main elements" of the doctrine.[6]

THE THREE MAIN ELEMENTS

Assurance or representation

9–003   O (or one of his predecessors in title[7]) must have given some encouragement to C to act in the way that he subsequently did. O's conduct may be active in that he has made an express assurance or representation to C. Or it may be passive in that he has stood silently by with knowledge that his own rights were more extensive than C believed them to be while C was acting on his mistaken belief by, for example, building on land not knowing that it was O's, or not knowing that O had a mortgage over it.[8]

In active encouragement cases it is unclear what degree of clarity the assurance or representation must have. The degree of clarity will have a bearing on whether it is reasonable for C to rely on it. In the leading case on this issue the House of Lords failed to give a clear answer. Lord Walker stated that the relevant assurance must be "clear enough" and that what amounts to sufficient clarity is hugely dependent on context. It must, however, be unambiguous and must appear to have been intended to be taken seriously. It must be a promise which one might reasonably expect to be relied upon by C. An offer of "financial security" will be too vague.[9] On the other hand a promise that C should inherit "the farm" was held to be sufficient, notwithstanding that the extent of the farm was liable to fluctuate from time to time.[10]

In passive encouragement cases C must normally prove that O knew that C had spent money[11] or had carried out or intended to carry out other detrimental acts[12] and that C was

---

[5]   *Taylors Fashions Ltd v Liverpool Victoria Trustees Co Ltd* [1982] 1 Q.B. 133N at 151–152 per Oliver J.

[6]   *Thorner v Major* [2009] UKHL 18 per Lord Walker at [29].

[7]   *Hopgood v Brown* [1955] 1 W.L.R. 213.

[8]   *Ramsden v Dyson* (1866) L.R. 1 H.L. 129; *Steed v Whitaker* (1740) Barn.Ch. 220; *Inwards v Baker* [1965] 2 Q.B. 29.

[9]   *Layton v Martin* [1986] 2 F.L.R. 227.

[10] *Thorner v Major* [2009] UKHL 18.

[11] *Swallow Securities Ltd v Isenberg* [1985] 1 E.G.L.R. 132.

[12] *Crabb v Arun District Council* [1976] Ch. 179.

acting under a mistaken belief that he had or would acquire an interest in or over O's land as O cannot be said to have encouraged a belief of which he is ignorant. [13]

Reasonable reliance on the assurance or representation

C must prove (i) that he relied on the assurance and (ii) that it was reasonable to do so.   **9–004**

Reliance

Whether C relied on O's assurance or representation is a question of fact but once an assurance or representation by O has been proved, it is presumed that C has relied on it and it is for O to rebut that presumption.[14]   **9–005**

Reasonableness

C's reliance on O's promise must be reasonable. [15] As stated above the question of whether C's reliance is reasonable may be closely related to the issue of whether the assurance is sufficiently clear. Consideration of this aspect will also overlap with consideration of whether O has acted unconscionably, since it will rarely be unconscionable for O to resile, when it was not reasonable for C to rely on the assurance. It may not be reasonable for C to rely on a representation where O makes clear that he may change his mind.[16] However, O cannot avoid liability by establishing that *he* did not intend C to rely on the assurances in question where it was reasonable for C to rely on them.[17]   **9–006**

It will not normally be reasonable for C to rely on representations made in "subject to contract" negotiations because both parties will understand that any assurances made will not be binding until a contract is executed.[18] Similarly in a commercial context where parties are negotiating a lease or a contract of sale it will not normally be reasonable for C to rely on any assurance made, as the parties will appreciate that it is necessary to have a contract in writing containing all the terms signed by both parties in order to comply with s.2 of the Law of Property (Miscellaneous Provisions) Act 1989.[19] Similarly if terms remain to be agreed, it may not be reasonable to rely on O's representations.[20]

Unconscionable disadvantage or detriment suffered by C

Detriment is not a narrow or technical concept. The detriment need not consist of the expenditure of money or other quantifiable financial detriment, so long as it is something   **9–007**

---

[13] *Brinnand v Ewens* (1987) 19 H.L.R 415.
[14] *Greasley v Cooke* [1980] 1 W.L.R. 1306.
[15] *Thorner v Major* [2009] UKHL 18.
[16] *Gillett v Holt* [2001] Ch. 210 at 227A 230A.
[17] *Thorner v Major* [2009] UKHL 18.
[18] *Attorney General of Hong Kong v Humphreys Estate (Queen's Gardens) Ltd* [1987] A.C. 114.
[19] *Yeoman's Row Management Ltd v Cobbe* [2008] UKHL 55.
[20] *Herbert v Doyle* [2010] EWCA Civ 1095.

substantial.[21] The issue of whether C has suffered a detriment is to be judged at the moment when O seeks to go back on the assurance.[22]

The most obvious form of detriment is where C has incurred expenditure, such as by spending money on improving property which in fact belongs to O. Thus C may have built a house on O's land[23]; or C may have built a mill on his own land in the belief that he would be able to take water for it from O's canal[24]; or C may have renovated and managed a property which he believed belonged to O on the basis that he would receive the two flats on the ground floor.[25]

Other acts of financial detriment also suffice. C may have sold part of his land, making the rest land-locked, in the belief that he would have an easement of way to the land-locked land over O's land[26]; or C may have given up his job and his council house to go and live near his father in a house provided by the father, believing that it would become C's[27]; or C, having initially been paid as a housemaid, may subsequently have cared for the members of the family without receiving wages on the basis of assurances that she could remain in the house for the remainder of her life.[28]

In another case C, who had helped her mother and her stepfather throughout her adult life without remuneration on the basis that she would inherit her stepfather's property, had incurred sufficient detriment to receive his entire estate when he died intestate.[29] And C, who had worked for O, a gentleman farmer, for almost 40 years on the basis of assurances that the bulk of the farming business would be left to him in O's will, had incurred sufficient detriment to be able to claim one of O's farms outright as financial compensation for the loss of other farms, once O attempted to transfer all his assets to a third party.[30]

In considering what detriment C has suffered it is always necessary to take into account any countervailing benefit C has received from O. Thus C's enjoyment of O's property rent-free has been held to outweigh any detriment he may have incurred in expending money.[31] But the court must make a broad enquiry and the fact that C may have derived considerable, permanent social and financial benefit from his relationship with O does not preclude a finding of detriment.[32] C must have prejudiced himself by acting to his detriment. It is for O to prove that C's detrimental acts have not caused C to suffer unconscionable disadvantage.[33]

In passive encouragement cases C must normally prove that O knew that the property was his. If O wrongly thought that the property belonged to C then he has not acquiesced and his conduct is not unconscionable.[34] It will normally not be unconscionable for

---

[21] *Gillett v Holt* [2001] Ch. 210 at 232D–E.
[22] *Gillett v Holt*, above.
[23] *Inwards v Baker* [1965] 2 Q.B. 29.
[24] *Rochdale Canal Co v King (No.2)* (1853) 16 Beav. 630.
[25] *Yaxley v Gotts* [2002] Ch. 162.
[26] *Crabb v Arun D.C.* [1976] Ch. 179.
[27] *Jones v Jones* [1977] 1 W.L.R. 438; and see *Pascoe v Turner* [1979] 1 W.L.R. 431.
[28] *Greasley v Cooke* [1980] 1 W.L.R. 1306.
[29] *Re Basham (dec'd)* [1986] 1 W.L.R. 1498.
[30] *Gillett v Holt* [2001] Ch. 210. at 237–238. See also similar facts in *Thorner v Major* above.
[31] *Lee-Parker v Izzet (No.2)* [1972] 1 W.L.R. 775.
[32] *Gillett v Holt* [2001] Ch. 210
[33] *Greasley v Cooke* [1980] 1 W.L.R. 1306.
[34] *Armstrong v Sheppard & Short Ltd* [1959] 2 Q. B. 384.

a minor in a passive encouragement case to later assert his right because there is no true acquiescence,[35] although the position may be different if the minor acted fraudulently.[36]

NO BAR TO EQUITABLE RELIEF

In order to make out a case for proprietary estoppel there must be no bar to equitable relief **9–008** being given to C.

The doctrine of estoppel may not be invoked to render valid a transaction which the legislature, on grounds of general public policy, has enacted is to be invalid or void.[37] However, it has been held that failure to comply with s.2 of the Law of Property (Miscellaneous Provisions) Act 1989 will not always be a bar to a claim for proprietary estoppel, as s.2(5)(c) expressly provides that the existence or operation of a constructive trust would not be affected by the application of that section and a constructive trust is a remedy which the court may impose to satisfy a claim in proprietary estoppel.[38] The exact circumstances within which proprietary estoppel will afford a remedy to a party to a contract for the sale of land which would otherwise be void for non-compliance with s.2 are uncertain. Context is important. The courts are less likely to allow circumvention of s.2 in a commercial context and/or where the parties intend to proceed by way of contract than in a familial or other informal context.[39] Where the parties expected to proceed by way of formal contract it may be that only where O has expressly or impliedly promised not to rely on the lack of formality that proprietary estoppel will succeed.[40]

Where C's interest should have been protected by registration but has not been, C can claim the benefit of a proprietary estoppel in the obviously exceptional situation where both O and C have wrongly proceeded on the basis that C's interest was not registrable.[41] However, no proprietary estoppel can protect C against a third party from his failure to register an interest which was clearly registrable.[42]

It may also be inequitable for C to be given relief because of his own misconduct,[43] as where he attempts to support his claim by putting forward what he knows to be wholly false particulars of his expenditure on O's property[44] or where O's assurances are only made on the basis of C's dishonest conduct towards O.[45]

Another implication of this rule is that as statutory body cannot act outside its powers, relief will be barred if it would fetter the statutory discretion or statutory duty of a statutory body.[46]

---

[35] *Duke of Leeds v Earl of Amherst* (1846) 2 Ph. 117 at 123.

[36] *Savage v Foster* (1723) 9 Mod. 35.

[37] *Yaxley v Gotts* [2000] Ch. 162 per Clark L.J. at 181.

[38] *Yaxley v Gotts* [2000] Ch. 162.

[39] See the reasoning in *Cobbe v Yeoman's Row Management Ltd* [2008] UKHL 55 in relation to the commercial context and *Thorner v Major* [2009] UKHL 18 in relation to an informal context.

[40] *Kinane v Mackie-Conteh* [2005] EWCA Civ 45.

[41] *Taylors Fashions Ltd v Liverpool Victoria Trustees Co Ltd* [1982] Q.B. 133N (option to renew a lease which, prior to *Beelsy v Hallwood Estates* [1960] 1 W.L.R. 549, was generally thought not to be registrable).

[42] *Lloyds Bank Plc v Carrick* [1996] 4 All E.R. 630 (estate contract—unregistered land).

[43] See *Williams v Staite* [1979] Ch. 291 at 299, 300.

[44] *J. Willis & Son v Willis* [1986] 1 E.G.L.R. 62.

[45] *Murphy v Rayner* [2011] EWHC 1 (Ch).

[46] *Chalmers v Pardoe* [1963] 1 W.L.R. 677; *Western Fish Products Ltd v Penwith D.C.* [1981] 2 All E.R. 204 (town planning).

SATISFACTION OF THE EQUITY

9–009   Where an equity is established, the next question which has to be considered is the extent of the equity.[47] The maximum extent of the equity arising from proprietary estoppel is that of the belief or expectation of C that O encouraged: C will not be given more than that.[48] The court has a wide discretion as to the remedy and will analyse the minimum equity to do justice.[49] The minimum equity does not always mean satisfying the belief or expectation of C that O encouraged, as the court may as an alternative order payment of money to compensate C for any detriment he has suffered. Whether it is appropriate to give effect to C's expectation or to award compensation is highly dependent on context.[50] The court will consider the proportionality of the detriment suffered by C compared to the expectation encouraged by O[51] and the compensation may be significantly less than the value of the expectation encouraged by O.[52]

Where the terms of a proposed lease or contract have been agreed, C and O probably regarded the expected benefit and the accepted detriment as being proportionate and the court is more likely to vindicate C's expectation.[53] It can even extend to interlinked transactions. Thus, where C and O arranged that O would buy C's building and that C would erect a new building on O's land, which he duly did, O was compelled to purchase C's building.[54] Difficulties may arise where O and C have agreed what C is to obtain but not the nature of his interest. An agreement that C was to receive the ground floor of a building could have been an agreement for the grant either of a freehold or of a long lease; C claimed the latter and was awarded a lease for 99 years rent-free.[55]

The remedy will not correspond with the belief or expectation of C that O encouraged if that would overcompensate C. Thus no order was made satisfying C's expectation that he would be able to live in a house for the rest of his lifetime when an order to that effect would have made C a tenant for life under the Settled Land Act 1925 with all the powers (including the power of sale) conferred on a tenant for life by that Act.[56] However, the parties could have avoided any risk of this by substituting a lease at a nominal rent determinable on death[57] and, since the enactment of the Trusts of Land and Appointment of Trustees Act 1996, a person in C's position will have no such powers anyway unless the land is already settled under the Settled Land Act 1925 because his interest will take effect behind a trust of land.[58]

The cases show the wide range of remedies employed by the court. At one extreme, it

---

[47]   *Crabb v Arun District Council* [1976] Ch.179 at 193 per Scarman L.J.
[48]   *Dodsworth v Dodsworth* [1973] E.G.D. 233.
[49]   *Crabb v Arun DC* above.
[50]   *Jennings v Rice* [2003] 1 P. & C. R. at [42]–[52] per Walker L.J.
[51]   *Jennings v Rice* [2003] 1 P. & C. R. at [50] per Walker L.J.
[52]   *Jennings v Rice* [2003] 1 P. & C.R. 100; *Wayling v Jones* (1993) 69 P. & C.R. 170.
[53]   *Att-Gen. of Hong Kong v Humphreys Estate (Queen's Gardens) Ltd* [1987] A.C. 114; *J.T. Developments Ltd v Quinn* (1990) 62 P. & C.R. 33.
[54]   *Salvation Army Trustee Co Ltd v West Yorkshire Metropolitan CC* (1981) 41 P. & C.R. 179.
[55]   *Yaxley v Gotts* [2000] Ch. 162.
[56]   *Dodsworth v Dodsworth* [1973] E.G.D. 233 at 236, pointing out that this had been overlooked in *Inwards v Baker* [1965] 2 Q.B. 29. See above, para.7–006 for the Settled Land Act 1925.
[57]   *Griffiths v Williams* [1977] E.G.D. 919 at 925, pointing out what had been overlooked in *Dodsworth v Dodsworth* [1973] E.G.D. 233.
[58]   Above, para.7–017.

may suffice simply to dismiss any proceedings by O for possession[59] or to grant an injunction, such as restraining O from obstructing C's improved ancient lights.[60] At the other extreme, O may be ordered to convey his land to C gratuitously, as where C has built a house[61] or carried out improvements[62] on land which O had ineffectually given to him. O has also been ordered to grant lesser interests to C, such as leases,[63] easements[64] and rights of occupation.[65]

Monetary compensation has also been ordered, ranging from the return of the sums expended by C[66] through the value of the interest which C expected to receive with interest thereon[67] to the sum which C had to pay in order to acquire from a third party the strip of land on which his building was encroaching.[68] Grants of a right in or a right to occupy land have also been combined with grants of monetary compensation. Thus C has been required to pay a reasonable purchase price for O's property after deducting the amount expended on improvements.[69] On the other hand, assurances that the bulk of O's farming business would be left to C in O's will were given effect to by granting C both one of O's farms outright and financial compensation for the loss of the others.[70]

In the exercise of its wide discretion, the court does not restrict itself to the circumstances which initially gave rise to the equity or to the amount of C's expenditure, but considers the whole of the circumstances down to the time of the action. Thus where proprietary estoppel would otherwise have entitled C to an easement on paying a reasonable sum for that right, prolonged obstructive conduct by O may result in C being awarded the easement without payment.[71] Again, where O knew that C's improvements to the house in which she lived were being made in the belief that O had given it to her, the circumstances justified an order that O should convey the house to C gratuitously, even though C's expenditure had been relatively modest.[72] On the other hand, where C had expected to be allowed to stay rent-free in a house for the rest of his life, his minimum equity was held to have expired where he had lived there rent-free for over 18 years, his use of the property was minimal, he was in employment and capable of paying for his own accommodation, and O was in financial difficulties and had an urgent need for the property herself.[73] In this field, equity is both inventive and flexible.

---

[59] *Inwards v Baker* [1965] 2 Q.B. 19; *Williams v Staite* [1979] Ch. 291.
[60] *Cotching v Bassett* (1862) 32 Beav. 101.
[61] *Dillwyn v Llewelyn* (1862) 4 De G.F. & J. 517, where O had died.
[62] *Pascoe v Turner* [1979] 1 W.L.R. 431.
[63] *Griffiths v Williams* (1977) 248 E.G. 947.
[64] *Crabb v Arun District Council* [1976] Ch. 179.
[65] *Greasley v Cooke* [1980] 1 W.L.R. 1306; *Matharu v Matharu* [1994] 2 F.L.R. 597.
[66] *Dodsworth v Dodsworth* [1973] E.G.D. 233 (as a pre-condition of O obtaining an order for possession); *Unity Joint Stock Mutual Banking Association v King* (1858) 25 Beav. 72 (lien on O's property for his outlay).
[67] *Wayling v Jones* (1995) 69 P. & C.R. 170.
[68] *Wilson Bowden Properties v Milner* (1997) New Law Digest, Property Communication 128.
[69] *Lim Teng Huan v Ang Swee Chuan* [1992] 1 W.L.R. 113.
[70] *Gillett v Holt* [2001] Ch. 210 at 237–238.
[71] *Crabb v Arun D.C.* [1976] Ch. 179.
[72] *Pascoe v Turner* [1979] 1 W.L.R. 431.
[73] *Sledmore v Dalby* (1996) 72 P. & C.R. 196.

PROPRIETARY ESTOPPEL AND THIRD PARTIES

9–010   Where O is ordered to convey his land to C, C will become its registered proprietor. Where, on the other hand, C's equity has been satisfied by the grant of a lesser interest in land, that interest will have to be protected in the appropriate way if it is to be enforceable against third parties.

Prior to any such satisfaction, C's interest might be thought to be enforceable only against O and his personal representatives. However, it has been held that an interest which is protected by proprietary estoppel is also capable of binding the successors in title of the party originally estopped.[74] It has also been stated that this decision is binding on all courts other than the House of Lords.[75] Further, the Land Registration Act 2002 specifically so provides,[76] thus resolving any challenge in the case of registered land and indicating the likely outcome of any challenge in the case of unregistered land.

However, that does not mean that an interest protected by proprietary estoppel will bind the whole world. Estoppel interests in unregistered land are governed by the equitable doctrine of notice.[77] Unless C has an interest which overrides registration[78] by virtue of his actual occupation of the land[79] or his open exercise and enjoyment of an easement,[80] estoppel interests in registered land require protection on the register.

Further, an interest which is protected by proprietary estoppel is just as capable of being overreached as it would be if it had been formally created. Consequently, if C has a family interest, such as a right of occupation, his interest will not be binding as against any purchaser or mortgagee who acquires O's property under an overreaching conveyance.[81] However, a commercial interest held by C, such as a lease or an easement, would not have been capable of being overreached if it had been formally created and, if otherwise enforceable against O's successors in title, will continue to be binding notwithstanding the fact that they have acquired O's property under an overreaching conveyance.

SUMMARY OF KEY CASES

- *Taylor Fashions Ltd v Liverpool Victoria Friendly Society* [1979] EWHC Ch1, [1982] 1 Q.B. 133
- *Yaxley v Gotts* [1999] EWCA Civ 3006, [2000] Ch. 162
- *Gillett v Holt* [2000] EWCA Civ 66, [2001] Ch. 210

---

[74] *Hopgood v Brown* [1955] 1 W.L.R. 213; *Inwards v Baker* [1965] 2 Q.B. 29; *E.R. Ives Investment Ltd v High* [1967] 2 Q.B. 379.

[75] *Lloyds Bank Plc v Carrick* [1996] 4 All E.R. 630.

[76] LRA 2002 s.116.

[77] *E.R. Ives Investment Ltd v High* [1967] 2 Q.B. 379.

[78] Above, paras 5–022 et seq.

[79] LRA 2002 Sch.1 para.3, Sch.3 para.3.

[80] *Celsteel Ltd v Alton House Holdings Ltd* [1986] 1 W.L.R. 512; [1985] 1 W.L.R. 204; *Thatcher v Douglas* (1996) 146 N.L.J. 282.

[81] *Birmingham Midshires Mortgage Services Ltd v Sabherwal* (2000) 80 P. & C.R. 256.

- *Yeoman's Row Management Ltd v Cobbe* [2008] UKHL 55
- *Thorner v Major* [2009] UKHL 18
- *Crabb v Arun DC* [1976] Ch. 179 (CA)
- *Joyce v Epsom and Ewell BC* [2012] EWCA Civ 1398

FURTHER READING

- M. Dixon, "Invalid contracts, estoppels and constructive trusts" [2005] Conv. 247
- B. McFarlane, *The Structure of Property Law*, (Hart Publishing, 2008) pp.443–474
- B. McFarlane, "Proprietary Estoppel and Third Parties After the Land Registration Act 2002" (2003) 62 C.L.J. 661
- M. Dixon, "Proprietary Estoppel and Formalities in Land Law and the Land Registration Act 2002: A Theory of Unconscionability" in *Modern Studies in Property Law: Vol 1*, E Cooke, ed. (Hart Publishing, 2001)
- M. Dixon, "Defining and confining estoppel" (2010) 30 L.S.
- E. Cooke, "Estoppel and the protection of expectations" (1997) 17 L.S. 258
- P. Milne, "Proprietary estoppel in a procrustean bed" (2011) M.L.R. 412
- "Proprietary estoppel: A return to principle?" [2009] Conv. 260
- Prof. John Mee "Proprietary estoppel and inheritance: Enough is enough?" [2013] Conv. (4) 280

Chapter 10

LICENCES

CHAPTER SUMMARY

The main legal controversies in relation to licences have been the extent to which they are revocable by the licensor and whether they bind third parties.

In essence, a licence is a mere permission given by the occupier of land to a person to do **10–001** something on that land which would otherwise be a trespass.[1] The scope of licences is great. They range from a simple oral permission given to a boy to fetch his ball from the garden to an elaborate deed granting exclusive possession of a large building for an indefinite period which would have been a lease if the period had been definite.[2] At common law, most licences could be revoked at any time, though if the licensor did this in breach of contract he would be liable in damages. A licence created no interest in the land, so that if V sold his lodging house to P, the lodgers could not resist eviction by P, and their only remedy was to sue V for damages. Normally a licence gave no right to the exclusive possession of the land.

Although it is said that the licence creates no interest in the land it has been held that a licensee can maintain a possession action against a trespasser, even though the licensee has no estate in the land,[3] but the position is not beyond doubt.[4]

TYPES OF LICENCES

Some licences give the licensee the right to the exclusive occupation of the land. At one **10–002** point, this became increasingly common for flats and other dwellings where owners were seeking to avoid the occupier of the land obtaining statutory protection from eviction, which is available only to tenants and not to licensees.[5] However, the courts now ignore any provisions in the agreement between the parties which are pretences or shams.[6] Consequently,

---

[1] See *Thomas v Sorrell* (1673) Vaugh. 330 at 351.
[2] See below, para.11–024.
[3] *Manchester Airport Plc v Dutton* [2000] Q.B. 133.
[4] Note the discussion of this case in *Mayor of London v Hall* [2011] 1 W.L.R. 504, per Lord Neuberger at 515.
[5] Below, para.11–009.
[6] Below, 11–011.

where a person has exclusive occupation of the land, he will now only be a licensee if the other essentials of a lease or tenancy are not present.[7]

Other licences confer a right of occupation but not exclusive possession, as with lodgers and guests in a hotel.[8] There is also a wide range of miscellaneous licences, such as leave to use a concert hall for a few days[9]; permission to put pleasure boats on a canal[10]; permission to erect an advertisement hoarding or electrical sign[11]; the grant of the "front of the house rights" in a theatre, i.e. the exclusive right to supply refreshments and to use the refreshment rooms[12]; and permission to see a race or cinema performance.[13]

Four main categories of licence[14] require consideration: the first two are relatively straightforward, but the other two are more complex, especially as regards revocability and as to whether successors in title will be bound.

Bare licence

10–003   A bare licence is the simplest form of licence. It is a licence not granted for valuable consideration, such as a gratuitous permission to enter a house or cross a field. Even if it is granted by deed, the licensor can revoke it at any time without being liable in damages,[15] though the licensee will not become a trespasser until he has been given a reasonable time to withdraw.[16] He cannot resist the licensor's claim by denying the latter's title, as he will be estopped from doing this as long as he is in possession,[17] but thereafter he is free to do so.[18] A revocable licence is automatically revoked by the death of the licensor or by any disposition by him of his interest in the land.[19]

Licence coupled with an interest

10–004   A licence may be coupled with an interest in the land or chattels thereon. Thus rights to enter another's land to hunt and take away the deer killed, or to cut down a tree and remove it can both take effect as profits á prendre[20]; they consequently involve the grant of an interest in the land in question, the profit á prendre, and also a licence annexed to that interest to come onto the land.[21] The interest must be a recognised interest in property,[22] and it must have been validly created. Thus at law a right to take game or minerals, being

---

[7]   Below, 11–006.

[8]   Below, 11–010.

[9]   See *Taylor v Caldwell* (1863) 3 B. & S. 826.

[10]   *Hill v Tupper* (1863) 2 H. & C. 121; above, para.15–004

[11]   *Wilson v Tavener* [1901] 1 Ch. 578; *Walton Harvey Ltd v Walker and Homfrays Ltd* [1931] 1 Ch. 274.

[12]   *Frank Warr & Co Ltd v L.C.C.* [1904] 1 K.B. 713.

[13]   *Wood v Leadbitter* (1845) 13 M. & W. 838; *Hurst v Picture Theatres Ltd* [1915] 1 K.B.1.

[14]   This classification may not be exhaustive.

[15]   *Wood v Leadbitter* (1845) 13 M. & W. 838; *Aldin v Latimer Clark, Muirhead & Co* [1894] 2 Ch. 437.

[16]   *Minister of Health v Bellotti* [1944] K.B. 298.

[17]   *Terunnanse v Terunnanse* [1968] A.C. 1086; and see above, para.11–035.

[18]   *Government of the State of Penang v Beng Hong Oon* [1972] A.C. 425.

[19]   *Terunnanse v Terunnanse* [1968] A.C. 1086 at 1095.

[20]   See below, para.15–020.

[21]   See *Thomas v Sorrell* (1673) Vaugh. 331 at 351; *Wood v Leadbitter* (1845) 13 M. & W. 838 at 845.

[22]   See *Hounslow L.B.C. v Twickenham Garden Developments Ltd* [1971] Ch. 233 at 244, 254, doubting *Vaughan v Hampson* (1875) 33 L.T.15 ("interest" in attending a meeting).

a profit á prendre,[23] must have been created by deed or prescription[24] and properly registered, whereas no formalities are required for the grant of a right to take away chattels, such as felled timber or cut hay. Equity will give effect to a specifically enforceable agreement to grant an interest, so that a licence coupled with a profit á prendre granted merely in writing but for value may be protected by injunction.[25]

A licence[26] coupled with an interest is irrevocable[27] and also assignable, though only with the interest with which it is coupled. It binds successors in title to the land in the same way as that interest.

Contractual licence

A contractual licence is a licence granted for value, such as a ticket for the theatre or for a football match, or an agreement to house lodgers or hotel guests. The rights under such licences primarily depend on the terms of the contract. At common law, such licences were inherently revocable even where revocation would be a breach of contract: the power of revocation was not taken away by a contract not to exercise it. At common law, such licences created no interest in the land, and like other personal contracts they did not bind successors in title to that land. As will be seen below, each of these propositions has now been substantially modified. A contractual licence is not a separate entity from the contract conferring it but takes effect as part of it, according to its terms.[28]

10–005

Licence by estoppel

A licence by estoppel is a licence which the licensor is precluded by estoppel from revoking or otherwise failing to put into effect. There were a number of cases in the past where the courts satisfied a claim in proprietary estoppel by the grant of such a licence. Thus where at a licensor's request the licensee extended a jetty and erected a warehouse on the licensor's land, the licensor was estopped from revoking the licence.[29] Such a licence was held to be capable of binding a third party who took with notice.[30] That decision tends to blur the essential distinction between leases which create interests in land and licences which do not.[31] Licences by estoppel have probably had their day and it is likely that in future courts will satisfy claims in proprietary estoppel in other ways.[32]

10–006

---

[23] Below, para.15–020.

[24] *Duke of Somerset v Fogwell* (1826) 5 B. & C. 875.

[25] *Frogley v Earl of Lovelace* (1859) Johns. 333.

[26] *James Jones & Sons Ltd v Earl of Tankerville* [1909] 2 Ch. 440 at 442.

[27] *Muskett v Hill* (1836) 5 Bing. N.C. 694 at 707, 708.

[28] *Millennium Productions Ltd v Winter Garden Theatre (London) Ltd* [1946] 1 All E.R. 678, not affected in H.L. [1948] A.C. 173.

[29] *Plimmer v Mayor, etc. of the City of Wellington* (1884) 9 App.Cas. 699. See also *Inwards v Baker* [1965] 2 Q.B. 29.

[30] *Inwards v Baker* [1965] 2 Q.B. 29.

[31] *Ashburn Anstalt v Arnold* [1989] Ch. 1.

[32] See further *Megarry & Wade: The Law of Real Property* (London: Sweet & Maxwell), paras 16–006 and 34–022 for effect on third parties.

CREATION OF LICENCES

10–007   No formalities are required for the creation of a licence. It may arise not only from a docu-ment but also from the spoken word or the tacit acceptance of a state of affairs. But when a licence is coupled with an interest, such as a profit á prendre, that interest must comply with any requirements for its creation[33]; otherwise the creation of licences is free from formalities.

REVOCATION OF LICENCES

Bare licences

10–008   As has been seen above,[34] a bare licence is revocable at any time, either expressly or by the death of the licensor or by a disposition of the land.

Licences coupled with interests

10–009   As has also been seen above,[35] a licence coupled with an interest is irrevocable.[36]

Contractual licences

10–010   Where the parties intended that the contractual licences should not be able to be revoked in breach of contract then the licensee can enforce the contract. This is entirely a ques-tion of the true construction of the agreement between them.[37] Where this is found to be the case, the contractual licence will be capable of enforcement; an injunction will be granted to restrain a threatened revocation of the licence or the enforcement of a wrongful revocation,[38] and specific performance of the licence may be decreed.[39] An injunction to restrain a breach of contract may be granted to enforce a licence of very short duration (e.g. a day) where the licensor purports to revoke the licence.[40]

In the absence of an express agreement that a contractual licence should not be able to be revoked in breach of contract, the courts sometimes infer the existence of an agree-ment restricting the revocation of a licence, particularly where there is some informal family arrangement. Thus where a man brought a house as a home for himself, his mistress and their children, and the mistress gave up a rent controlled flat in order to move into the house, it was held that she had been given an implied contractual licence to remain in the house as long as the children were of school age and the house was reasonably needed to

---

[33] Below, 15–033.
[34] Below, 10–033.
[35] Above, 10–004.
[36] Above, 10–004.
[37] *Winter Garden Theatre (London) Ltd v Millenium Productions Ltd* [1948] A.C. 173; no such intention was found.
[38] *Millenium Productions Ltd v Winter Garden Theatre (London) Ltd* [1946] 1 All E.R. 678 at 685 (this conclusion was not affected by the subsequent appeal ([1948] A.C. 173).
[39] *Verrall v Great Yarmouth BC* [1981] Q.B. 202.
[40] See *Verrall v Great Yarmouth BC* [1981] Q.B. 202 where, however, the contract was specifically enforceable.

house her and them.[41] Again, where a mother bought a house for her son and his wife to occupy for £7 a week, and the son later left his wife, the court inferred that the couple had been granted a joint contractual licence determinable only for good reason, such as the wife taking another man to live with her in the house.[42] However, in these cases it is often difficult to say whether any contract can really be inferred, and if it is, what its terms are.[43] In such circumstances it is now better to rely on the more flexible doctrine of estoppel.[44]

A licence which has been acted on

There is a common law rule which is akin to but separate from proprietary estoppel to the effect that once a licence is given it cannot be revoked if it has been acted upon. Thus where a landowner gives permission to another to lay a sewer on his land, he may not revoke it once the sewer is laid.[45] The same result would usually be achieved by reliance on proprietary estoppel but it would seem that the common law rule applies even where the licensor is ignorant of his ownership of the land.[46]   **10–011**

Determination of licences by licensee

A licensee may determine his licence in accordance with its terms, or by abandoning it. No formalities are required for abandonment: it suffices if the licensee so conducts himself as to justify the licensor in acting on the assumption that the licence has been abandoned.[47]   **10–012**

TRANSMISSION OF BENEFIT

In general, the benefit of a licence is assignable unless the contrary appears from its nature or some provision in it. This is so even for bare licences,[48] though these may more readily indicate that they are not assignable (such as an invitation to tea, or to play tennis) than will most contractual licences or licences coupled with an interest.[49] A bare licensee probably cannot grant a sub-licence,[50] but for other licences this seems to depend on the nature and terms of the licence. It is possible to extend the benefit of a contractual licence under the Contracts (Rights of Third Parties) Act 1999.[51]   **10–013**

---

[41] *Tanner v Tanner* [1975] 1 W.L.R. 1346; contrast *Horrocks v Forray* [1976] 1 W.L.R. 230 (no licence).
[42] *Hardwick v Johnson* [1978] 1 W.L.R. 683; and see *Chandler v Kerley* [1978] 1 W.L.R. 693 (implied contractual licence determinable on reasonable notice: 12 months).
[43] See *Horrocks v Forray* [1976] 1 W.L.R. 230; *Chandler v Kerley* [1978] 1 W.L.R. 693.
[44] See, e.g. *Maharaj v Chand* [1986] A.C. 898.
[45] *Armstrong v Sheppard* [1959] 2 Q. B. 384.
[46] *Armstrong v Sheppard* [1959] 2 Q. B. 384 per Lord Evershed at 401.
[47] *Bone v Bone* [1992] E.G.C.S. 81.
[48] See *Mellor v Watkins* (1874) L.R. 9 Q.B. 400.
[49] See *Shayler v Woolf* [1946] Ch. 320.
[50] See *Goldsack v Shore* [1950] 1 K.B. 708 at 714.
[51] s.1.

TRANSMISSION OF BURDEN

Bare licences

10–014   As has been seen above,[52] the burden of a bare licence does not pass with the land[53]; on the contrary, it is automatically revoked if the licensor disposes of his interest in the land.[54]

Licences coupled with an interest

10–015   As has also been seen above,[55] the burden of a licence coupled with an interest will pass with the land in the same way as the burden of the interest will pass with it. Thus the burden of a licence coupled with a profit á prendre will pass with the land unless the profit requires protection against the purchaser in question and has not been protected in the appropriate way.[56]

Contractual licences

Principle

10–016   In principle, a contractual licence, like all other contracts, will bind the parties to it but will not bind third parties; the burden of the licence will not run with the land. Thus where A contracted to give B the right to fix posters to the flank walls of A's cinema for four years, but then sold the cinema to P before the four years had run, P took free from the licence, though A was liable to B for breach of his contract.[57]

Binding successors in title

10–017   For a time this basic position was altered by a line of cases beginning with *Errington v Errington*,[58] in which contractual licences were held to be binding on successors in title. In that case a father bought a house on mortgage, and allowed his son and daughter-in-law to live in it, promising to convey the house to them if they remained in occupation and paid all the instalments under the mortgage. Before they had done this the father died, leaving all his property (including the house) to his widow. She was held to be bound by the licence on the basis that it constituted an equitable interest in the unregistered land in question that would bind the whole world except a bona fide purchaser for value without notice.[59]

---

[52]   Above, para.10–003.
[53]   *Wallis v Harrison* (1838) 4 M. & W. 538; and see *Terunnanse v Terunnanse* [1968] A.C. 1086 at 1095.
[54]   *Terunnanse v Terunnanse* [1968] A.C. 1086 at 1095.
[55]   Above, para.10–004.
[56]   See below, para.15–033.
[57]   *King v David Allen & Sons, Billposting, Ltd* [1916] 2 A.C. 54; and see *Clore v Theatrical Properties Ltd* [1936] 3 All E.R. 483 ("front of house" rights: above, para.10–003).
[58]   [1952] 1 K.B. 290. See (1952) 68 L.Q.R. 337 (H.W.R. Wade).
[59]   *Errington v Errington* [1952] 1 K.B. 290 at 294, 298, 299.

No interest in land

It was right to hold that the licence bound the widow, either on the basis that it was also a **10–018** licence by estoppel and binding on her as such[60] or because it amounted to an estate contract[61] which was also binding on her.[62] However, it is now accepted that it was wrong to reach this conclusion on the grounds that a contractual licence is an interest in land.[63] The assertion that it created such an interest in land, made without regard to binding authorities to the contrary, now has the status of a heresy that has received its quietus,[64] like the so-called deserted wife's equity.[65]

When a licence will bind a successor

The circumstances in which a licence will bind a successor are limited to those cases where **10–019** the conscience of the successor in title is affected, so that it would be inequitable to allow him to deny the claimant's interest in the property.[66] In such cases the court will impose a remedial constructive trust. In relation to title to land, certainty is of prime importance, and neither inferences from slender material nor bare assertions will suffice to establish such a trust.[67] A licence is not given any greater efficacy, or made binding on a purchaser, merely because the land is sold "subject to" it. The circumstances would have to show that the transferee promised to honour the licence.[68] Where that is the case the circumstances of the sale, coupled with these words, may establish a constructive trust that binds the purchaser to give effect to the licence.[69] Thus where the trustees of an estate agreed to allow the widow of an employee to occupy her cottage rent free for her life, repairing it and cultivating the garden, and the trustees then sold it subject to her rights, and at a reduced price because of them, it was held that the purchaser was bound by a constructive trust to give effect to her rights, so that they could not evict her.[70]

---

[60] Above para.10–006.

[61] At that time an oral contract which had been part performed sufficed; above, para.6–002.

[62] She was not a purchaser for money or money's worth and so was bound by that contract despite its non-registration.

[63] *Ashburn Anstalt v Arnold* [1989] Ch. 1.

[64] *Ashburn Anstalt v Arnold* [1989] Ch. 1; *I.D.C. Group Ltd v Clark* [1992] 1 E.G.L.R. 187.

[65] See above, para.6–070.

[66] *Ashburn Anstalt v Arnold* [1989] Ch. 1 at 22, 25.

[67] *Ashburn Anstalt v Arnold* [1989] Ch. 1 at 24 (commenting on *D.H.N. Food Distributors Ltd v Tower Hamlets LBC* [1976] 1 W.L.R. 852), 26.

[68] *IDC Group Ltd v Clark* [1992] 1 E. G. L. R. 187 at 190 per Browne Wilkinson V.C.

[69] *Lyus v Prowsa Developments Ltd* [1982] 1 W.L.R. 1044; *Ashburn Anstalt v Arnold* [1989] Ch. 1 at 24, 25, disapproving *Binions v Evans* [1972] Ch. 359 at 368.

[70] *Binions v Evans* [1972] Ch. 359; *Ashburn Anstalt v Arnold* [1989] Ch. 1 at 23.

SUMMARY OF KEY CASES

- *Street v Mountford* [1985] A.C. 809
- *A.G. Securities v Vaughan* [1990] 1 A.C. 417
- *Antoniades v Villiers* [1990] 1 A.C. 417
- *Bruton v London and Quadrant Housing Trust* [2000] 1 A.C. 406
- *Winter Garden Theatre (London) Ltd v Millenium Productions Ltd* [1948] A.C. 173
- *Ashburn Anstalt v Arnold* [1989] Ch. 1

FURTHER READING

- G. Battersby, "Contractual and estoppel licenses as proprietary interests in land" [1991] Conv. 36

Chapter 11

NATURE AND CREATION OF LEASE

CHAPTER SUMMARY

Before considering leases and tenancies in detail, some mention will be made of their history and terminology. The chapter then looks at how leases are created and the formalities involved. The chapter proceeds to look at different types of tenancy and lastly at how they may be assigned. The chapter covers the perennial issue of the difference between licences and leases. It also looks at the requirement for certainty in relation to the duration of a leasehold term.

PART 1   INTRODUCTION

HISTORY

Leases

A lease, as generally understood today, is a document creating an interest in land for a fixed period of certain duration,[1] usually but not necessarily in consideration of the payment of rent. This has not always been so.

11–001

Leases for lives

The owner of a life estate in land was able to recover the land itself if he was dispossessed, whereas until the end of the fifteenth century a tenant for a term of years could not do so if he was dispossessed by someone other than his landlord. One result of this was that in early times it was a common practice for a lessee to take a lease of land for the duration of a specified number of lives, instead of for a specified term of years. Thus, instead of a lease for 99 years, a tenant would take a lease for the life of the survivor of X, Y and Z. The tenant had an estate *pur autre vie*, which, being an estate of freehold and classified as real property,[2]

11–002

---

[1] See above, para.2–006.
[2] *Weigall v Brome* (1833) 6 Sim. 99; above.

entitled him to recover the land if he was dispossessed. The disadvantage of the uncertainty of the period was outweighed by the advantages it gave to the tenant and sometimes to the landlord. The rent payable was usually fairly small, but a lump sum, technically known as a fine, was paid when the lease was granted. A further fine was payable when, on the dropping of the lives, the tenant exercised the right the lease invariably gave him to replace them and so extend the lease. If the lessor was a corporation such as a monastery or college, the fines were treated as income by the then members of the corporation, to the disadvantage of their successors. Leases for life finally lost their popularity when legislation in the first half of the nineteenth century compelled corporations to add such fines to their capital.[3] Nowadays a lease for life is converted into a 90-year determinable term.[4]

Leases for fixed terms of years

11–003   Leases for fixed terms of years were in the past used for more purposes than one. The usual type of lease is the occupational lease, where the tenant holds at a rent or in consideration of a fine, or both, and occupies the property himself, as his residence or as his place of business, or sub-lets it. This type of lease is dealt with in this chapter. In the past leases were granted as a mere conveyancing device without a fine and at no rent, in order to provide security for the payment of money. This was known as a mortgage by demise. This method of creating mortgages has not been possible since the Land Registration Act 2002 came into force.[5]

Statutory intervention

11–004   The modern tendency has been to enact legislation designed to protect tenants against their landlords. At common law, the matter was in general one of contract: provided a landlord did not contravene the terms of his bargain, he might at will evict his tenant, or under the threat of eviction secure his agreement to pay an increased rent of whatever amount he could exact. The two crucial matters in any scheme for protecting tenants are protection against eviction, and control of rent. Legislation has been piecemeal. Apart from some relatively mild provisions concerning agricultural land, beginning with the Agricultural Holdings (England) Act 1875, no real system of control existed until the first of the Rent Acts was enacted in 1915. There is little common design to be found in the various statutes: protection against eviction is provided by a wide variety of devices, and so is control of rent. There are three main categories, depending on the nature of the tenancy. They are:

(i)   business premises;
(ii) agricultural land; and
(iii) dwellings.

Full consideration of the numerous Acts which give security of tenure and/or rent protection in each of the above areas is beyond the scope of this book, but it is important to remember when

---

[3]   See Radcliffe, *Real Property*, 2nd edn (1928), p.28.
[4]   LPA 1925 s.149(6).
[5]   LRA 2002 s.23(1).

reading what follows that in many cases the common law rules set out below will be subject to a statutory overlay. By way of example contrary to the position at common law a business tenancy which is protected by the Landlord and Tenant Act 1954 will not necessarily terminate at the end of the term, it will, if certain conditions are fulfilled, continue by virtue of statute.

TERMINOLOGY

It is important to be familiar with the terms used in the law of leases. A lease is sometimes referred to as a "demise" and the premises in question as the "demised premises". The term "tenancy" is normally used for interests lasting for a relatively short period only, while "lease" usually indicates a more enduring interest. There is no hard-and-fast division, and in this chapter "lease" normally includes "tenancy". "Lease" and "term of years" are virtually synonymous terms today (before 1926 a term of years could only be regarded as one kind of lease, since leases for lives were by no means unknown but today they have nearly all disappeared[6]). "Lease" is often used interchangeably for the document and the "term of years" or "leasehold interest" created by it, although strictly it merely means the document.   **11–005**

The grantor of a lease is known as the lessor, the person to whom it is granted as the lessee. On the grant of a lease, the lessor retains a reversion, which he may assign. Similarly, the lessee may assign the lease, provided that this has not been prohibited. Instead of assigning the lease (i.e. transferring the property for the whole of the period for which it is held), the owner of the lease may grant a sub-lease (or underlease) for some shorter period, the parties to this sub-lease being known as the sub-lessor and sub-lessee respectively. Where the original lessor and original lessee have both assigned their interests, the new owners of the reversion and the lease are sometimes called the lessor and lessee, although it is better to keep these expressions for the original parties to the lease, and refer to the owners for the time being, whether original or by assignment, as the landlord and the tenant.

These expressions may be illustrated as follows:

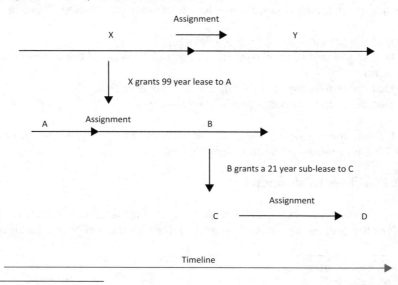

---
[6]   Below, para.11–031.

This diagram is the usual way of representing the following events. X grants a 99 years' lease to A and then assigns the reversion to Y. B takes an assignment of A's lease and grants a sub-lease to C for 21 years, C assigning his sub-lease to D. As to the 99 years' lease, X is the "lessor", Y is the "assignee of the reversion" or "landlord", and A the "lessee". B is in a dual position; as to the 99 years' lease, he is the "assignee" or "tenant" and as to the 21 years' lease he is the "sub-lessor" or "landlord". C is the "sub-lessee", and D the "assignee" of the sub-lease, or the "sub-tenant".

For the purpose of enforcing covenants in leases created before 1996, it is important to note that "privity of contract" exists between X and A and between B and C, whilst "privity of estate" potentially exists between Y and A, and then Y and B (having the same estates as were originally vested in X and A), and between B and D. However, "privity of estate" will only actually exist if all the relevant grants and assignments have been carried out with the formalities required by the common law rather than merely having taken effect in equity.[7] The enforcement of covenants in leases granted after 1995 is instead governed by the Landlord and Tenant (Covenants) Act 1995 ("the 1995 Act"). In the absence of contrary agreement, covenants in such leases are enforceable only as between current landlords and current tenants, so only as between Y and B and between B and D, and this is the case whether or not all the relevant grants and assignments have been carried out with the formalities required by the common law.[8]

PART 2   CREATION OF LEASES AND TENANCIES

ESSENTIALS OF A LEASE OR TENANCY

11–006   No lease or tenancy can be created unless four conditions are satisfied. They are:

(i) that the premises are sufficiently defined;
(ii) that the tenant has the right to exclusive possession of the premises during the term;
(iii) that the requirements as to duration are satisfied; and
(iv) that the proper formalities have been observed.

Under a tenancy there is nearly always a requirement to pay rent, but this is not actually essential.[9] The four heads will be considered in turn.

Premises sufficiently defined

11–007   A lease or tenancy can exist only in relation to defined premises, which is called the "demise", or the "demised premises". Thus a contract by the owner of a building to store

---

[7]   See below, para.11–018.
[8]   See below, para.11–021.
[9]   *Ashburn Anstalt v Arnold* [1989] Ch. 1; and see LPA 1925 s.205(1)(xxvii).

goods in them, though with liberty to change the rooms in which they are stored, at his convenience, cannot create a tenancy since no rights are given over any particular area.[10] But where the premises are clearly defined, the mere imposition of severe restrictions on the use that can be made of them will not negative a tenancy.[11]

Right to exclusive possession

In determining whether a tenancy has been granted, the essential question is whether there has been the grant of a right to occupy the premises and exclude all others including the landlord. This right is known as the right to exclusive possession of the premises. If there has, then provided the other requirements for a tenancy are satisfied, a tenancy will have been created.[12] It is the right to exclusive possession which distinguishes a lease from a licence, a distinction which was crucial under the Rent Act 1977 (and its precursors) as the former gave the tenant the protection of the Act and the latter did not.[13]

11–008

Right

The question is not whether it was intended to confer a right to exclusive possession, nor whether exclusive possession is in fact enjoyed, but whether a right to exclusive possession has in fact been given[14]; and this has to be determined from the substance of the transaction as a whole, though disregarding any provisions which are mere pretences or shams[15]; such provisions are inserted in order to try to prevent the occupier from obtaining statutory protection against eviction. "The manufacture of a five-pronged implement for manual digging results in a fork even if the manufacturer, unfamiliar with the English language, insists that he intended to make and has made a spade"[16] and "A cat does not become a dog because the parties have agreed to call it a dog".[17] What must be considered is what the parties have in fact done, and not what they intended, or pretended, to do. The courts will look at the substance and not the form. In *Berrisford v Mexfield Housing Co-operative Limited*[18] Lord Neuberger reiterated the reasoning in *Street v Mountford* that "the legal consequences of what the parties have agreed is a matter of law rather than dependant on what the parties intended."[19]

11–009

---

[10] *Interoven Stove Co Ltd v Hibbard* [1936] 1 All E.R. 263; and see *Wells v Kingston-upon-Hull Corp* (1875) L.R. 10 C.P. 402.

[11] *Joel v International Circus and Christmas Fair* (1920) 124 L.T. 459.

[12] *Street v Mountford* [1985] A.C. 809. The authorities are fully considered in Megarry's *Rent Acts* 11th edn (1989 and subsequent Supplements). For a recent analysis, see Bright, "*Street v Mountford* Revisited", in S. Bright (ed), *Landlord and Tenant Law: Past, Present and Future* (Oxford: Hart Publishing, 2006).

[13] "If exclusive possession at a rent for a term does not constitute a tenancy then the distinction between a contractual tenancy and a contractual licence of land becomes wholly unidentifiable." Per Lord Templemant in *Street v Mountford* [1985] A.C. 908 at 825.

[14] *Street v Mountford* [1985] A.C. 809.

[15] See below, para.11–011.

[16] *Street v Mountford* [1985] A.C. 809 at 819.

[17] *Antoniades v Villiers* [1990] 1 A.C. 417 at 444.

[18] [2011] UKSC 52.

[19] [2011] UKSC 52 at [17].

Exclusive possession

11–010   The right must be to "exclusive" possession, entitling the tenant to exclude all others (including the landlord) from the premises during the term.[20] Lodgers are not tenants, because the owner and his staff have unrestricted access to the room or rooms to provide attendance or services, and although the lodger has the right to be there he cannot call the place his own.[21] The same applies to occupants of retirement or nursing homes,[22] a local authority's hostel for homeless men,[23] and hotel rooms and bed-sitting rooms, or other places where no one else is entitled to live, but where the grantor retains control of the premises.[24] On the other hand, the fact that bathroom and lavatory facilities are shared with other persons does not prevent the occupier from having exclusive possession of the room or rooms that he occupies provided he can exclude all others from those premises during the term.[25] In technical terms, his lease of those premises will be coupled with an easement or a licence to use the bathroom and lavatory. The same would be true of shared kitchen facilities. However, in the context of whether or not the occupier has statutory protection from eviction, shared kitchen facilities,[26] but not shared bathroom and lavatory facilities,[27] prevent his accommodation from being a dwelling; but the fact that he has no cooking facilities and never eats there does not have this effect[28] nor does the fact that the premises have no bed, provided that he does normally sleep there.[29]

Pretences or shams

11–011   In determining whether or not a tenancy has been granted, the court will ignore any provisions in the agreement which are mere pretences or shams seeking to negative a tenancy.[30] Thus provisions in a "licence" to occupy a small room which negated any right to exclusive possession, allowed the licensor (who retained a set of keys) to use and authorise others to use the room, and conferred no right to occupy the room from 10.30 until noon each day have been held to be mere pretences which did not prevent a tenancy arising.[31] Again, where a cohabiting couple simultaneously made separate agreements to occupy a small flat on terms that they had no exclusive possession and that the use of the flat was to be in common with the landlord and others authorised by him, the two agreements, being interdependent, were held to make the couple the joint holders of a lease.[32] But independ-

---

[20]   *Street v Mountford* [1985] A.C. 809.
[21]   *Street v Mountford* [1985] A.C. 809 at 818.
[22]   *Abbeyfield (Harpenden) Society Ltd v Woods* [1968] 1 W.L.R. 374.
[23]   *Westminster City Council v Clarke* [1992] 2 A.C. 288.
[24]   *Luganda v Services Hotels Ltd* [1969] 2 Ch. 209 at 219; *Esso Petroleum Co Ltd v Fumegrange Ltd* [1994] 2 E.G.L.R. 90; *National Car Parks Ltd v Trinity Development Co (Banbury) Ltd* [2001] EWCA Civ 1686. [2002] 2 P. & C.R. 18.
[25]   *Westminster City Council v Clarke* [1992] 2 A.C. 288.
[26]   *Neale v Del Soto* [1945] K.B. 144.
[27]   *Neale v Del Soto* [1945] K.B. 144; *Westminster City Council v Clarke* [1992] 2 A.C. 288.
[28]   *Uratemp Ventures Ltd v Collins* [2001] 3 W.L.R. 806.
[29]   *Uratemp Ventures Ltd v Collins* [2001] 3 W.L.R. 806; see S. Bright [2002] C.L.J. 146.
[30]   *Street v Mountford* [1985] A.C. 809 at 825; *A.G. Securities v Vaughan* [1990] 1 A.C. 417 at 462.
[31]   *Aslan v Murphy (No.1)* [1990] 1 W.L.R. 766; and see *Street v Mountford* [1985] A.C. 809 at 825.
[32]   *Antoniades v Villiers* [1990] 1 A.C. 417. But consider *Mikeover Ltd v Brady* (1989) 21 H.L.R. 513 (no joint tenancy as no joint obligation to pay the rent: *sed quaere*).

ent agreements made at different times and on different terms which gave four persons the exclusive right to use a flat in common with each other made them mere licensees; and, lacking the four unities,[33] they could not in any case have been joint tenants.[34]

Status of landlord

It does not even matter that the grantor of the right had no title to grant a lease if, as between himself and the grantee, he is estopped from denying the existence of a right to exclusive possession. In *Bruton v London & Quadrant Housing Trust* [2000] 1 A.C. 406 the House of Lords held that if the grantor is a mere licensee but enters into a contract which gives the grantee the right to exclusive possession for a term, there will be a lease, albeit a lease which is not capable of binding third parties.   **11–012**

Exceptions

The intention to create a tenancy is negatived if the parties did not intend to enter into legal relationships at all (perhaps in a family situation), or where the relationship between the parties was that of vendor and purchaser, or employer and service occupier. The intention of the parties is important in deciding whether or not they intended to enter into legal relations, or whether the transaction was a mere family arrangement or act of friendship or generosity.[35]   **11–013**

Requirements as to duration

The general nature of an estate less than freehold has already been considered,[36] and details of the requisite duration of each particular type of lease or tenancy are set out below.[37] A lease cannot be for an uncertain period such as the duration of a war.[38]   **11–014**

Requisite formalities and legal issues

To create a legal estate after 1925, a lease or tenancy must not only grant a term of years absolute within s.1(1) of the Law of Property Act 1925[39] but must also be made with the proper formalities.   **11–015**

Leases and tenancies

A lease cannot create a legal estate unless it is made by deed.[40]   **11–016**
But there is an exception for a lease which:

---

[33] See above, para.8–005.
[34] *A.G. Securities v Vaughan* [1990] 1 A.C. 417.
[35] *Street v Mountford* [1985] A.C. 809 at 826.
[36] Above, para.2–001.
[37] Below, para.11–024.
[38] Below, para.11–025.
[39] Above, paras 4–016 et seq.
[40] LPA 1925 ss.52(1), 205(1)(ii), (xxiii).

    (i) takes effect in possession (i.e. starts immediately);

    (ii) is for a term not exceeding three years, whether or not the lessee is given power to extend the term; and

    (iii) is at the best rent reasonably obtainable without taking a fine (i.e. a premium).[41]

If all three conditions are complied with, a legal lease or tenancy can be created either orally or by writing which does not satisfy the requirements of a deed.

Contracts for leases and tenancies

11–017   Since September 26, 1989,[42] the general rules has been that a contract to grant a lease or tenancy is void unless it is actually made in writing and signed by all the parties.[43] However, contracts for leases or tenancies within the above exception are also exempt from this requirement,[44] and so may be made either orally or by writing which does not satisfy this requirement.

Requisite formalities and equitable leases

Informal lease void at law

11–018   A lease which did not satisfy the above requirements was void at law and passed no legal estate. However, although at law the lease was ineffective to create any tenancy, a tenancy at law might arise independently of the lease. For if the tenant took possession with the landlord's consent, a tenancy at will arose; and as soon as rent was paid and accepted, the tenancy at will was converted into a yearly or other periodic tenancy (depending on the way the rent was paid[45]), on such of the terms of the lease as were consistent with the periodic tenancy created. Thus if in 1920 a lease for 99 years was granted orally or merely in writing, the largest estate which the tenant could claim in a court of law was usually a yearly tenancy; and his claim to this depended not on the lease but upon his possession and the payment and acceptance of rent.

Effect as contract

11–019   Although such a lease itself failed to create any legal estate, it was not entirely ineffective, for it might be treated as a contract to grant the lease. A lease is clearly distinct from a contract to grant a lease: the difference is between "I hereby grant you a lease" and "I hereby agree that I will grant you a lease". Nevertheless, both law and equity concurred in treating an imperfect lease as a contract to grant a lease, provided it was made for value and was sufficiently evidenced in writing, or, so far as equity was concerned, was supported

---

[41]   LPA 1925 ss.52(1), (2)(d), 54(2). The Localism Act 2011 s.156 has created further exceptions to the categories of tenancies excluded from the general rule. See also LPA 1925 s.205(1)(xxiii) for the definition of "fine".

[42]   For the pre-existing law, see above, para.6–002.

[43]   LP(MP)A 1989 s.2; see above, para.6–005.

[44]   LP(MP)A 1989 s.2(5)(a).

[45]   *Martin v Smith* (1874) L.R. 9 Ex. 50; below, para.11–027.

by a sufficient act of part performance.[46] Today, the requirements of evidence in writing or part performance have been replaced by a requirement that the lease should actually be in writing and have been signed by all the parties.[47] The attitude of equity was particularly important, for under the doctrine of *Parker v Taswell*[48] equity would first treat an imperfect lease as a contract to grant the lease, and then order specific performance of that contract.[49] Once the actual lease had been granted in pursuance of the decree of specific performance, the position of the parties was the same for the future as if the lease had been a legal lease granted by deed in the first place.

Walsh v Lonsdale[50]

The rights of the parties under an imperfect lease were thus clear whenever specific performance had been decreed. What was not so clear was the position if, as was far more often the case, no decree of specific performance had been granted but the parties were entitled to obtain one. In equity, the principle is "equity looks on that as done which ought to be done", so that the parties were treated as if the lease had been granted. But there was no such principle at law, and, indeed, it would have been strange if the positive requirements of statute could have been so easily circumvented. Yet equity might intervene to restrain the parties from exercising their legal rights in opposition to their equitable obligations, and the Judicature Act 1873[51] provided that where the rules of law and equity conflicted, the rules of equity should prevail. Accordingly, in *Walsh v Lonsdale*[52] it was held that the relationship of the parties was the same as if the lease had actually been granted.

11–020

In that case L agreed in writing to grant by a deed a lease of a mill to T for seven years, one of the terms being that T should on demand pay a year's rent in advance. No deed was executed, but T was let into possession and for a year and a half paid rent quarterly, although not in advance. L then demanded a year's rent in advance, and on T's refusal to pay, exercised his right to enforce payment by distress (distress is the right of a landlord to enter the leased premises and enforce payment of any rent which is due by seizing and selling enough of any goods that are found there[53]).

T then brought an action for damages for wrongful distress, and for specific performance of the agreement. T contended that distress was a legal, and not an equitable, remedy, and that as at law he was only a yearly tenant with no obligation to pay rent in advance, L could not distrain for the rent.[54] It was held, however, that since the distress would have been legal had the lease agreed upon been granted by deed, and since equity treated the parties as if this had been done, the distress was lawful in equity. The equitable rule prevailed over the rule at law and so even at law T could not complain of the distress. This principle applies even if the lease to T was granted while L had no

---

[46] See *Tidey v Mollett* (1864) 16 C.B.(N.S.) 298; but see *Harte v Williams* [1934] 1 K.B. 201.
[47] LP(MP)A 1989 s.2, applying to contracts made after September 26, 1989: see above, para.6–005.
[48] (1858) 2 De G. & J. 559.
[49] *Zimbler v Abrahams* [1903] 1 K.B. 577.
[50] (1882) 21 Ch.D. 9.
[51] s.25(11), then JA 1925 s.44, now Supreme Court Act 1981 s.49.
[52] See above.
[53] See below, para.13–027.
[54] See *Manchester Brewery Co v Coombs* [1901] 2 Ch. 608 at 617, 618.

legal estate in the land but only a contract to purchase it; for equity would enforce both contracts.[55]

Differences between legal and equitable leases

11–021   The effect of *Walsh v Lonsdale* is to render an enforceable agreement for a lease very nearly as good as a legal lease, and the same applies to an imperfect lease which is enforceable as an agreement for lease. There are still, however, some points of difference.

Specific performance: The rule depends upon the willingness of equity to grant the discretionary remedy of specific performance, so that if an agreement for a lease is one of which the court will not grant specific performance (as where the tenant is in breach of his obligations to the landlord and so does not come to equity with clean hands[56]), the position under it will be precarious. Further, if the court lacks jurisdiction to order specific performance,[57] a tenant will not be able to enforce the agreement in that court,[58] though he could defend proceedings by the landlord which ignored the agreement, as the court can give effect to an equitable defence.[59] But in any event a tenant who has gone into possession and paid rent may rely on his yearly or other periodic tenancy.[60]

Easements: Certain easements and similar rights may be created on a grant of a legal estate which will not be created by a mere contract.[61]

The burden of covenants: In respect of leases granted before 1996, an agreement for a lease which is enforceable under *Walsh v Lonsdale* is not as good as a lease as regards third parties, but only as regards the actual parties to the agreement. As between the actual parties, there is privity of contract; and as the benefit of a contract is assignable, an assignee from either of them can take the benefit of the covenants in the lease. But assignees will not be bound by the covenants, for the burden of a contract does not bind assignees, and there is no privity of estate which can make the burden run with the estate, as it would if a lease (and so an estate) had been granted.[62] However, where a yearly or other periodic tenancy has arisen from the tenant taking possession and paying rent, the burden of any covenants that are consistent with such a tenancy will run with it.[63] This disadvantage does not occur in respect of leases granted after 1995, since the burden of the covenants in the lease will run whether the lease is legal or enforceable under *Walsh v Lonsdale*.[64]

Third parties: The rights of a tenant under an agreement for a lease, being merely equitable, are subject to the same frailty as all equitable interests, namely, they will not necessarily bind third-party purchasers from the landlord. If L agrees to grant a lease for five years

---

[55]   *Industrial Properties (Barton Hill) Ltd v Associated Electrical Industries Ltd* [1977] Q.B. 580.
[56]   *Coatsworth v Johnson* (1886) 55 L.J.Q.B. 220 at 222. But see (1987) 7 Oxf. J.L.S. 60 (S. Gardner).
[57]   See, e.g. County Courts Act 1984 s.23(d).
[58]   *Foster v Reeves* [1892] 2 Q.B. 255; contrast *Cornish v Brook Green Laundry Ltd* [1959] 1 Q.B. 394.
[59]   *Kingswood Estate Co Ltd v Anderson* [1963] 2 Q.B. 169.
[60]   *Bell Street Investments Ltd v Wood* [1970] E.G.D. 812.
[61]   Under LPA 1925 s.62: see below, para.15–042.
[62]   See below, para.14–049.
[63]   *Doe d. Thomson v Amey* (1840) 12 A. & E. 476.
[64]   L&T(C)A 1995 ss.3(1), 28(1); see below, para.14–059.

to T and then conveys the legal fee simple to X or, for that matter grants a legal lease or a legal mortgage to him, X is capable of taking the land or his interest therein free of T's rights.

Unregistered Land

In the case of unregistered land, X will take free of T's rights if he is a bona fide purchaser **11–022** of a legal estate in the land without notice. Whether X has notice will be determined by whether T has protected his agreement as a Class C(iv) land charge. Registration of that land charge is deemed to be notice to the whole world so that X will be bound; but failure to register will render the agreement void against a purchaser for money or money's worth of a legal estate in the land, which X will necessarily be.[65] The fact that X has actual knowledge of T's agreement is immaterial in these cases.[66] Failure to register the agreement may be defeated by the purchaser, even though the tenant is in possession of the land.[67]

Registered Land

In the case of registered land, T is in a much better position because X will be bound by the **11–023** agreement if T has protected it by the entry of a notice on the register of the landlord's estate, regardless of the length of term granted.[68] Even where an agreement for a lease is not registered, it may be protected as an overriding interest where the tenant is in actual occupation of the property.[69]

TYPES OF LEASES AND TENANCIES

Classification

Leases and tenancies may be classified under the five following heads. **11–024**

Leases for a fixed period **11–025**

Certainty of term: A lease may be granted for any certain period of certain duration, no matter how long or short. Leases for a week or for 3,000 years are equally valid. Both the commencement and the duration of the term must either be certain or else be rendered certain before the lease takes effect.[70] Thus a lease for 99 years from January 1 next complies with this rule but a tenancy granted during wartime "for the duration of the war" does not.[71] An Act of 1944[72] converted tenancies granted during the Second World War into

---

[65] LCA 1972 s.4(6), (7), replacing LCA 1925 s.13(2); *Hollington v Rhodes* [1951] 2 TLR 691; for land charges, see above, para.1–026.
[66] Above, para.6–079.
[67] See *Lloyd's Bank Plc v Carrick* [1996] 4 All E.R. 630.
[68] LRA 2002 s.32(1).
[69] LRA 2002 s.29; Sch.3 para.2
[70] *Harvey v Pratt* [1965] 1 W.L.R. 1025.
[71] *Lace v Chantler* [1944] K.B. 368.
[72] Validation of War-Time Leases Act 1944.

valid tenancies for 10 years determinable after the war by (usually) one month's notice; but there is nothing in that Act to rescue tenancies for other uncertain periods, such as until the landlord requires the land for road widening,[73] or "so long as the company is trading",[74] from the rule that makes them void.

The requirement as to certainty of duration was considered in detail by the Supreme Court in *Berrisford v Mexfield Housing Co-operative Limited*.[75] In that case the court revisited the House of Lord's decision in *Prudential Assurance Co Ltd v London Residuary Body* [1992] 2 A.C. 386. Lord Neuberger summarised the effect of *Prudential* in five principles[76]:

   (i) an agreement for a term, whose maximum duration can be identified from the inception can give rise to a valid tenancy;

  (ii) an agreement which gives rise to a periodic arrangement determinable by either party can also give rise to a valid tenancy;

 (iii) an agreement could not give rise to a tenancy as a matter of law if it was for a term whose maximum duration was uncertain at the inception;

 (iv) (a) a fetter on a right to serve notice to determine a periodic tenancy was ineffective if the fetter is to endure for an uncertain period, but (b) a fetter for a specified period could be valid.

Despite their Lordships being of the view that the law is not in a satisfactory state,[77] and that there is "no apparent practical justification for holding that an agreement for term of uncertain duration cannot give rise to a tenancy",[78] they chose not to depart from the certainty requirement. Prior to 1926 where a lease of uncertain duration was granted to an individual it could take effect as a tenancy for life under the principle in *Parker v Taswell*.[79] Where it would have taken effect as a tenancy for life it will now take effect as a tenancy for a term of 90 years, determinable on the defendant's death pursuant to s.149(6) of the Law of Property Act 1925.

The rule applies even if each party has been given power to determine the tenancy during the uncertain period.[80] Where the rule invalidates a lease but a periodic tenancy arises from the payment and acceptance of rent, that tenancy will not incorporate any provisions for determination in the void lease that are inconsistent with the periodic tenancy.[81]

Reversionary leases: A lease which is granted to take effect in the future is known as a reversionary lease. Before 1926, there was no restriction upon the length of time that might elapse before the term began.[82] But since 1925 the grant of a term to take effect more than 21 years from the instrument creating it is void if at a rent or in consideration of a fine; so

[73] *Prudential Assurance Co Ltd v London Residuary Body* [1992] 2 A.C. 386.
[74] *Birrell v Carey* (1989) 58 P. & C.R. 184.
[75] [2011] UKSC 52.
[76] [2011] UKSC 52.
[77] See Lord Neuberger at 34; Lady Hale at 93; and Lord Dyson at 115.
[78] Lord Neuberger at 34.
[79] See above, para.11–019.
[80] *Prudential Assurance Co Ltd v London Residuary Body* [1992] 2 A.C. 386, overruling *Ashburn Anstalt v Arnold* [1989] Ch. 1.
[81] *Prudential Assurance Co Ltd v London Residuary Body* [1992] 2 A.C. 386.
[82] There were no restrictions before 1926; see *Mann, Crossman & Paulin Ltd v Registrar of Land Registry* [1918] 1 Ch. 202.

is any contract made after 1925 to create such a term.[83] Thus the grant of a lease in 2014 to commence in 2044, or a contract made in 2014 to grant in 2015 a lease to commence in 2044 is void. However, there is nothing to invalidate a contract made in 2014 to grant in 2044 a lease which is then to commence immediately, for that lease is not reversionary.[84] An option in a lease for 35 years to renew it on its determination is similarly not invalidated.[85]

Determination: The general rule is that a lease for a fixed period automatically determines when the fixed period expires; but there are statutory exceptions to this rule.[86]

Yearly tenancies   **11–026**

Creation: A yearly tenancy is one which continues from year to year indefinitely until determined by proper notice, notwithstanding the death of either party or the assignment of his interest. Continuation each year depends on the will of the parties as shown by their omission to serve a notice to quit; and in retrospect it is considered a single tenancy and not a succession of tenancies.[87] Such a tenancy may be created either expressly or by implication. Thus an express grant to A "from year to year" or "as a yearly tenant" will create a yearly tenancy. It should be noted, however, that a grant "to X for one year and thereafter from year to year" will give X a tenancy for at least two years; for he has been given a definite term of one year followed by a yearly tenancy which can be determined only at the end of the first year of the latter tenancy.[88]

A yearly tenancy arises by implication whenever a person occupies land with the owner's consent in circumstances indicating a tenancy, and rent measured with reference to a year is paid and accepted, unless there is sufficient evidence to show that some other kind of tenancy was intended.[89] A yearly tenancy also arises when a tenant under a lease for a fixed term holds over (i.e. remains in possession at the end of his term) and, in circumstances indicating a tenancy,[90] rent is paid and accepted on a yearly basis. In this case, the tenant will hold under such of the terms of the expired lease as are not inconsistent with a yearly holding.[91] Thus covenants to repair,[92] or to carry on some specified trade on the premises[93] and provisos for re-entry by the landlord on non-payment of rent[94] may be implied in a yearly tenancy. But a covenant to paint every three years[95] and a provision for two years' notice to quit[96] are inconsistent with a yearly tenancy and cannot be implied in this way.

The payment of rent at more frequent intervals than a year will not prevent a yearly

---

[83] LPA 1925 s.149(3).
[84] (1947) 63 L.Q.R. 20; *Re Strand and Savoy Properties Ltd* [1960] Ch. 582; *Weg Motors Ltd v Hales* [1962] Ch. 49.
[85] *Re Strand and Savoy Properties Ltd* [1960] Ch. 582.
[86] See below.
[87] *Hammersmith and Fulham LBC v Monk* [1992] 1 A.C. 478; for joint tenants, see above.
[88] *Re Searle* [1912] 1 Ch. 610.
[89] *Kemp v Derrett* (1814) 3 Camp. 510; *Javad v Aqil* [1991] 1 W.L.R. 1007; *Walji v Mount Cook Land Ltd* [2002] 1 P. & C. R. 13.
[90] *Clarke v Grant* [1950] 1 K.B. 104; *Longrigg, Burrough & Trounson v Smith* [1979] E.G.D. 472.
[91] *Dougal v McCarthy* [1893] 1 Q.B. 736.
[92] *Wyatt v Cole* (1877) 36 L.T. 613.
[93] *Sanders v Karnell* (1858) 1 F. & F. 356.
[94] *Thomas v Packer* (1857) 1 H. & N. 669
[95] *Pinero v Judson* (1829) 6 Bing. 206.
[96] *Tooker v Smith* (1857) 1 H. & N. 732.

tenancy from arising by implication. The test is the period by reference to which the parties calculated the rent. Thus an agreement for "£10,400 per annum payable weekly" prima facie creates a yearly tenancy; had the agreement been for "£200 per week", a weekly tenancy would be presumed, despite the fact that in each case the tenant would in fact have made the same payments, namely £200 every week.[97]

Determination: A yearly tenancy may be determined by such notice and at such time as the parties agree.[98] Different periods for the landlord and tenant may be agreed, and it may be provided that the landlord should be entitled to give notice only in certain circumstances,[99] such as if he requires the premises for his own occupation.[100] But a term that one party should not be entitled to give notice at all is void as repugnant to the nature of a periodic tenancy.[101] In default of such agreement, the tenancy can be determined by at least half a year's notice expiring at the end of a completed year of the tenancy. The meaning of "half a year" depends on the day upon which the tenancy began. If the tenancy began on one of the usual quarter-days (Lady Day (March 25), Midsummer Day (June 24), Michaelmas (September 29)[102] or Christmas (December 25)), "half a year" means "two quarters"; otherwise "half a year" means 182 days.[103] Thus, if a yearly tenancy began on March 25, notice to quit given on or before September 29 is good, although it is less than 182 days[104]; and if a yearly tenancy began on September 29, notice must be given on or before March 25, even though it is more than 182 days. In each of these cases, the tenancy began on a quarter-day[105]; had it started on some other day, for instance March 26, at least 182 days' notice would have been required.[106] It will be noted that in neither case is the period of the notice necessarily six months, although of course the parties may agree that such shall be the notice required.

As has been seen,[107] a notice to quit for a periodic tenancy is not invalid merely because it has been given by only one of joint landlords or joint tenants.

Weekly, monthly and other periodic tenancies

11–027   A tenancy from week to week, month to month, quarter to quarter, and the like (including a tenancy for some artificial period, such as for successive periods of 364 days[108]) can be created in a similar way to a yearly tenancy, namely either by express agreement or by inference, such as that arising from the payment and acceptance of rent measured with reference to a week, month or quarter, as the case may be, in circumstances indicating a tenancy.[109] In general, the position of the parties under such a tenancy is similar

---

[97]   See *Adler v Blackman* [1953] 1 Q.B. 146.
[98]   *Re Threlfall* (1880) 16 Ch.D. 274 at 281, 282.
[99]   *Re Midland Railway Co's Agreement* [1971] Ch. 725.
[100] As in *Breams Property Investment Co Ltd v Stroulger* [1948] 2 K.B. 1.
[101] *Centaploy Ltd v Matlodge Ltd* [1974] Ch. 1.
[102] A mnemonic is that for these three the last digit is the same as the number of letters in the month.
[103] Anon. (1575) 3 Dy. 345a.
[104] *Doe d. Durant v Doe* (1830) 6 Bing. 574.
[105] *Morgan v Davies* (1878) 3 C.P.D. 260.
[106] Co.Litt. 135b.
[107] Above, para.8–006.
[108] *Land Settlement Association Ltd v Carr* [1944] K.B. 657.
[109] *Cole v Kelly* [1920] 2 K.B. 106 at 132; *Clarke v Grant* [1950] 1 K.B. 104; *Longrigg, Burrough & Trounson v Smith* [1979] E.G.D. 472.

to that under a yearly tenancy; save that notice of termination is not half a period, but a full period, expiring at the end of a completed period, subject to any contrary agreement between the parties.[110] This is the "corresponding date" rule, under which "month" normally means calendar month, despite the differing lengths.[111] Thus in the absence of any contrary agreement, a weekly tenancy commencing on a Monday can be determined either by notice given on or before one Monday to expire on the following Monday,[112] or, since a week starting on a Monday is complete at midnight on the following Sunday, by notice given on or before one Sunday to expire on the following Sunday.[113] But for dwellings, not less than four weeks' notice in writing must be given, containing (if given by the landlord) prescribed information relating to orders for possession and legal advice; and this now extends to residential licences, with certain exceptions, such as rent free or family sharing licences.[114]

Tenancies at will

A tenancy at will arises whenever a tenant, with the consent of the landlord, occupies qua tenant (and not merely as a servant or agent) on the terms that either party may determine the tenancy at any time. In some cases the tenant holds rent free, as where the vendor of a fee simple, owing to some delay in completion, lets the purchaser into possession of the property before the conveyance has been executed.[115] But unless the parties agree that the tenancy shall be rent free, the landlord is entitled to compensation for the use and occupation of the land[116]; and if a rent is fixed the landlord may distrain for it in the usual way.

    11–028

A tenancy at will comes to an end when either party does any act incompatible with the continuance of the tenancy, as where the tenant commits voluntary waste,[117] or the landlord enters the land and cuts trees or carries away stone,[118] or either party gives notice to the other determining the tenancy. The tenancy is also determined if either party dies or assigns his interest in the land.[119] Essentially, the tenancy is a personal relation between the landlord and his tenant.[120]

If a tenancy at will is created without any agreement as to payment of rent, and rent is subsequently paid and accepted upon some regular periodical basis, a yearly, monthly or other periodical tenancy will normally arise under the rules set out under heads (b) and (c) above, unless the circumstances indicate otherwise.[121]

---

[110] *Queen's Club Gardens Estates Ltd v Bignell* [1924] 1 K.B. 117; *Lemon v Lardeur* [1946] K.B. 613.

[111] See *Dodds v Walker* [1981] 1 W.L.R. 1027; *E. J. Riley Investments Ltd v Eurostile Holdings Ltd* [1985] 1 W.L.R. 1139.

[112] *Newman v Slade* [1926] 2 K.B. 328.

[113] *Bathavon R.D.C. v Carlile* [1958] 1 Q.B. 461.

[114] Protection from Eviction Act 1977 ss.3A, 5; HA 1988 ss.31, 32; SI 1988/2201; *Schnabel v Allard* [1967] 1 Q.B. 627.

[115] *Howard v Shaw* (1841) 8 M. & W. 118. See also *Hagee (London) Ltd v A. B. Erikson & Larson* [1976] Q.B. 209.

[116] Distress for Rent Act 1737 s.11; *Howard v Shaw* (1841) 8 M. & W. 118.

[117] Countess of Shrewsbury's Case (1600) 5 Co.Rep. 13b.

[118] *Turner v Doe d. Bennett* (1842) 9 M. & W. 643.

[119] *Pinhorn v Souster* (1853) 8 Exch. 763 at 772.

[120] *Wheeler v Mercer* [1957] A.C. 416 at 427, 428.

[121] *Javad v Aqil* [1991] 1 W.L.R. 1007.

Tenancies at sufferance

11–029   A tenancy at sufferance arises where a tenant, having entered upon land under a valid tenancy, holds over without the landlord's assent or dissent.[122] Such a tenant differs from a trespasser in that his original entry was lawful, and from a tenant at will in that his tenancy exists without the landlord's assent. No rent, as such, is payable, but the tenant is liable to pay compensation for his use and occupation of the land.[123] The tenancy may be determined at any time, and may be converted into a yearly or other periodic tenancy in the usual way, such as if rent is paid and accepted with reference to a year in circumstances where the parties intended there to be a tenancy.

There are statutory penalties for tenants who hold over after giving or receiving notice to quit:

Double annual value: If the landlord gives the tenant written notice to quit and the tenant is a tenant for life or for years, the tenant is liable to pay the landlord a sum calculated at double the annual value of the land in respect of the period for which he holds over after the notice expired. This can be enforced by action but not otherwise, for example not by distress.[124] This provision applies to tenancies from year to year as well as to tenancies for fixed terms of years or for a year certain, but not to weekly,[125] or, no doubt, to other periodic tenancies.

If the tenant gives the landlord written or oral notice to quit, then, whatever the type of tenancy, the tenant is liable to pay double rent in respect of the period for which he holds over after the notice expired; payment can be enforced by action or distress.[126]

The curiously differing terms of these aged provisions will be noticed. The rent and the annual value may be the same, but they often differ, as where premises have been let at a reduced rent in consideration of a fine.

Statutory modifications

11–030   Although the parties to a lease can in general create a lease for such periods as they think fit, statute has made some modifications to this position.

Leases for lives

11–031   By the Law of Property Act 1925,[127] a lease at a rent or a fine for life or lives, or for a term of years determinable with a life or lives or on the marriage of the lessee, is converted into a term of 90 years, whether it was granted before or after 1925. A contract for such a lease is treated in a similar way. The lease continues even after the death or marriage, as the case may be, although either party may determine it thereafter (but not before) by serving on the other one month's written notice to expire on one of the

---

[122] See *Remon v City of London Real Property Co Ltd* [1921] 1 K.B. 49 at 58.
[123] *Leigh v Dickeson* (1884) 15 QBD 60.
[124] L & TA 1730 s.1.
[125] *Lloyd v Rosbee* (1810) 2 Camp. 453.
[126] Distress for Rent Act 1737 s.18. For a recent discussion of this statute see *Ballard (Kent) Ltd v Oliver Ashworth (Holdings) Ltd* [2000] Ch. 12.
[127] s.149(6).

quarter-days applicable to the tenancy, or, if no special quarter-days are applicable, on one of the usual quarter-days. Thus leases at a rent or fine granted "to A for life", "to B for 10 years if he so long lives", and "to C for 99 years if he so long remains a bachelor" are all converted into terms which will continue for 90 years unless by the proper notice they are determined on any quarter-day (not necessarily the first) after the event has occurred. But these provisions do not apply to a lease which takes effect in equity under a settlement.[128]

Perpetually renewable leases

A perpetually renewable lease was a lease which gave the tenant the right to renew it for another period as often as it expired; usually the tenant had to make some payment on exercising this right. A lease will be perpetually renewable if there is a covenant to renew it on the terms of the existing lease "including this covenant for renewal",[129] but not if the inclusion of the covenant for renewal is part of a separate obligation.[130] By the Law of Property Act 1922,[131] all such leases existing at the end of 1925 were converted into terms of 2000 years, calculated from the beginning of the existing terms; and perpetually renewable leases granted after 1925 take effect as terms of 2000 years from the date fixed for the commencement of the term. Any perpetually renewable sub-lease created out of a perpetually renewable lease is converted into a term of 2000 years less one day. The 2000-year lease is subject to the same terms as the original lease, with the following modifications. **11–032**

Termination: The tenant for the time being (but not the landlord) may terminate the lease on any date upon which, but for the conversion by the Act, the lease would have expired if it had not been renewed, provided he gives at least 10 days' written notice to the landlord.

Assignment: Every assignment or devolution of the lease must be registered with the landlord or his solicitor or agent within six months, and a fee of one guinea paid.

Breach of covenant: A tenant who assigns the lease is not liable for breaches of covenant committed after the assignment. In leases granted before 1996, the general rule is that the original lessee is liable for all breaches occurring during the term, even if they occur after he has assigned the lease[132]; perpetually renewable leases are a statutory exception to this rule which has been abolished for leases granted after 1995.[133]

Fine: Any fine or other payment for renewal for which the lease provides is converted into additional rent and spread over the period between the renewal dates, except where the lease is granted after 1925, when the obligation for payment is void.

It should be noted that the landlord has no right to determine the lease at the renewal dates. Before 1926, if L granted T a lease for 21 years with a perpetual right of renewal, it was T alone who had the right to decide each 21 years whether or not to renew the lease.

---

[128] LPA 1925 ss.149(6)(a), 205(1)(xxvi); SLA 1925 s.117(1)(xxiv).
[129] *Parkus v Greenwood* [1950] Ch. 644; *Caerphilly Concrete Products Ltd v Owen* [1972] 1 W.L.R. 372.
[130] *Marjorie Burnett Ltd v Barclay* (1980) 258 E.G. 642.
[131] s.145 and Sch.15.
[132] See below, para.14–004.
[133] See below, para.14–014.

This position is preserved, save that now the lease continues unless determined, instead of requiring renewal.

Over-lengthy renewals

11–033   A contract made after 1925 to renew a lease for over 60 years from its termination is void.[134] This is aimed at single renewals, not perpetual renewals.

Reversionary leases

11–034   A lease at a rent or a fine to commence at too distant a future date or a contract to create such a lease cannot be granted after 1925. This has already been dealt with.[135]

Estoppel

Estoppel

11–035   On the grant of a lease or tenancy, both landlord and tenant and their successors in title are in general mutually estopped from denying the validity of the transaction. Neither landlord nor tenant will be permitted to assert that the tenancy which they have purported to create is invalid,[136] and this is so even if the landlord had no title to grant a lease[137] or if the tenancy is merely oral.[138] The tenant is still estopped from denying his landlord's title after going out of possession and so can still be sued on repairing covenants, unless evicted by title paramount, that is to say by someone with a title superior to that of the landlord.[139] But except in the case of companies within the Companies Acts,[140] this doctrine does not prevent a corporation from contending that it had no power to grant or receive a tenancy, for estoppel cannot validate an ultra vires act.[141]

Tenancy by estoppel

11–036   One consequence of this rule is that if the landlord in fact has no estate in the land, then although the lease or tenancy can confer no actual estate on the tenant, and cannot be effective against third parties,[142] it is good between the parties to it and their successors in title.[143] Both landlord and tenant will be estopped from denying the validity of their lease or tenancy; they cannot "blow hot and cold" by claiming that the transaction was valid when entered into, and yet asserting subsequently that it was a nullity.

No tenancy by estoppel arises, however, if the lessor had a legal interest (as distinct from

---

[134] LPA 1922 Sch.15.
[135] Above, para.11–025.
[136] See *Cuthbertson v Irving* (1859) 4 H. & N. 742; (1860) 6 H. & N. 135.
[137] *Bruton v London & Quadrant Housing Trust* [2000] 1 A.C. 406; see M. Dixon [2000] C.L.J. 25.
[138] *E.H. Lewis & Son Ltd v Morelli* [1948] 2 All E.R. 1021.
[139] *Industrial Properties (Barton Hill) Ltd v Associated Electrical Industries Ltd* [1977] Q.B. 580.
[140] Companies Act 1985 (CA 1985) s.35, as substituted by Companies Act 1989 s.108.
[141] *Rhyl U.D.C. v Rhyl Amusements Ltd* [1959] 1 W.L.R. 465.
[142] *Tadman v Henman* [1893] 2 Q.B. 168.
[143] See *E.H. Lewis & Son Ltd v Morelli* [1948] 2 All E.R. 1021.

an equitable interest[144]) in the land when he granted the lease. If his interest was greater than the tenancy, the lease takes effect in the ordinary way; if it was equal to or smaller than the tenancy, the grant of the lease operates as an assignment of the lessor's interest.[145] Thus if L grants T a lease for 99 years, T will take a lease for 99 years by estoppel if L had no interest in the land when the lease was granted. But if L had a lease for 10 years at that time, the lease for 99 years will operate as an assignment to T of L's lease for 10 years.

Feeding the estoppel

If there is a tenancy by estoppel, and subsequently the landlord acquires an interest in the land out of which the tenancy could have been created (such as the fee simple), this is said to "feed the estoppel". From that moment the lease becomes fully effective, giving the tenant an actual estate in the land.[146] This formerly created difficulties if the landlord purchased the land on mortgage. Theoretically, the legal estate vested in the landlord an instant before he mortgaged the land; and in that instant the estoppel was fed, and so the tenancy would bind the mortgagee.[147] But theory has yielded to convenience, and now the transactions are treated as being simultaneous, so that the mortgagee takes free from the tenancy.[148]

11–037

PART 3   ASSIGNMENT OF LEASES AND TENANCIES

In order to effect a legal assignment of a lease, a deed must be employed,[149] even if the lease has been created by word of mouth, such as a yearly tenancy in possession at a rack rent.[150] However, on principles similar to those applicable to the creation of leases,[151] an assignment in writing will be effective in equity. In respect of leases granted before 1996, such an assignment is effective only as between assignor and assignee. Thus, unless estopped from so doing, the assignee may deny liability to the landlord on the covenants of the lease since there will be no privity of estate between them save in respect of any periodic tenancy that arises from the payment and acceptance of rent.[152] This does not apply to leases granted after 1995, since the burden of the covenants in the lease will run whether the lease is assigned by deed or by writing.[153] On an assignment the assignor can reserve a right of entry to ensure compliance by the assignee and his successors with covenants in

11–038

---

[144] *Universal Permanent B.S. v Cooke* [1952] Ch. 95 at 102 (tenancy by estoppel on letting by purchaser before completion).
[145] *Beardman v Wilson* (1868) L.R. 4 C.P. 57; *Wollaston v Hakewill* (1841) 3 Man. & G. 297 at 323.
[146] *Mackley v Nutting* [1949] 2 K.B. 55.
[147] *Church of England B.S. v Piskor* [1954] Ch. 553.
[148] *Abbey National B.S. v Cann* [1991] 1 A.C. 56.
[149] LPA 1925 s.52(1), replacing RPA 1845 s.3.
[150] *Crago v Julian* [1992] 1 W.L.R. 372.
[151] Above.
[152] *Rodenhurst Estates Ltd v W. H. Barnes Ltd* [1936] 2 All E.R. 3.
[153] L&T(C)A 1995 ss.3(1), 28(1); see below, para.14–009.

the assignment, the effect of which is to create an equitable right of entry.[154] Other matters concerning assignments are dealt with below.[155]

The grant of sub-leases is governed by the rules relating to the grant of leases.[156]

SUMMARY OF KEY CASES

- *Street v Mountford* [1985] A.C. 809
- *A.G. Securities v Vaughan* [1990] 1 A.C. 417
- *Antoniades v Villiers* [1990] 1 A.C. 417
- *Bruton v London and Quadrant Housing Trust* [2000] 1 A.C. 406
- *Lace v Chantler* [1944] K.B. 368
- *Prudential Assurance Co Ltd v London Residuary Body* [1992] A.C. 386
- *Mexfield v Berrisford* [2011] UKSC 52; [2012] 1 A.C. 955

FURTHER READING

- E. Cooke, *Land Law* (OUP, 2006), Ch.7
- S. Bright, "The uncertainty of certainty in leases" (2012) 128 L.Q.R. 337
- S. Bridge, "Former tenants, future liabilities and the privity of contract principle: The Landlord and Tenant (Covenants) Act 1995" [1996] 55 C.L.J. 313
- S. Bridge, "Landlord and tenant law", in L. Tee, (ed.) *Essays in Land Law*, (Devon: Willan, 2002)

---

[154] *Shiloh Spinners Ltd v Harding* [1973] A.C. 691.
[155] Below, para.11–016, Ch.14 et seq.
[156] Above, paras 11–025 et seq.

Chapter 12

DETERMINATION OF TENANCIES

CHAPTER SUMMARY

This Chapter sets out the various ways in which a tenancy can be determined as well as the means in which it can be resurrected or replaced.

A lease or tenancy may come to an end in the following ways:

1) By expiry
2) By notice
3) By forfeiture
4) By surrender
5) By merger
6) By becoming a satisfied term
7) By enlargement
8) By disclaimer
9) By frustration
10) By repudiation
11) By rescission

Whilst this chapter sets out the ways in which the common law treats the termination of leases, in most cases statute intervenes to continue the lease or tenancy in the same or similar form, to provide a right of renewal or to limit the ways in which physical possession can be obtained.

For short term residential tenancies, in most cases, either the Housing Act 1980 (public sector) or the Housing Act 1988 (private sector) will apply. For long residential leases the Local Government and Housing Act 1989 applies, in addition to rights conferred on a tenant to extend a lease under the Leasehold Reform Act 1967 (leases of houses) or the Leasehold Reform, Housing and Urban Development Act 1993 (leases of flats). Whilst in the commercial sphere, business leases are on the whole protected by the Landlord and Tenant Act 1954.

BY EXPIRY

12–001   As has been seen,[1] a lease or tenancy for a fixed period automatically determines when the fixed period expires. In some cases the tenant may be entitled to be granted a new lease or to remain in possession as a statutory tenant.[2]

BY NOTICE

12–002   A lease or tenancy for a fixed period cannot be determined by notice unless this has been expressly agreed. A lease for a substantial term such as 21 years often contains a break clause which enables the tenant or landlord to determine it at the end of a specified period (i.e. after the seventh or fourteenth year), in which case the length of the notice required, the time when it is to be given, and other matters of this kind, depend on the terms of the lease. In the absence of any such provision the lease will continue for the full period.

Yearly, weekly, monthly and other periodical tenancies can be determined by notice. These provisions, and the determination of tenancies at will and at sufferance, have already been considered.[3]

Many periodic tenants have statutory protection against eviction.[4]

BY FORFEITURE

12–003   Forfeiture is the right of the landlord to terminate the lease prior to the expiry of the term.

Right to forfeit

12–004   A landlord's right to forfeit a lease (i.e. enforce a forfeiture of it) may arise under three heads.

Denial of title

12–005   If a tenant clearly and unambiguously denies his landlord's title to the whole (and not merely part) of the land,[5] as by asserting that he or some third party is the true owner, the landlord is entitled to forfeit the tenancy.[6] This is based on terms implied into the lease for the purposes of s.146(1) of the Law of Property Act 1925 and is treated as analogous to a unilateral repudiatory breach of contract, so that the landlord can elect whether to accept the repudiation and end the lease or reject it and bind the tenant to the term.[7]

---

[1]   Above, para.11–025.
[2]   Above, see the introduction to this chapter.
[3]   Above, paras 11–025 et seq.
[4]   See Protection from Eviction Act 1977.
[5]   *W. G. Clarke (Properties) Ltd v Dupre Properties Ltd* [1992] Ch. 297.
[6]   *Wisbech St. Mary Parish Council v Lilley* [1956] 1 W.L.R. 121. Quaere whether the provisions as to notice and relief apply: see below, para.12–013.
[7]   See *Abidogun v Frolan Health Care Ltd* [2001] EWCA Civ 1821.

The modern tendency is to treat the doctrine narrowly and so it is not easy to successfully invoke it.[8]

Express forfeiture clauses, breach of covenant

Nearly every lease contains a list of things which the tenant shall and shall not do, and these may be framed as conditions or as covenants. In most cases they are framed as covenants (such as "The tenant hereby covenants with the landlord as follows . . ."). When this is done, save for certain circumstances,[9] the landlord has no right to forfeit the lease merely because the covenants are broken. He can only do so if the lease contains an express provision for forfeiture on breach of the specific covenant which has been breached or on breach of the covenants in the lease in general.[10] Every well-drawn lease contains a forfeiture clause which, in a legal lease, creates a legal right of re-entry, making the lease voidable at the landlord's option if a covenant is broken, subject to compliance with any relevant statutory restraints.

12–006

  If no lease has actually been granted but the parties have either agreed that a lease containing the "usual covenants" will be granted, or have entered into an agreement for a lease containing no reference to the covenants which it should contain, then, subject to any contrary agreement by the parties, the lease must contain whatever covenants and conditions may be "usual" in the circumstances.[11]

Breach of condition

In rarer cases, the tenant's obligations are worded as conditions, (such as if the lease is granted "upon condition that" or "provided always that" certain things are done or not done). If so, the lease may be forfeited on breach of condition even if there is no forfeiture clause.[12] In such a case, the continuance of the lease has been made conditional upon the tenant performing his obligations, and upon breach of one of them the lease becomes voidable at the landlord's option; but if the landlord does not treat the lease as forfeited, the tenant cannot set up his own breach in order to avoid his liabilities under the lease.[13]

12–007

Waiver of breach

A landlord, by waiver, may lose the right to forfeit for a particular instance of breach either before or after they have decided to forfeit. Waiver may be express or implied. It will be implied if:

12–008

---

[8] See *Eastaugh v Crisp* [2007] EWCA Civ 638.
[9] See below para.12–026: for when a breach will amount to a repudiation and therefore not require a forfeiture clause.
[10] *Doe d. Willson v Phillips* (1824) 2 Bing. 13. For proposals for reforming the law of forfeiture, see (2006) Law Com. No. 303.
[11] See *Hampshire v Wickens* (1878) 7 Ch.D. 555.
[12] See *Doe d. Lockwood v Clarke* (1807) 8 East 185.
[13] See *Doe d. Bryan v Bancks* (1821) 4 B. & Ald. 401; *Roberts v Davey* (1833) 4 B. & Ad. 664.

(i)   the landlord is aware of the acts or omissions of the tenant giving rise to the right of forfeiture; and

(ii) the landlord does some unequivocal act recognising the continued existence of the lease.[14]

To constitute a waiver, both elements must be present. The landlord will be treated as having the knowledge of his managing agents[15]; but mere suspicion is not knowledge.[16] A waiver will be implied where a landlord, with knowledge of the breach, distrains (exercises his right to distress) for rent, whether due before or after the breach,[17] or demands or sues for or accepts rent falling due after the breach,[18] even if the rent is accepted "without prejudice"[19] or by the mistake of the landlord's agents.[20] Waiver is a matter of law, not intention.[21] Other acts, such as negotiating a variation of terms of the lease and so recognising its continuance, may amount to a waiver, though not against a background of threatened proceedings for forfeiture[22]; and there can be no waiver once the landlord has shown his final decision to treat the lease as forfeited, as by commencing an action for possession.[23]

As would be expected, a waiver extends only to the particular breach in question, and does not operate as a general waiver of all future breaches and the same applies to a licence granted to the tenant to do any act.[24] All that is waived is the right of forfeiture for the breach, and not the breach itself.[25] A waiver is no bar to an action for damages for breach of the covenant.[26]

Mode of forfeiture

12–009   The normal method of enforcing a forfeiture is by issuing and serving a claim form seeking possession; such a claim form usually contains an unequivocal demand for possession, so that its service operates to determine the lease.[27] Alternatively, unless the premises are let as a dwelling[28] and some person is lawfully residing in it or in any part of

---

[14] *Matthews v Smallwood* [1910] 1 Ch. 777 at 786; *Greenwood Reversions Ltd v World Entertainment Foundations Ltd* [2008] EWCA Civ 47.

[15] *Metropolitan Properties Co Ltd v Cordery* (1980) 39 P. & C.R. 10.

[16] *Chrisdell Ltd v Johnson* (1987) 54 P. & C.R. 257. Compare *Van Haarlam v Kasner* [1992] 36 E.G. 135 (knowledge of tenant's arrest enough).

[17] *Ward v Day* (1863) 4 B. & S. 337 at 353; 5 B. & S. 364.

[18] *Goodright d. Charter v Cordwent* (1795) 6 T.R. 219; *David Blackstone v Burnetts (West End) Ltd* [1973] 1 W.L.R. 1487 (rent payable in advance).

[19] *Davenport v R.* (1877) 3 App. Cas. 115; *Segal Securities Ltd v Thoseby* [1963] 1 Q.B. 887.

[20] *Central Estates (Belgravia) Ltd v Woolgar (No.2)* [1972] 1 W.L.R. 1048.

[21] See *Matthews v Smallwood* [1910] 1 Ch. 777 at 786.

[22] *Expert Clothing Service & Sales Ltd v Hillgate House Ltd* [1986] Ch. 340; and see *Church Commissioners for England v Nodjoumi* (1986) 51 P. & C.R. 155.

[23] *Grimwood v Moss* (1872) L.R. 7 C.P. 360.

[24] LPA 1925 ss.143, 148, replacing earlier provisions which altered the law laid down in *Dumpor's Case* (1603) 4 Co.Rep. 119b.

[25] See *Greenwich LBC v Discreet Selling Estates Ltd* (1991) 61 P. & C.R. 405.

[26] *Stephens v Junior Army and Navy Stores Ltd* [1914] 2 Ch. 516.

[27] *Elliott v Boynton* [1924] 1 Ch. 236, as explained in *Canas Property Co Ltd v.K.L. Television Services Ltd* [1970] 1 Q.B. 433.

[28] Which includes leases of mixed residential/retail premises following *Patel v Pirabakaran* [2006] 1 W.L.R. 3112, CA.

it,[29] the landlord can enforce his right of forfeiture by making peaceable re-entry onto the land.[30] It is usually inadvisable for a landlord to adopt this method. Although reasonable force may be used, it is a criminal offence if any violence is used or threatened when the landlord knows that there is someone on the premises who is opposed to the entry.[31] In practice, peaceable re-entry is therefore limited to premises which have been abandoned by the tenant and to commercial premises outside working hours. Physically entering and changing the locks is not the only form of peaceable re-entry, the grant of a new tenancy or entering into a direct tenancy with a sub-tenant in occupation can also constitute an act of forfeiture. Only if peaceable re-entry is made unlawfully[32] does the tenant have any remedy in damages.[33] However, peaceable re-entry does not deprive the tenant of any right which he may have to relief against forfeiture.[34] It is this fact, coupled with the fact that the tenant agreed to the right of re-entry being inserted into the lease when he acquired it, that is likely to defeat any challenge to peaceable re-entry which may be made under the Human Rights Act 1998.[35]

Conditions for forfeiture: general

The conditions under which a right of forfeiture can be enforced depend upon whether the right arises from breach of the covenant or condition to pay rent or from breach of any other provision. Further, statute has intervened so as to place further hurdles in the path of a landlord who seeks to forfeit residential leases.   **12–010**

In each case, first, equity, and later, statute, have intervened so as to allow tenants to obtain relief from forfeiture in certain circumstances.[36]

Conditions for forfeiture: forfeiture for non-payment of rent

Where a landlord has the right to forfeit a lease for non-payment of rent, two important points to be considered are the landlord's formal demand for the rent and the tenant's right to relief.   **12–011**

Landlord's formal demand

Before commencing proceedings, whether in the High Court[37] or in the County Court,[38] the landlord must either have made a formal demand for the rent, or else be exempted from making such a demand.   **12–012**

---

[29] Protection from Eviction Act 1977 (PEA 1977) s.2.
[30] See, e.g. *Billson v Residential Apartments Ltd* [1992] 1 A.C. 494.
[31] Criminal Law Act 1977 (CLA 1977) s.6, replacing statutes from 1381 onwards. For another disadvantage, see *R. v Hussey* (1924) 18 Cr.App.R. 160 (getting shot).
[32] See Housing Act 1988 (HA 1988) s.27.
[33] *Hemmings v Stoke Poges Golf Club* [1920] 1 K.B. 720.
[34] *Billson v Residential Apartments Ltd* [1992] 1 A.C. 494.
[35] See A. Bruce [2000] N.L.J. 462.
[36] For the equitable jurisdiction, see *Shiloh Spinners Ltd v Harding* [1973] A.C. 691; *Billson v Residential Apartments Ltd* [1992] 1 A.C. 494.
[37] Common Law Procedure Act 1852 s.210.
[38] County Courts Act 1984 s.139(1).

Formal demand: To make a formal demand, the landlord or his authorised agent must demand the exact sum due on the day when it falls due at such convenient hour before sunset as will give time to count out the money, the demand being made upon the demised premises and continuing until sunset.[39]

Exemption from formal demand: To avoid the technicalities of a formal demand, every well-drawn lease provides that the lease may be forfeited if the rent is a specified number of days in arrear, "whether formally demanded or not". The words quoted exempt the landlord from making a formal demand. However, even if a lease contains no such clause, a formal demand is dispensed with in any action for forfeiture if:

(i)   half a years rent is in arrears; and
(ii) either Commercial Rent Arrears Recovery is not exercisable to recover the arrears or there are not sufficient goods available upon the premises to satisfy all the arrears by CRAR.[40]

Residential tenancies: There are two further requirement in the case of residential long leases for rent to become payable. Firstly, an address for service of notices in England and Wales on the landlord must be provided.[41] Secondly, the landlord must give the tenant prescribed notice setting out the tenant's rights and stating a date for payment between 30 and 60 days after service.[42] A failure to adhere to either of these requirements will mean that rent is not payable, whether or not the requirement of a formal demand has been provided for under the lease. Further statutory protection is given to long residential tenancies by prohibiting forfeiture in cases where the sum does not exceed a prescribed amount and/or has not been outstanding for a prescribed period.[43]

Right to relief of tenant

12–013   The tenant may be able to claim relief against the forfeiture. Equity considered that a right of forfeiture was merely security for payment of the rent, so that if:

(i)   the tenant paid the rent due by the date on which relief against forfeiture was ordered and interest thereon; and
(ii) the tenant paid any expenses to which the landlord had been put; and
(iii) it was just and equitable to grant relief,

equity would restore the tenant to his position despite the forfeiture of the lease.[44] These remain the financial prerequisites of relief against forfeiture being granted. This is the

---

[39] See 1 Wms. Saund. (1871) 434 et seq.
[40] See either s.210 Common Law Procedure Act 1852 (High Court) or s.139(1) County Courts Act 1984 (county Court). Following the Tribunal, Courts and Enforcement Act 2007, the Commercial Rent Arrears Recovery came into force on April 6, 2014 and replaced the common law of distress.
[41] Landlord and Tenant Act 1987 s.48.
[42] Commonhold and Leasehold Reform Act 2002 s.166.
[43] Commonhold and Leasehold Reform Act 2002 s.167.
[44] See *Howard v Fanshawe* [1895] 2 Ch. 581.

case even where the rent is merely a ground rent; the tenant is not obliged to pay an occupation rent in respect of the period between forfeiture and relief being granted.[45] However, where the landlord has gone back into possession prior to relief against forfeiture being granted, he must account for the value of his occupation. Consequently, an occupation rent will be deduced from the rent, interest and expenses payable by the tenant.[46] Originally, there was no limit to the time within which application for relief had to be made, apart from the general principle that equity would give no assistance to stale claims.[47]

The position now differs depending on whether proceedings are brought in the High Court or the County Court. Proceedings must now be brought in the County Court unless they involve complicated disputes of fact or points of law of general importance.[48] The value of the property in question and the amount of rent due are relevant but are normally not alone enough to justify proceedings being brought in the High Court.[49]

Proceedings in the High Court are primarily governed by the Common Law Procedure Act 1852.[50] That Act provides that if, before trial, the tenant pays requisite amount,[51] the proceedings must be stayed. However, this provision is only applicable where at least half a year's rent is in arrears. Furthermore, where the landlord has obtained an order for possession and had that order executed, an application for relief must be made within six months of the execution of the order, in other words within six months of the landlord going back into possession. This is the case whether at least half a year's rent is in arrears[52] or not.[53] However, if the landlord has re-entered without obtaining an order for possession, the statute does not apply at all and the old equitable inherent jurisdiction of the court remains.[54] While the court tends to adopt the same time limit, it will not "boggle at a matter of days".[55]

Proceedings in the County Court are governed by the County Courts Act 1984.[56] If the tenant pays all the arrears and costs into court at least five days before the trial date, the proceedings must be stayed. If this is not done, the court will make an order for possession but will postpone the execution of that order so as to give the tenant a chance to pay; execution will be suspended for at least four weeks and the court has a discretion to make one or more further extensions. However, the power to grant relief against forfeiture to the tenant ends once the possession order has been executed and the landlord has gone

---

[45] *Escalus Properties Ltd v Dennis* [1996] Q.B. 231.

[46] *Bland v Ingrams Estates Ltd (No.2)* [2002] 2 W.L.R. 361 at [19]–[29].

[47] See *Hill v Barclay* (1811) 18 Ves. 56 at 59, 60.

[48] CPR Pt 55A P.D. paras 1.1 to 1.3.

[49] CPR Pt 55A P.D. para.1.4.

[50] ss.210–212, replacing L & TA 1730 ss.2, 4.

[51] *Standard Pattern Co Ltd v Ivey* [1962] Ch. 432, criticised in (1962) 78 L.Q.R. 168 (R.E.M.).

[52] Common Law Procedure Act 1852 s.210.

[53] Senior Courts Act 1981 s.38.

[54] *Thatcher v C. H. Pearce & Sons (Contractors) Ltd* [1968] 1 W.L.R. 748. Nor does the six months limit apply to a mortgagee of the lease who was not party to the proceedings for forfeiture: *United Dominions Trust Ltd v Shellpoint Trustees* [1992] 39 E.G. 144, examining the turgid statutory drafting.

[55] *Thatcher v C. H. Pearce & Sons (Contractors) Ltd* [1968] 1 W.L.R. 748 at 756 per Simon P.

[56] s.138, as amended by Administration of Justice Act 1985 s.55.

back into possession (this restriction does not apply to those claiming through the tenant who can claim relief whenever they first become aware of the forfeiture[57]).

If relief is granted, the tenant continues to holds under the old lease[58] and execution of a new document is not required. Relief takes effect subject to any legal lease granted by the landlord after the forfeiture to a lessee who takes without notice of the previous tenant's equity to seek relief.[59] However, where such a lessee has notice of that equity, his lease is interposed between the landlord and tenant, who becomes in effect his tenant and the sub-tenant of the landlord.[60] The rent payable by the tenant since the commencement of his lease will be payable to him rather than to the landlord less an occupation rent in respect of his own occupation.[61] In practice these sums are likely to cancel one another out.

Right to relief of those claiming through the tenant

12–014   Where a lease is forfeited, subsidiary interests in that lease will also be destroyed.[62] Consequently, those claiming through the tenant are also entitled to claim relief against forfeiture irrespective of whether the tenant himself is able to do so and can do so whenever they first become aware of the forfeiture.[63] In an effort to avoid late applications, rules of court oblige the landlord to serve a copy of his claim form on any persons claiming through the tenant of whose interests he is aware[64] but this will not necessarily always work.

The Law of Property Act 1925[65] specifically provides that a sub-tenant has the same right of applying for relief against forfeiture as the tenant under the head lease. Where relief is granted to a sub-tenant of only part of the premises, the court will grant the sub-tenant a term no longer than the term he held under his sub-lease[66] and will normally impose terms that will restore the landlord to his former position.[67] The sub-tenant will usually enter into a new lease direct with the former landlord under the forfeited lease on terms similar to (though not necessarily the same as) those of the old sub-lease.

The Common Law Procedure Act 1852[68] specifically provides that a mortgagee of a lease may obtain relief against forfeiture for six months after the landlord has executed a judgment for possession and a mortgagee can also obtain relief under the inherent jurisdiction and in a County Court.[69] It has also been held that a person who has registered a charging order against a lease can obtain relief against forfeiture, both in the High Court under the inherent jurisdiction and in the County Court.[70] However, he will have to do so in the name

---

[57]   *Croydon (Unique) Ltd v Wright* [1999] 4 All E.R. 257.
[58]   Common Law Procedure Act 1852 s.212; JA 1925 s.46; and see County Courts Acts 1984 (CCA 1984) s.139(2).
[59]   *Fuller v Judy Properties Ltd* [1992] 14 E.G. 106 (actually an authority on LPA 1925 s.146(2)).
[60]   *Bland v Ingrams Estates Ltd (No.2)* [2002] 2 W.L.R. 361 at [13].
[61]   *Bland v Ingrams Estates Ltd (No.2)* [2002] 2 W.L.R. 361 at [19]–[29].
[62]   *Great Western Ry v Smith* (1876) 2 Ch.D. 235 at 253.
[63]   *Croydon (Unique) Ltd v Wright* [1999] 4 All E.R. 257.
[64]   CPR Pt 55A, P.D. para.2.4.
[65]   s.146(4) as amended by LP(A)A 1929 s.1; see *Belgravia Insurance Co v Meah* [1964] 1 Q.B. 436.
[66]   See *Ewart v Fryer* [1901] 1 Ch. 499 at 515.
[67]   *Belgravia Insurance Co Ltd v Meah* [1964] 1 Q.B. 436.
[68]   s.210.
[69]   County Courts Act 1984 s.139(2).
[70]   *Bland v Ingrams Estates Ltd* [2001] 2 W.L.R. 1638.

of the tenant, if necessary by joining him as a defendant,[71] and relief will generally only be given on terms that the lease is immediately sold.[72]

Conditions for forfeiture: forfeiture for breach of other covenants or conditions

Forfeiture for breach of a covenant or condition other than for payment of rent is subject to the landlord's obligation to serve a notice in the statutory form and the tenant's right to relief against forfeiture. This is the case whether proceedings are to be brought in the High Court or the County Court but there are some exceptions to the general rule. The right to receive a notice and to apply for relief prevails over any stipulation to the contrary in the lease.[73] Hence a device such as an undated surrender executed by the tenant as a guarantee against breaches of covenant is void.[74]

    In the case of long residential leases, before either service of the statutory s.146 notice or exercising the right to forfeit,[75] the provisions of either s.81 of the Housing Act 1996 or s.168 of the Commonhold and Leasehold Reform Act 2002 must be complied with. Section 81 applies to forfeiture for non-payment of service charges or administration charges; s.168 applies to forfeiture for other breaches of covenant. Each section provides that there can be no forfeiture or forfeiture notice until there has been a determination of breach. This can be either by way of an admission or through court, First-tier Tribunal (Property Chamber) (Residential Property) or an arbitral tribunal.

12–015

General rule

12–016

Service of notice: Before proceeding to enforce a forfeiture either by action or re-entry, the landlord must serve on the tenant a statutory notice in writing under the Law of Property Act 1925, s.146.[76] The notice must:

    (i) specify the breach complained of; and
    (ii) require it to be remedied, if it is capable of remedy; and
    (iii) require the tenant to make compensation in money for the breach,[77] if the landlord requires such compensation.[78]

Capable of remedy: A breach of a positive covenant (i.e. to do something) is normally capable of remedy by doing what has been left undone, such as carrying out building

---

[71] *Bland v Ingrams Estates Ltd* [2001] 2 W.L.R. 638.
[72] *Bland v Ingrams Estates Ltd (No.2)* [2002] 2 W.L.R. 361 at [37].
[73] LPA 1925 s.146(12).
[74] *Plymouth Corp v Harvey* [1971] 1 W.L.R. 549; and see *Richard Clarke & Co Ltd v Widnall* [1976] 1 W.L.R. 845.
[75] As to whether it is necessary to serve a s.146 notice for non-payment of residential service charges reserved as rent, see the conflicting Court of Appeal decisions of *Freeholders of 69 Marina, St Leonards on Sea v Oram* [2012] H.L.R. 12 and *Escalus Properties v Robinson* [1995] 3 W.L.R. 524 (which was not cited in *Freeholders of 69 Marina*).
[76] Replacing CA 1881 s.14, and CA 1882 ss.2, 4.
[77] LPA 1925 s.146(1).
[78] *Lock v Pearce* [1893] 2 Ch. 271 (despite the words "in any case").

work[79] or painting,[80] even though this is done belatedly. If the covenant is negative (i.e. not to do something) whilst it had been said that it can never be remedied,[81] for "that which was done cannot be undone", [82] the modern approach is that at least some breaches of negative covenants, if not all, are capable of remedy.[83] Thus a breach of a covenant against assigning or sub-letting the premises is incapable of remedy.[84] However, an assignment is valid despite having been made in breach of covenant and so it is on the assignee that the statutory notice must be served.[85] Again, the use of the premises for prostitution in breach of a covenant against permitting user for any illegal or immoral purpose cannot be remedied merely by ceasing the prohibited use, for this will not remove the stigma attached to the premises.[86] But the breach is remediable where there is no notoriety and the immoral use by the sub-tenant can be suppressed by the tenant taking prompt action as soon as he discovers the breach.[87] The question seems to be whether the harm to the landlord done by the breach is for practical purposes capable of being retrieved.[88] The path of safety is for the statutory notice to require the specified breach to be remedied "if it is capable of remedy".[89] A notice may be valid even if it does no more than specify the breach, as where the breach is irremediable and the landlord seeks no compensation, perhaps to avoid soiling his hands with the fruits of prostitution, or other illegal or immoral activities.[90]

Time for compliance: After serving the notice, the landlord must allow the tenant a reasonable time for compliance with it. The Act does not define what is a reasonable time, but it will be measured by the time that it would take to perform the covenant, as by doing the requisite building work or decoration, or, if the covenant is negative, by terminating the breach.[91] For many positive covenants a period of three months is usually considered to be enough in normal circumstances. Even if the breach is irremediable, reasonable notice must be given so as to enable the tenant to consider his position. In such cases, two days notice has been held to be insufficient[92] although 14 days may be enough.[93] If within a reasonable time the notice has not been complied with, the landlord may proceed to enforce the forfeiture. This he may do either in person or by action.

---

[79] *Expert Clothing Service & Sales Ltd v Hillgate House Ltd* [1986] Ch. 340.

[80] See *Hoffmann v Fineberg* [1949] Ch. 245 at 257.

[81] *Rugby School (Governors) v Tannahill* [1934] 1 K.B. 695 at 701 (in C.A. [1935] 1 K.B. 87); and see *Scala House & District Property Co Ltd v Forbes* [1974] Q.B. 575 at 585.

[82] *Rugby School (Governors) v Tannahill* [1934] 1 K.B. 695 at 701 per MacKinnon J.

[83] *Scala House & District Property Co Ltd v Forbes* [1974] Q.B. 575, and see the further observations of Neuberger L.J. in *Akici v Butlin* [2006] 1 W.L.R. 201 and *Savva v Houssein* (1996) 73 P. & C.R. 150.

[84] *Scala House & District Property Co Ltd v Forbes* [1974] Q.B. 575; and see *Horsey Estates Ltd v Steiger* [1899] 2 Q.B. 79 (tenant in liquidation).

[85] *Old Grovebury Manor Farm Ltd v W. Seymour Plant Sales and Hire Ltd* [1979] 1 W.L.R. 1397.

[86] *Rugby School (Governors) v Tannahill* [1935] 1 K.B. 87; *British Petroleum Pension Trust Ltd v Behrendt* (1986) 52 P. & C.R. 117; and see *Hoffmann v Fineberg* [1949] Ch. 245 (illicit gaming); *Van Haarlam v Kasner* [1992] 36 E.G. 135 (using premises for spying).

[87] *Glass v Kencakes Ltd* [1966] 1 Q.B. 611.

[88] *Expert Clothing Service & Sales Ltd v Hillgate House Ltd* [1986] Ch. 340.

[89] See *Glass v Kencakes Ltd* [1966] 1 Q.B. 611 at 629.

[90] *Rugby School (Governors) v Tannahill* [1935] 1 K.B. 87.

[91] *Expert Clothing Service & Sales Ltd v Hillgate House Ltd* [1986] Ch. 340 at 357.

[92] *Horsey Estate Ltd v Steiger* [1899] 2 Q.B. 79.

[93] *Scala House & District Property Co Ltd v Forbes* [1974] Q.B. 575.

Exceptional cases

As has already been mentioned, the above provisions concerning the necessity for serving **12–017** a notice and the tenant's right to apply for relief govern all covenants and conditions (other than those for payment of rent) with few exceptions. These are as follows:

Mining leases: Cases where there has been a breach of a covenant in a mining lease providing for inspection of the books, accounts, weighing machines or other things, or of the mine itself.[94] Since the rent reserved on such a lease usually varies with the quantity of minerals extracted, such a covenant is most important to the landlord. There is consequently no restriction upon the landlord forfeiting the lease without serving a notice, and no provision enabling the tenant to obtain relief.

Bankruptcy or execution: Cases where there has been a breach of a condition against the tenant's bankruptcy (or, for a corporation, insolvent liquidation[95]) or the taking of the lease in execution[96]; the bankruptcy of a surety for the tenant is outside this provision.[97] This head must be divided into two.

(1) *No protection*. In five specified cases, on breach of such a condition, s.146 has no application at all; the lease can thus be forfeited at once without service of a notice and without possibility of relief.[98] These cases are those where the lease is of—

    (i) agricultural or pastoral land; or

    (ii) mines or minerals; or

    (iii) a public house or beershop; or

    (iv) a furnished house; or

    (v) property with respect to which the personal qualifications of the tenant are of importance for the preservation of the value or character of the property,[99] or on the ground of neighbourhood to the landlord or to any person holding under him.

(2) *Protection for one year and after*. In all other cases, on breach of such a condition, the protection of s.146 applies for one year from the bankruptcy, liquidation or taking in execution; if during that year the landlord wishes to forfeit the lease, he must serve the notice and the tenant can apply for relief. But once the year has elapsed, the tenant is no longer protected; the landlord can forfeit the lease without serving notice and the court has no power to grant relief.[100] Yet if the tenant's lease is sold during the year, the protection of s.146 continues indefinitely.[101] This allows the trustee in bankruptcy to dispose of the lease to a purchaser at a reasonable price, for if the lease were liable to be forfeited after the year without the service of notice or the chance of relief, it would be difficult to find a purchaser.

---

[94] LPA 1925 s.146(8).
[95] LPA 1925 s.205(1)(i).
[96] LPA 1925 s.146(9).
[97] *Halliard Property Co Ltd v Jack Segal Ltd* [1978] 1 W.L.R. 377.
[98] LPA 1925 s.146(9).
[99] See *Bathurst (Earl) v Fine* [1974] 1 W.L.R. 905.
[100] LPA 1925 s.146(10)(b).
[101] LPA 1925 s.146(10)(a).

Breach of repairing covenant: Leasehold Property (Repairs) Act 1938. Where there are more than three years left to run on a lease with a term of seven years or more, any s.146 notice seeking to forfeit for breach of a repairing covenant, must inform the tenant of their right to serve a counter-notice under the 1938 Act in which case the landlord will not be able to forfeit without the permission of the court.

Right to relief of tenant

12–018   While the landlord "is proceeding" to enforce the forfeiture by action or otherwise, the tenant may apply to the court for relief, either in any action by the landlord to enforce the forfeiture or by making a separate application.[102] "Is proceeding" is here used in the sense of "proceeds",[103] or "has proceeded"[104]; and a tenant may seek relief as soon as the landlord has served the statutory notice,[105] though usually it will be better to wait and see whether or not the landlord actually decides to proceed to forfeiture. Where the forfeiture is being enforced by action, the right to apply for relief is exercisable at any time before the landlord has taken possession under a judgment in his favour.[106] Thereafter no relief can be granted, even within six months of the forfeiture.[107] Where the forfeiture is enforced in person, the right to apply for relief continues for an indefinite period after the landlord's entry, though in deciding whether to grant relief the court will take into account all the circumstances, including any delay by the tenant in applying.[108]

The court may grant relief on such terms as it thinks fit[109]; and if relief is granted the effect is as if the lease had never been forfeited.[110] Relief is usually granted where the breach has been remedied, though it may be refused if the tenant's personal qualifications are important and he has proved unsatisfactory.[111] But where the breach involves immoral use, relief will be refused except in very exceptional circumstances.[112] Where premises are physically divided and separately occupied, and the breaches are confined to one part only, relief may be granted in respect of the other part.[113] Relief takes effect subject to any legal lease granted by the landlord after the forfeiture to a lessee who takes without notice of the previous tenant's equity to seek relief.[114] However, where such a lessee has notice of that equity, his lease is interposed between the landlord and tenant, who becomes in effect his tenant and the sub-tenant of the landlord.[115]

---

[102] LPA 1925 s.146(2).

[103] *Billson v Residential Apartments Ltd* [1992] 1 A.C. 494.

[104] *Billson v Residential Apartments Ltd* [1992] 1 A.C. 494 at 539.

[105] *Billson v Residential Apartments Ltd* [1992] 1 A.C. 494 at 539, 540, 544.

[106] *Billson v Residential Apartments Ltd* [1992] 1 A.C. 494 at 540.

[107] Contrast non-payment of rent: above, para.12–013.

[108] *Billson v Residential Apartments Ltd* [1992] 1 A.C. 494 at 540, 543.

[109] LPA 1925 s.146(2).

[110] *Dendy v Evans* [1909] 2 K.B. 894.

[111] *Bathurst (Earl) v Fine* [1974] 1 W.L.R. 905 (stately home); and see LPA 1925 s.146(9).

[112] *Central Estates (Belgravia) Ltd v Woolgar (No.2)* [1972] 1 W.L.R. 1048 (short-lived homosexual brothel: tenant aged and sick: value of premises not diminished); *Ropemaker Properties Ltd v Noonhaven Ltd* [1989] 2 E.G.L.R. 50 (valuable lease of West End clip joints); *Van Haarlam v Kasner* [1992] 36 E.G. 135.

[113] *G.M.S. Syndicate Ltd v Gary Elliott Ltd* [1982] Ch. 1 (ground floor shop; immoral "club" in basement).

[114] *Fuller v Judy Properties Ltd* [1992] 14 E.G. 106.

[115] *Bland v Ingrams Estates Ltd (No.2)* [2002] 2 W.L.R. 361 at [13] (actually a case on forfeiture for non-payment of rent).

Right to relief of those claiming through the tenant

As in the case of forfeiture for non-payment of rent,[116] those claiming through the tenant **12–019** are also entitled to claim relief against forfeiture irrespective of whether the tenant himself is able to do so and can do so whenever they first become aware of the forfeiture.[117] It will be recalled that, in an effort to avoid late applications, rules of court oblige the landlord to serve a copy of his claim form on any persons claiming through the tenant of whose interests he is aware[118] but this will not necessarily always work.

It has been held that a sub-tenant and a mortgagee have the same right as the tenant[119] to apply to the court for relief against forfeiture while the landlord "is proceeding" to enforce the forfeiture by action or otherwise.[120] This decision supplements the specific provision that a sub-tenant has the same right of applying for relief against forfeiture as the tenant under the head lease.[121] Where relief is granted to a sub-tenant of only part of the premises, the court will grant the sub-tenant a term no longer than the term he held under his sub-lease[122] and will normally impose terms that will restore the landlord to his former position.[123] The sub-tenant will usually enter into a new lease direct with the former landlord under the forfeited lease on terms similar to (though not necessarily the same as) those of the old sub-lease. A mortgagee is treated as a sub-tenant for these purposes even if his mortgage is not by way of sub-lease[124]; and a person who has registered a charging order against a lease also has a right to relief against forfeiture,[125] presumably the same right as he has in the case of forfeiture for non-payment of rent.[126]

BY SURRENDER

If a tenant surrenders his lease to his immediate landlord, who accepts the surrender, the **12–020** lease merges in the landlord's reversion and is extinguished. The surrender must be to the immediate landlord; a transfer of the lease to a superior landlord does not work as a surrender but operates merely as an assignment of the lease. Thus if L leases land to T for 99 years and T sub-leases to S for 21 years, S's sub-lease will be extinguished by surrender if The transfers it to T but not if he transfers it to L. A surrender by an assignee which releases him from all liabilities under the lease will also release prior assignees, even if liable under direct covenants with the landlord.[127] But a surrender takes effect subject to the rights of others in the lease surrendered, and so they will be binding for as long as those rights

---

[116] Above, at para.12–014.
[117] *Croydon (Unique) Ltd v Wright* [1999] 4 All E.R. 257.
[118] CPR Pt 55A, P. D. para.2.4.
[119] Under LPA s.146(2).
[120] *Escalus Properties Ltd v Dennis* [1996] Q.B. 231.
[121] LPA 1925 s.146(4).
[122] See *Ewart v Fryer* [1901] 1 Ch. 499 at 515.
[123] *Chatham Empire Theatre Ltd v Ultrans Ltd* [1961] 1 W.L.R. 817; *Belgravia Insurance Co Ltd v Meah* [1964] 1 Q.B. 436.
[124] *Grand Junction Co Ltd v Bates* [1954] 2 Q.B. 160.
[125] *Croydon (Unique) Ltd v Wright* [1999] 4 All E.R. 257.
[126] *Bland v Ingrams Estates Ltd* [2001] 2 W.L.R. 1638.
[127] *Deanplan Ltd v Mahmoud* [1993] Ch. 151.

would have lasted.[128] A surrender cannot be a unilateral act and it is for the tenant to show that the landlord has unequivocally accepted the surrender to avoid liability under the lease.[129] Abandonment of the premises by the tenant without more does not operate as a surrender.[130]

Surrender may be either express or by operation of law. For an express surrender, at law a deed is required.[131]

There will be surrender by operation of law if the parties do some act showing an intention to terminate the lease, and the circumstances are such that it would be inequitable for them to rely on the fact that there has been no surrender by deed.[132] Surrender by operation of law has been found to have taken place where:

(i)   the tenant accepts a fresh lease from his immediate reversioner, even though the new lease is for a shorter term than the old one or starts at a future date[133]; and

(ii) the tenant sells the freehold as trustee of it forgetting that he also has a lease of it.[134]

Variation of a lease by extending the term or enlarging (but not reducing) the demise, operates by way of surrender and regrant.[135] Other variations, such as an agreed increase of rent, do not necessarily bring about a surrender and regrant.[136]

There will also be a surrender by operation of law if the tenant gives up possession of the premises and the landlord accepts it.[137] The acceptance of keys by the landlord may not be sufficient evidence of acceptance. In each case it is a question of fact as to whether the landlord has intended to determine the tenancy.[138]

BY MERGER

12–021   Merger is the counterpart of surrender. Under a surrender, the landlord acquires the lease, whereas merger is the consequence of the tenant retaining the lease and acquiring the reversion, or of a third party acquiring both lease and reversion. The principle is the same in both surrender and merger: the lease is absorbed by the reversion and destroyed.

For merger to be effective, the lease and the reversion must be vested in the same person in the same right with no vested estate intervening.[139] Merger may take place even if the immediate reversion consists of a lease shorter than the lease merged.[140] Thus if A, a

---

[128] *E. S. Schwab & Co Ltd v McCarthy* (1976) 31 P. & C.R. 196.

[129] *Relvok Properties Ltd v Dixon* (1973) 25 P. & C. R. 1.

[130] *Bellcourt Estates Ltd v Adesina* [2005] EWCA Civ 208, citing *Megarry & Wade* with approval.

[131] LPA 1925 s.52.

[132] See *Glynn v Coghlan* [1918] 1 I.R. 482 at 485.

[133] *Ive's Case* (1597) 5 Co.Rep. 11a.

[134] *Allen v Rochdale BC* [2000] Ch. 221.

[135] *Baker v Merckel* [1960] 1 Q.B. 657.

[136] *Jenkin R. Lewis & Son Ltd v Kerman* [1971] Ch. 477.

[137] See *Oastler v Henderson* (1877) 2 QBD 575; but see *Chamberlain v Scally* [1992] E.G.C.S. 90 (no unequivocal conduct by the parties).

[138] *Artworld Financial Corp v Safaryan* [2009] EWCA Civ 303.

[139] See *Chambers v Kingham* (1878) 10 Ch.D. 743.

[140] *Hughes v Robotham* (1593) Cro.Eliz. 302.

tenant in fee simple, leases land to B for 1000 years and a few years later leases the same land to C for 400 years, the result is to give C for 400 years the reversion on B's lease. If X then acquires both C's reversion and B's lease, the 1000 year lease will merge in the 400 year reversion and leave X with but 400 years.[141] There is no merger if the person in whom the two interests vest doesn't intend that to occur.[142]

BY BECOMING A SATISFIED TERM

If a lease is granted as security for the payment of money, the term becomes satisfied and the lease automatically ceases when all the money has been paid.[143]   **12–022**

BY ENLARGEMENT

Under certain conditions, not frequently encountered in practice, a lease may be enlarged into a fee simple by the tenant executing a deed of enlargement. Under the Law of Property Act 1925[144] this can be done only if—   **12–023**

- (i)   there is not less than 200 years of the lease unexpired; and
- (ii)   the lease was originally granted for at least 300 years; and
- (iii)   no trust or right of redemption[145] exists in favour of the reversioner; and
- (iv)   the lease is not liable to be determined by re-entry for condition broken; and
- (v)   no rent of any money value is payable. A rent of "one silver penny if lawfully demanded" is a rent of no money value, but a rent of three shillings is not.[146] A rent under such a lease which does not exceed £1 per annum and which has not been paid for a continuous period of 20 years (five having elapsed since 1925) is deemed to have ceased to be payable and can no longer be recovered.

For a sub-lease to be capable of enlargement under the section, it must be derived out of a lease which is itself capable of enlargement.

A fee simple acquired by enlargement is subject to all the provisions which affected the term of years out of which it arose. This seems to be one of the few ways of making positive covenants run with freehold land.[147] There is some uncertainty as to whether enlargement actually extinguishes the landlord's estate or whether it continues in parallel to the new freehold. This has led the Land Registry to alter their practice on enlargement so that when it occurs, two titles will be recorded; the new enlarged freehold title and the pre-existing one.[148]

---

[141] *Stephens v Bridges* (1821) 6 Madd. 66.
[142] See LPA 1925 s.185 and *EDF Energy Networks (EPN) Plc v BOH Ltd* [2011] EWCA Civ 19.
[143] See below, para.17–009.
[144] s.153.
[145] e.g. a right of redemption under a mortgage; see below, para.17–055.
[146] *Re Chapman and Hobbs* (1885) 29 Ch.D. 1007; *Re Smith and Stott* (1883) 29 Ch.D. 1009n.
[147] See below, Ch.16.
[148] See *Harrison* "Enlargement of long leases under s.153 LPA" Landlord and Tenant Review 2013, 17(6), 216–217.

BY DISCLAIMER

12–024   Most rights to disclaim a lease arise under statute. Thus tenants whose premises were rendered unfit by war damage were given a statutory power to disclaim their tenancies.[149] Similar rights were given to certain tenants of premises which were requisitioned under emergency powers.[150] The effect of valid disclaimers of this type is the same as if there had been a surrender.

Not all statutory provisions for disclaimer take effect in this way; most significantly a trustee in bankruptcy or the liquidator of an insolvent company may disclaim an onerous lease[151] but by so doing they only terminate any future liability of themselves and the insolvent person.[152] This disclaimer does not destroy the lease and subject to the provisions of the Insolvency Act, the rights and liabilities of third parties continue.[153] Therefore a landlord can rely on a surety to the lease notwithstanding the disclaimer.[154] The landlord can claim in the insolvency for the whole of the remaining rent payable under the lease subject to a discount for early payment and to giving credit for the value of what he has received back after taking into account the cost of any necessary repairs to the premises.[155]

BY FRUSTRATION

12–025   Leases are more than mere contracts in that they create estates in land. Nevertheless, the doctrine of frustration of contracts applies in principle to leases, though only rarely will it operate.[156] Thus a lease of a warehouse for 10 years will not be frustrated by the closure of the only means of access to it for 20 months when some five years of the term have elapsed.[157] But a lease might perhaps be ended by frustration[158] if the land were physically destroyed (such as by being engulfed by the sea), or if the lease were merely incidental to a commercial contract that had been frustrated, or where the lease was a short lease of a holiday villa which was totally destroyed by lightning before the term begins. Agreements for a lease and covenants in a lease may similarly, but not readily, be held to have been frustrated.[159]

---

[149] Landlord and Tenant (War Damage) Acts 1939 and 1941.

[150] Landlord and Tenant (Requisitioned Land) Acts 1942 and 1944.

[151] Insolvency Act 1986 ss.178, 315.

[152] *Re Thompson and Cottrell's Contract* [1943] Ch. 97 at 99.

[153] *Hindcastle Ltd v Barbara Attenborough Associates Ltd* [1997] A.C. 70.

[154] And in cases where an assignee has become insolvent, the landlord may also be able to rely on covenants entered into by the original tenant—but note the impact of the Landlord and Tenant (Covenants) Act 1995.

[155] *Re Park Air Services Plc* [2000] 2 A.C. 172 (the rent payable under the lease was four times the market value).

[156] *National Carriers Ltd v Panalpina (Northern) Ltd* [1981] A.C. 675.

[157] *National Carriers Ltd v Panalpina (Northern) Ltd* [1981] A.C. 675.

[158] *National Carriers Ltd v Panalpina (Northern) Ltd* [1981] A.C. 675; *Cricklewood Property and Investment Trust Ltd v Leighton's Investment Trust Ltd* [1945] A.C. 221; see the various dicta.

[159] *National Carriers Ltd v Panalpina (Northern) Ltd* [1981] A.C. 675.

BY REPUDIATION

The determination of a tenancy by repudiation has the same enigmatic quality as that of determination by frustration. A tenancy will not normally be determined by repudiation, i.e. by one party accepting a breach of a fundamental term of the tenancy by the other as being a repudiation of the tenancy.[160] Thus a landlord's derogation from grant in not preventing other tenants from parking on a forecourt in breach of the tenant's exclusive right so to do, will not constitute a repudiatory breach entitling the tenant to determine the lease.[161] Nor, apparently, will a tenant's prolonged refusal to pay rent entitle the landlord to determine, as distinct from forfeit, the lease. However, a landlord has been held have committed repudiatory breaches entitling the tenant to determine the lease where he wilfully and persistently refused to repair defects which had made the premises unfit for habitation[162] and where he made the tenant's unit dark and virtually unusable as a result of having leased adjoining premises to a pawnbroker.[163] It therefore now seems to be accepted that a breach of the terms of a lease can amount to a repudiatory breach but only in extreme cases.

12–026

BY RESCISSION

A lease may be set aside by the court where it was granted as a result of the fraud of one of the parties[164] or where it constitutes an unconscionable bargain.[165]

12–027

SUMMARY OF KEY CASES

- *Billson v Residential Apartments Ltd* [1992] 1 A.C. 494
- *Thomas v Ken Thomas Ltd* [2006] EWCA Civ 1504

FURTHER READING

- Law Commission No.303 Termination of Tenancies for Tenant Default
- "Forfeiture—a long overdue reform?" (2007) 11(5) L.&T.R. 140

---

[160] *Total Oil Great Britain Ltd v Thompson Garages (Biggin Hill) Ltd* [1972] 1 Q.B. 318, not citing *Wilson v Finch Hatton* (1877) 2 Ex.D. 336.
[161] *Nynehead Developments Ltd v R.H. Fibreboard Containsers Ltd* [1999] 1 E.G.L.R. 7.
[162] See *Hussein v Mehlman* [1992] 32 E.G. 59.
[163] *Chartered Trust Plc v Davies* [1997] 2 E.G.L.R. 83.
[164] *Killick v Roberts* [1991] 1 W.L.R. 1146 (fraud by the tenant).
[165] *Boustany v Piggott* (1993) 69 P. & C.R. 298 (claim by the landlord).

Chapter 13

RIGHTS AND DUTIES OF THE PARTIES UNDER A LEASE OR TENANCY

CHAPTER SUMMARY

The rights and duties of the landlord and tenant under a lease or tenancy fall under five heads.

- First, the lease may be silent as to everything except the essential terms as to parties, premises, rent and duration. This is not infrequently the case with weekly and other periodic tenancies.
- Secondly, the parties may have agreed to be bound by the "usual covenants".
- Thirdly, the lease may provide in the orthodox way not only for the matters dealt with by the "usual covenants" but also for a number of other matters.
- Fourthly, there are a number of statutory provisions relating to the rights and duties of the parties to a lease.

Last, there are fixtures: these have already been considered.

This chapter deals with the first three of those heads. The question how far covenants in a lease can be enforced between persons other than the original lessor and original lessee is considered separately.

POSITION IN THE ABSENCE OF EXPRESS PROVISION

Except so far as the lease or tenancy agreement otherwise provides, the position of the parties is as set out below.   **13–001**

Position of the landlord

Quiet enjoyment

A covenant by the landlord for quiet enjoyment (or a corresponding agreement if the tenancy is not created by deed[1]) is automatically implied from the mere relationship of   **13–002**

---

[1] *Baynes & Co v Lloyd & Sons* [1895] 1 Q.B. 820 at 826 (in C.A. [1895] 2 Q.B. 610); *Budd-Scott v Daniell* [1902] 2 K.B. 351.

landlord and tenant,[2] unless it is displaced by the presence of an express covenant for quiet enjoyment,[3] which may differ in its terms. The implied covenant extends to all acts of the landlord and any lawful acts of those claiming under him, but not the acts of others, such as someone claiming by title paramount (such as a superior landlord[4]), nor to acts of the land-lord himself if he is acting under statutory authority,[5] nor to matters caused by factors in existence prior to the commencement of the tenancy.[6] The covenant is not one for "quiet" enjoyment in the acoustic sense; the landlord undertakes not that the tenant will be free from the nuisance of noise, but that he will be free from disturbance by adverse claimants to the property.[7] The covenant is broken if a person to whose acts it extends causes subsid-ence to the land by working minerals under it,[8] or in some other way physically and sub-stantially interferes with the tenant's enjoyment of the land[9]; and this includes persistent intimidation of the tenant to induce her to leave.[10] No exemplary damages can be awarded merely for breach of the covenant,[11] though they can be if the tort of trespass has been committed.[12] In addition, a residential occupier now has a right to statutory damages if he is unlawfully evicted from his premises, whether directly or indirectly.

No derogation from grant

13–003   It is a principle of general application that a grantor must not derogate from his grant.[13] He must not seek to take away with one hand what he has given with the other. In the case of leases, the covenant for quiet enjoyment will extend to many of the acts which might be construed as a derogation from the lessor's grant; but acts not amounting to a breach of the covenant may nevertheless be restrained as being in derogation of the grant. Thus, if land is leased for the express purpose of storing explosives, the lessor and those claiming under him will be restrained from using adjoining land so as to endanger the statutory licence necessary for storing explosives.[14]

There must, however, be some act making the premises substantially less fit for the purposes for which they were let. No action will lie if the landlord, having let the premises for some particular trade, such as for a wool shop only, lets adjoining premises for purposes which offer trade competition; for the original premises are still fit for use as a wool shop even if the profits will be diminished.[15] Nor will mere invasion of privacy, as by erecting an external staircase passing the windows of the flat demised, amount to a breach of the

---

2   *Budd-Scott v Daniell* [1902] 2 K.B. 351; *Markham v Paget* [1908] 1 Ch. 697; *Kenny v Preen* [1963] 1 Q.B. 499.
3   *Miller v Emcer Products Ltd* [1956] Ch. 304.
4   *Baynes & Co v Lloyd & Sons* [1895] 2 Q.B. 610; *Jones v Lavington* [1903] 1 K.B. 253.
5   *Commissioners of Crown Lands v Page* [1960] 2 Q.B. 274 (requisitioning).
6   *Southwark LBC v Mills* [2001] 1 A.C. 1.
7   *Hudson v Cripps* [1896] 1 Ch. 265 at 268.
8   *Markham v Paget* [1908] 1 Ch. 697.
9   *Owen v Gadd* [1956] 2 Q.B. 99 (adjacent scaffolding).
10   *Kenny v Preen* [1963] 1 Q.B. 499.
11   *Perera v Vandiyar* [1953] 1 W.L.R. 672; *Branchett v Beaney* [1992] 3 All E.R. 910.
12   *Drane v Evangelou* [1978] 1 W.L.R. 455.
13   *Palmer v Fletcher* (1663) 1 Lev. 122; and see (1964) 80 L.Q.R. 244 (D. W. Elliott).
14   *Harmer v Jumbil (Nigeria) Tin Areas Ltd* [1921] 1 Ch. 200.
15   *Port v Griffith* [1938] 1 All E.R. 295.

obligation,[16] although interference with the stability of the house by vibrations caused by powerful engines on adjoining land may suffice, and so may excessive noise, such as that caused in altering another flat in the same building.[17]

In certain cases, obligations as to fitness and repair

In general, the landlord gives no implied undertaking that the premises will be fit for habitation,[18] nor is he liable to repair them. But this rule is subject to five qualifications, which to some extent overlap.

13–004

Furnished lettings: Where a house is let furnished, the landlord impliedly undertakes that it is fit for human habitation when let.[19] If this is not the case, the tenant may repudiate the tenancy and recover damages for any loss he has suffered.[20] But if the premises are fit for human habitation when let, the landlord need do no more. He is under no obligation to keep them in this condition.[21] The tenant is not deemed to warrant his fitness to occupy the premises, such as that he is free from contagious diseases.[22]

Houses let at a low rent: Under the Landlord and Tenant Act 1985,[23] if a house is let for human habitation at a low rent, then, notwithstanding any stipulation to the contrary, there is:

(i) an implied condition that it is fit for human habitation at the beginning of the tenancy; and

(ii) an implied undertaking by the landlord that he will keep it in this condition throughout the tenancy.

This liability applies only to defects of which the landlord has notice,[24] though it extends to minor matters such as a broken sash-cord, for the question is not how difficult it is to repair the defect but whether by ordinary use of the premises damage may be naturally caused to the occupier.[25] Yet these provisions are of limited importance today as they still apply only if the rent does not exceed £80 a year in London and £52 elsewhere.[26]

Short leases of dwellings: In any lease or agreement for a lease[27] of a dwelling-house granted on or after October 24, 1961, whatever the rent or rateable value, a covenant by the landlord to do certain repairs is implied if the term is less than seven years (unless the tenant can

---

[16] *Browne v Flower* [1911] 1 Ch. 219.
[17] *Newman v Real Estate Debenture Corp Ltd* [1940] 1 All E.R. 131.
[18] *Hart v Windsor* (1844) 12 M. & W. 68.
[19] *Smith v Marrable* (1843) 11 M. & W. 5 (bugs).
[20] *Wilson v Finch Hatton* (1877) 2 Ex.D. 336; *Charsley v Jones* (1889) 53 J.P. 280; cp.
[21] *Sarson v Roberts* [1895] 2 Q.B. 395.
[22] *Humphreys v Miller* [1917] 2 K.B. 122.
[23] s.8, replacing earlier legislation.
[24] *McCarrick v Liverpool Corp* [1947] A.C. 219.
[25] *Summers v Salford Corp* [1943] A.C. 283 (tenant injured when other sash-cord broke).
[26] L & TA 1985 s.8; and see ss.8(5).
[27] *Brikom Investments Ltd v Seaford* [1981] 1 W.L.R. 863.

extend it to seven years or more) or if the landlord can determine it within seven years.[28] The covenant cannot be excluded or limited by any agreement to the contrary unless the county court has authorised this as being reasonable; and any covenant by the tenant to repair or pay money in lieu thereof is of no effect so far as it is covered by the landlord's covenant.

The obligations of the landlord under the implied covenant are as follows.

(1) *Structure and exterior*: to keep the structure and exterior of the dwelling in repair.[29] This includes the drains, gutters and external pipes,[30] and also the outside walls (even if excluded from the demise[31]) and any outside steps which form an essential part of the means of access to the dwelling,[32] but not a backyard.[33] The obligation does not extend to defects such as condensation which arise from faulty design rather than disrepair.[34] It does extend, however, to the plasterwork forming part of the walls and ceilings and the landlord is therefore liable for damage to that plasterwork caused by damp and mould.[35]

(2) *Installations*: to keep in repair and proper working order the installations in the dwelling:

    (i) for the supply of water, gas and electricity, and for sanitation, including basins, sinks, baths and sanitary conveniences, but not other appliances for making use of water, gas and electricity; and

    (ii) for space heating and heating water.[36]

Initially, the statute was drafted narrowly so that the section did not apply to installations or structures not within the dwelling. Where a lease is granted after January 14, 1989, and the dwelling forms part only of a building, the landlord's statutory covenant is extended so as to apply to any part of the building in which he has an estate or interest. It also applies to any installations which directly or indirectly serve the dwelling if they are owned by him or are under his control, or if they are part of any part of the building in which he has an estate or interest. But it is a defence if he shows that he made reasonable endeavours to obtain adequate access to do the works, and failed.[37]

An ill-designed water closet cistern in a maisonette which floods the floor whenever used is not in "proper working order".[38]

There are two main limitations on these obligations of the landlord. First, they do not apply to works or repairs for which the tenant is liable by virtue of his duty to use the premises in a tenant-like manner,[39] such as his duty to take reasonable precautions against burst

---

[28] L & TA 1985 ss.11 (as amended by HA 1988 s.116), 1214, 36, 38.
[29] L & TA 1985 s.11(1)(a).
[30] L & TA 1985 s.11(1)(a).
[31] *Campden Hill Towers Ltd v Gardner* [1977] Q.B. 823.
[32] *Brown v Liverpool Corp* [1969] 3 All E.R. 1345.
[33] *Hopwood v Cannock Chase D.C.* [1975] 1 W.L.R. 373. See further *Irvine v Moran* (1990) 24 H.L.R. 1.
[34] *Quick v Taff Ely BC* [1986] Q.B. 809; contrast *Stent v Monmouth D.C.* (1987) 19 H.L.R. 269.
[35] *Grand v Gill* [2011] 1 W.L.R. 2253, CA.
[36] L & TA 1985 s.11(1)(b).
[37] L & TA 1985 s.11(1A), (3A), inserted by Housing Act 1988 s.116.
[38] *Liverpool CC v Irwin* [1977] A.C. 239.
[39] L & TA 1985 s.11(2)(a); and see (b), (c). For the tenant's duty, see below, para.13–012.

pipes when leaving the premises unoccupied during winter.[40] Secondly, the obligations do not apply to any defect in the demised premises unless the landlord has notice or knowledge of the defect, either specifically or from facts that would put a reasonable man on inquiry.[41]

Where the statutory covenant applies to the landlord, there is an implied covenant by the tenant to permit the landlord to enter and view the premises at reasonable times of the day on 24 hours' prior notice in writing to the occupier.[42]

Duty of care: In some cases a landlord owes to all persons who might reasonably be expected to be affected by defects in the state of any part of the premises let[43] a statutory duty to take reasonable care in all the circumstances[44] to see that they and their property are reasonably safe from injury or damage. This duty arises where the landlord is under an obligation to the tenant for the maintenance or repair of the premises, or has a right to enter the premises to maintain and repair them, and he knows or ought to have known of the defect.[45] The landlord cannot contract out of his liability under this provision.[46] However, the tenant will be guilty of contributory negligence if he has been put on inquiry that there was a real risk that the defects have occurred.[47]

Implied terms: In some cases the court may imply a covenant or obligation by the landlord as to the physical condition of the premises. Thus where a flat in a tower block is let on terms which impose obligations on the tenant but not on the landlord, the landlord will be held to be under an implied obligation to take reasonable care to maintain the common parts of the block (i.e. the lifts, the stairs and the lighting on the stairs) in a state of reasonable repair and efficiency, thereby supplementing the incomplete terms of the tenancy.[48] Again, where a tenant has covenanted to keep the interior of a house in good repair, the landlord may be subject to an implied covenant to keep the exterior in good repair, thus giving the tenant's covenant business efficacy by imposing a correlative obligation that will preserve the interior from the elements.[49] But where the lease sets out the full obligations of both parties, terms will be implied in it only if it is necessary to do so in order to give the lease business efficacy, and not merely because they seem reasonable.[50]

Local housing authorities: Local housing authorities have extensive powers of compelling the person who has control of a house (usually the owner or his agent) to enforce housing

---

[40] *Wycombe Health Authority v Barnett* (1982) 47 P. & C.R. 394 (two days' absence: not liable); criticised (1984) 81 L.S.G. 3408 (M. P. Thompson), discussing lagging.

[41] *O'Brien v Robinson* [1973] A.C. 912; *Dinefwr BC v Jones* (1987) 19 H.L.R. 445; *Hall v Howard* (1988) 20 H.L.R. 566.

[42] L & TA 1985 s.11(6).

[43] *Smith v Bradford Metropolitan Council* (1982) 44 P. & C.R. 171 (patio).

[44] *Sykes v Harry* (2001) 82 P. & C.R. 35.

[45] Defective Premises Act 1972 s.4. See, e.g. *McAuley v Bristol CC* [1992] 1 Q.B. 134 (defective garden step). See also *Targett v Torfaen BC* [1992] 3 All E.R. 27 (liability of builder at common law for negligent design or construction).

[46] Defective Premises Act 1972 s.6(3).

[47] *Sykes v Harry* (2001) 82 P. & C.R. 35.

[48] *Liverpool CC v Irwin* [1977] A.C. 239; and see *King v South Northamptonshire DC* (1992) 64 P. & C.R. 35 (access to rear entrance).

[49] *Barrett v Lounova (1982) Ltd* [1990] 1 Q.B. 348. Contrast *Demetriou v Poolaction Ltd* [1991] 1 E.G.L.R. 100, where there was no such obligation.

[50] *Liverpool CC v Irwin* [1977] A.C. 239; *Duke of Westminster v Guild* [1985] Q.B. 688.

standards and eliminate hazards.[51] Tenants can attempt to avoid the burden of directly enforcing their rights by setting the local housing authority in motion.

Position of the tenant

Obligation to pay rent

13–005 This is discussed below.[52]

Obligation to pay rates and taxes

13–006 The tenant is under an obligation to pay all rates and taxes except those for which the landlord is liable. A landlord is liable to income tax on the rent.[53] The tenant is liable for council tax[54] (on residential property) and non-domestic rates (on commercial property)[55].

Obligation not to commit waste

13–007 A tenant's liability for waste depends upon the nature of his tenancy. A tenant for a fixed term of years is liable for both voluntary and permissive waste, and must therefore keep the premises in proper repair.[56] A yearly tenant is similarly liable save that liability for permissive waste is limited to keeping the premises wind- and water-tight.[57] A weekly tenant, on the other hand, is not liable for permissive waste as such, though they must use the premises in a tenant-like manner, and so must take proper care of them, for example by keeping the drain pipes unblocked.[58] The same rule probably applies to monthly and quarterly tenants. A tenant at will is not liable for permissive waste,[59] although if they commit voluntary waste the tenancy is thereby terminated and they are liable to an action for damages.[60] A tenant at sufferance is liable for voluntary waste,[61] though probably not for permissive waste.

Landlord's right to view

13–008 A landlord may by statute or by the terms of the tenancy be expressly authorised to enter the premises; and if he is liable to repair the premises he has an implied right to enter them for this purpose.[62] Otherwise, he has no right to enter the premises so long as the tenancy endures.[63]

---

[51] Housing Act 2004.
[52] Below, para.13–015.
[53] Income Tax (Trading and Other Income) Act 2005.
[54] Local Government and Finance Act 1992 (LGFA 1992).
[55] LGFA 1992.
[56] *Yellowly v Gower* (1855) 11 Exch. 274; for waste, see above, para.4–012.
[57] *Wedd v Porter* [1916] 2 K.B. 91.
[58] *Warren v Keen* [1954] 1 Q.B. 15.
[59] *Harnett v Maitland* (1847) 16 M. & W. 257.
[60] *Countess of Shrewsbury's Case* (1600) 5 Co.Rep. 13b.
[61] *Burchell v Hornsby* (1808) 1 Camp. 360.
[62] *Saner v Bilton* (1878) 7 Ch.D. 815.
[63] *Stocker v Planet Building Society* (1879) 27 W.R. 877.

POSITION UNDER A LEASE CONTAINING THE USUAL COVENANTS

Effect of agreement

If a lease has actually been granted, the obligations of the parties in the absence of any contrary provision in the lease are as set out above. If, on the other hand, the parties have either agreed that a lease containing the "usual covenants" shall be granted, or have entered into an agreement for a lease containing no reference to the covenants which it should contain, then, subject to any contrary agreement by the parties, the lease must contain whatever covenants and conditions may be "usual" in the circumstances, and if it does not, it may be rectified to accord with the agreement. Except in so far that they cover the same ground, the obligations imposed by the "usual" covenants and conditions are additional to those set out under the heading "Position in the absence of express provision" above.[64]   **13–009**

The usual covenants

The following covenants and conditions are always "usual".[65]   **13–010**

On the part of the landlord

This is a covenant for quiet enjoyment in the usual qualified form, i.e. extending only to the acts of the lessor or the rightful acts of any person claiming from or under him.   **13–011**

On the part of the tenant   **13–012**

- (i) a covenant to pay rent;
- (ii) a covenant to pay tenant's rates and taxes, i.e. all rates and taxes except those which statute requires the landlord to bear;
- (iii) a covenant to keep the premises in repair and deliver them up at the end of the term in this condition;
- (iv) a covenant to permit the landlord to enter and view the state of repair, if he is liable to repair; and
- (v) a condition of re-entry for non-payment of rent, but not for breach of any other covenant.

Usual by custom or usage

In addition to the above provisions, which are always "usual", other covenants may be "usual" in the circumstances of the case, by virtue, for example, of the custom of the neighbourhood or trade usage. In each case, this is a question of fact for the court, taking into account the nature of the premises, their situation, the purpose for which they are being let, the length of the term, the evidence of conveyancers and the contents of books of prec-   **13–013**

---

[64] Above, para.13–001.
[65] See *Hampshire v Wickens* (1878) 7 Ch.D. 555.

edents.[66] Today, a right of re-entry for breach of any covenant will normally be "usual".[67] In the absence of such special circumstances, however, many covenants which in practice are usually inserted in leases and are therefore literally "usual" are nevertheless not deemed to be "usual" in the technical sense of the word. Examples are covenants against assignment, covenants against carrying on specified trades, and provisos for forfeiture if the tenant has a bankruptcy order made against him or enters into liquidation or suffers any distress or process of execution to be levied upon his goods or makes any assignment or composition for the benefit of his creditors. Such provisions are frequently inserted when (as is usually the case) no contract to take a lease has been made and the terms of the lease are a matter for negotiation between the parties. But if a contract for a lease has been made, no covenant can be inserted in the lease without the concurrence of both parties unless either the contract provides for it or the covenant is technically a "usual" covenant.

POSITION UNDER CERTAIN COVENANTS USUALLY FOUND IN LEASES

13–014 A number of covenants have already been considered, but certain other covenants must be mentioned as well.

Covenant to pay rent

13–015 Unless the lease provides for payment in advance, rent is normally payable in arrear.[68] It continues to be payable even if the premises cannot be used, for example owing to destruction by fire[69] or other calamity, or seizure by military authorities for the occupation of troops,[70] save in the exceptional case of the lease being frustrated.[71] However, this stern common law rule is frequently mitigated by an express provision in the lease, and in the case of war damage and requisitioning (but not other events) the tenant has been given a statutory right to disclaim his tenancy.[72]

The landlord may enforce payment of the rent:

(i) directly, by:
    (a) an action for the money; or
    (b) distress;
(ii) indirectly, by the threat of forfeiture if the lease contains a forfeiture clause. Forfeiture has already been dealt with,[73] and there is no need to discuss an action for the money. The availability of distress has been become increasingly restricted with the introduction of Commercial Rent Arrears Recovery.[74]

---

[66] See *Flexman v Corbett* [1930] 1 Ch. 672.
[67] *Chester v Buckingham Travel Ltd* [1981] 1 W.L.R. 96. See [1992] Conv. 18 (L. Crabb).
[68] *Coomber v Howard* (1845) 1 C.B. 440.
[69] *Belfour v Weston* (1786) 1 T.R. 310.
[70] *Whitehall Court Ltd v Ettlinger* [1920] 1 K.B. 680.
[71] See above, para.12–025.
[72] See above, para.12–024.
[73] Above, para.12–003 et seq.
[74] See Tribunals, Courts and Enforcement Act 2007 and Taking Control of Goods Regulations 2013 (2013/1894).

Covenant against assigning, underletting or parting with possession (alienation)

The tenant's rights

If the lease is silent on the matter the tenant is entitled to assign, underlet or part with pos-   **13–016**
session of the premises without the landlord's consent; for during the term the property
is the tenant's. However, a covenant against assignment, underletting or parting with possession of all or any part of the premises is often inserted in leases; and although an assignment or sub-lease made in breach of covenant is valid,[75] the breach will usually give rise to
forfeiture or a claim for damages.

Unreasonable withholding of consent

If the covenant is absolute, the landlord can enforce it if he wishes; and, although he   **13–017**
may waive a breach in any particular instance, he cannot be compelled to do so, even if
his attitude is entirely unreasonable. But if the covenant is one against assigning or sub-
letting "without licence or consent" (often called a "qualified covenant") the Landlord and
Tenant Act 1927[76] provides that notwithstanding any provision to the contrary the covenant is deemed to be subject to a proviso that the licence or consent is not to be unreasonably withheld. This does not permit the tenant to assign or sub-let without seeking the
landlord's consent: if he does so, he is in breach of covenant even if the landlord, if asked,
could not properly have withheld his consent.[77] But if he seeks consent and it is unreasonably withheld he may forthwith assign or sub-let without the consent,[78] or else pursue
the safer but slower course of seeking a declaration from the court of his right to do so.[79]

The Landlord and Tenant Act 1988 has now strengthened the position of the tenant, particularly against dilatory or evasive landlords.[80] If the tenant serves a written application for
consent on the landlord, the landlord is under a duty to give his consent unless it is reasonable not to do so; and, if consent is withheld or is granted subject to conditions, he must give
written notice of the reasons for withholding the consent or imposing the conditions, and
this notice must be given within a reasonable time.[81] The burden of proof on these matters
now lies on the landlord,[82] and any breach of duty under the Act now sounds in damages.[83]

These provisions do not apply to a term in a lease requiring that before seeking to assign
the lease the tenant must offer to surrender it to the landlord gratis; for in effect this is

---

[75] *Old Grovebury Manor Farm Ltd v W. Seymour Plant and Hire Ltd (No.2)* [1979] 1 W.L.R. 1397.
[76] s.19(1).
[77] *Eastern Telegraph Co Ltd v Dent* [1899] 1 Q.B. 835.
[78] *Treloar v Bigge* (1874) L.R. 9 Ex. 151.
[79] *Young v Ashley Gardens Properties Ltd* [1903] 2 Ch. 112.
[80] See *29 Equities Ltd v Bank Leumi (UK) Ltd* [1986] 1 W.L.R. 1490 at 1494.
[81] L & TA 1988 s.1(3), (4). See, e.g. *Midland Bank Plc v Chart Enterprises Inc* [1990] 2 E.G.L.R. 59
(delay).
[82] L & TA 1988 s.1(5).
[83] L & TA 1988 s.4.

a condition precedent to there being any right to assign, rather than the withholding of consent under an existing right.[84] Such a term requires protection by registration.[85]

Reasonableness

13–018   In determining whether the withholding of consent is reasonable, the question is whether, having regard to the purpose of the covenant, the landlord can show[86] that the withholding was reasonable.[87] He cannot rely on matters unconnected with the relationship of landlord and tenant,[88] and although he need consider only his own relevant interests, it is unreasonable to withhold consent where the detriment to the tenant would be extreme, and disproportionate to the benefit to the landlord[89]; and contra, if vice versa.[90] The landlord now appears to be confined to the reasons given in response to the tenant's application,[91] and in any event he cannot rely on any reason which did not in fact influence his mind when withholding consent.[92] If any of the reasons given is plainly bad, this may establish unreasonableness.[93] Usually no withholding of consent will be reasonable unless it is based on the person of the assignee or the proposed use of the premises,[94] and this includes the impact of supervening statutes which would confer additional protection on the tenant.[95] If the reason for refusing consent amounts to discrimination on the grounds of race, religion, sexual orientation, sex, disability or gender reassignment, then as well as being unreasonable it will be unlawful.[96] Unless the lease provides for it, the landlord may not require the payment of a fine or other valuable consideration for giving his consent.[97]

Breach

13–019   To amount to a breach of covenant against assignment on underletting, there must in general be some voluntary dealing with the property inter vivos. Thus a bequest of the lease is no breach,[98] nor is the involuntary vesting of the lease in the trustee in bankruptcy upon the tenant's bankruptcy,[99] or the compulsory sale of the lease under statutory provisions,[100]

---

[84]   *Bocardo SA v S. & M. Hotels Ltd* [1980] 1 W.L.R. 17.
[85]   Above, para.5–024.
[86]   L & TA 1988 s.1(5).
[87]   *Leeward Securities Ltd v Lilyheath Properties Ltd* (1983) 17 H.L.R. 35.
[88]   *Houlder Bros v Gibbs* [1925] Ch. 575.
[89]   *International Drilling Fluids Ltd v Louisville Investments (Uxbridge) Ltd* [1986] Ch. 513, cited with approval in *Ashworth Frazer Ltd v Gloucester CC* [2001] 1 W.L.R. 2180.
[90]   *Deverall v Wyndham* [1989] 1 E.G.L.R. 57.
[91]   See L & TA 1988 s.1(3), (5).
[92]   *Bromley Park Garden Estates Ltd v Moss* [1982] 1 W.L.R. 1019.
[93]   See *Berenyi v Watford BC* (1980) 256 E.G. 271.
[94]   See *Viscount Tredegar v Harwood* [1929] A.C. 72.
[95]   *West Layton Ltd v Ford* [1979] Q.B. 593. Consider, e.g. the Leasehold Reform Act 1967 and the Rent Act 1977.
[96]   Equality Act 2010.
[97]   LPA 1925 s.144, replacing CA 1892 s.3.
[98]   *Fox v Swann* (1655) Sty. 482.
[99]   *Re Riggs* [1901] 2 K.B. 16.
[100]   *Slipper v Tottenham & Hampstead Junction Ry* (1867) L.R. 4 Eq. 112.

as distinct from a voluntary sale by the tenant's trustee in bankruptcy.[101] A mortgage made by the grant of a sub-lease is a breach, but one made by a mere deposit of the title deeds is not, nor is a declaration of trust made by the tenant for the benefit of his creditors.[102] A covenant merely against underletting is perhaps not broken by an assignment or by letting lodgings.

Covenant to repair

Construction of covenant

In long leases, the tenant usually covenants to do all repairs; in short leases, the landlord frequently assumes liability for external and structural repairs, and in some cases is compelled by statute to do so.[103] Subject to this, in every case, the matter is one for negotiation. If no provision is made for repairs, neither party is liable for them, apart from statute and the general law relating to waste. The extent of the liability of any party under a repairing covenant depends, of course, upon the wording of the covenant, but expressions such as "tenantable repair", "sufficient repair", or "good and substantial repair" seem to add little to the meaning of the word "repair".[104] On a letting of premises that are out of repair, a covenant to "keep" them in good repair requires them to be put into good repair.[105] If the covenant is qualified by words such as "fair wear and tear excepted", they exclude liability for defects due to reasonable use of the premises or the action of the elements, but not for consequential damage caused, for example by rain entering through an unrepaired skylight.[106]

13–020

Repair

"Repair" is not confined to restoring the original structure but extends to replacing subsidiary parts of the building which can no longer be repaired, as by rebuilding a wall,[107] replacing the roof,[108] or providing new drainpipes for old. It is often difficult to draw the line between "repair" and "renewal" or "improvement". The matter is essentially one of degree, and in particular whether the works will so change the character of the building as to restore to the landlord a building that is wholly different from that demised.[109] The basic question is whether in all the circumstances of the case the requisite work as a whole can fairly be called a repair. It may be so substantial as to be beyond anything that a reasonable person could contemplate as being a repair.[110] The circumstances to be considered include the terms of the lease; the nature of the building; its state when let; the nature and extent of the repair; the nature, extent and cost of the works to be done,

13–021

---

[101] *Re Wright* [1949] Ch. 729.
[102] *Gentle v Faulkner* [1900] 2 K.B. 267.
[103] Above, para.13–004.
[104] *Anstruther-Gough-Calthorpe v McOscar* [1924] 1 K.B. 716 at 722, 723.
[105] *Proudfoot v Hart* (1890) 25 QBD 42 at 50.
[106] *Regis Property Co Ltd v Dudley* [1959] A.C. 370.
[107] *Lurcott v Wakely* [1911] 1 K.B. 905.
[108] *Elite Investments Ltd v T. I. Bainbridge Silencers Ltd* [1986] 2 E.G.L.R. 43.
[109] *Ravenseft Properties Ltd v Davstone (Holdings) Ltd* [1980] Q.B. 12.
[110] *Brew Brothers Ltd v Snax (Ross) Ltd* [1970] 1 Q.B. 612.

and who is to do them; the value and life-span of the building, and the effect of the works on them; and the comparative cost of alternative remedial works, their effect on the occupants and the likelihood of a recurrence in each case: and the weight to be attached to these factors will vary from case to case.[111] Thus to remedy an inherent defect may or may not be repair. Curing dampness in a modern high-class flat by inserting a silicone damp course will be a repair,[112] whereas it is not a repair where the damp in an aged cellar with porous bricks can be cured only by constructing new walls.[113] Premises that are still in the same physical condition as they were when first let are not out of repair merely because through some inherent structural defect the basement has been flooded, though without doing any harm.[114]

Enforcement

13–022   As has already been seen,[115] the court has statutory power to order specific performance of the landlord's repairing covenants in favour of a tenant of a dwelling-house[116] and it can do so in favour of a tenant of any type of property under its inherent jurisdiction.[117] The court may also order specific performance of the tenant's repairing covenants in favour of the landlord but it will only do so where damages would be an inadequate remedy. An example is where the lease contains no proviso for re-entry and forfeiture, where the property is deteriorating and the landlord has no right of access to carry out the repairs himself.[118] In other circumstances, he will have to elect between forfeiture and an award of damages. (Both require leave to sue in respect of any property (other than an agricultural holding) let for a term of years certain of not less than seven years which has at least three years unexpired[119] and special rules govern the measure of damages.[120])

Measure of damages

13–023   The measure of damages recoverable by a tenant for the breach of a repairing covenant is the cost of carrying out the repairs. However, the measure of damages recoverable by a landlord for such a breach formerly varied according to the time of the breach. If the breach occurred during the term, damages were calculated on the decrease in the value of the reversion caused by the breach,[121] i.e. on the difference between the value of the landlord's interest with the repairs done and its value without. Thus the longer the lease had to run, the less would be the damages. But if the breach occurred at the end of the term, the cost

---

[111] *Holding and Management Ltd v Property Holding Plc* [1990] 1 All E.R. 938 at 945 (omitted from [1989] 1 W.L.R. 1313).
[112] *Elmcroft Developments Ltd v Tankersley-Sawyer* (1984) 15 H.L.R. 63.
[113] *Pembery v Lamdin* [1940] 2 All E.R. 434.
[114] *Post Office v Aquarius Properties Ltd* [1987] 1 All E.R. 1055.
[115] Above, para.13–004.
[116] L & TA 1985 s.17.
[117] *Jeune v Queen's Cross Properties Ltd* [1974] Ch. 97.
[118] *Rainbow Estates Ltd v Tokenhold Ltd* [1999] Ch. 64.
[119] Leasehold Property (Repairs) Act 1938, as extended by L & TA 1954 s.51.
[120] See below.
[121] *Ebbetts v Conquest* [1895] 2 Ch. 377 (affirmed [1896] A.C. 490).

of repairing the premises was recoverable by the landlord[122] even if he did not propose to spend the money in making the repairs but intended to demolish the premises instead. Now, however, by the Landlord and Tenant Act 1927,[123] damages for breach of a repairing covenant are not to exceed the diminution in the value of the reversion, though if the repairs are going to be done, that diminution will usually be measured by the cost of the repairs.[124] Further, no damages are recoverable if the premises are to be demolished, or structurally altered in such a way as to make the repairs valueless, at or soon after the end of the term. There are special provisions enabling the court in certain cases to relieve the tenant from liability for internal decorative repairs.[125]

Leave to sue

There are also provisions which protect the tenant of any property (except agricultural holdings) let for a term of years certain of not less than seven years which has at least three years unexpired.[126] The lack of any provision for relief against claims for damages for non-repair often enabled landlords to force tenants to surrender their leases prematurely, and so the Leasehold Property (Repairs) Act 1938[127] provides that no action for damages for breach of a covenant to repair the property can be brought unless the landlord has first served on the tenant a notice in the form required by the Law of Property Act 1925 s.146,[128] and one month has elapsed thereafter. Further, whether the landlord is claiming damages or forfeiture, he cannot proceed without the leave of the court in such cases if within 28 days the tenant serves on the landlord a counter-notice claiming the protection of the Act; and the notice served by the landlord must inform the tenant of his right to serve a counter-notice. The court can grant leave only on certain specified grounds, such as that the cost of immediate repair would be small compared with the cost of repair in the future. The Act does not apply where the landlord, under a power in the lease, enters and carries out the repairs, and sues the tenant for the cost, for his claim against the tenant is for a debt, and not for "damages" within the Act.[129]

13–024

Deducting cost of repairs from rent

A tenant who does repairs for which the landlord is liable is entitled to deduct the cost from the present or future rent,[130] though this should not be done without prior notification to the landlord.[131]

13–025

---

[122] *Joyner v Weeks* [1891] 2 Q.B. 31.
[123] s.18(1).
[124] *Smiley v Townshend* [1950] 2 K.B. 311.
[125] LPA 1925 s.147.
[126] Leasehold Property (Repairs) Act 1938, as extended by L & TA 1954 s.51.
[127] s.1.
[128] See above, para.12–017.
[129] *Hamilton v Martell Securities Ltd* [1984] Ch. 266; *Colchester Estates (Cardiff) v Carlton Industries Plc* [1986] Ch. 80.
[130] *Lee-Parker v Izzet* [1971] 1 W.L.R. 1688; *Asco Developments Ltd v Gordon* [1978] E.G.D. 376.
[131] See [1981] Conv. 199 (A. Waite) for this and other precautions.

Covenant to insure

13–026   A covenant to insure against fire is broken if the premises are uninsured for any period, however short, even if no fire occurs.[132]

REMEDY

13–027   The basic remedy available for breach of covenant is damages, although distress (the right to enter the premises and enforce payment by seizing and selling enough of any goods which are found there) is in some cases an alternative remedy for unpaid rent.133

However, a landlord cannot either claim damages or levy distress when he has successfully forfeited the lease. The court has statutory power to order specific performance of the landlord's repairing covenants in favour of a tenant of a dwelling-house[134] and it can do so in favour of a tenant of any type of property under its inherent jurisdiction.[135] The court may also order specific performance of the tenant's repairing covenants in favour of the landlord but it will only do so where damages would be an inadequate remedy. An example is where the lease contains no proviso for re-entry and forfeiture, where the property is deteriorating and the landlord has no right of access to carry out the repairs himself.[136]

In other circumstances, he will have to elect between forfeiture and an award of damages. The court will not generally order specific performance of other types of positive covenants, particularly where whether or not the order has been complied with is likely to be contentious. Thus, because of the difficulties of drawing an order with sufficient precision to avoid continuous and wasteful litigation, specific performance was denied where the tenant breached a covenant to keep the premises open as a supermarket. There would have been a risk of the landlord being enriched at the tenant's expense whereas an award of damages would bring the matter to an end.[137] However, the court will generally grant an injunction restraining any breach of a negative covenant, typically a covenant which is restrictive of the user of the land.

SUMMARY OF KEY CASES

- *Southwark LBC v Mills* [2001] 1 A.C. 1

---

[132] *Penniall v Harborne* (1848) 11 Q.B. 386.
[133] As of April 2014, distress for most commercial premises is abolished and replaced with Commercial Rent Arrears Recovery.
[134] L & TA 1985 s.17.
[135] *Jeune v Queen's Cross Properties Ltd* [1974] Ch. 97.
[136] *Rainbow Estates Ltd v Tokenhold Ltd* [1999] Ch. 64.
[137] *Co-operative Insurance Ltd v Argyll Stores (Holdings) Ltd* [1998] A.C. 1.

FURTHER READING

- J. Gaunt QC, "Where the law went wrong: Joyner v Weeks" (2013) 17(6) L.&T.R. 202
- P. Clark, "The RICS small business retail lease" Conv. 2012 5, 355–362
- Equality Act 2010, JHL 2011, 14(4), D83–84

Chapter 14

LEASEHOLD COVENANTS

CHAPTER SUMMARY

This chapter covers the enforceability, or "running", of covenants in leases if the landlord, or the tenant, or both, dispose of their interest in one way or another. The chapter also considers the position of third parties to leases such as sureties and management companies in these situations.

This is an important topic because leases are commonly granted for far longer fixed terms than many other types of contract, and so one or both of the parties often disposes of their interest during the term.

As a result of the enactment of the Landlord and Tenant (Covenants) Act 1995 ("the 1995 Act"),[1] the law now differs depending on whether the lease in question was created before January 1, 1996[2] ("an old lease") or after that date ("a new lease"). Because the two regimes are quite distinct, with little overlap, the structure of this Chapter is to consider the two regimes separately. The rules will first be summarised and then considered in detail.

PART 1   GENERAL PRINCIPLES

WHAT IS A "COVENANT" FOR THIS PURPOSE?

Usually, the expression "covenant" means a promise contained in a deed; but in the law of landlord and tenant the expression "covenant" also includes other enforceable agreements.[3] In respect of new leases, "covenant" is a defined expression[4] including any term, condition or obligation, express or implied, or imposed by law[5], and extending to collateral agreements.

14–001

---

[1] Based on Law Com. No.174; see S. N. Bridge [1996] C.L.J. 313.
[2] The date that the Landlord and Tenant (Covenants) Act 1995 came into force.
[3] See *Weg Motors Ltd v Hales* [1961] Ch. 176 at 193; [1962] Ch. 49 at 73.
[4] 1995 Act s.28(1).
[5] 1995 Act s.2(1).

Contrast with the general law of contract

14–002   Unless a contract is expressly agreed to be personal, or non-assignable, then as a general rule a contracting party can "assign the contract".[6] But what is assignable is the benefit of the contract. The burden of the contract cannot as a general rule be assigned other than by agreement of the other party; novation is the usual result if that happens. Broadly speaking the "benefit" of a covenant is the right to sue on the covenant and the "burden" is the obligation to perform it. These general principles of the law of contract were long recognised by the common law as being inadequate for leases, given that they are not simply contracts but also create an estate in land. Some covenants therefore bind successors in title of the original parties; the burden may pass with the interest of landlord or tenant. Similarly, the benefit of certain covenants may pass without express assignment. In respect of new leases, and again in contrast with the general law of contract, assignment may have the effect of releasing the assignor from the burden of his covenant obligations.

Two regimes

14–003   As noted above, it is crucial to identify whether the lease is an old lease or a new lease. The basic rule is that a lease created after January 1, 1996 is a new lease. However, there are two minor exceptions to this rule: a lease which is granted pursuant to an agreement or to a court order made before January 1, 1996[7] or pursuant to the exercise of an option granted before that date, no matter when that option is exercised,[8] is an old lease.

PART 2   INTRODUCTION TO ENFORCEABILITY UNDER OLD LEASES AND NEW LEASES—THE TWO REGIMES CONTRASTED

INTRODUCTION TO ENFORCEABILITY OF COVENANTS IN OLD LEASES

14–004   The law governing the enforceability of covenants in old leases is a complex and not entirely coherent mixture of common law principles and various provisions of the Law of Property Act 1925.[9] Some very broad propositions can be set out as a framework upon which the detailed treatment which follows is built. The basic principles are these:

(a) all covenants are enforceable if there is privity of contract between the parties;
(b) the benefit, but not the burden, of any covenant may be assigned;
(c) if privity of contract is absent, but there is privity of estate, then covenants which "touch and concern the land" are enforceable;

---

[6]   And see LPA 1925 s.136 on legal assignments and which applies to all contracts, not just contracts relating to land.
[7]   LT(C)A 1995 s.1(3).
[8]   LT(C)A 1995 s.1(6).
[9]   LT(C)A 1995 ss.17 and 19 apply to old leases as well as new leases.

(d) if none of the above apply, but the covenant is a restrictive covenant, the benefit and burden can run in accordance with the general law applicable to restrictive covenants;

(e) otherwise, covenants are not enforceable.

The first two of those principles are simply the general law of contract translated into the landlord and tenant context. "Privity of contract" means that the parties are the original parties to the lease; the general rule is that the benefit of any contractual right may be assigned[10] but the burden may not. The original landlord and original tenant thus remain liable no matter times their interest is assigned on.

"Privity of Estate" means that the relationship of landlord and tenant exists between the parties; in other words there is privity of estate between the current landlord and current tenant. But the relationship must be one of legal tenure: there is no privity of estate between a landlord and an equitable assignee of the tenant or between the (head) landlord and a sub-tenant.

As to which covenants "touch and concern" the land, this is a somewhat technical subject discussed in detail later, but very broadly it means covenants to do with the relationship of landlord and tenant in respect of the land demised.

Summary enforceability of covenants in old leases

Enforcement against the parties to an old lease

As between the original parties to a lease, there is privity of contract simply because the parties concerned have made a legally enforceable agreement.[11] Clearly, if two people have agreed to do or not to do certain things, their obligations bind them, whether or not their contract has anything to do with land, and whether the covenant is negative or positive. The covenants can be enforced both at law, by an action for damages, and in equity, by an injunction or specific performance. Consequently, covenants can be enforced against an original party to a lease throughout its entire term, irrespective of the fact that he has assigned his interest to a third party. However, the ability of the landlord for the time being to recover "fixed charges" (rent, service charges and any other liquidated sums) from the original lessee has now been restricted. He can now only do so if he serves notice on the original lessee of his intention so to do within six months of each fixed charge becoming due.[12] Where a covenant is enforceable under privity of contract, there is no need to look further.

14–005

Against an assignee of an original party

Where either the landlord for the time being or the tenant for the time being (or both of them) is not an original party to the lease, there is no privity of contract but there is said to be privity of estate between the parties to the lease for the time being provided that it has been created and assigned with the necessary formalities.[13] In this case, any covenants in

14–006

---

[10] LPA 1925 s.136.
[11] See the diagram below at para.14–040.
[12] LT(C)A 1995 s.17.
[13] See the diagram below at para.14–040.

the lease which touch and concern the land, such as repairing covenants, are enforceable both at law and in equity. But covenants which do not relate to the land are not enforceable under this head nor is the burden of any covenant in a lease which has been created or assigned only in equity. Where a covenant is enforceable under privity of estate, there is no need to look further.

Against a guarantor

14–007   Any guarantor, whether of an original party or of an assignee, is in the same position as the person whose liability he is guaranteeing.

INTRODUCTION TO ENFORCEABILITY OF COVENANTS IN NEW LEASES

14–008   The 1995 Act lays down a new and largely self-contained statutory scheme for the transmission of covenant liability. There must of course be an initial contractual liability between landlord and tenant but beyond that the concepts of privity of contract, privity of estate and "touching and concerning" the land have no place under the 1995 Act.
   In very broad terms:

    (a) the benefit and burden of all covenants other than those which are "personal" or those which do not relate to the land demised will pass on assignment of the lease or of the reversion;

    (b) tenants and their guarantors are released from liability on assignment (although they may in certain cases be required to guarantee the assignee's performance of covenants);

    (c) landlords are not automatically released on assignment but may apply for release.

Summary enforcability of convenants in new leases

Against the landlord and tenant for the time being

14–009   Liability under all covenants by the original lessor and the original lessee passes on the lawful assignment of their respective interests to the persons to whom those interests are successively assigned no matter how the lease was created and assigned. The only exceptions relate to unlawful assignments or assignments by operation of law, to those covenants which are expressed to be personal to the person who entered into them, to those which require registration under the Land Charges Act 1972 or the Land Registration Act 2002, and to those which are no longer enforceable.

Against former landlords and tenants

14–010   Where any tenant, whether the original lessee or a subsequent assignee, assigns his lease, he will thereupon be released from the burden of any covenants which would otherwise have bound him (a subsequent assignee would only have been liable anyway where he has covenanted directly with the landlord for the time being). He will also cease to be entitled to the benefit of the covenants entered into by the landlord. However, a landlord can have recourse to the tenant who held the lease immediately before the tenant for the time being if the lease contains a covenant requiring the consent of the landlord to any assignment. In these circumstances, the landlord may give his consent on condition that the assigning tenant guarantees the performance of the covenants by the tenant to whom he is assigning (such an agreement is known as an "authorised guarantee agreement" or an "AGA"). However, the landlord will only be able to recover a fixed charge under an AGA if he serves notice on the former tenant that he proposes to do so within six months of the sum becoming due.

On the other hand, where the original lessor assigns his interest, he is not automatically released from liability under his covenants, but he may normally, before or within four weeks of the assignment taking place, apply to the tenant for the time being to be released. If the tenant refuses his consent, the lessor may apply to the court for a declaration that it is reasonable for the covenant to be released. A subsequent landlord is not liable under his covenants anyway once he has assigned on.

Against a guarantor

Any guarantor, whether of the landlord and tenant for the time being or of former landlords   **14–011**
and tenants, is in the same position as the person whose liability he is guaranteeing.

Enforcement against others

Direct enforcement

Where covenants are not enforceable under the rules which have just been discussed, the   **14–012**
general rule is that covenants concerning the land are not directly enforceable. This is the case as between a landlord and a sub-tenant and as between the vendor of freehold land and a person who subsequently buys it from the purchaser; this is also the case as between the landlord for the time being of an old lease and a tenant other than the original lessee where the lease has been created or assigned only in equity. To this rule there are three exceptions, the second of which is of great importance.

Benefit: First, even the common law allowed the benefit of certain covenants (i.e. the right to sue on the covenant) to be assigned with land; and equity followed the law. One example already mentioned[14] is that of covenants for title, the benefit of which runs with the land, so that whoever is entitled to the land is entitled to the benefit of the covenants. But the burden of a covenant (i.e. the liability to be sued upon it) cannot be assigned; at law, if there is no privity of estate the covenantor alone can be sued on a covenant.

Restrictive covenants in equity: Secondly, equity allows the transmission of the burden (as well as the benefit) of restrictive covenants affecting the land, i.e. covenants which are negative in nature, restraining the doing of some act, such as building on the land. As usual, however, a purchaser of a legal estate for value takes free from such burdens if he takes without notice or if the covenants are void against him for want of registration.[15]

Mutual benefit and burden: Thirdly, equity sometimes allows the transmission of the burden (as well as the benefit) of positive covenants under the principle of mutual benefit

---

[14] Above, para.6–050.
[15] See above, para.6–070; and see below, paras 14–054 et seq.

and burden. If land cannot be enjoyed without the use of a particular benefit, the burden of any corresponding obligation can be enforced against the person who is benefitting. Thus, a covenant to contribute to the costs of maintenance of the footpaths and roads of a private estate can be enforced against the owners of all the houses on it since they cannot reach their properties without using the footpaths and roads.[16]

Where a covenant is enforceable under one of these three heads, there is no need to look further. Where it is not, it may be able to be enforced indirectly.

Indirect enforcement

14–013   Where a leasehold covenant cannot be enforced directly, it may sometimes be enforced indirectly by virtue of a forfeiture clause in the lease. Thus if L leases land to T, and T sub-lets it to S, L cannot directly enforce the covenants in the lease against S. However, proceedings for forfeiture of the lease will normally impel S to comply with the covenant (such as by doing the requisite repairs), and so avoid losing his interest; for, if a lease is forfeited, the sub-tenancy falls with it. Unlike direct enforcement, this indirect enforcement is subject to the important powers of the court to grant relief against forfeiture.[17] Yet often it will be better to perform the covenant than to face the uncertainty, delay and cost of seeking relief. There seems to be nothing to confine this type of enforcement to covenants which are enforceable against T; and forfeiture clauses may be imposed on the assignment of a lease or on the grant of a fee simple.[18]

PART 3   OLD LEASES

POSITION OF THE ORIGINAL PARTIES TO AN OLD LEASE

Basic position—original tenant

14–014   If a lease is granted by L to T, there is privity of contract between them. The effect of this is not only that L may enforce all the covenants in the lease against T while he retains it, but also that T remains liable on the covenants for the whole term, notwithstanding any assignment of the lease.[19] Thus if T takes a lease for 99 years, he makes himself liable for 99 years, even if he assigns the lease after only one year has run; thus, L may accordingly sue T for unpaid rent or for damages if the covenant to repair is not observed by the assignee.

---

[16] Below, para.16–019.
[17] Above, paras 12–014 et seq.
[18] See below, para.16–017. *Shiloh Spinners v Harding* [1973] A.C. 691.
[19] *Thursby v Plant* (1670) 1 Wms.Saund. 230. The rule does not apply to perpetually renewable leases; see above, para.11–032.

Events after assignment which may release the tenant

When a covenant has not been performed[20], the defences available to the original parties are few:

14–015

    (i)   There may have been such a change in the terms of the original lease that there will be held to have been a surrender and a re-grant, in which case both parties will be released. However, this will only be held where the variation affects the legal estate and increases either the extent of the premises or the term in a manner not envisaged by the original lease.[21]

   (ii)   Other variations which are not envisaged by the terms of the lease will not bind the original parties but they will remain bound by the original terms of the lease; consequently, an increase in rent other than as a result of the valid exercise of a rent review clause in the original lease will not bind the original lessee but he will remain liable for rent at the original rate.[22]

 (iii)   A release of an assignee from liability may also release the original lessee.[23] However, the release only of a surety of an assignee will not do so.[24]

 (iv)   Where a lease is continued by statute beyond its original term, the liability of the original lessee will cease unless, obviously, he is still the tenant in occupation or, less obviously, the lease contains clear words to the contrary effect.[25]

Events after assignment which do not release the tenant

Save as indicated above, the rule is strict:

14–016

    (i)   An original lessee remains liable on covenants which, after assigning the lease, he is powerless to perform,[26] unless by apt wording in the lease he has limited his liability to the time while the lease is vested in him.[27] Otherwise he must rely on his rights to indemnity from subsequent assignees,[28] and these may prove to be of little worth.[29]

   (ii)   Similarly, T remains liable even though the breach may be committed not by the person to whom he assigned (T2), but a subsequent assignee (T3, or T4; it matters not how many assignments there are)

 (iii)   As has already been indicated, if the lease contains a rent review clause, he will be

---

[20] Performance by someone else, such as surety, will discharge the original tenant from liability.

[21] *Friends Provident Life Office v British Railways Board* [1996] 1 All E.R. 336 and in respect of variations since January 1, 1996. LLT(C)A 1995 s.18.

[22] *Friends Provident Life Office v British Railways Board* [1996] 1 All E.R. 336.

[23] *Deanplan Ltd v Mahmoud* [1993] Ch. 151.

[24] *Allied London Investments Ltd v Hambro Life Assurance Ltd* (1983) 269 E.G. 41.

[25] *City of London Corp v Fell* [1994] 1 A.C. 458.

[26] *Thames Manufacturing Co Ltd v Perrotts (Nichol & Peyton) Ltd* (1985) 50 P. & C.R. 1.

[27] See *Johnsey Estates Ltd v Webb* [1990] 1 E.G.L.R. 80 (sureties).

[28] See below, para.14–040.

[29] See, e.g. *Weaver v Mogford* [1988] 2 E.G.L.R. 48.

liable for any increased rent that has been properly fixed under the clause, even though he has had no say in the increase.[30]

(iv) T remains liable if the assignee becomes insolvent and the trustee in bankruptcy of an individual tenant, or liquidator of a company tenant, disclaims the lease.[31]

(v) Even though L may be (and usually is) entitled to forfeit against the assignee, T cannot make L do so. L is entitled simply to keep pursuing T, for rent every quarter for example.[32]

Liability of original tenant to an assignee of the landlord's reversion

14–017   At common law L2 could not sue the original tenant, but it is now generally accepted that L's right to sue T passes automatically on assignment of the reversion to L2.[33]

Basic position—original landlord

14–018   The position of the original lessor is the same as that of the tenant. There is privity of contract with T and so L remains liable on his covenants even after assigning his reversion.[34]

Reform of original tenant liability under old leases

14–019   The original party liability rule is obviously more likely adversely to affect original lessees than original lessors and its stringency, ill-understood by many lessees, was emphasised in the years immediately prior to the enactment of the 1995 Act when there was a slump in property values and rents being paid by tenants under existing leases substantially exceeded the rent payable under new leases. Assignees of leases, particularly companies holding commercial premises, would simply stop paying the rent and go into insolvent liquidation. Their liquidator would then disclaim the lease and their landlords would then claim the rent from the original lessees, who might have assigned the lease many years before. This was one of the principal reasons why the 1995 Act was enacted.

As noted earlier, the main thrust of the 1995 Act was to replace the existing law with a wholly new regime applicable to New Leases. That part of the 1995 Act was not retrospective. But it also introduced two significant reforms which do apply to Old Leases as well as New Leases and which are intended to temper the effect of original tenant liability:

(i) the "section 17 notice" procedure;
(ii) the right to an overriding lease.

---

[30] *Centrovincial Estates Plc v Bulk Storage Ltd* (1983) 46 P. & C.R. 393; *Selous Street Properties Ltd v Oronel Fabrics Ltd* (1984) 270 E.G. 643.

[31] *Hindcastle v Barbara Attenborough Associates* [1997] A.C. 70.

[32] T may now be entitled to claim an overriding lease under the 1995 Act s.19.

[33] *Centrovincial Estates Plc v Bulk Storage Ltd* (1983) 46 P. & C.R. 393; LPA 1925 s.141.

[34] *Stuart v Joy* [1904] 1 K.B. 368; LPA 1925 s.142(2); *Hua Chiao Commercial Bank Ltd v Chiaphua Industries Ltd* [1987] A.C. 99.

Section 17 notices

The ability of the landlord for the time being of an old lease to recover "fixed charges" (rent, service charges and any other liquidated sums) from the original lessee is now subject to provisions in the 1995 Act[35] which apply to both old leases and new leases. A landlord can now only recover such fixed charges from a former tenant if he serves notice, in a prescribed form, on that tenant within six months of any fixed charge becoming due. This notice informs the former tenant that the sum is due and that the landlord intends to recover that sum from him. A notice of this kind is often referred to as a "section 17 notice" and is sufficiently served if it is sent by registered post to the last known abode of the original lessee.[36]

14–020

"Fixed charge" includes rent, service charges, and sums payable under a liquidated damages clause. Where rent is subject to a rent review clause and the reviewed rent is back-dated, the reviewed rent does not "become due" for the purposes of s.17 until the revised rent has been agreed or determined.[37]

Right to an overriding lease

An original lessee[38] who pays in full any sum so claimed under a s.17 notice is entitled to what the 1995 Act describes as an "overriding lease", a lease for three days longer than the original lease (unless the landlord is himself a lessee and the landlord's interest would thereby be displaced[39]) which contains the same covenants as the original lease save for those expressed to be personal between the landlord and tenant or those which have ceased to be binding. This overriding lease is a reversionary lease and so is interposed between the interest of the landlord and the lease of the tenant for the time being[40]; the original lessee therefore becomes the landlord of the tenant for the time being. Consequently, any breach of covenant by the tenant for the time being will enable the original lessee to forfeit the lease, assuming of course that there is a right of re-entry or forfeiture, and thereby cause his overriding lease to come into possession. An overriding lease held by the original lessee of an old lease is itself an old lease,[41] so he will remain liable to the landlord for the time being for the whole of the remainder of his term. However, he will normally be able to cover the amount of any liability by assigning or sub-letting, although this will not be the case in the event of another slump in property values of the type which occurred in the years immediately prior to the enactment of the 1995 Act.

14–021

Direct covenants by assignees

It should also be mentioned that many covenants not to assign the lease without the lessor's consent provide that consent will not be forthcoming unless the assignee of the lease

14–022

---

[35] s.17.
[36] *Commercial Union Life Assurance Co Ltd v Moustafa* [1999] 2 E.G.L.R. 44.
[37] *Scottish & Newcastle Plc v Raguz (No.3)* [2008] UKHL 65; [2008] 1 W.L.R. 2494.
[38] Intermediate assignees, and guarantors have the same rights. It is possible for more than one person to be entitled to claim an overriding lease; if so then the first to apply has priority.
[39] In which case T obtains an overriding lease for the term of the landlord's interest less three days.
[40] LT(C)A 1995 ss.19–20.
[41] LT(C)A 1995 s.20(1).

covenants directly with the lessor to observe all the tenant's covenants for the remainder of the term. A refusal of consent in the absence of such a direct covenant is reasonable. Where an assignee does covenant directly in this way, he will from then on be in exactly the same position as the original lessee[42] and will be liable to the landlord for the time being for any breach of the tenant's covenants for the rest of the term. Where following a further assignment a landlord wishes to recover fixed charges from such an assignee, he is obliged to serve a s.17 notice on the assignee.

Liability of guarantors

14–023   Any guarantor of an original party to an old lease or of an assignee of the lease who has covenanted directly with the lessor is in exactly the same position as the person whose liability he is guaranteeing. Where a landlord wishes to recover fixed charges from the guarantor of the original lessee of an old lease, he is obviously obliged to serve a s.17 notice on the guarantor but is not also obliged to serve one on the original lessee.[43]

POSITION WHERE THE ASSIGNMENT OF AN OLD LEASE IS EFFECTIVE AT LAW

14–024   This section considers the position where an old lease has been created and assigned with the formalities required by the law and has neither been created nor assigned only in equity.[44] In this context the rights and liabilities of assignees of the lease or of the reversion depend on:

    (i) whether the covenants "touch and concern" the land;
    (ii) whether there is privity of estate.

Covenants which do not touch and concern the land do not run even if there is privity of estate, so this issue will be considered first before turning to the privity of estate rules which govern the transmission of the benefit and burden of such covenants.

Covenants touching and concerning the land

14–025   The rights and liabilities of assignees of an old lease, either of the lease or of the reversion, depend on whether or not the covenant in question "touches and concerns the land" or, to use more modern phraseology, has "reference to the subject-matter" of the lease.[45] Any covenant which affects the landlord in his capacity as landlord or the tenant in his capacity as tenant may be said to touch and concern the land.[46]

    It has been suggested that, as a satisfactory working test, a covenant by a tenant touches and concerns the land if: (i) it is beneficial only to the reversioner for the time being; (ii)

---

[42] *Deanplan Ltd v Mahmoud* [1993] Ch. 151 (release of one such assignee by the release of a later assignee).
[43] *Cheverell Estates Ltd v Harris* [1998] 1 E.G.L.R. 27.
[44] Above, paras 11–015 et seq. For covenants in equitable leases, see para.11–021.
[45] LPA 1925 ss.141(1), 142(1).
[46] *Breams Property Investment Co Ltd v Strougler* [1948] 2 K.B. 1.

it affects the nature, quality, mode of user or value of the reversioner's land; and (iii) it is not expressed to be personal in nature[47]; and correspondingly for covenants by a landlord. However, it must be noted that the benefit may pass even if the burden is intended to be personal, and vice versa.

Despite these attempts to impose some structure on the "touch and concern" principle, the rules have been assailed as being "purely arbitrary" and the distinctions as mostly being "quite illogical".[48] It was the proposals of the Law Commission that this test should be abandoned[49] which eventually led to the enactment of the 1995 Act.[50]

Given the uncertain and arbitrary nature of the "principle", it necessary to refer to decided examples of the operation of the test[51]: covenants in the left-hand columns below have been held to touch and concern the land, while those in the right-hand columns have been held not to do so.

Covenants by a lessee of an old lease

14–026

1 To pay rent
2 To repair
3 To pay the landlord £40 towards redecoration[52]
4 To use as a private dwelling-house only

5 Not to assign the lease without the lessor's consent
6 To pay an annual sum to a third party[53]
7 To repair and renew the tools of a smithy standing on the land[54]
8 Not to employ persons living in other parishes to work in the demised mill[55]

Covenants by a lessor of an old lease

14–027

1 To renew the lease[56]
2 To supply the demised premises with water
3 Not to build on certain parts of the adjoining land
4 To give the lessee the first refusal if adjoining land is sold[57]

5 To pay at the end of the lease for chattels not amounting to fixtures
6 To pay the tenant £500 at the end of the lease unless a new lease is granted[58]
7 To repay to the tenant money deposited as security against breaches of covenant[59]

---

[47] *P. & A. Swift Investments v Combined English Stores Group Plc* [1989] A.C. 632 at 642; and see *Horsey Estates Ltd v Steiger* [1899] 2 Q.B. 79 at 89. It is possible to have a covenant which is somewhere in between—a covenant which is expressed to be personal but assignable on conditions; that may touch and concern the land: *Aviva Life & Pensions UK v Linpac Mouldings* [2010] L. & T.R. 10 at [44].
[48] See *Grant v Edmondson* [1931] 1 Ch. 1 at 29 per Romer L.J.
[49] (1988) Law Com. No.174 at p.17.
[50] Other factors determined the timing of the enactment; see above, para.14–019.
[51] See *London Diocesan Board v Phithwa* [2005] UKHL 70; [2005] 1 W.L.R. 3956.
[52] *Mayho v Buckhurst* (1617) Cro.Jac. 438.
[53] *Williams v Earle* (1868) L.R. 3 Q.B. 739.
[54] *Boyer v Warbey* [1953] 1 Q.B. 234.
[55] *Congleton Corp v Pattison* (1808) 10 East 130.
[56] *Richards v Sydenham* (1703) 2 Vern. 447. The inclusion of this is regarded as somewhat anomalous: *Woodall v Clifton* [1905] 2 Ch. 257 at 279.
[57] *Collison v Lettsom* (1815) 6 Taunt. 224.
[58] *Re Hunter's Lease* [1942] Ch. 124.
[59] *Hua Chiao Commercial Bank Ltd v Chiaphua Industries Ltd* [1987] A.C. 99.

Covenants by a guarantor

14–028 Covenants by a person who guarantees the liability of either a lessee or a lessor of an old lease touch and concern the land and are enforceable by assignees of the reversion and the lease to the extent that those liabilities arise under covenants which themselves touch and concern the land.[60]

Estate contracts

14–029 The enforceability of covenants in an old lease which also constitute estate contracts is not determined by whether or not they touch and concern the land but by whether or not they are enforceable as estate contracts. Covenants giving the lessee the right to renew his lease[61] or to purchase the freehold or leasehold reversion[62] are estate contracts by the lessor. So are notices by lessees exercising statutory rights to purchase the freehold or to take an extended lease.[63] On the other hand, covenants obliging the lessee to offer to surrender his lease to the lessor before seeking to assign it are estate contracts by the lessee.[64]

In the case of unregistered land, failure to protect such estate contracts by the registration of a Class C(iv) land charge will render them void against any assignee of the party burdened by the covenant.[65] In the case of registered land, an estate contract should be protected by notice. A degree of protection is given by virtue of actual occupation[66] but lessors and lessees who have sub-let are not in actual occupation. Lessors and lessees who have neither protected their estate contracts nor have interests which override registration are in the same position as in the case of unregistered land and lose the benefit of their estate contracts as against any assignee for value

It should be noted that where a covenant which constitutes an estate contract is not enforceable against a successor in title to the party burdened by it, the original lessor or lessee will nevertheless be liable for damages for breach of that contract to whoever has the benefit of the estate contract. It is not a defence to such an action that the estate contract would have been enforceable against the successor in title had it been protected by registration in the appropriate way.[67] While the measure of damages is likely to be minimal in the case of options, unless the option was to acquire the interest in question at less than the market rate, the measure may well be very substantial when the claimant is a lessee who has been unable to exercise a statutory right to purchase the freehold or to take an extended lease or a lessor who has been unable to take advantage of a covenant obliging the lessee to offer to surrender his lease to the lessor before seeking to assign it.

---

[60] *P. & A. Swift Investments v Combined English Stores Group Plc* [1989] A.C. 632; *Coronation Street Industrial Properties Ltd v Ingall Industries Plc* [1989] 1 W.L.R. 304.
[61] *Phillips v Mobil Oil Ltd* [1989] 1 W.L.R. 888.
[62] *Midland Bank Trust Co Ltd v Green* [1981] A.C. 513.
[63] Leasehold Reform Act 1967 s.5; see also para.12–002.
[64] *Greene v Church Commissioners for England* [1974] Ch. 467.
[65] *Midland Bank Trust Co Ltd v Green* [1981] A.C. 513; *Greene v Church Commissioners for England* [1974] Ch. 467; *Phillips v Mobil Oil Ltd* [1989] 1 W.L.R. 888.
[66] Above, para.5–023.
[67] *Wright v Dean* [1948] Ch. 686.

Principles of transmission

Having considered which covenants touch and concern the land, the rights and liabilities **14–030** of assignees and their guarantors must next be examined.[68] As in every case when the question of enforcing legal liabilities arises, two separate questions must be considered:

  (i) whether the potential defendant is liable; and
  (ii) whether the potential claimant is entitled to sue.

In the case of the rights and liabilities of assignees under covenants concerning land and their guarantors, these questions may be expressed in the following form:

  (i) whether the burden of the covenant has passed to the potential defendant; and
  (ii) whether the benefit of the covenant has passed to the potential claimant.

These questions are governed by the common law where the lessee assigns his lease, but by statute where the lessor assigns his reversion. The rules are somewhat incoherent, hence their replacement with a statutory regime for New Leases under the 1995 Act.

Where the lessee assigns his lease

If L grants a legal lease to T, and T assigns it by deed to T2, the common law rule laid down **14–031** in *Spencer's Case*[69] is that T2 is entitled to the benefit, and subject to the burden, of all covenants and conditions touching and concerning the land; for there is privity of estate. In short, both the benefit and the burden of the covenants run with the land. In applying this rule, the following points should be noted.

The lease must be in due form

Originally, the benefit and burden of covenants ran only with a lease by deed, but it can now **14–032** run with a lease for three years or less made by unsealed writing.[70] A legal oral tenancy for less than three years has been held not to suffice,[71] but this rule may no longer be law.[72]

There must be a legal assignment of the whole term   **14–033**

Legal assignment: The benefit and burden of covenants run with the lease only in the case of a legal assignment of the whole of the remainder of the term.[73] Where instead of an assignment there has been a sub-lease, the sub-lessee takes neither the benefit nor the burden of the covenants in the lease, even if his sub-lease is only one day shorter than the

---

[68] See generally (1991) 11 Leg.Stud. 47 (R. Thornton).
[69] (1583) 5 Co.Rep. 16a.
[70] See *Boyer v Warbey* [1953] 1 Q.B. 234.
[71] *Elliot v Johnson* (1866) L.R. 2 Q.B. 120.
[72] See *Boyer v Warbey* [1953] 1 Q.B. 234 at 246; and see above, para.11–016, for the tenancies which can be created orally; see also below, para.14–042.
[73] *West v Dobb* (1869) L.R. 4 Q.B. 634.

head lease. Thus if L leases land to T1 for 99 years, T1 assigns the lease to T2, and T2 sub-leases the land to S for the residue of the term of 99 years less one day, S is not an assignee and there is privity neither of contract nor of estate between L and S. T2 is still the tenant under the lease for 99 years, and until he assigns it, he remains liable upon it. Consequently if S does some act which is contrary to a covenant in the 99 years' lease, L cannot sue S but can sue T2 or forfeit the lease.[74] In practice, the covenants inserted in a sub-lease are always at least as stringent as those in the head lease, so that if a sub-tenant does some act forbidden by the head lease, this will constitute a breach of the covenants in the sub-lease and thus make the sub-tenant liable to the tenant, though not to the head lessor.

No legal assignment: If there is no legal assignment, the benefit and burden of covenants in a lease do not run with it under the Rule in *Spencer's Case*. Thus as a legal assignment can be made only by deed,[75] the covenants will not run where the assignment is made in some other way (such as by a contract to assign) and so takes effect only in equity.[76] However, the benefit (but not the burden) of the covenants can be expressly assigned.[77]

Squatters: A squatter on leasehold land is not even an assignee of the lease, and so he can neither sue nor be sued on the covenants.[78] But both an equitable assignee and a squatter may be estopped from denying liability on the covenants in the lease.[79] In the case of registered land, privity of estate will be established once the squatter has become registered as proprietor of the lease in place of the person whose title he has barred.[80]

Liability of personal representatives

14–034 When T[81] dies the lease devolves by operation of law upon T's personal representative(s).[82] The extent of the personal representative's liability may be a personal liability or merely a representative liability depending on his actions. If an original lessee or one of his assignees dies and his personal representatives take possession of the demised premises (something which the personal representatives of their guarantors cannot of course do), the personal representatives occupy the position of assignees of the lease and so become personally liable on the covenants.[83] However, as regards the payment of rent (but not as regards other covenants) a personal representative may by proper pleading limit his liability to the yearly value of the premises.[84]

---

[74] Assuming there is a proviso for re-entry, which there almost invariably is. Forfeiture of T2's lease also terminates S's sub-lease; see paras 12–014, 12–019.

[75] Above, para.11–038.

[76] *Cox v Bishop* (1857) 8 De G.M. & G. 815; *Friary Holroyd and Healey's Breweries Ltd v Singleton* [1899] 1 Ch. 86 (reversed on other grounds [1899] 2 Ch. 261).

[77] Above, para.14–002.

[78] *Tichborne v Weir* (1892) 67 L.T. 735; below, para.18–047.

[79] See *Rodenhurst Estates Ltd v W. H. Barnes Ltd* [1936] 2 All E.R. 3 (equitable assignee); *Ashe v Hogan* [1920] 1 I.R. 159 (squatter); and see above, para.11–036.

[80] On application to the land Registry after not less than 10 years' adverse possession, see LRA 2002 Sch.6 para.9(2). Contrast unregistered land where under LA 1980 ss.15, 17 the squatter extinguishes T's title and obtains a different possessory title for himself.

[81] Or the last survivor of joint tenants.

[82] His executors, if testate.

[83] *Tilney v Norris* (1700) 1 Ld.Raym. 553.

[84] *Rendall v Andreae* (1892) 61 L.J.Q.B. 630.

Personal representatives of the original lessee and of his assignees who do not take possession of the premises, and personal representatives of the guarantors[85] incur no personal liability upon any covenant[86]; their liability is only representative. On the death of any of them, his personal representatives have exactly the same liability as the person whom they represent but only to the extent of the assets of the deceased in their hands.[87]

Protection

If the deceased was an original party to an old lease or his guarantor, the personal representatives are in a difficult position since they cannot tell what breaches of covenant may occur in the future. This is also the case where the deceased either held a new lease immediately before the tenant, for the time being, and entered into an AGA, or is a former landlord of a new lease who has not yet been released, or has guaranteed the liabilities of any such person. Although it has long been settled that the personal representatives need not put aside part of the estate as an indemnity fund for future breaches,[88] their position used to be precarious in other respects. In order to make it unnecessary for personal representatives to seek the protection of the court in such cases, the Trustee Act 1925[89] provides that if personal representatives who are liable as such under any covenant in a lease or any guarantee given in respect of any such liability:

14–035

    (i)   satisfy any existing liabilities which have been claimed;
    (ii) set aside any fixed sum agreed to be laid out on the premises; and
    (iii) assign the lease to the person entitled under the will or intestacy; or to a purchaser,

they cease to have representative liability in respect of the assets which came to their hands. This also now applies to any liability under an AGA.[90] This does not render the assets immune from liability, for they may be followed into the hands of the beneficiaries[91]; but the personal representatives need not concern themselves with this. These provisions do not of course protect personal representatives from their personal liability if they have taken possession of the premises. However, they may set aside a fund from the estate by way of indemnity,[92] to be distributed when no longer needed.[93]

Part assignments

In the case of an assignment of part of the land demised by a lease, covenants which run with the land will bind the assignee of part if and insofar as they relate to the part which has been assigned to him. The part assignee can be sued only for the rent attributable to his part but distress can be levied for the whole rent.

14–036

---

[85] Personal representatives of the original lessor and of his assignees also incur representative liability only.
[86] *Wollaston v Hakewill* (1841) 3 Man. & G. 297 at 320.
[87] *Helier v Casebert* (1665) 1 Lev. 127; *Youngmin v Heath* [1974] 1 W.L.R. 135 (weekly tenancy).
[88] *King v Malcott* (1852) 9 Hare 692.
[89] s.26(1), replacing LPAA 1859 s.27.
[90] s.26 (1A) added by L & T(C) A 1995.
[91] s.26(2).
[92] *Re Owers* [1941] Ch. 389.
[93] *Re Lewis* [1939] Ch. 232.

Things in posse: The burden of a covenant relating to a thing *in posse*, requiring the lessee to do something entirely new (such as to erect a building) formerly ran with the land only if the lessee had expressly covenanted for himself and his assigns that the covenant would be performed.[94] This rule still applies to leases granted before 1926. However, although many leases granted before 1926 are still in existence, it is hardly likely that any such covenants remain unperformed. The rule does not apply to leases granted after 1925[95] and it has never applied to covenants relating to things *in esse* (in existence).

Extent of the liability of assignees

14–037   Although the original lessee is liable by virtue of privity of contract for all breaches of covenant throughout the term of the lease, an assignee is liable only for breaches committed while the lease is vested in him i.e. for the duration of the privity of estate. He is under no liability for breaches committed either before the lease was assigned to him[96] or after he has assigned it[97]; but if a covenant is broken while the lease is vested in him, his liability for this breach continues despite any assignment.[98] In the case of a continuing breach (such as disrepair) which begins before assignment, the assignee is liable to remedy the breach, and the lease in the hands of the assignee may be forfeit, but any damages will cover only the period after assignment. Thus while the original lessee of an onerous lease cannot divest himself of liability for future breaches, an assignee can do so by assigning the lease, such as to a pauper,[99] though he will remain liable to indemnify the tenant who assigned the lease to him.[100]

Tenant's rights to sue for breaches by the landlord

14–038   The assignor retains the right to sue for breaches of covenant by the landlord committed before assignment of the lease.[101] If a landlord's breach is a continuing breach, the assignee will be able to enforce compliance after assignment, but will not be able to recover damages for any period of breach before assignment.[102] The right to sue may, however, be assigned expressly.[103]

Liability of guarantors

14–039   Where the assignment of an old lease is effective at law, any guarantor of an assignee of that lease is in the same position as the person whose liability he is guaranteeing.[104]

---

[94] *Spencer's Case* (1583) 5 Co.Rep. 16a; but see *Minshull v Oakes* (1858) 2 H. & N. 793 (conditionally *in posse*).

[95] LPA 1925 s.79.

[96] *Granada Theatres Ltd v Freehold Investment (Leytonstone) Ltd* [1959] Ch. 592.

[97] *Paul v Nurse* (1828) 8 B. & C. 486; but see L & TA 1985 s.3(3A), inserted by L & TA 1987 s.50 (dwellings: liability of outgoing landlord continues until tenant is notified of new landlord).

[98] *Harley v King* (1835) 2 Cr.M. & R. 18.

[99] *Hopkinson v Lovering* (1883) 11 QBD 92.

[100] See below, para.14–040.

[101] *City & Metropolitan Properties Ltd v Greycroft Ltd* [1987] 1 W.L.R. 1085.

[102] *City & Metropolitan Properties Ltd v Greycroft Ltd* (above).

[103] *Trendtex Trading Corp v Credit Suisse* [1982] A.C. 679.

[104] *P. & A. Swift Investments v Combined English Stores Group Plc* [1989] A.C. 632; *Coronation Street Industrial Properties Ltd v Ingall Industries Plc* [1989] 1 W.L.R. 304.

Indemnities from assignees

Implied indemnity: If a covenant has been broken, the lessee and the assignee entitled to the lease at the time of the breach are each liable to be sued by the lessor. But although the lessor may sue either or both, he can only have one satisfaction: he has no right to recover twice.[105] The primary liability is that of the assignee, and if the original lessee is sued, he may claim indemnity from the assignee in whom the lease was vested at the time of the breach, whether that assignee obtained the lease from the lessee or from some other assignee.[106]

Express indemnity: In addition to this implied obligation to indemnify the original lessee, it is usual for each assignee to enter into an express covenant to indemnify his assignor against future breaches of covenant; and by statute[107] in any assignment for value made after 1925 such a covenant is implied.[108]

Effect: The effect of these rights of indemnity may be illustrated thus:

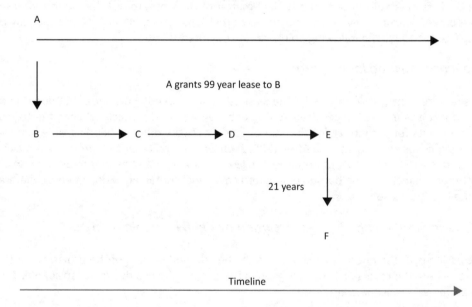

A has leased land to B for 99 years; by successive assignments E has become entitled to the lease and has granted a sub-lease to F for 21 years. If F does some act which is contrary to a covenant in the head lease, A can sue either B (privity of contract) or E (privity of estate). If A sues B, B has an implied right to indemnity against E. Alternatively, if on the assignment to C a covenant of indemnity was given to B, he may claim indemnity from C. C in turn may

---

[105] *Brett v Cumberland* (1619) Cro.Jac. 521.

[106] *Wolveridge v Steward* (1833) 1 Cr. & M. 644; *Moule v Garrett* (1872) L.R. 7 Ex. 101. The claim is probably to be categorised as a restitutionary claim: *Electricity Supply Nominees v Thorn EMI* (1991) 63 P. & C.R. 143.

[107] LPA 1925 s.77(1)(c); Sch.2, Pt IX; in the case of registered leases LRA 2002 s.134(2) and Sch.12 para.20.

[108] Note that these covenants are not implied in the case of New Leases, the separate regime applying to which is considered later.

claim indemnity from D, and D from E, provided in each case that a covenant for indemnity was given on the assignment. The importance of these various rights is emphasised if one of the parties is insolvent or has disappeared. Apart from the rules relating to restrictive covenants,[109] F incurs no liability to anyone except so far as his act was a breach of a covenant in the sub-lease and so makes him liable to E.

Where the lessor assigns his reversion

14–041   If L, a tenant in fee simple, leased his land to T, and then L conveyed his fee simple, subject to the lease, to R, the common law rule was that with the exception of "implied covenants" (i.e. certain covenants which the law implied, such as to pay rent),[110] neither the benefit nor the burden of the covenants in the lease ran with the reversion: R was neither able to sue nor liable to be sued. But since the Grantees of Reversions Act 1540, ss.1 and 2, the benefit and burden of all covenants and provisions contained in a lease which touch and concern the land (or have reference to the subject-matter of the lease, to use the modern phrase) have passed with the reversion. The current provisions are ss.141 and 142 of the Law of Property Act 1925. The following points should be noted.

The lease must be in due form

14–042   This requirement will be satisfied if the lease is made by deed[111] or, under the doctrine of *Walsh v Lonsdale*,[112] is a specifically enforceable agreement[113] which satisfies the formal requirements for a contract for the sale of land.[114] (These differ depending on when the agreement was entered into.[115]) After 1925, even a mere oral tenancy is probably sufficient for, under s.154 of the Law of Property Act 1925, ss.141 and 142 extend to an underlease "or other tenancy".[116] The burden of landlord covenants contained in documents collateral to the lease will also pass.[117]

The reversion may have been assigned by deed in whole or in part

14–043   The assignee of the entire reversion takes the benefit and burden of the provisions in the lease. Where the reversion is not assigned in its entirety, the position is not so simple. Two separate cases must be considered.

Severance as regards the estate: Where the assignee has part of the reversion, as where a fee simple reversioner grants a lease of his reversion to X, the reversion is severed as regards the estate. In this case, X, as the person entitled to part of the reversion, falls within

---

[109] Below, para.14–054.

[110] See *Vyvyan v Arthur* (1823) 1 B. & C. 410.

[111] *Smith v Egginton* (1874) L.R. 9 C.P. 145.

[112] Above, para.11–020.

[113] *Rickett v Green* [1910] 1 K.B. 253.

[114] *Rye v Purcell* [1926] 1 K.B. 446; *Weg Motors Ltd v Hales* [1962] Ch. 49.

[115] See above, paras 6–002 et seq.

[116] Contrast above, para.14–033.

[117] *Weg Motors v Hales* [1962] Ch. 49 (collateral option); *System Floors Ltd v Ruralpride Ltd* [1995] 1 E.G.L.R. 48 (side letter); *Lotteryking v AMEC* [1995] 2 E.G.L.R. 13 (collateral contract).

the statutory provisions, so that the benefit and burden of both covenants and conditions pass to him as the immediate reversioner.[118]

Severance as regards the land: Where the assignee has the reversion of part, as where a fee simple reversioner conveys the fee simple in half the land to X, the reversion is severed as regards the land. All conditions and rights of re-entry now become severable on the severance of the reversion.[119] The tenancy itself, however, continues as one tenancy.[120]

Rights of an assignee of the reversion to sue and forfeit for previous breaches

After an assignment of the reversion, the assignee is now alone entitled to sue the tenant for rent or for breaches of covenant, whether such rent accrued or such breaches occurred before or after the assignment.[121] This is brought about by the Law of Property Act 1925 (the law was formerly different).[122] This Act also provides that rights of re-entry are enforceable by the new reversioner, provided they have not been waived. Waiver may be express or implied.[123] Waiver will not be implied merely because the reversion is assigned "subject to and with the benefit of" the lease[124]; it is "the merest *res inter alios acta*", without any impact on the tenant.[125]   **14–044**

Liability of an assignee for assignor's breach

The assignee of the reversion is not liable for breaches of covenant committed by the assignor[126] and the tenant has no right of set-off against rent falling due after the assignment.[127] If a landlord's breach is a continuing breach, the assignee will be liable to comply with the covenant but will not be liable in damages for any period of breach before assignment.   **14–045**

Liability of an assignor of the reversion after assignment

As in the case of tenants, the general rule is that an assignor of the reversion (who is not the original landlord) is not liable for breaches committed after assignment of the reversion. There is an exception where the lease is of a dwelling-house: in that case the assignor remains liable (jointly and severally with the assignee) until notice of the assignment is given to the tenant.[128]   **14–046**

---

[118] *Wright v Burroughes* (1846) 3 C.B. 685.

[119] LPA 1925 s.140(1). The position is different if the lease was made before 1882 and the reversion was severed before 1926.

[120] *Jelley v Buckman* [1974] Q.B. 488.

[121] *Re King* [1963] Ch. 459; *London and County (A. & D.) Ltd v Wilfred Sportsman Ltd* [1971] Ch. 764.

[122] s.141, replacing CA 1911 s.2.

[123] For waiver, see above, paras 12–006 et seq.

[124] *London and County (A. & D.) Ltd v Wilfred Sportsman Ltd* [1971] Ch. 764.

[125] *London and County (A. & D.) Ltd v Wilfred Sportsman Ltd* [1971] Ch. 764 at 782 per Russell L.J.

[126] *Duncliffe v Caerfelin Properties Ltd* [1989] 2 E.G.L.R. 38.

[127] *Edlington Properties v Fenner* [2006] EWCA Civ 403; [2006] 1 W.L.R. 1583.

[128] LTA 1985 s.3(3A) and 3(3B).

Merger or surrender of the reversion

14–047   Where the landlord's reversion is itself leasehold (a head-lease), the benefit and burden of covenants is preserved on a merger or surrender of the head-lease and is transmitted to the interest into which the head-lease is merged or surrendered.[129]

Liability of guarantors

14–048   Where the assignment of an old lease is effective at law, any guarantor of an assignee of the reversion is in the same position as the person whose liability he is guaranteeing.[130]

Enforcement after assignment

14–049   The liability of the original parties to a lease during the whole term of the lease[131] is not destroyed by assignment. Thus for covenants touching and concerning the land an original lessor remains liable even after he has assigned the reversion[132]; and an original lessee who assigns his term remains liable even to a subsequent assignee of the reversion with whom he has never had any privity of estate.[133] Further, a tenant's right to sue his landlord for existing breaches of covenant continues to exist after he has assigned the lease.[134]

POSITION WHERE THE ASSIGNMENT OF AN OLD LEASE IS EFFECTIVE ONLY IN EQUITY

14–050   An assignment of an old lease may be effective only in equity, either because the lease was not created with the formalities required by the law (such as because of the lack of a deed[135]) and for that reason takes effect only in equity or because, as has already been seen,[136] a legal lease has not been assigned by deed[137] and for that reason the assignment of it takes effect only in equity.[138] In such circumstances, the rules for the running of the benefit and burden of covenants which touch and concern the land, as considered above, are only partly applicable. That does not alter the fact that the original parties are bound by privity of contract in the manner which has already been considered.[139]

---

[129] LPA 1925 s.139.

[130] *P. & A. Swift Investments v Combined English Stores Group Plc* [1989] A.C. 632; *Coronation Street Industrial Properties Ltd v Ingall Industries Plc* [1989] 1 W.L.R. 304.

[131] Above, para.14–014.

[132] *Celsteel Ltd v Alton House Holdings Ltd (No 2)* [1986] 1 W.L.R. 666 at 672, 673; [1987] 1 W.L.R. 291 at 296.

[133] *Arlesford Trading Co Ltd v Servansingh* [1971] 1 W.L.R. 1080.

[134] *City and Metropolitan Properties Ltd v Greycroft* (1987) 54 P. & C.R. 266.

[135] See above, paras 11–012 et seq.

[136] Above, para.14–032.

[137] Above, para.11.038. This may be deliberate: a "virtual assignment", *Clarence House v Natwest* [2009] EWCA Civ 1311; [2010] 1 W.L.R. 1216.

[138] *Cox v Bishop* (1857) 8 De G.M. & G. 815; *Friary Holroyd and Healey's Breweries Ltd v Singleton* [1899] 1 Ch. 86 (reversed on other grounds [1899] 2 Ch. 261).

[139] Above, para.14–016.

Covenants running with the lease

The common law rule in *Spencer's Case*[140] under which an assignee of the tenancy takes the benefit and burden of such covenants does not appear to apply.[141] **14–051**

If L grants an equitable tenancy to X and X assigns it to Y, L cannot enforce the covenants against Y,[142] for there is no privity of estate which will carry the burden to Y. It would be convenient if equity were to follow the law and make the burden of the covenants run with the land, and there are dicta supporting the view that it does.[143] There is also a broad principle that he who takes the benefit must also bear the burden.[144] But authorities to the contrary[145] have yet to be disposed of satisfactorily.[146]

The benefit of such covenants is less confined. If L grants an equitable tenancy to X, who then assigns it to Y, Y may be able to enforce the covenants against L, since the benefit of the covenants, being assignable, can be passed to Y.[147]

Covenants running with the reversion

Where the reversion on an equitable tenancy is assigned, the position is substantially the same as where the tenancy is legal: for the statutory provisions[148] for the running of the benefit and burden with the reversion are applicable. "Lease" in the statute is defined as including an underlease "or any other tenancy", and this makes the benefit and burden run with the reversion in the same way as if the tenancy were legal.[149] **14–052**

Liability of guarantors

Where an assignment of an old lease is effective only in equity, there is no authority as to the liability of any guarantors of the assignees but their liability is presumably the same as that of the person whose liability they are guaranteeing. **14–053**

RESTRICTIVE COVENANTS IN AN OLD LEASE

Where covenants are not enforceable under the rules which have already been discussed, the basic rule at law is that no covenants can be enforced. Thus if L grants a lease to T, who grants a sub-lease to S, there is no privity of contract or estate between L and S, and so the covenants in the lease and sub-lease cannot be enforced between them. Again, when V **14–054**

---

[140] (1583) 5 Co.Rep. 16a; above, para.14–031.
[141] *Marquis Camden v Batterbury* (1860) 7 C.B.N.S. 864; *Elliott v Johnson* (1866) L.R. 2 Q.B. 120.
[142] See *Austerberry v Corp of Oldham* (1885) 29 Ch.D. 750.
[143] See *Boyer v Warbey* [1953] 1 Q.B. 234 at 246, 247.
[144] *Tito v Waddell (No.2)* [1977] Ch. 106 at 299–302.
[145] See, e.g. *Elliott v Johnson* (1866) L.R. 2 Q.B. 120; and see the authorities on equitable assignments, above, para.14–050.
[146] See the general survey of equitable leases and equitable assignments at [1978] C.L.J. 98 (R. J Smith).
[147] See *Griffith v Pelton* [1958] Ch. 205, where, however, the lease was legal.
[148] LPA 1925 ss.141, 142, replacing CA 1881 ss.10, 11.
[149] *Rickett v Green* [1910] 1 K.B. 253; *Rye v Purcell* [1926] 1 K.B. 446.

sells his freehold land to P, and P then sells it to Q, there is no privity of contract or estate between V and Q.

Restrictive covenants relating to the demised premises

14–055   Restrictive covenants in a head lease that comply with the relevant rules may usually be enforced in equity against sub-tenants. In the case of unregistered land, such covenants are not registrable as land charges. Consequently, their enforceability depends on the equitable doctrine of notice. If the sub-tenant has the right to see the head lease when he took his sub-lease, which will be the case where he was the original sub-lessee,[150] he will inevitably have notice of any restrictive covenants therein and so will be bound by them. But an assignee of a sub-lease has no right to see the head lease as a matter of law.[151] Consequently, unless he is entitled to do so under the terms of the contract of assignment or actually knows of the existence of the restrictive covenant in question, he will not have notice of them[152] and will consequently take free of them. This is also the position of a sub-under-lessee and his assignees. However, in the case of registered land, any type of sub-lessee and his assignees will automatically be bound by any restrictive covenants in the head lease.

Relating to land other than the demised premises

14–056   But, although a restrictive covenant entered into by the original lessor in respect of land which is not comprised in the lease is enforceable against him indefinitely, it is not enforceable against a purchaser or a tenant of the land not comprised in the lease. The enforceability of such covenants against such persons depends on the general law applicable to restrictive covenants. By way of brief summary:

(a)   Unregistered land: The enforceability of such covenants under the general law is, in the case of unregistered land, governed by the equitable doctrine of notice[153]; thus in the normal case the purchaser or tenant of the land not comprised in the lease will take free of the covenant.

(b)   Registered land: restrictive covenants made between a lessor and a lessee are registrable insofar as they do not apply to the demised premises.[154]

It should also be recalled that covenants in a head lease, whether restrictive or not, may be indirectly enforceable against sub-tenants by virtue of the existence of a forfeiture clause in the head lease.[155]

---

[150] LPA 1925 s.44(4).
[151] LPA 1925 s.44(3).
[152] LPA 1925 s.44(5).
[153] *Dartstone Ltd v Cleveland Petroleum Co Ltd* [1969] 1 W.L.R. 1807.
[154] LRA 2002 s.33(c). The position was different under the previous LRA 1925, see *Oceanic Village Ltd v United Attractions Ltd* [2000] Ch. 234 (a new lease case but equally applicable to old leases on this point).
[155] Above, paras 12–014 et seq.

PART 4   NEW LEASES

INTRODUCTION

Key concepts under the 1995 Act

The concepts of privity of contract and privity of estate do not apply to new leases. **14–057**
Enforceability of covenants under new leases is entirely governed by the 1995 Act. Although
leases governed by the 1995 Act are referred to as "new leases", within the Act the word
"tenancy" is used, and which is defined as including sub-tenancies and agreements for lease
i.e. equitable leases.

It is essential to consider carefully the statutory definitions; in particular of "covenant"
and "assignment"

"covenant" is a defined expression[156] including any term, condition or obligation, express
or implied, or imposed by law,[157] and extending to collateral agreements.

The 1995 Act concerns itself with the transmission of "landlord covenants" and "tenant
covenants", each of which is a defined expression.[158]

"tenancy" (lease) is defined as including an agreement for tenancy (lease). But this does
not include an option for the grant of a lease which has not been exercised.[159]

"assignment" is a defined expression in s.28. It includes equitable assignments, assignments in breach of covenant and assignments by operation of law. Unlike the position in
respect of old leases, not every disposal of the landlord's reversion is an "assignment"
for the purposes of the 1995 Act; for example, the grant of a concurrent lease is not an
assignment of the landlord's interest.[160]

Attempts to exclude the operation of the 1995 Act

The 1995 Act contains very broad anti-avoidance provisions. Any agreement which excludes, **14–058**
modifies or otherwise frustrates the operation of any provision of the 1995 Act is void,[161]
as is any agreement which provides for the determination of any tenancy or the imposition
of any penalty, disability or liability on any tenant in the event of, in connection with, or in
consequence of the operation of any provision of that Act.[162] A clause which releases the
landlord from liability on the landlord covenants upon assignment of the reversion is not
inconsistent with the aims of the Act and is valid.[163]

---

[156] 1995 Act s.28(1).
[157] LT(C)A 1995 Act s.2(1).
[158] Conditions precedent to the grant of a lease are not within the statute: *Ridgewood Properties
Group v Valero Energy* [2013] EWHC 98 (Ch) [2013] Ch. 525 at [55].
[159] *Ridgewood Properties Group v Valero Energy* [2013] EWHC 98 (Ch) [2013] Ch. 525 at [51].
[160] LT(C)A 1995 s.15 governs concurrent leases.
[161] LT(C)A 1995 s.25(1).
[162] LT(C)A 1995 s.25(2), (3). It is the objective effect of any term which needs to be considered: *K/S
Victoria Street v House of Fraser* [2011] EWCA Civ 904; [2011] 2 P. & C.R. 15.
[163] *London Diocesan Fund v Phithwa* [2005] UKHL 70; [2005] 1 W.L.R. 3956.

POSITION OF LANDLORD AND TENANT FOR THE TIME BEING OF A NEW LEASE

The basic rule

14-059   The basic rule under the 1995 Act is that the burden and the benefit of all covenants in a new lease entered into by the original lessor and the original lessee (respectively described in the 1995 Act as the "landlord covenants" and the "tenant covenants"[164]) passes on the assignment of their respective interests to the persons to whom those interests are successively assigned[165]; there is no longer any requirement that the covenants should touch and concern the land.[166] This is the case even when the assignment of a new lease is effective only in equity[167]; as has already been seen,[168] this may be either because the lease was not created with the formalities required by the law (for example because of the lack of a deed[169]) and for that reason takes effect only in equity or because a legal lease has not been assigned by deed[170] and for that reason the assignment of it takes effect only in equity.[171]

The exceptions

14-060   The basic rule is subject to the following exceptions.

Personal covenants

14-061   The burden and benefit of any covenant in a new lease 'which (in whatever terms) is expressed to be personal to any person' does not pass when that person assigns his interest.[172] "Personal" does not mean "non-transferable" but means not intended to bind the person from time to time entitled to the tenancy.[173] This formula requires that the language of tenancy, read in its context, expresses or otherwise conveys the intention that the covenant shall be personal in the sense that it is not to be annexed to the tenancy or reversion. There is no requirement as to how the intention is to be expressed: the tenancy does not have to spell it out in terms that the covenant is to be personal. The intention may be expressed explicitly or implicitly deduced from the language used read in its proper context.[174] As the statutory formulation indicates, it is possible for a covenant to be personal to only one of the parties to it, in which case its burden, or more usually its benefit, will pass when the other party assigns his interest.

---

[164] LT(C)A 1995 s.28(1).
[165] LT(C)A 1995 ss.2(1), 3(1).
[166] LT(C)A 1995 s.2(1).
[167] LT(C)A 1995 s.28(1).
[168] Above, para.11–038.
[169] Above, paras 11–016 et seq.
[170] Above, para.11–038. This may be deliberate: a "virtual assignment", *Clarence House v Natwest* [2009] EWCA Civ 1311; [2010] 1 W.L.R. 1216.
[171] As in *Cox v Bishop* (1857) 8 De G.M. & G. 815.
[172] LT(C) A 1995 s.3(6)(a).
[173] *First Penthouse Ltd v Channel Hotels & Properties (UK) Ltd* [2003] EWHC 2713 (Ch); [2004] L. & T.R. 16 (the point was not considered on appeal at [2004] EWCA Civ 1072; [2004] L. & T.R. 27).
[174] *First Penthouse Ltd v Channel Hotels & Properties (UK) Ltd* at [49].

Covenant no longer binding

Where a covenant in a new lease has ceased to be binding on the assignor prior to the   **14–062**
assignment, because it has been released or has expired, it will not revive on assignment.[175] However, waivers of covenant which are expressed to be personal to a particular landlord or tenant will not prevent that covenant being enforced following an
assignment.[176]

Estate contracts

As in the case of old leases, the enforceability of covenants in a new lease which also   **14–063**
constitute estate contracts is not determined by the normal rules but by whether they
are enforceable as estate contracts. The 1995 Act has no effect on the enforceability of
covenants which are required to be registered under the Land Charges Act 1972 or the Land
Registration Act 2002.[177] It has already been seen[178] that covenants giving the lessee the
right to renew his lease[179] or to purchase the freehold or leasehold reversion[180] are estate
contracts by the lessor, as are notices by lessees exercising statutory rights to purchase
the freehold or to take an extended lease,[181] while covenants obliging the lessee to offer
to surrender his lease to the lessor before seeking to assign it are estate contracts by the
lessee.[182] Failure to protect such estate contracts by registration will continue to render
them void against any assignee of the party burdened by the covenant who takes free of
them; thus an assignee of unregistered land for money or money's worth will do so[183] and
an assignee of registered land for value will do so unless the party with the benefit of the
covenant has an interest which overrides registration,[184] something which no lessor or
lessee who has sub-let has had since the Land Registration Act 2002 came into force.[185]

Principles of transmission

General

The benefit and burden of all landlord and tenant covenants which pass to assignees will   **14–064**
pass on an assignment either of the whole or of any part of the interest in question.[186] This
is also the case with any right of re-entry and forfeiture.[187]

---

[175] LT(C)A 1995 s.3(2), (3).
[176] LT(C)A 1995 s.3(4).
[177] LT(C)A 1995 s.3(6)(b).
[178] Above, para.14–026.
[179] *Phillips v Mobil Oil Ltd* [1989] 1 W.L.R. 888.
[180] *Midland Bank Trust Co Ltd v Green* [1981] A.C. 513.
[181] Leasehold Reform Act 1967 s.5.
[182] *Greene v Church Commissioners for England* [1974] Ch. 467.
[183] *Midland Bank Trust Co Ltd v Green* [1981] A.C. 513; *Greene v Church Commissioners for England*
[1974] Ch. 467; *Phillips v Mobil Oil Ltd* [1989] 1 W.L.R. 888.
[184] *Webb v Pollmount Ltd* [1966] Ch. 584.
[185] See above, para.5–023.
[186] LT(C)A 1995 s.3(1).
[187] LT(C)A 1995 s.4.

Where former landlord or tenant has not been released

14–065 In the event that the assignor is not released from the burden of the covenants in question for one of the reasons considered below, he remains liable to the other party (jointly and severally with the assignee). The unreleased assignor will also remain liable (jointly and severally with the assignee) to anyone to whom the other party assigns.[188]

Who may tenant covenants be enforced against?

14–066 The tenant covenants are enforceable against:

(a) any tenant who is bound by them; and
(b) any mortgagee of his interest who is in possession.[189]

Who may enforce tenant covenants or a right of re-entry?

14–067 The tenant covenants are enforceable by:

(a) any landlord who has their benefit[190];
(b) a lessee of the reversion[191] (such as the holder of an overriding lease[192]); and
(c) a mortgagee of the reversion who is in possession of the reversion.[193]

In principle a tenant can be sued by both the grantor of his lease and a holder of an overriding lease. That will be the case if a breach of covenant causes damage to both the overriding lessee and the grantor. But in other situations, such as a failure to pay rent, the grant of the overriding lease will estop the grantor from enforcing.

Who may landlord covenants be enforced against?

14–068 The landlord covenants are enforceable against:

(a) any landlord who is bound by them;
(b) any lessee of the reversion; and
(c) any mortgagee in possession of the reversion.[194]

---

[188] Because "landlord covenant" and "tenant covenant" include covenants binding on a former landlord or tenant who has not been released and so are transmitted on any assignment by the other party.
[189] LT(C)A 1995 s.15(4).
[190] LT(C)A 1995 s.15(1), (6).
[191] LT(C)A 1995 s.15(1)(a).
[192] See below.
[193] LT(C)A 1995 s.15(1)(b).
[194] LT(C)A 1995 s.15(2).

Where this gives the tenant a number of persons to sue, all those persons are jointly and severally liable to the tenant[195] but between themselves the liable parties will be entitled to an indemnity from the party actually responsible for the breach.[196]

Who may enforce landlord covenants?

The landlord covenants are enforceable by:

14–069

(a) any tenant who has their benefit; and
(b) any mortgagee of his interest who is in possession.[197]

Partial assignments

When a lease or a reversion is assigned only in part, the position is as follows:

14–070

Attribution

Whether and to what extent any covenant is enforceable against the assignee depends on whether it is attributable to any specific part of the land in question or whether it is applicable to the whole of the land.[198] Where it is so attributable, it must be complied with by whoever holds the interest in that part of the land.[199] Where it is applicable to the whole of the land, as in the case of a covenant to pay rent or service charges, both the assignor and the assignee are jointly and severally liable for the whole amount due unless and until the liability is apportioned.[200] However, one may seek contribution from the other.[201]

14–071

Apportionment

The 1995 Act permits apportionment where this is agreed by all the relevant parties.[202] In default of agreement, the assignor and assignee can agree an apportionment and, before or within four weeks of the partial assignment taking place,[203] apply to the other party to the lease to make that apportionment binding.[204] This is done by serving a notice on the other party in a specified form,[205] informing him of the assignment and the request that the apportionment should become binding on him.[206] The apportionment will then become binding unless the other party serves a written counter-notice within four weeks. If he does

14–072

---

[195] LT(C)A 1995 s.13(1).
[196] For example a landlord who has granted an overriding lease will be entitled to be indemnified by the overriding lessee.
[197] LT(C)A 1995 s.15(3).
[198] LT(C)A 1995 s.9(6).
[199] LT(C)A 1995 s.3(2), (3).
[200] LT(C)A 1995 s.13(1).
[201] LT(C)A 1995 s.13(3), applying the provisions of Civil Liability (Contribution) Act 1978.
[202] LT(C)A 1995 s.26(1).
[203] LT(C)A 1995 s.10(1).
[204] LT(C)A 1995 s.9.
[205] LT(C)A 1995 s.27; SI 1995/2964.
[206] LT(C)A 1995 s.10(1).

so, there will be no apportionment unless either the assignor and the assignee apply to the court for, and obtains, a declaration that it is reasonable for the apportionment to become binding or the other party withdraws his objections in writing.[207] Any apportionment is effective from the date of the partial assignment.[208]

Forfeiture and disclaimer

14–073   The 1995 Act also provides that, where there has been a partial assignment, rights of re-entry and forfeiture are exercisable only against the part of the land whose tenant is in breach of covenant[209] and that rights of disclaimer are exercisable only in respect of the part of the land whose tenant is insolvent.[210]

Pre-assignment breaches

Liability

14–074   As in the case of old leases, neither the landlord nor the tenant of a new lease is liable for a breach of covenant committed before he took his assignment.[211]

Right to sue

14–075   Neither the landlord nor the tenant of a new lease can sue in respect of breaches of covenant committed before he took his assignment[212] (by contrast the landlord but not the tenant of an old lease is entitled to do this). However, the right to sue for past breaches can be expressly assigned[213] and if it is the assignee can sue. Such assignments are common-place, particularly on an assignment of the reversion.[214]

Right to forfeit

14–076   Notwithstanding that the right to sue for pre-assignment breaches does not automatically pass, the landlord for the time being is entitled to exercise any right to re-enter and forfeit the lease in respect of a breach committed before the assignment to him.[215] Where he seeks to do so in respect of arrears of rent which existed at the date of the assignment to him, any sums paid by the tenant in respect of those arrears and interest thereon in order to obtain relief against forfeiture will have to be paid to him rather than to the person actually entitled to them, the assignor. Since it is thought that the latter will not be entitled to sue for them thereafter, he may be able to recover them either by a restitutionary claim or in

---

[207] LT(C)A 1995 s.10(2).
[208] LT(C)A 1995 s.10(3).
[209] LT(C)A 1995 s.21(2).
[210] LT(C)A 1995 s.23(1).
[211] LT(C)A 1995 s.23(1).
[212] LT(C)A 1995 s,23(1)
[213] LT(C)A 1995 s.23(2).
[214] *Megarry & Wade: The Law of Real Property* (2012), p.992.
[215] LT(C)A 1995 s.23(3).

equity, particularly if the assignee paid less for the reversion because the assignor did not also assign the right to sue for these arrears.[216]

Liability of guarantors

The guarantors of the landlord and tenant for the time being of a new lease are in the same position as the person whose liability they have guaranteed.   **14–077**

POSITION OF FORMER LANDLORDS AND TENANTS OF A NEW LEASE

The basic rule for former tenants

Former tenants are released from liability under the tenant covenants when they assign their lease[217] but may remain liable to the landlord until the next assignment under an authorised guarantee agreement.   **14–078**

Release from liability

When the original lessee of a new lease assigns his lease, he will thereupon be released from the burden of the tenant covenants and will cease to be entitled to the benefit of the landlord covenants.[218] If the assignment is of part, then to the extent that covenants fall to be complied with in respect of the part assigned the same applies.[219] A subsequent tenant of a new lease does not as such require the assistance of the 1995 Act to be released from his tenant covenants when he assigns on. However, as has already been seen,[220] many covenants not to assign the lease without the lessor's consent provide that consent will not be forthcoming unless the assignee of the lease covenants directly with the lessor to observe all the tenant covenants for the remainder of the term. Where an assignee does covenant directly in this way, he will from then on be in exactly the same position as the original lessee.[221] Consequently, he does require the assistance of the 1995 Act to be released from his liability to the landlord for the time being for any breach of the tenant covenants for the rest of the term; its provisions relating to release and, for that matter, those relating to authorised guarantee agreements apply to him in the same way as they apply to an original lessee.[222]   **14–079**

Release from a covenant liability does not affect any liability for breach of covenant committed before the release takes effect.[223] Where a person ceases to be entitled to enforce

---

[216] *Megarry & Wade: The Law of Real Property* (2012), p.993.
[217] Except where the assignment is in breach of covenant or in the case of assignments by operation of law; see LT(C)A 1995 s.11.
[218] LT(C)A 1995 s.5(2).
[219] LT(C)A 1995 s.5(3).
[220] Above, para.14–022.
[221] *Deanplan Ltd v Mahmoud* [1993] Ch. 151 (release of one such assignee by the release of a later assignee).
[222] "Tenant covenant" includes covenants in collateral agreements such as a licence to assign or a collateral deed of covenant by an assignee: see LT(C)A 1995 s.28(1).
[223] LT(C)A 1995 s.24(1).

a covenant, this does not affect the entitlement to sue for breach of covenant committed before the release takes effect.[224]

Authorised guarantee agreements

14–080   A landlord can have recourse to the tenant who held the lease immediately before the tenant for the time being if the lease contains a covenant requiring the consent of the landlord to any assignment; in these circumstances, the landlord may give his consent on condition that the assigning tenant guarantees the performance of the covenants by the tenant to whom he is assigning. Such an agreement is known as an "authorised guarantee agreement" or "AGA".[225] Where the covenant against assignment is absolute, the landlord can refuse consent as of right and so is entitled to grant consent only on the basis that the assigning tenant enters into an authorised guarantee agreement.[226] Where the covenant against assignment is qualified, the landlord will be able to do so as of right only if the lease is not a residential lease and he has stipulated that entering into such an agreement is a prerequisite of consent being given.[227] (Such a stipulation will normally be in the lease itself but there is nothing in the 1995 Act to prevent the landlord and the tenant making a subsequent agreement to this effect.) Where the landlord has not so stipulated, he can only require the tenant to enter into an authorised guarantee agreement if it is reasonable for him to do so.[228] Since the 1995 Act came into force, it has become standard practice for landlords to include such stipulations in commercial leases. However, when the tenant of an old lease exercises a statutory right to obtain a new lease, typically in the case of a business tenancy,[229] his previous lease will contain no such stipulation and the result will turn entirely on reasonableness.[230]

All or any of the following liabilities can be imposed on the assigning tenant by an authorised guarantee agreement:

(i)   liability as sole or principal debtor in respect of the tenant covenants while his assignee remains tenant[231] (this renders him liable even if the terms of the lease are varied);

(ii)   liability as guarantor of his assignee's compliance with the tenant covenants provided that that liability is not more onerous than liability under (i) would be[232]; and

(iii)   in the event that the lease is disclaimed on his assignee's insolvency, an obligation to take a new lease whose duration and covenants are not more onerous than those of the lease which he is assigning.[233]

---

[224] LT(C)A 1995 s.24(4). The cause of action may be assigned, LT(C)A 1995 s.23(2).
[225] LT(C)A 1995 s.16.
[226] LT(C)A 1995 s.16(3).
[227] LTA 1927 s.19(1A) inserted by LT(C)A 1995 s.22.
[228] LTA 1988 s.1 (this applies because the condition has to be lawfully imposed; see LT(C)A 1995 s.16(3)(b).
[229] See above, para.11–005.
[230] *Wallis Fashion Group Ltd v CGU Life Assurance Ltd* [2000] 2 E.G.L.R. 49.
[231] LT(C)A 1995 s.16(5)(a).
[232] LT(C)A 1995 s.16(5)(b).
[233] LT(C)A 1995 s.16(5)(c).

An agreement will not be an authorised guarantee agreement if it purports to guarantee performance of the obligations of anyone other than the assignee or to impose liability on the tenant in respect of any covenants from which the assignee is released.[234] Any such agreement is void.[235] In this way the 1995 Act ensures that the assignor's liability ceases when the assignee further assigns.

Section 17 notices

However, the ability of the landlord for the time being to recover "fixed charges" (rent, service charges and any other liquidated sums) from a former tenant who has entered into an authorised guarantee agreement is now subject to his obligation to serve a notice, often referred to as a "section 17 notice". As has already been seen, a landlord can now only recover such fixed charges from a former tenant if he serves notice, in a prescribed form, on that tenant within six months of any fixed charge becoming due. This notice informs the former tenant that the sum is due and that the landlord intends to recover that sum from him.[236] A s.17 notice is sufficiently served if it is sent by registered post to the last known abode of the former tenant.[237]

14–081

Overriding leases

A former tenant who pays in full any sum so claimed under a problem notice is entitled to what the 1995 Act describes as an "overriding lease", a lease for three days longer than the original lease (unless the landlord's interest would thereby be displaced) which contains the same covenants as the original lease. This overriding lease is a reversionary lease and so is interposed between the interest of the landlord and the lease of the tenant for the time being[238]; the former tenant therefore becomes the landlord of the tenant for the time being. Consequently, any future failure to pay a fixed charge by the tenant for the time being will enable the former tenant to forfeit the lease and cause his overriding lease to come into possession. An overriding lease held by a former tenant of a new lease is itself an new lease[239]; so he will remain liable to the landlord for the time being only while he remains the tenant of the overriding lease and for the duration of any authorised guarantee agreement which he may be obliged to sign pursuant to any covenant requiring the landlord's consent to an assignment. However, he will normally be able to cover the amount of any liability by assigning or sub-letting, although this will not be the case in the event of another slump in property values of the type which occurred in the years immediately prior to the enactment of the 1995 Act.

14–082

The basic rule for former landlords

A former landlord of a new lease other than the original lessor does not require the assistance of the 1995 Act to be released from his landlord covenants and there is in practice no

14–083

---

[234] LT(C)A 1995 s.17.
[235] LT(C)A 1995 s.19.
[236] LT(C)A 1995 s.17.
[237] *Commercial Union Life Assurance Co Ltd v Moustafa* [1999] 2 E.G.L.R. 44.
[238] LT(C)A 1995 ss.19–20.
[239] LT(C)A 1995 s.20(1).

possibility that he will have covenanted directly with the lessee to observe all the landlord covenants for the remainder of the term. Where the original lessor of a new lease assigns his interest, however, his position differs from that of original tenants. An original landlord is not automatically released from liability under the landlord covenants. He not only retains the right to enforce the tenant covenants but also remains liable to the tenant for the time being on the landlord covenants. However, except in those cases where the assignment is by operation of law (as on his death or bankruptcy),[240] he may, before or within four weeks of the assignment taking place, apply to the tenant for the time being to be released.[241] This is done by serving a notice on the tenant in a specified form,[242] informing him of the assignment and the request that the landlord covenants be released.[243] The landlord covenants will then be released unless the tenant serves a written counter-notice within four weeks. If he does so, there will be no release unless either the landlord applies to the court for, and obtains, a declaration that it is reasonable for the landlord covenants to be released or the tenant withdraws his objections in writing.[244] If he does not or cannot seek a release or fails to obtain one, he may apply in the same way to be released on any subsequent assignment of the reversion.[245] A release has effect from the date of the assignment in question[246] and also deprives the landlord of the right to enforce the tenant covenants as from that date. If the assignment is of part only of the reversion, then to the extent that covenants fall to be complied with in respect of the part assigned the same applies.

Release from a covenant liability does not affect any liability for breach of covenant committed before the release takes effect.[247] Where a person ceases to be entitled to enforce a covenant, this does not affect the entitlement to sue for breach of covenant committed before the release takes effect.[248]

The exceptions to the basic rules

14–084   The basic rules are subject to the following exceptions.

Express release clause

14–085   A clause which releases the landlord from liability on the landlord covenants upon assignment of the reversion is not inconsistent with the aims of the Act and is valid.[249]

Personal covenants

14–086   The burden and benefit of any covenant in a new lease "which (in whatever terms) is expressed to be personal to any person" does not pass when that person assigns his inter-

---

[240] LT(C)A 1995 s.11.
[241] LT(C)A 1995 s.6(2).
[242] LT(C)A 1995 s.27; SI 1995/2964.
[243] LT(C)A 1995 s.8(1).
[244] LT(C)A 1995 s.8(2).
[245] LT(C)A 1995 s.7(1), (2).
[246] LT(C)A 1995 s.8(3).
[247] LT(C)A 1995 s.24(1).
[248] LT(C)A 1995 s.24(4). The cause of action may be assigned, LT(C)A 1995 s.23(2).
[249] *London Diocesan Fund v Phithwa* [2005] UKHL 70; [2005] 1 W.L.R. 3956.

est.[250] Consequently, the original lessor and the original lessee will remain liable on or will be able to enforce any covenant which is personal to them throughout the term. The fact that the original lessor is released from the landlord covenants in the way just described does not release him from liability under any personal covenant.[251]

Estate contracts

In the event that a covenant in a new lease which also constitutes an estate contract is not enforceable against a successor in title to the party burdened by it, the original lessor or lessee will, just as in the case of an old lease, nevertheless be liable for damages for breach of that contract to whoever has the benefit of the estate contract. It is not a defence to such an action that the estate contract would have been enforceable against the successor in title had it been protected by registration in the appropriate way.[252] While the measure of damages is likely to be minimal in the case of options, unless the option was to acquire the interest in question at less than the market rate, the measure may well be very substantial when the claimant is a lessee who has been unable to exercise a statutory right to purchase the freehold or to take an extended lease or a lessor who has been unable to take advantage of a covenant obliging the lessee to offer to surrender his lease to the lessor before seeking to assign it.

14–087

Excluded assignments

An excluded assignment is one which takes effect by operation of law (as on the death or bankruptcy of the landlord or tenant) or which is made in breach of covenant[253] (in practice only feasible in the case of an assignment of a lease in breach of an absolute or qualified covenant against assignment; covenants restricting assignment *by the landlord* are never encountered). A party to a lease who makes an excluded assignment remains liable on his own covenants, but can enforce those of the other party, until the next assignment of the interest in question.[254] In the case of a tenant, fixed charges can only be recovered following the service of a s.17 notice and a tenant who pays a fixed charge in full is entitled to an overriding lease. No authorised guarantee agreement can arise on the occasion of an excluded assignment.[255] However, on the next assignment of the lease, the landlord who is entitled to demand an authorised guarantee agreement is able to demand one both from the tenant who made the excluded assignment and from his assignee. Nor, where an excluded assignment is partial, can the parties to it apply for an agreed apportionment to become binding on the other party to the lease until the next assignment.[256]

14–088

---

[250] LT(C)A 1995 s.3(6)(a). As to what constitutes a personal covenant see *First Penthouse Ltd v Channel Hotels & Properties (UK) Ltd* [2003] EWHC 2713 (Ch); [2004] L&TR 16 discussed at para.14–061 above.

[251] *BHP Petroleum Great Britain Ltd v Chesterfield Properties Ltd* [2002] Ch. 194 approved by *London Diocesan Board v Phithwa* [2005] UKHL 70; [2005] 1 W.L.R. 3956 at [23].

[252] *Wright v Dean* [1948] Ch. 686.

[253] LT(C)A 1995 s.11(1).

[254] LT(C)A 1995 s.11(2)–(4).

[255] LT(C)A 1995 s.16(1).

[256] LT(C)A 1995 s.11(5)(b), (6).

Contrary intention

14–089   The Court of Appeal has indicated that there is nothing in the 1995 Act to fetter the freedom of contracting parties to place a limit on the transmissibility of the benefit or burden of obligations under a tenancy.[257] Parties can obviously prevent the burden of covenants running by classifying them as personal. However, if this indication means that parties can provide that the burden of covenants will not be released on assignment, the whole policy of the 1995 Act will have been undermined. Lessors could require lessees to enter into the usual transmissible covenant to pay the rent and a personal covenant to pay the rent throughout the term, thus retaining the right to sue both the original lessee and the current tenant. However, it is likely that any such personal covenant would be regarded as an agreement which excludes, modifies or otherwise frustrates the operation of a provision of the 1995 Act and is consequently void.[258] The answer may be to say that any personal covenant which mirrors a transmissible covenant is void; this would give the original parties a choice between transmissibility and non-transmissibility but no possibility of having both.

Indemnity

14–090   In those limited circumstances where a former landlord or tenant of a new lease remains liable on covenants post-assignment, and discharges the liability of the landlord and tenant for the time being, indemnity covenants are no longer applied.[259] Where the assignor does so, he has an implied right to restitution from the assignee.[260]

Pre-assignment breaches

14–091   As has already been seen, neither the landlord nor the tenant of a new lease is liable for a breach of covenant committed before he took his assignment[261] nor can either the landlord or the tenant of a new lease sue in respect of breaches of covenant committed before he took his assignment.[262] Such breaches of covenant remain actionable by and against the former tenant or landlord as the case may be unless the right to sue for the past breaches has been expressly assigned.[263]

Liability of guarantors[264]

14–092   Where a tenant is released from tenant covenants on assignment, any guarantor of the performance of those covenants is released to the same extent as the tenant[265] and any

---

[257] *BHP Petroleum Great Britain Ltd v Chesterfield Properties Ltd* [2002] Ch. 194.
[258] LT(C)A 1995 s.25(1).
[259] LT(C)A 1995 s.14.
[260] See *Moule v Garrett* (1872) L.R. 7 Ex. 101.
[261] LT(C)A 1995 s.23(1).
[262] LT(C)A 1995 s.23(1).
[263] LT(C)A 1995 s.23(2).
[264] Guarantees of landlord's liability are not common so this paragraph considers matters from the perspective of a guarantor of the tenant.
[265] LT(C)A 1995 s.24(2) and see *Good Harvest Partnership LLP v Centaur Services Ltd* [201] EWHC 330 (Ch); [2010] Ch. 426.

provision which purports to maintain the guarantee of performance of the covenants after release of the tenant is void.[266] However, the guarantors of former tenants of a new lease can validly be required to guarantee the obligations of the assigning former tenant under any AGA which the former tenant enters into on assignment. Such a further guarantee is not itself an AGA but does not offend the release provisions in the Act because the guarantor is still released to the same extent as the assigning former tenant.[267]

Management companies

Properties of a single landlord which are in multiple occupation are often managed by a management company which will be a party to each lease and will be obliged to perform services such as the provision of porterage and the maintenance and cleaning of the common areas in consideration of a covenant by each tenant to pay the appropriate proportion of the cost. Such companies are brought within the 1995 Act in order to ensure that tenants can neither sue nor be sued on their covenants following the assignment of their leases.[268] This is achieved by deeming covenants which are exercisable by or against a third party of this type[269] to be tenant covenants where they are exercisable by the landlord or against the tenant and to be landlord covenants where they are exercisable by the tenant or against the landlord.[270] Thus former tenants will automatically be released in the normal way and former landlords can apply to be released in the normal way. The 1995 Act does not deal with the situation where such a third party seeks to assign its rights, or its burdens. Leases with management companies as parties often do not permit such assignment; if they do then the general law applies.

14–093

RESTRICTIVE COVENANTS IN A NEW LEASE

Relating to the demised premises

All covenants in new leases which are restrictive of the user of the leased land are enforceable against any assignee of the lease or the reversion and any owner or occupier of the land to which the covenant relates, even if there is no express provision to this effect in the lease or sub-lease in question.[271] Consequently, any type of sub-lessee and his assignees, any licensee and any squatter will be bound by all the restrictive covenants in a head lease.

14–094

It should also be recalled that covenants in a head lease, whether restrictive or not, may be indirectly enforceable against sub-tenants by virtue of the existence of a forfeiture clause in the head lease.[272]

---

[266] LT(C)A 1995 s.25(1); *K/S Victoria Street v House of Fraser* [2011] EWCA Civ 904; [2011] 2 P. & C.R. 15.

[267] *K/S Victoria Street v House of Fraser* (above) at [46].

[268] LT(C)A 1995 s.12.

[269] Guarantors and others who have undertaken a financial liability referable to the performance or non-performance of a covenant by another party are not within s.12: LT(C)A 1995 s.12(1)(b).

[270] LT(C)A 1995 s.12(2), (3).

[271] LT(C)A 1995 s.3(5).

[272] See above, paras 12–014 et seq.

Relating to land other than the demised premises

14–095   However, although a restrictive covenant entered into by the original lessor in respect of land which is not comprised in the lease is a landlord covenant and is enforceable against the landlord for the time being, it is not by virtue of the 1995 Act enforceable against a purchaser or a tenant of the land not comprised in the lease.[273] The enforceability of such a covenant depends on the general law applicable to restrictive covenants.[274] By way of brief summary:

(a)   Unregistered land: the enforceability of such covenants under the general law is, in the case of unregistered land, governed by the equitable doctrine of notice[275]; thus in the normal case the purchaser or tenant of the land not comprised in the lease will take free of the covenant.

(b)   Registered land: restrictive covenants made between a lessor and a lessee are registrable insofar as they do not apply to the demised premises.[276]

SUMMARY OF KEY CASES

- *In re King (deceased); Robinson v Gray* [1963] Ch. 459
- *Oceanic Village Ltd v United Attractions Ltd* [2000] Ch. 234
- *London Diocesan Fund v Phithwa* (sometimes referred to as *"Avonridge v Mashru"*) [2005] UKHL 70, [2005] 1 W.L.R. 3956

FURTHER READING

- R. Thornton, "Enforceability of leasehold covenants: More questions than answers" (1991) 11 L.S. 47
- P. Walter, "The Landlord and Tenant (Covenants) Act 1995: A legislative folly" [1996] Conv. 432

---

[273]   *Oceanic Village Ltd v United Attractions Ltd* [2000] Ch. 234.
[274]   *Oceanic Village Ltd v United Attractions Ltd* (above).
[275]   *Dartstone Ltd v Cleveland Petroleum Co Ltd* [1969] 1 W.L.R. 1807.
[276]   LRA 2002 s.33(c). The position was different under the previous LRA 1925, see *Oceanic Village Ltd v United Attractions Ltd* [2000] Ch. 234.

Chapter 15

EASEMENTS, PROFITS AND INCORPOREAL HEREDITAMENTS

CHAPTER SUMMARY

This chapter covers the principal types of incorporeal hereditament, namely easements and profits á prendre. Very broadly, easements are private rights over a neighbour's land, such as a right of way. Profits á prendre are rights to take something from land, such as a right to catch fish. This Chapter considers the characteristics of easements and profits, how easements and profits are created, transferred and extinguished, and the particular features of some of the more common types of easement and profit. At the end of the Chapter is a short section dealing with rentcharges and mention of the other types of incorporeal hereditament. It has already been seen that incorporeal hereditaments are rights in land which do not give the owner present physical possession of the land.[1] There are two quite distinct classes of incorporeal hereditaments:

(i) those which are merely rights over the land of another and can never become corporeal hereditaments, such as easements, profits and rentcharges; and

(ii) those which may ripen into corporeal hereditaments. Thus a grant to A for life with remainder to B in fee simple gave B an incorporeal hereditament which became corporeal after A's death.

The second class has already been dealt with.[2] It is with incorporeal hereditaments in the first class that this chapter is concerned. The only incorporeal hereditaments which need to be considered at length are easements, profits and rentcharges.[3] They do not form a homogeneous class. Some, such as easements, can exist only for the benefit of other land, while others, such as rentcharges, lead an independent existence. In one sense, those in the former category are not hereditaments at all, for they cannot be inherited or dealt with except as appendages to the land which they benefit.

---

[1] Above, para.3–030.
[2] Above, paras 1–014, 2–035, 3–023.
[3] There are others which are either obsolete or of little importance in connection with the modern law of real property, such as titles of honour, advowsons and tithes.

PART 1   EASEMENTS AND PROFITS

NATURE OF EASEMENTS

15–001   An easement may be defined as a right to use, or restrict the use of, the land of another person in some way. This definition is not exact, for it includes certain rights which are not easements, such as restrictive covenants, and it does not illustrate what sort of a right an easement is. Examples of easements are rights of way, the right of a flat-owner to use a communal garden, and rights of light. The best way in which to amplify this imperfect definition is to examine:

> (i)   the essentials of an easement; and
> (ii) the distinction between easements and certain analogous rights.

Essentials of an easement

Summary

15–002   There are four essential characteristics of an easement:
1. There must be a dominant tenement and a servient tenement.[4]
2. The easement must "accommodate" i.e. confer a benefit on the dominant tenement.
3. The dominant and servient tenements must be owned or occupied by different persons.
4. The easement must be capable of forming the subject-matter of a grant.
The fourth characteristic may appear somewhat circular but what it means is that:

> (a)   the easement must be the sort of right which could validly be granted by Deed (even if it is claimed to arise by implication or prescription);
> (b)   the owner of the servient tenement must be capable of granting an easement and the owner of the dominant tenement must be capable of receiving the easement. As to what sorts of rights could validly be granted by Deed and thus exist as an easement, the following general principles can be stated:
> > (i)   the right must be sufficiently definite;
> > (ii)   the right must not be too extensive;
> > (iii) the right must not require expenditure by the owner of the servient tenement;
> > (iv)   the right must be within the general nature of rights recognised as being capable of existing as easements.

There must be a dominant and a servient tenement[5]

15–003   If X owns Greenacre and grants a right to use a path across it to the owner for the time being of the neighbouring plot of Whiteacre, Greenacre is the servient tenement and Whiteacre

---

4   Often referred to as "dominant land" and "servient land" although this is not strictly accurate and can lead to confusion when considering easements created by lease

5   *Hawkins v Rutter* [1892] 1 Q.B. 668. It may be noted that this is one requirement which distinguishes easements from profits: profits need not be appurtenant to a dominant tenement.

the dominant tenement. Had X granted the right to A who owned no land at all, A would have acquired a licence to walk over Greenacre, but his right could not exist as an easement, for a dominant tenement is lacking. Put technically, an easement cannot exist in gross[6] (independently of the ownership of land) but only as appurtenant (attached) to a dominant tenement.[7] On any transfer of the dominant tenement, the easement will pass with the land, so that the occupier for the time being can enjoy it,[8] even if he is a mere lessee.[9]

The easement must accommodate the dominant tenement

A right cannot exist as an easement unless it confers a benefit on the dominant tenement as   **15–004**
a tenement. It is not enough that the right should give the owner for the time being some personal advantage unconnected with his land, such as a right to use a wall on the servient tenement for advertising generally and not merely in connection with a business carried on upon the dominant tenement.[10] The test is whether the right makes the dominant tenement a better and more convenient tenement, for example a right to affix to adjoining premises a signboard for a public house.[11] There has to be some nexus between the enjoyment of the right and the use of the dominant tenement, so that the grant to a purchaser of the right free of charge to attend a nearby zoo or cricket ground cannot create an easement.[12]

Again, if X owns land in Northumberland, he cannot burden it with an easement of way in favour of land in Kent, for although it may be very convenient for the owner of the Kentish land to walk across X's Northumberland estate when he goes north, the right of way does not improve the Kentish land as a tenement.[13] This does not mean that a right cannot exist as an easement unless the dominant and servient tenements are contiguous; even if they are separated by other land,[14] an easement can still exist, provided it in fact confers some benefit upon the dominant tenement as such,[15] as does a right for the dominant owner to enjoy a nearby pleasure ground or garden.[16] Nor will a right be any the less an easement merely because it benefits other land as well as the dominant tenement.[17]

In *Ackroyd v Smith*[18] it was held that a right of way granted "for all purposes" to the tenant of Whiteacre and his successors in title was not an easement, for the grant permitted

---

[6] *Rangeley v Midland Ry* (1868) 3 Ch.App. 306 at 310; *London & Blenheim Retail Parks* [1994] 1 W.L.R. 31. The rule can be criticised, see (1980) 96 L.Q.R. 557 (M.F. Sturley).

[7] See *Re Salvin's Indenture* [1938] 2 All E.R. 498 (dominant tenement partly incorporeal); *Wall v Collins* [2007] Ch. 390 (easement created by lease survives merger of the lease with the freehold reversion).

[8] LPA 1925 s.187(1); *Leech v Schweder* (1874) 9 Ch.App. 463 at 474, 475.

[9] *Thorpe v Brumfitt* (1873) 8 Ch.App. 650.

[10] *Clapman v Edwards* [1938] 2 All E.R. 507.

[11] *Moody v Steggles* (1879) 12 Ch.D. 261.

[12] *Re Ellenborough Park* [1956] Ch. 131 at 174.

[13] See *Bailey v Stephens* (1862) 12 C.B. (N.S.) 91 at 115.

[14] e.g. where the dominant tenement is separated from the terminus of a right of way by land over which permission would be required to cross, as in *Huckvale v Aegean Hotels* (1989) 58 P. & C.R. 163. Cf. the "road to nowhere" in *Beech v Kennerley* [2012] EWCA Civ 158.

[15] *Todrick v Western National Omnibus Co Ltd* [1934] Ch. 561; *Pugh v Savage* [1970] 2 Q.B. 373.

[16] *Re Ellenborough Park* [1956] Ch. 131 (park in a square).

[17] *Simpson v Mayor of Godmanchester* [1897] A.C. 696.

[18] (1850) 10 C.B. 164.

the way to be used for purposes not connected with Whiteacre. Had the grant been worded "for all purposes connected with Whiteacre" it could have created an easement. Probably the words used would be construed in this sense if the case arose today.[19]

In *Hill v Tupper*[20] the owner of a canal leased land on the bank of the canal to Hill, and granted him the sole and exclusive right of putting pleasure boats on the canal. Tupper, without any authority, put rival pleasure boats on the canal. The question was whether Hill could successfully sue Tupper. If Hill's right amounted to an easement, he could sue anyone who interfered with it, for it was a right in land. If it was not an easement, then it could only be a licence,[21] i.e. a mere personal arrangement between Hill and the canal owner not amounting to an interest in land, so that Hill would have no right to sue those interfering with it.[22] It was held that since the right did not improve Hill's land qua land, but gave him a mere personal advantage, it was not an easement and so he could not sue Tupper. The result would have been different if the right granted had been to cross and recross the canal to get to and from Hill's land. The canal owner, of course, could have sued Tupper for trespassing on the canal.[23]

The dominant and servient tenements must be owned or occupied by different persons

15–005   An easement is essentially a right *in alieno solo* (in the soil of another): therefore a person cannot have an easement over his own land.[24] "When the owner of Whiteacre and Blackacre passes over the former to Blackacre, he is not exercising a right of way in respect of Blackacre; he is merely making use of his own land to get from one part of it to another."[25]

It should be noted, however, that the same person must not only own both tenements but also occupy both of them before the existence of an easement is rendered impossible. Thus if an easement over Greenacre is appurtenant to Whiteacre, it will not be affected by the fee simple in each plot being vested in one person if the plots are occupied by different lessees[26]; unity of ownership without unity of possession is not fatal to an easement. Similarly, if the fee simple in each plot is owned by different persons, the easement will not be destroyed if the plots are leased to the same tenant, creating unity of possession without unity of ownership; during the currency of the lease the easement is suspended but it will revive when the lease ends.[27]

The name "quasi-easements" is often used to describe rights habitually exercised by a man over part of his own land which, if the part in question were owned and occupied by

---

[19] See *Todrick v Western National Omnibus Co Ltd* [1934] Ch. 561 at 583–585; and see *Clapman v Edwards* [1938] 2 All E.R. 507.

[20] (1863) 2 H. & C. 121.

[21] For licences, see Ch.10.

[22] Note that a licensee with possession may be able to take proceedings to evict trespassers: *Manchester Airport v Dutton* [2000] Q.B. 133. Hill's right did not amount to possession.

[23] See *Lord Chesterfield v Harris* [1908] 2 Ch. 397 at 412 (affirmed [1911] A.C. 623).

[24] Among other cases see *Sovmots Investments v Secretary of State* [1979] A.C. 144 at 169.

[25] *Roe v Siddons* (1888) 22 QBD 224 at 236 per Fry L.J.

[26] *Richardson v Graham* [1908] 1 K.B. 39; and see *Buckby v Coles* (1814) 5 Taunt. 311 at 315. This situation is actually very common, as in the case of flats with easements over common parts.

[27] *Thomas v Thomas* (1835) 2 Cr.M. & R. 34 (see especially at 40).

another, would be easements. These are of some importance, for in certain circumstances they may become true easements.[28]

The easement must be capable of forming the subject-matter of a grant

No right can exist as an easement unless it could have been granted validly by deed. This involves the following points.   **15–006**

The right must be sufficiently definite: The extent of the right claimed must be capable of reasonable definition. This principle lies behind many of the exclusions discussed later. Thus, although there can be an easement of light where a defined window receives a defined amount of light,[29] there can be no easement of unrestricted light to the claimant's land,[30] nor of privacy,[31] nor of prospect (the right to a view), for "the law does not give an action for such things of delight".[32] Similarly, although an easement for the passage of air through a defined channel may exist,[33] there can be no easement for the general flow of air over land to a windmill or chimney.[34] Again, although an easement to receive an undiminished flow of water through a defined channel may exist,[35] there can be no easement either to receive[36] or to discharge[37] percolating water such as rainwater, for any advantage or disadvantage produced thereby is a product of nature. However, sometimes rights which cannot take effect as easements may be obtained by means of simple contract, the imposition of restrictive covenants[38] or under the rule against derogation from grant.[39]

The right must not be too extensive: An easement is a right over the land of another, and not a right to it. A right which effectively gives the grantee possession or sole use of the servient land is too extensive to be recognised as an easement. This issue has frequently arisen in the context of rights to park. Thus the continuous occupation of the whole of a strip of land for the storage and repair of vehicles cannot be an easement, for it amounts to virtually the whole beneficial use of the land.[40] Similarly an exclusive right to a defined parking place cannot be an easement if it renders the ownership of the owner of the servient tenement illusory[41]; whether it does so or not is a question of degree.[42] This doctrine is often referred to as "the ouster principle": is the servient owner "ousted" from his land by the easement such that he is left unable to make any reasonable use of the servient

---

[28] As when the land is sold in separate parts. Discussed below.
[29] *Easton v Isted* [1903] 1 Ch. 405.
[30] *Colls v Home and Colonial Stores Ltd* [1904] A.C. 179.
[31] *Browne v Flower* [1911] 1 Ch. 219.
[32] *Aldred's Case* (1610) 9 Co.Rep. 57b at 58b, per Wray C.J.
[33] *Bass v Gregory* (1890) 25 QBD 481; *Cable v Bryant* [1908] 1 Ch. 259.
[34] *Webb v Bird* (1862) 13 C.B. (N.S.) 841; *Bryant v Lefever* (1879) 4 C.P.D. 172.
[35] *Dickinson v Grand Junction Canal Co Ltd* (1852) 7 Exch. 282 at 301.
[36] *Chasemore v Richards* (1859) 7 H.L. Cas. 349.
[37] *Palmer v Bowman* [2000] 1 All E.R. 23.
[38] Covenants are dealt with in Ch.16.
[39] See below, para.15–017.
[40] *Copeland v Greenhalf* [1952] Ch. 488, in which *Wright v Macadam* [1949] 2 K.B. 744 was not cited.
[41] *Batchelor v Marlow* (2001) 82 P. & C.R. 36 (exclusive parking for 10 hours a day from Monday to Friday).
[42] *London & Blenheim Estates Ltd v Ladbroke Retail Parks Ltd* [1992] 1 W.L.R. 1298 (affirmed [1994] 1 W.L.R. 31).

tenement himself. The question is addressed to the area over which the easement is claimed, not the entirety of the servient tenement.[43] But the ordinary parking of cars is a discontinuous process[44] and the right to park a car intermittently anywhere in a defined area can be an easement.[45] Other situations in which the issue of the extent of the easement has arisen, and where quite extensive rights have been upheld as easements include the right of the tenant of part of a house to store coal in a shed in the garden[46] and the right to graze horses.[47]

The right must not require expenditure by the owner of the servient tenement: Subject only to some minor and anomalous exceptions, if a right involves the expenditure of money by the owner of the servient tenement, it will not be recognised as an easement. To put it another way, easements do not encompass rights to require something to be done.

It follows from this that there is no obligation on the servient owner to maintain the subject matter of the easement; what is implied into the grant is that the owner of the dominant tenement has the right to enter the servient tenement to repair the subject matter of the easement. For example, the grant of a right to cross a bridge or take water from pipes and a pump does not oblige the servient owner to repair it and nor does it entitle the dominant owner to a flow of water.[48] But the owner of the dominant tenement is entitled as of right to repair the bridge, pipes or pump himself.[49] The servient owner is also prohibited from doing anything which might prevent the dominant owner from carrying out repairs.[50]

The principal exception to the "no expenditure" principle is the obligation to fence land in order to keep out cattle.[51] This has been described as "in the nature of a spurious easement",[52] or, more kindly, as "in the nature of an easement"[53]; and it may also arise by custom.[54]

The right must be within the general nature of rights capable of existing as easements: Although most easements fall under one of the well-known heads of easements, such as

---

[43] *Moncrieff v Jamieson* [2007] 1 W.L.R. 2620 (HL) in which the utility of the ouster principle was criticised. It has also been criticised by the Law Commission.

[44] *Williams v Usherwood* (1983) 45 P. & C.R. 235 at 251; and see *Pavledes v Ryesbridge Properties Ltd* (1989) 58 P. & C.R. 459 (car park for factory).

[45] *London & Blenheim Estates Ltd v Ladbroke Retail Parks Ltd* [1992] 1 W.L.R. 1298 (affirmed [1994] 1 W.L.R. 31); *Hair v Gillman and Inskip* (2000) 80 P. & C.R. 108. The logic of a rule which holds that there can be an easement to park, but not in the very common situation of a right to park in a single defined space, was questioned in *Moncrieff v Jamieson* (above) but for the moment that remains the position.

[46] Held to be a valid easement in *Wright v Macadam* [1949] 2 K.B. 744; contrast *Copeland v Greenhalf* [1952] Ch. 488.

[47] Right to graze 10 horses for 12 hours a day during 8 months of the year on under an acre of land: held to be a valid easement in *Polo Woods Foundation v Shelton-Agar* [2010] 1 P. & C.R. 12.

[48] *Rance v Elvin* (1985) 50 P. & C.R. 9 (right to passage of water through pipe but not to a supply of water).

[49] *Jones v Pritchard* [1908] 1 Ch. 630.

[50] In *Goodhart v Hyett* (1883) 25 Ch. D 182 an injunction was granted to the dominant owner to stop the owner of the servient tenement from building on top of pipes in respect of which there was an easement.

[51] *Crow v Wood* [1971] 1 Q.B. 77; *Egerton v Harding* [1975] Q.B. 62.

[52] *Lawrence v Jenkins* (1873) L.R. 8 Q.B. 274 at 279 per Archibald J.

[53] *Crow v Wood* [1971] 1 Q.B. 77 at 85 per Lord Denning M.R.

[54] *Egerton v Harding* [1975] Q.B. 62.

rights of way, light, support and so on, the list of easements is not closed. "The category of servitudes[55] and easements must alter and expand with the changes that take place in the circumstances of mankind."[56] But there are limits. "It must not therefore be supposed that incidents of a novel kind can be devised and attached to property, at the fancy or caprice of any owner."[57] Today, new rights are unlikely to be recognised as easements if they prevent the servient owner from doing things on his land, in the way that rights of light do, as distinct from requiring him merely to suffer something to be done on his land.[58] Nor are rights likely to be accepted as easements if they involve the servient owner in the expenditure of money, for no recognised easement (with the anomalous exception of fencing easements) does this.[59] But new rights which do not involve the servient owner in expenditure have from time to time been recognised as easements, for example in 1896 the right to go upon the land of another to open sluice gates,[60] in 1915 a right to store casks and trade produce on land,[61] in 1955 the right to use a neighbour's lavatory,[62] in 1956 the right to enjoy a park[63] in 1973 the right to use an airfield[64] and in 1982 the right to park in the curtilage of a block of flats[65] were all recognised as being capable of existing as easements.

There must be a capable grantor: There can be no claim to an easement if at the relevant times the servient tenement was owned by someone incapable of granting an easement, for example a statutory corporation with no power to grant easements[66] or a tenant who lacks the power to bind the reversion.[67] An express grant naturally requires for its validity that all necessary grantors join in, as with land in joint ownership where all the joint owners must be party to the Deed.

There must be a capable grantee: An easement can be claimed only by a legal person capable of receiving a grant. Thus a claim by a company with no power to acquire easements must fail[68]; similarly, a fluctuating body of persons, such as "the inhabitants for the time being of the village of X", cannot claim an easement, for no grant could be made to them. But such bodies may claim similar rights by showing that there is a custom to that

---

55 "servitude" is the equivalent of an easement in Scots Law; servitudes are discussed in a number of the House of Lords cases (*Moncrieff v Jamieson* [2007] 1 W.L.R. 2620 being a recent example, but are not part of the law of England and Wales.
56 *Dyce v Hay* (1852) 1 Macq. 205 at 312 per Lord St. Leonards L.C.
57 *Keppell v Bailey* (1833) 2 My. & K. 517 at 535 per Lord Brougham L.C.
58 See *Phipps v Pears* [1965] 1 Q.B. 76 (protection of wall from weather by adjoining house: no easement); contrast *Sedgwick Forbes Bland Payne Group Ltd v Regional Properties Ltd* (1979) 257 E.G. 64 at 70 (building divided horizontally) and *Hunter v Canary Wharf Ltd* [1997] A.C. 655 (right to receive television signal and so prevent building envisaged as easement).
59 See *Pomfret v Ricroft* (1669) 1 Wms.Saund. 321; *Rance v Elvin* (1985) 50 P. & C.R. 9 (right to passage of water through pipe but not to a supply of water).
60 *Simpson v Mayor of Godmanchester* [1896] 1 Ch. 214; [1897] A.C. 696.
61 *Att.-Gen. of Southern Nigeria v Holt* [1915] A.C. 599. The headnote calls the right an irrevocable licence, but it was clearly recognised as an easement: see at 617.
62 *Miller v Emcer Products Ltd* [1956] Ch. 304.
63 *Re Ellenborough Park* [1956] Ch. 131.
64 *Dowty Boulton Paul Ltd v Wolverhampton Corp (No.2)* [1976] Ch. 13.
65 *Newman v Jones* (March 22, 1982, an unreported decision of Sir Robert Megarry V.C.).
66 See *Re Salvin's Indenture* [1938] 2 All E.R. 498.
67 *Derry v Saunders* [1919] 1 K.B. 223.
68 *National Guaranteed Manure Co v Donald* (1859) 4 H. & N. 8.

effect, such as a customary right of way across land to reach the parish church,[69] or a customary right to play games[70] or to dry nets on certain land.[71] There may also be a customary duty, such as a duty binding the frontagers to a common to fence against cattle grazing the common.[72]

Distinction between easements and certain analogous rights

15–007   The nature of easements may be further illuminated by contrasting them with certain other rights.

Natural rights

15–008   Like easements, "natural rights" are not easy to define. A "natural right" is a right attaching to land in its natural state, which is recognised by the common law, and which arises automatically without the need for an express or implied grant. Breach of such natural rights may give rise to liability in nuisance at the suit of the owner of the land for the time being.

The natural right most commonly encountered is the right of support. In addition to his rights over his own land, every landowner has a natural right to support, i.e. a right that the support for his land provided by his neighbour's land should not be removed,[73] whether directly or by causing the subsoil to liquefy.[74] A similar right exists in cases where the surface of the land and the soil underneath are owned by different persons; the owner of the surface has a natural right to have it supported by the subjacent soil[75] unless this right is excluded by clear words or necessary implication in some statute or agreement.

This natural right extends only to land in its natural state; there is no natural right to support for buildings or for the additional burden on land which they cause.[76] Similarly, there is no natural right to have buildings supported by neighbouring buildings.[77] If no more damage is done than is necessary, a man may pull down his house without having to provide support for his neighbour's house.[78] However, there are limits to a landowner's freedom of action. If support is withdrawn, and the land would have fallen even it had not been built upon, an action lies in respect of any damage to the buildings.[79] Also, the "measured duty of care" discussed below may be broken "if a neighbour does something which would foreseeably cause damage to a neighbouring owner or fails to take action to avoid such damage".[80]

---

[69]   *Brocklebank v Thompson* [1903] 2 Ch. 344.

[70]   *New Windsor Corp v Mellor* [1974] 1 W.L.R. 1504.

[71]   *Mercer v Denne* [1905] 2 Ch. 538.

[72]   *Egerton v Harding* [1975] Q.B. 62.

[73]   *Backhouse v Bonomi* (1861) 9 H.L.C. 503.

[74]   *Lotus Ltd v British Soda Co Ltd* [1972] Ch. 123 where the defendant had been extracting brine. It will be interesting to see whether "fracking" for shale gas gives rise to similar claims in future.

[75]   *London & North Western Ry v Evans* [1893] 1 Ch. 16 at 30.

[76]   *Wyatt v Harrison* (1823) 3 B. & Ad. 871.

[77]   *Peyton v Mayor of London* (1829) 9 B. & C. 725.

[78]   The right to have buildings supported by land or by other buildings can, however, be acquired as an easement

[79]   *Stroyan v Knowles* (1861) 6 H. & N. 454; *Lotus Ltd v British Soda Co Ltd* [1972] Ch. 123.

[80]   *Gale on Easements*, 19th edn (London: Sweet & Maxwell) at para.10–38 relying on *Holbeck Hall Hotel v Scarborough BC* [2000] Q.B. 836, a case concerning failure to maintain a sea wall leading to cliff erosion.

In a relatively recent development, the common law has recognised a "measured duty of care" on a landowner to take reasonable steps to abate a naturally occurring nuisance which he did not create himself.[81] The duty lies on the occupier to do ". . .what is reasonable to expect of him in his individual circumstances".[82] The inherent flexibility in this approach is to be contrasted with the law applicable to easements. It has been held that an occupier may be in breach of this duty and hence liable in nuisance for failing to take reasonable steps to prevent slippage of his land onto a neighbour's land below it.[83] Where an owner or occupier carries out reasonable works to abate a nuisance, the cost may be recoverable from the neighbour responsible.[84]

Rights of water may exist as natural rights or as easements, depending on the circumstances. There is a natural right to water flowing naturally in a defined channel[85] but not to water percolating naturally through the ground without a defined channel.[86] It follows that to dam or divert a stream or river is an actionable nuisance[87]; however, the right to a dam or diversion may be the subject matter of an easement.[88]

There is no "natural right" to light, presumably because if all land were in its natural state, light would not be blocked. An easement of light can, however, be acquired for windows in a building.

Public rights

An easement must always be appurtenant to land; it is a right exercisable by the owner for the time being by virtue of his estate in the land. On the other hand, a public right, is a right exercisable by anyone, whether he owns land or not, merely by virtue of the general law.[89]   **15–009**

The public rights which most closely resemble easements are public rights of way. The land over which a public right of way exists is known as a highway, and although most highways have been made up into roads, and most easements of way exist over footpaths, the presence or absence of a made road has nothing to do with the distinction.[90] There may be a highway over a footpath, while a well-made road may be subject only to an easement of way, or may exist only for the landowner's benefit and be subject to no easement at all. A highway need not lead to any other highway or public place.[91] Unlike a private right of way, creation of a highway maintainable at public expense effects a transfer in ownership. The

---

[81] *Goldman v Hargrave* [1967] 1 A.C. 645 (PC) concerning a botched attempt to extinguish a fire started by lightning strike.

[82] *Goldman v Hargrave* (above).

[83] *Leakey v National Trust* [1980] Q.B. 485.

[84] *Delaware Mansions v Westminster CC* [2002] 1 A.C. 321 (HL) (tree roots causing subsidence).

[85] *Palmer v Bowman* [2000] 1 All E.R. 22. It may not be easy to identify what is natural and what derives from human intervention; see *Green v Lord Somerleyton* [2004] 1 P. & C.R. 33.

[86] *Acton v Blundell* (1843) 12 M.&W. 324; *Bradford Corp v Pickles* [1895] A.C. 587.

[87] *Swindon Waterworks Co v Wilts and Berks Canal Navigation Co* (1875) L.R. 7 HL 697.

[88] Rights to do something which would otherwise be a nuisance are a recognised category of easement.

[89] This definition of "public right" was approved in *Overseas Investment Services Ltd v Simcobuild Construction* (1995) 70 P. & C.R. 322 at p.328.

[90] For a discussion of the different kinds of highway recognised by the common law see *Suffolk CC v Mason* [1979] A.C. 705.

[91] Whereas a "road to nowhere" is unlikely to be recognised as an easement, see *Beech v Kennerley* [2012] EWCA Civ 158.

surface of the highway together with as much sub-soil and airspace above as is required, vests in the highway authority.[92]

Public rights also differ from easements in their mode of creation. The mode of creation of public highways is discussed after the section on creation of easements.[93]

Restrictive covenants

15–010 Easements and restrictive covenants[94] are similar in that an easement, like a restrictive covenant, may entitle a landowner to restrict the use that his neighbour makes of his land; thus the owner of an easement of light may prevent the servient owner from obstructing his light by erecting a building on the adjoining land. There are other resemblances, such as the need for dominant and servient tenements, and in general the law of restrictive covenants may be regarded as being an equitable extension of the law of easements. Nevertheless, restrictive covenants are best regarded as a very different kind of interest from easements or profits, as demonstrated by the following characteristics

Scope

15–011 Restrictive covenants are wider in scope and more flexible than easements. As has been seen, there can be no easement entitling the dominant owner to a view or the general flow of air.[95] But by means of suitable restrictive covenants preventing his neighbour from building, a landowner can enjoy both the view and a general flow of air.

Visibility

15–012 An inspection of the land will suggest the existence of many easements, but it is otherwise with restrictive covenants. Thus footpaths suggest an easement of way and pipes, an easement of drainage, but no inspection of the land will reveal the existence of a covenant against trading upon it.

Existence at law

15–013 An easement may exist at law[96] or in equity, whereas the burden of a restrictive covenant runs *only* in equity.

Prescription

15–014 An easement may be acquired by prescription; not so a restrictive covenant.

---

[92] Highways Act 1980 s.263. The highway authority's interest is a fee simple determinable if the land ceases to be used as a highway, see *Wiltshire CC v Frazer* (1983) 47 P. & C.R. 69.

[93] Below para.15–063.

[94] For restrictive covenants, see below, Ch.16.

[95] Above, para.15–006.

[96] Most easements are legal interests.

Positive nature

A restrictive covenant is entirely negative; it neither entitles the dominant owner nor binds the servient owner to do any positive act. Easements similarly do not bind the servient owner to do any positive act,[97] but as regards the dominant owner certain easements (called "positive easements") entitle the owner to do positive acts, for example easements of way, while others (called "negative easements") do not; for example, easements of light. Certain easements thus contain a positive element which is lacking in restrictive covenants.[98]

15–015

Licences

Licences resemble easements in that they authorise the use of the land of another in some way. But licences, which cannot exist as legal estates or interests or, probably, as equitable interests, are far more flexible and less restricted than easements. Thus they may be created without formality; they require no dominant tenement; and they may authorise the occupation of land.[99] On the other hand, they are, as a general rule, personal rights and not binding on successors in title of the licensor. Whether or not a grant is an easement or a licence is firstly dependent on the purported grant satisfying the requirements of an easement and secondly is a matter of construction of the deed creating the right.[100]

15–016

Rights arising under the rule against derogation from grant

A grantor may not "derogate from his grant": in other words, where he sells or leases land, knowing that the grantee intends to use it for a particular purpose, neither he nor his successors in title may do anything to impede such purposed use, and the grantee obtains corresponding rights.[101] The rule "merely embodies in a legal maxim a rule of common honesty"[102] that one cannot give with one hand and take away with the other.[103] Thus, where a lease was granted to a timber merchant who needed a free general flow of air to dry his timber, a purchaser of the lessor's adjoining land could not build upon it so as to obstruct the ventilation required by the lessee.[104] Although the doctrine is most often encountered in landlord and tenant cases, it applies to all forms of grant including sales of land, and even sales of personal property.[105] The rule may be considered to confer a species of property right because it is enforceable by successors in title of the grantee against successors in title of the grantor.[106]

15–017

---

[97] But see the obligation to fence: above, para.15–006.

[98] There can of course be positive covenants, but as a general proposition positive covenants only bind successors in title when they are leasehold covenants.

[99] For licences, see Ch.10.

[100] *IDC Group v Clark* [1992] 2 E.G.L.R. 184.

[101] For discussions of the principle see (1964) 80 L.Q.R. 244 (D.W. Elliott) and the judgment in *Johnston & Sons v Holland* [1988] 1 E.G.L.R. 264.

[102] *Harmer v Jumbil (Nigeria) Tin Areas Ltd* [1921] 1 Ch. 200.

[103] *Carter v Cole* [2009] 2 E.G.L.R. 15.

[104] *Aldin v Latimer Clark, Muirhead & Co* [1894] 2 Ch. 437. There could be no easement on these facts because the air did not flow through an identifiable channel or opening.

[105] See *Johnston & Sons v Holland* [1988] 1 E.G.L.R 264.

[106] Again see *Johnston & Sons v Holland* (above).

Customary rights of fluctuating bodies

15–018   It was mentioned earlier that rights in favour of such bodies cannot exist as easements.[107] Customary rights are recognised if they are ancient,[108] certain,[109] reasonable and continuous. Customary rights differ from easements in that they are exercisable by all who are included within the custom,[110] independently of ownership of a dominant tenement or of any grant. Thus the custom may extend to all the inhabitants of a particular locality, whether or not they own land.[111] Examples include the right to hold a fair or wake[112] or for fishermen to dry nets.[113]

Quasi-easements

15–019   As already explained,[114] rights exercised by a landowner over his own land which, if he did not own that land, could exist as easements, are sometimes called quasi-easements.

NATURE OF A PROFIT Á PRENDRE

15–020   A profit á prendre has been described as "a right to take something off another person's land. It may be more fully defined as a right to enter another's land to take some profit of the soil, or a portion of the soil itself, for the use of the owner of the right".[115] The thing taken must be something taken out of the soil,[116] i.e. it must be either the soil, the natural produce thereof, or the wild animals existing on it; and the thing taken must at the time of taking be susceptible of ownership.[117] A right to "hawk, hunt, fish and fowl" may thus exist as a profit,[118] for this gives the right to take creatures living on the soil which, when killed, are capable of being owned. But a right to take water from a spring or a pump, or the right to water cattle at a pond, may be an easement though it cannot be a profit; for the water, when taken, was not owned by anyone nor was it part of the soil.[119] A right to take water stored in an artificial receptacle, such as a tank, is not an easement but may perhaps exist either as a profit or a mere licence, probably the latter.[120] In the same way that there can be

---

[107] Above, para.15–006.
[108] Meaning dating back to 1189, but this may be presumed if there has been long use and there is no evidence of later origin.
[109] Although the nature of the custom can change with the times, e.g. a custom which allows for the playing of games may include cricket, even though cricket had not been invented in 1189: *R v Oxfordshire CC Ex p. Sunningwell PC* [2000] 1 A.C. 335.
[110] But only by those within the custom, such as inhabitants of a parish or town, and not by the general public.
[111] *Race v Ward* (1855) 4 E. & B. 702.
[112] *Wyld v Silver* [1963] Ch. 243.
[113] *Mercer v Denne* [1905] 2 Ch. 538.
[114] Above, para.15–005.
[115] *Polo Woods Foundation v Shelton-Agar* [2010] 1 P. & C.R. 12 at [19]–[20]; *Duke of Sutherland v Heathcote* [1892] 1 Ch. 475 at 484 per Lindley L.J.
[116] *Manning v Wasdale* (1836) 5 A. & E. 758 at 764.
[117] *Race v Ward* (1855) 4 E. & B. 702 at 709; *Lowe v J. W. Ashmore Ltd* [1971] Ch. 545 at 557.
[118] *Wickham v Hawker* (1840) 7 M. & W. 63.
[119] See *Mason v Hill* (1833) 5 B. & Ad. 1 at 24; *Manning v Wasdale* (1836) 5 A. & E. 758 at 764.
[120] See (1938) 2 Conv. (N.S.) 203. (J.S. Fiennes).

"quasi-easements", there can be "quasi-profits" where rights in the nature of a profit are exercised by a person over his own land.

Classification of profits á prendre

Profits á prendre may be classified in two ways: as to ownership, and in respect of its relationship to land (because, unlike an easement a profit need not be appurtenant to land).   **15–021**

Classification of profits á prendre as to ownership

A profit á prendre may be enjoyed: **15–022**

(i) by one person to the exclusion of all others; this is known as a several profit; or
(ii) by one person in common with others; this is known as a profit in common, or a common.

Classification of profits á prendre in relation to land

A profit is not necessarily appurtenant to land, as is the case with easements. It may exist in the following three principal forms[121]:   **15–023**

(i) Profit appurtenant;
(ii) Profit appendant;
(iii) Profit in gross.

In addition, there are profits pur cause de vicinage.

A profit appurtenant

This is a profit, whether several or in common, attached to land by act of parties. A profit appurtenant may be acquired either by grant or by prescription. In general, there must be compliance with the four conditions necessary for the existence of an easement, which can exist only as appurtenant to land.[122] Thus a profit of piscary appurtenant cannot be exploited for commercial purposes; the number of fish taken must be limited to the needs of the dominant tenement.[123]   **15–024**

A profit appendant

This is a profit annexed to land by operation of law; probably it exists only in the form of a common of pasture.[124] If before the Statute Quia Emptores 1290 the lord of a manor sub-infeudated arable land to a freeholder, the freeholder obtained, as appendant to the arable lands, the right to pasture, on the waste land of the manor, animals to plough and   **15–025**

---

[121] *Polo Woods Foundation v Shelton-Agar* [2010] 1 P. & C.R. 12 at [20].
[122] Above, para.15–002.
[123] *Harris v Earl of Chesterfield* [1911] A.C. 623.
[124] See 6 *Halsbury* (4th edn), pp.199, 220; but see Tudor L.C.R.P., pp.713–716.

manure the land granted to him.[125] This right was known as a common of pasture appendant and was limited both as to the kind and number of animals which could be depastured. It extended only to horses and oxen (to plough the land) and cows and sheep (to manure it),[126] and only to the number of these "levant and couchant" on the land to which the right was appendant, i.e. the number which the dominant tenement was capable of maintaining during the winter.[127] It was immaterial that the land was at any particular time used for purposes temporarily rendering the maintenance of cattle impossible, for the test was not the number actually supported but the number which the land could be made to support.

No common appendant could be created after 1290,[128] for a conveyance of freehold land in a manor after that date resulted in the grantee holding of the grantor's lord, and the land passed out of the manor altogether.

A profit in gross

15–026   This is a profit, whether several or in common, exercisable by the owner independently of his ownership of land; there is no dominant tenement. Thus a right to take fish from a canal without stint (i.e. without limit) can exist as a profit in gross,[129] but not, as already seen, as a profit appurtenant. A profit in gross is an interest in land which will pass under the owner's will or intestacy or can be sold or dealt with in any of the usual ways.

A profit pur cause de vicinage

15–027   This exists only in the form of a common of pasture. If two adjoining commons are open to each other, there is a common *pur cause de vicinage* if the cattle put on one common by the commoners have always been allowed to stray to the other common, and vice versa.[130] The claim fails if in the past the cattle have been driven off one common by the commoners thereof,[131] or if the commons have been fenced off,[132] or if the two commons are not contiguous to each other, even if they are separated only by a third common.[133]

Distinctions between profits á prendre and certain analogous rights

Quasi-profits

15–028   The principles that apply to quasi-profits are similar to those that govern quasi-easements.[134]

---

[125] *Earl of Dunraven v Llewellyn* (1850) 15 Q.B. 791 at 810.
[126] *Tyrringham's Case* (1584) 4 Co.Rep. 36b at 37a.
[127] *Robertson v Hartopp* (1889) 43 Ch.D. 484 at 516.
[128] See above, para.1–055.
[129] *Staffordshire & Worcestershire Canal Navigation v Bradley* [1912] 1 Ch. 91.
[130] *Pritchard v Powell* (1845) 10 Q.B. 589 at 603.
[131] *Heath v Elliott* (1838) 4 Bing.N.C. 388.
[132] *Tyrringham's Case* (1584) 4 Co.Rep. 36b.
[133] *Commissioners of Sewers v Glasse* (1874) L.R. 19 Eq. 134.
[134] Above, para.15–005.

Other natural rights

The same applies. An example is the right of a riparian owner to the unimpeded passage of fish from neighbouring portions of the stream.[135]

15–029

Public rights

The public right which most closely resembles a profit is the right of the public to fish in the sea and all tidal waters.[136] However, since in theory the right is the Crown's, it was formerly possible for the Crown to grant to an individual the exclusive right to fish in a specified part of the sea or tidal waters; such a franchise was known as a free fishery.[137] In short, the public may fish in all tidal waters except a free fishery. But it has been held that the effect of Magna Carta 1215 was to prevent the Crown from creating any new free fisheries,[138] although any already existing remain valid and transferable to this day.

15–030

The right to fish in non-tidal water is dealt with below.[139]

Rights of fluctuating bodies

There can be no custom for a fluctuating body of persons to take a profit.[140] The reason is said to be that otherwise the subject-matter would be destroyed.[141] However, if in fact such a right has been enjoyed for a long time as of right the courts will endeavour to find a legal origin for it. Two methods have been evolved.

15–031

Presumed incorporation by Crown grant: The reason why a fluctuating body cannot own a profit is that the body is not a legal person to which a grant could be made.[142] However, the Crown is able to incorporate any body of persons (i.e. make them into a corporation), and so could, for example, grant a charter to a village making it a city or borough. Consequently there is nothing to prevent the Crown from making a grant of a profit to the inhabitants of a district and providing therein that for the purposes of the grant they should be treated as a corporation, though for other purposes they remain unincorporated. In fact, such grants have been made but rarely.[143] Their chief importance is that the court will presume that a grant of rights of this kind owned by the Crown at the time of the supposed grant has been made, provided:

    (i) long enjoyment is proved; and

   (ii) those claiming the grant, and their predecessors, have always regarded themselves

---

[135] See *Barker v Faulkner* (1898) 79 L.T. 24.

[136] *Anderson v Alnwick DC* [1993] 1 W.L.R. 1156 which records that bait-digging on the foreshore is included in the right

[137] 3 Cru.Dig. 261; see, e.g. *Stephens v Snell* [1939] 3 All E.R. 622.

[138] *Malcolmson v O'Dea* (1863) 10 H.L.C. 593 at 618; but see Theobald, *Land*, pp.58 et seq.

[139] Below, para.15–093.

[140] *Alfred F. Beckett Ltd v Lyons* [1967] Ch. 449.

[141] *Race v Ward* (1855) 4 E. & B. 702 at 705, 709.

[142] *Fowler v Dale* (1594) Cro.Eliz. 362.

[143] See, e.g. *Willingale v Maitland* (1866) L.R. 3 Eq. 103.

as a corporation and have acted as such as regards the right, as by holding meetings or appointing some officer to supervise the right.[144]

Presumed charitable trust: Even when the court cannot presume incorporation by Crown grant because the claimants have not acted as a corporation, if long enjoyment is shown the court may be able to find a legal origin for the right by presuming a grant of the profit to some corporation, subject to a trust or condition that the corporation should allow the claimants to exercise the rights claimed. Thus in *Goodman v Mayor of Saltash*[145] the free inhabitants of certain ancient tenements had for 200 years enjoyed an oyster fishery from Candlemas (February 2) to Easter Eve each year. This right had been shared by the local corporation, which had enjoyed the right all the year round from time immemorial. The House of Lords refused to presume a grant incorporating the inhabitants for the purpose of the grant, but held that the corporation was entitled to a profit subject to a trust or condition in favour of the free inhabitants. Such a trust is charitable and so is not subject to the rule against inalienability.[146]

CREATION OF EASEMENTS AND PROFITS

Easements and profits may exist as legal interests or equitable interests

15–032   An easement or profit may take effect at law, or merely in equity. Equitable easements and profits may not bind successors in title, particularly in respect of registered land since the Land Registration 2002 came into force.

Easements and profits as legal interests

15–033   An easement or profit can exist as a legal interest in land only if:

(i)   it is held for an interest equivalent to a fee simple absolute in possession or term of years absolute[147]; and

(ii) it is created either by statute, deed or prescription; and

(iii) in the case of an express grant or reservation in respect of registered land, that it is completed by registration.[148]

An express grant of a legal easement or profit must be by deed.[149]

Easements and profits taking effect in equity

15–034   If the conditions for the existence at law of an easement of profit are not satisfied, then it will take effect in equity only. So a document which is not a deed which creates an ease-

---

[144] See *Re Free Fishermen of Faversham* (1887) 36 Ch.D. 329; *Lord Rivers v Adams* (1878) 3 Ex.D. 361.
[145] (1882) 7 App. Cas. 633.
[146] (1882) 7 App. Cas. 633.
[147] Law of Property Act 1925 s.1(2); above, para.1–010.
[148] Land Registration Act 2002 s.27.
[149] *Duke of Somerset v Fogwell* (1826) 5 B. & A. 875.

ment may create a valid equitable easement or profit if made for value. But because an easement or profit is an interest in land, the document must (unless the court is prepared to find a constructive trust) comply with the signed writing requirements for a contract for the sale of land.[150] Similarly, an easement over registered land created by deed remains an equitable easement if it is not registered.

The methods of creation of an easement or profit á prendre

The various methods of creation (or "acquisition" as some of the cases call the process) of easements and profits must now be considered. The methods are: **15–035**

    (1) By statute
    (2) By express grant or express reservation
    (3) By implied reservation or implied grant
    (4) By virtue of s.62 of the Law of Property Act 1925
    (5) By prescription or presumed grant

By statute

Easements created by statute are most frequently found in the case of local Acts of Parliament, such as an Act giving a right of support to a canal constructed under statutory powers.   **15–036**

By express grant or reservation

The meanings of "grant" and "reservation" are best illustrated by considering a landowner who sells part of his land and retains the rest. He may reserve for himself easements or profits over the land sold, and grant the purchaser rights over the land retained. However, as explained below, for historical reasons "reservations" actually operate as grants.   **15–037**

Express grant

The ordinary case of an easement or profit created by the express words of a deed needs little discussion. The word "grant", though usual, is no longer essential; but not even the "grant" of a mere "licence" will create an easement.[151] A grant need not be part of a conveyance on sale. The question is one of substance, not form, so easements may be created by deeds, however the deed describes itself. Easements may be created by provisions which purport to be covenants, for example. The dominant tenement, if not sufficiently identified, may be inferred from the circumstances.[152]   **15–038**

---

[150] Law of Property (Miscellaneous Provisions) Act 1989 s.2. Oral agreements for value could formerly do the same if they were supported by sufficient evidence in writing or part performance see, e.g. *Mason v Clarke* [1955] A.C. 778.
[151] LPA 1925 s.51(1); *I.D.C. Group Ltd v Clark* [1992] 1 E.G.L.R. 187.
[152] *The Shannon Ltd v Venner Ltd* [1965] Ch. 682.

Express reservation

15–039   Before 1926, a legal easement or profit could not be created by a simple reservation in favour of the grantor. Being a new right it could be only be created by grant, and a person could not grant to himself. If, however, the conveyance reserved the right to the grantor, and the grantee also executed the conveyance, it operated as a conveyance to the grantee followed by the re-grant of the easement or profit by the grantee to the grantor.[153] The effect of a simple reservation not executed by the grantee was merely to create an equitable easement or profit.[154]

Since 1926 it has not been necessary for the grantee to execute the conveyance, as statute has provided that the reservation of a legal estate or interest shall be effective at law without any execution of the conveyance by the grantee "or any regrant by him".[155] It seems, however, that despite these words, the change merely goes to formalities.[156] The so-called reservation is still deemed to operate as a grant by the purchaser, which may have significant consequences.[157] Where land held on trust was sold, and conveyed to the purchaser by the legal and equitable owners, a reservation by the equitable owners took effect as a grant of an legal easement by the purchaser and not as a reservation of a mere equitable easement by the vendor of the equitable interest.[158] Another consequence lies in the operation of the rule that where grants are ambiguous they are construed against the grantor, which in the case of a reservation of an easement on sale, means they are construed against the *purchaser*.[159]

By implied reservation or grant

Implied reservation

15–040   A grant is normally construed against the grantor and in favour of the grantee. Further, a grantor must not derogate from his grant. Consequently the general rule is that no easements will be implied in favour of a grantor[160]; if he wishes to reserve any easements he must do so expressly.[161] To this rule there are two narrow exceptions: easements of necessity and easements giving effect to intended use.

---

[153] *Durham & Sunderland Ry v Walker* (1842) 2 Q.B. 940 at 967.

[154] *May v Belleville* [1905] 2 Ch. 605.

[155] LPA 1925 s.65; see also *Wiles v Banks* (1985) 50 P. & C.R. 80 (conveying "subject to" a right may make it an easement.

[156] *St. Edmundsbury and Ipswich Diocesan Board of Finance v Clark (No.2)* [1975] 1 W.L.R. 468 at 478–480, commenting on *St. Edmundsbury and Ipswich Diocesan Board of Finance v Clark (No.2)* [1973] 1 W.L.R. 1572 at 1587–1591, where the view that the change is one of substance was maintained.

[157] The Law Commission recently considered the law in respect of reservations to be illogical but did not recommend any change: Law Com No.327 (2011) at para.2.53

[158] *Johnstone v Holdway* [1963] 1 Q.B. 601.

[159] *Bulstrode v Lambert* [1953] 1 W.L.R. 1064 at 1068; *St. Edmundsbury and Ipswich Diocesan Board of Finance v Clark (No.2)* [1975] 1 W.L.R. 468 at 477–480; but see *Cordell v Second Clanfield Properties Ltd* [1969] 2 Ch. 9.

[160] Because it would derogate from the grant, see e.g. *Holaw (470) Ltd v Stockton Estates* (2001) 81 P. & C.R. 29 at [82].

[161] *Wheeldon v Burrows* (1879) 12 Ch.D. 31 at 49.

Easements of necessity: If a grantor conveys the whole of a plot of land except a piece in the middle which, being completely surrounded by the part conveyed, is inaccessible, a way of necessity over the part conveyed will be implied in favour of the part retained.[162] This is so even if some of the surrounding land belongs to third parties, though it is essential that the necessity should exist at the time of the conveyance and not merely arise later.[163] The question is not whether the way is necessary for the reasonable enjoyment of the land retained, but whether the land cannot be used at all without the way.[164] Thus no such way will be inferred if there is some other means of access (such as by water[165]), even if it is difficult and inconvenient.[166] The right is based on the inference that unless otherwise provided the parties did not intend to make the land inaccessible.[167] The former owner of both plots may select the particular way to be enjoyed, provided it is convenient[168]; but, once selected, it cannot be changed except by agreement.[169] It seems that if an easement of necessity is acquired, it does not cease even if the necessity later ceases (for example if the landlocked owner buys another adjoining piece of land).[170]

Easements giving effect to intended use: Easements required to carry out the common intention of the parties as to the use of the retained land will be implied in favour of the grantor even though not expressed in the conveyance.[171] Thus in the common case of the grant (sale) of one of two houses supported by each other, the mutual grant and reservation of easements of support will be implied if (as is usual) such an intention can be inferred.[172] But in more fact-specific cases, a grantor who wishes to show that a reservation was mutually intended has a heavy onus of proof to discharge in establishing both the intention that the retained land be used in a specific manner and that the claimed easement is necessary to that use. Thus a landlord will not impliedly reserve any right to advertise on his tenant's outside walls[173] nor will a vendor impliedly reserve the right to construct and to use an intended extension to an existing road marked as such on the conveyance in question.[174]

Implied grant

By comparison with implied reservation, the grant of easements by implication is more easily established because the grant should be construed in favour of the grantee. If the owner of two plots conveys one of them, certain easements over the land retained are implied in favour of the land conveyed. The express grant of the land is said to be accompanied by the implied grant of the easements. Rights which will arise by implied grant are as follows:

15–041

---

[162] *Pinnington v Galland* (1853) 9 Exch. 1.
[163] *Midland Ry. v Miles* (1886) 33 Ch.D. 632.
[164] *Union Lighterage Co v London Graving Dock Co* [1902] 2 Ch. 557 at 573.
[165] *Manjang v Drammeh* (1991) 61 P. & C.R. 194.
[166] *M.R.A. Engineering Ltd v Trimster Co Ltd* (1988) 56 P. & C.R. 1 (public footpath but no road).
[167] *Nickerson v Barraclough* [1981] Ch. 426, rejecting public policy.
[168] See *Pearson v Spencer* (1861) 1 B. & S. 571 at 585; affirmed (1863) 3 B. & S. 761.
[169] *Deacon v South Eastern Ry* (1889) 61 L.T. 377.
[170] See most recently *Huckvale v Aegean Hotels* (1989) 58 P. & C.R. 163.
[171] *Pwllbach Colliery Co Ltd v Woodman* [1915] A.C. 634.
[172] *Richards v Rose* (1853) 9 Exch. 221.
[173] *Re Webb's Lease* [1951] Ch. 808.
[174] *Chaffe v Kingsley* [2002] 1 E.G.L.R. 104.

    (i)   easements of necessity;

   (ii)   easements giving effect to intended use;

  (iii)   ancillary easements;

  (iv)   easements within *"The Rule in Wheeldon v Burrows"*.

Easements of necessity and intended easements: The rules which apply in these two cases are similar to those in the case of implied reservation. However, in practice a court will be much more ready to imply easements in favour of the grantee than it is to imply a reservation to the grantor.[175] In *Moncrieff v Jamieson*[176] it was said that this rule and the Rule in *Wheeldon v Burrows* are no more than examples of the application of the contractual principles for the implication of terms.

Thus where a landlord let his basement for use as a restaurant, and from the outset such a use was not lawful unless a proper ventilation system was installed, the tenant was held to be entitled to install and use a ventilation duct attached to the outside of the landlord's premises as an easement of necessity.[177] The letting of a flat in a block of flats impliedly carries with it the right to use the stairs corridors and lifts to reach the door of the flat.[178]

Ancillary easements: These are easements necessary for the enjoyment of some right expressly granted. Thus if there is a grant of an easement of the right to draw water from a spring, a right of way to the spring will be implied.[179]

Easements within the rule in Wheeldon v Burrows: In *Wheeldon v Burrows*[180] it was laid down that upon the grant of part of a tenement, there would pass to the grantee as easements all quasi-easements over the land retained which:

    (i)   were "continuous and apparent",

   (ii)   were necessary to the reasonable enjoyment of the land granted; and

  (iii)   had been, and were at the time of the grant, used by the grantor for the benefit of the part granted.

In short, this rule is about creating legal easements in favour of a purchaser of part of a vendor's land which are necessary for reasonable use of the purchased part and which reflect the previous common use by the vendor. It is a branch of the principle against derogation from grant.[181] Because of that, the rule can apply to create a more extensive easement even where the conveyance expressly creates a limited easement, but it cannot apply where the claimed easement would be inconsistent with an expressly granted easement.[182]

A "continuous" easement is one giving the right to do some act of a continuous and constant nature and which does not require personal activity for its enjoyment. An "apparent" easement is one which is evidenced by some sign on the servient tenement discoverable on

---

[175] See *Adealon International v London Borough of Merton* [2007] EWCA Civ 362 [2007] 1 W.L.R. 1898 at [14] – [16].

[176] [2007] UKHL 42; [2007] 1 W.L.R. 2620 at 2657.

[177] *Wong v Beaumont Property Trust Ltd* [1965] 1 Q.B. 173.

[178] *Liverpool City Council v Irwin* [1977] A.C. 239 (HL).

[179] *Pwlbach Colliery Co Ltd v Woodman* [1915] A.C. 634 at 646.

[180] (1879) 12 Ch.D. 31.

[181] *Sovmots Investments v Secretary of State for the Environment* [1979] A.C. 144 at 168H.

[182] *Millman v Ellis* (1995) 71 P. & C.R. 158.

a careful inspection by a person ordinarily conversant with the subject.[183] Thus a drain into which water from the eaves of a house runs,[184] a watercourse through visible pipes,[185] and windows enjoying light,[186] all indicate the existence of continuous and apparent easements. On the other hand, a right to take water from a neighbour's pump from time to time[187] or a right to project the bowsprit of ships when in dock over the land of another[188] have been held to be outside the meaning of "continuous and apparent"[189] easements. Rights of way do not in general fall within the definition, but a way over a made road, or one which betrays its presence by some indication such as a worn track, will pass under the rule in *Wheeldon v Burrows* despite the fact that a way strictly speaking is not "continuous".[190]

An easement is "necessary to the reasonable enjoyment of the land" if the land cannot be reasonably enjoyed without it; the test is much less stringent than for an easement of necessity which arises only where property cannot be enjoyed at all without the easement.[191] It is still not clear whether this requirement and the requirement of "continuous and apparent" user are alternatives or, probably, cumulative,[192] with the first requirement being based on conveyancing convenience and the second on the rule against derogation from grant.[193]

Use "by the grantor" probably means by the grantor himself and not, for example, by a tenant of the land.[194]

These rules apply to contracts to make a grant[195] as well as to grants. They also apply where the grantor, instead of retaining any land himself, makes simultaneous grants to two or more grantees. Each grantee obtains the same easements over the land of the other as he would have obtained if the grantor had retained it[196]; and similarly for two or more gifts that are made by the same will.[197]

By operation of section 62 of the Law of Property Act 1925

An easement or profit á prendre may be created by express grant even though it is not mentioned in any deed. The Law of Property Act 1925 s.62(1)[198] provides that any conveyance   **15–042**

---

[183] *Pyer v Carter* (1857) 1 H. & N. 916 at 922.

[184] *Pyer v Carter* (1857) 1 H. & N. 916.

[185] *Watts v Kelson* (1870) 6 Ch.App. 166.

[186] *Phillips v Low* [1892] 1 Ch. 47 at 53.

[187] *Polden v Bastard* (1865) L.R. 1 Q.B. 156.

[188] *Suffield v Brown* (1864) 4 De G.J. & S. 185.

[189] On the origin of the phrase, see (1967) 83 L.Q.R. 240 (A.W.B. Simpson).

[190] See *Hansford v Jago* [1921] 1 Ch. 322; *Robinson Webster (Holdings) v Agombar* [2002] 1 P. & C.R. 20 at [76].

[191] Above, para.15–040 and see *Wheeler v JJ Saunders Ltd* [1996] Ch. 19.

[192] The more recent cases treat them as separate, cumulative requirements; see for example their separate treatment in *Robinson Webster (Holdings) v Agombar* [2002] 1 P. & C.R. 20 at [81]–[82]

[193] See *Sovmots Investments Ltd v Secretary of State for the Environment* [1979] A.C. 144 at 168, 169, 175; (1977) 41 Conv. 415 at 422 (C. Harpum).

[194] Per *Kent v Cavanagh* [2006] EWCA Civ 162; [2007] Ch.1, at [45]. LPA 1925 s.62 may well apply in this situation.

[195] *Borman v Griffith* [1930] 1 Ch. 493.

[196] *Swansborough v Coventry* (1832) 2 M. & S. 362.

[197] *Schwann v Cotton* [1916] 2 Ch. 459.

[198] Replacing CA 1881 s.6(1): see also LPA 1925 s.62(2). It applies to both registered and unregistered land.

made after 1881 shall, subject to any contrary intention expressed in the conveyance,[199] operate to convey with the land a wide range of things and rights,[200] including all privileges, easements, rights and advantages appertaining or reputed to appertain to the land or any part of it.[201] Thus, if a landlord grants his tenant a mere licence to use a coal shed for domestic purposes,[202] or to go through the landlord's house to reach the premises demised,[203] or to park intermittently anywhere in a defined area,[204] a subsequent conveyance to the tenant will operate to grant him the right as an easement unless the landlord revokes the licence prior to the conveyance. A right to require a neighbour to maintain fences may similarly arise.[205]

Nature of rights: The section will not elevate into easements or profits rights which the grantor has no power to create by express grant,[206] or rights which cannot exist as legal easements or profits.[207] Thus it will not apply to a "right" to have a house protected from the weather by a contiguous house,[208] or to have central heating and hot water,[209] nor to a "right" of way over a courtyard during business hours when not inconvenient to the landlord,[210] or to use the landlord's passageway only while he is in occupation.[211] Nor will it apply where it is apparent that the "right" is merely temporary. Thus the first purchaser of a house in a housing development will not have the access of light to his windows transformed into an easement of light that would prevent adjoining plots of land from being built upon.[212]

Diversity of occupation or continuous and apparent: The general rule is that s.62 will apply only where at the time of the grant the two tenements are in different occupation. What a landowner does on his own land he does as owner and not by virtue of any "right" in respect of one part of it over another.[213] But where one part is occupied by a tenant and he has been enjoying "rights" over the other part while it was occupied by the landlord, s.62 can apply to make those "rights" into easements if the landlord then grants the tenant a formal lease.[214] By way of exception to the general rule requiring diversity of occupation,

---

[199] LPA 1925 s.62(4).
[200] Note that the section is not concerned with the transmission on sale of pre-existing easements appurtenant to the land: these pass to the purchaser automatically and in the case of registered land vest in the registered proprietor pursuant to ss.11 and 12 of the LRA 2002.
[201] See *Graham v Philcox* [1984] Q.B. 747 (enlarged dominant tenement—a right of way to a flat became a right of way for the building containing the flat).
[202] *Wright v Macadam* [1949] 2 K.B. 744.
[203] *Goldberg v Edwards* [1950] Ch. 247.
[204] *Hair v Gillman and Inskip* (2000) 80 P. & C.R. 108.
[205] *Crow v Wood* [1971] 1 Q.B. 77. For this "spurious easement", see above, para.15–006.
[206] *Quicke v Chapman* [1903] 1 Ch. 659 (grantor a mere licensee); *M.R.A. Engineering Ltd v Trimster Co Ltd* (1988) 56 P. & C.R. 1 (s.62 did not create rights over land previously sold by grantor).
[207] *International Tea Stores Co v Hobbs* [1903] 2 Ch. 165 at 172.
[208] *Phipps v Pears* [1965] 1 Q.B. 76.
[209] *Regis Property Co Ltd v Redman* [1956] 2 Q.B. 612.
[210] *Green v Ashco Horticulturist Ltd* [1966] 1 W.L.R. 889. But note that the law will not fail to recognise an easement simply because it is only exercisable between certain times of day: *Lawrence v Fen Tigers* [2014] UKSC 13; [2014] 2 W.L.R. 433 at [33].
[211] *Goldberg v Edwards* [1950] Ch. 247.
[212] *Godwin v Schweppes Ltd* [1902] 1 Ch. 926; and see *Green v Ashco Horticulturist Ltd*, above.
[213] See *Sovmots Investments Ltd v Secretary of State for the Environment* [1979] A.C. 144 at 169, 176.
[214] *Wright v Macadam* [1949] 2 K.B. 744; *Goldberg v Edwards* [1950] Ch. 247.

the section may also apply to a "right" which is reputed to appertain to the land as being continuous and apparent,[215] such as windows enjoying a "right" of light,[216] a watercourse through visible pipes,[217] or a hard-beaten road.[218]

Operation of the section: The section applies to any "conveyance of land",[219] and this includes any assurance of property by an instrument, including leases, mortgages and assents,[220] but not a will or contract, nor an oral tenancy.[221] Where the section applies, the "right" in question becomes a legal easement or profit. Sometimes the section operates unexpectedly. A landlord who renews a lease[222] or sells the reversion to the tenant[223] may find that he has transformed into easements "rights" over his adjoining land which he has merely permitted the tenant to enjoy. Again, a vendor who lets the purchaser into possession before completion may find that "rights" over his adjoining land which the purchaser has enjoyed on sufferance have become easements on completion.[224] These unintended grants may be avoided by the insertion of suitable provisions into contracts, conveyances and leases, excluding the operation of the section; and most standard forms of contract do this,[225] though sometimes the subsequent conveyance inadvertently fails to do so.[226]

Relation between section 62 and implied grant

The importance of the rules relating to implied grant has been considerably reduced by the operation of s.62 of the Law of Property Act 1925. Yet implied grants have not been superseded by the section: the provisions overlap but are by no means identical in their operation. They may be compared as follows.   **15–043**

Width: The section is wider than the rules for implied grant. The section applies to "all . . . rights . . . appertaining or reputed to appertain" to the land, and is not limited to rights that are necessary for the reasonable enjoyment of the land. Further, unlike implied grants, the section can apply to profits á prendre.

Contracts: The rules for implied grants apply not only to conveyances but also to contracts and wills. The section applies only to a "conveyance", and widely though that word is defined,[227] it does not include contracts[228] or wills. Nor does it apply to a lease in writing for

---

[215] The Court of Appeal confirmed that continuous and apparent quasi-easements could pass under s.62 despite lack of diversity of occupation in *P&S Platt v Crouch* [2003] EWCA Civ 1110; [2004] 1 P. & C.R. 18 at [42]. See also *Long v Gowlett* [1923] 2 Ch. 177; [1979] Conv 113 (C. Harpum).
[216] *Broomfield v Williams* [1897] 1 Ch. 602.
[217] *Watts v Kelson* (1870-71) L.R. 6 Ch.App. 166.
[218] *Bayley v G.W.R.* (1884) 26 Ch.D. 434.
[219] LPA 1925 s.62(1).
[220] LPA 1925 s.205(1)(ii).
[221] *Rye v Rye* [1962] A.C. 496.
[222] *Wright v Macadam* [1949] 2 K.B. 744.
[223] *International Tea Stores Co v Hobbs* [1903] 2 Ch. 165.
[224] See *Lyme Valley Squash Club Ltd v Newcastle under Lyme BC* [1985] 2 All E.R. 405.
[225] See *Squarey v Harris-Smith* (1981) 42 P. & C.R. 119; and see the Standard Conditions of Sale 1990, Condition 3.4 (Encyclopedia of Forms and Precedents (5th edn), Service Volume C (vol.35), Form 21.1, para.442.7).
[226] See *Lyme Valley Squash Club Ltd v Newcastle under Lyme BC* [1985] 2 All E.R. 405.
[227] See Ch.6.
[228] *Re Peck and the School Board for London* [1893] 2 Ch. 315.

over three years, not being by deed, for such a lease can take effect only as a contract to grant a lease, which is no conveyance.[229]

Section 62 may be excluded by a term of a contract[230] or a "contrary intention" implied from circumstances[231]; if it is excluded by express term then recourse may be had to the rules for an implied grant.

Restriction and rectification: It will be seen that a conveyance will sometimes convey more than the purchaser is entitled to under the contract. If both contract and conveyance are silent as to easements, the narrower rules for implied grant will limit the purchaser's rights under the contract, while the more ample operation of the section may give him wider rights. Thus a non-apparent way may be outside the doctrine of implied grant but within the section.[232] In such cases the vendor can insist on the conveyance being worded so as to restrict it to the rights which the contract gives the purchaser.[233] If the conveyance has been executed, a vendor who acts promptly may seek to have it rectified,[234] except as against a purchaser without notice of the equity of rectification.

By presumed grant, or prescription

Introduction and general principles

15–044   The basis of prescription is that if long enjoyment of a lawful "right" is shown, the court will uphold the right[235] by presuming that it had a lawful origin, i.e. that there once was an actual grant of the right, even though it is impossible to produce any evidence of such a grant. However, it is not enough to show long user by itself: user of a particular kind is required.

Three methods of prescription

15–045   There are three types of prescription, each of which needs to be considered separately:

(1) prescription at common law;
(2) prescription under the doctrine of "lost modern grant"; and
(3) prescription under the Prescription Act 1832.

This is an unsatisfactory state of affairs that calls for simplification by Parliament.[236] The Law Commission recently reviewed this area of the law; it recommended replacement of

---

[229] *Borman v Griffith* [1930] 1 Ch. 493.
[230] LPA 1925 s.62(4): the section applies ". . .only if and so far as a contrary intention is not expressed in the conveyance".
[231] *Alford v Hannaford* [2011] EWCA Civ 1099 at [38]–[40].
[232] See *Ward v Kirkland* [1967] Ch. 194.
[233] *Re Walmsley and Shaw's Contract* [1917] 1 Ch. 93.
[234] See *Clark v Barnes* [1929] 2 Ch. 368.
[235] Because it is important that long-established de facto enjoyment of rights in the nature of easements or profits should not be disturbed; see the explanation given in *R v Oxfordshire CC Ex p. Sunningwell PC* [2000] 1 A.C. 335.
[236] See *Tehidy Minerals Ltd v Norman* [1971] 2 Q.B. 528 at 543.

the existing system with a single new statutory scheme for the acquisition of easements by prescription.[237]

The particular kind of user which must be shown

Except so far as the Act otherwise provides, a claim to an easement or profit under any head must be supported by user complying with the following conditions.   **15–046**

User as of right

The user must be "as of right"[238] which means that it must have been enjoyed *nec vi, nec clam, nec precario* (without force, without secrecy, without permission).[239] The claimant must show that he has used the right as if he were entitled to it.[240] The whole law of prescription rests upon acquiescence[241]; and mere toleration is enough.[242]   **15–047**

Forcible user (*vi*) occurs not only where the dominant owner breaks down barriers or commits other acts of violence, but also where the user is continued despite the servient owner making continuous and unmistakable protests.[243]

Secret user (*clam*) occurred where a dock had been supported by invisible rods sunk under the servient tenement,[244] or where there had been intermittent and secret discharges of injurious chemicals into a sewer.[245] So, too, no easement can be established against an owner who, owing to absence or other reason, is able to prove that he had no knowledge of the user.[246]

Permissive user (*precario*) occurs where the use is with the permission of the servient owner.[247] If the servient owner has given the claimant the right to use the easement or profit claimed, so that there has been an actual grant of such a right, the user is not *precario*, and the claimant can rely upon his grant without resorting to prescription. But if the claimant has been given permission to use the right claimed "until further notice", or

---

[237] Law Com. No.327 (2011). The Commission recommended complete abolition of any rights to acquire profits á prendre by prescription.

[238] See *R (Lewis) v Redcar and Cleveland BC* (No.2) [2010] 2 A.C. 70 at [20].

[239] *Solomon v Mystery of Vintners* (1859) 4 H. & N. 585 at 602 (common law prescription); *Sturges v Bridgman* (1879) 11 Ch.D. 852 at 863 (lost modern grant); Prescription Act 1832 ss.1, 2 and *Tickle v Brown* (1836) 4 A. & E. 369 at 382 (prescription under the Act). In *R(Beresford) v Sunderland CC* [2003] UKHL 60; [2004] 1 A.C. 889 Lord Bingham said at [3] that "as of right" was defined by this Roman law maxim.

[240] In *R(Beresford) v Sunderland CC* above at [72] Lord Walker said that "as of right" means "as *if* of right". If the claimant actually had an express grant of the right claimed there would be no prescription required.

[241] *Dalton v Angus & Co* (1881) 6 App. Cas. 740 at 773, 803.

[242] The servient owner must not "suffer in silence" *R(Beresford) v Sunderland CC* above at [77]; [81]; *Mills v Silver* [1991] Ch. 271.

[243] *Dalton v Angus & Co* (1881) 6 App. Cas. 740 at 786. See, e.g. *Newnham v Willison* (1988) 56 P. & C.R. 8; *Dennis v Ministry of Defence* [2003] Env L.R. 34 (protests against military aircraft noise).

[244] *Union Lighterage Co v London Graving Dock Co* [1902] 2 Ch. 557.

[245] *Liverpool Corp v H. Coghill & Son Ltd* [1918] 1 Ch. 307.

[246] *Diment v N. H. Foot Ltd* [1974] 1 W.L.R. 1427.

[247] Permission or consent is the opposite of acquiescence or "suffering in silence"; the former negatives prescription whereas the latter is an essential component of the claim: see *R(Beresford) v Sunderland CC* above at [81].

has had to seek permission anew each year, the user is *precario* and no easement or profit can rise from it by prescription.[248] Similarly, if applications for permission to use a way have been made by the claimant from time to time,[249] or he has made annual payments for his enjoyment, there is evidence that the user was *precario*, for such acts are inconsistent with the claimant having a right to the easement or profit claimed.

User during unity of possession, i.e. while the claimant was in possession of both dominant and servient tenements, is not user as of right,[250] As a general proposition, the claimant's subjective beliefs are not relevant.[251] Hence proof that the claimant exercised his right under the mistaken belief that a valid easement or profit had already been granted to him will not prevent the user from being as of right.[252] The principle involved is that the right must have been exercised *qua* easement or profit and not, for example, under any actual or supposed right of an occupant of both tenements.

User in fee simple

15–048   The user must be by or on behalf of a fee simple owner against a fee simple owner who both knows of the user and is able to resist it. In general, only easements or profits in fee simple can be acquired by prescription.[253] An easement or profit for life or for years, for example, may be expressly granted but cannot be acquired by prescription, for the basis of prescription is a presumed grant by the owner of the servient tenement, and only a grant in fee simple will be presumed. Consequently the claimant must show either that he is the fee simple owner himself or that he claims on behalf of the fee simple owner. A tenant under a lease must thus prescribe on behalf of the fee simple owner and not merely on his own behalf.[254]

As prescription rests on acquiescence,[255] a claim will generally fail if user can be proved only when the servient land was occupied by a tenant for life[256] or for years,[257] for while the land is let the fee simple owner may well not have knowledge[258] and even if he does he will probably be unable to contest the user. But if the user began against the fee simple owner it will not become ineffective because the land is later settled or let.[259]

Further, if A leases two plots of his land to two tenants, one tenant cannot prescribe for an easement against the other, for otherwise the result would be that A would acquire an easement over his own land.[260]

---

[248] However, if a personal licence expires, it does not follow that continued use by a successor in title is taken to be permitted: *Tara Hotel v Kensington Close Hotel* [2010] EWHC 2749 (Ch).

[249] *Monmouth Canal Co v Harford* (1834) 1 Cr.M. & R. 614.

[250] *Bright v Walker* (1834) 1 Cr.M. & R. 211 at 219.

[251] *R v Oxfordshire CC Ex p. Sunningwell PC* [2000] 1 A.C. 335 at pp.355–356

[252] *Earl de la Warr v Miles* (1881) 17 Ch.D. 535; *Bridle v Ruby* (1988) 56 P. & C.R. 155; but see [1989] Conv. 261 (G. Kodilinye).

[253] See, e.g. *Kilgour v Gaddes* [1904] 1 K.B. 457 at 460.

[254] *Gateward's Case* (1607) 6 Co.Rep. 59b; *Dawnay v Cashford* (1697) Carth. 432.

[255] *Dalton v Angus & Co* (1881) 6 App. Cas. 740 at 773, 774.

[256] *Roberts v James* (1903) 89 L.T. 282; *Llewellyn (deceased) v Lorey* [2011] EWCA Civ 37.

[257] *Daniel v North* (1809) 11 East 372.

[258] If the freeholder is out of possession both when the user began and during the period of use relied upon the court is unlikely to impute knowledge of the use to the freeholder: *Williams v Sandy Lane (Chester) Ltd* [2006] EWCA Civ 1738; [2007] 1 P. & C.R. 27 (CA).

[259] *Pugh v Savage* [1970] 2 Q.B. 373.

[260] *Kilgour v Gaddes* [1904] 1 K.B. 457; *Simmons v Dobson* [1991] 1 W.L.R. 720.

There are certain modifications of this rule. First, profits in gross may be acquired by prescription at common law,[261] or under the doctrine of lost modern grant. In this case, the right is claimed not in respect of any estate but on behalf of the claimant personally. Such prescription is known as prescription in gross. The claimant must show that he and his predecessors in title to the profit (often his ancestors) have enjoyed the right,[262] instead of showing that he and his predecessors in title to the dominant tenement have enjoyed it.[263] There can be no prescription in gross for easements (which cannot exist in gross), nor can a profit in gross be claimed under the Prescription Act 1832.[264] Secondly, certain modifications are made in claims under the Prescription Act 1832. Thus under the Act easements of light can be acquired by one tenant against another tenant of the same landlord.[265] This is anomalous; it applies only to light and only to claims under the Act. Other modifications under the Act will be noted later.

Continuous user

The claimants must show a continuity of enjoyment. This is interpreted reasonably; in the case of easements of way it is clearly not necessary to show ceaseless user by day and night. User whenever circumstances require it is normally sufficient,[266] provided the intervals are not excessive; but merely casual use, dependent on tolerance, is not enough.[267] Continuity is not broken if the user is varied by agreement, as where the parties vary the line of a way for convenience.[268]

    15–049

    The three types of prescription must now be considered in turn.

Prescription at common law

Length of user

User of the nature discussed above must be shown to have continued since time immemorial, namely since 1189. If this is shown, the court presumes that a grant was made prior to that date. The reason for 1189 being adopted is that from time to time limits were fixed within which actions for the recovery of land were to be brought. Instead of adopting a specified period of years, events such as the beginning of the reign of Henry I or the last voyage of Henry II to Normandy were periodically selected. The last choice to be made was the beginning of the reign of Richard I, namely 1189. These periods originally had nothing to do with prescription, but the courts adopted the last date as the period of time immemorial upon which all claims based on custom or prescription depended. Modern legislation has

    15–050

---

[261] *Johnson v Barnes* (1873) L.R. 8 C.P. 527.
[262] *Welcome v Upton* (1840) 6 M. & W. 536.
[263] Such prescription is *"in the que estate"*: the user is by the claimant and *"ceux que estate il ad"* (those whose estate he has). See Litt. 183.
[264] *Shuttleworth v Le Fleming* (1865) 19 C.B. (N.S.) 687.
[265] See below, para.15–060.
[266] *Dare v Heathcote* (1856) 25 L.J. Ex. 245.
[267] *Ironside, Crabb and Crabb v Cook, Cook and Barefoot* (1981) 41 P. & C.R. 326 (occasional deviations from a way onto a roadside verge).
[268] *Davis v Whitby* [1974] Ch. 186.

altered the rule for claims to land, but 1189 remained the essential date for custom and prescription.[269]

Presumption

15–051   It is clearly impossible in most cases to show continuous user since 1189, and so the courts adopted the rule that if unexplained user for 20 years or more is shown, the court would presume that that user has continued since 1189[270]; user for less than 20 years requires supporting circumstances to raise the presumption.[271] However, this presumption may be met by showing that at some time since 1189 the right could not or did not exist.[272] Thus an easement of light cannot be claimed by prescription at common law for a building which is shown to have been erected since 1189.[273] Consequently it was virtually impossible to establish a claim to light at common law, and many claims based on enjoyment lasting for centuries were liable to be defeated by evidence that there could have been no enjoyment of the right in 1189. Again, if it could be shown that any time since 1189 the dominant and servient tenements had been in the same ownership and occupation, any easement or profit would have been extinguished and so any claim at common law would fail.[274] To meet this state of affairs, the courts invented what has been called the "revolting fiction"[275] of the lost modern grant.

Lost modern grant

The presumption

15–052   The weakness of common law prescription was that the claim failed if it was shown that user had begun at some date after 1189. The doctrine of lost modern grant avoided this by presuming from long user that an actual grant of the easement or profit had been made at some time subsequent to 1189 but prior to the user supporting the claim, and that unfortunately this grant had been lost.[276] "Juries were first told that from user, during living memory, or even during 20 years, they might presume a lost grant or deed; next they were recommended to make such presumption; and lastly, as the final consummation of judicial legislation, it was held that a jury should be told, not only that they might, but also that they were bound to presume the existence of such a lost grant, although neither judge nor jury, nor anyone else, had the shadow of a belief that any such instrument had ever really existed."[277] In their anxiety to find a legal origin for a right of which there had been open and uninterrupted enjoyment for a long period, unexplained in any other way, the courts presumed that a grant had been made, and so made it immaterial that enjoyment had

---

[269] See generally *Bryant v Foot* (1867) L.R. 2 Q.B. 161 at 180, 181.

[270] *R v Oxfordshire CC Ex p. Sunningwell PC* [2000] 1 A.C. 335 at 350. According to Lord Hoffmann the 20 year period derives from the time limit for possessory actions in the long-since repealed Limitation Act 1623.

[271] *Bealey v Shaw* (1805) 6 East 208 at 215.

[272] *Hulbert v Dale* [1909] 2 Ch. 570 at 577.

[273] *Duke of Norfolk v Arbuthnot* (1880) 5 C.P.D. 390.

[274] See below, para.15–071.

[275] *Angus & Co v Dalton* (1877) 3 QBD 85 at 94 per Lush J.

[276] See, e.g. *Dalton v Angus & Co* (1881) 6 App. Cas. 740 at 813.

[277] *Bryant v Foot* (1867) L.R. 2 Q.B. 161 at 181 per Cockburn C.J.

not continued since 1189. User for 20 years normally sufficed to raise the presumption[278]; and unlike prescription under the Act, once the period has run, the easement comes into existence and is not affected by any subsequent cessation of the user.[279]

Evidence

Rather stronger evidence of user is required to induce the court to presume a lost modern grant than is required for prescription at common law.[280] In theory, the doctrine can be invoked only if something prevents the application of common law prescription[281] but in modern times the Courts have permitted both claims to be run together.[282] Since the doctrine is admittedly a fiction, the claimant will not be ordered to furnish particulars of the fictitious grant (for example as to the parties), but he must plead whether the grant is alleged to have been made before or after a particular date.[283] Crucially, the presumption cannot be rebutted by evidence that no grant was in fact made.[284] But the claim is defeated by proof that during the entire period when the grant would have been made there was nobody who could lawfully have made it, as for instance where the claimed use is contrary to a public statute and thus would be unlawful even if carried on by the servient owner.[285] The court has refused to presume a lost grant of a way where the land had been in strict settlement (under which there was no power to make a grant) from the time when the user began down to the time of action.[286]

15–053

Prescription Act 1832: Easements (except rights of light) and profits

The Prescription Act 1832 ("the 1832 Act") was passed to meet the difficulties and uncertainties mentioned above, and in particular the difficulty of persuading juries to presume grants to have been made when they knew this was not the case. It is ill-drafted,[287] but in many cases it has substituted certainty for uncertainty. The 1832 Act makes special provision for easements of light, so that the other rights under the 1832 Act will be dealt with first, and then easements of light. The 1832 Act is perhaps best dealt with by giving a summary of the effect of each section and then annotating the sections in groups.

15–054

---

[278] *Penwarden v Ching* (1829) Moo. & M. 400.

[279] *Mills v Silver* [1991] Ch. 271; below, para.15–056.

[280] *Tilbury v Silva* (1890) 45 Ch.D. 98 at 123.

[281] *Bryant v Lefever* (1879) 4 C.P.D. 172 at 177.

[282] See *Mills v Silver* (above).

[283] *Tremayne v English Clays Lovering Pochin & Co Ltd* [1972] 1 W.L.R. 657, not following *Gabriel Wade & English Ltd v Dixon & Cardus Ltd* [1937] 3 All E.R. 900.

[284] *Tehidy Minerals Ltd v Norman* [1971] 2 Q.B. 528.

[285] *Bakewell v Brandwood* [2004] UKHL 14; [2004] 2 A.C. 519 explaining a line of earlier cases beginning with *Neaverson v Peterborough R.D.C.* [1902] 1 Ch. 557 and including *George Legge & Son v Wenlock Corp* [1938] A.C. 204 (no easement to discharge sewage into a stream where such discharge was illegal pollution).

[286] *Roberts v James* (1903) 89 L.T. 282. See now SLA 1925 s.49(1).

[287] The Law Commission has recommended repeal and replacement; Law Com. No.327 (2011).

15–055   *Sections 1 to 4 of the 1832 Act*

Section 1: profits: No claim to a profit is to be defeasible by showing that user commenced after 1189 if 30 years' uninterrupted enjoyment as of right is shown. If 60 years' uninterrupted enjoyment as of right is shown, the right is deemed to be absolute unless it has been enjoyed by written consent or agreement.

Section 2: easements except rights of light: The section makes exactly similar provisions for all easements except the easement of light, though the periods are 20 and 40 years respectively instead of 30 and 60.[288]

Section 3: rights of light: Easements of light are dealt with below.[289]

Section 4: periods and interruptions: All periods of enjoyment under the 1832 Act are those periods next before some action in which the claim is brought into question. Further, no act is to be deemed an interruption until it has been submitted to or acquiesced in for one year after the party interrupted had notice both of the interruption and of the person making it.

15–056   *The chief points to note on this group of sections*

"Next before some action": The 1832 Act does not say that an easement or profit comes into existence after 20, 30, 40 or 60 years' user in the abstract; all periods under the 1832 Act are those next before some action in which the right is questioned. Thus until some action is brought, there is a mere inchoate right to an easement or profit, however long the user.[290] Further, even if there has been user for longer than the statutory periods, the vital period is always that period (such as of 20 years) next before some action. Thus if user commenced 50 years ago but ceased five years ago, a claim will fail if the action is commenced today, for there has not been continuous user during the 20 or 40 years next before the action.[291] Similarly a claim under the 1832 Act will fail if there has been unity of possession for a substantial period immediately before the action, for there has not been user as an easement during the whole of the vital period.[292]

"Without interruption": The user must be "without interruption"; but a special meaning is given to "interruption". If D has used a way over S's land for over 20 years, and then a barrier is erected barring his way, D can still succeed in establishing an easement, provided that at the time an action is brought he has not acquiesced in the obstruction for one year after he has known both of the obstruction and of the person responsible for it.[293]

"Interruption" means some hostile obstruction and not mere non-user.[294] A complaint or protest against an interruption suffices to negative acquiescence if it is communicated to

---

[288] The difference between the longer and shorter periods is discussed in its own section, at para.15–057 below.

[289] Below, para.15–058 et seq.

[290] *Colls v Home and Colonial Stores* [1904] A.C. 179 at 189–190; *Hyman v Van den Bergh* [1908] 1 Ch. 167.

[291] *Parker v Mitchell* (1840) 11 A. & E. 788; contrast lost modern grant: above.

[292] *Aynsley v Glover* (1875) 10 Ch.App. 283.

[293] *Seddon v Bank of Bolton* (1882) 19 Ch.D. 462.

[294] *Smith v Baxter* [1900] 2 Ch. 138 at 143.

the servient owner; and its effect normally endures for some time after it has been made, so that there is no acquiescence in an interruption for a year merely because a year has elapsed since the last protest was made.[295]

User for 19 years and a day followed by 364 days' interruption is thus, for the purposes of the 1832 Act, 20 years' user upon which a claim will succeed. But this does not mean that 364 days is in fact deducted from the periods in the 1832 Act. To say that user for 19 years and a day is as good as user for 20 years is inaccurate, for:

(i) no action can be brought to establish an easement if only 19 years and a fraction have elapsed since the user began,[296] whereas after 20 years' user, an action can be started forthwith; and

(ii) if an interruption commences after user for 19 years and a day, not until it has lasted for 364 days can the dominant owner commence an action to establish his easement, for not until then is there a period of 20 years.[297] If he waits another day, the interruption will have lasted for a year and his claim must fail. Thus he has only one day on which to issue his claim, whereas if he has enjoyed user for 20 years when an interruption commences, he may issue his claim on any of the next 364 days.

User "as of right": Sections 1 and 2 provide that the enjoyment must be by a "person claiming right thereto", and s.5 provides that it is sufficient to plead enjoyment "as of right". The effect is that claims under the 1832 Act must be based on user which would have sufficed at common law, i.e. *nec vi, nec clam, nec precario*.[298]

At common law, any consent or agreement by the servient owner, whether oral or written, rendered the user *precario*. Under the 1832 Act, this rule applies to the shorter periods (20 years for easements, 30 years for profits); but in the case of the longer periods (40 years for easements, 60 years for profits) a special meaning is given to *precario* by providing that the right is to be absolute unless enjoyed by written consent or agreement. A mere oral consent given at the beginning of the period and not renewed will thus not defeat a claim based on one of the longer periods, although it would be fatal at common law. However, oral consents repeatedly given during a period will defeat a claim based even on the longer periods.[299]

Effect of consents: The effect of consents may be summarised thus[300]:

(i) any consents, whether oral or written, which have been given intermittently during the period make the user *precario* and defeat a claim based on either the shorter or longer periods;

(ii) a written consent given at the beginning of the user (and extending throughout) defeats a claim based on either the shorter or longer periods; and

(iii) an oral consent given at the beginning of the user (and extending throughout)

---

[295] *Davies v Du Paver* [1953] 1 Q.B. 184; *Dance v Triplow* (1991) 63 P. & C.R. 1 (2.5 years too much).
[296] *Lord Battersea v Commissioners of Sewers for the City of London* [1895] 2 Ch. 708.
[297] *Reilly v Orange* [1955] 1 W.L.R. 616.
[298] *Gardner v Hodgson's Kingston Brewery Co Ltd* [1903] A.C. 229 at 238, 239.
[299] *Gardner v Hodgson's Kingston Brewery Co Ltd* [1903] A.C. 229; *Jones v Price* (1992) 64 P & CR 404.
[300] See *Tickle v Brown* (1836) 4 A. & E. 369; *Healey v Hawkins* [1968] 1 W.L.R. 1967.

defeats a claim based on the shorter periods but not a claim based on the longer periods.

If user commences by consent, the question whether it continues by consent is one of fact.[301] In the case of a written consent or agreement, signature by the servient owner is not essential; a document signed by the dominant owner or his leasehold tenant may suffice.[302]

Sections 5 to 8 of the 1832 Act

15–057   Section 5 deals with pleadings.

Section 6 provides that enjoyment for less than the statutory periods shall give rise to no claim. This does not prevent a lost grant being presumed from user for less than a statutory period if there is some evidence to support it in addition to the enjoyment.[303]

Section 7 provides that any period during which the owner of the servient tenement has been a child, mental patient or tenant for life shall automatically be deducted from the shorter periods; further, the period during which an action is pending and actively prosecuted is also to be deducted.

Section 8 provides that if the servient tenement has been held under a "term of life, or any term of years exceeding three years from the granting thereof", the term shall be excluded in computing the period of 40 years in the case of a "way or other convenient [sic] watercourse or use of water", provided the claim is resisted by a reversioner upon the term within three years of its determination.

No more need be said about ss.5 and 6. Sections 7 and 8 are complicated and can conveniently be dealt with together.

Deduction: Where either s.7 or s.8 applies, the period deducted is excluded altogether when calculating the period next before action. Thus if there has been enjoyment of a profit for 45 years in all, consisting of 25 years' user against the fee simple owner, then 19 years against the life tenant, and then a further year against the fee simple owner, the claim fails; for by s.7 the period of the life tenancy is deducted when calculating the period next before action brought, and thus less than 30 years' user is left. But if the user continues for another four years, the claim would succeed, for there is 30 years' user consisting of 25 years before and five years after the life tenancy; since the period of the life tenancy is disregarded, the 30-year period is, for the purposes of the Act, next before action within s.4.[304] The sections in effect connect the periods immediately before and after the period deducted, but they will not connect two periods separated in any other way, such as by a period of unity of possession.[305]

Application: Section 7 applies to the shorter periods both for easements and profits; but s.8 does not apply to profits at all, and applies to the longer period only in the case of easements of way "or other convenient watercourse or use of water". Probably "convenient"

---

[301] *Gaved v Martyn* (1865) 19 C.B. (N.S.) 732; *Healey v Hawkins* [1968] 1 W.L.R. 1967.
[302] *Hyman v Van den Bergh* [1908] 1 Ch. 167; *Paragon Finance Plc v City of London Property Co Ltd* [2002] 1 P. & C.R. 470.
[303] *Hanmer v Chance* (1865) 4 De G.J. & S. 626 at 631.
[304] *Clayton v Corby* (1842) 2 Q.B. 813.
[305] *Onley v Gardiner* (1838) 4 M. & W. 496.

is a misprint for "easement", and the phrase should read "or other easement, watercourse or use of water" as in s.2. If so, s.8 applies to all easements (except light): but the point is unsettled.[306]

Ambit: Section 7 applies to the servient owner being a child, mental patient or tenant for life: s.8 applies where the servient tenement has been held under a term for over three years, or for life. Thus a life tenancy can be deducted under both sections, but infancy or mental illness affect only the shorter periods. If D has enjoyed a way against S's land for 25 years, but S has been mentally ill for the last 15 of those years, s.7 defeats D's claim. If D continues his user for another 15 years, however, his claim succeeds even though S's mental illness continues throughout.

Further, it will be observed that the only provision for deduction of leasehold terms is in s.8. Thus, where there had been user of a way for 20 years, the servient land being under lease for 15 of the 20 years, but free from any lease at the beginning and end of the period, an easement was established[307]: for s.7 makes no mention of leaseholds, and s.8 does not apply to the 20-year period. It will be noted that here the user commenced against the fee simple owner who, by leasing the land, voluntarily put it out of his power to resist the user: had the lease been granted before the user commenced and continued throughout, the position would have been different, for no user as against a fee simple owner able to resist it could be shown.[308] In short, a lease may affect a claim in two ways:

    (i) by showing that there has been no user against a fee simple owner who knows of it and can resist it; and

    (ii) by falling within the provisions of s.8 allowing deduction.

The first of these is a common law rule not affected by the 1832 Act; the second is a creature of the statute and can apply only to claims under the 1832 Act based on the 40-year period.

Right to deduct: In s.7, the provision for deduction is absolute: in s.8, it is conditional, the condition being that the reversioner resists the claim within three years of the determination of the term of years or life. Thus if the reversioner fails to resist the claim within three years, he has no right of deduction. Further s.8 extends only to a reversioner and not to a remainderman,[309] so that it will rarely apply to the usual kind of settlement.

It will be seen from this that s.7 is wide in its scope, giving an absolute right of deduction from the shorter periods for both easements and profits; s.8, on the other hand, is very narrow, giving only a reversioner a conditional right of deduction from the 40-year period in the case of (possibly) only two classes of easements.

Difference between longer and shorter periods: In the case of the shorter periods, the only benefits which the 1832 Act confers upon a claimant are that the period for which he must show user is clearly laid down, and that he cannot be defeated by proof that his enjoyment began after 1189. The nature of the user required is still substantially the same, so that

---

[306] See *Laird v Briggs* (1881) 19 Ch.D. 22 at 33.

[307] *Palk v Shinner* (1852) 18 Q.B. 568; *Pugh v Savage* [1970] 2 Q.B. 373.

[308] *Bright v Walker* (1834) 1 Cr.M. & R. 211.

[309] *Symons v Leaker* (1885) 15 QBD 629. But see *Holman v Exton* (1692) Carth. 246 (remainderman "within the equity" of a statute applicable to reversioners).

the claimant must show continuous, uninterrupted user as of right by or on behalf of a fee simple owner against a fee simple owner who both knew of the user and could resist it.

In the case of the longer periods, however, although uninterrupted user as of right is expressly required, and easements can be acquired only on behalf of a fee simple owner, the 1832 Act provides that the right becomes absolute after the required period next before action has elapsed. User against a fee simple owner who both knew of it and was able to resist it is therefore not required[310]; the only exceptions to this are those provided by s.8. Thus user of a way for 20 years against land held under a life tenancy will give no claim under the 1832 Act,[311] but user for 40 years will suffice, subject to s.8.[312] It seems, therefore, that although all prescription is, in general, founded upon the presumption of a grant, there is no need to presume a grant in the case of claims based on the longer periods under the 1832 Act. Logically that would mean that a prescriptive right could be acquired against a servient owner with no power to grant, for instance where the servient owner is a corporation with no power of grant. However, the Court of Appeal has now clarified that a prescriptive right cannot be acquired against such a servient owner[313] except in the case of claims to rights of light under the 1832 Act.[314] The difference between the longer and the shorter periods may be summarised thus:

(i) a presumption of a grant is required in the case of the shorter periods, though possibly not in the case of the longer periods;

(ii) an oral consent given at the beginning of the period defeats a claim based on one of the shorter periods, but not one based on one of the longer periods;

(iii) the shorter periods are subject to the provisions of s. 7 but not s.8: the 40 years' period is subject to s.8 in the case of easements of way and water alone, it seems, but otherwise the longer periods are subject to neither section.

Prescription Act 1832: Easements of light

15–058   Easements of light are in some respects on a footing different from that of other rights under the 1832 Act. Section 3 provides in effect that after the actual enjoyment of the access of light to a "dwelling-house, workshop, or other building" (which includes a greenhouse[315]) has continued for 20 years without interruption, the right is deemed absolute unless enjoyed by written consent or agreement. On the effect of this, the main points to note are the following.

---

[310] *Wright v Williams* (1836) 1 M. & W. 77.

[311] *Bright v Walker* (1834) 1 Cr.M. & R. 211.

[312] *Wright v Williams* (1836) 1 M. & W. 77, not cited in *Davies v Du Paver* [1953] 1 Q.B. 184.

[313] *Housden v Conservators of Wimbledon & Putney Commons* [2008] EWCA Civ 200; [2008] 1 W.L.R. 1172 applying *Proprietors of the Staffordshire & Worcester Canal Navigation v Proprietors of the Birmingham Canal Navigation* (1866) L.R. 1 HL 254.

[314] Rights to light would appear to remain governed by *Tapling v Jones* (1865) 11 H.L.C. 290 at 304, see *Housden* (above) at [66]. The same three Law Lords decided both *Tapling v Jones* and the *Staffs Canal* case (above) so the different result must be taken to be deliberate. The fact that actual enjoyment confers an easement of light, whereas user as of right is required for other easements, is some indication that it is light alone which requires no presumption of a grant.

[315] *Clifford v Holt* [1899] 1 Ch. 698.

Resemblances

Light resembles other rights claimed under the 1832 Act in two respects.   **15–059**

Section 4 applies: Consequently, the period in question is that next before action,[316] and, with the modification noted below, "interruption" has the same meaning as in other cases[317].

Written consent: the rules relating to written consent are the same as for other claims under the 1832 Act. The rules have to be applied in different situations, however, as for example to tenancies.[318] Where the terms of a tenancy are such that enjoyment of light is permissive or capable of curtailment by the adjoining owner, there can be no prescription.[319]

Differences

Light differs from other rights claimed under the 1832 Act in six respects.   **15–060**

Only one period: There is only one period for light, namely 20 years.

Disabilities: Sections 7 and 8 do not apply.

Obstruction: Wartime restrictions and later planning control made it difficult to interrupt the enjoyment of inchoate rights of light with screens or other erections. Instead, a servient owner may now provide a notional obstruction.[320] He must first obtain from the Lands Tribunal a certificate either of exceptional urgency or that due notice has been given to those likely to be affected. He may then register as a local land charge a notice identifying the dominant and servient tenements and specifying the size and position of the notional obstruction; and for a year this notice takes effect as an obstruction known to and acquiesced in by all concerned. While the notice is in force, the dominant owner may sue for a declaration as if his light actually had been obstructed, and for the cancellation or variation of the registration. Further, for this purpose he may treat his enjoyment as having begun a year earlier than it did; this avoids the "19 years and a day" type of problem.[321]

Actual user suffices: User as of right is not required[322]: actual enjoyment suffices, provided there has been no written consent. Thus the provision that written consent defeats the claim is the only fragment of *nec vi, nec clam, nec precario* which is left in claims to light under the 1832 Act; oral consent is no bar, even though evidenced by annual payments.[323] But there must be enjoyment of the light *qua* easement: enjoyment during unity of possession is not enough.[324]

---

[316] *Hyman v Van den Burgh* [1908] 1 Ch. 167.
[317] *Smith v Baxter* [1900] 2 Ch. 138.
[318] As noted below, because "user as of right" is unnecessary, rights of light can be acquired by tenants against landlords and other tenants.
[319] *RHJ Ltd v FT Patten (Holdings) Ltd* [2008] EWCA Civ 151; [2008] Ch. 341.
[320] Pursuant to the Rights of Light Act 1959.
[321] Rights of Light Act 1959 ss.2, 3.
[322] *Colls v Home & Colonial Stores Ltd* [1904] A.C. 179 at 205.
[323] *Plasterers' Co v Parish Clerk's Co* (1851) 6 Exch. 630.
[324] *Ladyman v Grave* (1871) 6 Ch.App. 763.

No grant: There is no need to presume a grant, because the 1832 Act provides that 20 years' actual enjoyment confers an absolute right[325]; in other words, it is not necessary to show user by or on behalf of one tenant in fee simple against another. Thus the mere fact that the servient tenement has been under lease for the whole period does not prevent the acquisition under the Act of an easement of light valid against the reversioner.[326] This has been taken to its logical conclusion, so that under the Act one tenant can acquire an easement of light over land occupied by another tenant of the same landlord,[327] or by the landlord himself.[328] In the former case, on the expiration of the lease of the servient tenement, the easement is effective against the landlord and all subsequent owners of the land.[329]

Crown not bound: Sections 1 and 2 mention the Crown: s.3 does not. A statute does not bind the Crown unless it so provides either expressly or by necessary implication,[330] and so an easement of light cannot be acquired under the Act against the Crown[331]; but other easements and profits can.

Prescription Act 1832: Limits to the 1832 Act

15–061   The 1832 Act does not enable claimants to establish as easements or profits rights which could not be established as such at common law. Thus a claim by the freemen and citizens of a town to enter land and hold races thereon on Ascension Day cannot be established under the 1832 Act.[332] Nor has the 1832 Act abolished the other methods of prescription. Consequently, it is usual to plead all three methods of prescription, although the claimant does this at his own risk as to costs, such as if this form of pleading needlessly increases the other party's expenses.[333] If a claim is made solely under the 1832 Act, it is liable to be defeated by showing unity of possession at any time during the period[334]; this is not so under the doctrine of lost modern grant[335] or at common law.[336] Again, if the claim is made solely at common law, it will be defeated if it is shown that the enjoyment started after 1189. But as seen already, this would not defeat a claim by lost modern grant or under the 1832 Act. Nor should a claim be based on lost modern grant alone, for the court will not presume a modern grant if the right can be established in any other way.[337] However, a method of prescription under which it is legally impossible for a claim to succeed should never be pleaded. Thus a profit in gross should not be claimed under the 1832 Act,[338] although it may be claimed by prescription at common law.[339]

---

[325] *Tapling v Jones* (1865) 11 H.L.C. 290 at 304, 318.
[326] *Simper v Foley* (1862) 2 J. & H. 564.
[327] *Morgan v Fear* [1907] A.C. 425.
[328] *Foster v Lyons & Co Ltd* [1927] 1 Ch. 219 at 227.
[329] *Morgan v Fear* [1907] A.C. 425.
[330] *Perry v Eames* [1891] 1 Ch. 658 at 665.
[331] *Wheaton v Maple & Co* [1893] 3 Ch. 48.
[332] *Mounsey v Ismay* (1865) 3 H. & C. 486.
[333] *Harris v Jenkins* (1883) L.R. 22 Ch.D. 481 at 482.
[334] *Damper v Bassett* [1901] 2 Ch. 350.
[335] *Hulbert v Dale* [1909] 2 Ch. 570; and see *Mills v Silver* [1991] Ch. 271 (cessation of user: above, para.15–049).
[336] *Dalton v Angus & Co* (1881) 6 App. Cas. 740 at 814.
[337] *Gardner v Hodgson's Kingston Brewery Co Ltd* [1903] A.C. 229 at 240.
[338] *Shuttleworth v Le Fleming* (1865) 19 C.B. (N.S.) 687.
[339] *Johnson v Barnes* (1873) L.R. 8 C.P. 527.

Creation and extinguishment of public rights of way

The purpose of this section is not to set out an extensive treatment of the law of highways **15–062** but to identify the ways in which the creation and extinction of public rights of way differ from the creation and extinction of easements and profits.

Creation

Public rights of way[340] are created in a quite different way to easements and profits. A public **15–063** right of way may be created in the following ways.

By statute: This needs no explanation.

By dedication and acceptance: (1) *At common law*. To establish a highway at common law by dedication and acceptance, it must be shown:

- (i) that the owner of the land dedicated the way to the public; and also
- (ii) that the public accepted that dedication, the acceptance normally being shown by user by the public.[341]

Dedication may be formal, although this is comparatively infrequent. It is usually inferred from long user by the public, the user thus being effective to prove both dedication and acceptance.[342] But to raise a presumption of dedication, there must have been open use as of right for so long a time that it must have come to the notice of the landowner that the public were using the way as of right, thus justifying the inference that the landowner consented to this user.[343] User with the landowner's licence is not user as of right,[344] for it acknowledges that the way is being used not because the public has a right to do so but because the landowner has agreed not to treat it as a trespass in the particular case in question. Further, the use must have been without interruption by the owner. A practice frequently adopted to disprove any intention to dedicate is to close the way for one day in each year, for this openly asserts the landowner's right to exclude the public at will.[345]

The length of the enjoyment to be shown depends on the circumstances of the case. Where the circumstances have pointed to an intention to dedicate, 18 months have been held to be enough,[346] while where the circumstances are against dedication, a substantially greater period may be insufficient.

(2) *Under the Highways Act 1980*. The Rights of Way Act 1932 (now replaced by provisions in the Highways Act 1980[347]) simplified the position to some extent by laying down a definite period of use that will suffice to show that a right of way exists. The public can still

---

[340] For a discussion of the different types of highway see *Suffolk CC v Mason* [1979] A.C. 705 at 710.
[341] See *Cubitt v Lady Caroline Maxse* (1873) L.R. 8 C.P. 704 at 715.
[342] The development of the principles of dedication is explained by Lord Hoffmann in *R(Godmanchester Town Council) v Secretary of State* [2008] 1 A.C. 221 at [4]–[7].
[343] *Greenwich District Board of Works v Maudslay* (1870) L.R. 5 Q.B. 397 at 404.
[344] *R. v Broke* (1859) 1 F. & F. 514.
[345] See *British Museum Trustees v Finnis* (1833) 5 C. & P. 460; and see [1986] Conv. 161 (A. Samuels).
[346] *North London Ry v The Vestry of St. Mary, Islington* (1872) 27 L.T. 672.
[347] s.31.

rely on the common law to claim a right of way based on use for a shorter period than that laid down by the Act if an intent to dedicate can be inferred.[348]

The Act of 1980 provides that a way over land (not including a river[349]) is to be deemed to have been dedicated as a highway if it "has been actually enjoyed by the public as of right[350] and without interruption for a full period of 20 years", unless "there is sufficient evidence that there was no intention during that period to dedicate it".[351] "Interruption" means interruption in fact, and not, for instance the mere closing of the way only at times when nobody used it or was likely to do so.[352] The absence of any intention to dedicate can be shown either in one of the usual ways, as by closing the way for one day in each year, or in one of the special ways provided by the Act, namely, by exhibiting a notice visible to those using the way, or by depositing a map with the local council with a statement of what ways the landowner admits to be highways and lodging statutory declarations at intervals of not more than six years, stating whether any other ways have been dedicated. A reversioner or remainderman upon an interest for life or *pur autre vie* is entitled to the same remedies against the public as if he were in possession.[353]

The 20-year period is to be calculated as that next before the time when the right to use the way was brought into question by a notice exhibited to the public negativing the dedication or otherwise.[354]

Extinguishment

15–064   When a highway has been established, it can be stopped up or diverted only by natural causes[355] or an order made under certain statutory provisions.[356] The mere obstruction of the highway or the failure by the public to use it will not destroy the rights of the public, for "once a highway always a highway".[357] And a mere closing order for a highway leaves unaffected any easement over the route of the highway.[358]

---

[348] s.31(9); *Wild v Secretary of State* [2010] EWCA Civ 1406 at [26].

[349] *Att.-Gen. ex rel. Yorkshire Derwent Trust Ltd v Brotherton* [1992] 1 A.C. 425 (right of navigation cannot be acquired under the Act).

[350] "as of right" bears the same meaning as it does in respect of the acquisition of easements: *R v Oxfordshire CC Ex p. Sunningwell PC* [2000] 1 A.C. 335.

[351] Highways Act 1980 (HA 1980) s.31(1). This is an objective test; it requires evidence of "overt acts" to show the public at large that there is no intention to dedicate: *R (Godmanchester Town Council) v Secretary of State* (above).

[352] *Lewis v Thomas* [1950] 1 K.B. 438.

[353] HA 1980 s.33.

[354] HA 1980 s.31(2).

[355] For example, cliff erosion.

[356] e.g. HA 1980 ss.116–123; Town and Country Planning Act 1990 ss.247–260.

[357] *Dawes v Hawkins* (1860) 8 C.B. (N.S.) 848 at 858 per Byles J.; *R (Smith) v Land Registry* [2011] Q.B. 413 at [50] (no adverse possession of a highway).

[358] *Walsh v Oates* [1953] 1 Q.B. 578.

EXTINGUISHMENT OF EASEMENTS AND PROFITS

By statute

An Act of Parliament may extinguish an easement or profit expressly or by implication.[359] By contrast with restrictive covenants, there is no power in a court or tribunal to modify or discharge easements or profits.[360] Historically, rights of common could be extinguished by statutory rights of approvement, and by inclosure. These methods have recently been abolished[361] but they remain relevant as they may historically have operated to extinguish a right of common.

15–065

Approvement

The lord of a manor had a common law right to "approve" the manorial waste over which the tenants exercised rights of pasture. Approvement was effected by the lord taking part of the waste for his separate enjoyment. The Statutes of Merton 1236[362] and Westminster II 1285[363] confirmed this practice, but obliged the lord to leave sufficient land for the commoners. The onus of proving sufficiency was on the lord, and there had to be enough pasture for all the animals which the commoners were entitled to turn out, and not merely for those in fact turned out in recent years.[364]

15–066

Inclosure

Inclosure involves the discharge of the whole manorial waste from all rights of common, whereas approvement applies only to commons of pasture appendant or appurtenant, and discharges only part of the land. From the middle of the eighteenth century, a large number of private Inclosure Acts were passed. The policy of Parliament was to encourage the efficient production of food, which was hardly possible under the relics of the feudal system. The Inclosure (Consolidation) Act 1801 and the Inclosure Act 1845 facilitated inclosures, but public opinion was aroused by the disappearance of open spaces, and the Inclosure Act 1852 prevented inclosures being made without the consent of Parliament.

15–067

By release

Express release

At law, a deed is required for an express release.[365] In equity, however, an informal release will be effective provided it would be inequitable for the dominant tenant to claim that

15–068

---

[359] But as to implication, see *Jones v Cleanthi* [2007] 1 W.L.R. 1604 – servient owner ordered by local authority under Pt XI of the Housing Act 1985 to block up a right of way; held not to extinguish the easement for all time.

[360] As to the powers of the Upper Tribunal (Lands Chamber) pursuant to s.84 of the LPA 1925 see paras 16–034 et seq.

[361] By the Commons Act 2006.

[362] c. 4, now called the Commons Act 1236: Statute Law Revision Act 1948, Sch.2.

[363] c. 46, now called the Commons Act 1285: Statute Law Revision Act 1948, Sch.2.

[364] *Robertson v Hartopp* (1889) 43 Ch.D. 484.

[365] Co.Litt. 264b.

the right still exists, as where he has orally consented to his light being obstructed and the servient tenant has spent money on erecting the obstruction.[366]

Implied release

15–069 **Abandonment:** If the dominant owner shows an intention to release an easement or profit, it will be extinguished by implied release. But abandonment will not readily be inferred.[367] Mere non-user is never enough by itself: an intention to abandon the right must be shown.[368] There is no presumption that abandonment may be presumed from non-user for over 20 years; abandonment will not be inferred even from long disuse where there has been no occasion for any user.[369]

It is a question of fact whether an act was intended as an abandonment. Alterations to the dominant tenement which make the enjoyment of an easement or profit impossible or unnecessary may show an intent to abandon the right. Thus if a mill to which an easement of water is appurtenant is demolished without any intent to replace it, or a canal to which an easement of water is appurtenant is turned in to a railway, the easement is released.[370] On the other hand, bricking up a door for 30 years may not show abandonment of a right of way, as it can be unbricked.[371] Similarly the demolition of a house to which an easement of light is appurtenant may amount to an implied release, unless it is intended to replace the house by another building.[372] It is not essential that the new windows should occupy exactly the same positions as the old, provided they receive substantially the same light[373]; the test is identity of light, not identity of aperture. Acquiescence in obstructions in the servient land may show an intent to abandon, but not if it can be explained, such as by the use of an alternative but precarious way.[374]

15–070 **Excessive user:** The better view is that excessive use is a nuisance which can be restrained by injunction but does not extinguish the easement. If the dominant tenement is so altered that the burden of the easement is substantially increased, the right *may* be extinguished altogether.[375] Merely erecting new buildings is not enough.[376]

---

[366] *Waterlow v Bacon* (1866) L.R. 2 Eq. 514.

[367] *Snell & Prideaux v Dutton Mirrors* [1995] 1 E.G.L.R. 259 at 261.

[368] Meaning that it is intended by the person who holds the right that he will never in any circumstances use it again and nor will any successor in title: *Swan v Sinclair* [1924] 1 Ch. 254; affirmed [1925] A.C. 227; and see *Tehidy Minerals Ltd v Norman* [1971] 2 Q.B. 528.

[369] *Moore v Rawson* (1824) 3 B. & C. 332 at 339; *Benn v Hardinge* (1992) 66 P. & C.R. 246 (175 years non-use but no physical change to the land; no abandonment).

[370] *Liggins v Inge* (1831) 7 Bing. 682 at 693 (mill) *National Guaranteed Manure v Donald* (1859) 4 H&N 8 (canal).

[371] *Cook v Mayor and Corp of Bath* (1868) L.R. 6 Eq 177. See also *Jones Cleanthi* (above).

[372] *Ecclesiastical Commissioners for England v Kino* (1880) 14 Ch.D. 213.

[373] *Scott v Pape* (1886) 31 Ch.D. 554.

[374] *Treweeke v 36 Wolseley Road Pty Ltd* (1973) 128 C.L.R. 274; and see *Ward v Ward* (1852) 7 Exch. 838.

[375] *Ankerson v Connelly* [1906] 2 Ch. 544; affirmed [1907] 1 Ch. 678; and see *Ray v Fairway Motors (Barnstaple) Ltd* (1969) 20 P. & C.R. 261 (extra burden insufficient).

[376] *McAdams Homes v Robinson* [2004] EWCA Civ 214; [2005] 1 P. & C.R. 30.

Frustration: Extinguishment by frustration seems to be possible but improbable.[377]

By unity of ownership and possession

If the dominant and servient tenements come into the ownership and possession of the same person, any easement[378] or profit[379] is extinguished. Unity of possession without unity of ownership is not enough[380]: the right is merely suspended until the unity of possession ceases. Similarly, unity of ownership without unity of possession effects no extinguishment[381]: the right continues until there is also unity of possession. Thus if both dominant and servient tenements are under lease, the easement or profit will not be extinguished merely by both leases being assigned to X, not will it be extinguished merely by Y purchasing both reversions; but if both leases and both reversions become vested in Z, the right is gone.   **15–071**

SPECIES OF EASEMENTS

In this section, there is a detailed consideration of some of the more common types of easement and the particular issues which arise in respect of each of them.   **15–072**

Rights of way

Extent of easements of way

An easement of way may be either general or limited. A general right of way is one which may be used by the owner of the dominant tenement at any time and in any manner.[382] A limited right of way is one which is subject to some restriction. The restriction may be as to time, such as a way which can be used only in the daytime[383] or in case of fire,[384] or it may be as to the mode in which the way can be used, such as a way limited to foot passengers, or to cattle and other animals in the charge of a drover, or to wheeled traffic,[385] and the like. In construing the size and location of the right of way, the court is entitled to take into account: the terms of the conveyance and grant; the physical characteristics of the area at the time of the grant; and, where the conveyance and grant are giving effect to a contract of sale, the terms of that contract (but not any statements made by an auctioneer at the time when it was being entered into).[386]   **15–073**

---

[377] See *Huckvale v Aegean Hotels Ltd* (1989) 58 P. & C.R. 163.
[378] *Buckby v Coles* (1814) 5 Taunt. 311.
[379] *Tyrringham's Case* (1584) 4 Co.Rep. 36b at 38a; *White v Taylor* [1969] 1 Ch. 150.
[380] *Canham v Fisk* (1831) 2 Cr. & J. 126.
[381] *Richardson v Graham* [1908] 1 K.B. 39.
[382] See *Moncrieff v Jamieson* [2007] UKHL 42; [2007] 1 W.L.R. 2620 at 2632. Use by the dominant owner of course includes use by his visitors, or his tenants if the dominant tenement is let.
[383] *Collins v Slade* (1874) 23 W.R. 199.
[384] *I.D.C. Group Ltd v Clark* [1992] 1 E.G. L.R. 187.
[385] *Ballard v Dyson* (1808) 1 Taunt. 279.
[386] *Peacock v Custins* (2001) 81 P. & C.R. 34.

A right of way can normally be used only as a means of access to the dominant tenement.[387] A right to pass over Plot A to reach Plot B cannot also be used as a means of access to Plot C lying beyond Plot B.[388] However, in some circumstances it may not be outside the scope of the grant to use the right of way to access Plot B and then go off Plot B onto Plot C for some incidental or ancillary activity such as picnicking or strolling on Plot C.[389]

In the absence of a contrary agreement[390] or special circumstances,[391] it is for the grantee of a way, not the grantor, to construct the way and to repair it when constructed[392]; the grantee may enter the servient tenement for these purposes.[393] If the way becomes impassable, there is no right to deviate from it unless the servient owner has obstructed it.[394]

Effect of mode of acquisition

15–074   The extent of an easement of way depends upon how it was acquired.

Express grant or reservation: Here the question is primarily one of construction of the grant.[395] If the intention is not made clear, a grant is construed most strongly against the person making it, in accordance with the general rule, while a reservation is construed in his favour, for it takes effect as a regrant by the other party.[396] Thus an easement granted in general terms is not confined to the purpose for which the land is used at the time of the grant.[397] A right of way for general purposes granted as appurtenant to a house can accordingly be used for the business of an hotel if that house is subsequently converted into an hotel.[398]

If a way is granted "as at present enjoyed", prima facie these words refer to the quality of the user (for example on foot or with vehicles) and do not limit the quantity of the user to that existing at the time of the grant.[399] In cases of difficulty, the surrounding circumstances must be considered: thus both the condition of the way (for instance whether it

---

[387] *Harris v Flower* (1905) 74 L.J. Ch. 127; *Peacock v Custins* [2002] 1 W.L.R. 1815.

[388] See for example *Das v Linden Mews* [2003] 2 P. & C.R. 4. The result may be different if at the date of grant plot B was in active use as the access to plot C, in which case the grant may be construed as permitting access to plot C; see the first instance decision in *Nickerson v Barraclough* [1980] Ch. 325 at 336.

[389] *Peacock v Custins* (above).

[390] The grant of the right of way might be expressed such that use of the way is conditional upon the grantee contributing to the cost of maintenance; if so the grantee may be restrained from using the way if he defaults on payment; see *Carter v Cole* [2006] EWCA Civ 398 applying the "benefit and burden" principle.

[391] See *Saint v Jenner* [1973] Ch. 275 (failure to repair results in obstruction).

[392] See *Miller v Hancock* [1893] 2 Q.B. 177 (not affected by *Fairman v Perpetual Investment Building Society* [1923] A.C. 74 on the duty to the dominant owner).

[393] *Newcomen v Coulson* (1877) 5 Ch.D. 133. Note that the owner of the servient tenement may repair the way if he wishes to: *Transco v Stockport MBC* [2003] UKHL 61; [2004] 2 A.C. 1 at [80].

[394] *Selby v Nettlefold* (1873) 9 Ch.App. 111.

[395] The grant is a contract and therefore is construed in its factual matrix.

[396] For this rule, see above, para.15–039.

[397] *South Eastern Ry v Cooper* [1924] 1 Ch. 211.

[398] *White v Grand Hotel, Eastbourne Ltd* [1913] 1 Ch. 113 (affirmed on another point, 84 L.J. Ch. 938); and see *Alvis v Harrison* (1990) 62 P. & C.R. 10.

[399] *Hurt v Bowmer* [1937] 1 All E.R. 797.

is a footpath or a metalled road) and the nature of the dominant tenement (for example whether it is a dwelling-house or a factory) may be of assistance.[400]

Implied grant or reservation: A way of necessity is limited to the necessity existing at the time the right arose; thus if an encircled plot is used for agricultural purposes at the time of the grant, the way of necessity over the surrounding land is limited to agricultural purposes and cannot be used for carting building materials.[401]

In other cases of implied grant, the circumstances of the case must be considered. Thus where a testator devised adjoining plots of land to different persons and one plot was bought by a railway company for conversion into a railway station, it was held that a way which had been used in the testator's lifetime for domestic purposes and for the purposes of warehouses on the land could not be used as a public approach to the station.[402]

Prescription: Where an easement of way is acquired by long user, the extent of the way is limited by the nature of the user. Thus a way acquired by long user for farming purposes cannot be used for mineral purposes or for the cartage of building materials.[403] It has been held that user during the prescriptive period as a carriageway does not authorise user for cattle,[404] although it covers use as a footway[405] (since prima facie the greater includes the less) and it extends to use for motor traffic even if the user proved was for horse-drawn vehicles alone.[406] Moreover, unless there is a radical change in the nature of the dominant tenement, the user is not limited to the number or frequency of vehicles or pedestrians using the way during the prescriptive period.[407]

Rights of light

No natural right

There is no natural right of light; a landowner may so build on his land as to prevent any light from reaching his neighbour's windows,[408] unless his neighbour has an easement of light or some other right such as a restrictive covenant against building. The access of light to windows is sometimes deliberately obstructed in order to prevent an easement of light being acquired by prescription.[409]

15–075

---

[400] *Cannon v Villars* (1878) 8 Ch.D. 415 at 420, 421; *St. Edmundsbury & Ipswich Diocesan Board of Finance v Clark (No.2)* [1973] 1 W.L.R. 1572 at 1591–1596; affirmed [1975] 1 W.L.R. 468.

[401] *Corp of London v Riggs* (1880) 13 Ch.D. 798.

[402] *Milner's Safe Co Ltd v Great Northern and City Ry* [1907] 1 Ch. 208.

[403] *Wimbledon Conservators v Dixon* (1875) 1 Ch.D. 362.

[404] *Ballard v Dyson* (1808) 1 Taunt. 279.

[405] *Davies v Stephens* (1836) 7 C. & P. 570.

[406] *Lock v Abercester Ltd* [1939] Ch. 861.

[407] *British Railways Board v Glass* [1965] Ch. 538; *Woodhouse & Co Ltd v Kirkland (Derby) Ltd* [1970] 1 W.L.R. 1185.

[408] *Tapling v Jones* (1865) 11 H.L.C. 290.

[409] See above, para.15–060.

Quantum of light

15–076   The amount of light to which the dominant owner is entitled was finally settled in *Colls v Home and Colonial Stores Ltd*[410]: this amount is enough light according to the ordinary notions of mankind for the comfortable use of the premises as a dwelling, or, in the case of business premises, for the beneficial use of the premises for ordinary shop or other business purposes. The quantum of light is greater where it is needed for the ordinary beneficial use of the particular building, and for a greenhouse it includes the direct access of the sun's rays.[411] In each case the test is that of the ordinary use of the dominant tenement: the dominant owner is not entitled to object even to a substantial diminution in his light, provided enough is left for the ordinary purposes. The test is not "How much light has been taken away?" but "How much light is left?"[412] An easement for more light than is required for ordinary purposes may be acquired by enjoyment of it for 20 years for purposes known by the servient owner to require it.[413] But the quantum of light to which the dominant owner is entitled is not affected by the fact that he has used the room in question for purposes requiring but little light,[414] for a right of light is a right to have the access of light for all ordinary purposes to which the room may be put,[415] including any sub-division of it that might reasonably be expected.[416]

Alteration of apertures

15–077   An easement of light can exist only in respect of a window or other aperture in a building, such as a skylight.[417] If the dominant owner alters the size or position of the window, the burden on the servient owner cannot be increased; an obstruction which would not have been actionable before the alteration will not be actionable even if it deprives the altered window of most of its light.[418] But if it is established that an obstruction is an infringement of an easement of light for one set of windows, and another set of windows (for which no easement exists) is also obstructed by it, the dominant owner can recover damages in respect of both sets of windows; for the obstruction is illegal and the damage to both sets of windows is the direct and foreseeable consequence of it.[419]

Standard of light

15–078   The standard of light varies to some extent from neighbourhood to neighbourhood,[420] the test in each case being that laid down in *Colls' case*. There is no "45 degrees" rule, i.e. no rule that an interference with light is actionable only if the obstruction rises above a line

---

[410] [1904] A.C. 179.
[411] *Allen v Greenwood* [1980] Ch. 119.
[412] *Higgins v Betts* [1905] 2 Ch. 210 at 215.
[413] *Allen v Greenwood* [1980] Ch. 119.
[414] *Price v Hilditch* [1930] 1 Ch. 500.
[415] *Yates v Jack* (1866) 1 Ch.App. 295.
[416] *Carr-Saunders v Dick McNeil Associates Ltd* [1986] 1 W.L.R. 922.
[417] *Easton v Isted* [1903] 1 Ch. 405.
[418] *Ankerson v Connelly* [1907] 1 Ch. 678.
[419] *Re London, Tilbury & Southend Ry, etc.* (1889) 24 QBD 326.
[420] *Fishenden v Higgs & Hill Ltd* (1935) 153 L.T. 128.

drawn upwards and outwards from the centre of the window at an angle of 45 degrees; at most, the test provides a very slight presumption.[421] Modern standards of lighting have risen, too.[422]

Other sources

In considering whether an easement of light has been obstructed, other sources of light of which the dominant owner cannot be deprived must be taken into account, such as vertical light through a skylight.[423] In one case[424] a room was lit though two sets of windows, one set facing A's land and the other facing B's land. It was held that the light received by both sets of windows had to be considered, but that A could not obscure the greater part of the light passing over his land in reliance upon B supplying a large quantity of light. Neither servient owner could build to a greater extent than, assuming a building of like height on the other servient tenement, would still leave the dominant tenement with sufficient light according to the test in *Colls' case*. The fact that the occupiers of the dominant tenement generally use artificial light, as with modern offices, is not material to the question of whether there has been a substantial diminution in natural light, but may be relevant to the relief granted for the interference.[425]

15–079

Rights of support

It has already been seen[426] that the natural right which every landowner has a natural right to support extends only to land in its natural state; there is no natural right to support for buildings or for the additional burden on land which they cause.[427] Similarly, there is no natural right to have buildings supported by neighbouring buildings.[428] If no more damage is done than is necessary, a man may pull down his house without having to provide support for his neighbour's house. However, the right to have buildings supported by land or by other buildings can, however, be acquired as an easement, particularly by implied reservation, implied grant and presumed grant. Once acquired, even by prescription, an easement of support will not be lost by reason of a change of use of a building in the dominant tenement unless that change is such as to increase substantially the burden on the servient tenement[429]; in this respect the rules governing rights of support are different from those which govern rights of way and rights of light.[430]

15–080

---

[421] *Fishenden v Higgs & Hill Ltd* (1935) 153 L.T. 128. For scientific tests as to "sill ratio", "grumble points" and 50% adequacy, see *Charles Semon & Co Ltd v Bradford Corp* [1922] 2 Ch. 737; *Fishenden v Higgs & Hill Ltd* (1935) 153 L.T. 128; *Ough v King* [1967] 1 W.L.R. 1547.

[422] *Ough v King* [1967] 1 W.L.R. 1547.

[423] *Smith v Evangelisation Society (Incorporated) Trust* [1933] Ch. 515.

[424] *Sheffield Masonic Hall Co Ltd v Sheffield Corp* [1932] 2 Ch. 17.

[425] *Midtown v City of London Real Property Co* [2005] EWHC 33; [2005] 1 E.G.L.R.65; *Tamares (Vincent Square) Ltd v Fairpoint Properties (Vincent Square) Ltd* [2006] EWHC 3589; [2007] 1 W.L.R. 2148.

[426] Above, para.15–008.

[427] *Wyatt v Harrison* (1823) 3 B. & Ad. 871.

[428] *Peyton v Mayor of London* (1829) 9 B. & C. 725.

[429] *Ray v Fairway Motors (Barnstaple) Ltd* (1969) 20 P. & C.R. 261.

[430] See *Attwood v Bovis Homes Ltd* (2000) 82 P. & C.R. 2.

Rights of water

15–081   A variety of easements may exist in connection with water, such as rights:

(i)   to take water from a pump, spring or river, though this is now subject to statutory restrictions[431];

(ii)   to water cattle at a pond[432];

(iii)   to take more water from a natural watercourse than would be permitted by the natural rights of ownership[433];

(iv)   to receive an undiminished flow of water through a defined channel[434];

(v)   to receive water through a pipe situated on the servient tenement[435];

(vi)   to receive the discharge of water from the land of another,[436] although there can be no easement to receive the discharge of percolating water such as rainwater[437];

(vii)   to enter the land of another to open sluice gates[438];

(viii)   to pollute the waters of a stream or river[439];

(ix)   to discharge water onto the land of another[440] ("easement of drainage"), although there can be no easement to discharge percolating water such as rainwater[441]; and

(x)   to be able to permit rain water to drop from a roof on to a neighbour's land ("easement of eavesdrop").

Easements of drainage and easements of eavesdrop are in the same position as easements of support in so far as increases in the amount of water being discharged or dropped are concerned.[442] This is presumably also the case for rights to pollute waters. Rights to take water from, as distinct from rights to discharge water onto, the servient tenement also appear to be in the same position.[443]

Rights of air

15–082   Although an easement for the passage of air through a defined channel may exist,[444] there can be no easement for the general flow of air over land to a windmill or chimney.[445]

---

[431] See *Cargill v Gotts* [1981] 1 W.L.R. 441.

[432] *Manning v Wasdale* (1836) 5 A. & E. 758.

[433] *McCartney v Londonderry & Lough Swilly Ry* [1904] A.C. 301 at 313.

[434] *Dickinson v Grand Junction Canal Co Ltd* (1852) 7 Exch. 282 at 301.

[435] *Rance v Elvin* (1985) 50 P. & C.R. 9.

[436] *Ivimey v Stocker* (1866) 1 Ch.App. 396.

[437] *Chasemore v Richards* (1859) 7 H.L.Cas. 349.

[438] *Simpson v Mayor, etc. of Godmanchester* [1897] A.C. 696.

[439] *Baxendale v McMurray* (1867) 2 Ch.App. 790; see *Scott-Whitehead v National Coal Board* (1987) 53 P. & C.R. 263, considered [1987] Conv. 368 (S. Tromans).

[440] *Mason v Shrewsbury & Hereford Ry.* (1871) L.R. 6 Q.B. 578 at 587.

[441] *Palmer v Bowman* [2000] 1 All E.R. 23.

[442] *Attwood v Bovis Homes Ltd* (2000) 82 P. & C.R. 2.

[443] *Cargill v Gotts* [1981] 1 W.L.R. 441.

[444] *Bass v Gregory* (1890) 25 Q.B.D. 481; *Cable v Bryant* [1908] 1 Ch. 259.

[445] *Webb v Bird* (1862) 13 C.B. (N.S.) 841; *Bryant v Lefever* (1879) 4 C.P.D. 172.

However, sometimes such rights may be obtained by means of the imposition of restrictive covenants[446] or under the rule against derogation from grant.[447]

Miscellaneous easements

There are a variety of miscellaneous easements, such as rights: **15–083**

- (i) to create a nuisance by the discharge of gases, fluids or smoke, or by making noises[448] or vibrations;
- (ii) to hang clothes on a line passing over another's land[449];
- (iii) to mix manure on the servient tenement for the benefit of the adjoining farm;
- (iv) to use a wall for nailing trees thereto or for supporting a creeper;
- (v) to extend the bowsprits of ships over a wharf[450];
- (vi) to use a coal shed for domestic purposes[451];
- (vii) to store casks and trade produce on the servient tenement;
- (viii) to let down the surface of land by mining operations under it;
- (ix) to use an airfield[452];
- (x) to enter the servient tenement to repair buildings on the dominant tenement[453];
- (xi) to park a car[454];
- (xii) to receive electricity via a cable[455]; and
- (xiii) to enjoy a garden or park (a *jus spatiandi*).[456]

Certain rights are not easements but resemble them. A right to use a pew in a church has been described as not being an interest in land but an interest of a peculiar nature in the nature of an easement created by Act of Parliament[457]; and the right to require a neighbouring landowner to repair his fences exists as a "spurious easement".[458]

SPECIES OF PROFITS Á PRENDRE

The following are the main types of profit á prendre. Some are usually met with as commons,   **15–084**
and some as several profits.

---

[446] See Ch.16.
[447] Above, para.15–017.
[448] Discussed in *Lawrence v Fen Tigers* [2014] UKSC 13; [2014] 2 W.L.R. 433 at [28]–[46].
[449] *Drewell v Towler* (1832) 3 B. & Ad. 735.
[450] *Suffield v Brown* (1864) 4 De G.J. & Sm. 185.
[451] *Wright v Macadam* [1949] 2 K.B. 744.
[452] *Dowty Boulton Paul Ltd v Wolverhampton Corp (No.2)* [1976] Ch. 13.
[453] *Ward v Kirkland* [1967] Ch. 194.
[454] For example *Hair v Gilman* (2000) 80 P. & C.R. 108; *Moncrieff v Jamieson* [2007] UKHL 42; [2007] 1 W.L.R. 2620.
[455] *Duffy v Lamb* (1997) 75 P. & C.R. 364.
[456] *Re Ellenborough Park* [1956] Ch. 131; *Barrie House Freehold Ltd v Merie Bin Mahfouz Group* [2012] EWHC 353 (Ch).
[457] *Brumfitt v Roberts* (1870) L.R. 5 C.P. 224 at 233.
[458] *Coaker v Willcocks* [1911] 2 K.B. 124; *Crow v Wood* [1971] 1 Q.B. 77.

Profit of pasture

15–085   A profit of pasture may exist in the following forms.

Appendant

15–086   A profit of pasture appendant is limited to horses, oxen, cows and sheep, the numerical test being levancy and couchancy.[459]

Appurtenant

15–087   A profit of pasture appurtenant is not confined to any particular animals, but depends on the terms of the grant or, in the case of prescription, the animals habitually turned out to pasture. The number of animals may either be tested by levancy and couchancy, or be fixed; it cannot be unlimited.[460] A right limited by levancy and couchancy cannot be severed from the land to which it is appurtenant but a fixed right can[461]; the registration of a right limited by levancy and couchancy under the Commons Registration Act 1965[462] is thereby converted into a fixed right and may thereafter also be severed.[463]

Pur cause de vicinage

15–088   Under a common of pasture *pur cause de vicinage*, the commoners of one common may not put more cattle upon it than it will maintain. Thus, if Common A is 50 acres in extent and Common B 100 acres, the commoners of A must not put more cattle on A than the 50 acres will support, in reliance on their cattle straying to B.[464]

In gross

15–089   A profit of pasture in gross may exist for a fixed number of animals or *sans nombre*. The last phrase means literally "without number" (an alternative form is "without stint"), but such a right is limited to not more cattle than the servient tenement will maintain in addition to any existing burdens.

Limitation of numbers

15–090   Rights of common registrable under the Commons Registration Act 1965 must be registered for a definite number of animals. After registration has become final, the right is exercisable only in relation to the number so registered.[465]

---

[459] Above, para.15–025.
[460] *Benson v Chester* (1799) 8 T.R. 396 at 401.
[461] *Bettison v Langton* [2001] UKHL 24; [2002] 1 A.C. 27.
[462] s.15(1).
[463] *Bettison v Langton* (above).
[464] *Corbet's Case* (1585) 7 Co.Rep. 5a.
[465] Commons Registration Act 1965 s.15.

Profit of turbary

A profit of turbary is the right to dig and take from the servient tenement peat or turf for use as fuel in a house on the dominant tenement. It may exist as appurtenant, or, where it is limited to some specified quantity, in gross.[466] Where it is appurtenant, the turves can be used only for the benefit of the dominant tenement and not, for example for sale, even if the dominant owner is entitled to a fixed quantity.[467]   **15–091**

Profit of estovers

A profit of estovers is the right to take wood from the land of another as house-bote, plough-bote or hay-bote. It may exist as appurtenant, or, if limited to a specified quantity, in gross.   **15–092**

Profit of piscary and other sporting rights

A profit of piscary is a right to catch and take away fish. It can exist in gross (when it may be unlimited) or as appurtenant (when it must be limited to the needs of the dominant tenement). Other sporting rights, such as a right of hunting, shooting, fowling and the like, may also exist as profits á prendre.[468] It is no infringement of such a right for the servient owner merely to cut timber in the ordinary way, even if he thereby drives away game[469]; but it is otherwise if fundamental changes in the land are made, as where the whole or a substantial part of the land is built upon or converted into racing stables.[470]   **15–093**

Profit in the soil

A profit in the soil is the right to enter the servient tenement and take sand, stone, gravel and the like.[471] It may exist as appurtenant or in gross.   **15–094**

RIGHTS OF ACCESS

At common law

At common law, there is no right of access by a landowner onto a neighbour's land for the purposes of repairing his property, or for improving it. Such a right can exist as an easement; otherwise, the neighbour's permission must be obtained.   **15–095**

---

[466] *Mellor v Spateman* (1669) 1 Wms.Saund. 339 at 346.
[467] *Hayward v Cunnington* (1668) 1 Lev 231.
[468] *Ewart v Graham* (1859) 7 H.L.C. 331 at 345.
[469] *Gearns v Baker* (1875) 10 Ch.App. 355.
[470] *Peech v Best* [1931] 1 K.B. 1.
[471] Co.Litt. 122a.

Statutory rights

15–096   The lack of any such rights at common law is inconvenient so Parliament has intervened to provide landowners with certain statutory rights of entry.

The Party Walls (etc.) Act 1996 includes a statutory right of entry to maintain a party wall.

Under the Access to Neighbouring Land Act 1992, the court can make an "access order", giving a landowner the right of access to adjoining or adjacent land. This can be done so as to enable the landowner to do works that are reasonably necessary for the preservation of his land (or part of it),[472] but only if the works cannot be carried out (or would be substantially more difficult to carry out) without entering the servient land.[473] An application for an order is a pending land action.[474] An access order binds successors in title to the servient land, subject to registration as a land charge in the register of writs or orders affecting land, or, for registered land, protection by a notice on the register.

PART 2   RENTCHARGES

NATURE OF RENTCHARGES

Rentcharges and rent services

15–097   In order to understand what a "rent charge" or "rentcharge" is, one has to understand what "rent" may be if not a "rent charge". "Rent" is essentially a periodical payment in respect of land; and there are two main types of rent: "rent service" and "rentcharge". Where the relationship of lord and tenant exists between the parties, any rent payable by virtue of that relationship by the tenant to the lord is a rent service. Rent payable under a lease, which is paid to the lord of that land, or "landlord" as we now say, is a rent service. If there is no relationship of lord and tenant, the rent is a rentcharge.

Thus if L grants a lease to T at £5,000 per annum and X charges his fee simple estate with the payment of £2,000 per annum to Y, L has a rent service and Y a rentcharge. Since the Statute Quia Emptores 1290 it has been impossible for a grantor to reserve any services on a conveyance of freehold land in fee simple, for the grantee holds of the grantor's lord, and not of the grantor. Consequently, no rent reserved on a conveyance of freehold land in fee simple after 1290 can be a rent service. Although at law services could be reserved when an owner in fee simple granted a life estate[475] or a fee tail, it was most unusual to do so. The only rent service now met with in practice is the rent reserved upon the grant of a lease

---

[472] It is important to note that the right does not cover works of improvement. This is a serious limitation on the scope of the Act.

[473] Access to Neighbouring Land Act 1992 s.1.

[474] Access to Neighbouring Land Act 1992 ss.4, 5.

[475] A grant for life at a rent now creates a term of 90 years: see above, para.11–031.

for a term of years. A rent service is annexed to a reversion, while a rentcharge stands on its own. In some parts of the country (including Manchester, Bath and Bristol) rentcharges were for long used wholly or partly instead of paying a capital sum on the purchase of property.[476]

The person to whom the rent is payable under a rentcharge is often referred to as "the rent owner"; the owner of the land charged with the rentcharge is often referred to as "the terre tenant".

Other types of rent relevant to rentcharges

Rent seck

This was a rentcharge with no power of distress. It is now obsolete.   **15–098**

Chief rent

This was a rent service reserved on the subinfeudation of freehold land in fee simple. The Statute Quia Emptores 1290 for the most part prevented such rents being created.[477] Any chief rents existing in 1925 were extinguished by the end of 1935. In some parts of the country, such as Manchester, rentcharges are sometimes called chief rents.   **15–099**

Fee farm rent

This was the name originally used for chief rents; latterly, it has been applied to rentcharges reserved on a conveyance in fee simple.   **15–100**

Quit rent

This was a rent service payable by a copyholder to his lord, whereby he went quit of his obligation to perform agricultural services; and chief rents were sometimes called quit rents. Quit rents existing in 1925 were extinguished by the end of 1935.   **15–101**

Rents of assize

This term is rarely encountered today; it was applied both to chief rents and quit rents.   **15–102**

Legal and equitable rentcharges

A rentcharge is real property, so that both at law and in equity it could be held for any of the usual estates or interests.[478] However, since 1925 an interest in a rentcharge can be legal only if it is: **15–103**

---

[476] See generally (1975) Law.Com. No.68.
[477] Above, para.1–058.
[478] See, e.g. *Chaplin v Chaplin* (1733) 3 P.Wms. 229 (entail); *Re Fraser* [1904] 1 Ch. 726 (term of years).

    (i) in possession; and

    (ii) either perpetual or for a term of years absolute.

Further, a rentcharge cannot exist at law unless the proper formalities have been employed for its creation.[479]

Rentcharge on a rentcharge

15–104   At common law, a rentcharge could be charged only upon a corporeal hereditament. There could be no rentcharge charged upon another rentcharge or other incorporeal hereditament[480]; a right of distress would clearly be inappropriate in such cases. However, since 1925 a rentcharge charged upon another rentcharge has been valid, even if created before 1926; and special provisions have been made for enforcing payment.[481]

Restrictions on rentcharges

15–105   The Rentcharges Act 1977[482] severely curtailed most rentcharges, excepting those few types which still performed a useful service. Apart from the exceptions, the Act:

    (i) prevented the creation of any rentcharge after August 21, 1977; and

    (ii) provided for the extinguishment of existing rentcharges after 60 years.

The exceptions are as follows:

    (i) a "family rentcharge", i.e. where land is charged for the life of a person or a shorter period whether under a settlement under the Settled Land Act 1925, a trust of land or otherwise[483];

    (ii) a rentcharge imposed under an order of the court or a statutory rentcharge for works on land[484]; and

    (iii) an "estate rentcharge", of which there are two types:

        – a rentcharge for a nominal amount which is subject to a right of re-entry imposed as a means of enforcing covenants or other obligations relating to land[485];

        – a rentcharge (a "variable estate rentcharge") for the sums due in respect of the performance by the holder of the rentcharge of covenants made by him for the provision of services to, for the maintenance or repair of,

---

[479] See below.

[480] *Re The Alms Corn Charity* [1901] 2 Ch. 750 at 759.

[481] LPA 1925 s.122: below, para.15–113.

[482] s.2(1), (2).

[483] The Rentcharges Act 1977 s.2(3)(a), (b) as substituted by TLATA 1996 Sch.3 para.15(1), (2).

[484] The Rentcharges Act 1977 s.2(3)(d).

[485] The Rentcharges Act 1977 s.2(3)(c), (4)(a), (5).

or for the insurance of the land charged.[486] The sum payable must be reasonable in relation to the services.[487]

Both types of estate rentcharges have important practical uses, particularly in schemes of development where plots are to be sold freehold but there is much "common use" land. The first type of estate rentcharge can be used to make the burden of positive covenants run with freehold land. The second type provides for something very like a "service charge", which is commonplace in long leases, to function in respect of freehold land; allowing for an estate company to maintain common areas and recover the costs from the freeholders of the various plots in the scheme.[488]

CREATION AND TRANSFER OF RENTCHARGES

Creation

Subject to the Rentcharges Act 1977, a rentcharge can be created only as follows.   **15–106**

By statute

A rentcharge may be created either by statute, or by virtue of powers conferred thereby.[489]   **15–107**

By instrument inter vivos

Apart from statute, a legal rentcharge can be created inter vivos only by a deed[490]; but a document merely in writing may create an equitable rentcharge.[491]   **15–108**

By will

A will now operates only in equity,[492] so that if a rentcharge is created or devised by will, the beneficiary gets no legal interest until the personal representatives have assented to the gift.   **15–109**

---

[486] The Rentcharges Act 1977 s.2(3)(c), (4)(b), (5). The benefit to the land charged can be indirect: *Johnson Security Ltd v Orchard Trading Estate Management* [2002] EWCA Civ 406; [2002] 2 E.G.L.R. 1 (payment of rates on the estate roads etc.); *Canwell Estate Co v Smith Bros Farms Ltd* [2012] EWCA Civ 237; [2012] 1 W.L.R. 2626 (covenant to maintain all the roads on an estate including those over which the land charged has no right of way).

[487] The Rentcharges Act 1977 s.2(5). If a sum claimed is unreasonable, s.2(5) means that the rentcharge cannot be relied upon to collect the unreasonable sum. It does not mean that the rentcharge itself is void: *Canwell Estate Co v Smith Bros Farms Ltd* (above).

[488] *Johnson Security Ltd v Orchard Trading Estate Management* (above); *Canwell Estate Co v Smith Bros Farms Ltd* (above).

[489] See, e.g. Improvement of Land Act 1864.

[490] See *Hewlins v Shippam* (1826) 5 B. & C. 221 at 229.

[491] *Jackson v Lever* (1792) 3 Bro.C.C. 605; LPA 1925 s.53.

[492] See LPA(Am)A 1924 Sch.IX.

Words of limitation

15–110   If an existing rentcharge is being transferred by deed or will, the normal rule for corporeal hereditaments applies and the whole interest in the rentcharge passes without words of limitation unless a contrary intention is shown.[493] But if a rentcharge is being created by will or (perhaps) by deed, only a life interest will be created unless an intention is shown to create some larger interest.[494]

Rentcharges in respect of registered land

15–111   As the registered proprietor has the power to make a disposition of any sort permitted by the general law, he may grant a rentcharge or transfer the registered land subject to the reservation of a rentcharge[495]—provided of course that it is one of the types of rentcharge which survive the Rentcharges Act 1977. The grant of a rentcharge is a registrable disposition.[496] A legal rentcharge has its own title[497] and whoever is registered as proprietor of that title is in law the rent owner; the rentcharge is also noted against the title to the land charged.[498]

Apportionment

15–112   If part only of land charged by a rentcharge is sold, the basic rule is that each part remains charged with the whole rent; consequently the owner of each part is liable for the full amount. An agreement to apportion the rent may be made, but this only binds the rent owner if the rent owner is party to the agreement.[499] There is a procedure for the compulsory legal apportionment of a rentcharge, involving an application to the Secretary of State.[500]

MEANS OF ENFORCING PAYMENT

Rentcharge charged on land

15–113   There are four remedies available to the owner of a rentcharge charged on land if it is not paid. The first remedy, namely an action for the money arises at common law; the other three are created by statute,[501] and replace remedies formerly expressly conferred by most instruments creating rentcharges.

---

[493] Above, paras 2–017 et seq.
[494] See *Nichols v Hawkes* (1853) 10 Hare 342; *Grant v Edmondson* [1930] 2 Ch. 245 at 254; [1931] 1 Ch. 1; above.
[495] LRA 2002 ss.23–24.
[496] LRA 2002 s.27(2)(e).
[497] LRR 2002 r.2(2).
[498] LRA 2002 Sch.2 para.6.
[499] In which case it is known as "a legal apportionment". An agreement between the seller and purchaser of part of the land charged, and to which the rent owner is not party, is "an equitable apportionment".
[500] Rentcharges Act 1977 s.13(1).
[501] LPA 1925 s.121, replacing CA 1881 s.44.

Action for the money

A personal action for the rent will lie against the *terre tenant* (the freehold tenant of the land upon which the rent is charged) even if the rent was not created by him[502] and exceeds the value of the land.[503] If the land has been divided, the *terre tenant* of any part is liable for the full amount[504]; but a mere lessee for a term of years is not liable,[505] for the action lies only against the freeholder.   **15–114**

Although the right to sue and the liability to be sued run with the rentcharge and the land respectively, the benefit of an express covenant for payment does not run with the rentcharge without express assignment.[506] Thus if a rentcharge created by A in favour of X is conveyed to Y and the land to B, Y cannot sue A on his covenant for payment if B fails to pay.

Distress

If an express power of distress is given by the instrument creating the rentcharge, the extent of the right is a question of construction. If there is no such express power, and the rentcharge was created before 1882, the rentcharge owner can distrain upon the land as soon as the rent or any part of it is in arrear.[507] If the rentcharge was created after 1881, then, subject to any contrary intention, the rentcharge owner can distrain as soon as the rent or any part of it is 21 days in arrear.[508]   **15–115**

Entry into possession

If a rentcharge was created after 1881 and shows no contrary intention, the rentcharge owner may, when the rent or any part of it is 40 days in arrear, enter and take possession of the land without impeachment of waste and take the income until he has paid himself all rent due with costs.[509]   **15–116**

Demise to a trustee

If the rentcharge was created after 1881 and shows no contrary intention, the rentcharge owner may, if the rent or any part of it is 40 days in arrear, demise the land to a trustee for a term of years, with or without impeachment of waste, on trust to raise the money due, with all costs and expenses, by creating a mortgage, receiving the income or any other reasonable means.[510] If a rentcharge owner has only an equitable interest, he can grant only an equitable lease to the trustee, but the estate owner can be compelled to clothe the equitable lease with the legal estate.[511]   **15–117**

---

[502] *Thomas v Sylvester* (1873) L.R. 8 Q.B. 368.
[503] *Pertwee v Townsend* [1896] 2 Q.B. 129.
[504] *Christie v Barker* (1884) 53 L.J.Q.B. 537.
[505] *Re Herbage Rents* [1896] 2 Ch. 811.
[506] See *Grant v Edmondson* [1931] 1 Ch. 1, criticised (1931) 47 L.Q.R. 380 (W. Strachan).
[507] LTA 1730 s.5.
[508] LPA 1925 s.121(2).
[509] LPA 1925 s.121(3).
[510] LPA 1925 s.121(4).
[511] LPA 1925 ss.3(1), 8(2).

If the rentcharge was created before July 15, 1964 the last three statutory remedies were expressly excepted from the rule against perpetuities, together with similar express powers conferred by an instrument.[512] Other, wider, provisions were not considered to be excepted from the rule, for example a clause which is sometimes inserted entitling the rentcharge owner to effect a permanent forfeiture of the land if the rent is unpaid for a specified period.[513] If the rentcharge was created after July 15, 1964, but before April 6, 2010 the rule against perpetuities did not apply to any powers or remedies for enforcing it.[514] The rule against perpetuities does not apply to rentcharges created after April 5, 2010.

Rentcharge charged on another rentcharge

15–118   Instead of the statutory remedies of distress, entry into possession and demise to a trustee, the owner of a rentcharge charged upon another rentcharge may appoint a receiver if the rent or any part of it is 21 days in arrear.[515] The receiver has all the powers of a receiver appointed by a mortgagee.[516] Thus if Greenacre is charged with a rent of £100 per annum and that rentcharge is charged with a rent of £25 per annum in favour of X, a receiver of the £100 can be appointed by X if the £25 is unpaid for 21 days.

EXTINGUISHMENT OF RENTCHARGES

15–119   A rentcharge may be extinguished by release, statutory discharge, merger, limitation or the expiry of the 60-year period under the Rentcharges Act 1977.

Release

15–120   The owner of a rentcharge may by deed release the land from the rent, either wholly or in part. A partial release may take the form of releasing all the land from part of the rent,[517] or releasing part of the land from the whole of the rent.[518] An informal release may be valid in equity.

Statutory redemption

15–121   Land will be discharged from a rentcharge if the landowner obtains a "redemption certificate" from the Secretary of State for the Environment (or Wales) certifying that he has paid the owner of the rentcharge a sum representing the capital value as certified by the Secretary of State.[519]

---

[512] LPA 1925 s.121(6).
[513] See *Re Trustees of Hollis' Hospital and Hague's Contract* [1899] 2 Ch. 540, criticised in Challis R.P. 190.
[514] Perpetuities and Accumulations Act 1964 s.11, amending LPA 1925 s.121(6).
[515] LPA 1925 s.122(2), (3).
[516] LPA 1925 s.122(2); below, para.17–029.
[517] Co.Litt. 148a.
[518] LPA 1925 s.70.
[519] Rentcharges Act 1977, ss.8-10, replacing LPA 1925 s.191.

Merger

At common law, if a rentcharge became vested in the same person as the land upon which **15–122** it was charged, the rentcharge became extinguished by merger, even if this was not the intention.[520] For this to occur, both the rent and the land must have been vested in the same person at the same time and in the same right.[521] This automatic rule of the common law no longer applies, for, by the Law of Property Act 1925,[522] there is to be no merger at law except in cases where there would have been a merger in equity, and the equitable rule is that merger depends upon the intention of the parties.[523] Even if an intention that there should be no merger cannot be shown, there will be a presumption against merger if it is to the interest of the person concerned to prevent it.[524]

Limitation

If a rentcharge is not paid for 12 years and no sufficient acknowledgment of the owner's **15–123** title is made, it is extinguished under the Limitation Act 1980.[525]

Elapse of 60 years

With certain exceptions, every rentcharge will be extinguished, without compensation, **15–124** when 60 years have elapsed since it was first payable or since July 21, 1977 (i.e. on July 21, 2037), whichever is the later.[526] But this does not apply to variable rentcharges, nor to any rentcharge, whenever created, that is of the kind excluded from the prohibition against creation.[527]

Other types of incorporeal hereditament

Aside from easements, profits and rentcharges, there are further species of incorporeal **15–125** hereditament, but none of are of sufficient importance to the study of the law of real property to warrant more than a mention here:

   (i) Tithes and chancel repair liability: the liability of "lay rectors"—the current owners of certain former Church lands—to repair the chancel of the local church[528].
   (ii) Advowsons: the perpetual right of "presentation to an ecclesiastical living" i.e. (in simplified terms) the right to nominate the local priest.
   (iii) Annuities: payment of an annual sum not charged against land.
   (iv) Franchises: a royal privilege which is either perpetual or for a term of years, held by grant of the Crown. Many of these ancient franchises still exist, including the

---

[520] *Capital and Counties Bank Ltd v Rhodes* [1903] 1 Ch. 631 at 652.
[521] *Re Radcliffe* [1892] 1 Ch. 227.
[522] s.185, replacing JA 1873 s.25(4).
[523] *Ingle v Vaughan Jenkins* [1900] 2 Ch. 368.
[524] *Re Fletcher* [1917] 1 Ch. 339.
[525] See below, para.18–028.
[526] Rentcharges Act 1977 s.3(1).
[527] Rentcharges Act 1977 s.3(3), (4), (5); above, para.15–106.
[528] See *Aston Cantlow PCC v Wallbank* [2003] UKHL 37, [2004] 1 A.C. 546.

right to a market (which prohibits any rival market, including a car boot sale, within a certain radius), but also rights to fairs, rights of wreck, rights to treasure and to "free fishery".

SUMMARY OF KEY CASES

- *In re Ellenborough Park* [1956] Ch. 131
- *Graham v Philcox* [1984] Q.B. 747
- *Moncrieff v Jamieson* [2007] UKHL 42, [2007] 1 W.L.R. 2620

FURTHER READING

- Hill-Smith, "Rights of Parking and the Ouster Principle after *Batchelor v Marlow*" [2007] 71 Conv. 223
- Tee, "Metamorphoses and Section 62 of the Law of Property Act 1925" [1998] 62 Conv. 115
- Barnsley, "Equitable Easements—Sixty Years On" (1999) 115 L.Q.R. 89

Chapter 16

FREEHOLD COVENANTS

CHAPTER SUMMARY

Landlords are able to control use of land by means of covenants in the lease. Control of a freehold owner's use of land is less straightforward and understandably so; the law is reluctant to fetter the use of land in the hands of a freehold owner. This chapter deals with covenants over freehold titles and the difficulties in trying to make them endure in the face of successive owners.

The majority of freehold covenants are restrictive covenants. That is covenants which restrict the actual use to which land is put or development of it. The other type of covenant, positive covenants, impose an obligation on the owner of land to do something, usually to fence or contribute to the cost of maintenance of nearby land over which the owner has some rights.

As has been seen,[1] lawful covenants in a lease are enforceable as between landlord and tenant whether they are positive or negative. What must be considered in this chapter is the position where covenants are entered into between freehold owners of adjacent land. Thus if V conveys part of his land to P, and P enters into covenants with V relating to the rest of V's land, V can of course enforce those covenants against P. But if V then sells his remaining land to W, and P sells his land to Q, the position is more complex. Whether W can enforce P's covenants against Q depends on two different questions, namely:

    (i) whether the benefit of P's covenants has passed to W; and
    (ii) whether the burden of P's covenants has passed to Q.

Only if both questions are answered in the affirmative can the covenants be enforced: the claimant must be entitled to sue, and the defendant must be liable to be sued. If either of them is an original party to the covenant, then obviously only one of these questions will arise. If V had not conveyed the rest of his land to W, the question whether the benefit of the covenant had passed to him would not arise.

LAW AND EQUITY

In answering these questions, equity has partly followed the law and partly diverged sharply from it.

---

[1]   Above, Ch.14.

In broad terms, the *benefit* of a covenant, whether positive or negative, will run with land if it touches and concerns it, and has been annexed to it. This is the rule at law, and equity has followed the law, though with some relaxations and considerable complexity in the details.

The *burden* of the covenant is another matter. At law, the burden of the covenant would not pass with the land affected.[2] On the other hand, equity developed a doctrine known as the rule in *Tulk v Moxhay*[3] under which the burden of a covenant attached to the covenantor's land would run with it, provided the covenant was negative in nature and not positive. The law of covenants other than as between landlord and tenant thus came to be the equitable law of restrictive covenants. This law grew up soon after the outburst of building and increase of population associated with the Industrial Revolution. Restrictive covenants became analogous to negative equitable easements[4]; like them,[5] they are extinguished when there is unity of ownership and possession for both plots of land,[6] with one important exception.[7] Most easements (other than rights of light) entitle a landowner to do positive acts affecting neighbouring land; but restrictive covenants, like easements of light, prohibit certain acts on that land. Throughout the subject, two questions must always be asked:

(i) whether the claimant has the benefit of the covenant so that they are entitled to sue; and

(ii) whether the defendant is subject to the burden of the covenant so that they are liable to be sued.

These questions will be considered separately, first at law and then in equity. For completeness, the position of the original parties to the covenant will also be considered, although the covenant will, of course, be enforceable as between them as a matter of contract.

PART 1   BENEFIT

THE BENEFIT AT LAW

The original covenantee

16–001   A covenant taken for the benefit of land may of course be worded so as to apply only for so long as the covenantee himself owns the land. Where this is not the case, an original covenantee who has not assigned the benefit of the covenant can always enforce it against

---

[2] Though this rule can be mitigated by certain devices, see below, paras 16–014 et seq.

[3] (1848) 2 Ph. 774; below, para.16–025.

[4] See *Re Nisbet and Potts' Contract* [1906] 1 Ch. 386 at 409; *Kelly v Barrett* [1924] 2 Ch. 379 at 405; *Newton Abbot Co-operative Society Ltd v Williamson & Treadgold Ltd* [1952] Ch. 286 at 293.

[5] Above, para.15–068.

[6] *Re Tiltwood, Sussex* [1978] Ch. 269.

[7] Below, para.16–013.

the original covenantor, even if the covenantee has parted with the land for whose benefit the covenant was taken[8] (as in the case of easements, this land is generally described as the dominant tenement and the land intended to be burdened by the covenant is known as the servient tenement).

Anyone who is actually named as a party to the deed creating the covenant will be an original covenantee. By virtue of the Contracts (Rights of Third Parties) Act 1999, the covenant can now also be enforced by anyone for whose benefit a party named in the deed expressly contracted.[9] However, such a person is not converted into an original covenantee for the purposes of the transmission of the benefit to an assignee. More significant for the latter purpose is the fact that under s.56 of the Law of Property Act 1925[10] a person may now take a benefit under a deed even if he is not named as a party to it. For this to occur, the deed must purport to be made with the person in question,[11] and not merely to be made for his benefit.[12] Where A and B are the only parties to a deed, the difference is between A covenanting with B for the benefit of C, and A covenanting directly with C. In the former case C is within the Contracts (Rights of Third Parties) Act 1999. In the latter case C is within s.56.

The effect of s.56 is that, if V sells land to P and P binds his land by a covenant expressed to be with V and the owners for the time being of certain adjoining plots of land, these adjoining owners can sue on the covenant as original covenantees, even though they were not parties to the conveyance creating the covenant.[13] In such a case, the adjoining owners are clearly identifiable persons in existence at the time of the conveyance. However, even if the covenant is expressed to be made with the successors in title of those adjoining owners as well, those successors in title are not original covenantees, for at the date of the conveyance they are not ascertained or ascertainable.[14] Similarly, if a covenant is made expressly for the benefit of the present owner of a plot of land and his successors in title, the owner at the time of the conveyance is an original covenantee but future owners are not. They, like the successors in title to the adjoining owners, can enforce the covenant only under the rules relating to assignees.

Assignees

If V sells part of his land to P in fee simple and P enters into covenants binding the land which he buys, the benefit of P's covenant may run at law with V's fee simple estate in the land which he retains, so that a subsequent purchaser of V's land can enforce the covenant against P. It is immaterial whether the covenant is negative (not to do something) or positive (to do something). Thus the common law doctrine applies equally to a covenant not

16–002

---

[8]   See *LCC v Allen* [1914] 3 K.B. 642 at 664. Damages will be only nominal.
[9]   This has overtaken the controversy as to whether s.56 itself enables a third party to enforce a contract made for his benefit. See *Megarry & Wade: The Law of Real Property*, para.32–007 and *Amsprop Trading Ltd v Harris Distribution Ltd* [1997] 1 W.L.R. 1025.
[10] Replacing RPA 1845 s.5; see *Beswick v Beswick* [1968] A.C. 58 at 102–107.
[11] *White v Bijou Mansions Ltd* [1937] Ch. 610 at 625; [1938] Ch. 351 at 365; *Lyus v Prowsa Developments Ltd* [1982] 1 W.L.R. 1044 at 1049.
[12] See *Re Miller's Agreement* [1947] Ch. 615.
[13] *Dyson v Forster* [1909] A.C. 98. See also *Re Ecclesiastical Commissioners for England's Conveyance* [1936] Ch. 430 (where liability was equitable).
[14] *Westhoughton UDC v Wigan Coal and Iron Co Ltd* [1919] 1 Ch. 159 at 169, 170.

to build on the land purchased by P or a covenant to supply pure water to the land retained by V.[15] It is also immaterial that the covenant has nothing to do with P's land or, indeed, that the covenantor has no land.[16] For a covenant to be enforceable in this way, the following conditions must be satisfied.

The covenant must touch and concern land of the covenantee[17]

16–003 It is essential that the covenant should be made for the benefit of land owned by the covenantee (i.e. V in the above examples) at the time of the covenant. In general, the test for determining whether a covenant touches and concerns the land is similar to that which is applicable to covenants in a lease created before 1996.[18] Thus if in a lease a surety enters into a covenant with the landlord which touches and concerns the land, the benefit of the covenant will run with the reversion.[19]

Annexation of covenant

16–004 The benefit of the covenant must be annexed to a legal estate in the land of the covenantee. Where the covenant benefits the land, no formal words of annexation are needed.[20] But at law, it is not enough to show that the covenantee has an equitable interest in the land retained. It must be shown that the covenant was made for the benefit of some legal estate into whomsoever's hands it might come, and not for the mere personal advantage of the covenantee.[21]

Ownership of the land

16–005 An assignee who seeks to enforce a covenant made before 1926 must show that he has the legal estate to which the benefit of the covenant was attached.[22] But a covenant made after 1925 is deemed to be made with the covenantee and his successors in title, and the persons deriving title under him or them,[23] and so is enforceable by those claiming under the covenantee. Thus whether a mere tenant under a lease can enforce a covenant annexed to the legal fee simple depends on the date of the covenant. It is immaterial whether the person enforcing the covenant knew of its existence when he obtained the land[24]: what is annexed to the land passes with the land.

---

[15] See *Shayler v Woolf* [1946] 1 All E.R. 464 at 467 (affirmed [1946] 2 All E.R. 54).
[16] *Smith v River Douglas Catchment Board* [1949] 2 K.B. 500. See, e.g. *The Prior's Case*, Y.B. 42 Edw. 3, Hil., pl. 14 (1368) (covenant to sing).
[17] *Rogers v Hosegood* [1900] 2 Ch. 388.
[18] Above, paras 14–024 et seq.
[19] *P. & A. Swift Investments v Combined English Stores Group Plc* [1989] A.C. 632; *Coronation Street Industrial Properties Ltd v Ingall Industries Plc* [1989] 1 W.L.R. 304.
[20] See *Westhoughton UDC v Wigan Coal and Iron Co Ltd* [1919] 1 Ch. 159 at 170.
[21] *Rogers v Hosegood* [1900] 2 Ch. 388.
[22] *Westhoughton UDC v Wigan Coal and Iron Co Ltd* [1919] 1 Ch. 159.
[23] LPA 1925 s.78.
[24] *Rogers v Hosegood* [1900] 2 Ch. 388.

THE BENEFIT IN EQUITY

As mentioned above,[25] the rules in equity for the passing of the benefit of a covenant are similar to those at law. Yet although they are rather less strict, they are considerably more complicated.[26]

16–006

The original covenantee

The position of the original covenantee in equity is similar to that at law. In particular, s.56 of the Law of Property Act 1925 applies.[27] However, if the original covenantee parts with the land for the benefit of which it was taken, equity will not enforce it against the covenantor's successor in title, since enforcement would no longer be for the protection of land.[28]

16–007

Assignees

For anyone except an original covenantee to be entitled to enforce a covenant in equity he must show, first, that the covenant touches and concerns land, and, secondly, that the benefit of the covenant has passed to him.

16–008

Touching and concerning land

The covenant must touch and concern land of the covenantee. Equity follows the law, and the legal rules apply.[29] By analogy with easements,[30] it may be said that the covenant must accommodate the dominant tenement.

16–009

Entitled to benefit of covenant

The claimant must establish that he is entitled to the benefit of the covenant. He may do this by showing either:

16–010

    (i)   that the benefit of the covenant has been annexed to land and that he owns some interest in that land; or

   (ii)   that the benefit of the covenant has been assigned to him and that he owns some interest in the land for the benefit of which the covenant was made; or

  (iii)   that there is a building scheme or other scheme of development.

---

[25] Above, para.16–001.

[26] For a general survey, see (1938) 6 C.L.J. 339 (S.J. Bailey); and see (1971) 87 L.Q.R. 539 (D.J. Hayton); [1972B] C.L.J. 157 (H.W.R. Wade).

[27] Above, para.16–001.

[28] *Chambers v Randall* [1923] 1 Ch. 149 at 157, 158.

[29] *Re Union of London and Smith's Bank Ltd's Conveyance* [1933] Ch. 611.

[30] See above, para.15–004.

Annexation to land

16–011   The rules developed by equity have two requirements: first, that the benefit of the covenant has been annexed to land, and, secondly, that the claimant owns some interest in that land. Equity's rules for annexation have now been supplemented by statute.

Annexation in equity: A landowner who obtains a covenant from another landowner may do so merely for his own personal advantage, or he may do so for the benefit of his land, enjoying the advantage so long as the land is his. Covenants of the first kind will not automatically run with the covenantee's land, but those of the second type normally will. The question is whether the covenant sufficiently indicates the land with which the benefit is to run, and also whether it shows that it is made either for the benefit of that land or else with the covenantee in his capacity of owner of it.[31] A covenant with the vendors "their heirs, executors, administrators, and assigns" will not suffice, for it indicates no land.[32] A classic formulation is "with intent that the covenant may enure to the benefit of the vendors their successors and assigns and others claiming under them to all or any of their lands adjoining or near to" the land conveyed.[33] Where the precise land is not identified, it may be ascertained by extrinsic evidence.[34] Express words of annexation are desirable, but they are not required if from the words of the covenant and the surrounding circumstances it appears that annexation was intended.[35]

Annexation by statute: By s.78 of the Law of Property Act 1925 ("section 78"),[36] a covenant made after 1925 "relating to any land of the covenantee shall be deemed to be made with the covenantee and his successors in title and the persons deriving title under him or them, and shall have effect as if such successors and other persons were expressed". For restrictive covenants, the words "successors in title" include the owners and occupiers for the time being of the covenantee's land intended to be benefited.[37] This provision, and in particular the phrase "successors in title", is plainly apt to show that the covenant is intended to be for the benefit of the covenantee's land rather than himself personally, and so is to be annexed to the land. Yet for over 50 years s.78 remained in obscurity until in 1979 the *Federated Homes* case[38] gave it full effect. For covenants made after 1925 it is no longer necessary to show from other sources that it was intended to annex the benefit of the covenant to the covenantee's land: instead, it will be automatically annexed by virtue of s.78 unless a contrary intention appears, as where the benefit is expressly made transmissible only by express assignment.[39] Though much criticised,[40] the decision seems sound; and it is plainly convenient. As at law, the benefit of a covenant duly annexed to identifiable[41] land

---

[31] See *Drake v Gray* [1936] Ch. 451 at 466.
[32] *Renals v Cowlishaw* (1878) 9 Ch.D. 125; affirmed (1879) 11 Ch.D. 866.
[33] See *Rogers v Hosegood* [1900] 2 Ch. 388 at 389.
[34] See [1972B] C.L.J. 157 at 166–168 (H.W.R. Wade).
[35] *Shropshire CC v Edwards* (1983) 46 P. & C.R. 270; *J. Sainsbury Plc v Enfield L.B.* [1989] 1 W.L.R. 590.
[36] Replacing CA 1881 s.58, where the wording was different.
[37] LPA 1925 s.78(1).
[38] *Federated Homes Ltd v Mill Lodge Properties Ltd* [1980] 1 W.L.R. 594.
[39] *Roake v Chadha* [1984] 1 W.L.R. 40.
[40] See (1980) 43 M.L.R. 445 (D.J. Hayton); (1981) 97 L.Q.R. 32 (G.H. Newsom); [1982] Legal Studies 53 (D.J. Hurst).
[41] The land must be identifiable either by express reference or by necessary implication from

passes to successors in title even if they know nothing of it; and the successors in title take only by succession and not as original covenantees.[42]

It is improbable that the benefit of a covenant not annexed to land could pass under s.62 of the Law of Property Act 1925 ("section 62"),[43] for it is difficult to see how it could be a right "appertaining or reputed to appertain" to land.[44]

Area: The benefit of a covenant is annexed to each part of the covenantee's land, so that it will pass with parts of that land,[45] but indications to the contrary are readily found.[46] Even if a covenant is made for the benefit of an area of land too great to be reasonably benefited, the benefit will be annexed to it, if the covenant is expressed to be for the benefit of the land "or any part" of it.[47]

Ownership of land: In addition to showing that the benefit of the covenant has been annexed to land, the claimant must establish that he owns some interest in that land. He need not show that he has succeeded to the covenantee's estate in the land, nor that he has the whole of it.[48]

Assignment with land

Express assignment: Where the benefit of a covenant has not been annexed to land, it can nevertheless be expressly assigned.[49] Such an assignment, like other assignments of rights under a contract, enables the assignee to enforce the covenant against the original covenantor. But successors in title to the covenantor are liable only in equity under the rule in *Tulk v Moxhay*,[50] and equity will permit an assignee of the covenantee to enforce the covenant only if the benefit of it has been assigned to him together with some or all of the land protected by it. That land must be properly identified, if not from the wording of the deed,[51] then from the surrounding circumstances.[52]   **16–012**

Time of assignment: The assignment must, it seems, be made at the time of the conveyance of the land which is to be protected.[53] An express assignment is not required if the circumstances show that the benefit of the covenant was intended to be included

---

the actual conveyance, see *Crest Nicholson Residential (South) Ltd v McAlister* [2004] EWCA Civ 410.

[42] Above, para.16–001.
[43] Considered above, para.15–032.
[44] See *Roake v Chadha* [1984] 1 W.L.R. 40 at 47.
[45] *Federated Homes Ltd v Mill Lodge Properties Ltd* [1980] 1 W.L.R. 59; although prior to this case the opposite was considered true so that it was only annexed to the whole of the land, see *Re Union of London and Smith's Bank Ltd's Conveyance* [1933] Ch. 611 at 628; *Re Jeff's Transfer (No.2)* [1966] 1 W.L.R. 841.
[46] *Drake v Gray* [1936] Ch. 451; *Re Selwyn's Conveyance* [1967] Ch. 674.
[47] *Marquess of Zetland v Driver* [1939] Ch. 1.
[48] *Formby v Barker* [1903] 2 Ch. 539.
[49] *Re Union of London and Smith's Bank Ltd's Conveyance* [1933] Ch. 611.
[50] (1848) 2 Ph. 744.
[51] *Re Union of London and Smith's Bank Ltd's Conveyance* [1933] Ch. 611 at 625, 631.
[52] *Newton Abbot Co-operative Society Ltd v Williamson & Treadgold Ltd* [1952] Ch. 286; *Marten v Flight Refuelling Ltd* [1962] Ch. 115.
[53] *Chambers v Randall* [1923] 1 Ch. 149.

in the sale.[54] But once the land has been sold, the benefit of the covenant cannot be assigned: one purpose of the covenant is to make the covenantee's land more readily saleable, and if he has succeeded in disposing of the whole of his land without assigning the benefit of the covenant, it ceases to be assignable.[55] If only part of his land has been disposed of, he can assign the benefit of the covenant when he sells any of the parts still retained, but he cannot assign it to those who have already purchased parts of the land.[56]

Subsequent assignment: The assignment need not necessarily be made by the original covenantee. If, for example, the original covenantee dies, both the covenant and the land that it benefits will devolve on his personal representatives, who may hold it as bare trustees for a devisee under the covenantee's will or for some other successor to the land. As owner in equity, the successor can sue on the covenant without joining the personal representatives,[57] and can assign it to a purchaser.[58] Subsequent owners of the land have been held to be entitled only if there is a complete chain of assignments of the benefit of the covenant to them[59]; but the better view is that the first assignment of the benefit together with the land operates as a "delayed annexation" of the benefit, so that it will thereafter run with the land without further assignment.[60]

16–013   Schemes of development

Mutual enforceability: Where land has been laid out in lots which are to be sold to purchasers and built upon, restrictions are often imposed on the purchasers of each lot for the benefit of the estate generally, such as covenants restraining trading on the estate, prohibiting the erection of cheap buildings and the like. In the ordinary way, these covenants would be enforceable only by the vendor. But much of the purpose of the covenants given by a purchaser of one lot would be lost if they could not be enforced:

   (i)   by those who have previously bought lots; and
   (ii) by those who subsequently buy the unsold lots.

Each of these results could be achieved without any special rules for schemes of development. The first would be achieved if the purchaser's covenants were expressly made with those who had previously bought lots as well as with the vendor. The second could be achieved by the covenant being expressed to be for the benefit of the whole or any part of the land retained by the vendor, and so attaching the benefit of them to each lot sold in the future, or by the vendor expressly assigning the benefit of the covenants with each lot sold.[61]

---

[54] *Renals v Cowlishaw* (1878) 9 Ch.D. 125 at 129.
[55] *Re Rutherford's Conveyance* [1938] Ch. 396.
[56] *Re Union of London and Smith's Bank Ltd's Conveyance* [1933] Ch. 611 at 632.
[57] *Earl of Leicester v Wells-next-the-Sea UDC* [1973] Ch. 110.
[58] *Newton Abbot Co-operative Society Ltd v Williamson & Treadgold Ltd* [1952] Ch. 286.
[59] *Re Pinewood Estate, Farnborough* [1958] Ch. 280.
[60] See (1968) 84 L.Q.R. 22 at 31, 32 (P.V. Baker).
[61] See above, para.16–006.

Principle of schemes: It is, however, unnecessary for these arrangements to be made. There is a wide principle that where an owner of a defined[62] area of land deals with it on the footing of imposing restrictive obligations on the use of various parts of it as and when he sells them off, for the common benefit of himself (insofar as he retains any land) and of the various purchasers *inter se*, and the purchasers buy on this footing, then the common intention gives rise to an independent equity which binds each owner (including the vendor) as soon as the first part is sold[63]; at that point, the scheme crystallises.[64] This common intention may appear either expressly from the terms of a deed of mutual covenant[65] or of a series of conveyances, or else impliedly from extrinsic evidence which satisfies the conditions for a building scheme.[66] "Building schemes", though important, are but a species of the genus of "scheme of development".[67]

Building schemes: The conditions of a building scheme were for most part laid down in *Elliston v Reacher*.[68] These are as follows:

(i) the claimant and the defendant must each have derived title from a common vendor or a successor in title who is bound in equity by the obligations of the common vendor[69];

(ii) previously to the sale of the claimant's and defendant's plots, the common vendor must have laid out or intended to lay out the estate in lots subject to restrictions which were intended to be imposed on all of them and were consistent only with some general scheme of development;

(iii) the common vendor must have intended the restrictions to be for the benefit not merely of himself but of all lots sold[70];

(iv) the claimant's and the defendant's plots must both have been bought from the common vendor on the footing that the restrictions were to be for the benefit of the other lots; and

(v) the area to which the scheme extends must be clearly defined.[71]

The whole essence of a building scheme is that each purchaser should know when he buys his plot from the common vendor that the covenants given by him are to be enforceable by the owners of all the other lots.[72] It is not necessary to prove an express undertaking by

---

[62] *Lund v Taylor* (1975) 31 P. & C.R. 167.

[63] *Baxter v Four Oaks Properties Ltd* [1965] Ch. 816 at 825; *Re Dolphin's Conveyance* [1970] Ch. 654; *Brunner v Greenslade* [1971] Ch. 993 at 1003–1005, stating the principles.

[64] *Brunner v Greenslade* [1971] Ch. 993 at 1003.

[65] *Baxter v Four Oaks Properties Ltd* [1965] Ch. 816.

[66] See *Re Dolphin's Conveyance* [1970] Ch. 654 at 662, 663; (1971) 87 L.Q.R. 539 at 546-551 (D.J. Hayton).

[67] See *Brunner v Greenslade* [1971] Ch. 993 at 999.

[68] [1908] 2 Ch. 374 at 384; affirmed [1908] 2 Ch. 665. The first real hint of the doctrine was in *Western v MacDermott* (1866) L.R. 1 Eq. 499; but see *Re Pinewood Estate, Farnborough* [1958] Ch. 280 at 286, 287.

[69] *Re Dolphin's Conveyance* [1970] Ch. 654.

[70] Which may be hard to prove: see, e.g. *Tucker v Vowles* [1893] 1 Ch. 195.

[71] This last condition was added by *Reid v Bickerstaff* [1909] 2 Ch. 305: see *Kelly v Barrett* [1924] 2 Ch. 379 at 401.

[72] See *Jamaica Mutual Life Assurance Society v Hillsborough Ltd* [1989] 1 W.L.R. 1101.

him that this should be so, provided the circumstances show that he must have realised it. If before his purchase he saw some plan of the estate with the restrictions endorsed thereon, as in *Elliston v Reacher*, this suffices; but the absence of a proper plan may be fatal.[73] A scheme establishes a "local law" for a defined area, and the landowners within it have both community of interest and reciprocity of obligation.[74] The reservation by the common vendor of a power to release all or part of the land from the restrictions does not negative a building scheme, nor is it essential that the restrictions imposed on each plot should be identical: it suffices if there is some general scheme of development.[75]

Sub-schemes: Where a lot has been divided into sub-lots, the scheme may be enforceable by and between the purchasers of the sub-lots.[76] Furthermore, one result of the "local law" established by a scheme is that where two or more lots come into the same hands, the covenants are not pro tanto extinguished but become enforceable between the owners of the lots if and when they are again separated.[77]

Buildings already erected: If a fully-built upon estate is disposed of in sections, and conditions analogous to those laid down for building schemes are satisfied, the covenants will be enforceable as in building schemes.[78] Again, the principle of a building scheme has been applied to a block of residential flats, preventing the landlord from letting or using any of them otherwise than for residential purposes[79]; but the court will be slow to infer a letting scheme from the mere similarity of the covenants when each floor of a large house is sub-let separately.[80]

PART 2   BURDEN

THE BURDEN AT LAW

The rule

16–014   As already mentioned,[81] the rule at law is that the burden of a covenant will not pass with freehold land.[82] Despite the inconvenient consequences of this rule, which contrasts both with the rule for leaseholds, where the benefit and burden of covenants run at law with the lease and the reversion,[83] and with the rule in equity, where the burden of restrictive

---

[73] e.g. *Osborne v Bradley* [1903] 2 Ch. 446; *Harlow v Hartog* (1977) 245 E.G. 140.
[74] *Reid v Bickerstaff* [1909] 2 Ch. 305 at 319, 323.
[75] *Pearce v Maryon-Wilson* [1935] Ch. 188; *Reid v Bickerstaff* [1909] 2 Ch. 305 at 319.
[76] *Brunner v Greenslade* [1971] Ch. 993.
[77] *Texaco Antilles Ltd v Kernochan* [1973] A.C. 609. Contrast other restrictive covenants: above.
[78] *Torbay Hotel Ltd v Jenkins* [1927] 2 Ch. 225 at 241.
[79] See *Hudson v Cripps* [1896] 1 Ch. 265.
[80] *Kelly v Battershell* [1949] 2 All E.R. 830.
[81] Above, see the introduction to this chapter.
[82] *Austerberry v Corp of Oldham* (1885) 29 Ch.D. 750 at 781–785; *E. & G.C. Ltd v Bate* (1935) 79 L.J. News. 203; *Cator v Newton* [1940] 1 K.B. 415 (registered land).
[83] Above, Ch.14.

covenants can run with freehold land,[84] it has been confirmed by the House of Lords.[85] Its rationale has been stated to be that:

> "equity cannot compel a owner to comply with a positive covenant entered into by his predecessors in title without flatly contradicting the common law rule that a person cannot be made liable upon a contract unless he is a party to it."[86]

Nevertheless, there are certain means whereby what cannot be achieved directly can be accomplished indirectly. There are five heads.

Chain of covenants

If V sells land to P, and P covenants, for example, to erect and maintain a fence, P will remain liable to V on the covenant by virtue of privity of contract even if P sells the land to Q. P will accordingly protect himself by extracting from Q a covenant of indemnity against future breaches of the covenant to fence. If Q then fails to maintain the fence, V cannot sue Q, but he can sue P, and P can then sue Q on the covenant for indemnity. In theory, liability can be maintained indefinitely in this way; but with each sale of the land the chain of covenants of indemnity becomes longer, and more liable to be broken by the insolvency or disappearance of one of the parties to it. This indirect enforcement of covenants by means of indemnities is thus an imperfect substitute for the direct enforcement which the common law refuses to allow.   **16–015**

Right of entry annexed to rentcharge

A right of entry annexed "for any purpose" to a legal rentcharge is a legal interest in the land.[87] A rentcharge may include covenants to build, repair, and so on which are ancillary to an obligation to pay what may be only a nominal sum. It is possible, therefore, to secure the performance of those covenants by reserving a rentcharge and annexing to it a right of entry, allowing the proprietor to enter and make good any default in the observance of the covenants, and to charge the cost to the owner in possession.[88] The efficacy of such a scheme is judicially untested but was recognised by the Rentcharges Act 1977. That Act [89] places some limitation on the creation of rentcharges, but specifically excepts those created for the purpose of making covenants enforceable in this way.   **16–016**

Right of re-entry in gross

It has been said to be "indisputable" that a vendor of a freehold can reserve a right of re-entry in order to enforce positive covenants made by his purchaser.[90] Such a right will take   **16–017**

---

[84] Below, para.16–022.
[85] *Rhone v Stephens* [1994] 2 A.C. 310.
[86] *Rhone v Stephens* [1994] 2 A.C. 310 at 318 per Lord Templeman.
[87] Above, para.4–020.
[88] See Law Com. No.68 (1975), para.49.
[89] s.2(3)(b), (4); see above, para.15–097.
[90] *Shiloh Spinners v Harding* [1973] A.C. 691 at 717 per Lord Wilberforce (the decision actually concerned an assignment by a lessee).

effect as an equitable rather than a legal right of entry.[91] Given the possibility of using estate rentcharges, rights of re-entry in gross only need to be used in the case of covenants whose performance does not relate in any way to the land in question and thus fall outside the class of rentcharges permitted by the Rentcharges Act 1977.

Enlarged long lease

16–018   A more effective but artificial method is to insert the covenant in a lease which can be enlarged into a fee simple pursuant to s.153 of the Law of Property Act 1925, and then to enlarge the lease.[92]

Conditional benefit

16–019   A man who claims the benefit of a conveyance or other deed must submit to its burdens. Thus if a conveyance of land on a housing estate gives the purchaser the right to use the estate roads but imposes on him a liability to contribute to the cost of their upkeep, a successor in title cannot use the roads without paying the contributions.[93] Similarly, it has been held that a right of way granted in exchange for not objecting to a minor trespass by the grantor's foundations could not be withdrawn unless the trespass was remedied.[94] The liability is thus not absolute but conditional; he who does not enjoy need not submit although often there will be little choice.

The principle was subsequently extended to a case in which grants of mining rights were made to a company in return for covenants to replant the land. The company's successors in title were held liable on the covenants as having taken the benefit of the grants of mining rights.[95] However, the "pure principle of benefit and burden" (as distinct from conditional benefit and burden) distilled from this case, which would have left little of the common law rule against the burden of covenants running with land intact,[96] has since been rejected by the House of Lords, who have restricted the doctrine to cases where the condition is "relevant to the exercise of the right".[97] The party in question must, "at least in theory", be able to choose between enjoying his right with the consequential duty to perform his obligation and renouncing his right with the consequential release from that duty.[98] Consequently, the fact that A's roof was supported by B's property did not entitle B to enforce a positive covenant to repair the roof made by A's predecessor in title. Quite where that leaves the person granted the right of way is unclear; could he really compel the grantor to remove his foundations by surrendering his right of way?

---

[91]   LPA 1925 s.1(2)(e). In the case of registered land, this will require protection on the Land Register.
[92]   See above, para.12–023; *Re M'Naul's Estate* [1902] 1 I.R. 114; (1958) 22 Conv (n.s.) 101 (T.P.D. Taylor).
[93]   *Halsall v Brizell* [1957] Ch. 169.
[94]   *E.R. Ives Investment Ltd v High* [1967] 2 Q.B. 379.
[95]   *Tito v Waddell (No.2)* [1977] Ch. 106 at 289–311 (the "Ocean Island" case).
[96]   See the seventh edition of this work at p.419.
[97]   *Rhone v Stephens* [1994] 2 A.C. 310 at 322 per Lord Templeman; see *Elwood v Goodman* [2013] EWCA Civ 1103, N.P. Gravells (1994) 110 L.Q.R. 346, J. Snape [1994] Conv. 477.
[98]   *Rhone v Stephens* [1994] 2 A.C. 310 at 322 see also *Thamesmead Town Ltd v Allotey* [1998] 3 E.G.L.R. 97 and *Wilkinson v Kerdene Ltd* [2013] EWCA Civ 44.

Summary of the position at law

Enforcement

It will be observed that only within narrow limits does the common law enforce covenants **16–020** outside the confines of privity of contract or the leasehold context. As will be seen shortly, equity became far more flexible and would enforce covenants in many cases where the common law would not.

This does not, however, render the rules at law obsolete, for if a covenant is enforceable at law, the claimant, on proving his case, is entitled as of right to a judgment for damages (even though they may be nominal), whereas if a covenant is enforceable only in equity the court has a discretion in deciding whether to give any remedy at all. However, since the equitable remedy of an injunction is the one usually desired, this point is not of great practical importance. Yet it should be remembered that at law it is quite immaterial whether the covenantor has any land or whether the covenant is negative or positive, and that in the case of a positive covenant, damages will usually be the most suitable remedy.

Reform

The present rule against the burden of covenants running with the land at law still creates **16–021** many problems. The methods of indirect enforcement of such covenants, considered above,[99] are not entirely satisfactory, and although the burden of covenants will run with land in equity if they are negative, the burden of positive covenants will not. It is now clear that the situation cannot be remedied without legislation.[100] A number of proposals have been made from time to time for enabling the burden of positive covenants to run with land.[101] The only one which has so far been enacted is of relatively limited scope, namely for the introduction of a new tenure called "commonhold".[102] Another,[103] for the introduction of "land obligations", is understood to be still under active consideration.[104]

Commonhold: Commonhold is a wholly new freehold tenure created by the Commonhold and Leasehold Reform Act 2002.[105] It is not a new estate, but a form of land holding of a freehold estate. Since its introduction in September 2004, it has failed to spark the interest of those involved with the development of land and the creation of interests. In the first five years of its creation, there were only 12 commonhold developments (totalling 97 residential units) compared to the many hundreds of thousands of leasehold interests that were created in the same period. The description which follows is no more than an outline; much of the detail of how this new tenure will work is contained in statutory instruments.[106]

---

[99] Above, para.16–014.

[100] *Rhone v Stephens* [1994] 2 A.C. 310 at 321 per Lord Templeman.

[101] See Law Com. No.11 (1967); Law Com. No.127 (1984); (1987) Cmnd. 179 & (1990) Cmnd. 1345 (the Aldridge Committee).

[102] Commonhold and Leasehold Reform Act 2002.

[103] Law Com. No 127 (1984).

[104] *Megarry & Wade: The Law of Real Property*, para.32–093.

[105] See N. Roberts [2002] N.L.J. 338.

[106] See Commonhold Regulations 2004 (2009/2363) (as amended) and the Commonhold (Land Registration) Rules 2004 (2004/1830).

Commonhold can be created in respect of registered land held for an estate in fee simple[107] and that land has to have contact with the ground[108] (so there is no possibility of "flying commonholds" with ground floor shops excluded). It creates a means of providing for freehold ownership of buildings such as blocks of flats which are horizontally divided with individuals owning different units on one or more floors. The owner of each unit has a freehold registered title,[109] subject to the provisions of the "commonhold community statement",[110] a document which will have to be in a prescribed form,[111] although there is no requirement for standard wording. This regulates the maintenance and user of the common parts and specifies the percentage of the annual "commonhold assessment",[112] a term which replaces, what in the case of units owned under long leases, is known as the service charge, payable by each unit-holder. It is this document that ensures that the burden of what is, in effect, positive covenants will run.[113]

Each owner of a "commonhold unit" is automatically be a member of the "commonhold association",[114] a company limited by guarantee whose Memorandum and Articles of Association is in prescribed form.[115] The commonhold association owns the common parts[116] and sets the annual "commonhold assessment".[117] This will assess each year the funds necessary for, at the very least, the repair and insurance of the common parts. In practice, at least in the cases of blocks of flats, it is likely that the commonhold assessment will also provide the funds for the repair and insurance of the foundations, the main structure, the roof and the maintenance of them and of the common parts.

The directors of the commonhold association[118] are able to recover payments due from unit-holders through the courts and both they and other unit holders are able to restrain and recover compensation for other breaches of the commonhold community statement.[119] However, there is no possibility of forfeiture of a unit, no matter how blatant the breach.[120] Although court proceedings in respect of arrears may ultimately lead to the imposition of a charging order on the unit in question, that charge will not enjoy priority over pre-existing mortgages. (This contrasts starkly with the situation under leasehold system, where the inevitable existence of a right of re-entry and forfeiture in each lease enables the landlord to demand payment of arrears of service charges from mortgagees as a condition of not forfeiting, thus giving the arrears priority over the mortgage debts.) However, the directors of the community association are not obliged to take proceedings if they reasonably think that inaction is the best course to follow and they must have regard to the desirability of using alternative dispute resolution.[121]

---

[107] Commonhold and Leasehold Reform Act 2002 (CLRA 2002) s.1.
[108] CLRA 2002 s.4, Sch.2 para.1.
[109] CLRA 2002 s.9(3)(b), (c).
[110] CLRA 2002 s.9(3)(e).
[111] CLRA 2002 ss.31–33.
[112] CLRA 2002 s.38.
[113] CLRA 2002 s.31(3)(b).
[114] CLRA 2002 ss.34–46.
[115] CLRA 2002 s.34(2) Sch.3, Pt I.
[116] CLRA 2002 s.9(3)(a).
[117] CLRA 2002 s.38.
[118] CLRA 2002 s.35.
[119] CLRA 2002 s.37.
[120] CLRA 2002 s.31(8).
[121] CLRA 2002 s.38.

Unit-holders have an absolute right to transfer their units and will cease to be liable to the commonhold association for payments due in respect of any period after the transfer.[122] Nor can the creation of interests in the whole or part of a unit or of charges over the whole of a unit be prohibited.[123] However, it is not possible to create interests other than leases in the whole or part of a commonhold unit unless at least 75 per cent of the members of the community association consent.[124] Further, the type of leases which can be granted will be restricted in order to prevent the reintroduction of the problems which commonhold was intended to resolve.[125]

Save in the relatively unlikely case where leaseholders do unanimously agree to convert, the decision as to whether or not to utilise commonhold will be entirely that of the developer.

Where a developer does decide to use commonhold, they must apply to the relevant Land Registrar for the registration of a freehold estate in land as a freehold estate in commonhold land[126]; the certificate of incorporation, memorandum and articles of association of the commonhold association and the commonhold community statement must accompany the application.[127] The commonhold may initially be registered without unit holders in which case the developer will retain control of the commonhold until the first person other than the developer becomes entitled to be registered as a unit-holder.[128] At that point the commonhold association will become entitled to be registered as proprietor of the common parts and the commonhold community statement will come into effect.[129] However, no unit-holder will become registered until a full list of the commonhold units is provided giving details of the proposed initial unit-holders.[130] (In practice it is likely that this list will accompany the initial application, in which case the commonhold association will immediately be registered as proprietor of the common parts and the commonhold community statement will immediately come into effect.[131])

Provision is also made for the termination of commonhold in the event of a decision to this effect by a solvent community association,[132] in the event that the commonhold association becomes insolvent,[133] and in the event of compulsory purchase.[134] It will also be necessary to dissolve a community association in the event that the unit-holders wish to sell their commonholds for redevelopment.

Land obligations: Under the scheme of "land obligations" proposed by the Law Commission,[135] a new interest in land, which could be legal, would be created similar to an easement and, like an easement, requiring both a dominant and a servient tenement.

---

[122] CLRA 2002 s.16.

[123] CLRA 2002 s.20(1).

[124] CLRA 2002 s.20((3), (4).

[125] CLRA 2002 ss.17, 18.

[126] CLRA 2002 s.2.

[127] CLRA 2002 Sch.1.

[128] CLRA 2002 s.7(1), (2).

[129] CLRA 2002 s.7(3).

[130] CLRA 2002 s.9(2).

[131] CLRA 2002 s.9(3).

[132] CLRA 2002 ss.43–48.

[133] CLRA 2002 ss.50–54.

[134] CLRA 2002 s.60.

[135] (2011) Law Com No.327, Making Land Work: Easements Covenants and Profits á Prendre: (1984) Law Com. No.127, as modified by (1990) Cmnd. 1345, para.3.49. See *Megarry & Wade: The Law of Real Property*, pp.1010–1011.

It would cover both negative obligations and three specific positive obligations and the burden of both would run with the land. The present rules for the running of the benefit of positive covenants would be abolished other than the rules governing conditional benefit. However, their benefit could nevertheless be expressly assigned and this would clearly be necessary in the case of covenants which fell outside the scheme because there was no servient tenement.[136] The three specific positive obligations would be:

(i)   the carrying out on either the servient or the dominant tenement of works which would benefit the dominant tenement or any part of it;

(ii) the provision of services for the benefit of the dominant tenement or any part of it; and

(iii) the reimbursement of expenditure incurred in performing either of the obligations already set out.

THE BURDEN IN EQUITY

Liability general

16–022   It has been seen[137] that the rules in equity as to the benefit of a covenant are in the main merely a more relaxed and detailed version of the rules at law. As to the burden of the covenant, however, the rules in equity came to be completely different. Until *Tulk v Moxhay*[138] was decided in 1848 (a time when the full effects of the vast expansion in industrial and building activities were being felt), equity had gone no further than the common law.[139] In that case it was decided that a covenant to maintain the garden in the centre of Leicester Square in London uncovered with any buildings would be enforced by injunction against a purchaser of the land who had bought with notice of the covenant.

For some while the question was thought to be solely one of notice: a person who took land with notice that it had been bound by some restriction could not disregard that restriction. On this footing, it was immaterial whether the restriction had been imposed to benefit other land or merely the covenantee personally: it sufficed that there was some contractual restriction on the use of the land and that the land had been acquired with notice of it.[140] But since 1882[141] it has been accepted that equity will enforce a restrictive covenant against a purchaser only if it was made for the protection of some other land. Restrictive covenants came to resemble easements as being rights over one plot of land ("the servient tenement") existing for the benefit of another plot of land ("the dominant tenement"). In short, at a leap, the law of restrictive covenants passed from the sphere of contract to the sphere of property.

---

[136] As in *Smith v River Douglas Catchment Board* [1949] 2 K.B. 500.
[137] Above, para.16–066.
[138] (1848) 2 Ph. 774.
[139] Despite *Whatman v Gibson* (1838) 9 Sim. 196, the question was regarded as still being open in *Bristow v Wood* (1844) 1 Coll.C.C. 480.
[140] See *Luker v Dennis* (1877) 7 Ch.D. 227.
[141] See *London & South Western Ry v Gomm* (1882) 20 Ch.D. 562 at 583.

Liability the original covenantor

The original covenantor usually remains liable on the covenant, even if he has parted with the servient tenement, for the common form of covenant extends to the acts of persons claiming under him[142]; but today, words limiting the ambit of the covenant to the period of his ownership of the servient tenement are often inserted.[143]

16–023

Liability assignees

An assignee of land of the original covenantor is bound by the covenant only if three conditions are fulfilled.

16–024

The covenant must be negative in nature

After a few cases in which the court was prepared to enforce positive covenants, the rule was settled in 1881 that none except negative covenants would be enforced by equity.[144] The question is whether in substance[145] the covenant is negative in nature: it is immaterial whether the wording is positive or negative. Thus the covenant in *Tulk v Moxhay*[146] itself was positive in wording, but part of it was negative in nature (to keep the land in Leicester Square "in an open state, uncovered with any buildings"), so that this part merely bound the covenantor to refrain from building, without requiring him to do any positive act.

16–025

   The test is generally whether the covenant requires expenditure of money for its proper performance; if the covenant requires the covenantee to put his hand in his pocket, it is not negative in nature.[147] A covenant to give the first refusal of a plot of land is negative in nature, for in effect it is a covenant not to sell to anyone else until the covenantee has had an opportunity of buying. But a covenant "not to let the premises get into disrepair", despite its apparently negative form, is in substance positive, for it can be performed only by the expenditure of money on repairs. Among the restrictive covenants most frequently met with in practice are covenants against building on land, against carrying on any trade or business (or certain specified trades or businesses[148]) on the premises concerned, and against using residential property for any purpose other than that of a single private dwelling-house.

---

[142] *LCC v Allen* [1914] 3 K.B. 642 at 660, 673; and see LPA 1925 s.79(1).

[143] See *Morrells of Oxford Ltd v Oxford United Football Club Ltd* [2001] Ch. 459.

[144] *Haywood v Brunswick Permanent Benefit BS* (1881) 8 QBD 403. See [1981] Conv. 55 (C.D. Bell); [1983] Conv. 29 (R. Griffith).

[145] *Shepherd Homes Ltd v Sandham (No.2)* [1971] 1 W.L.R. 1062.

[146] See above.

[147] *Haywood v Brunswick Permanent Benefit B.S.* (1881) 8 QBD 403 at 409, 410.

[148] Such covenants are apparently not subject to the doctrine of restraint of trade when given on the acquisition of property: *Esso Petroleum Co Ltd v Harper's Garage (Stourport) Ltd* [1968] A.C. 269 at 298, 309, 316, 325, 334; and see *Cleveland Petroleum Co Ltd v Dartstone Ltd* [1969] 1 W.L.R. 116 (covenant in lease). But it is not clear whether this is still the case as from April 6, 2011 land agreements are no longer excluded from the Competition Act 1998. See the Competition Act 1998 (Land Agreements Exclusion Revocation) Order 2010, SI 2010/1709.

At the date of the covenant, the covenantee must own land that will benefit from the covenant

16–026   Here again, as mentioned above, the rule was not settled at first. It is now accepted, however, that with statutory exceptions in favour of local authorities,[149] a restrictive covenant is similar to an equitable easement, and that the burden of the covenant will run with land only if the covenant was made for the protection of land belonging to the covenantee. As with easements,[150] there must be a dominant tenement which the covenant will benefit (or accommodate).[151] Thus covenants binding land in Hampstead will be too remote to benefit land in Clapham,[152] and if the covenantee retains no other land, a purchaser of the Hampstead land will take free from the covenant. Yet a landlord's reversion on a lease is a sufficient interest to entitle him to enforce the covenant against a sub-tenant, even though he has no other adjoining land.[153]

The burden of the covenant must have been intended to run with the covenantor's land

16–027   A covenant may be confined, either expressly or by implication, so as to bind the covenantor alone.[154] In this case, assignees of the covenantor's land are not bound by the covenant. But if the covenant was made by the covenantor for himself, his heirs and assigns, the burden will normally be attached to his land. Although covenants relating to the covenantor's land which are made after 1925 are deemed to have been made by the covenantor on behalf of himself, his successors in title, and the persons deriving title under him or them,[155] their burden will nevertheless run only if the parties so intend; the difference since 1925 has been that such an intention will be presumed unless the contrary is expressed.[156] There is no need for the contrary intention to be expressed in so many words; a stark contrast between the wording of the relevant covenant and that of other covenants in the same deed will suffice.[157]

Effect

16–028   If these conditions are satisfied, the effect is that the burden of the covenant runs in equity. There are two main consequences of this.

---

[149] See, e.g. Housing Act 1985 (HA 1985) s.609; Town and Country Planning Act 1990 s.106.
[150] Above, para.15–001.
[151] See *Formby v Barker* [1903] 2 Ch. 539; *LCC v Allen* [1914] 3 K.B. 642; (1971) 87 L.Q.R. 539 at 545 (D.J. Hayton).
[152] *Kelly v Barrett* [1924] 2 Ch. 379 at 404.
[153] *Regent Oil Co Ltd v J. A. Gregory (Hatch End) Ltd* [1966] Ch. 402 at 433.
[154] See *Re Fawcett and Holmes' Contract* (1889) 42 Ch.D. 150; *Re Royal Victoria Pavilion, Ramsgate* [1961] Ch. 581.
[155] LPA 1925 s.79(1).
[156] *Rhone v Stephens* [1994] 2 A.C. 310 at 321–322; *Morrells of Oxford Ltd v Oxford United Football Club Ltd* [2001] Ch. 459.
[157] *Morrells of Oxford Ltd v Oxford United Football Club Ltd* [2001] Ch. 459.

Equitable remedies

Only equitable remedies, which are of course discretionary, are available. The two possibili-   **16–029**
ties are an injunction and damages in lieu of an injunction under the Chancery Amendment
Act 1858.[158] The person with the benefit of the covenant will normally seek an injunction.
However, they will not obtain either an injunction or damages if, knowing of the breach,
they have taken no action for several years; in these circumstances, they will have acquiesced in the breach.[159] They are not, as in an action at law, entitled to insist upon some
damages being awarded just because they have made out their case. On the other hand,
lesser acts of acquiescence such as a failure to seek interim relief is only likely to deprive
them of an injunction.[160] In such circumstances and also where the claimant has not sought
an injunction, the primary measure of recovery is any loss in value suffered by his land.
Where, on the other hand, his land has suffered no such loss in value, the assessment of
damages involves the court ascertaining the sum of money which might reasonably have
been demanded by the claimant from the defendant as a quid pro quo for releasing the
covenant to the extent that it has been breached.[161] This is done by ascertaining the sum
that would have been arrived at in negotiations between the parties, if each had made
reasonable use of his respective bargaining position without holding out for unreasonable
amounts.[162]

Possibility of purchaser taking free of the covenant

The covenant suffers from the infirmity of all equitable interests, namely that it is possible   **16–030**
for a purchaser to take free of it, in which case it will not be enforced against him.

Unregistered land: In unregistered conveyancing, covenants made before 1926, many of
which are still in force, are subject to the old rules as to notice and will not bind a bona fide purchaser for value of a legal estate without notice of the covenant, or someone claiming through
such a person.[163] So are covenants in leases, whenever made, although the only persons
capable of taking free of them are assignees of old sub-leases,[164] original holders and assignees of old sub-under-leases,[165] and purchasers of interests in adjoining land also owned by
the lessor.[166] A restrictive covenant made after 1925 other than between a lessor and a lessee
must be registered as a Class D-II land charge.[167] If registered it will bind the whole world.[168]

---

[158] Senior Courts Act 1981 s.50. The jurisdiction survived the repeal of the Act of 1858: *Leeds Industrial
Co-operative Society Ltd v Slack* [1924] A.C. 851.
[159] *Gafford v Graham* [1999] 3 E.G.L.R. 75.
[160] *Gafford v Graham* [1999] 3 E.G.L.R. 75.
[161] *Wrotham Park Ltd v Parkside Homes Ltd* [1974] 1 W.L.R. 798; *Jaggard v Sawyer* [1995] 1 W.L.R.
269; *Gafford v Graham* [1999] 3 E.G.L.R. 75; see also *Attorney-General v Blake* [2001] 1 A.C. 268;
HKRUK II (CHC) ltd v Heaney [2010] EWHC 2245 (Ch).
[162] *Amec Developments Ltd v Jury's Hotel Management (UK) Ltd* (2001) 82 P. & C.R. 286.
[163] *Wilkes v Spooner* [1911] 2 K.B. 473.
[164] See above, paras 14–054 and 14–057.
[165] See above, paras 14–054 and 14–057.
[166] *Dartstone Ltd v Cleveland Petroleum Co Ltd* [1969] 1 W.L.R. 1807.
[167] Above, para.6–070.
[168] *White v Bijou Mansions Ltd* [1937] Ch. 610.

If not registered, it will be void against a subsequent purchaser for money or money's worth of a legal estate in the land.[169]

Registered land: In registered conveyancing, covenants in leases, whenever made, cannot be protected on the Land Register but will nevertheless bind all types of sub-lessees and their assignees.[170] However, a bona fide purchaser for value claiming under a registered disposition of an interest in adjoining land also owned by the lessor will automatically take free of them.[171] A restrictive covenant other than between a lessor and a lessee must be protected on the Land Register. It should be protected by a notice, either agreed or unilateral.[172]

PART 3   ENFORCEMENT

DETERMINATION

16–031   The enforceability of a restrictive covenant may be decided in any of three ways:

- (i) in an action to enforce the covenant;
- (ii) on application to the court for a declaration; or
- (iii) on application to the Lands Tribunal for the discharge or modification of the covenant.

Action to enforce the covenant

16–032   Prima facie, a restrictive covenant remains enforceable indefinitely.[173] In certain cases, however, the court may refuse to enforce an action brought by the person entitled to the benefit of a covenant. Thus, if the person entitled to enforce the covenant has remained inactive in the face of open breaches for so long and in such circumstances that a reasonable person would believe that the covenant no longer applies, the court will not enforce it.[174] The same applies if the neighbourhood is so completely changed (as from a residential to a shopping area) that an action to enforce the covenant would be unmeritorious, not bona fide and brought with some ulterior motive.[175]

Declaration by the court

16–033   Sometimes a landowner will be content to break a covenant and rely upon being able to establish one of the above defences if an action is brought. This, however, will not always

---

[169] See above, para.6–079.
[170] See above, para.14–057.
[171] *Oceanic Village Ltd v United Attractions Ltd* [2000] Ch. 234.
[172] LRA 2005 s.32(1).
[173] See *Mackenzie v Childers* (1890) L.R. 43 Ch.D. 265 at 279.
[174] *Chatsworth Estates Co v Fewell* [1931] 1 Ch. 224.
[175] *Chatsworth Estates Co v Fewell* [1931] 1 Ch. 224; *Westripp v Baldock* [1939] 1 All E.R. 279.

be satisfactory, as where it is desired to sell or lease the land and the purchaser or lessee wishes to be assured that he is in no danger from the covenant. Consequently, provision has now been made permitting an application to the court for a declaration whether any freehold land is affected by any restriction, and if so, the nature, extent and enforceability of it.[176] This provision is often used in respect of the many covenants created in the nineteenth century which are today unenforceable through non-compliance with the more modern rules governing the transfer of the benefit of the covenants. There is no power under this head to modify or discharge a valid covenant.

Discharge or modification by the (Upper Tribunal) Lands Chamber

In some cases a covenant may still be enforceable, but it may be undesirable for this state of affairs to continue. Consequently, a discretionary[177] power has been given to the Upper Tribunal (Lands Chamber)[178] to modify or discharge the restrictive covenant, with or without the payment of compensation; and an order may be refused unless the applicant accepts reasonable alternative restrictions.[179] An applicant is not disqualified merely because he recently bound himself by the covenant, though this is a factor to be considered.[180] He must bring his case within one of four heads.   **16–034**

Obsolete

By reason of changes in the character of the property or neighbourhood or other material circumstances the restriction ought to be deemed obsolete.   **16–035**

Obstructive

The continued existence of the restriction would impede some reasonable use of the land for public or private purposes, and either it confers no practical benefit[181] of substantial value or advantage, or it is contrary to the public interest, and (in either case) any loss can be adequately compensated in money.[182]   **16–036**

Agreement

The persons of full age and capacity entitled to the benefit of the restrictions have agreed, either expressly or by implication, by their acts and omissions, to the discharge or modification sought.   **16–037**

---

[176] LPA 1925 s.84(2). See s.84(7), below.
[177] *Driscoll v Church Commissioners for England* [1957] 1 Q.B. 330.
[178] LPA 25 s.84(1).
[179] *Jones v Rhys-Jones* (1974) 30 P. & C.R. 451.
[180] LPA 1925 s.84(1), (1C); LPA 1969 s.28.
[181] *Gilbert v Spoor* [1983] Ch. 27 (a view).
[182] See the questions as formulated in *Re Bass Ltd's Application* (1973) 26 P. & C.R. 156 and discussed in (1979) 129 N.L.J. 523 (H.W. Wilkinson).

No injury

16–038   The discharge or modification would not injure the persons entitled to the benefit of the covenant.

These powers apply to restrictions whenever made, but do not apply to restrictions imposed on a disposition made either gratuitously or for a nominal consideration for public purposes.[183] They apply to restrictions on freehold land and to restrictions on leasehold land if the lease was made for more than 40 years and at least 25 have expired,[184] but they do not apply to mining leases.[185]

There is also provision for the county court to authorise the conversion of a house into two or more tenements in contravention of a restrictive covenant or a provision in a lease if owing to changes in the neighbourhood the house cannot readily be let as a whole, or if planning permission for the conversion has been granted.[186]

Implications for the Land Register

16–039   Any release, waiver, discharge or modification of a restrictive covenant should be noted on the Land Register. Where the court has refused to enforce the covenant by injunction or declared that it is no longer enforceable, the entry on the Land Register will simply be cancelled. Where the Lands Chamber or the court has discharged or modified the covenant, the entry on the Land Register will be cancelled or modified as the case may be.

TOWN PLANNING

16–040   In recent years, the extension of town and country planning control has to some extent reduced the importance of restrictive covenants. If planning control imposes restrictions which will preserve the amenities of a neighbourhood, landowners have little incentive to impose or enforce restrictive covenants with the same object. Nevertheless, restrictive covenants have not been superseded by planning control. A landowner must see that what he proposes to do will contravene neither the private system of restrictive covenants nor the public system of planning control; and restrictive covenants sometimes extend to matters not usually dealt with by planning law. Further, a covenantee has the enforcement of the covenant under his control, whereas a landowner may be disappointed in the way in which the local planning authority imposes or enforces planning control against his neighbours. Nevertheless, the practical advice to give a landowner whose neighbour's activities are objectionable is often not to launch proceedings to enforce any apposite restrictive covenant, with consequent delay, expense and uncertainty, but to encourage the local planning authority to exercise its powers of enforcing planning control.

---

[183] LPA 1925 s.84(7).
[184] *Ridley v Taylor* [1965] 1 W.L.R. 611.
[185] LPA 1925 s.84(12), as amended by LTA 1954 s.52.
[186] HA 1985 s.610. See *Josephine Trust Ltd v Champagne* [1963] 2 Q.B. 160.

SUMMARY OF KEY CASES

- *Halsall v Brizell* [1957] Ch. 169.
- *Tulk v Moxhay* (1848) 1 H & Tw 105
- *Federated Homes Ltd v Mill Lodge Properties Ltd* [1980] 1 W.L.R. 594.
- *Crest Nicholson Residential (South) Ltd v McAllister* [2004] 1 W.L.R. 2409
- *Rhone v Stevens* [1994] 2 A.C. 310.
- *Elliston v Reacher* [1908] 2 Ch. 374

FURTHER READING

- Law Com No.327, *Making Land Work: Easements, Covenants and Profits à Prendre*
- Editor's note, "Is there any value in restrictive covenants?" [2007] Conv. 70 (on *Small*)
- Law Commission, *"Easements, Covenants and Profits á prendre"*, Consultation Paper No.186, March 2008
- J. Martin, "Remedies for breach of restrictive covenants" [1996] Conv. 329

Chapter 17

MORTGAGES

CHAPTER SUMMARY

A mortgages is a security for a debt, whether secured over personalty or realty. However, here we are only concerned with mortgages of real property. In essence it is a contract made under deed between two parties to secure a debt over the borrower's property. The borrower is known as the mortgagor and the lender is known as the mortgagee. Colloquially it is often said that a bank gives a mortgage to a borrower. However, the converse is true and the borrower gives the lender a mortgage over his property in exchange for a mortgage loan.

This chapter will examine the following:

- the nature of a mortgage and its historical origins;
- the creation of mortgages in both registered and unregistered land;
- the rights of a party under a mortgage;
- transfer of those rights; and
- priority of mortgages.

PART 1   NATURE OF A MORTGAGE

SECURITY

Mortgages provide lenders with security for their money. Where a loan is made without security, the lender has a right to sue for the money due if it is not repaid in accordance with the terms of his agreement with the borrower but that is all. If the borrower becomes insolvent, the lender is likely to lose part or all of his money. But if the borrower gives the lender some security of adequate value for the loan, the lender is protected even if the borrower becomes insolvent, for the lender's claim to the security takes precedence over the claims of the borrower's other creditors.

A mortgage is only one type of security but it is the most important one. The essential nature of a mortgage is that it is a conveyance of a legal or equitable interest in property, with a provision for redemption, i.e. that upon repayment of a loan or the performance

17–001

of some other obligation the interest created will be cancelled. The borrower is known as the "mortgagor" (the person who creates the mortgage); the lender is known as the "mortgagee" (the person who receives the mortgage).[1]

Mortgages today are principally regarded as the means by which an owner-occupier is able to borrow the funds necessary for him to buy the property in which he lives. However, mortgages taken out by owner-occupiers became common only in the second half of the twentieth century; the overwhelming majority of the law governing mortgages had by then already been developed in the context of commercial loans secured in order to fund business enterprises. A number of interventions by the legislature have therefore been necessary to adapt the law to the special needs of owner-occupiers.[2]

Any loan secured by a mortgage will usually be for less than the total value of the mortgaged property; otherwise it would not provide sufficient security for repayment. It should be noted that the amount by which the value of the property exceeds the amount needed to redeem the mortgage is often colloquially referred to as the mortgagor's "equity" in the property. However, this is not a technical term. In the event that the value of the mortgaged land subsequently becomes insufficient to redeem the mortgage (this usually happens as a result of the land falling in value but can also happen as a result of the building up of substantial arrears of interest and of interest on the interest), the mortgagor is colloquially said to be in "negative equity".

Other transactions

17–002   A mortgage must be distinguished from a lien, a pledge and a charge.

Lien

17–003   A lien may arise at common law, in equity or under certain statutes. A common law lien is the right to retain possession of the property of another until a debt is paid; thus a garage proprietor has a common law lien upon a motor-car repaired by him.[3] This lien is a mere passive right of retention, giving no right to sell or otherwise deal with the property,[4] and is extinguished if the creditor parts with possession to the debtor or his agent.[5]

An equitable lien is not dependent upon a continued possession of the property[6] and in this respect resembles a mortgage. But it differs from a mortgage, inter alia, in that a mortgage is a right founded on contract whereas an equitable lien arises from general principles of equity which do not permit a person who has acquired property under a contract to keep it without payment.[7] Thus a vendor of land who has conveyed away that land without receiving the full purchase price has an equitable lien upon it for the balance unpaid.[8]

---

[1]   The Law Commission has recommended fundamental changes in the law of mortgages: see (1986) Law Com.W.P. No. 99; (1991) Law Com. No.204.
[2]   For example, s.8 of the Administration of Justice Act 1976.
[3]   *Green v All Motors Ltd* [1917] 1 K.B. 625.
[4]   But see Torts (Interference with Goods) Act 1977 ss.12, 13 Sch.1, replacing Disposal of Uncollected Goods Act 1952.
[5]   *Pennington v Reliance Motor Works Ltd* [1923] 1 K.B. 127.
[6]   *Wrout v Dawes* (1858) 25 Beav. 369.
[7]   See *Mackreth v Symmons* (1808) 15 Ves. 329 at 340.
[8]   *Chapman v Tanner* (1684) 1 Vern. 267.

A statutory lien is the creature of the statute under which it arises, and the rights which it confers depend on the terms of that statute. Railways, shipowners and solicitors have been given such rights.

Pledge

A pledge or pawn is the loan of money in return for the delivery of possession of chattels to the lender. Although the lender has certain powers of sale, the general property in the goods remains in the borrower and the lender has possession. In a mortgage, on the other hand, the lender acquires ownership of the mortgage and the borrower usually retains possession of the property mortgaged.

17–004

Charge

For most practical purposes, a charge is regarded as a species of mortgage, and is dealt with accordingly in this chapter. Nevertheless, there is an essential difference between a mortgage and a charge. A mortgage is a conveyance of an interest in property subject to a right of redemption, whereas a charge conveys nothing and merely gives the chargee certain rights over the property concerned as security for the loan.[9]

17–005

PART 2   CREATION OF MORTGAGES

LEGAL MORTGAGES AND CHARGES OF UNREGISTERED LAND

The modern law under the Law of Property Act 1925 and the Land Registration Act 2002 can only be understood in the light of the law prior to the 1925 legislation.

17–006

Mortgages of freeholds before 1926

Before 1926, a legal mortgage of freehold land was usually created by conveying the estate in fee simple to the mortgagee subject to a covenant by the latter to reconvey the property to the mortgagor if the principal sum lent and the agreed interest was repaid on the due date. Although at law the mortgagee was entitled to keep the estate in fee simple if that payment was not made on time, equity took the view that the property mortgaged was merely a security for the money lent, and that it was unjust that the mortgagor should lose his property merely because he was late in repaying the loan. Therefore, even if the date fixed for repayment had long passed, equity compelled the mortgagee to reconvey the property to the mortgagor on payment of the principal sum together with interest and costs. In effect the mortgagor had two separate rights of redemption:

17–007

---

[9] See *London County and Westminster Bank Ltd v Tompkins* [1918] 1 K.B. 515.

(i) a legal right to redeem on the fixed day (at law, a mortgagor has no right to redeem either before or after the date fixed by the mortgage for redemption, but on that one day alone); and

(ii) an equitable right to redeem thereafter (equity allowed the mortgagor an equitable right to redeem on any day after the date fixed for redemption by the mortgage, a right which can be exercised only on equitable terms).

Once equity's intervention had become established, the fixed day on which the legal right to redeem arose tended to be six months after the date of the mortgage, even though there was no real expectation by either party that the money would be repaid then. In practice a mortgagor relied entirely on his rights in equity, the sum total of which was and is known as his equity of redemption.

It is important to distinguish the mortgagor's equity of redemption from his equitable right to redeem. The latter does not exist until the legal date for redemption is past and is but one of the adjuncts of the equity of redemption. In contrast the equity of redemption exists as soon as the mortgage is made.[10] It is the mortgagor's right of ownership of the property subject to the mortgage,[11] and is an interest in land which can be granted, devised and, in short, dealt with like any other interest in land.[12] It has already been seen[13] that the equity of redemption is usually of considerable value. Consequently, the equity of redemption can itself be mortgaged. But as before 1926 the interest of the mortgagor in the equity of redemption was merely equitable, any mortgage of it was necessarily effective only in equity; no legal mortgage could be created over something which existed only in equity. Consequently before 1926 only one legal mortgage could exist over freehold property; all second and subsequent mortgages were necessarily equitable.

Mortgages of freeholds after 1925

17-008   The Law of Property Act 1925 provided[14] that freeholds can no longer be mortgaged by means of a conveyance of the fee simple. Only two methods were then possible:

(i) by the grant of a very long lease in the case of a mortgage of a freehold, or a sub-lease if the mortgaged interest were a lease, subject to a provision for that lease to cease to exist when the mortgage is redeemed ("a mortgage by demise"); or

(ii) by the grant by deed of a charge which is expressed to be by way of legal mortgage.

However, in reality, the only method by which a legal mortgage is now created is by way of charge. The creation of a mortgage by way of demise has long been obsolescent. This method may now only be used in unregistered land because on the coming into force on

---

[10] *Brown v Cole* (1845) 14 Sim. 427; *Kreglinger v New Patagonia Meat and Cold Storage Co Ltd* [1914] A.C. 25 at 48.

[11] *Re Wells* [1933] Ch. 29 at 52.

[12] See *Casborne v Scarfe* (1738) 1 Atk. 603 at 605.

[13] Above, para.17–001.

[14] s.85(1).

October 13, 2003, the Land Registration Act provided that, in relation to registered land, a legal mortgage may only be created by way of charge.[15] A mortgage of unregistered land will, in reality, take effect by way of legal charge because its creation is a trigger for compulsory first registration.[16]

Mortgage by demise

When this method was employed, the term of years granted to the mortgagee was usually **17–009** a long term, for example 3,000 years. The provision for that lease to cease to exist when the mortgage was redeemed was really unnecessary, for on repayment the term becomes a satisfied term and automatically ceased.[17] In other respects, the position was much as it was before 1926. A fixed redemption date was still named, and it was still usually six months after the date of the mortgage. Thereafter the mortgagor had an equitable right to redeem in lieu of his legal right. The difficulty that a mortgagee by demise had no right to the title deeds was obviated by an express provision giving a first mortgagee the same right to the deeds as if he had the fee simple.[18]

The principal change brought about by the 1925 legislation was that the mortgagor retained the legal fee simple. This does not mean that the equity of redemption lost its importance; a fee simple giving the right to possession of land only when a lease for 3,000 years has expired is of little value compared with the right to insist that the fee simple shall forthwith be freed from the term of 3,000 years on payment of the money due. Indeed, the term "equity of redemption" is now sometimes used to include the mortgagor's legal estate. But the change meant that the mortgagor had, in addition to his equity of redemption, a legal fee simple out of which a further term of years could be granted. Consequently, second and subsequent mortgages could all be legal. Thus A, the fee simple owner of Blackacre, could create successive legal mortgages in favour of X, Y and Z. The term he granted to each mortgagee was usually at least one day longer than the term under the previous mortgage. Thus X may be given 2,000 years, Y 2,000 years and a day, and Z 2,000 years and two days, so that each mortgagee had a reversion upon the prior mortgage term.

The rights of Y and Z, though seemingly rather nebulous, were in fact quite substantial. Thus if A defaulted and the property were sold by X under his power of sale,[19] the money was paid first to X to discharge his mortgage, the balance to Y to discharge his, the balance to discharge Z's mortgage, and any surplus to A. In short, the parties rank in the order X, Y, Z, A. Further, any mortgagee always had the right, upon giving proper notice, to insist upon redeeming any prior mortgage.[20] Thus Y might insist upon buying up X's mortgage and so succeeding to X's position.

An attempt to create a first mortgage by conveyance of the fee simple operated as the grant of a term of 3,000 years without the mortgagee being liable to be impeached for waste but subject to the usual provision for the lease to cease to exist when the mortgage

---

[15] LRA 2002 s.23(1)(a).
[16] LRA 2002 s.4(1)(g).
[17] See above, para.12–021.
[18] LPA 1925 s.85(1).
[19] Below, paras 17–027 et seq.
[20] Below, para.17–058.

were redeemed.[21] An attempt to create a second or subsequent mortgage in the same way took effect as the grant of a term one day longer than the preceding term.[22] The system was thus foolproof.

The grant by deed of a charge expressed to be by way of legal mortgage

17-010   As has been stated, this is now the only method of creating a mortgage over registered land after the commencement of the Land Registration Act 2002. This was a new creation of the Law of Property Act 1925[23] and for brevity is usually called a "legal charge". To be effective, it must be:

(i)   made by deed (a charge merely in writing will have no effect at law);

(ii)   expressed to be by way of legal mortgage (the deed must contain a statement that the charge is made by way of legal mortgage)[24]; and

(iii)   in respect of registered land, it must be registered in accordance with the Land Registration Act 2002.[25]

The effect of such a charge of freehold land is that the chargee (whether first or subsequent) gets the same protection, powers and remedies as if he had a term of 3,000 years without being liable to be impeached for waste.[26] Although he gets no actual legal term of years, he is as fully protected as if he had one.[27] The name "charge" is thus a little misleading because although a legal charge is by nature a charge and not a mortgage, for all practical purposes it is indistinguishable from a mortgage.

Mortgages of leaseholds before 1926

17-011   Before 1926 a legal mortgage of leasehold land could be made in either of two ways:

(i)   by assignment of the lease to the mortgagee subject to a covenant by the latter to reassign that lease to the mortgagor if the principal sum lent and the agreed interest was repaid on the due date; or

(ii)   by the grant to the mortgagee of a sub-lease at least one day shorter than the lease subject to a provision for that lease to cease to exist when the mortgage was redeemed.

The first method was rarely employed, for it meant that the mortgagee became liable on such of the covenants in the lease as touched and concerned the land. This was not so if the second method was employed, for then the mortgagee was only an under-lessee and there

---

[21]   LPA 1925 s.85(2).

[22]   LPA 1925 s.85(2).

[23]   s.87.

[24]   *Cityland and Property (Holdings) Ltd v Dabrah* [1968] Ch. 166; *Ruoff & Roper: Registered Conveyancing* (London: Sweet & Maxwell), para.23.07.

[25]   LRA 2002 s.27 and Sch.2 para.8.

[26]   LPA 1925 s.87(1).

[27]   See *Regent Oil Co Ltd v J.A. Gregory (Hatch End) Ltd* [1966] Ch. 402.

was privity neither of contract nor of estate between him and the lessor.[28] Whichever form was employed, the mortgage normally contained the usual provision that the loan should be repaid on a fixed date six months ahead, and thereafter the mortgagor had an equitable right to redeem.

Where a mortgage had been made by assignment, second and subsequent mortgages were made by a mortgage of the mortgagor's equity of redemption. Where the prior mortgage had been made by sub-lease, subsequent mortgages were made by the grant of further sub-leases, each normally being one day longer than the previous one.

Mortgages of leaseholds after 1925

The Law of Property Act 1925 provides[29] that leaseholds can no longer be mortgaged by assignment. After the Law of Property Act 1925 and before commencement of the Land Registration Act 2002, only two methods were possible. The two methods were: **17–012**

(i) by the grant of a sub-lease for a term of years absolute, subject to a provision for that sub-lease to cease to exist when the mortgage is redeemed, the term of the sub-lease being at least one day shorter than the leasehold term vested in the mortgagor; or

(ii) by the grant by deed of a charge which is expressed to be by way of legal mortgage.

The grant of a sub-lease for a term of years absolute

The term of the sub-lease had to be at least one day shorter than the term of the lease which is being mortgaged, otherwise it would operate as an assignment.[30] If the lease required the tenant to obtain the landlord's licence before a sub-lease by way of mortgage was made, the licence could not be unreasonably refused.[31] The first mortgagee had the same rights to the deeds as if his mortgage had been made by assignment.[32] It was usual to make the sub-lease 10 days shorter than the lease, so as to allow room for second and subsequent mortgages. Thus if T mortgaged a 50-year lease, the first mortgage would be secured by a sub-lease for 50 years less 10 days, any second mortgage by a sub-lease for 50 years less nine days, and so on. But this was not essential, for the old rule[33] that a lease may take effect in reversion upon another lease of the same or greater length was confirmed by the Law of Property Act 1925.[34] Thus, if the first mortgage was made by a sub-lease for 50 years less one day, the second mortgage would be secured by a sub-lease of the same length and so on; each mortgage would take effect in its proper order. **17–013**

An attempted mortgage by way of assignment after 1925 operated as a sub-lease for a term of years absolute subject to that sub-lease ceasing to exist when the mortgage was

---

[28] Above, paras 14–002 et seq.
[29] s.86(1).
[30] *Beardman v Wilson* (1868) L.R. 4 C.P. 57; above, para.8–045.
[31] LPA 1925 s.86(1).
[32] LPA 1925 s.86(1).
[33] *Re Moore & Hulme's Contract* [1912] 2 Ch. 105.
[34] s.149(5).

redeemed. A first or only mortgagee takes a term 10 days shorter than the lease mortgaged. Second and subsequent mortgages took terms one day longer than under the previous mortgage, if this was possible. In every case, however, the sub-term had to be at least one day shorter than the term mortgaged.[35]

The grant by deed of a charge expressed to be by way of legal mortgage

17–014   The grant by deed of a charge expressed to be by way of legal mortgage gives the mortgagee (whether first or subsequent) the same rights and remedies as if he had a sub-lease one day shorter than the term vested in the mortgagor.[36] As in the case of freeholds,[37] he gets no actual term of years but is as fully protected as if he had one, so that he may seek relief against forfeiture in the same way as a sub-lessee.[38]

Mortgages of registered title under the Land Registration Act 2002

17–015   A registered charge may be effected by any deed charging the land with the payment of money.[39] It does not take effect at law until it has been registered,[40] although it takes effect in equity in the meantime.[41] However, the mortgage security will not be affected by any interest which overrides registration when that interest arises between the creation of the charge and its registration.[42] On registration, an entry is made in the charges register giving the name of the person in whose favour the charge is made, together with particulars of it.

A registered chargee has all the powers of a legal mortgagee, unless the register otherwise provides.[43] The priority of registered charges is governed by the order of entry in the register, unless it otherwise provides.[44] The rules which govern the ways in which that order of priorities can be altered as a result of a mortgagee making a further advance will be considered later on.[45]

Section 23 of the Land Registration Act 2002 permits the owner of registered land to make any disposition of any kind permitted by the general law, other than a legal sub-mortgage.[46] That section also permits the owner to charge the land with the payment of money indebtedness and to secure it by the registered charge.[47] The effect of this section is that it is now impossible to create a legal charge of registered land unless the owner executes and registers a legal charge.

---

[35]   LPA 1925 s.86(2). See *Grangeside Properties Ltd v Collingwoods Securities Ltd* [1964] 1 W.L.R. 139.
[36]   LPA 1925 s.87(1).
[37]   Above, para.17–010.
[38]   Above, para.12–014.
[39]   LRA 2002 s.23(1)(b).
[40]   *Grace Rymer Investments Ltd v Waite* [1958] Ch. 831; and see *Lever Finance Ltd v Needleman's Trustee* [1956] Ch. 375.
[41]   *Mortgage Corp Ltd v Nationwide Credit Corp Ltd* [1994] Ch. 49.
[42]   *Abbey National B.S. v Cann* [1991] 1 A.C. 56.
[43]   LRA 2002 s.52(1).
[44]   LRA 2002 s.48(1).
[45]   See below, paras 17–083 et seq.
[46]   LRA 2002 s.23(2)(a).
[47]   LRA 2002 s.23(2)(b).

Advantages of legal charges

Although there is nothing in the Law of Property Act 1925 to suggest any reason why a legal **17–016** charge, either of freeholds or leaseholds, should be preferred to a mortgage by demise, it always has been in practice. There seem to be three practical advantages in using a legal charge:

(i) it is a convenient way of mortgaging freeholds and leaseholds together; the deed is shortened by stating that all the properties specified in the schedule are charged by way of legal mortgage, instead of setting out the length of the mortgage terms in each case;

(ii) the grant of a legal charge over a lease probably does not amount to a breach of any covenant in that lease against sub-letting, for the charge creates no actual sub-lease in favour of the mortgagee but merely gives him the same rights as if he had a sub-lease; and

(iii) the form of a legal charge is short and simple.

Compulsory registration

Since April 1, 1998, a first legal mortgage of an estate in fee simple or a term of years abso- **17–017** lute in unregistered land has triggered compulsory registration of that freehold or leasehold title.[48] As has been discussed the mortgage must then be created by the grant of a legal charge and it will therefore take effect as a registered charge.[49]

EQUITABLE MORTGAGES AND CHARGES

Equitable mortgages of equitable interests

If the mortgagor has no legal estate but only an equitable interest, any mortgage he effects **17–018** must necessarily be equitable. Thus beneficiaries under a trust have merely equitable interests and so can create only equitable mortgages.

The 1925 legislation has not affected the form of equitable mortgages of equitable interests. Such mortgages are still made by a conveyance of the equitable interest to the mortgagee with a provision for reconveyance of that interest to the mortgagor when the mortgage is redeemed. The actual form of words employed is immaterial provided that the meaning is plain.[50] Nor need the mortgage be made by deed, as is essential for a legal mortgage; but it must either be in writing signed by the mortgagor or his agent authorised in writing, or else be made by will.[51] The mortgagee should give notice to whoever holds the legal title to the property in question, in practice one or more trustees, in order to secure priority over later equitable mortgages of the same interest under what is known as the rule in *Dearle v Hall*.[52]

---

[48] Above, para.5–016.
[49] Below.
[50] See *William Brandt's Sons & Co v Dunlop Rubber Co Ltd* [1905] A.C. 454 at 462.
[51] LPA 1925 s.53(1).
[52] (1828) 3 Russ. 1; below, para 17–083.

Where a mortgagor purports to create a legal mortgage or charge but fails to do so because he has not yet acquired legal title to the property in question; in such circumstances, the mortgagee obviously does not acquire a legal mortgage. Where the mortgagor has already contracted to buy the property in question, he will already have an equitable interest therein so the mortgagee will immediately acquire an equitable mortgage. But in any event he acquires a mortgage by estoppel. Consequently, if the mortgagor subsequently acquires the legal title which he purported to mortgage or charge, that acquisition "feeds" the estoppel and the mortgagee will immediately acquire a legal mortgage or charge; this is the case whether the land in question is unregistered[53] or registered.[54]

Mortgages which are equitable because they are informal

17–019   Under the same principles as apply to leaseholds,[55] equity treats an enforceable contract to create a legal mortgage,[56] or an imperfect legal mortgage,[57] as being an actual mortgage. To be enforceable, the transaction was formerly required to be supported either by sufficient evidence in writing or by a sufficient act of part performance. However, for transactions after September 26, 1989, neither evidence in writing nor part performance will suffice; instead, the contract will be valid only if it is made in writing, containing all the terms, and is signed by all parties to it.[58] If it is, the contract will need to be protected as an estate contract in the usual way if it is to be enforceable against all third parties.

It is important to note that the formalities for a contract for a mortgage and the creation of the mortgage are different. It is a common mistake that the creation of a legal mortgage must comply with s.2 of the Law of Property (Miscellaneous Provisions) Act 1989. It is only equitable mortgages that must comply with such formalities. Section 2 is concerned with contracts for the creation or sale of legal estates or interests in land, not with the documents which actually create or transfer such estates or interests. A transfer, conveyance or assignment, a lease or legal mortgage are not within the scope of s.2.[59]

Mortgages by deposit of documents of title

17–020   Prior to this change in the law in 1989, a mere deposit of the title deeds to unregistered land which could not be accounted for in any other way would be taken to be part performance of a contract to create a mortgage,[60] even if not a word about such a contract had been uttered,[61] so that an equitable mortgage was created by such a deposit.[62] The deposit had to have been made for the purpose of giving a security, so that delivery of the deeds

---

[53]   *Right d. Jefferys v Bucknell* (1831) 2 B. & Ald. 278.
[54]   *First National Bank Plc v Thompson* [1996] Ch. 231.
[55]   *Walsh v Lonsdale* [1882] 21 Ch. D 9.
[56]   See *Ex p. Wright* (1812) 19 Ves. 255 at 258.
[57]   *Parker v Housefield* (1834) 2 My. & K. 419 at 420.
[58]   Law of Property (Miscellaneous Provisions) Act 1989 s.2.
[59]   See *Helden v Strathmore Ltd* [2011] EWCA Civ 542 at [27] per Neuberger M.R.
[60]   *Russel v Russel* (1783) 1 Bro.C.C. 269.
[61]   *Bozon v Williams* (1829) 3 Y. & J. 151 at 161.
[62]   *Bank of New South Wales v O'Connor* (1889) 14 App.Cas. 273 at 282; *Re Wallis & Simmonds (Builders) Ltd* [1974] 1 W.L.R. 391.

by mistake, or to enable a mortgage to be drawn up, created no mortgage.[63] But it was not essential that all the deeds should have been deposited, provided that those that were delivered were material evidence of title.[64] The mortgagee had no lien on the deeds apart from his right to retain them under the mortgage, so that if the mortgage contract was void, the deeds had to be given up.[65]

Until the commencement of the Land Registration Act 2002, in registered conveyancing the land certificate could take the place of the title deeds to unregistered land, and a lien could be created by deposit of the land certificate. The holder of a registered charge could similarly create a lien on his charge by deposit of his charge certificate.[66] The mere possession of the certificate provided some protection,[67] though not against transactions for which production of the certificate was not requisite, such as certain leases.[68] The lender, however, could have a notice of the existence of the deposit entered on the charges register of the land affected. A lien could also be created by giving the registrar a notice of intention to deposit the land certificate.[69] The latter procedure was useful where a loan was made in connection with the purchase of the land. Naturally the land certificate was not available until the transfer had been registered after completion of the purchase. Once registered, the land certificate would then be delivered by the registrar to the person named in the notice.

It has not been possible to create these types of mortgage by deposit of documents since the Land Registration Act 2002 came into force. The Land Registry no longer issues land or charge certificates and instead, upon registration of an estate or interest, the Land Registry issues an official copy of the register and a Title Information Document. The issuing of these documents is confirmation that the estate or interest has been registered.

Equitable charges

An equitable charge is created where specific property is appropriated to the discharge of some debt or other obligation without there being any change in ownership either at law or in equity.[70] Thus if A signs a written contract agreeing that he thereby charges some specific land of his with the payment of £5,000 to B, an equitable charge over that land is created.[71] The same applies where a will or voluntary settlement charges money on land.[72] An enforceable contract to create a legal charge also creates an equitable charge.[73]   **17–021**

---

[63] *Norris v Wilkinson* (1806) 12 Ves. 192.
[64] *Lacon v Allen* (1856) 3 Drew. 579.
[65] *Re Molton Finance Ltd* [1968] Ch. 325.
[66] LRA 1925 s.66 (repealed).
[67] *Barclays Bank Ltd v Taylor* [1974] Ch. 137.
[68] See *Strand Securities Ltd v Caswell* [1965] Ch. 958.
[69] LRR 1925 rr.240–242.
[70] *London County and Westminster Bank Ltd v Tompkins* [1918] 1 K.B. 515 at 528.
[71] *Matthews v Goodday* (1861) 31 L.J. Ch. 282 at 282, 283.
[72] *Re Owen* [1894] 3 Ch. 220.
[73] *Swiss Bank Corp v Lloyds Bank Ltd* [1979] Ch. 548; on appeal, [1982] A.C. 584; and see above, para.11–017.

PART 3   RIGHTS OF THE PARTIES UNDER A MORTGAGE OR CHARGE

17–022   The rights of the parties under a mortgage or charge will be considered under four heads:

   (i) the rights of the mortgagee or chargee;
  (ii) rights common to both parties;
 (iii) the right of the mortgagor or chargor to redeem; and
 (iv) the other rights of the mortgagor or chargor.

RIGHTS OF THE MORTGAGEE OR CHARGEE REMEDIES FOR ENFORCING PAYMENT

17–023   Unless the parties have otherwise agreed, a mortgagee or chargee has five remedies available for enforcing payment. Three of the remedies are primarily directed to recovering the capital due and putting an end to the security: these are an action for the money, foreclosure, and sale. The other two remedies are taking possession and appointing a receiver. These primarily seek merely to recover the interest due, though possession is now usually sought so as to facilitate sale with vacant possession. The right of sale and the right to appoint a receiver are given by statute[74] but the rights are commonly amplified by covenants in the mortgage. The other remedies are inherent in the nature of the transaction. Today, actions for foreclosure have become rare.[75] A mortgagee will not be restrained from enforcing payment merely because the mortgagor has some large cross-claim against him,[76] even if it is for a larger amount than the sum due to the mortgagee.

It may be noted that two of the mortgagee's remedies are derived from the common law (an action on the covenant, and the right to take possession), one is equitable (foreclosure) and two were formerly contractual and are now statutory (sale, and the appointment of a receiver).

A mortgagee is not obliged to take any steps to realise his security; he can sit back and do nothing.[77] However, if he does take some steps to exercise his rights, he must act fairly towards the mortgagor.[78] Thus, where a mortgagee refused to consent to a sale by the mortgagor which, because of a fall in property values, would not raise enough money to discharge the mortgage and instead sought an order for possession with a view to letting the house until such time as property values had risen again, he was held not to be acting fairly. This was because the rent obtained would be substantially less than the interest on the mortgage which would continue to be debited to the mortgagor. Sale was therefore ordered on the application of the mortgagor[79] on the basis that the mortgagee would be

---

[74] LPA 1925 s.101(1).
[75] See *Palk v Mortgage Services Funding Plc* [1993] Ch. 330.
[76] *Samuel Keller (Holdings) Ltd v Martins Bank Ltd* [1971] 1 W.L.R. 43; *Ashley Guarantee Plc v Zacaria* [1993] 1 W.L.R. 62; *Albany Home Loans Ltd v Massey* [1997] 2 All E.R. 609.
[77] *China and South Sea Bank Ltd v Tan* [1990] 1 A.C. 538 at 545.
[78] *Palk v Mortgage Services Funding Plc* [1993] Ch. 330 at 338.
[79] Under LPA 1925 s.91(2).

free to purchase the property itself if it wanted to take the risk of what would happen to property values in the future. This decision was made in the aftermath of a substantial generalised fall in property values. Such falls in value and the consequential appearance of negative equity on a large scale have, historically, been extremely rare. Consequently in normal circumstances it is not likely that mortgagees will find themselves constrained in this way.

Where a mortgagee does decide to act, the remedies available differ according to whether the mortgage or charge is legal or equitable.

Legal mortgagees or chargees

A legal mortgagee or legal chargee has the following remedies for enforcing his security.   **17–024**

To sue for the money due

At any time after the date fixed for payment the mortgagee may sue for the money lent.[80]   **17–025**
This remedy is, of course, in no way peculiar to mortgages. It is perfectly proper for the mortgage to sue for the money due in an attempt to bankrupt the mortgagor and obtain possession of the property via his trustee in bankruptcy[81] even though the mortgagee has failed to obtain possession of the property by virtue of being a secured creditor.[82]

To foreclose   **17–026**

The nature of foreclosure: By giving the mortgagor an equitable right to redeem after he had lost his legal right of redemption, equity interfered with the bargain made between the parties. But equity prescribed limits to the equity of redemption which it created; the mortgagor's equitable right to redeem could in appropriate circumstances be extinguished. The process, for which an order of the court was and is necessary, is known as "foreclosure". On foreclosure "the court simply removes the stop it has itself put on"[83]; equity's interference to prevent the conveyance of the legal fee simple from having its full effect comes to an end.

Before 1926, a legal first mortgagee of freehold land had the estate in fee simple vested in him anyway so an order extinguishing the equity of redemption was of itself sufficient to leave the mortgagee as owner of the property both at law and in equity. Since 1925, a mortgagee has not had the whole legal estate of the mortgagor vested in him. Consequently it is no longer sufficient for an order for foreclosure merely to destroy the mortgagor's equity of redemption; the Law of Property Act 1925[84] therefore provides that, in the case of both mortgages and charges, a final order for foreclosure (technically, a foreclosure order absolute) vests the mortgagor's fee simple or lease in the mortgagee.

The right to foreclose does not arise until the legal right to redeem has ceased to exist, i.e. until the legal date for redemption has passed[85] or until there is a breach of a condition

---

[80] See *Bolton v Buckenham* [1891] 1 Q.B. 278.
[81] See above, para.8–045.
[82] *Alliance & Leicester Plc v Slayford* [2001] 1 All E.R. (Comm.) 1.
[83] *Carter v Wake* (1877) 4 Ch.D. 605 at 606 per Jessel M.R.
[84] ss.88(2), 89(2).
[85] *Williams v Morgan* [1906] 1 Ch. 804.

required for keeping the legal right of redemption alive.[86] Once this has happened, the mortgagee may commence foreclosure proceedings unless he has agreed not to do so[87] (sometimes a mortgagee will contract not to enforce the security by foreclosure or other means until he has given some specified notice or until the mortgagor has broken one of his covenants in the mortgage). If no redemption date is fixed or if the loan is repayable on demand, the right to foreclose arises when a demand for repayment has been made and a reasonable time thereafter has elapsed.[88]

Parties to a foreclosure action: An action for foreclosure can be brought by any mortgagee of property, whether he is the original mortgagee or an assignee, and whether he is a first or subsequent mortgagee. The effect of a foreclosure order absolute in an action brought by the first mortgagee is to make him the sole owner both at law and in equity, free from any subsequent mortgages. If the action is brought by a second or subsequent mortgagee, he will hold the property subject to prior incumbrances, but free from all subsequent incumbrances. Where trustees foreclose, they hold the land on a trust of land.[89]

As will be seen shortly,[90] a foreclosure action gives the mortgagor and all others interested in the equity of redemption an opportunity of redeeming the mortgage. Consequently, all persons interested in the equity of redemption must be made parties to the action. Thus if X has made successive mortgages of his property to A, B and C, and B starts foreclosure proceedings, A's mortgage security will not be affected by those proceedings and so there is no need for A to be made a party to the action. But if the action is successful, C will lose his mortgage security and X his equity of redemption, and so both must be made parties to the action.

Foreclosure orders nisi: The first step in a foreclosure is to obtain from the court a foreclosure order nisi. This provides that if the mortgagor repays the money lent on a fixed day (usually six months from the accounts being settled by the relevant court officer), the mortgage shall be discharged, but that if this is not done, the mortgage shall be foreclosed. If there are several mortgagees and the first mortgagee is foreclosing, each mortgagee is given the alternative of either losing his security or else redeeming (paying off) the first mortgage. Sometimes the court will give the mortgagees successive periods to effect this redemption, but usually there will be only one period for all of them.[91] At the request of the mortgagee or of any person interested (such as the mortgagor) the court may order a sale of the property instead of foreclosure.[92]

Foreclosure orders absolute: If no order for sale is made and the property is not redeemed on the date fixed, a foreclosure order absolute is made. This destroys the mortgagor's equity of redemption and transfers his fee simple or term of years to the mortgagee,[93] who thus becomes sole owner at law and in equity, subject only to prior incumbrances. In the

---

[86] *Twentieth Century Banking Corp Ltd v Wilkinson* [1977] Ch. 99.
[87] *Ramsbottom v Wallis* (1835) 5 L.J.Ch. 92.
[88] *Toms v Wilson* (1863) 4 B. & S. 453.
[89] LPA 1925 s.31, as amended by TLATA 1996 Sch.2, para.1; above, paras 7–003 et seq.
[90] See below.
[91] *Platt v Mendel* (1884) 27 Ch.D. 246.
[92] LPA 1925 s.91(2); *Twentieth Century Banking Corp Ltd v Wilkinson* [1977] Ch. 99.
[93] LPA 1925 ss.88(2), 89(2); LRA 1925 s.34(3) (repealed); there is no explicit provision in LRA 2002 but the law remains the same.

case of registered land, the mortgagee is registered as proprietor of the land and his charge is cancelled.

Re-opening a foreclosure absolute: Although a foreclosure order absolute appears to be final, it is not necessarily so, for the court will sometimes re-open the foreclosure absolute. Circumstances which may influence the court to do this are the fact that the mortgagor was prevented from raising the money by an accident at the last moment, any special value which the property has to the mortgagor (such as if it was an old family estate), a marked disparity between the value of the property and the amount lent, and the promptness of the application. Even if the mortgagee has sold the property on after obtaining his fore-closure order absolute, the court may still re-open the matter. This is unlikely, however, if the purchaser bought the property some time after foreclosure and without notice of any circumstances which might induce the court to interfere.[94]

To sell   17–027

History: There is no right, either at common law or in equity, for a mortgagee to sell the mortgaged property free from the equity of redemption, although of course he can freely transfer the estate which is vested in him subject to the equity of redemption. Consequently, an express power was usually inserted in mortgage deeds enabling the mort-gagee to sell the property free from the equity of redemption if certain specified events occurred. However, a satisfactory power of sale is now contained in the Law of Property Act 1925.[95]

The power: Every mortgagee whose deed of mortgage shows no contrary intention has a power of sale, provided:

   (i) the mortgage was made by deed (all legal mortgages must be anyway); and
  (ii) the mortgage money is due, i.e. the legal date for redemption has passed[96] (if the mortgage money is payable by instalments, the power of sale arises as soon as any instalment is in arrear).[97]

When these conditions have been fulfilled, the statutory power of sale arises. Nevertheless, the power does not become exercisable unless one of the three following conditions has been satisfied[98]:

   (i) notice requiring payment of the mortgage money has been served on the mort-gagor and default has been made in payment of part or all of it for three months thereafter; or
  (ii) some interest under the mortgage is two months or more in arrears; or
 (iii) there has been a breach of some provision contained in the Law of Property Act 1925 or in the mortgage deed (other than the covenant for payment of the

[94] *Campbell v Holyland* (1877) 7 Ch.D. 166 at 172, 173.
[95] ss.101–107, applicable to mortgages made after 1881.
[96] LPA 1925 s.101.
[97] *Payne v Cardiff R.D.C.* [1932] 1 K.B. 241.
[98] LPA 1925 s.103.

mortgage money or interest) which should have been observed or performed by the mortgagor or by someone who concurred in making the mortgage.

Protection of purchasers: The difference between the power of sale arising and becoming exercisable is as follows. If the power has not arisen, the mortgagee has no statutory power of sale at all; the most he can do is to transfer his mortgage. But if the power of sale has arisen, he can make a good title to a purchaser free from the equity of redemption even if the power has not become exercisable. The title of a purchaser in good faith is not impeachable merely because none of the three specified events has occurred or the power of sale has in some way been irregularly or improperly exercised. Any person injured by an unauthorised, improper or irregular exercise of the power has a remedy in damages against the person exercising it.[99] Thus while a purchaser from a mortgagee must satisfy himself that the power of sale has arisen, he need not inquire whether it has become exercisable. However, if he has actual knowledge (as distinct from merely constructive notice) that the power is not exercisable or that there is some impropriety in the sale, he will not take free from the mortgagor's interest[100]; nor is he likely to if he turns a blind eye to suspicious circumstances.

Mode of sale: In general, the statutory power of sale is exercisable without any order of the court being required and without first taking possession.[101] The mortgagee may sell by public auction or by private contract, and has a wide discretion as to the terms and conditions upon which the sale is made, including making the sale subject to conditions.[102] The power is unaffected by any disposition by the mortgagor, so that a contract of sale entered into by the mortgagee will prevail over an earlier contract of sale made by the mortgagor.[103] The power becomes exercised as soon as a contract, albeit conditional, is made, so that thereupon the equity of redemption is suspended unless and until the contract goes off.[104] To prevent the mortgagee entering into such a contract, the mortgagor must tender the sum necessary to redeem the mortgage in full.[105]

It has already been seen that the mortgagee must act fairly towards the mortgagor when exercising his rights[106] but, save where there is generalised negative equity, it is not likely that mortgagees will often find themselves constrained in this way. In any event, the mortgagee is not a trustee for the mortgagor of his power of sale,[107] for the power is given to the mortgagee for his own benefit to enable him the better to realise his security. Thus he need not delay the sale in the hope of obtaining a better price,[108] nor does he have to attempt to sell by auction before selling by private contract.[109] Moreover, his motive for selling, such

---

[99] LPA 1925 s.104(2).
[100] *Bailey v Barnes* [1894] 1 Ch. 25 at 30; *Lord Waring v London & Manchester Assurance Co Ltd* [1935] Ch. 310 at 318.
[101] *Horsham Properties v Clark* [2009] 1 W.L.R. 1255.
[102] LPA 1925 s.101(1), (2); *Silven Properties v Royal Bank of Scotland* [2004] 1 W.L.R. 997.
[103] *Duke v Robson* [1973] 1 W.L.R. 267.
[104] *Property & Bloodstock Ltd v Emerton* [1968] Ch. 94.
[105] *Payne v Cardiff R.D.C.* [1932] 1 K.B. 241.
[106] *Palk v Mortgage Services Funding Plc* [1993] Ch. 330 at 338.
[107] *Kennedy v De Trafford* [1897] A.C. 180.
[108] *Bank of Cyprus (London) Ltd v Gill* [1980] 2 Lloyd's Rep. 51; and see *China & South Sea Bank Ltd v Tan Soon Gin* [1990] 1 A.C. 531.
[109] *Davey v Durrant* (1857) 1 De G. & J. 535 at 553, 560.

as spite against the mortgagor, is immaterial.[110] But the sale must be a true sale: a "sale" by the mortgagee to himself, either directly or through an agent, is no true sale and may be set aside or declared void.[111] The mortgagee must act in good faith and use his powers for proper purposes.[112]

However, the mortgagee is under a duty to take reasonable care to obtain a proper price,[113] so that he will be liable to the mortgagor if he advertises the property for sale by auction without mentioning a valuable planning permission,[114] or if he sells the property on a "crash sale" basis without exposing it to the market for a proper period of time.[115] However, he will not be in breach if he takes a commercial decision to sell at a particular time, even though a higher price might have been obtained by delaying.[116] The duty to obtain a proper price for the property, which may be excluded by an appropriately drafted term in the mortgage,[117] is owed not merely to the mortgagor but also to a surety for the loan,[118] though not to an equitable co-owner of the land.[119] If the mortgagee sells to an associated person or company, the onus is on him to show that a proper price was obtained.[120]

Proceeds of sale: Although the mortgagee is not a trustee of his power of sale, he is a trustee of the proceeds of sale. After discharging any payments properly due, any balance must be paid to the next subsequent incumbrancer,[121] or, if none, to the mortgagor.[122] A mortgagee who has a surplus will be liable to any subsequent mortgagee of whom he had actual or constructive notice who is prejudiced by the payment of the surplus to the mortgagor.[123] In the case of unregistered land, he should therefore search in the land charges register[124] to discover the existence of any subsequent mortgages since registration constitutes actual notice. If the mortgagee pays money to the mortgagor he will be liable to any subsequent mortgagee who is thereby prejudiced.[125] In the case of registered land the mortgagee must search the register of the property since registration constitutes notice for this purpose.[126] Any mortgagee who fails to do so will be liable in the same way as a mortgagee or unregistered land. But a sale by a mortgagee does not affect any prior mortgage: the purchaser takes the property subject to any such mortgage, though free from the rights of the vendor,

---

[110] *Nash v Eads* (1880) 25 S.J. 95.

[111] *Downes v Grazebrook* (1871) 3 Mer. 200; *Williams v Wellingborough BC* [1975] 1 W.L.R. 1327.

[112] *Burgess v Auger* [1998] 2 B.C.L.C. 478 at 482.

[113] For building societies the duty is statutory: Building Societies Act 1986 Sch.4, replacing earlier legislation.

[114] *Cuckmere Brick Co Ltd v Mutual Finance Ltd* [1971] Ch. 949.

[115] *Predeth v Castle Phillips Finance Co Ltd* [1986] 2 E.G.L.R. 144.

[116] *Meftah v Lloyds TSB Bank Plc* [2001] 2 All E.R. (Comm.) 741.

[117] *Bishop v Bonham* [1988] 1 W.L.R. 742 at 752.

[118] *Standard Chartered Bank Ltd v Walker* [1982] 1 W.L.R. 1410.

[119] *Parker-Tweedale v Dunbar Bank Plc* [1991] Ch. 12.

[120] *Tse Kwong Lam v Wong Chit Sen* [1983] 1 W.L.R. 1394.

[121] See *Samuel Keller (Holdings) Ltd v Martin's Bank Ltd* [1971] 1 W.L.R. 43.

[122] LPA 1925 s.105; see *Thorne v Heard* [1895] A.C. 495. See below for the effect of the Limitation Act 1980.

[123] *West London Commercial Bank v Reliance Permanent B.S.* (1885) 29 Ch.D. 954.

[124] See above, para.6–070.

[125] *West London Commercial Bank v Reliance Permanent BS* (1885) 28 Ch. D 954.

[126] LRA 2002 s.54.

subsequent mortgagees, and the mortgagor.[127] In other words, if A mortgages his property to B, C and D and C then sells under the power of sale, the purchaser will take the property free of the interests of A, C and D but subject to B's mortgage.

17–028   ## To take possession

The right: Since a legal mortgage gives the mortgagee a term of years, he is entitled, subject to any contrary indication in the mortgage, to take possession of the mortgaged property as soon as the mortgage is made, even if the mortgagor is guilty of no default[128]; a legal chargee has a corresponding statutory right.[129] The mortgagee or chargee may do so without a court order,[130] even where the subject-matter of the mortgage is a dwelling-house occupied by the mortgagor although in those circumstances the court can grant relief to the mortgagor.[131] If the property is already lawfully let to tenants, the mortgagee cannot take physical possession, but instead takes possession by directing the tenants to pay their rents to him instead of to the mortgagor.[132] However, an order for possession may be refused if the mortgagee is not acting as such but is acting merely as an agent for a mortgagor who is trying to evict a tenant.[133] The mortgagee's right to possession may also be affected by the rights of co-owners of the mortgaged property, which are considered below.[134]

The practice: A mortgagee who is exercising his rights in respect of a property which is the home of the mortgagor will generally need to take possession of it in order to be able to sell it with vacant possession. In such circumstances, institutional mortgagees will, despite their right to take possession without a court order, normally seek such an order if the mortgagor is in occupation so that he has an opportunity of claiming statutory relief. Mortgagees sometimes also need to take possession in the case of commercial property. But except where there is to be a sale in the immediate future or where the property is already fully let to tenants,[135] mortgagees are generally slow to take possession. This is because, if they do so, they will be liable to account to the mortgagor for the use of the property on an extremely strict basis, namely on what is known as the footing of wilful default. This means that they must account not only for everything that they actually receive but also for everything that they could conceivably have received.[136]

This is not a problem where the whole of the property is already let since the mortgagee will simply have to account to the mortgagor for the rents which he receives from the existing tenants; that is why there is little risk in taking possession of fully let property. However,

---

[127] LPA 1925 s.104(1).

[128] *Birch v Wright* (1786) 1 T.R. 378 at 383; *Four-Maids Ltd v Dudley Marshall (Properties) Ltd* [1957] Ch. 317 at 320.

[129] LPA 1925 s.87(1).

[130] *Ropaigealach v Barclays Bank Plc* [2000] Q.B. 263.

[131] See below, para.17–028.

[132] *Horlock v Smith* (1842) 6 Jur. 478.

[133] *Quennell v Maltby* [1979] 1 W.L.R. 318.

[134] Below, para.17–073.

[135] The Mortgage Repossessions (Protection of Tenants etc) Act 2010 offers tenants of an unauthorised tenancy of mortgaged residential property limited protection by giving the court the power to suspend the delivery of possession for a period not exceeding two months.

[136] *Chaplin v Young (No.1)* (1863) 33 Beav 330 at 337, 338.

where this is not the case, the potential problems are considerable. Where a mortgagee was a brewer and the mortgaged property was a "free" house, a mortgagee who took possession and let the property as a "tied" house was held liable for the additional rent which he would have obtained if he had let the property as a "free" house.[137] Similarly, if a mortgagee occupies the property himself instead of letting it, he will be liable to account to the mortgagor for a fair occupation rent.[138] However, he need pay no rent if through decay or otherwise the land is incapable of being beneficially occupied.[139]

Powers while in possession: While in possession, a mortgagee whose mortgage was made by deed may cut and sell timber and other trees ripe for cutting which were not planted or left standing for shelter or ornament, or contract for this to be done within 12 months of the contract.[140] Although he is not liable for waste, he will be liable if he improperly cuts timber; and despite his right to work mines already opened, he may not open new mines. However, if the property becomes insufficient security for the money due, the court will not interfere if he cuts timber and opens mines, provided he is not guilty of wanton destruction.[141]

A mortgagee in possession must effect reasonable repairs,[142] and may without the mortgagor's consent effect reasonable but not excessive improvements; the cost will be charged to the mortgagor in the accounts.[143]

Relief of mortgagor:

(1) *Inherent jurisdiction.* The court has a very limited inherent jurisdiction to grant a short adjournment of proceedings for possession in order to give the mortgagor a chance of paying off the mortgage in full or otherwise satisfying the mortgagee, unless there is no reasonable prospect of this occurring.[144] The court also has inherent jurisdiction to adjourn proceedings for possession pending sale of the property so that the mortgagor rather than the mortgagee can have the conduct of the sale[145] (a sale by a mortgagor in possession is likely to yield a higher price than a sale by a mortgagee who has repossessed the property). However, this only appears to be possible where the sale price will be enough to discharge the mortgagor's debt.

(2) *Consumer credit agreements.* Where a mortgage is regulated by the Consumer Credit Act 1974 (as amended by the Consumer Credit Act 2006), the court has discretion to suspend an order for possession[146] and/or to make a "time order" for the payment of any sums owed by such instalments as it considers reasonable, having regard to the means of the debtor.[147] There is no formal requirement for payment within a reasonable time but the court can take this into account when exercising its discretion.

---

[137] *White v City of London Brewery Co* (1889) 42 Ch.D. 237.

[138] *Marriott v Anchor Reversionary Co* (1861) 3 De G.F. & J. 177 at 193.

[139] *Marshall v Cave* (1824) 3 L.J. (o.s.) Ch. 57, not cited in *Fyfe v Smith* [1975] 2 N.S.W.L.R. 408 (hotel: occupation so as to preserve its business).

[140] LPA 1925 s.101(1).

[141] *Millett v Davey* (1863) 31 Beav. 470 at 475, 476.

[142] *Richards v Morgan* (1853) 4 Y. & C.Ex. 570.

[143] *Shepard v Jones* (1882) 21 Ch.D. 469.

[144] *Birmingham Citizens Permanent B.S. v Caunt* [1962] Ch. 883; contrast *Quennell v Maltby* [1979] 1 W.L.R. 318 at 322, obiter.

[145] *Cheltenham & Gloucester Plc v Booker* (1997) 73 P. & C.R. 412.

[146] CCA 1974 s.135

[147] CCA 1974 s.129.

(3) *Dwelling-houses.* Where the property mortgaged consists of or includes a dwelling-house, the court has a wide statutory jurisdiction in claims for possession (other than in proceedings for foreclosure in which possession is also claimed and in the case of mortgages regulated by the Consumer Credit Act 1974). Whether the property consists of or includes a dwelling-house is determined at the time the claim for possession is made, not at the time the mortgage was granted.[148] However, the existence of this statutory jurisdiction does not deprive the mortgagee of his right to take possession of the mortgaged property and, if he does so, that jurisdiction is not applicable.[149] Furthermore, if the mortgagee sells to a purchaser without first seeking a possession order, the mortgagor cannot invoke the statutory restriction because the purchaser is not the mortgagee.[150] However, institutional mortgagees nevertheless normally seek an order for possession if the mortgagor is in occupation.

Where the mortgagor seeks relief, the court may adjourn the proceedings, or stay or suspend execution of any judgment or order for possession for a defined or ascertainable period,[151] or postpone the date for delivery of possession.[152] Where the mortgagor is in arrears with his payments, the jurisdiction is only exercisable where it appears to the court that "the mortgagor is likely to be able within a reasonable period to pay any sums due under the mortgage", or to remedy any other default under it.[153] The court has power to impose conditions as to the payment of arrears and current sums and as to the remedying of defaults.[154] A common form of relief is therefore to suspend the order for possession on the basis of a revised schedule of payments gradually eradicating the arrears. Where this is done, the mortgagee may seek leave to enforce the order at any time[155] and will obviously do so if the mortgagor fails to keep to the revised schedule.

The "reasonable period" for the payments of sums due under the mortgage is normally the entire balance of the mortgage term,[156] although shorter periods are likely to be imposed where the mortgagor is not in a position to make any periodical payments or is in breach of some other provision of the mortgage such as letting the property to a tenant in breach of covenant. In the case of instalment mortgages (as most mortgages of dwelling-houses are), or mortgages which otherwise permit deferred payment,[157] the "sums due" are merely the instalments or payments in arrear, and not the whole capital sum, even if (as is usual) the mortgage makes this payable in full on any default by the mortgagor.[158] In deciding whether the mortgagor is likely to be able to pay the sums due within a reasonable

---

[148] *Royal Bank of Scotland Plc v Miller* [2001] 3 W.L.R. 523.
[149] *Ropaigealach v Barclays Bank Plc* [2000] Q.B. 263.
[150] *Horsham Properties v Clark* [2009] 1 W.L.R. 1255.
[151] *Royal Trust Co of Canada v Markham* [1975] 1 W.L.R. 1416.
[152] Administration of Justice Act 1970 (AJA 1970) s.36.
[153] AJA 1970 s.36(1).
[154] AJA 1970 s.36(3).
[155] *Abbey National Mortgages Plc v Bernard* (1996) 71 P. & C.R. 257.
[156] *Cheltenham and Gloucester B.S. v Norgan* [1997] 1 W.L.R. 343.
[157] See *Bank of Scotland v Grimes* [1986] Q.B. 1179 (endowment mortgage included); *Habib Bank Ltd v Tailor* [1982] 1 W.L.R. 1218. See [1984] Conv. 91 (S. Tromans).
[158] AJA 1970 s.8(1); *First Middlesbrough Trading and Mortgage Co Ltd v Cunningham* (1974) 28 P. & C.R. 69.

time, the court must take into account not only the arrears[159] but also the sums accruing.[160] The court will have regard to probabilities such as an impending sale of the property,[161] but not to remote possibilities such as hoped-for legacies or winnings from the pools,[162] or the fruits of a counterclaim against the mortgagee.[163]

Where it is clear that the mortgagor is not able to pay the arrears and sums accruing within a reasonable time, the court is often asked to suspend an order for possession pending sale of the property so that the mortgagor rather than the mortgagee can have the conduct of the sale.[164] (It can do so both under its inherent jurisdiction and under the statutory jurisdiction.[165]) While this benefits the mortgagor, in that a sale by a mortgagor in possession is likely to yield a higher price than a sale by a mortgagee who has repossessed the property, the court has to bear in mind the possibility that the mortgagor may attempt to delay matters.[166] Further, it has no jurisdiction to suspend an order pending sale where it is clear that the sale price will not be enough to discharge the mortgagor's debt.[167]

The statutory jurisdiction also appears to be exercisable where the mortgagor is not in arrears with his payments but is in default under the mortgage in some other way.[168] In these circumstances also the court can impose conditions as to the remedying of the default. However, serious non-financial defaults, such as unauthorised lettings of the mortgaged property, are generally irremediable,[169] in which case an order for possession will be both made and executed.

Once a possession order has actually been executed, the court's discretion under the statutory jurisdiction comes to an end; it cannot thereafter either suspend the order or set it aside and make a new order for possession.[170]

Spouses, civil partners and "connected persons": Where the spouse or civil partner of a mortgagor is entitled to occupy a dwelling-house by virtue of the Family Law Act 1996,[171] the Act makes any payment by that spouse or civil partner in respect of mortgage payments as good as if made by the mortgagor.[172] The spouse or civil partner can thus avert proceedings for possession by the mortgagee. He or she is entitled to be made party to any proceedings by the mortgagee if the court sees no special reason against it and is satisfied that the spouse may be expected to make such payments or do such things as might affect the exercise of the court's statutory jurisdiction to grant relief.[173] These rights have now

---

[159] See *Town & Country B.S. v Julien* (1991) 24 H.L.R. 312 (arrears over £190,000).
[160] AJA 1973 s.8(2).
[161] *Royal Trust Co of Canada v Markham* [1975] 1 W.L.R. 1416; and see *Target Home Loans v Clothier* [1994] 1 All E.R. 439.
[162] See *Hastings & Thanet B.S. v Goddard* [1970] 1 W.L.R. 1544 at 1548.
[163] *Citibank Trust Ltd v Ayivor* [1987] 1 W.L.R. 1157.
[164] *Cheltenham & Gloucester Plc v Booker* (1996) 73 P. & C.R. 412.
[165] Both inherent and statutory; see *Royal Trust Co of Canada v Markham* [1975] 1 W.L.R. 1416.
[166] *Cheltenham & Gloucester Plc v Krausz* [1997] 1 W.L.R. 1558.
[167] *Cheltenham & Gloucester Plc v Krausz* [1997] 1 W.L.R. 1558.
[168] This was the majority view in *Western Bank Ltd v Schindler* [1977] Ch. 1.
[169] *Britannia Building Society v Earl* [1990] 1 W.L.R. 422.
[170] *National and Provincial B.S. v Ahmed* [1995] 2 E.G.L.R. 127.
[171] See above, para.1–023.
[172] Family Law Act 1996 (FLA 1996) s.30(3).
[173] FLA 1996 s.55.

been extended in certain circumstances[174] to "connected persons" such as former spouses, former civil partners, cohabitants, and former cohabitants. If the spouse or civil partner's statutory right of occupation has actually been registered,[175] the mortgagee must serve notice of any proceedings on him or her.[176]

Attornment clauses: At one time many legal mortgages contained an attornment clause, by which the mortgagor attorned, or acknowledged himself to be, a tenant at will or from year to year of the mortgagee, usually at a nominal rent such as a peppercorn or five pence. Formerly this was inserted because a speedy procedure in the High Court was available to enable landlords to recover possession of the demised property from their tenants, and no such procedure was available for mere mortgagees; the attornment clause enabled mortgagees to sue for possession qua landlords. But changes to the rules of court in 1933, 1936 and 1937 made the speedy procedure available to mortgagees as such, so that this reason for the use of attornment clauses has long since gone and they are now not much used. A surviving advantage of such clauses is that covenants by the mortgagor in the mortgage relating to the premises will be enforceable by the mortgagee against an assignee of the mortgagor under the rules governing the running of covenants in leases.[177] Where an attornment clause has been used, the tenancy created thereby must in the absence of contrary provision be determined by notice to quit before proceedings for possession are commenced.[178] However, no statutory protection against eviction is conferred on the tenant-mortgagor, for the relevant legislation is concerned only with true tenancies.[179]

Limitation: Formerly if the mortgagee went into possession of unregistered mortgaged land and remained there for 12 years, or, in respect of registered land, had been in possession for the 12 year limitation period before October 13, 2003, without either acknowledging the mortgagor's title or receiving any payments from him, the mortgagor's equity of redemption would be extinguished and the mortgagee would acquire title to the land.[180] Since the Land Registration Act 2002 came into force on October 13, 2003, unless the mortgagee had been in possession for 12 years before that date then no period of limitation will run[181] and the provisions of Sch.6 of the 2002 Act apply.

17–029   To appoint a receiver

History: In order to avoid the dangers of taking possession and yet achieve much the same result, mortgages used to provide for the appointment of a receiver with extensive powers of management of the mortgaged property. At first, the appointment was made by the mortgagor at the request of the mortgagee, but later, mortgagees began to reserve a

---

[174] FLA 1996 ss.35(13), 36(15).
[175] Above, para.1–023.
[176] FLA 1996 s.56.
[177] *Regent Oil Co Ltd v J.A. Gregory (Hatch End) Ltd* [1966] Ch. 402. All leases created by attornment clauses are "old leases", no matter when they were actually made.
[178] *Hinckley & Country B.S. v Henny* [1953] 1 W.L.R. 352.
[179] *Steyning and Littlehampton B.S. v Wilson* [1951] Ch. 1018; *Alliance B.S. v Pinwill* [1958] Ch. 788.
[180] Limitation Act 1980 (LA 1980) s.16; *Young v Clarey* [1948] Ch. 191.
[181] LRA 2002 s.96(2).

power for themselves, acting in theory as agents for the mortgagor, to appoint a receiver. In such circumstances the receiver was deemed the agent of the mortgagor, and the mortgagee was not liable to account strictly[182] in the same way as would have been the case if he had taken possession or if the receiver had been his own agent. A satisfactory power to appoint a receiver is conferred by the Law of Property Act 1925.[183] In the case of registered land, it cannot be exercised until the mortgagee has been registered as proprietor of his charge.[184]

The power: The statutory power to appoint a receiver arises and becomes exercisable in the same circumstances as the power of sale.[185] The mortgagee makes the appointment by writing, and may remove or replace the receiver in the same way. The receiver is deemed to be the agent of the mortgagor, who is solely responsible for his acts unless the mortgage otherwise provides,[186] or unless the mortgagee represents him as being the mortgagee's agent.[187] The corollary of this is that the receiver owes duties to the mortgagor and anyone else with an interest in the equity of redemption which include but are not necessarily confined to a duty of good faith.[188] While his primary duty is to bring about a situation in which interest can be paid and the capital repaid, if he manages the mortgaged property he must do so with due diligence,[189] although this does not actually oblige him to carry on a business previously carried on by the mortgagor.

The receiver has power to recover the income of the property by action, distress or otherwise, and to give valid receipts for it. The income so received by the receiver and any profit obtained by managing the mortgaged property is first used to discharge outgoings, to pay interest due on prior incumbrances, and to pay the receiver's commission and other expenses. Thereafter, it is used to pay the interest due under the mortgage. If the mortgagee so directs in writing, any surplus may be applied towards discharge of the principal money lent on mortgage if that is due; otherwise, the surplus is payable to the person who would have been entitled to it had the receiver not been appointed, normally the mortgagor.[190]

Limitation: Unlike a mortgagee in possession, a receiver can obtain no title against the mortgagor under the Limitation Act 1980 for he is the mortgagor's agent.

The mortgagee's remedies are cumulative

A mortgagee is not bound to select one of the above remedies and pursue that and no   **17–030**
other: subject to his not recovering more than is due to him, he may employ any or all of the remedies to enforce payment.[191] Thus if he sells the property for less than the mortgage debt, he may then sue the mortgagor upon the personal covenant for repayment for the

---

[182] Above, para.17–027.
[183] s.101.
[184] *Lever Finance Ltd v Needleman's Trustees* [1956] Ch. 375.
[185] LPA 1925 ss.101(1), 109(1).
[186] LPA 1925 s.109(2); *White v Metcalf* [1903] 2 Ch. 567.
[187] *Chatsworth Properties Ltd v Effiom* [1971] 1 W.L.R. 144.
[188] *Medforth v Blake* [2000] Ch. 86.
[189] *Medforth v Blake* [2000] Ch. 86.
[190] LPA 1925 s.109.
[191] *Palmer v Hendrie* (1859) 27 Beav. 349 at 351.

balance.[192] This is so even if the sale was by the court and the mortgagee, bidding by leave of the court, has purchased the property.[193] The limitation period for recovering the capital sum is 12 years because the debt is created by deed and is therefore a speciality.[194]

However, if he wishes to sue after foreclosure, he can do so only on condition that he re-opens the foreclosure[195]; for, despite the foreclosure, he is treating the mortgage as being still alive. Consequently, if by disposing of the property after foreclosure the mortgagee has put it out of his power to re-open the foreclosure, he cannot sue upon the personal covenant for repayment.[196] This is one of the reasons that foreclosure is considered an unattractive remedy.

Equitable mortgagees or chargees

17–031   The extent to which the foregoing remedies are exercisable by an equitable mortgagee or chargee is as follows.

To sue for the money due

17–032   The position is the same as for a legal mortgage.

To foreclose

17–033   An equitable mortgagee may foreclose in the same way as a legal mortgagee, save that the court order will direct the mortgagor to convey the legal title to the mortgagee.[197] An equitable chargee, however, has no right of foreclosure,[198] for a charge effects no conveyance of a legal or equitable interest.

17–034   ### To sell

Unregistered land: For unregistered land, the statutory power of sale[199] applies wherever the mortgage or charge was made by deed[200]; other mortgagees or chargees have no power of sale, though they may apply to the court for an order for sale.[201] Although an equitable mortgagee or chargee by deed has the statutory power of sale, this probably does not enable him to convey the legal estate to the purchaser.[202] To overcome this defect, either or both of two conveyancing devices are employed.

---

[192] *Rudge v Richens* (1873) L.R. 8 C.P. 358.
[193] *Gordon Grant & Co Ltd v Boos* [1926] A.C. 781.
[194] *West Bromwich Building Society v Wilkinson* [2005] 1 W.L.R. 2303; LA 1980 s.8.
[195] *Perry v Barker* (1806) 13 Ves. 198; and see above, para.17–027.
[196] *Palmer v Hendrie* (1859) 27 Beav. 349.
[197] *James v James* (1873) L.R. 16 Eq. 153.
[198] *Re Lloyd* [1903] 1 Ch. 385.
[199] Above, paras 17–027 et seq.
[200] LPA 1925 s.101(1).
[201] LPA 1925 s.91(2).
[202] *Re Hodson and Howes' Contract* (1887) 35 Ch.D. 668; contrast *Re White Rose Cottage* [1965] Ch. 940 at 951.

(1) *Power of attorney*. An irrevocable power of attorney is inserted in the deed empowering the mortgagee or his assigns to convey the legal estate.[203]

(2) *Declaration of trust*. A clause is inserted in the deed whereby the mortgagor declares that he holds the legal estate on trust for the mortgagee, and empowers the mortgagee to appoint himself or his nominee as trustee in place of the mortgagor. The mortgagee can thus vest the legal estate in himself or the purchaser.

Registered land: For registered land, only a mortgagee or chargee who has been registered as a chargee has the statutory power of sale[204]; but equitable mortgagees may use the above conveyancing devices to sell the legal estate.[205]

Possible right to take possession

Although it is usually said that an equitable mortgagee, having no legal estate, has no right to possession, on principle there seems no reason why, like a tenant under an equitable lease, he should not be entitled to it[206]; and a provision in the mortgage may give him the right to it. If the land is let, he cannot collect the rent from the tenant, for that is payable to the legal reversioner[207] to whom the tenant is bound under the rules governing leasehold covenants. An equitable chargee, who has not even the benefit of a contract to create a legal mortgage, cannot even claim possession.   **17–035**

To appoint a receiver

As in the case of the power of sale, the statutory power to appoint a receiver[208] exists only if the mortgage or charge was made by deed and, in the case of registered land, only if the mortgage or charge has been registered as a charge.[209] In other cases, a receiver can be obtained only by applying to the court.   **17–036**

OTHER RIGHTS OF A MORTGAGEE

Certain other rights of a mortgagee must now be considered. The position of these and other matters is in general the same for both mortgages and charges, whether legal or equitable, and "mortgage" will accordingly be used hereafter to include all such incumbrances unless the contrary is indicated.   **17–037**

---

[203] These powers are now regulated by the Powers of Attorney Act 1971 (PAA 1971) ss.4(1), 5(3).

[204] LRA 2002 s.51.

[205] See, e.g. *Re White Rose Cottage* [1964] Ch. 483 at 495, 496; [1965] Ch. 940 at 955, 956.

[206] See *Walsh v Lonsdale* (1882) 21 Ch. D 9.

[207] *Finck v Tranter* [1905] 1 K.B. 427.

[208] Above, para.17–029.

[209] *Lever Finance Ltd v Needleman's Trustee* [1956] Ch. 375.

Right to fixtures

17–038   It is a question of construction to determine what property is included in a mortgage. However, subject to any contrary intention, a mortgage includes all fixtures attached to the land either at the date of the mortgage or thereafter; the exceptions as between landlord and tenant do not apply.[210]

Right to possession of the documents of title

Unregistered land

17–039   A first mortgagee of unregistered land has the same right to the title deeds as if he had the fee simple or an assignment of the lease which has been mortgaged, as the case may be[211]; but under all mortgages made since 1881, the mortgagor is entitled to inspect and make copies of the deeds, despite any contrary agreement.[212] However, first mortgages of registered land made on or after April 1, 1998 trigger first registration of title so in the case of such mortgages the deeds will have to be sent to the Land Registry for the title to be registered and thereafter the mortgagor will have a registered title. These triggers for compulsory first registration still exist under the Land Registration Act 2002.

If the land is still unregistered when the mortgage is redeemed by the mortgagor (this can only be the case if the mortgage was created prior to April 1, 1998), the mortgagee must deliver the deeds to him unless he has notice of some subsequent incumbrance, in which case the deeds should be delivered to the incumbrancer next in order of priority of whom the mortgagee has notice. Contrary to the general rule that registration is notice, registration under the Land Charges Act 1972 is not notice for this purpose,[213] although as has been seen a mortgagee is bound to search before he distributes any surplus after a sale.[214] If a mortgage becomes statute-barred by lapse of time,[215] the mortgagee must return the deeds even if no part of the mortgage debt has been or will be paid.[216]

Right to insure against fire at the mortgagor's expense

17–040   Under the Law of Property Act 1925[217] a mortgagee or registered chargee may insure the mortgaged property against fire and charge the premiums on the property in the same way as the money lent. This power, which is given only where the mortgage was made by deed, is exercisable as soon as the mortgage is made. The amount of the insurance must not exceed the amount specified in the deed, or, if none, two-thirds of the amount required to restore the property in case of total destruction. But the mortgagee cannot exercise his power if:

---

[210] Above, para.2–042.
[211] LPA 1925 ss.85(1), 86(1).
[212] LPA 1925 s.96(1).
[213] LPA 1925 s.96(2), added by LP(Am)A 1926 Sch.
[214] Above, para.17–027.
[215] Below, Ch.18.
[216] *Lewis v Plunket* [1937] Ch. 306; and see above, para.17–018.
[217] ss.101(1), 108, replacing CA 1881 ss.19(1), 23.

(i) the mortgage deed declares that no insurance is required; or

(ii) the mortgagor keeps up an insurance in accordance with the mortgage deed; or

(iii) the mortgage deed is silent as to insurance and the mortgagor keeps up an insurance to the amount authorised by the Act with the mortgagee's consent.

Right to consolidate

The right

Consolidation may be described as the right of a person in whom two or more mortgages are vested to refuse to allow one mortgage to be redeemed unless the other or others are also redeemed. In its basic form, the principle is simple. If A has mortgaged both Greenacre and Whiteacre to X, each property being worth £500,000 and each loan being £400,000, it would be unfair, if the value of Greenacre subsequently sinks to £350,000 and the value of Whiteacre doubles, to allow A to redeem Whiteacre and leave Greenacre unredeemed. In such a case, equity permits X to consolidate, and so to oblige A to redeem both mortgages or neither. In seeking redemption, A is asking for the assistance of equity, and equity puts its own price upon its interference, saying that he who seeks equity must do equity.   **17–041**

This simple concept has been elaborated to some extent; different considerations may arise where third parties are concerned, such as by transfer of a mortgage. The rules on the subject may be stated as follows.

Conditions

There can be no consolidation unless the following four conditions are satisfied.   **17–042**

(i) Reservation of right: Unless both the mortgages were made before 1882 or unless at least one of the mortgages reserves the right to consolidate or shows an intention to allow consolidation, s.93 of the Law of Property Act 1925 provides that there is no right to consolidate. It is common practice for mortgages to contain a clause excluding the operation of s.93, so permitting consolidation. Where there is a right of consolidation, the Land Registration Rules 2003 makes provision for an application to be made for an entry to be made on the register in respect of that right.[218]

(ii) Redemption dates passed: In the case of both mortgages, the legal dates for redemption must have passed.[219] Consolidation is an equitable doctrine and does not come into play unless and until only equitable rights to redeem are concerned.

(iii) Same mortgagor: Both mortgages must have been made by the same mortgagor.[220] Mortgages made by different mortgagors can never be consolidated, even if both properties later come into the same hands. This is so even if X makes one mortgage and Y, as trustee for X, makes the other, or if A makes one mortgage and A and B jointly make the other.[221] But it is immaterial whether or not the mortgages were made to the same mortgagees.

---

[218] LRR 2003 r.110.
[219] *Cummins v Fletcher* (1880) 14 Ch.D. 699.
[220] *Sharp v Rickards* [1909] 1 Ch. 109.
[221] *Thorneycroft v Crockett* (1848) 2 H.L.C. 239.

(iv) Simultaneous unions of mortgages and equities: There must have been a time when both the mortgages were vested in one person and simultaneously both the equities of redemption were vested in another person.[222] If this state of affairs exists at the time when redemption is sought, the mortgagee can consolidate, subject to the other conditions being fulfilled. Even if this state of affairs has ceased to exist by the time redemption is sought because the equities of redemption are then owned by different persons, a mortgagee who still holds both mortgages can consolidate.

Illustrations

17–043   There is no need to illustrate (i) and (ii), but the following examples may be given of the operation of (iii) and (iv).
   This represents the following steps:

   (1)   A mortgages one estate to X.
   (2)   B mortgages another estate to X.
   (3)   C purchases the equities of redemption of both properties.

There can be no consolidation here, even though Condition (iv) is satisfied, for the mortgages were made by different mortgagors.

   (1)   A mortgages one estate to X.
   (2)   A mortgages another estate to Y.
   (3)   Z purchases both mortgages.

Here Z can consolidate, provided Conditions (i) and (ii) are satisfied. Condition (iii) is satisfied and so is Condition (iv).

   (1)   A mortgages one estate to X.
   (2)   A mortgages another estate to Y.
   (3)   C purchases the equity on the first estate.
   (4)   D purchases the equity on the second estate.
   (5)   Z purchases both mortgages.

There can be no consolidation here, for Condition (iv) is not satisfied. It is true that at one stage (after Step (2)) both equities were in one person's hands, and that an another stage (Step (5)) both mortgages were in another person's hands; but at no one moment have both these conditions obtained. The equities separated before the mortgages came together.
   If C instead of D had purchased the equity on the second estate, Z could have consolidated, even though at the time of C's purchase no right to consolidate had arisen; the purchaser of two or more equities takes subject to the risk of the mortgages coming into the same hand and so permitting consolidation. This represents the same position as the previous example, except that Steps (3) and (5) have changed places. As Z has now

---

[222] See *Pledge v White* [1896] A.C. 187 at 198.

purchased both mortgages before A parted with either equity, Z may consolidate the mortgages provided Conditions (i) and (ii) are satisfied. In this event, if C seeks to redeem his mortgage, Z can refuse redemption unless C purchases the mortgage on D's property as well as redeeming his own mortgage.

More than two mortgages

These rules of consolidation apply equally when it is sought to consolidate more than two mortgages. Sometimes it will be found that while Mortgage I can be consolidated with Mortgages II and III, there is no right to consolidate Mortgages II and III with each other, for example if only Mortgage I contains a consolidation clause. Examples containing more than two mortgages are best worked out by taking the mortgages in pairs and applying the rules to each pair in turn.

17–044

Extent of doctrine

The nature of the mortgages or the property mortgaged is immaterial. There can be consolidation even if one mortgage is legal and one equitable, or if both are equitable, or if one mortgage is of personalty and the other of realty,[223] or if both are mortgages of personalty. The doctrine has even been applied to two mortgages on the same property.[224] Further, it is immaterial whether the equity of redemption has been conveyed *in toto* or whether it has merely been mortgaged; a mortgagee of an equity of redemption is a purchaser pro tanto, i.e. to the extent of his interest. Thus if a mortgagee has a right of consolidation, it is effective against subsequent mortgagees of the property as well as the mortgagor.

17–045

Purchasers

The doctrine of consolidation makes it dangerous to buy property which is subject to a mortgage by which the purchaser will be bound after completion without first making careful inquiries. If a right to consolidate has once arisen, a person who subsequently acquires one or both of the equities of redemption is liable to have the mortgages consolidated against him. And even if no right to consolidate has arisen, a person who acquires two equities of redemption is liable to have the mortgages consolidated if one person acquires both of them. But a person who acquires only one equity of redemption at a time when no right to consolidate has arisen normally suffers no risk of consolidation.[225]

17–046

Right to tack

This is considered below.[226]

17–047

---

[223] *Tassell v Smith* (1858) 2 De G. & J. 713.
[224] *Re Salmon* [1903] 1 K.B. 147; *sed quaere*.
[225] *Harter v Coleman* (1882) 19 Ch.D. 630.
[226] Below, paras 17–098 et seq.

RIGHTS COMMON TO BOTH PARTIES

Power of leasing

Leases not binding

17–048   The most important right common to both parties is the right of granting a lease of the mortgaged property. Apart from any statutory or contractual provisions, a mortgagor can grant a lease which is binding on himself. Even if his mortgage has taken the form of the grant of a long term of years so that he has no legal right to possession, he will be unable subsequently to deny the validity of that lease and eject the tenant because of the doctrine of estoppel. However, he cannot grant a lease which is binding on the mortgagee[227] nor can a mortgagee grant a lease which will be binding on the mortgagor following redemption.[228]

   Thus at common law, once property had been mortgaged, a satisfactory lease could be made only if both mortgagor and mortgagee concurred in granting it, or if the mortgage gave either or both of the parties power to grant binding leases. However, statute has materially altered this position; the provisions discussed below apply to all mortgages made after 1881 unless the parties have expressed a contrary intention, either in the mortgage itself or in some other written document.[229] (It is in fact common for mortgages of residential property to preclude the mortgagor from exercising any power to grant leases or tenancies; a lease granted by the mortgagor in breach of such a provision in the mortgage deed will not bind the mortgagee,[230] unless he subsequently adopts the tenancy, as by accepting rent from the tenant.[231])

Power to lease

17–049   A power to grant leases which will be binding on both mortgagor and mortgagee is exercisable by the mortgagee, if he is in possession or has appointed a receiver who is still acting; otherwise, by the mortgagor if he is in possession.

Term of lease

17–050   A lease may be granted for not more than 50 years for agricultural or occupation purposes or 999 years for building where the mortgage in question was granted after 1925.[232]

---

[227] *Rogers v Humphreys* (1835) 4 A. & E. 299 at 313.
[228] See *Chapman v Smith* [1907] 2 Ch. 97 at 102.
[229] LPA 1925 s.99, replacing CA 1881 s.18.
[230] *Dudley & District Benefit B.S. v Emerson* [1949] Ch. 707; *Britannia B.S. v Earl* [1990] 1 W.L.R. 422.
[231] See *Stroud B.S. v Delamont* [1960] 1 W.L.R. 431.
[232] LPA 1925 s.99(3). In the case of mortgages granted before 1926, the periods were 21 years and 99 years respectively.

Conditions of lease

To fall within the statutory powers, any lease granted must comply with the following conditions: **17–051**

(i) it must be limited to take effect in possession not later than 12 months after its date;

(ii) it must reserve the best rent reasonably obtainable, and with certain qualifications no lump sum payment may be taken;

(iii) it must contain a covenant by the lessee for payment of rent and a condition of re-entry on the rent not being paid for a specified period not exceeding 30 days; and

(iv) a counterpart of the lease must be executed by the lessee and delivered to the lessor and a counterpart of any lease granted by the mortgagor must be delivered within one month to the mortgagee.[233]

These conditions do not preclude the grant of oral leases in exercise of the statutory power[234]; such leases need not comply with the last two conditions.[235] Neither the statutory power of leasing nor any provision in the mortgage excluding these powers (as is common in the case of a mortgagor of residential property) deprives either party of his common law right to grant a lease but that lease will not bind the other unless adopted by him.[236] Further, the parties may extend the statutory powers by an agreement in writing, whether or not that agreement is contained in the mortgage.[237]

Power of accepting surrenders of leases

If the parties have not expressed a contrary intention, either in the mortgage or otherwise in writing, statute[238] enables a surrender of any lease or tenancy to be effected, binding the parties to the mortgage, on the following terms.   **17–052**

Power to accept

The surrender may be accepted by the mortgagee, if he is in possession or has appointed a receiver who is still acting; otherwise, by the mortgagor if he is in possession.   **17–053**

Conditions of surrender

For the surrender to be valid: **17–054**

(i) an authorised lease of the property must be granted to take effect in possession within one month of the surrender;

---

[233] See *Public Trustee v Lawrence* [1912] 1 Ch. 789.
[234] LPA 1925 s.99(17). For oral leases, see above, para.11–016.
[235] *Rhodes v Dalby* [1971] 1 W.L.R. 1325 at 1331, 1332.
[236] *Rust v Goodale* [1957] Ch. 33; contrast *Taylor v Ellis* [1960] Ch. 368.
[237] LPA 1925 s.99(14).
[238] LPA 1925 s.100, replacing CA 1911 s.3.

(ii) the term of the new lease must not be shorter than the unexpired residue of the surrendered lease; and

(iii) the rent reserved by the new lease must not be less than the rent reserved by the surrendered lease.

The statutory power of accepting a surrender is thus exercisable only for the purpose of replacing one lease by another,[239] but the power may be extended by an agreement in writing, whether or not that agreement is contained in the mortgage.

RIGHT OF THE MORTGAGOR OR CHARGOR TO REDEEM

Protection of the mortgagor

17–055 One aspect of equity's protection of the mortgagor's equity of redemption is to be found in the maxim "once a mortgage, always a mortgage". This is applied in two ways.

The test of a mortgage is substance, not form

17–056 If a transaction is in substance a mortgage, equity will treat it as such, even if it is dressed up in some other guise, as by the documents being cast in the form of an absolute conveyance.[240] Thus, if a mortgage is expressed in the form of a conveyance with an option for the mortgagor to repurchase the property in a year's time, the mortgagor is entitled to redeem it even after the year has expired.[241]

No clogs on the equity

17–057 There must be no clog or fetter on the equity of redemption. This means not only that the mortgagor cannot be prevented from eventually redeeming his property, but also that he cannot be prevented from redeeming it free from any conditions or stipulations in the mortgage.

No irredeemability: It is impossible to provide that a mortgage shall be totally irredeemable[242] or that the right of redemption shall be confined to certain persons or to a limited period.[243] A provision in a mortgage that the property shall become the mortgagee's absolutely when some specified event occurs is void.[244] In all such cases, the owner of the equity of redemption may redeem as if there had been no such restriction. But once the mortgage has been made, equity will not intervene if the mortgagor, by a separate and independent transaction, gives the mortgagee an option of purchasing the property and thus of depriving

---

[239] See *Barclays Bank Ltd v Stasek* [1957] Ch. 28.

[240] *Barnhart v Greenshields* (1853) 9 Moo.P.C. 18.

[241] *Waters v Mynn* (1850) 15 L.T.(o.s.) 157; and see *Grangeside Properties Ltd v Collingwoods Securities Ltd* [1964] 1 W.L.R. 139.

[242] *Re Wells* [1933] Ch. 29 at 52.

[243] *Salt v Marquess of Northampton* [1892] A.C. 1.

[244] *Toomes v Conset* (1745) 3 Atk. 261.

the mortgagor of his equity of redemption.[245] While the mortgagor is in the defenceless position of seeking a loan, or arranging for a transfer of the mortgage,[246] equity will protect him; but once he has obtained the loan or secured the transfer, this protection is not needed.

A provision postponing the date of redemption until some future period longer than the customary six months, such as for 40 years, is valid, provided the mortgage as a whole is not so oppressive and unconscionable that equity would not enforce it, and provided it does not make the equitable right to redeem illusory.[247] In one case, a lease for 20 years was mortgaged on conditions which prevented its redemption until six weeks before the end of the term. Such a provision rendered the equitable right to redeem illusory and so was held void.[248] Generally, however, the court will not interfere with a bargain made between two parties on an equal footing, even if this does postpone redemption for a considerable period.

Limited companies are not protected by this rule, for by statute a debenture may be made wholly or partly irredeemable, and even an ordinary mortgage by a company is a debenture.[249]

Redemption free from conditions in the mortgage: The mortgagor cannot be prevented from redeeming exactly what he mortgaged, i.e. the property free from all conditions or stipulations in the mortgage. The essence of a mortgage is a loan of money in return for security. Sometimes terms are inserted in a mortgage which give the mortgagee some other advantage in addition to his security. If this advantage is obtained by fraud or oppression, it will be set aside, but otherwise there is no objection to an advantage which ceases whenever the mortgage is redeemed, such as a provision making the mortgaged property, a public house, a "tied" house until redemption.[250] The general enforceability of advantages which end on redemption represents an advance on the attitude which the courts had at one time adopted, rendering all collateral advantages for the mortgagee void on the basis that they were a disguised form of interest contravening the usury laws.[251] After the last of the statutes dealing with usury was repealed in 1854, the courts gradually became more liberal and it is now settled that in certain cases a collateral advantage may remain effective even after redemption.

The chief difficulty in stating the present position lies in trying to reconcile the clog held void in *Bradley v Carritt*[252] with the collateral advantage held valid in *Kreglinger v New Patagonia Meat and Cold Storage Co Ltd*.[253] In *Bradley's* case the substance of the transaction was a mortgage of shares in which the mortgagor bound himself to endeavour to induce the company to employ the mortgagee as broker, and if the company did not, to

---

[245] *Reeve v Lisle* [1902] A.C. 461 (option 12 days after mortgage, unlike *Samuel v Jarrah Timber and Wood Paving Corp Ltd* [1904] A.C. 323, where the mortgage deed contained the option).
[246] *Lewis v Frank Love Ltd* [1961] 1 W.L.R. 261.
[247] *Knightsbridge Estates Trust Ltd v Byrne* [1939] Ch. 441 (affirmed on other grounds: [1940] A.C. 613). Both parties were bound to allow the full 40-year period.
[248] *Fairclough v Swan Brewery Co Ltd* [1912] A.C. 565. Contrast *Santley v Wilde* [1899] 2 Ch. 474, which seems unsound: see *Noakes & Co Ltd v Rice* [1902] A.C. 24 at 31, 34.
[249] CA 2006 s.739; *Knightsbridge Estates Trust Ltd v Byrne* [1940] A.C. 613.
[250] *Biggs v Hoddinott* [1898] 2 Ch. 307; *Noakes & Co Ltd v Rice* [1902] A.C. 24.
[251] See *Jennings v Ward* (1705) 2 Vern. 520 at 521; *Noakes & Co Ltd v Rice* [1902] A.C. 24 at 33.
[252] [1903] A.C. 253.
[253] [1914] A.C. 25.

pay the mortgagee an amount equivalent to the broker's fees. In *Kreglinger's* case the substance of the transaction was a loan of money to a meat company in return for an option for five years on any sheepskins which the company had for sale. The differing results in these cases can be explained in two ways. In *Bradley's* case the shares returned were fettered by the practical restriction that they could not be sold without retaining so much of the voting rights attached to them as allowed the mortgagor to continue to control the appointment, whereas in *Kreglinger's* case the property was returned unfettered. Alternatively it can be said that in *Bradley's* case the agreement fettering the mortgagor was a mere clause put in a mortgage, and so void, the basis of the agreement being a mortgage and nothing else. In *Kreglinger's* case, on the other hand, the transaction was substantially the grant of an option in return for a loan of money, with the result that the option was not merely a part of the mortgage but a separate and independent transaction and so valid.[254] The courts are reluctant to allow the doctrine which forbids clogs on the equity of redemption to upset a freely negotiated commercial contract.[255]

Unconscionable terms: The court has a general jurisdiction to grant relief against terms in a mortgage which are oppressive or unconscionable.[256] Thus where a property company sold one of its houses to the tenant, lending him £2,900 on a mortgage of the house which required repayment of £4,553 over six years, the transaction was held to be unconscionable, and the tenant was held to be entitled to redeem the mortgage on paying £2,900 with interest of seven per cent as fixed by the court.[257] Nor do the provisions commonly found entitling the mortgagee to vary the rate of interest from time to time give him a completely unfettered power to do so. There is an implied term that he cannot do so dishonestly, for an improper purpose, capriciously, arbitrarily or in a way that no reasonable mortgagee, acting reasonably, would do.[258] However, raising interest rates by more than standard market rates had risen because of commercial considerations in order to overcome financial difficulties did not amount to a breach of that implied term.[259] Further, if provisions in a mortgage, though unreasonable, are not initially unconscionable, subsequent events will not invalidate them. Thus, where a commercial mortgage for ten years was indexed to the Swiss franc, and there was then an unforeseen fall in the value of the pound by two-thirds, the court refused to intervene.[260]

Regulated mortgages: The Consumer Credit Act 2006 has amended the Consumer Credit Act 1974 by repealing ss.127 to 140, relating to extortionate credit bargains, and making significant changes to the Act generally. In place of the provisions relating to extortionate credit bargains the 2006 Act has introduced new provisions relating to unfair relationships.[261] The court may make an order under s.140B of the Act in connection with a credit agreement if it determines that the relationship between them is unfair to the debtor because of: (i) any

---

[254] See *Re Petrol Filling Station, Vauxhall Bridge Road, London* (1968) 20 P. & C.R. 1.
[255] *Kreglinger's Case* [1914] A.C. 25 at 46; *Samuel v Jarrah Timber and Wood Paving Corp Ltd* [1904] A.C. 323 at 327.
[256] *Knightsbridge Estates Trust Ltd v Byrne* [1939] Ch. 441 at 457; in H.L., [1940] A.C. 613.
[257] *Cityland and Property (Holdings) Ltd v Dabrah* [1968] Ch. 166, as explained in *Multiservice Bookbinding Ltd v Marden* [1979] Ch. 84 at 109, 110.
[258] *Paragon Finance v Nash* [2002] 1 W.L.R. 685.
[259] *Paragon Finance v Nash* [2002] 1 W.L.R. 685.
[260] *Multiservice Bookbinding Ltd v Marden* [1979] Ch. 84.
[261] CCA 1974 ss.140A–140.

of the terms of the agreement or related agreement; (ii) the way in which the creditor has exercised or enforced any of his rights under the agreement; or (iii) because of any other thing done (or not done) by, or on behalf of the creditor.[262] The new provisions give the court wide powers to order the repayment in whole or part the sum paid by the debtor, the return of property, alteration of the terms of the agreement, or to set it aside altogether.[263]

Most ordinary mortgages for house purchase are outside these provisions, which are aimed at improvident second mortgages by house owners for personal expenditure. The Financial Services and Markets Act 2000 regulates purchase mortgages. Where the 1974 Act (as amended) applies there are detailed provisions requiring a mortgage within the Act to be in a prescribed form, signed by both parties, which makes the mortgagor aware of his rights and duties, and the protection given by the Act; and the mortgagor must be sent a copy of the proposed mortgage at least seven days before he is sent a copy for signature, thus giving him a "consideration period".[264] The mortgagor may repay the sums due at any time, despite any agreement to the contrary[265]; and mortgages within the Act are enforceable only on an order of the court.[266]

Restraint of trade: A provision in a mortgage which is not oppressive, unconscionable or extortionate nor a clog on the equity of redemption may nevertheless be void on other grounds. Thus it may be invalid under the ordinary law of contract as being in unreasonable restraint of trade.[267]

Who can redeem?

Redemption is usually sought by the mortgagor; but the right to redeem is not confined to him and may be exercised by any person interested in the equity of redemption.[268] Thus the right to redeem extends to assignees of the equity of redemption, subsequent mortgagees, and even a lessee under a lease granted by the mortgagor but not binding on the mortgagee.[269]   **17–058**

Effect of redemption

Where redemption is effected by the only person interested in the equity of redemption, and the mortgage redeemed is the only incumbrance on the property, the effect of redemption is to discharge the mortgage and leave the property free from incumbrances. But if there are several mortgages on the property, the effect of redemption will normally be that the person paying the money takes a transfer of the mortgage, as where a second mortgagee redeems the first mortgage. If several incumbrancers seek to redeem a mortgage, the first in order of priority has the best claim.[270] However, if the mortgagor redeems   **17–059**

---

[262] CCA 1974 s.140A.
[263] CCA 1974 s.140B.
[264] CCA 1974 ss.58–61.
[265] CCA 1974 ss.94, 173.
[266] CCA 1974 ss.126, 173(3).
[267] *Esso Petroleum Co Ltd v Harper's Garage (Stourport) Ltd* [1968] A.C. 269.
[268] *Pearce v Morris* (1869) 5 Ch.App. 227 at 229.
[269] *Tarn v Turner* (1888) 39 Ch.D. 456.
[270] *Teevan v Smith* (1882) 20 Ch.D. 724 at 730.

a mortgage which has priority over one or more subsequent mortgages, the redemption discharges the mortgage and the mortgagor cannot claim to have it kept alive to the prejudice of the subsequent mortgagees.[271] For his mortgage to them included all the rights he had, including those against the prior mortgagee. But no such rule binds his successors in title.[272]

An incumbrancer who is entitled to redeem a mortgage may usually, instead of redeeming, insist upon the mortgagee transferring the mortgage to the incumbrancer's nominee.[273]

Terms of redemption

17–060   A mortgage may be redeemed either in court or out of court; the latter is the more usual. If a mortgagee unreasonably refuses to accept a proper tender of the money due and so makes an action for redemption necessary, he may be penalised in costs.[274]

The mortgagor may redeem on the legal date for redemption without giving notice of his intention to do so. After that date, when he is forced to rely upon his equitable right to redeem, it is a rule of practice that he must either give the mortgagee reasonable notice of his intention to redeem (six months usually sufficing), or else pay him six months' interest in lieu thereof.[275] It is only fair that the mortgagee should have a reasonable opportunity of finding another investment for his money. But the mortgagee is not entitled to any notice or interest in lieu thereof:

  (i) if he has taken steps to enforce his security, as by taking possession, or commencing foreclosure proceedings, or giving the mortgagor notice to repay the loan so as to entitle the mortgagee to sell on default being made[276]; or
  (ii) if the loan is merely of a temporary nature, as is usually the case in an equitable mortgage by deposit of documents of title.[277]

If the mortgagor gives six months' notice and fails to pay on the proper day, he must usually give a further six months' notice or pay six months' interest in lieu thereof,[278] unless he can give a reasonable explanation of his failure to pay, in which case it suffices to give reasonable notice, such as three months.[279]

Even if the mortgage makes no provision for interest, the mortgagor must pay it at a rate which the court will, if necessary, fix.[280]

---

[271] *Otter v Lord Vaux* (1856) 6 De G.M. & G. 638, recognised by LPA 1925 s.115(3); *Parkash v Irani Finance Ltd* [1970] Ch. 101.
[272] *Whiteley v Delaney* [1914] A.C. 132.
[273] LPA 1925 s.95.
[274] *Graham v Seal* (1918) 88 L.J.Ch. 31.
[275] *Johnson v Evans* (1889) 61 L.T. 18. The mortgage deed may provide to the contrary.
[276] See *Bovill v Endle* [1896] 1 Ch. 648.
[277] *Fitzgerald's Trustee v Mellersh* [1892] 1 Ch. 385.
[278] *Re Moss* (1886) L.R. 31 Ch.D. 90 at 94.
[279] *Cromwell Property Investment Co Ltd v Western* [1934] Ch. 322.
[280] See *Cityland and Property (Holdings) Ltd v Dabrah* [1968] Ch. 166.

"Redeem up, foreclose down"

The maxim "redeem up, foreclose down" applies where there are several incumbrancers **17–061** and one of them seeks by action to redeem a superior mortgage. The effect is best shown by an example. X has mortgaged his property successively to A, B, C, D, and E, the mortgages ranking in that order. X thus ranks last, for example in claiming any surplus if the property is sold. Suppose that D wishes to redeem B's mortgage and, owing to the complexity of the accounts or some other circumstance, an action for redemption is commenced. Before B's mortgage can be redeemed, the exact amount due to him must be settled by the court. This amount, however, does not affect only B and D, for C, E and X are all concerned with the amount which has priority to their interests; thus if the property were to be sold, C, E and X would all wish to know whether what B was entitled to was, say, £60,000 or £70,000, for upon that figure might depend their chances of receiving anything from the proceeds of sale. Consequently, the court will insist upon their being made parties to D's action for redemption so that they can be represented in the taking of the accounts between B and D, and thus be bound by the final result.

However, it would be unfair to give C, E and X the trouble and expense of taking part in the action merely to watch accounts being taken,[281] with the risk of a similar event taking place in the future, and so the court insists that the rights of all parties concerned in the action shall be settled once and for all. A is not concerned: it is immaterial to him what is due to B, for A's mortgage has priority to B's.[282] But all the other parties are concerned, and the order of the court will be that D shall redeem not only B's mortgage, but also C's mortgage, for both those mortgages have priority to D's. Further, the rights of E and X must be foreclosed: that is, each of them will have the opportunity of saving his rights by paying off the prior mortgages concerned in the action, but if he fails to do so, he will be foreclosed. Thus if E and X fail to redeem and are foreclosed, the final result will be that D, at the price of redeeming B and C, now holds the equity of redemption subject only to the first mortgage in favour of A.

The principle may be stated thus: a mortgagee who seeks to redeem a prior mortgage by action must not only redeem any mortgages standing between him and that prior mortgage,[283] but must also foreclose all subsequent mortgagees and the rights of the mortgagor[284]; in short, "redeem up, foreclose down".

It should be noted that this rule does not apply to redemptions out of court,[285] and that there is no rule "foreclose down, redeem up"; a mortgagee who forecloses is under no obligation to redeem any prior mortgages,[286] although he must foreclose all subsequent mortgagees as well as the rights of the mortgagor.[287] In other words, for foreclosure the rule is simply "foreclose down": a mortgagee cannot foreclose a subsequent mortgagee or the rights of the mortgagor unless he forecloses everyone beneath him.

---

[281] *Ramsbottom v Wallis* (1835) 5 L.J.Ch. 92.

[282] *Brisco v Kenrick* (1832) 1 L.J.Ch. 11.

[283] *Teevan v Smith* (1882) 20 Ch.D. 724 at 729.

[284] *Farmer v Curtis* (1829) 2 Sim. 466.

[285] See *Smith v Green* (1844) 1 Coll.C.C. 555.

[286] *Richards v Cooper* (1842) 5 Beav. 304.

[287] *Anderson v Stather* (1845) 2 Coll.C.C. 209.

Termination of equity of redemption

17–062   An equity of redemption may be extinguished against the wishes of the mortgagor:

> (i)   by foreclosure[288];
> (ii)   by sale[289]; or
> (iii)   by lapse of time.[290]

In addition, the mortgagor may himself extinguish his equity of redemption by releasing it to the mortgagee, or by redeeming.

OTHER RIGHTS OF THE MORTGAGOR OR CHARGOR

17–063   The mortgagor has various other rights, including the right to have the property sold by the court, the right to inspect the title deeds where the land in question is unregistered, the right to compel a transfer of the mortgage[291] and the right to bring actions. As to the right to bring actions, even if the mortgage has taken the form of the grant of a long term of years so that the mortgagor has no legal right to possession but merely the freehold reversion, provided that the mortgagee has not given notice of his intention to take possession or enter into receipt of the rents and profits, by statute[292] the mortgagor in possession may sue in his own name for possession or for the rents and profits. He may bring an action to prevent, or recover damages for, any trespass or other wrong, and he may enforce all covenants and conditions in any leases or tenancies of the property.

PART 4   TRANSFER OF RIGHTS

DEATH OF MORTGAGOR

17–064   On the death of a person who holds realty or personalty subject to a mortgage or charge, the person who is entitled under that person's will or intestacy will take the property subject to the mortgage or charge unless the deceased has shown a contrary intention[293] in any document, whether or not a will.[294] This rule was finally established by the Administration of Estates Act 1925.[295] However, it does not apply to a person who takes not

---

[288]   Above, paras 17–024 et seq.
[289]   Above, paras 17–027 et seq.
[290]   Below, para.18–029.
[291]   LPA 1925 ss.91, 95, 96.
[292]   LPA 1925 ss.98, 141, replacing earlier legislation.
[293]   See *Re Wakefield* [1943] 2 All E.R. 29; *Re Neeld* [1962] Ch. 643.
[294]   AEA 1925 s.35.
[295]   s.35.

as a legatee or devisee but, for instance as a purchaser under an option given to him by the will.[296]

These provisions do not affect any rights the mortgagee may have against the estate of the mortgagor. They merely ensure that as between the person taking the mortgaged property and the other beneficiaries, the burden of the mortgage should fall upon the former, in the absence of any contrary intention.

DEATH OF MORTGAGEE

Death of sole mortgagee

Under the Administration of Estates Act 1925[297] the mortgagee's right to the money lent and his interest in the mortgaged property both pass to his personal representatives. **17–065**

Death of one of several mortgagees

At law

Where two or more persons lent money on mortgage of freeholds or leaseholds, the legal estate was usually conveyed to them as joint tenants. On the death of one, his interest passed to the others by virtue of the rule of survivorship and the survivors could reconvey the legal estate to the mortgagor when he redeemed. **17–066**

In equity

In equity, however, there is a presumption of a tenancy in common where two or more together lend money on mortgage.[298] Accordingly, in the absence of any provision to the contrary, when one of the mortgagees died his share passed to his personal representatives, and if the mortgagor redeemed they would have to join in the transaction. If the mortgagees were trustees lending trust money, the disclosure of this fact would be sufficient to rebut the presumption, for trustees are always joint tenants[299]; but this would have the disadvantage of bringing the trusts on to the title.[300] **17–067**

Joint account clause

The practice accordingly grew up of inserting a "joint account clause" in mortgages where two or more persons lent money. This clause rebutted the presumption of a tenancy in common so far as the mortgagor was concerned and made it safe for him to pay his money to the surviving mortgagees. Since 1881 such a clause has not actually been necessary, for statute[301] **17–068**

---

[296] *Re Fison's W.T.* [1950] Ch. 394.
[297] AEA 1925 ss.1(1), 3(1).
[298] Above, para.8–030.
[299] Above, para.8–002.
[300] See, e.g. *Re Blaiberg and Abrahams* [1899] 2 Ch. 340.
[301] CA 1881 s.61, replaced by LPA 1925 s.111.

has provided that as between the mortgagor and the mortgagees, the mortgagees are deemed to have advanced the money on a joint account unless a contrary intention appears. The result is that the survivor or survivors can give a complete discharge for all moneys due, notwithstanding any notice of severance which the mortgagor may have. This, however, is mere conveyancing machinery; it does not affect the position of the mortgagees *inter se*, and if they are beneficially entitled and not trustees, the survivors must account to the personal representatives of the deceased mortgagee for his share.[302] Although a joint account clause in a mortgage today is thus strictly unnecessary, it is often inserted out of an abundance of caution.

TRANSFER OF EQUITY OF REDEMPTION INTER VIVOS

17–069   A mortgagor may at any time without the mortgagee's consent make a conveyance of his property subject to the mortgage, and the mortgagee cannot prevent an order for sale being made under the court's discretionary power[303] merely because the price is less than the sums due under the mortgage.[304] Notwithstanding any such conveyance, the mortgagor remains personally liable on the covenant to pay the money.[305] He therefore usually takes an express covenant for indemnity from the transferee, although such an obligation is implied.[306]

A mortgagor who wishes to sell free from the mortgage may do so:

  (i) if he redeems; or
 (ii) if the mortgagee consents (as he may well do if the security is adequate or if some other property is substituted for the property in question); or
(iii) if the mortgagor takes advantage of the statutory provision enabling the court to declare property free from an incumbrance upon sufficient money being paid into court.[307]

An assignee of the equity of redemption in general steps into the shoes of the mortgagor; but he does not merely by the assignment become personally liable to the mortgagee to pay the mortgage debt.[308]

TRANSFER OF MORTGAGES INTER VIVOS

In general

17–070   A mortgagee may transfer his mortgage at any time without the concurrence of the mortgagor. However, for various reasons it is advisable for the mortgagor's concurrence to be

---

[302] See *Re Jackson* (1887) 34 Ch.D. 732.
[303] Under LPA 1925 s.91(2).
[304] *Palk v Mortgage Services Funding Plc* [1993] Ch. 330.
[305] *Kinnaird v Trollope* (1888) 39 Ch.D. 636.
[306] *Bridgman v Daw* (1891) 40 W.R. 253.
[307] LPA 1925 s.50, replacing CA 1881 s.5(1).
[308] *Re Errington* [1894] 1 Q.B. 11.

obtained, such as in order to obtain his admission of the state of accounts showing the amount still due under the mortgage.[309]

Once the transfer has been made, the transferee should give notice of it to the mortgagor, unless the mortgagor has notice already, such as because he was a party to the transfer. If the mortgagor has no actual or constructive notice, the transferee cannot complain if the mortgagor pays to the transferor money due under the mortgage.[310]

Sub-mortgages

A sub-mortgage is a mortgage of a mortgage. A mortgagee may, instead of transferring his mortgage, borrow money upon the security of it. A well-secured debt can itself be good security for a loan to the creditor. Thus if X has lent £20,000 upon a mortgage made by B, and X then wishes to raise a temporary loan of £2,000 himself, it would clearly be inadvisable for X to transfer the mortgage to Y for £20,000 or to call in the whole of his loan. Consequently, X would raise the money by mortgaging his mortgage, i.e. by making a sub-mortgage.   **17–071**

Before 1926, a sub-mortgage was effected by a transfer of the mortgage subject to a proviso for redemption. In the case of unregistered land, this form is still available if the mortgage is equitable or is a legal charge. But where it has been created by the grant of a term of years, a legal sub-mortgage can be made only by the grant of a sub-lease or by a legal charge.[311] In general, the sub-mortgagee takes over the mortgagee's rights of enforcing payment under the original mortgage; thus he may sell the property. Alternatively, he may exercise his remedies against the mortgage itself, as by selling it. In the case of registered land, it is no longer possible to create a sub-mortgage.[312] However, the proprietor of a registered charge is able to charge his registered charge by way of sub-charge[313] and the holder of any sub-charge and of any sub-sub-charge has the same powers as the holder of the registered charge and any superior sub-chargee.[314]

DISCHARGE OF MORTGAGES

Since 1925, in the case of any mortgage of unregistered land, a receipt indorsed on or annexed to the mortgage deed, signed[315] by the mortgagee and stating the name of the person paying the money, normally discharges the mortgage.[316] Where the mortgage has been created by the grant of a term of years absolute, that term will either be surrendered or reconveyed. Where the mortgage has been created by charge, the charge will simply be cancelled. But if the receipt shows that the person paying the money was not entitled to the immediate equity of redemption and makes no provision to the contrary, that receipt   **17–072**

---

[309] See *Turner v Smith* [1901] 1 Ch. 213.
[310] *Dixon v Winch* [1900] 1 Ch. 736 at 742.
[311] LPA 1925 s.86(1), (3).
[312] LRA 2002 s.23(2)(a), (3).
[313] LRA 2002 s.23(2)(b).
[314] LRA 2002 s.53.
[315] See *Simpson v Geoghegan* [1934] W.N. 232.
[316] LPA 1925 s.115(1).

operates as a transfer of the mortgage to him.[317] Building society mortgages may still be discharged by a special form of receipt, indorsed on the mortgage, which does not state who paid the money and cannot operate as a transfer of the mortgage.[318] There are certain advantages in such a receipt.[319]

Quite apart from these provisions, once a mortgage created by the grant of a term of years absolute has been redeemed, the term becomes a satisfied term and ceases forthwith.[320] But although, when coupled with this provision, it might be thought that an ordinary receipt (i.e. one not complying with the conditions relating to indorsed receipts) would operate as a sufficient discharge, conveyancers do not in practice rely upon such a receipt, for it is only prima facie proof of payment.

In the case of registered land, a registered charge is discharged by the removal of the entry on the register. An application to remove a registered charge from the register must be made on the correct form[321] and may be executed by deed.[322] Charges may also be removed electronically[323]

PART 5   PRIORITY OF MORTGAGES

17–073   The expression "priority of mortgages" has traditionally referred to the situation where there is more than one mortgage on the same property. In such circumstances, the proceeds of sale of the property may not be sufficient to satisfy all the mortgages, in which case it will be necessary to determine their priority. The complex rules which have been evolved for determining priorities of mortgages are mainly applications of the rules relating to competing legal and equitable interests. These rules, which differ depending on whether the land in question is registered or unregistered, are subject to any agreement between the mortgagees, for they can alter them as they wish, without the mortgagor's consent, unless the mortgages otherwise provide.[324] In addition to these rules, there is also a process known as "tacking", which alters the priorities settled under the general rules. However, questions of priority also arise as between mortgagees and the holders of beneficial interests in the land in question. These rules, which do not depend on whether the land is registered or unregistered, will be considered first.

---

[317] LPA 1925 s.115(2). See *Cumberland Court (Brighton) Ltd v Taylor* [1964] Ch. 29.
[318] Building Societies Act 1986 (BSA 1986), Sch.4, para.2.
[319] Wurtzburg & Mills, *Building Society Law*, paras 6.44–6.46.
[320] LPA 1925 ss.5, 116; above, para.17–007.
[321] LRR 2003 r.114.
[322] LRR 2003 r.114.
[323] LRR 2003 r.115. See further *Ruoff & Roper: Registered Conveyancing* (London: Sweet & Maxwell), para.28-012.
[324] *Cheah Theam Swee v Equiticorp Finance Group Ltd* [1992] 1 A.C. 472.

PRIORITIES AS BETWEEN MORTGAGEES AND BENEFICIAL CO-OWNERS

A mortgagee derives title through his mortgagor. Consequently, he will virtually always be bound by any commercial interests in or over the land in question, such as leases, easements and restrictive covenants. Only where any interest has not been protected in the appropriate way will the mortgagee, as the purchaser for value of an interest in the land, have any possibility of being in a better position than his mortgagor. However, the position as between mortgagees and the holders of family interests in the land is more complex. When difficulties arise, they almost invariably arise as between a mortgagee and a beneficial co-owner of the land, usually (but not always[325]) in respect of a house occupied by a married couple or by unmarried partners.

17–074

Overreaching

The intention of the 1925 property legislation was that on any mortgage the interests of the beneficial co-owners would be overreached into the proceeds of the mortgage advance. This will indeed happen when there is a disposition by two trustees or a trust corporation whether the beneficiaries wish their interests to be overreached or not.[326] This is so even as to any of the beneficiaries who are in "actual occupation" of registered land. (Their interests, having been overreached, are no longer "subsisting" in the land, and so cannot override registration of the title of the purchaser.[327]) Where overreaching occurs, the interest of the mortgagee will enjoy priority over the interests of all the beneficial co-owners.

17–075

No overreaching

Effect

Where a mortgage is granted by a sole trustee of land who is not a trust corporation, the interests of beneficial co-owners will not be overreached but the 1925 property legislation did not state what will happen to them. However, the courts have decided that in these circumstances the overreachable but unoverreached interests of the beneficial co-owners are treated as if they were commercial interests rather than family interests.[328] Consequently, those interests will be destroyed as against a mortgagee of unregistered land who has no notice of them and will be destroyed as against a mortgagee of registered land unless they have been protected on the register or override the registration of the mortgagee's charge.

17–076

Possibility

However, it is only likely that there will be a sole trustee of land where a resulting or constructive trust has arisen as a result of contributions to the purchase price or common

17–077

---

[325] See, e.g. *Coldunell Ltd v Gallon* [1986] Q.B. 1184 (parents and son); *Bank of Baroda v Shah* [1988] 3 All E.R. 24 (brother and sister).

[326] See *City of London B.S. v Flegg* [1988] A.C. 54.

[327] See *City of London B.S. v Flegg* [1988] A.C. 54 at 123, 124.

[328] *Caunce v Caunce* [1969] 1 W.L.R. 286 (unregistered land); *Willliams & Glyn's Bank Ltd v Boland* [1981] A.C. 487 (registered land).

intention coupled with some act of detrimental reliance.[329] Beneficiaries of resulting and constructive trusts of this type will generally be in occupation of the land. If this is the case, it is only in the most exceptional circumstances (such as where the trustee has removed all signs of a beneficiary's existence) that the mortgagee will not be bound by his interest; otherwise the mortgagee will in the case of unregistered land have constructive notice of that interest[330] and in the case of registered land that interest will override the registration of the mortgagee's charge.[331]

Incidence

17–078   However, a mortgage which finances the purchase of the property in question will automatically take priority over the interest of any beneficial co-owner.[332] Only where this is not the case is there any potential problem for mortgagees and in such circumstances they have been reluctant to make loans to sole owners of land unless they are completely satisfied that no one other than him is in occupation of the property in question; this approach has effectively eradicated the possibility of mortgages being obtained by sole trustees of land.

Partial overreaching

17–079   A mortgage which has on the face of things overreached the interests of all the beneficial co-owners will not in fact overreach all those interests in certain circumstances.

Forgery of co-owner's signature

17–080   It will not do so if the signature of one of the beneficial co-owners was forged on the mortgage deed.[333] In such cases the mortgage takes effect only against the beneficial interest of the other co-owners who obtained it. However, the beneficial interest of the co-owner whose signature was forged remains bound to the extent that any previous mortgage paid off out of the advance was binding on him or her.[334] The extent to which the remedies of the mortgagee are restricted in these circumstances has already been considered.[335]

Behind the back of co-owner

17–081   Nor will it do so if the mortgage was obtained behind the back of one of the other co-owners.[336] In such cases the position is exactly the same as where there has been a forgery. The mortgage takes effect only against the beneficial interest of the co-owners who were aware of it but the beneficial interest of the co-owner who was unaware of it remains bound to the extent that any previous mortgage paid off out of the advance was binding

---

[329] Above, paras 8–037 et seq.
[330] *Kingsnorth Finance Co Ltd v Tizard* [1986] 1 W.L.R. 783.
[331] *Williams & Glyn's Bank Ltd v Boland* [1981] A.C. 487.
[332] *Abbey National B.S. v Cann* [1991] 1 A.C. 56.
[333] *First National Securities Ltd v Hegarty* [1985] Q.B. 850; cp. *Paddington B.S. v Mendelsohn* (1985) 50 P. & C.R. 244.
[334] *Equity & Law Home Loans Ltd v Prestridge* [1992] 1 W.L.R. 137.
[335] Above, para.8–045.
[336] *Equity & Law Home Loans Ltd v Prestridge* [1992] 1 W.L.R. 137.

on him or her.[337] The restrictions on the remedies of the mortgagee are also the same. However, where a co-owner knows that the property in question cannot be purchased without the aid of a mortgage, the mortgagee will be taken to have been authorised and it will take priority.[338]

Undue influence over or misrepresentation to co-owner

The most common situation in which a mortgage which has on the face of things overreached **17–082** the interests of all the beneficial co-owners will not in fact do so is where the validity of the mortgage is affected by the fact that it was entered into as a result of the undue influence of one co-owner over the other[339] or of some misrepresentation by one co-owner to the other. In this event, the mortgage takes effect only against the beneficial interest of the co-owner who exerted the undue influence or made the misrepresentation although the beneficial interest of the other co-owner will be bound to the extent that he or she received a direct financial benefit from the advance.[340] But it has been held the beneficial interest of the latter is not subject to such of the terms of the transaction as he or she was aware of at the time it was entered into.[341] That interest may therefore not be bound to the extent that any previous mortgage paid off out of the advance was binding on him or her. However, that will not prevent the property from being sold by the trustee in bankruptcy of the co-owner who exerted the undue influence or made the misrepresentation if the mortgagee bankrupts him.[342]

Most of the examples of mortgages being obtained as a result of undue influence or some form of misrepresentation occurred in the late 1980s at a time when general financial difficulties produced a considerable fall in land values coupled with a substantial rise in interest rates. Many small businesses fell into financial difficulties and their owners came under pressure from their banks to secure their existing overdrafts and future facilities by guarantees secured on their matrimonial homes.

The facts of the first of a number of leading cases[343] were typical. The husband's company's bank manager agreed to an increased overdraft facility on the basis that the husband would guarantee the company's indebtedness and that this guarantee would be secured by a charge on the matrimonial home. The documents were sent by the bank to a branch near the matrimonial home with instructions fully to explain the transaction and the nature of the documentation and to advise the couple that if they were "in any doubt they should contact their solicitors before signing". The wife was told by the husband that liability under the charge was limited to £60,000 when it was in fact unlimited, the bank gave her neither explanation nor advice and she signed the documents without reading them. The mortgage was set aside as against her beneficial interest.

A much less typical variant was for an advance actually to be obtained on the security of the residential property ostensibly for the benefit of both co-owners when it was in fact

---

[337] *Equity & Law Home Loans Ltd v Prestridge* [1992] 1 W.L.R. 137.
[338] *Bristol and West B.S. v Henning* [1985] 1 W.L.R. 778; *Paddington B.S. v Mendelsohn* (1985) 50 P. & C.R. 244.
[339] *Royal Bank of Scotland Plc v Ettridge (No.2)* [2002] 2 A.C. 773.
[340] *Midland Bank Plc v Greene* [1994] 2 F.L.R. 827.
[341] *TSB Bank Plc v Camfield* [1995] 1 W.L.R. 430.
[342] Above, para.8–045.
[343] *Barclays Bank Plc v O'Brien* [1994] 1 A.C. 180.

to be used for the purposes of only one of them. Thus in another leading case[344] a couple obtained an advance on the security of their matrimonial home on the basis that its proceeds were to be used for the purchase of a holiday home. In fact the husband wished to purchase shares and had pressured his wife into signing the application and the charge, neither of which she read. Given that the mortgagee had no reason to think that both co-owners were not to benefit from the transaction, it was not placed on inquiry as to the possibility of any undue influence; its mortgage was consequently binding on the wife.

Precisely when will a mortgagee be affected by any undue influence which is found to have been exerted by the debtor or by any misrepresentation which he has made? The mortgagee will clearly be affected by any such conduct by the debtor where it has used him as its agent for the purposes of obtaining the signature of the surety. However, reliance on this agency argument is highly artificial since, in obtaining the signature of the surety, the debtor is acting for himself not for the mortgagee.[345] Therefore it is only in very unusual circumstances[346] that mortgagees will now be adversely affected by this argument. It is also theoretically possible, where mortgagee and surety have used the same solicitor, for information communicated by the surety to the solicitor to be imputed to the mortgagee. However, because any information is likely to have been communicated to the solicitor before he was instructed by the mortgagee[347] and, even if it was communicated to him thereafter, probably could not be revealed by him to the mortgagee anyway,[348] this is highly unlikely in practice. Consequently, in the normal case, a mortgagee will only be affected by any undue influence or misrepresentation if it is held to have notice of it.

A mortgagee was at one time[349] only put on inquiry as to the possibility of undue influence or misrepresentation where the relationship between the debtor and surety was an emotional relationship between cohabitees[350] or where the mortgagee was aware that the surety reposed trust and confidence in the debtor in relation to his or her financial affairs or was actually under the debtor's influence in other respects.[351] However, a mortgagee is now put on inquiry in every case where the relationship between the debtor and the surety is non-commercial.[352] In such circumstances, the mortgagee must always take reasonable steps to bring home to the individual surety the risks which he or more usually she is running by acting as such. If the mortgagee fails to take those steps, it will be deemed to have notice of any claim which the surety may have that the transaction was procured by undue influence or a misrepresentation on the part of the debtor.[353] This principle applies not only to co-owners who act as sureties but also to absolute owners of property who do so.[354]

---

[344] *CIBC Mortgages Plc v Pitt* [1994] 1 A.C. 200.

[345] *Barclays Bank Plc v O'Brien* [1994] 1 A.C. 180.

[346] An example was where the employees of the bank, its debtor and the guarantor were all members of the same religious sect; see *Shams v United Bank Ltd* (May 24, 1994) on Lexis.

[347] *Halifax Mortgage Services v Stepsky* [1996] Ch. 207 (CA).

[348] *Halifax Mortgage Services v Stepsky* [1996] Ch. 1 (Ch.D.).

[349] As a result of *Barclays Bank Plc v O'Brien* [1994] 1 A.C. 180.

[350] The requirement for cohabitation was not rigid; see *Massey v Midland Bank Plc* [1995] 1 All E.R. 929.

[351] *Credit Lyonnais Bank Nederland NV v Burch* [1997] 1 All E.R. 144.

[352] *Royal Bank of Scotland Plc v Etridge (No.2)* [2002] 1 A.C. 773.

[353] *Royal Bank of Scotland Plc v Etridge (No.2)* [2002] 1 A.C. 773, see also *Credit Lyonnais Bank Nederland NV v Burch* [1997] 1 All E.R. 144.

[354] As in *Credit Lyonnais Bank Nederland NV v Burch* [1997] 1 All E.R. 144 (the surety was the debtor's employee).

Where the mortgagee is put on inquiry, it need do no more than take reasonable steps to satisfy itself that the practical implications of the proposed transaction have been brought home to the surety in a meaningful way, so that he or she enters into the transaction with her eyes open so far as its basic elements are concerned. At one time, the mortgagee would satisfy its duty of inquiry if its representatives held a private meeting with the surety in the absence of the debtor, informing him or her as to potential liability and risk and urging him or her to take independent legal advice. Only in exceptional cases where the mortgagee knew further facts which made undue influence not only possible but probable was it necessary for the mortgagee to insist on independent advice.[355] However, mortgagees came increasingly to rely on the confirmation of solicitors that such advice had been given and it was held in 2001[356] that such confirmation will ordinarily suffice in respect of past transactions.

For transactions after 2001, the mortgagee is not required to satisfy its duty of inquiry by means of a personal meeting with the surety. Ordinarily it will be reasonable for the mortgagee to rely upon confirmation from a solicitor, acting for the surety, that he has advised her appropriately. Such a solicitor acts for the surety, not as the agent of the mortgagee, and any deficiencies in his advice are a matter between solicitor and surety. However, if the mortgagee knows that the solicitor has not duly advised the surety or knows facts from which it ought to have realised that the surety has not received appropriate advice, the mortgagee takes the mortgage at its own risk.

The process of obtaining confirmation from the solicitor has been formalised as a series of requirements.[357]

(i) The mortgagee should communicate directly with the surety, informing him or her that for its own protection it will require written confirmation from a solicitor acting for him or her, to the effect that the solicitor has fully explained the nature of the documents and their practical implications. The surety should be told that the purpose of this requirement is that thereafter the binding nature of the documents should not be able to be disputed. The surety should be asked to nominate a solicitor to advise him or her separately from the debtor, although the solicitor may be the solicitor who is representing the debtor.

(ii) The mortgagee must explain the existing financial situation of the debtor and the purposes and amount of any new facility either to the surety or to the solicitor; if the debtor will not consent to the release of this information, the transaction cannot proceed.

(iii) Where the mortgagee believes or suspects that the surety has been misled or is not entering into the transaction of his or her own free will, it must inform the surety's solicitor of the facts giving rise to its belief or suspicion.

Detailed guidelines have also been provided for the solicitor advising the surety.

Although transactions entered into before the process was formalised in this way are likely to come before the courts for some years yet, the existence of all these guidelines makes it unlikely that any mortgagees will be adversely affected by any undue influence

---

[355] *Barclays Bank Plc v O'Brien* [1994] 1 A.C. 180 at 196–197.
[356] As a result of *Royal Bank of Scotland Plc v Etridge (No.2)* [2002] 1 A.C. 773.
[357] *Royal Bank of Scotland Plc v Etridge (No.2)* [2002] 1 A.C. 773.

or misrepresentation by the debtor in respect of future transactions. Any remedy by the surety will instead be sought from the solicitor who advised him or her.

PRIORITIES AS BETWEEN MORTGAGES OF UNREGISTERED LAND

17–083   Where there are competing mortgages of unregistered land, there are two basic rules, depending on what has been mortgaged. If a legal estate in land has been mortgaged, the rules depend on whether or not the mortgage has been protected by a deposit of documents relating to the legal estate affected; normally these are the title deeds. Mortgages protected in this way stand outside the system of registration of land charges, and depend for priority on the rules before 1926, subject to the law of land charges. Mortgages that are not protected in this way are registrable as land charges and depend on this system for their priority. If an equitable interest in any property has instead been mortgaged, the rule in *Dearle v Hall*[358] applies, so that priority depends on the dates on which notice of the mortgages was received by the trustees or other legal owner. Additional rules govern tacking.

However, it must be borne in mind that the grant of a first legal mortgage is a trigger for first registration of title. Consequently, where the first of two or more competing mortgages is a legal mortgage created after that date, it is not likely that the later mortgages will have been created prior to the title being registered; if created thereafter, priorities will be determined by the rules that govern priority as between mortgages of registered land.

Mortgages of a legal estate the rules

Mortgages included

17–084   This head includes all mortgages of a legal estate in land, whether the mortgage itself is legal or equitable. The question is "Has a legal estate been mortgaged?", not "Is the mortgage legal or equitable?".

Principles

17–085   The two main principles[359] are as follows:

Mortgages protected by deposits of deeds: A mortgage protected "by a deposit of documents relating to the legal estate affected" is expressly excepted from the provisions of the 1925 legislation requiring registration of mortgages,[360] since the absence of the title deeds will proclaim the mortgage to anyone seeking to deal with the land[361]; "protected" probably means "originally protected", and not "continuously protected".

Mortgages not protected by deposits of deeds: A mortgage made after 1925 and not protected by a deposit of documents relating to the legal estate affected has to be registered as a

---

[358] (1828) 3 Russ. 1.
[359] There is a full discussion in (1940) 7 C.L.J. 243 (R.E.M.).
[360] LCA 1972 s.2(4), replacing LCA 1925 s.10. They are probably not registrable as Class C(iv) estate contracts.
[361] But see above, para.6–078 for leases.

land charge. If the mortgage is legal, it should be registered as a puisne mortgage (Class C(i)). If the mortgage is equitable, it should be registered as a general equitable charge (Class C(iii)).[362]

Reasons for registration

The reasons for registering a puisne mortgage or a general equitable charge are as follows: **17–086**

Priority: Section 97 of the Law of Property Act 1925 provides that every such mortgage "shall rank according to its date of registration as a land charge pursuant to the Land Charges Act 1925 or 1972".[363]

Void for want of registration: Section 4(5) of the Land Charges Act 1972 provides that a Class C land charge created after 1925 shall "be void as against a purchaser of the land charged therewith, or of any interest in such land, unless the land charge is registered in the appropriate register before the completion of the purchase".[364] In that Act, unless the context otherwise requires, "purchaser" means "any person (including a mortgagee or lessee) who, for valuable consideration, takes any interest in land or in a charge of land".[365] Thus a puisne mortgage or a general equitable charge, if unregistered, is void against a purchaser of the legal fee simple even if he had actual knowledge of it; for where an interest is void for non-registration a purchaser is not prejudicially affected by notice of it.[366]

Mortgages of a legal estate operation of the rules

The effect of these provisions must be considered under four possible heads. **17–087**

Each mortgage protected by a deposit of deeds

A mortgage will be protected by a deposit of deeds if the documents deposited are material **17–088**
parts of the title, even if they are not all the title deeds.[367] Thus two or more mortgages protected by a deposit of deeds may be created, as where the mortgagor has secretly withheld some of the deeds when creating the first mortgage,[368] or where he recovers the deeds from the mortgagee on some pretext, such as obtaining them on a short loan to show the dimensions of the property to a person concerned with a rebuilding project.[369] In such cases, the mortgages are not registrable. Four categories have to be considered:

- (i)   where both mortgages are legal;
- (ii) where the first is legal and the second equitable;
- (iii) where the first is equitable and the second legal; and
- (iv) where both are equitable.

---

[362] See above, para.6–070.
[363] See LCA 1972 s.18(6).
[364] Formerly LCA 1925 s.13(2).
[365] LCA 1972 s.17(1).
[366] Above, para.6–079.
[367] *Lacon v Allen* (1856) 3 Drew. 579 (equitable mortgage).
[368] *Lacon v Allen* (1856) 3 Drew. 579 (equitable mortgage); *Walker v Linom* [1907] 2 Ch. 104.
[369] *Peter v Russell* (1716) Gilb.Eq. 122 (the "Thatched House" case).

These will be considered in turn. However, it is particularly unlikely that it will be possible to have two mortgages both protected by a deposit of deeds when the first of those mortgages is legal and was created on or after April 1, 1998. The rules governing each category are subject to the rules for loss of priority considered below.[370]

Both mortgages legal: Where both mortgages are legal, priority will normally depend on the order of creation. Where two mortgages are granted by way of leases, the second will take effect in reversion on the first.[371]

Legal mortgage followed by equitable mortgage: Where a legal mortgage is followed by an equitable mortgage, the legal mortgage has a double claim to priority, both as being prior in time and because where the equities are equal, the law prevails.

Equitable mortgage followed by legal mortgage: Where an equitable mortgage is followed by a legal mortgage, the primary rule is that the mortgages rank in the order of creation; but this priority may be displaced by the superiority of the legal estate. For this to occur, the legal mortgagee must show that he is a bona fide purchaser for value of a legal estate without notice of the prior equitable mortgage.[372] The inability of the mortgagor to produce all the title deeds will usually amount to notice to the legal mortgagee that some prior mortgage already exists.[373] But if his inquiries for the deeds were met by a reasonable excuse, he can claim priority as having taken without notice. The court has accepted surprisingly frail excuses as being reasonable, such as that the mortgagor was busy but would produce the deeds later,[374] or that the deeds were in Ireland, where the property lay.[375] Instead of applying the normal rule that requires a purchaser to make a proper investigation of title, the courts have held that nothing save gross negligence will postpone the legal mortgagee,[376] and it is grossly negligent to accept the excuse that the deeds also relate to other property.[377]

Both mortgages equitable: Where both mortgages are equitable, priority depends on the order in which they were created, provided that the equities are equal in other respects.[378] Accordingly, a first mortgagee who failed to ask for the title deeds, or who, having obtained them, redelivered them to the mortgagor without pressing for their early return, may be postponed to a second mortgagee who took all proper precautions but was nevertheless deceived.[379]

Loss of priority: Before 1926 it was settled that even a legal mortgagee might lose his priority in three classes of case, and the principles appear to apply after 1925, though their application to the rules laid down by statute has yet to be considered. The cases, which

---

[370] Below.

[371] *Jones v Rhind* (1869) 17 W.R. 1091.

[372] *Pilcher v Rawlins* (1872) 7 Ch.App. 259; *Att.-Gen. v Biphosphated Guano Co* (1879) 11 Ch.D. 327.

[373] *Oliver v Hinton* [1899] 2 Ch. 264 at 268.

[374] *Hewitt v Loosemore* (1851) 9 Hare 449.

[375] *Agra Bank Ltd v Barry* (1874) L.R. 7 H.L. 135.

[376] *Hewitt v Loosemore* (1851) 9 Hare 449; *Oliver v Hinton* [1899] 2 Ch. 264; see below.

[377] *Oliver v Hinton* [1899] 2 Ch. 264.

[378] *Rice v Rice* (1853) 2 Drew. 73.

[379] *Farrand v Yorkshire Banking Co* (1888) 40 Ch.D. 182.

are stated in terms of a legal mortgage, seem equally applicable to equitable mortgages.[380] They are as follows.

(1) *Fraud*. If a legal mortgagee is guilty of some fraud whereby the equitable mortgagee is deceived into believing that there was no legal mortgage on the property, the legal mortgagee will be postponed to the equitable mortgagee.[381]

(2) *Estoppel*. If the legal mortgagee either expressly or by implication made some misrepresentation by which the equitable mortgagee was deceived, the legal mortgagee will be estopped from asserting his priority.[382] Thus if a legal mortgagee indorses a receipt for his money on the mortgage and somebody is thereby induced to lend money on an equitable mortgage of the property, the legal mortgagee cannot afterwards claim priority for his loan if in fact it has not been discharged.[383] Again, if the legal mortgagee parts with the deeds to the mortgagor to enable him to raise money, he will be postponed to any subsequent mortgagee who lent money without notice of the first mortgage, even if the mortgagor had agreed to inform the second mortgagee of the first mortgage, or had agreed to borrow only a limited amount which in fact he exceeded.[384] Once the mortgagee clothes the mortgagor with apparent authority to deal with the property freely, he cannot afterwards claim the protection of any undisclosed limits set to this authority.

(3) *Gross negligence in relation to the title deeds*. If the legal mortgagee is grossly negligent in failing to obtain the title deeds, he is postponed to a subsequent equitable mortgagee who exercises due diligence. Failure to ask for the deeds at all would postpone a legal mortgagee[385]; it is otherwise if he inquires for them and is given a reasonable excuse.[386] If the legal mortgagee obtains the deeds, it appears that no amount of carelessness in failing to keep them in safe custody will postpone him, as where the deeds were kept in a safe to which the mortgagor had a key as manager working for the mortgagee.[387] But this seems questionable.

Neither mortgage protected by a deposit of deeds

Where neither mortgage is protected by a deposit of title deeds, priority is determined by the Law of Property Act 1925 and the Land Charges Act 1972, subject to any question that may arise as to loss of priority.[388] The two statutes speak with united voice in some cases and discordant voices in others, depending on the order in which the competing mortgages have been made and registered.   **17–089**

Concord: No difficulty arises if the first mortgage is duly registered before the second is made. Even if the first is equitable and the second legal, the first prevails, for s.97 of the

---

[380] See *Rimmer v Webster* [1902] 2 Ch. 163; *Taylor v Russell* [1892] A.C. 244.
[381] *Peter v Russell* (1716) Gilb.Eq. 122.
[382] *Dixon v Muckleston* (1872) 8 Ch.App. 155 at 160.
[383] *Rimmer v Webster* [1902] 2 Ch. 163.
[384] *Perry Herrick v Attwood* (1857) 2 De G. & J. 21.
[385] *Walker v Linom* [1907] 2 Ch. 104; and see *Colyer v Finch* (1856) 5 H.L.C. 905.
[386] *Manners v Mew* (1885) 29 Ch.D. 725.
[387] *Northern Counties, etc. Insurance Co v Whipp* (1884) 26 Ch.D. 482.
[388] See above.

Law of Property Act 1925 expressly provides that they shall rank in order of registration, and the provision that registration amounts to notice prevents the legal mortgagee from claiming to be a purchaser without notice. Nor is there any difficulty if neither mortgage is registered. Even if the first mortgage is legal and the second equitable, under s.4(5) of the Land Charges Act 1972 the first is void against the second for want of registration, and so the second has priority. Indeed, if there are several successive registrable mortgages, none of which has been registered, the priority accorded by the date of creation will be reversed, for the last will rank first and so on.

Discord: The difficult case is where the first mortgage was registered after the creation of the second mortgage. For example:

January 1, 1998	A grants a mortgage to X
February 2, 1998	A grants a mortgage to Y
March 3, 1998	X registers
March 4, 1998	Y registers

In such a case, the order according to s.97 is X, Y; according to s. 4(5) it is Y, X, for X's mortgage is void against Y. It is not clear which section will prevail. In favour of s.97, the chief point is that it is expressly dealing with the priority of mortgages, whereas s.4(5) makes unregistered mortgages void against subsequent mortgages only by virtue of the provision that "purchaser" includes a mortgagee.[389] On the other hand, the provision in s.4(5) that an unregistered land charge is void against a subsequent purchaser makes it hard to see how the registration of X's mortgage can give priority to something which, as regards Y, has no existence.[390] The problem still awaits solution (now that the grant of a first legal mortgage triggers compulsory registration of title, it probably never will be). It is thought that s.4(5) will probably prevail, since Y will have been induced to lend his money by the fact that no earlier charge appeared to exist and X could easily have protected himself by speedier registration. Even more complicated problems can be constructed, including cases of circularity, as where X has priority over Y who has priority over Z who has priority over X; but these need not be discussed here.[391]

Priority notices and official searches: At the beginning of 1926, there was the difficulty that it was physically impossible to register a land charge the instant after it had been created. Thus there was a dangerous gap between the creation of a mortgage and its registration. Further, even if a search for prior incumbrances was made, the mortgagee could not be sure that no incumbrance had been registered between the time of his search and the completion of the mortgage. These difficulties have been met by the devices of the priority notice and the official search, which have been dealt with earlier.[392]

First but not second mortgage protected by a deposit of deeds

17–090   In this case, the first mortgage, by taking its priority from the date of its creation, will normally have priority over the second mortgage.

---

[389] LPA 1925 s.205(1)(xxi).
[390] See *Kitney v M.E.P.C. Ltd* [1977] 1 W.L.R. 981.
[391] See (1968) 32 Conv 325 (W.A. Lee).
[392] Above, para.6–080.

Second but not first mortgage protected by a deposit of deeds

Here, ss.4(5) and 97 work in harmony. If the first mortgage is registered before the second is made, the first ranks for priority "according to its date of registration" (s.97), i.e. prior to the second mortgage, and s.4(5) has no application. If the first mortgage is not registered when the second mortgage is made, the first mortgage is void against the second for want of registration; and even if it is subsequently registered, it takes priority from the date of registration.

17–091

Summary

17–092

Deposit of deeds: A mortgage protected by a deposit of deeds ranks according to the date on which it was created. The mortgagee may lose priority:

(i) by fraud, estoppel or gross negligence; or
(ii) if his mortgage is equitable, by a legal mortgage being made to a mortgagee for value without notice.

No deposit of deeds: A mortgage not protected by deposit of deeds should be protected by registration. If the mortgagee fails to do this, he will not, it seems, be protected against a subsequent mortgagee (s.4(5)), unless, perhaps, he registers before him (s.97). If he does register he will be protected against all mortgages made thereafter.

Mortgages of an equitable interest

The priority of mortgages of an equitable interest in any property, whether real or personal, depends on the rule in *Dearle v Hall*.[393] Only since 1925 has this rule extended it to mortgages of equitable interests in land.[394] The basic provision of the rule is that the priority of competing mortgages depends on the order in which notice of them is received by the trustees or other legal owner; but this is subject to the important qualification that a mortgagee who, when lending his money, has notice of a prior mortgage cannot gain priority over it by giving notice first.

17–093

Various reasons for the rule have been given, including the consideration that, as between two equally innocent incumbrancers, priority should be accorded to the one who, by giving notice, had prevented the mortgagor from representing that he was the unincumbered owner of the interest mortgaged, and so deceiving third parties.[395] Whatever the reasons, the rule is now a rigid rule.[396] As amended by the Law of Property Act 1925, the rule falls under the following heads.

No notice of prior mortgage

A mortgagee who had notice of a prior mortgage when he lent his money cannot gain priority over it by giving notice first,[397] for he has not been prejudiced by the failure of the prior

17–094

---

[393] 3 Russ. 1.
[394] s.137(1).
[395] See *Ward v Duncombe* [1893] A.C. 369 at 392.
[396] See *Re Dallas* [1904] 2 Ch. 385.
[397] *Re Holmes* (1885) 29 Ch.D. 786.

mortgagee to give notice and so it would be inequitable to give him priority. But if when he lent his money he had no notice of a prior mortgage, notice of it when he gives his notice is immaterial.[398] Indeed, it is just what will impel him to give notice.[399]

Priority depends on notice being received, not given

17–095 Priority depends on the order in which notice is received by the trustees or other legal owner, and not on whether or when the mortgagees gave notice. Where notices are received simultaneously, the mortgages rank in the order of their creation, as where competing notices are delivered to a bank, one late at night and the other as soon as it opens the next day.[400] Notice from any reliable source suffices.[401] Indeed, one first mortgagee kept his priority by virtue of notice of the mortgage given not by him but by a letter sent to the trustee by the second mortgagee before giving his own notice.[402]

Notice must be in writing

17–096 Since 1925 no notice given or received after 1925 will affect priorities unless it is in writing.[403] Before 1926, notice received through reading a notice in a newspaper sufficed to preserve priority against a subsequent mortgagee who then gave express notice,[404] though it would not gain priority for a later mortgage over an earlier mortgage[405]: less is required to preserve priority than to gain it. Whether such notice is still effective is doubtful, for although it is in writing it has not been "served".[406]

17–097 *Service of notice*

Persons to be served: The persons "to be served" with notice are[407]:

  (i)   in the case of land settled under the Settled Land Act 1925, the trustees of the settlement;
  (ii) in the case of a trust of land, the trustees; and
  (iii) in the case of any other land, the estate owner of the land affected.

The person to be served is normally the owner of the legal estate, except in the case of land settled under the Settled Land Act 1925. Notice to the tenant for life of such a settlement might well be no protection, as where it is his life interest that is being mortgaged. No special provision has been made for any other cases, and so in these notice must be given to the legal owner, as before 1926.

---

[398] *Mutual Life Assurance Society v Langley* (1886) 32 Ch.D. 460.
[399] See below, para.17–098.
[400] *Calisher v Forbes* (1871) 7 Ch.App. 109.
[401] *Re Worcester* (1868) 3 Ch.App. 555.
[402] *Ipswich Permanent Money Club Ltd v Arthy* [1920] 2 Ch. 257.
[403] LPA 1925 s.137(3).
[404] *Lloyd v Banks* (1868) 3 Ch.App. 488.
[405] *Arden v Arden* (1885) 29 Ch.D. 702.
[406] LPA 1925 s.137(2).
[407] LPA 1925 s.137(2).

Notice should be given to all the trustees: It has always been advisable to give notice to all the trustees for the following reasons.

(i) Notice given to all the existing trustees remains effective even though they all retire or die without communicating the notice to their successors.[408]

(ii) Notice given to one of several trustees is effective against all incumbrances created during his trusteeship, and remains effective despite his death or retirement.[409]

(iii) On the other hand, notice given to one of several trustees is not effective against incumbrancers who advance money after the death or retirement of that trustee without having communicated the notice to one or more of the continuing trustees.[410]

(iv) If the mortgagor is a trustee, priorities will not be affected by the notice of the mortgage that he has, for this will afford no protection to subsequent mortgages.[411] But if the mortgagee is a trustee, the notice of the mortgage that he has will affect priorities, for to protect his mortgage he will readily disclose its existence to any prospective incumbrancers.[412]

Notice by indorsement: If for any reason a valid notice cannot be served (such as where there are no trustees), or can be served only at unreasonable cost or delay, a purchaser may require that a memorandum be indorsed on or permanently annexed to the instrument creating the trust, and this has the same effect as notice to the trustees. In the case of settled land, the trust instrument, and in the case of a trust of land, the instrument creating the equitable interest, is the document to be used for this purpose.[413]

Notice to trust corporation: The instrument creating the trust, the trustees or the court may nominate a trust corporation to receive notices instead of the trustees. In such cases, only notice to the trust corporation affects priority; notice to the trustees has no effect until they deliver it to the trust corporation, which they are bound to do forthwith. Provision is made for the indorsement of notice of the appointment on the instrument upon which notices may be indorsed, for the keeping of a register of notices, for the inspection of the register, for the answering of inquiries and for the payment of fees therefor.[414] In practice, little use is made of these provisions.

Production of notices: Since 1925, on the application of any person interested in the equitable interest, the trustees have been obliged to produce any notices served on them or their predecessors.[415]

Distribution: In addition to securing priority, notice to the trustees safeguards the mortgagee by ensuring that his claims will not be disregarded when the funds are distributed. Trustees are not liable if they distribute the trust funds to the prejudice of a mortgagee of whom they are unaware.[416]

---

[408] *Re Wasdale* [1899] 1 Ch. 163.
[409] *Ward v Duncombe* [1893] A.C. 369.
[410] *Re Phillips' Trusts* [1903] 1 Ch. 183.
[411] *Lloyds Bank v Pearson* [1901] 1 Ch. 865.
[412] *Browne v Savage* (1859) 4 Drew. 635.
[413] LPA 1925 s.137(4), (5).
[414] LPA 1925 s.138.
[415] LPA 1925 s.137(8); see also (9).
[416] *Phipps v Lovegrove* (1873) L.R. 16 Eq. 80.

Tacking

17–098   Tacking is a process whereby the rules relating to priorities can be modified, both for realty and for personalty. The process consists of allowing a mortgagee with inferior priority to "tack" (or attach) his mortgage to a mortgage with superior priority and thus to give it priority over any intervening mortgages. Since 1925, there has only been one form of tacking, the tacking of further advances. The former type of tacking known as the *tabula in naufragio* ("a plank in a shipwreck") is relevant only because the wider principle of which it forms part remains in force. That is the principle whereby priority for equitable interests may be obtained by acquiring a legal estate. Consequently, an equitable mortgagee may obtain priority over a prior unregistered[417] option to purchase the land if he obtains a legal charge on the land under a power in the mortgage, provided that he had no notice of the option when he lent the money.[418]

The tacking of further advances envisages the possibility that, after lending the money, a mortgagee may make further advances to the mortgagor on the security of the same property. There are three cases in which the mortgagee can tack his further advance to his original mortgage and claim priority over an intervening incumbrancer for both loans.[419] It is immaterial whether or not the prior mortgage was made expressly for securing further advances, or whether the subsequent mortgage is legal or equitable.[420]

Agreement of intervening incumbrancer

17–099   The mortgagee can tack if the intervening incumbrancer agrees. Building estates sometimes provide examples of this: the owner requires more money for further building on his estate, thereby making it a better security. The second mortgagee, not wishing to lend any more money, may agree to the first mortgagee making a further advance to be expended on further building and to rank in priority to the second mortgage.

No notice of intervening incumbrance

17–100   Any mortgagee, whether legal or equitable, may tack a further advance if it was made without notice of the intervening mortgage. Where the intervening mortgage is protected by a deposit of deeds and is thus not registrable, the normal rules as to notice operate. If the mortgage is not protected in this way and so is registrable, the rule that registration amounts to notice will apply and thus protect it if it is registered. In one case, however, registration is not deemed to be notice; if the prior mortgage was made expressly for securing further advances, such as on a current account (for example an overdraft at a bank, where the debt is increased and decreased as sums are drawn out or paid in), registration alone is not deemed to be notice, unless the intervening mortgage was registered when the last

---

[417] Had the mortgage been legal, not equitable, the option would have been void against it for want of registration: above, paras 6–070, 6–078.

[418] *McCarthy & Stone Ltd v Julian S. Hodge & Co Ltd* [1971] 1 W.L.R. 1547, where there was held to be notice. See also [1972A] C.L.J. 34 (P.B. Fairest).

[419] LPA 1925 s.94(1).

[420] LPA 1925 s.94(1).

search was made by the mortgagee.[421] This applies to a spouse's right of occupation which is registered after a mortgage has been made.[422]

An example may make this clearer. Mortgages have been made to A (who took the deeds) and B, in that order, and A has made further advances. If when A made his further advances he had actual, constructive or imputed notice of B's mortgage, he cannot tack under this head even if his mortgage, without obliging him to make further advances, was stated to be security for any further advances he might choose to make. If he had no such notice of B's mortgage when he made his further advances, but B's mortgage was registered at that time, then if A's mortgage is silent as to further advances, the registration amounts to notice and prevents A from tacking. But if A's mortgage was expressed to be security for any further advances that he might make, the registration will not prevent him from tacking, and thus he need not search before making each further advance.

This points a practical moral. Even if a second mortgage has been duly registered, the mortgagee should give express notice of his mortgage to the first mortgagee, for this:

(i) prevents tacking under this head; and
(ii) compels the first mortgagee to hand over the deeds to him when the first mortgage is discharged.[423]

Obligation to make further advance

A further advance may be tacked if the prior mortgage imposes an obligation on the mortgagee to make it. In this case, not even express notice will prevent tacking.[424] If in return for a mortgage a bank binds itself to honour a customer's cheques up to an overdraft of £100,000 there is no question of the bank having to search before honouring each cheque, for not even express notice will prevent the bank from tacking each further advance.   **17–101**

PRIORITIES AS BETWEEN MORTGAGES OF REGISTERED LAND

Mortgages of a legal estate

A charge by way of legal mortgage should always be registered, but it is necessary to state the effect on priority where it is so registered and also where it is not.   **17–102**

Registered charges: Subject to any entry on the register,[425] registered charges rank in the order in which they are entered on the register, irrespective of the order of creation.[426] The registered chargees may change the priority of the charges by agreement between

---

[421] LPA 1925 s.94(2).
[422] Family Law Act 1996 s.31(12). For the Act, see above, para.6–070.
[423] Above, para.17–039.
[424] LPA 1925 s.94(1)(c), reversing *West v Williams* [1899] 1 Ch. 132.
[425] See *Ruoff & Roper: Registered Conveyancing* (London: Sweet & Maxwell), para.27–009.
[426] LRA 2002 s.48; LRR 2003 r.101.

themselves.[427] A registered charge created for valuable consideration has priority over any prior mortgage of any type which has not been protected by entry on the register.[428]

Charges which have not been registered: As a legal charge is a registrable disposition,[429] a charge which is not registered will lose its priority against a disposition for valuable consideration which is registered.[430] A charge which is not protected on the register takes effect an equitable interest. As between competing interests of this kind, the ordinary equitable rule applies. Thus the earlier interest will take priority over the later.[431]

17–103 **Mortgages of an equitable interest:** For mortgages of an equitable interest in registered land, the rule in *Dearle v Hall*,[432] which has already been considered,[433] now applies to registered land in the same way as it applies to unregistered land.[434]

Tacking

17–104 Provision for the tacking of further advances has been made only in the case of registered charges.[435] There are two categories.

Obligatory

17–105 Where the proprietor of a registered charge is under an obligation, noted on the register, to make a further advance, any subsequent registered charge will take effect subject to any such further advance.[436]

17–106 ### Optional

Under the Land Registration Act 2002: The proprietor of a registered charge is able to make a further advance on the security of an existing charge if in the meantime he has not received notice from another chargee that a subsequent charge has been created.[437] It is possible to tack a further advance where an earlier charge records a maximum figure for the total money lent provided that the amount due to the proprietor of the registered charge when the further advance is made does not exceed that maximum figure.[438]

---

[427] LRR 2003 r.102.
[428] LRA 2002 s.30.
[429] LRA 2002 s.27 (2) (f).
[430] LRA 2002 s.29 (1).
[431] *Barclays Bank Ltd v Taylor* [1974] Ch. 137.
[432] (1828) 3 Russ. 1.
[433] Above, para.17–093.
[434] LRA 1986 s.5(1); *Ruoff & Roper: Registered Conveyancing* (London: Sweet & Maxwell), paras 8–11, 8–12.
[435] LRA 2002 s.49.
[436] LRA 2002 s.49(3).
[437] LRA 2002 s.49(1).
[438] LRA 2002 s.49(4); see *Ruoff & Roper: Registered Conveyancing* (London: Sweet & Maxwell), para.27–014.

SUMMARY OF KEY CASES

- *First National Securities Ltd v Hegerty* [1985] Q.B. 850, [1984] 3 All E.R. 641
- *Edwards v Lloyds TSB Bank Plc* [2004] EWHC 1745 (Ch) at [28]–[31]
- *Mortgage Corp v Shaire* [2001] Ch. 743, [2001] 4 All E.R. 364
- *Four Maids Ltd v Dudley Marshall Ltd* [1957] Ch. 317, [1957] 2 All E.R. 35
- *Quennell v Maltby* [1979] 1 W.L.R. 318, [1979] 1 All E.R. 568
- *Abbey National B.S. v Cann* [1991] 1 A.C. 56
- *Cuckmere Brick Co Ltd v Mutual Finance Ltd* [1971] Ch. 949
- *Tse Kwong Lam v Wong Chit Sen* [1983] 1 W.L.R. 1349
- *Palk v Mortgage Services Funding* [1993] 2 W.L.R. 415
- *Silven Properties Ltd v Royal Bank of Scotland Plc* [2004] 1 W.L.R. 997

FURTHER READING

- P. Omar, "Equitable interests and the secured creditor" [2006] Conv. 50
- E. Mujih, "From manifest disadvantage to transactions that call for explanation: have the difficulties been eliminated ten years after Royal Bank of Scotland Plc v Etridge (No.2)?" [2012] JILBR 395
- L. Whitehouse, "The mortgage arrears pre-action protocol: an opportunity lost" (2009) 72 M.L.R. 793–814

Chapter 18

ADVERSE POSSESSION AND LIMITATION PERIODS

CHAPTER SUMMARY

This chapter deals with the limitation periods applicable to claims in respect of land, and the related area of adverse possession. The two fall to be considered together, because under English law, acquisition of title to land by long occupation is a branch of the law of limitation. The historical basis for adverse possession, and the policy considerations which attend it, are considered first. The Chapter then considers length of the limitation period or period of adverse possession, when time starts to run (i.e. what amounts to adverse possession); and the acquisition of title once sufficient time has elapsed.

INTRODUCTION

Every legal system needs to incorporate time limits for bringing claims, as the bringing of **18–001** stale claims is likely to lead to injustice. There is also a general public interest in ensuring that long-established de facto rights to land should not be disturbed. Prescription is one solution to this problem, which is the solution adopted at common law and subsequently by statute in respect of easements and profits, but in respect of title to land itself, the solution adopted was based on limitation and is entirely statutory in its basis.

To understand the development of the law of adverse possession, it is necessary to place the law into its historical perspective.

First, the fundamentals of English land law date back to the Norman Conquest; by comparison land registration is a recent innovation. Historically, land was unregistered.

Secondly, in respect of unregistered land in England and Wales, the basis of title to land is possession. Possession of land by itself gives a title to the land good against the whole world except a person with a better right to possession.[1] If X takes possession of A's land, X has a title which will avail against all save A; a title acquired by wrong is still a title. X has a fee simple, and so has A; but all titles are relative, and so although X's fee is good, A's is better.[2] If, however, A fails to take steps to recover the land in due time, his claim will

---

[1] *Asher v Whitlock* (1865) L.R. 1 Q.B. 1.
[2] See *Leach v Jay* (1878) 9 Ch.D. 42 at 44, 45; *Ocean Estates Ltd v Pinder* [1969] 2 A.C. 19 at 24, 25.

be barred by limitation, and X's fee, freed from the superior claims of A's fee, will be good against all the world.

Thirdly, in the absence of a system of land registration, it could, and sometimes did, become very difficult to trace the "true" or "paper" owner of land. Deeds could be lost; land could fall into disuse if the owner disappeared. Recognising a saleable title in someone who has had actual possession for a long period allows for neglected land to be "recycled" into the economy.

For these reasons, among others, limitation in respect of claims to the possession of land was developed beyond limitation in other contexts. In simple contract, limitation bars the claim, but does not destroy the underlying right. But in respect of claims to the possession of land, expiry of the limitation period not only bars the claim to possession, it extinguishes the title of the true owner and title is acquired by the person in possession. This is referred to as "adverse possession" and gaining "title by adverse possession", because the possession is wrongful and adverse to the true owner up to the moment that title is acquired by the adverse possessor.[3]

Title by adverse possession also plays an important part in the conveyancing of unregistered land, because it reduces the period of the vendor's title which a purchaser must investigate.[4] A break in the chain of known conveyances will not matter if it is sufficiently historic.

The Land Registration Act 1925 (as amended from time to time) applied the Limitation Act 1980 and its predecessors to registered land with only minor modifications. However, the conceptual justifications for title by adverse possession which apply to unregistered land have no application to registered land. The basis for legal title is the register, not possession, and establishing a vendor's title is largely a matter of checking the register. Indeed, adverse possession can be argued to be contrary to the ethos of registered land in a modern society where an absolute title register can be kept on computer and updated very easily. Nevertheless, there are some important, if limited, practical justifications. Registered proprietors can disappear. On death the beneficiaries may not register the change in title. Adverse possession performs a useful function in establishing or regularising boundaries between titles. These considerations were applied when the Land Registration Act 1925 was repealed and replaced by the Land Registration Act 2002. The 2002 Act retains the essential concept of "adverse possession",[5] but the mechanism for acquiring title is entirely different and the circumstances in which an adverse possessor is likely to acquire title are much restricted.

Two systems

18–002   It is probably easiest to think of the current state of the law as two systems – one for unregistered land, one for unregistered land – which are based on a common concept of "adverse possession". In respect of unregistered land, the statutory basis for limitation and adverse possession remains the Limitation Act 1980. Since it came into force on October 13, 2003,

---

[3]   More emotively, it is sometimes referred to as "squatter's title" or "squatter's rights" but this is a colloquialism which is best avoided. The term "squatter" is, however, an acceptable shorthand for "adverse possessor"; it is used in the Legal Aid Sentencing and Punishment of Offenders Act 2012 s.144.

[4]   15 years, see LPA 1969 s.23.

[5]   LRA 2002 Sch.6 para.11(1).

the statutory basis for limitation and adverse possession in respect of registered land has been the Land Registration Act 2002.

"Adverse possession" means the same thing under both Acts. It is the consequences of establishing the requisite number of years of adverse possession, and the mechanism for acquiring title, which differ markedly between the two contexts.

Policy

The fundamental principle of the Limitation Act 1980, which consolidates earlier legislation,[6] **18–003** is that unless claims are enforced within a limited time, they become barred.

The policy which underlies the Limitation Act 1980 and, for that matter its predecessors, is that it is more important that long and undisturbed possession of land should be protected, even if initially it was wrongful, than that the law should lend its aid to the enforcement of stale claims. The policy behind the Land Registration Act 2002 is different. Because the register is paramount, long and undisturbed possession will only be recognised as conferring title if the person against whom it has been maintained does not object to the registration of the possessor as proprietor, having been given notice of the application. It is also fair to say that this change was influenced by what the Law Commission has described[7] as "considerable public disquiet" over the operation of the existing law.

Human rights

Both under the Limitation Act 1980 and under the Land Registration Act 2002 what is crucial **18–004** is the inactivity of the person against whom the necessary long and undisturbed possession has been maintained. It has been contended that the deprivation of that person's property to which his inactivity gives rise breaches the right to his possessions conferred by the Human Rights Act 1998, that the deprivation of his property without compensation is disproportionate to any legitimate public interest and breaches the fair balance between his interests and the interests of society as a whole, and that the relevant limitation period (12 years) is too short. However, these arguments ultimately failed when they were considered by the European Court of Human Rights.[8] The Grand Chamber held that adverse possession constituted a control of the user of property rather than a deprivation of a possession and found that the system under the Limitation Act 1980 was not incompatible with Art.1 of the First Protocol to the Convention. The claim from which the case arose pre-dated the Land Registration Act 2002; there seems little doubt that the much more restricted circumstances in which title by adverse possession may be acquired under that Act are also Convention-compliant.

---

[6]   The Limitation Act 1939 as affecting land was amended by the Limitation Amendment Act 1980, and both were repealed and replaced by the present Act.

[7]   Law. Com. No.271, para.24.

[8]   *J.A. Pye (Oxford) Ltd v UK* (2007) 46 E.H.R.R. 1083 (Grand Chamber).

Limitation distinguished from prescription

18–005   Limitation must be distinguished from prescription.[9] Two differences may be mentioned.

Subject-matter

18–006   Limitation often, although not always, concerns the ownership of the land itself, whereas prescription is directed solely to the acquisition of easements and profits over the land of another.

Limitation operates negatively

18–007   Prescription operates positively so as to presume the grant of an easement or profit by the owner of the land; title is thus derived from him. Limitation, on the other hand, operates negatively so as to bar a claim to the land, thus leaving some other claimant to the land free from the competing claim. Limitation may operate differentially, barring one person but not another. Thus it may bar a tenant under a lease but not his landlord. However, it should be noted that under the Land Registration 2002, where a claim to adverse possession is made out the adverse possessor is registered as proprietor in place of the previous registered proprietor. This is, arguably, very much as "positive" as prescription.

Elements of limitation

18–008   Despite the fact that most land is now registered, for two reasons it remains convenient to consider first the law under the Limitation Act 1980, which continues to apply to unregistered land. First, because the Land Registration Act 2002 for the most part builds upon the existing principles established under the Limitation Act 1980. Secondly, there remain many cases where an adverse possessor may claim to have acquired title to registered land under the Limitation Act 1980 before October 13, 2003 when the Land Registration Act 2002 came into force.

In every case of limitation/adverse possession, three aspects must be considered, namely:

(i)   the length of the limitation period or period of adverse possession;
(ii)   when time starts to run (i.e. what amounts to adverse possession); and
(iii)   the effect of the lapse of time.

These will be taken in turn.

---

[9]   Above, paras 15–044 et seq. See generally *Buckinghamshire CC v Moran* [1990] Ch. 623 at 644.

PART 1   THE LENGTH OF THE PERIOD

Under the Limitation Act 1980

There are three main periods of limitation and certain additional special periods: **18–009**

    (i) a period of six years for actions on simple contracts (such as for money lent without security) or claims for rent, and actions in tort[10];

    (ii) a period of 12 years for actions on a specialty[11]; "specialty" includes deeds so includes for example claims to enforce a covenant in a lease or conveyance[12];

    (iii) a period of 12 years (formerly 20 years) for the recovery of land or of money charged on land, as by a mortgage,[13] and for money due under a covenant;

    (iv) a period of 30 years (formerly 60 years) in the case of Crown land[14] (the 60-year period has been retained in the case of foreshore owned by the Crown[15]); and

    (v) a period of 30 years in the case of a spiritual or eleemosynary (i.e. charitable) corporation sole, such as a bishop or the master of a hospital.[16]

Under the Land Registration Act 2002

No period of limitation runs under the Limitation Act 1980 in respect of any estate in land,   **18–010**
rentcharge or right of redemption the title to which is registered.[17] Instead:

    (i) when a person is in adverse possession of registered land or has been evicted from that land during the last six months by the registered proprietor and he and his predecessors in title have been in adverse possession for 10 years, he is entitled to apply to the registrar to be registered as proprietor[18];

    (ii) the registrar then notifies this application to the registered proprietor, any registered chargee, and the registered proprietor of any superior title.[19] Anyone who is notified is able to serve a notice on the registrar within a period laid down by Rules[20];

    (iii) if no one serves a notice, the applicant will be registered as proprietor[21];

    (iv) if anyone does serve a notice, the applicant will only be able to be registered as proprietor at this stage in one of the following three circumstances:

---

[10] Limitation Act 1980 (LA 1980) ss.2, 5, 19. Claims in tort are subject to the Latent Damage Act 1986; and three years is the normal period for personal injuries: s.11.

[11] LA1980 s.8.

[12] But rent is subject to the shorter six year period even if reserved by a Deed.

[13] LA 1980 ss.15, 20.

[14] LA 1980 s.15(1), Sch.1 para.10.

[15] LA 1980 para.11.

[16] LA 1980 para.10.

[17] LRA 2002 s.96.

[18] LRA 2002 Sch.6 para.1.

[19] LRA 2002 para.2.

[20] LRA 2002 para.3.

[21] LRA 2002 para.4.

    (a) if it would be unconscionable because of an equity by estoppel for the registered proprietor to seek to dispossess the applicant and the circumstances are such that the applicant ought to be registered as proprietor;

    (b) if he is for some other reason entitled to be registered as proprietor (examples will be being entitled under the will or intestacy of the deceased proprietor or having purchased the land without having taken a transfer); and

    (c) if he is the owner of adjoining property, the boundary has not been determined, and for the 10-year period he reasonably believed that the land to which the application relates belonged to him[22].

  (v) a further application by the same applicant or his successors in title to be registered as proprietor after a further two-year period of possession will be successful[23] (and even if he does not make a further application, earlier judgments for possession then become unenforceable against him and he has a defence to any future action for possession[24]).

The only special period which remains is in the case of foreshore owned by the Crown; 60 years' adverse possession will be needed before the first application.[25] First registered proprietors of land registered under the Land Registration Act 2002 are bound by interests already acquired under the Limitation Act 1980.[26]

PART 2   THE RUNNING OF TIME

18–011   Time therefore has to run both under the Limitation Act 1980 and under the Land Registration Act 2002. The Land Registration Act 2002 specifically provides that a person is in adverse possession for the purposes of that Act if he would have been in adverse possession under the Limitation Act 1980.[27] However, there are some exceptions to this basic rule[28] which will be referred to below. The running of time falls under three heads: first, when time begins to run; secondly, what will postpone this date; and thirdly, what will start time running afresh. In general, once time has begun to run, it runs continuously.[29]

---

[22] LRA 2002 para.5. The reasonable belief is that of the applicant for registration, not whether (for example) his Solicitor could reasonably have believed it: *IAM Group Plc v Chowdrey* [2012] EWCA Civ 505; [2012] 2 P. & C.R. 13 at [27].

[23] LRA 2002 paras 6, 7.

[24] LRA 2002 s.98(2), (3), (4).

[25] LRA 2002 Sch.6 para.13.

[26] LRA 2002 s.11(4)(c).

[27] LRA 2002 Sch.6 para.11(1).

[28] LRA 2002 paras 11(2), 12.

[29] *Bowring-Hanbury's Trustee v Bowring-Hanbury* [1943] Ch. 104.

WHEN TIME BEGINS TO RUN

In the case of actions for the recovery of unregistered land or capital sums charged on land, time begins to run in accordance with the following rules. The same rules apply to establishing the necessary period of adverse possession of registered land prior to making an application for title.   **18–012**

Owner entitled in possession

Time will begin to run against an owner of land who is entitled in possession only where: **18–013**

> (i) he has either been dispossessed or discontinued his possession; and
> (ii) adverse possession of the land has been taken by some other person.[30]

Dispossession or discontinuance

An owner is "dispossessed" when he has been driven out of possession by another,[31] though there may be dispossession even if the owner knows nothing of it.[32] It is not necessary for the squatter to "oust" the true owner; what is required is that the squatter takes possession in the ordinary sense of that word.[33] An owner has "discontinued" his possession when he has abandoned it,[34] though mere non-user will not necessarily be abandonment.[35] Neither dispossession nor discontinuance alone will start time running: there must be adverse possession as well. So in practice little if anything turns on the technical distinctions between "dispossession" and "discontinuance", and it is establishing adverse possession which is of paramount importance.[36]   **18–014**

Adverse possession

Adverse possession is a somewhat complex concept. It is not defined in the Limitation Act 1980 which requires possession *"by some person in whose favour the period of limitation can run"*.[37] The meaning was developed through successive judgments. It depends on the squatter having possession of the land in fact, and also on his having the necessary intention to possess (*"animus possidendi"*).[38] If the possession is with the permission[39] of the true owner, it cannot be adverse.   **18–015**

---

[30] LA 1980 Sch.1 paras 1, 8.
[31] *Rains v Buxton* (1880) 14 Ch.D. 537 at 539.
[32] *Powell v McFarlane* (1979) 38 P. & C.R. 452 at 480. Nor is it necessary that the adverse possession is objectively apparent per *Purbrick v Hackney LBC* [2004] 1 P. & C.R. 553 at 561.
[33] *J.A. Pye (Oxford) Ltd v Graham* [2002] UKHL 30; [2003] 1 A.C. 419 at [30].
[34] *Rimington v Cannon* (1853) 12 C.B. 18 at 33.
[35] *Tecbild Ltd v Chamberlain* (1969) 20 P. & C.R. 633.
[36] *Buckinghamshire CC v Moran* [1990] Ch. 623 at 645.
[37] LA1980 Sch.1 para.8(1).
[38] *Buckinghamshire CC v Moran* [1990] Ch. 623 at 636 confirmed in *J.A. Pye (Oxford) Ltd v Graham* [2002] UKHL 30; [2003] 1 A.C. 419 at [40]; [74].
[39] Permission cannot be *implied* but actual permission may be *inferred* from an overt act of the true owner which is probative of permission: *Zarb v Parry* [2011] EWCA Civ 1306.

Possession in fact: The squatter must establish:

(i) that he has a degree of physical control of the land which amounts to possession in fact[40];

(ii) that his possession is exclusive, and not in effect shared with the true owner[41]; and

(iii) That he has dealt with the land as an occupying owner might be expected to deal with it, and that no-one else has done so.[42]

The nature of the requisite acts will vary with the nature of the land: they will not be the same for a building, a narrow strip of land, open fields, moorlands or a swamp.[43]

For buildings, changing the lock of a flat and living in it thereafter as if it were the squatter's own is unequivocal evidence.[44] So is moving into the upper part of a house of which the squatter was tenant of the ground floor.[45] Adverse possession may be subterranean, such as of a cellar.[46] One half of a seven metre stretch of a party wall in Knightsbridge was possessed by the owner of the other half as a result of installing, at different times, a security camera, security lighting, an entry phone system, a wall safe and an overflow pipe and by putting a roof on top of it.[47]

For open land, "enclosure is the strongest possible evidence of adverse possession, but it is not indispensable"[48]; concreting over an enclosed area and using it as a car park clearly suffices[49] as does maintaining the garden of an enclosed area.[50] (That does not mean that enclosure will be decisive if *animus possidendi* is absent because a fence or gates were erected merely in order to prevent invasions by the public[51] or to keep animals in[52]) Relatively trivial acts such as using the land for children to play on, or for tethering ponies or grazing goats will usually be insufficient,[53] though when land is virtually useless save for shooting, shooting over it may suffice.[54] In many cases, in the nature of things, adverse possession cannot be continuous from day to day.[55] Acts may suffice even though they do not inconvenience or otherwise affect the owner.[56]

---

40 *Buckinghamshire CC v Moran* [1990] Ch. 623.

41 It follows that at least some of the acts of possession relied on must effectively exclude the true owner (whether or not the true owner has tried to exercise his rights): *Sava v SS Global Ltd* [2008] EWCA Civ 1308 at [72]–[75].

42 *Powell v McFarlane* (1979) 38 P. & C.R. 452 at 470–471 approved in *JA Pye (Oxford) Ltd v Graham* (above).

43 See *West Bank Estates Ltd v Arthur* [1967] 1 A.C. 665; *Treloar v Nute* [1976] 1 W.L.R. 1295 at 1302; *Trustees of the Michael Batt Charitable Trust v Adams* (2001) 82 P. & C.R. 406.

44 *Lambeth L.B.C. v Blackburn* (2001) 82 P. & C.R. 39.

45 *Pollard v Jackson* (1993) 67 P. & C.R. 327.

46 *Rains v Buxton* (1880) 14 Ch.D. 537.

47 *Prudential Assurance Co Ltd v Waterloo Real Estate* [1999] 2 E.G.L.R. 85.

48 *Seddon v Smith* (1877) 36 L.T. 168 at 169 per Cockburn C.J.; *Buckinghamshire CC v Moran* [1990] Ch. 623.

49 *Burns v Anthony* (1997) 74 P. & C.R. D41.

50 *Buckinghamshire CC v Moran* [1990] Ch. 623; *Hounslow LBC v Minchinton* (1997) 74 P. & C.R. 221.

51 *Littledale v Liverpool Corp* [1900] 1 Ch. 19; *George Wimpey & Co Ltd v Sohn* [1967] Ch. 487.

52 *Inglewood Investment Co v Baker* [2002] EWCA Civ 1733; [2003] 2 P. & C.R. 319.

53 *Tecbild Ltd v Chamberlain* (1969) 20 P. & C.R. 633; *Boosey v Davis* (1987) 55 P. & C.R. 83.

54 *Red House Farms (Thorndon) Ltd v Catchpole* [1977] E.G.D. 798.

55 *Bligh v Martin* [1968] 1 W.L.R. 804 at 811.

56 *Treloar v Nute* [1976] 1 W.L.R. 1295. This case concerned land set aside for building and for

Adverse possession can be effected by the grant of a tenancy or express licence: the tenant or licensee possesses the land on behalf of the grantor.[57]

"Adverse": Possession is "adverse" only if the squatter has an *animus possidendi*, intending to possess the land to the exclusion of all other persons, including the owner.[58] Certain aspects of intention have been clarified in the case law:

(i)   no intention to own or acquire ownership of the land is needed[59];

(ii) the intention to exclude "the world" must be by the squatter on his own behalf, not on behalf of another;

(iii) showing an intention to possess does not require showing an intention to *dispossess*[60];

(iv) it is enough that the squatter intends to possess for the time being; the squatter does not have to intend to exclude the true owner in all future circumstances[61]; and

(v)   the intention to possess must be demonstrated clearly and by unequivocal acts i.e. acts which objectively show an intention to possess.

Possession will not cease to be adverse merely because the owner, in ignorance of his title, accepts a tenancy from the squatter.[62] However, the distribution of keys to other persons entitled to use the land indicates a lack of *animus possidendi*.[63] A person acting openly as owner in the (incorrect) belief that he has good title has the requisite *animus possidendi*[64]; but a tenant who occupies land thinking that it is part of the land leased to him does not have sufficient *animus possidendi* to maintain adverse possession as against the true owner either for himself or for his landlord.[65] In an unusual case where the same piece of land was mistakenly registered under two titles, a claim to rectification of the register by one paper owner could not be defeated by a claim of adverse possession by the other.[66] An intermittent though persistent trespasser who does not seek to dispossess the owner is not in adverse possession.[67] Nor is possession adverse if it is enjoyed under a contract with the owner,[68] or under a licence granted by him,[69] even if the licensee, without rejecting it, never in terms accepted it.[70] However, the possession of a former licensee who has continued to

---

which the true owner had no immediate use, hence he was not in fact inconvenienced by the squatting.

[57] See for example *Sze To Chun Keung v Kung Kwok Wai David* [1997] 1 W.L.R. 1232.

[58] *Buckinghamshire CC v Moran* [1990] Ch. 623.

[59] *Buckinghamshire CC v Moran* [1990] Ch. 623, see also *Lambeth LBC v Blackburn* (2001) 82 P. & C.R. 39.

[60] So intention to possess is shown where the squatter thinks the squatted land is his own (*Pulleyn v Hall Aggregates* (1992) 65 P. & C.R. 276 at 282); or does not realise that he has trespassed across a boundary, as in *Prudential Assurance Co Ltd v Waterloo Real Estate* [1999] 2 E.G.L.R. 85.

[61] *Buckinghamshire CC v Moran* [1990] Ch. 623 at 642–643.

[62] *Bligh v Martin* [1968] 1 W.L.R. 804.

[63] *Battersea Freehold and Leasehold Property Co Ltd v Battersea LBC* (2001) 82 P. & C.R. 137.

[64] *Armbrister v Lightbourn* [2012] UKPC 40; [2013] 1 P. & C.R. 17 at [83].

[65] *Trustees of the Michael Batt Charitable Trust v Adams* (2001) 82 P. & C.R. 406.

[66] Because the occupation was lawful until the register was rectified: *Parshall v Hackney* [2013] EWCA Civ 240; [2013] Ch. 568.

[67] *Powell v McFarlane* (1979) 38 P. & C.R. 452 at 480.

[68] *Hyde v Pearce* [1982] 1 W.L.R. 560.

[69] *Hughes v Griffin* [1969] 1 W.L.R. 23.

[70] *B.P. Properties Ltd v Buckler* (1987) 55 P. & C.R. 337.

use the land without permission in the hope that its owner would accede to his requests for a new licence is sufficient.[71]

By contrast, the true owner's intentions are irrelevant.[72] It is possible that if a squatter knows that the true owner has some special purpose for the land this may affect the question of whether the acts of possession are to be viewed as unequivocal, but such cases will be rare. Older cases which suggested a special rule that possession is not adverse if the possession does not interfere with the true owner's plans for the land, are wrong.[73]

Property which may be possessed adversely

18-016   Most obviously, land, including buildings on land, can be adversely possessed. Adverse possession may be established over underground buildings[74] or sub-soil or minerals even where the true owner retains possession of the part above ground. Party walls may be possessed adversely.[75] Land can be possessed adversely where crossed by a public highway[76] but a public highway itself may not be possessed adversely.[77]

If a squatter is dispossessed by a second squatter, the same rule applies as against the true owner, but the second squatter is vulnerable to being sued for possession by the first squatter in whose favour a fresh Limitation period runs.[78]

Successive squatters

18-017   We are here concerned with the period during which adverse possession is accruing but the necessary time to bar the true owner has not yet run. Even before the statutory period has expired, a squatter has a title good against everyone except the true owner.[79] To hold otherwise would mean that a squatter who had not barred the true owner would have no remedy against a person who dispossessed him; this might lead to breaches of the peace by competing squatters. Consequently, if a squatter who has not barred the true owner sells the land he can give the purchaser a right to the land which is valid against all except the true owner.[80] The same applies to devises, gifts or other dispositions by the squatter; in each case the person taking the squatter's interest can add the squatter's period of possession to his own.[81] Thus if X, who has occupied A's land for eight years, sells the land to Y, A will be barred after Y has held the land for a further four years.

---

[71] *J.A. PyeOxford Ltd v Graham* (above).

[72] *Buckinghamshire CC v Moran* [1990] Ch. 623 at 645 approved in *J.A.Pye Oxford Ltd v Graham* (above) at [45].

[73] *J.A.Pye Oxford Ltd v Graham* (above).

[74] *Rains v Buxton* (1880) 14 Ch.D 537: adverse possession of a cellar.

[75] *Prudential Assurance Co Ltd v Waterloo Real Estate* [1999] 2 E.G.L.R. 85.

[76] *J.A. Pye Oxford Ltd v Graham* (above) where a public footpath crossed the land.

[77] *R(Smith) v Land Registry* [2010] EWCA Civ 200; [2011] Q.B. 413.

[78] Under the Limitation Act 1980 even if the freehold is registered land, because the squatter's possessory "right" is unregistered.

[79] *Perry v Clissold* [1907] A.C. 73.

[80] This happens frequently in cases where a landowner has trespassed over a boundary and later sells his land; the accruing "rights" over the area to which he is trespassing will pass to the purchaser on the sale.

[81] *Asher v Whitlock* (1865) L.R. 1 Q.B. 1. See also *Mount Carmel Investments Ltd v Peter Thurlow Ltd* (1989) 57 P. & C.R. 396.

Again, if a squatter who is acquiring title under the Limitation Act 1980 is himself dispossessed, the second squatter can add the former period of occupation to his own.[82] For example, if land owned by A has been occupied by X for eight years, and Y dispossesses X, A will be barred when 12 years have elapsed from X first taking possession. But although at the end of that time A is barred, X will not be barred until 12 years from Y's first taking possession, for Y cannot claim to be absolutely entitled until he can show that everybody with any claim to the land has been barred by the elapse of the full period.

However, a squatter who applies for registration under the Land Registration Act 2002 is not able to add the period of occupation of any squatter whom he himself has dispossessed unless that squatter had earlier dispossessed the applicant and the three periods of adverse possession are continuous.[83]

There is no right to add together two periods of adverse possession if a squatter abandons possession before the full period has run and some time elapses before another person takes possession of the land. During the interval, there is no person in adverse possession whom the true owner could sue; thus time begins to run afresh when the second squatter takes possession of the land.[84]

Future interests

Under the Limitation Act 1980

Under the Limitation Act 1980, a person entitled in reversion or in remainder at the time **18–018** when adverse possession is taken has alternative periods: he has 12 years from adverse possession being taken or six years from the falling of his interest into possession, whichever is the longer.[85] Thus if land is settled on A for life with remainder to B, and X dispossesses A 10 years before A dies, B has six years from A's death in which to sue; but if X had dispossessed A three years before A's death, B would have 12 years from the dispossession of A. If X had not taken adverse possession until after A's death, B's interest would no longer have been a future interest, and he would have the normal period of 12 years from the taking of adverse possession. Further, if A's interest had been an estate in fee tail, then if he had been dispossessed by X, B would have been barred 12 years later. The alternative six-year period does not extend to a reversioner or remainderman whose interest was liable to be barred by the barring of a prior interest in fee tail.[86]

Under the Land Registration Act 2002

No one will be regarded as having been in adverse possession during any period in which **18–019** the land has been held for persons by way of succession.[87] Consequently, in all the examples above, X will not be able to make his first application until he has been in adverse possession as against B for 10 years. This apparently applies even where B is a reversioner

---

[82] *Site Developments (Ferndown) Ltd v Cuthbury Ltd* [2010] EWHC 10 (Ch); [2011] Ch. 226.
[83] LRA 2002 Sch.6 para.11(2).
[84] *Trustees, Executors and Agency Co Ltd v Short* (1888) 13 App. Cas. 793; LA 1980, Sch.1 para.8(2).
[85] LA 1980 s.15(2) Sch.1 para.4.
[86] LA 1980 ss.15(3), 38(5).
[87] LRA 2002 Sch.6 para.12.

or remainderman whose interest is liable to be barred by the barring of a prior interest in fee tail. This may be an oversight.

Leaseholds

Position of the landlord where land which is let is adversely possessed

18–020   The above provisions do not apply to a freehold or leasehold reversioner on a lease for a term of years where the tenant has been ousted. Irrespective of when the dispossession occurred, time does not run against the reversioner until the lease expires, because, until then, he has no right to possession.[88] Thus if L grants T a lease for 99 years and T is dispossessed by X, the 12-year period runs against T from the dispossession but against L only from the determination of the lease.

Landlord as adverse possessor

18–021   A landlord can, as against his own tenant, adversely possess land he has let, and thus acquire his tenant's leasehold title notwithstanding the rule against derogation from grant.[89]

Tenant as adverse possessor

18–022   The essential rule is that a tenant cannot acquire title by adverse possession against his landlord during the term of his lease, because his occupation cannot be adverse to his landlord.

If a tenant takes adverse possession of adjoining land of a third party, and occupies it together with the demised land,[90] that is on the face of it[91] for the benefit of the landlord as well as the tenant[92] and it is the landlord who will acquire any freehold title by adverse possession.[93] However, the tenant must know that the land does not belong to his landlord or he will lack the necessary *animus possidendi*.[94]

If a tenant takes possession of adjoining land of the landlord (encroaches onto it), there is a rebuttable[95] presumption that he takes it as an extension of his lease,[96] and it becomes subject to the terms of the tenancy[97] after the lapse of the requisite period of time. This is not the acquisition of title by adverse possession as the tenant's rights will terminate with the lease; it is a doctrine based on estoppel[98] and is best referred to as "encroachment" to avoid confusion.

---

[88] LA 1980 Sch.1 para.4.
[89] *Sze To Chun Keung v Kung Kwok Wai David* [1997] 1 W.L.R. 1232.
[90] *Tower Hamlets LBC v Barrett* [2005] EWCA Civ 923; [2006] 1 P. & C.R. 132 at [31].
[91] It is possible to rebut this presumption by sufficient evidence of a different intention—*Smirk v Lyndale Developments Ltd* [1975] Ch. 317, reversed on appeal but not on this point.
[92] *King v Smith* [1950] 1 All E.R. 554.
[93] The tenancy will extend to the squatted land for the remaining term of the tenancy.
[94] *Trustees of the Michael Batt Charitable Trust v Adams* (2001) 82 P. & C.R. 406.
[95] See *Kingsmill v Millard* (1855) 11 Exch. 313 at 318, 319.
[96] *Smirk v Lyndale Developments Ltd* [1975] Ch. 317, reversed on appeal but not on this point.
[97] *J.F. Perrott & Co Ltd v Cohen* [1951] 1 K.B. 705.
[98] *J.F. Perrott & Co Ltd v Cohen* (above).

Non-payment of rent

Save in the case of oral yearly or other periodic tenancies, a tenant cannot acquire a title **18–023** to the land leased to him as against his landlord during the currency of the lease, even by prolonged failure to pay rent. There is one exception to this in the case of a lease capable of enlargement into a fee simple. If a rent not exceeding £1 per annum reserved by such a lease has not been paid for a continuous period of 20 years, five of which have elapsed since 1925, the rent ceases to be payable. Neither the arrears nor any future payment can be recovered, and the lease may be enlarged into a fee simple.[99]

Adverse possession through adverse receipt of rent

A landlord may be barred if adverse possession is taken not of the land but of the rent from **18–024** it; for if for 12 years the tenant under a lease in writing at a rent of at least £10 per annum pays the rent to some person who wrongfully claims the reversion, and no rent is subsequently paid to the landlord, this bars the landlord's right to the reversion.[100] This rule does not apply to registered land.[101]

Special provisions applicable to yearly or other periodic tenants

Periodic Tenancy in writing

Where there is a yearly or other periodic tenancy under a lease in writing, time runs in the **18–025** tenant's favour from the determination of the tenancy.[102]

Periodic tenancy not in writing

If there is no lease in writing,[103] time runs in the tenant's favour from the end of the first **18–026** year or other shorter period of the tenancy,[104] subject to extension[105] by written acknowledgement, or by payment of rent, in which case time runs from the last receipt of rent.[106] So an oral periodic tenancy will in due course entitle the tenant to claim title under the Limitation Act 1980 or to apply under the Land Registration Act 2002 if no rent is paid for long enough. This is also the case if the tenant thinks that he is paying rent but he is not in fact doing so[107] or where the parties thought that there was a written tenancy but due to oversight there was no such tenancy.[108]

---

[99]   LPA 1925 s.153; above, para.12–023.
[100] LA 1980 Sch.1 para.6.
[101] LRA 2002 Sch.6 para.11(3)(b).
[102] There is no need for the tenant to show that he has taken any additional steps to dispossess the landlord beyond failing to vacate: *Williams v Jones* [2002] EWCA Civ 1097; [2002] 3 E.G.L.R. 69.
[103] There must be an actual valid lease, not just evidence of a lease—*Long v Tower Hamlets LBC* [1998] Ch. 197.
[104] LA 1980 Sch.1 para.5(1). See, e.g. *Jessamine Investment Co v Schwartz* [1978] Q.B. 264.
[105] Below, para.18–043.
[106] LA 1980 Sch.1 para.5(2).
[107] *Lodge v Wakefield Metropolitan CC* [1995] 2 E.G.L.R. 124.
[108] See *Mitchell v Watkinson* [2013] EWHC 2266 (Ch).

Tenants at will and at sufferance, and licensees

18–027   Time begins to run in favour of a tenant at will on the determination of his tenancy,[109] and in favour of a tenant at sufferance on the commencement of his tenancy; for he has no true tenancy,[110] but is in adverse possession. Time does not run in favour of a licensee, for he holds by the owner's consent.[111]

Rentcharges

18–028   In the case of a rentcharge in possession, time runs from the last payment of rent to the owner of the rentcharge.[112] Thus the rent owner's rights are barred:

(i)   if no rent is paid for 12 years, in which case the rentcharge is extinguished; or

(ii)   if the rent is paid to a stranger for 12 years, in which case the rentcharge remains enforceable against the land but the former owner's claim to it is extinguished in favour of the stranger.

Similar rules apply to other rents not due under a lease. Rules provide how the provisions of the Land Registration Act 2002 applies to registered rentcharges.[113]

Mortgages

Mortgagee's right to enforce his charge

18–029   As regards the mortgagee's right to recover the money charged on the land, or to claim possession, or to foreclose, time runs against him from the date upon which the money was due,[114] and when he is barred, his mortgage ceases to exist.[115] In each case, any written acknowledgment or any payment on account of principal or interest starts time running afresh.[116] Charging orders, however, remain enforceable regardless of the lapse of time since they were made.[117] The position is the same in respect of registered land.[118]

---

[109] LA 1980 Sch.1 para.4.

[110] Above, para.11–029.

[111] *Hughes v Griffin* [1969] 1 W.L.R. 23.

[112] LA 1980 s.38(8).

[113] LRA 2002 Sch.6 para.14.

[114] LA 1980 s.20. The same is true where the mortgagee takes possession and sells, but there is a shortfall: the 12 year period for suing for the shortfall runs from when payment was due, not from the date of sale: *West Bromwich BS v Wilkinson* [2005] UKHL 44; [2005] 1 W.L.R. 2303.

[115] *Cotterell v Price* [1960] 1 W.L.R. 1097.

[116] LA 1980 s.29; below, para.18–043. and see *Ashe v Natwest Bank* [2008] EWCA Civ 55; [2008] 1 W.L.R. 710.

[117] *Yorkshire Bank Finance v Mulhall* [2008] EWCA Civ 1156; [2009] 1 P. & C.R. 345. Charging orders are treated as equitable charges for the purposes of enforcement.

[118] Claims for possession by registered chargees remain subject to the time limits in the LA 1980: see LRA 2002 s.96(1).

The right of redemption

If a mortgagee goes into possession, time begins to run against subsequent mortgagees **18–030** and the mortgagor. If the land is unregistered, their rights to redeem are barred after 12 years.[119] However, in respect of registered land, to bar the right of redemption the mortgagee must apply to the registrar in the usual way after 10 years.[120]

Claims through Crown or corporation sole

It has been seen that the Crown is at present entitled to a 30-year period instead of the **18–031** usual 12.[121] If a person against whom time has started to run conveys his land to the Crown, the only change is that the limitation period becomes 30 years from the dispossession instead of 12. But in the converse case, where time has started to run against the Crown and the Crown then conveys the land to X, the rule is that X is barred at the expiration of 30 years from the original dispossession or 12 years from the conveyance to him, whichever is the shorter.[122] Thus X is entitled to 12 years from the date of the conveyance unless at that time there were less than 12 years of the Crown period unexpired, in which case he merely has the residue of that period.

Similar rules at present apply[123] to the 30-year period for a spiritual or eleemosynary corporation sole.[124]

Since the Land Registration Act 2002 came into force neither of these special periods exists in the case of registered land.

Trusts

Adverse possession by stranger

Equitable interests under trusts of land or under settlements under the Settled Land Act **18–032** 1925 are in general treated as "land" and so as subject to the normal rules.[125]

However, adverse possession of trust property by a stranger under the Limitation Act 1980 does not bar the trustee's title to the property until all the beneficiaries have been barred.[126] Thus if land is held on trust for A for life with remainder to B, 12 years' adverse possession of the land by X bars A's equitable interest and, but for the provision just mentioned, would bar the title to the legal estate. But time will not start to run against B's equitable interest until A's death,[127] and the same accordingly applies to the trustee's legal estate. Consequently, after the 12 years have run, the legal estate will be held on trust for X for the life of A, and subject thereto on trust for B. This is so whether the legal estate is held

---

[119] LA 1980 s.16; see, e.g. *Young v Clarey* [1948] Ch. 191.
[120] LRA 2002 s.95(2); above, para.18–010.
[121] Above, para.18–009.
[122] LA 1980 Sch.1 para.12.
[123] LA 1980 Sch.1 para.12.
[124] Above, para.18–009.
[125] LA 1980 ss.18, 20.
[126] LA 1980 ss.18, 20s.18.
[127] Above, para.18–018.

by the trustee (as will be the case under a trust of land) or by A (as will usually be the case under a settlement under the Settled Land Act 1925).

No adverse possession is possible under the Land Registration Act 2002 of land which is held for persons by way of succession.[128] Consequently, in the example set out above, X will not be able to apply to be registered as proprietor until 10 years after A's death.

Adverse possession by trustee

18–033   Trustees cannot obtain a title against their beneficiaries by adverse possession of the trust property; for there is no period of limitation for an action by a beneficiary to recover from his trustees the trust property or its proceeds in their possession or converted to their use, or in respect of any fraud by the trustees.[129] Thus if land is conveyed to X and Y as trustees of land for themselves as tenants in common, X cannot obtain a title to the land as against Y, no matter how long he excludes Y from the land or its rents and profits; for X and Y hold the legal estate on trust for themselves as tenants in common,[130] and X is thus trustee for Y.[131] But subject to this, the limitation period in respect of breaches of trust (such as paying the income of the trust to the wrong person) is six years.[132]

In one case a trustee's liability may be curtailed if he is also a beneficiary. If on a distribution of trust funds such a trustee receives or retains for himself trust property or its proceeds in excess of his proper share, his liability will be restricted to that excess after six years have passed, provided he acted honestly and reasonably.[133] Thus, if in distributing the trust property T takes one-third of it for himself in the honest and reasonable belief that it is divisible equally between himself and two others, his liability on the subsequent appearance of a further beneficiary who is entitled to share equally will be limited to one-twelfth of the trust property, once the six years have run.

Adverse possession by beneficiary

18–034   Time does not begin to run against the trustees or other beneficiaries if land held on a trust of land or under a settlement subject to the Settled Land Act 1925 is in the possession of a beneficiary who is not solely and absolutely entitled to it.[134]

POSTPONEMENT OF THE PERIOD

18–035   The date from which time begins to run may be postponed or the running of time may be suspended for a number of reasons:

1. Disability;

---

[128] LRA 2002 Sch.6 para.12.
[129] LA 1980 s.21(1).
[130] Above, Ch.8.
[131] See *Re Landi* [1939] Ch. 828.
[132] LA 1980 s.21(3).
[133] LA 1980 s.21(2).
[134] LA 1980 s.21(2). Sch.1 para.9.

2. Fraud; deliberate concealment or mistake;
3. During wartime.

However, the issue of proceedings, whether or not they are served, which are not pursued (because, for example, they have been dismissed for breaches of the Civil Procedure Rules) does not stop time running.[135]

Disability under the Limitation Act 1980

If the owner of an interest in land is under disability when the right of action accrues, then even if the normal period of limitation expires, the period is extended to six years from the time when he ceases to be under a disability or dies, whichever happens first, with a maximum period in the case of land of 30 years from the date when the right of action first accrued.[136] Thus if X takes possession of A's land at a time when A is of unsound mind, A will have 12 years from the dispossession or six years from his recovery in which to bring his action, whichever period is the longer, subject to the limit of 30 years from the dispossession.   **18–036**

Meaning of "disability"

A person is under a disability for this purpose "while he is an infant or lacks capacity (within the meaning of the Mental Capacity Act 2005) to conduct legal proceedings".[137]   **18–037**

Supervening disability

A disability is immaterial unless it existed at the time when the cause of action accrued. Thus if A becomes unsound of mind the day before he is dispossessed, the provisions for disability apply, whereas if he becomes unsound of mind the day after he has been dispossessed, they do not.   **18–038**

Successive disabilities

In the case of successive disabilities, if a person is under one disability and before that ceases another disability begins, the period is extended until both disabilities cease, subject to the maximum of 30 years.[138] But if one disability comes to an end before another disability starts, or if the person under disability is succeeded by another person under disability, time runs from the ceasing of the first disability. For example, A is a child when the cause of action accrues. If later, during his minority, he becomes unsound of mind, the six years does not start to run until he is both sane and of full age. But if he reaches full age before he becomes unsound of mind, or if he dies a child, and B, a mental patient, becomes entitled to the land, the six years run from A's majority in the first case and his death in the second.[139]   **18–039**

---

[135] *Markfield Investments Ltd v Evans* (2001) 81 P. & C.R. 33; see also LRA 2002 Sch.6 para.11(3)(a).
[136] LA 1980 s.28.
[137] LA 1980 s.38(2).
[138] See LA 1980 s.28(1).
[139] LA 1980 s.28(3).

Disability under the Land Registration Act 2002

18–040   Under the Land Registration Act 2002, no one may apply to be registered as proprietor during any period during which the existing registered proprietor is unable because of mental disability to make decisions of the kind to which the application would give rise or is unable to communicate his decisions because of either mental disability or physical impairment.[140] Mental disability is defined as "a disability or disorder of the mind or brain, whether permanent or temporary, which results in an impairment or disturbance of mental functioning".[141]

Fraud, deliberate concealment and mistake

18–041   Where:

    (i)   an action is based on the fraud of the defendant or his agent, or of any person through whom he claims, or his agent; or

    (ii)   any fact relevant to the claimant's right of action has been deliberately concealed from him by any such person; or

    (iii)   the action is for relief from the consequences of a mistake,

then time does not begin to run against the landowner until he discovers the fraud, concealment or mistake, or could with reasonable diligence have discovered it.[142] The term "deliberately concealed" has removed the element of unconscionable conduct[143] that was required by the former words "concealed by . . . fraud".[144] There are two types of conduct which amount to deliberate concealment and prevent a limitation period from running:

    (a)   where the defendant takes active steps to conceal his own breach of duty after he becomes aware of it;

    (b)   the *deliberate* commission of a breach of duty in circumstances in which it is unlikely to be discovered for some time.[145]

The rule as to mistake applies only where mistake is the basis of the action, as where the action is to recover money paid under a mistake of fact. There is no general doctrine that making a mistake (for example as to the true position of a boundary) stops time running.[146]

---

[140] LRA 2002 Sch.6 para.8(2).

[141] LRA 2002 Sch.6 para.8(3).

[142] LA 1980 s.32(1). If the relevant concealment occurs after time has begun to run, the Limitation clock is turned back to zero and does not restart until the concealment is discovered: *Sheldon v RHM Outhwaite (underwriting Agencies) Ltd* [1996] A.C. 102.

[143] See *Bartlett v Barclays Bank Trust Co Ltd* [1980] Ch. 515 at 537.

[144] The words used in the LA 1939 s.26(b), now repealed. See the discussion in *Cave v Robinson Jarvis & Rolf* [2002] UKHL 18; [2003] 1 A.C. 384.

[145] LA 1980 s.32(2). Where there is a breach of duty but the defendant is unaware of the breach, as is generally the case with negligent advice, there is no "deliberate concealment": *Cave v Robinson Jarvis & Rolf* (above).

[146] See *Phillips-Higgins v Harper* [1954] 1 Q.B. 411.

Neither fraud nor mistake will postpone the running of time as against a subsequent purchaser for value who did not know or have reason to believe that there was fraud or mistake.[147]

During wartime

The running of time under the Limitation Act 1980 is suspended during any period in which   **18–042**
the owner is an enemy or is detained in enemy territory[148] and no application can be made under the Land Registration Act 2002 during any such period.[149]

STARTING TIME RUNNING AFRESH

Time may be started running afresh by: **18–043**

    (i) a signed acknowledgment in writing of the owner's title; or
   (ii) part payment of principal sums due or interest.[150]

The acknowledgment or payment must be:

   (a) made by the person in whose favour time is running, or by his agent[151]; and
   (b) it must be made to the person whose title is being barred, or to his agent[152]: and
   (c) signed by the person making it.

The acknowledgment must be of existing liability[153] and not merely of facts which might give rise to liability,[154] or merely that there might be a claim.[155] But an acknowledgment of title need only admit that the person with paper title has better title than the person making the acknowledgment[156]; it need not admit the true owner's immediate right to possession.[157] The acknowledgment may be implicit rather than express.[158] An order for

---

[147] LA 1980 s.32(3).
[148] Limitation (Enemies and War Prisoners) Act 1945.
[149] LRA 2002 Sch.6 para.8(1).
[150] LA 1980 s.29.
[151] The acknowledgment must be "open"; acknowledgments in "without prejudice" correspondence are inadmissible: *Ofulue v Bossert* [2009] UKHL 16; [2009] 1 A.C. 990.
[152] LA s.30. *Lambeth LBC v Archangel* [2002] 1 P. & C.R. 18.
[153] As in *Moodie v Bannister* (1859) 4 Drew. 432; *Dungate v Dungate* [1965] 1 W.L.R. 1477; *Lambeth LBC v Archangel* [2002] 1 P. & C.R. 18.
[154] *Re Flynn (No.2)* [1969] 2 Ch. 403.
[155] *Good v Parry* [1963] 2 Q.B. 418.
[156] *Allen v Matthews* [2007] EWCA Civ 216; [2007] 2 P & C.R. 441.
[157] *Ofulue v Bossert* [2009] UKHL 16; [2009] 1 A.C. 990 at [74]–[75].
[158] *Lambeth LBC v Archangel* [2002] 1 P. & C.R. 18 (letter from squatter to true owner referring to refurbishing the owner's property); *Rehman v Benfield* [2006] EWCA Civ 1392; [2007] 2 P. & C.R. 317 (recitals in a void lease); *Ofulue v Bossert* [2009] UKHL 16; [2009] 1 A.C. 990 (squatter's offer to buy the land from the true owner).

possession will start a fresh period of time running on the judgment,[159] but a mere demand for possession will not.[160]

There may be any number of repeated extensions of a limitation period by successive acknowledgments or payments within the limitation period. Once the full period has run, however, no payment or acknowledgment can revive a right to recover land, for the elapse of time will have extinguished not only the owner's remedies for recovering the land but also his right to it.[161] It is otherwise in the case of other actions, where lapse of time bars only the remedy and not the right. Yet by estoppel a squatter, like any other land-owner, may preclude himself from asserting his title.[162]

PART 3   THE EFFECT OF THE ELAPSE OF TIME

TITLE TO LAND

The squatter's title to unregistered land acquired under the Limitation Act 1980

No "parliamentary conveyance"

18–044   The operation of the Limitation Act 1980 is negative, not positive: it transfers nothing but extinguishes the owner's title. The owner's title is not transferred to the squatter, and so there is no "parliamentary conveyance" to him.[163] Instead, the squatter owns a new estate of his own which by limitation will progressively improve until all competing interests are barred and he has an unencumbered fee simple absolute.

Burdens binding the squatter

18–045   Even if a squatter acquires title to an estate in fee simple, he may not be able to take a clean title; for burdens which bound the land will continue to bind it in the hands of the squatter. For example, a squatter will be bound by a restrictive covenant attached to the land unless he can show that it is no longer enforceable, for instance, by lapse of time since a breach of it; for until a breach occurs the covenantee has no right of action and time does not run

---

[159] *B.P. Properties Ltd v Buckler* (1987) 55 P. & C.R. 337. Time continues to run in respect of the adverse possession itself unless and until the judgment is enforced (or the squatter vacates) so if the right to enforce the judgment becomes time-barred, and the squatter has by that stage accrued the necessary period of adverse possession, the true owner's title becomes barred.

[160] *Mount Carmel Investments Ltd v Peter Thurlow Ltd* (1989) 57 P. & C.R. 396.

[161] LA 1980 s.17; *Nicholson v England* [1926] 2 K.B. 93.

[162] *Colchester BC v Smith* [1992] Ch. 421 (compromise of a possession action against the squatter); *St Pancras & Humanist Housing Association v Leonard* [2008] EWCA Civ 1442 (squatter held a management position within the paper owner).

[163] *Tichborne v Weir* (1892) 67 L.T. 735 at 737.

against him. A squatter without notice is not a purchaser without notice.[164] He will also be bound by easements and profits á prendre unless they have been abandoned.[165] A squatter is bound by a mortgage created by the true owner before the adverse possession began[166] but not one created after that.[167]   A squatter may also be bound by rights over the land that arise during the period of dispossession, as where the owner, by entering the land from time to time to trim a hedge and clear a drain,[168] or to repair and maintain his adjoining house,[169] acquires rights in the nature of easements.

Where the squatter acquires title by adverse possession against a lessee

In this situation, the lessee's title is extinguished, but the landlord's title is unaffected[170] and the landlord will be entitled to claim possession at the end of the term of the lease. Despite the fact that the lessee's title is extinguished the landlord cannot claim possession against the squatter before the term date of the lease unless the landlord had a right to determine the lease or there is a surrender by the (barred) tenant. If the tenant surrenders his tenancy to the freeholder, this enables the freeholder to evict the squatter forthwith, for the surrender removes the only interest which prevented the freeholder from claiming possession of land that he owns.[171]

18–046

If a squatter bars a tenant but not the freeholder, and the tenant then acquires the freehold, time begins to run against the freehold; but until it has run, the tenant, by virtue of owning the freehold, may evict the squatter immediately, for the freehold is not barred, and the former tenancy has merged in the freehold.[172]

Liabilities of tenant and squatter under a lease where the lessee's title is extinguished by adverse possession

Pending merger or surrender, the better view is that the tenant who has been dispossessed and the freeholder remain liable to one another on all the covenants in the lease throughout the remaining term.[173] This will be the case whether the lease is an "old lease" or a "new lease".[174] In the case of an "old lease", the original tenant will also remain liable to the freeholder.

18–047

However, a squatter who acquires title to a lease but not a title to the freehold is not

---

[164] *Re Nisbet & Pott's Contract* [1906] 1 Ch. 386.
[165] Above, para.15–069.
[166] See for example *Carroll v Manek* (1999) 79 P. & C.R. 173.
[167] LA 1980 s.15(4).
[168] *Marshall v Taylor* [1895] 1 Ch. 641 at 648, 651.
[169] *Williams v Usherwood* (1983) 45 P. & C.R. 235.
[170] *Chung Ping Kwan v Lam Island Development Co* [1997] A.C. 38.
[171] *Fairweather v St. Marylebone Property Co Ltd* [1963] A.C. 510. The reasoning is that the lease remains valid between landlord and tenant even though the tenant's title has been extinguished; but see (1962) 78 L.Q.R. 33 (H.W.R. Wade).
[172] *Taylor v Twinberrow* [1930] 2 K.B. 16. So the tenant as new freeholder can immediately claim possession even though the landlord as previous freeholder could not.
[173] *Spectrum Investment Co v Holmes* [1981] 1 W.L.R. 221; cp. *Re Field* [1918] 1 I.R. 40. This so whether or not the tenant is the original tenant or an assignee, as between landlord and tenant there is still privity of estate despite the tenant's loss of his title by adverse possession.
[174] Because the assignment to the squatter will be an "excluded assignment"; LT(C)A 1995 s.11.

in the position of an assignee of that lease. An assignee is liable to be sued for a breach of covenant committed while he held the lease even if at the time of the action the lease has expired,[175] but a squatter cannot be sued for breaches of covenant committed while he was in possession of the land[176] (unless the covenants are restrictive covenants enforceable as such[177]). However, the landlord's rights to forfeit for breach of covenant and to distrain for non-payment of rent are enforceable against the squatter. So during the term of the lease, the squatter can in practice be forced to pay the rent and perform the lessee's covenants by the threat of distress for rent or, if the lease contains a forfeiture clause as it usually does, of forfeiture.[178] The squatter is particularly vulnerable to forfeiture because he has no right to apply for relief against forfeiture.[179]

If a squatter takes advantage of some clause in the lease, such as a proviso that the rent should be halved if the covenants are observed, he cannot "blow hot and cold". If he accepts the benefits of the lease, he cannot reject the burdens. Consequently, he will be estopped from denying that he is bound by the lease.[180] But the mere payment of rent under a lease with no such clause will not operate as an estoppel.[181]

The squatter's title to registered land acquired under the Land Registration Act 2002

A "parliamentary conveyance"

18–048   Under the Land Registration Act 2002, the existing title is transferred to the adverse possessor so that there is a "parliamentary conveyance". The adverse possessor is registered as proprietor in place of the former true owner.[182] Consequently, registration of the adverse possessor under the Land Registration Act 2002 extinguishes such title as he had by virtue of being in adverse possession at the time of his application.[183]

Burdens binding the squatter

18–049   The Land Registration Act 2002 specifically provides that the registration of an adverse possessor thereunder does not affect the priority of any interest affecting the estate.[184] The only exception to this is that the estate will be vested in the squatter free of any registered charges which affected it immediately prior to its registration.[185] This is because registered chargees are among the persons whom the registrar is obliged to notify of the application

---

[175] Above, para.14–037.
[176] *Tichborne v Weir* (1892) 67 L.T. 735.
[177] See above para.14–054.
[178] See above, paras 12–001 et seq. After April 6, 2014 distress is replaced by commercial rent arrears recovery; Tribunal Courts and Enforcement Act (TCEA) 2007 s.72.
[179] *Tickner v Buzzacott* [1965] Ch. 426.
[180] *Ashe v Hogan* [1920] 1 I.R. 159; *Tito v Waddell (No.2)* [1977] Ch. 106 at 299–302.
[181] *Tichborne v Weir* (1892) 67 L.T. 735.
[182] LRA 2002 Sch.6 para.1, 4, 5.
[183] LRA 2002 Sch.6 para.9(1).
[184] LRA 2002 para.9(2).
[185] LRA 2002 para.9(3).

of the squatter for registration.[186] If they do not object, there is no reason why they should retain their interests. However, in the three circumstances in which the squatter can be registered as proprietor despite an objection,[187] registered charges will remain binding on him if he is so registered.[188]

Where the squatter acquires title by adverse possession against a lessee

In this situation, the lessee's title is acquired by the squatter, but the landlord's title is unaffected[189] and the landlord will be entitled to claim possession at the end of the term of the lease (but not before unless the landlord had a right to determine the lease).   **18–050**

If a squatter acquires a tenant's registered title, but not the freeholder's title, and the tenant then acquires the freehold, the lease does not merge with the freehold because the lease itself is vested in the squatter. Nor will any purported surrender of the lease by the "true" tenant enable the freeholder to evict the squatter prior to the end of the term. The lease remains binding on the freeholder.[190]

Liabilities of tenant and squatter under a lease where the lessee's title is acquired by adverse possession

The lease is binding as between the squatter and the landlord who are liable to one another on all the covenants in the lease throughout the remaining term. Pending any acquisition of the freehold by the (dispossessed) tenant or any determination of the lease, the tenant who has been dispossessed and the freeholder remain liable to one another on all the covenants in the lease throughout the remaining term.[191] This will be the case whether the lease is an "old lease" or a "new lease"[192]. In the case of an "old lease", the original tenant will also remain liable to the freeholder.[193]   **18–051**

Proof of title to unregistered land

A good title to unregistered land cannot be shown merely by proving adverse possession of land, however long the period. If A and his predecessors in title have been in possession of land for 20, 50, or 100 years, that alone does not prove that A is entitled to it; for the true owner: **18–052**

   (i)   might have been under disability at a relevant time; or
   (ii) might have been the Crown; or
   (iii) might have been the reversioner or remainderman under a settlement; or
   (iv) might be the reversioner on a long lease.

---

[186] LRA 2002 Sch.6 para.2(1)(b).
[187] LRA 2002 Sch.6 para.5(1)–(3).
[188] LRA 2002 Sch.6 para.9(4).
[189] *Chung Ping Kwan v Lam Island Development Co* [1997] A.C. 38.
[190] *Spectrum Investment Co v Holmes* [1981] 1 W.L.R. 221 (decided under the old LRA 1925).
[191] *Spectrum Investment Co v Holmes* [1981] 1 W.L.R. 221; and see above, para.14–033.
[192] Because the assignment to the squatter will be an excluded assignment; Landlord and Tenant (Covenants) Act 1995 s.11.
[193] See above, para.14–014.

Consequently, to establish a good title by the operation of the Limitation Act 1980 it must be shown:

    (i) who was the true owner of the interest in land in question; and

    (ii) that he has been barred by lapse of time.

It is highly unlikely that a vendor will be able to do this unless the person dispossessed left the deeds in the property or can be identified and persuaded to part with them for a consideration. But a vendor who can show these two things can establish a title which the courts will force even an unwilling purchaser to accept.[194] In practice, a seller who relies on title by adverse possession will sell to a buyer who is prepared to contract on terms that he will accept the title which the seller can establish.

The issue does not arise under the Land Registration Act 2002 as the squatter acquires registered title which is entitled to deal with like any other registered proprietor.

PART 4   OTHER LIMITATION PERIODS RELEVANT TO LAND LAW

ARREARS OF INCOME

18–053   The recovery of arrears of income is distinct from the recovery of the land or capital money which produces it. The arrears of rent which the landlord or the owner of a rentcharge can recover by action or distress are limited to the arrears accrued due during the previous six years.[195] For agricultural holdings, distress is restricted to rent falling due during the previous year,[196] and for bankruptcy it is limited to six months' rent accruing due before the commencement of the bankruptcy.[197]

There is also a six-year period for arrears of mortgage interest.[198] But a mortgagee who exercises his power of sale may retain all arrears of interest out of the proceeds of sale, for this is not recovery by action.[199] A mortgagor who seeks to redeem can do so only on the equitable terms of paying all arrears, however old.[200]

---

[194] *Re Atkinson & Horsell's Contract* [1912] 2 Ch. 1; contrast *George Wimpey & Co Ltd v Sohn* [1967] Ch. 487.

[195] LA 1980 ss.19, 38(1). From April 6, 2014 distress is replaced by commercial rent arrears recovery under TCEA 2007 s.72.

[196] Agricultural Holdings Act 1986 s.16 and see TCEA 2007 s.80.

[197] IA 1986 s.347.

[198] LA 1980 s.20(5).

[199] *Re Marshfield* (1887) 34 Ch.D. 721.

[200] *Dingle v Coppen* [1899] 1 Ch. 726; *Holmes v Cowcher* [1970] 1 W.L.R. 834.

Equitable remedies

Except as set out in the section of this Chapter concerning trusts, there are no statu- **18–054**
tory time limits for claims to equitable remedies, such as specific performance,[201] injunctions, rectification of contracts or Deeds, or relief from the consequences of a mistake.[202]
However, such claims are subject to the equitable doctrine of laches[203], which requires that
claims be brought without unreasonable delay and so relief may be refused if it would be
unconscionable to permit the claimant to rely on his rights.[204]

SUMMARY OF KEY CASES

- *Buckinghamshire County Council v Moran* [1990] Ch. 623
- *J.A. Pye (Oxford) Ltd v Graham* [2002] UKHL 30, [2003] A.C. 419
- *Pye v U.K. Application No.44302/02)* [2005] ECHR 921, [2005] 49 E.G., 90; reversed
  [2007] ECHR 700

FURTHER READING

- R. Kerridge, and A.H.R. Brierley, "Adverse possession, human rights and land registra-
  tion" [2006] Conv. 552
- M. Dixon, "Adverse possession and registered land" [2009] Conv. 169
- M. Dockray, "Why do we need adverse possession?" [1985] Conv. 272

---

[201] *P&O Nedloyd BV v Arab Metals Co (No.2)* [2006] EWCA Civ 1717; [2007] 1 W.L.R. 2288.
[202] LA1980 s.36(1).
[203] Preserved by LA 1980 s.36(2).
[204] *Re Loftus (deceased)* [2006] EWCA Civ 1124; [2007] 1 W.L.R. 591.

INDEX